Build a New World

With New Thoughts

Agilhard Idland

authorHOUSE®

AuthorHouse™ UK Ltd.
500 Avebury Boulevard
Central Milton Keynes, MK9 2BE
www.authorhouse.co.uk
Phone: 08001974150

First published by AuthorHouse 1/15/2010

ISBN: 978-1-4490-6951-3 (sc)

Library of Congress Control Number: 2010900250

Weblog: Build a New World   http://agilhard.wordpress.com/
Website: www.diagramstar.org
Biblical Images, in color: http://bsm.museum.no/
Bergen Skolemuseum

This book is printed on acid-free paper.

Build a New World

With new thoughts

The new world of thoughts is with a whole new foundation, based on the history about the lost Motherland. This is not a religion; it is uncovered true world history. The origin of all the religions, legends, tales and myths in the world are the lost Motherland. The Bible is the Ark of the Covenant, and the golden chest is now open. The content is the Diagram Star, better known as the Bethlehem Star.

Agilhard Idland

The Order of Anthrop

A Global Parliament

The Diagram Star

Contents

The message hidden in the Bible

The message about how lasting peace can be restored on planet earth is hidden in the Bible, under the camouflage of religion. The many camouflaged stories make the Bible in to the real Ark of the Covenant. The camouflage of religion is an imposed verbal lid over the knowledge human's need in order to be able to build a new world with lasting peace.

The whole world population lives inside a strong mental wall of imposed religious belief that has to be broken down with knowledge about the lost world history, before the message from the Bible can be understood by everyone. The message is all about a lost Motherland, which is the true origin of all the religions, legends, tales and myths in the world. Understanding the past will truly restore the knowledge that will save mankind from destroying planet earth completely.

The stories in the Bible, when all evil is removed, are the true world history from the time before the Motherland was destroyed in a natural catastrophe some twelve thousand years ago. After the catastrophe the chaos of wars and conflicts started and just never stopped. The forces of evil have ruled over the common world of thoughts for a long time and in order to understand the magnitude of it all, dormant brain cells have to be activated or even rebuilt. The name of the dominating evil forces in the world is the three factors of the Original Sin. By definition they are a long lasting crime against mankind: (1) the many national states, (2) the global system of capitalism (3) and all the religions in the world.

A clear and true definition of God

A true definition of God will activate your dormant brain cells and make you think new thoughts that are difficult even to imagine. God is the twelve members of the superior Motherland council. They all died in a large catastrophe and were remembered by the whole world population.

Up until some twelve thousand years ago the whole world population was governed from one Motherland, with one common set of laws and rules. The superior Motherland council was omnipotent, omniscient and omnipresent in a paradise world with lasting peace. The Motherland parliament as a whole had twelve democratic elected members from every tribal population in the world. They were a global assembly and together they elected the twelve members forming the superior Motherland council.

This is how the whole world was created. It was the superior Motherland council who supervised the building of a world with lasting peace. The reason that the twelve members were connected to the creation of the universe is simply wrong translating from Hieroglyphs to the Hebrew language. They only knew how the universe came to be.

The official emblem of the superior Motherland council was and still is the Diagram Star. The diagram shaped like a bright shining star have the sun and the moon in the centre and the twelve Zodiac star signs in the sections around. The twelve Zodiac signs were the official emblems, one for each member of the superior Motherland council. Taken down on earth the signs together in a circle with the sun and the moon in the center were made in to the Diagram Star, the official emblem for the superior Motherland council as a whole. The diagram had a multitude of meanings and stories connected to it and shaped like a bright shining star it was used all over the world as a common source of education. The teachers in all the education centers were Masters, educated in the Motherland, and in this manner the long lasting world peace was secured.

In every village or tribal community the main activity for everyone was education. The population was proud, happy and hard working for the common good, knowing that the best students would end up as Masters, and that the best of the best could be chosen to sit in the superior Motherland council.

It was a world completely without imposed religious belief, without national states and without the global capitalistic system. All humans were equals, not one greater than others.

All the tribal people who emigrated from the Motherland, who lived in colonies, kingdoms and empires, were living with one common set of laws and rules. The land had no owners, and the people living on it were administrated by the superior Motherland council. The village councils, and any other tribal leaders all over the world, had the superior Motherland council as their high leader, their king of kings, and they all lived like brothers and friends.

The land could only feed a certain number of humans, and when a village population got to big, a whole tribe departed to settle on new land nearby. There was always enough food for everyone all over the world. They all lived with lasting peace and had no knowledge of any other way to live. Life was good.

Over time the tribal people from the Motherland populated the whole world and the colonies evolved in to kingdoms and empires. All the kings and leaders had to promise to live by the common set of laws and rules given by the superior Motherland council. The world was truly a paradise for a long, long time.

The superior Motherland council of twelve was the leaders of the world, and after the Motherland was destroyed in a natural catastrophe some twelve thousand years ago, they all died along with almost all the other humans living on the large continent. Without the superior leadership from the Motherland, the chaos of wars and conflicts started all over the world. Brothers started killing brothers for the ownership of land, riches and personal power.

The twelve dead Motherland council members were remembered by the whole world population. Legends and stories were told about them all, and they over time they became the many gods in the world. They became spirits in the Spirit World, also called God in Heaven. Their power had shifted from physical to spiritual.

Kings and leaders around the world soon discovered that they could break the laws and rules of the lost Motherland as much as they wanted without being punished for it, and soon the chaos of wars and conflicts started and never ended. Warrior kings and priesthoods started making their own laws and rules for living. The quest for fertile land, riches and personal power made the daily life for humans change from a living earthly paradise to a living earthly hell.

As the generations lived and died, the absent common education and global communication changed the whole world population dramatically. Legends, tales and myths turned in to the many religions in the world. The twelve members of the superior Motherland council were remembered as the twelve signs of the Zodiac like they always had been. The Zodiac signs were visible on the night sky, and the stories about them were many. The knowledge of the lost Motherland faded in the growing chaos of wars and conflicts. The warrior kings and priesthoods, who wanted to control the people, forced the people to believe in the many different dogmas and assumptions that everyone knew was wrong. But nobody could speak against the king and the priesthoods and expect to live.

The God of the religion Christianity, and all other religions in the world, is the superior council of the lost Motherland. The words spoken by God in the Bible are all originating from the spiritual superior Motherland council. Time has come to remove all religions in the world and restore knowledge about the lost Motherland history with the use of the Bible the Diagram Star and all the legends, tales and myths in the world.

Understanding the world you live in

In order to restore the message hidden in the Bible in your own world of thoughts, you have to activate dormant brain cells, or even grow new ones, and it takes time.

For most people it is very difficult to understand that the building of national states and enforcing heavy taxation on the population was extremely wrong back then when it was done, and along with the enforcement of the many religions in the world, the three factors truly are the Original Sin.

Think about it for a while. The three factors of the Original Sin is nothing but a long lasting crime against mankind. A few fundamental facts that no one can deny proves that you can begin to regard the history of your national state and the world as negative and evil. It is not a question about good and bad national leaders. It is the governing system with many national states in the world that are wrong, and have been wrong ever since the superior leadership from the Motherland council disappeared from the face of the earth.

These are a few fundamental facts that no one can deny: You were born in to the world, given a name and a number. Enforced education started early and after graduation you started a lifetime of working and paying taxes and dues to your nation. After a long life as a more or less willing working slave, soldier and servant to your nation, you will die, not knowing why you ever lived. But all the time through your life on earth, you have had an inner feeling that something is very wrong with the way the world is organized. But you didn't understand what was wrong. If you now are beginning to understand, it means that dormant brain cells have been activated, and you are connected.

Now, if you are able to see the world history and the history of your nation with an opposite sign of what you have been taught to, you have made significant progress. You cannot deny that your nation, just as all the other nations in the world, was built with the use of warfare and brutal force. You cannot deny the fact that your national state and all the national states in the world are regular prison camps for their populations, living inside strong and heavily guarded borders. Your freedom inside the border is dictated by the national laws and rules for living and is very restricted. Notice now that this is the life you were born in to and was taught to believe is right. The world leaders truly believes that they are doing everything as right as possible for the population, given the circumstances.

The circumstances are that the life you are born in to is a life with the three factors of the Original Sin dominating your world of thoughts from birth to death. If you read more in this book, you will learn that the ongoing crime against mankind, that you and the whole world is inheriting and passing on to coming generations, is fully explained as wrong. If you separate everything that is evil and wrong from everything that is good and right, you will find the full history about the lost Motherland.

Moses is the history about the lost Motherland and God speaking from the spirit world is the superior Motherland council. You know that the biblical Israelites time and time again broke the laws and rules given by the superior Motherland council and made their own.

One of the stories is the camouflaged story about Jacob, who was given the name Israel, and his twelve sons. They are a symbol for the twelve tribes that emigrated from the Motherland and populated the whole world. The biblical Israelites are a true symbol for the whole world population at present time.

The symbolism is strong, showing that the whole world population willingly went to settle in old Egypt in order to survive a long lasting famine. After some four hundred years they had become working slaves, soldiers and servants for the ruling regime of Pharaoh. This is the inheritance the whole world population have lived with up through the whole known world history. The prove is unquestionable: You and the whole world population is still working slaves, soldiers and servants under the control of the national set of dictating laws and rules for living.

The Spirit World is the common world of thoughts.

The definition of God and all the other Gods in the world is now defined to be the deceased superior Motherland council. The twelve democratically elected council members used to be a physical and real power in the time before the Motherland went under in a natural catastrophe. They were regular human beings, but their titles were everlasting, remembered by the twelve signs of the Zodiac with the sun and the moon in the centre. They were the government for the whole world population.

The cosmic Zodiac has existed always as star signs and with them as a model the Diagram Star was made to be the first book used in common education. All humans remembered the whole world history since the beginning of time and the future for mankind was clear. People lived with the deep and profound safety and happiness that knowing the past and the future gives. Everything humans by nature needed to know was in the Spirit World, in the common world of thoughts, accessible for everyone because of the common education.

By being remembered by the whole world population, the superior Motherland council and the many who died with them in the catastrophe, is in the common world of thoughts, namely in the Spirit World. Heaven is a religious camouflage over the Spirit World. By activating dormant brain cells or even build new ones, the whole world population can ones again be living their lives connected to the Spirit World and find the knowledge how to build a new world with lasting peace.

The only way to restore lasting peace on earth is to build a new Motherland and elect a new superior Motherland council. By use of only peaceful means the global system of government with one set of laws and rules for the whole world population have to be made known to the whole world population. The world leaders of present time need a common superior leadership to secure lasting peace. The Old Testament is all about the lost Motherland. The New Testament is all about how to build a new world with lasting peace.

Jesus Christ is the born again Motherland history, speaking about the global kingdom the world leaders for so long have denied ever existed. Do you begin to understand the magnitude of the history the religion is a camouflage over? The political and religious leaders in the world need the camouflage of religion in order to stay in power. The power of many world leaders fighting to be the greatest, the richest and the military strongest nation in the world will always be wrong. The world really needs a new democratically elected superior Motherland council.

Jesus Christ as the born again Motherland history is the spiritual force who is selecting his twelve apostles from a multitude of disciples. Under the camouflage of religion the twelve apostles are symbolizing the new superior Motherland council that never came to be. Now you and the whole world population have to restore the lost world history and build a new world with lasting peace. The only help you will get is knowledge about the history about the lost Motherland.

The three women named Mary in the life of Jesus is a symbol for the lost Motherland. The large continent was divided in three kingdoms.

Virgin Mary is a symbol for the Motherland that was destroyed in the natural catastrophe. The Motherland and its history were remembered by all the colonies, kingdoms and empires all over the world as a spiritual heaven. The superior Motherland council died in the catastrophe and became powerless as spiritual beings. The forces of evil entered the world and took control.

Mary Magdalene is a symbol for the new Motherland that never came to be built some two thousand years ago. The temple ruin in Jerusalem, not a stone upon a stone, is a theatrical symbol for the state the world has been in for the last some twelve thousand years. Mary Magdalene is a symbol for the misused planet earth you all live on. Like her, you don't recognize Jesus now, meaning that you don't recognize the born again Motherland history even when it is explained to you. The three factors of the Original Sin is still controlling every minute of your lifetime on planet earth.

Carpenter Jacob is a symbol for the knowledge the whole world population needs in order to be able to build a new world with lasting peace.

The Cross is a symbol derived from the Diagram Star, the official emblem of the lost Motherland. By crucifying Jesus the born again Motherland history became symbolical nailed to the official emblem of the superior Motherland council. This is a good example of how terrible wrong the Hieroglyphs were translated in to the Hebrew language.

The camouflaged story about Jesus was written by a Master who knew the full Motherland history and used the badly translated stories for a reason. As long as all the religions continue to live on planet earth as a part of everyone's thoughts, the history about the lost Motherland will be there for humans to discover and recover. If it isn't done now, it might be too late to save the parts of the modern world that humans need to be able to build a new world with lasting peace.

Heaven and Hell

Heaven and Hell is easy to explain. The whole world used to be completely without the many national states, without the global system of capitalism and without all the religions. All humans lived in self supported villages and had education as their main activity. The whole world was truly a paradise, and the Motherland was the cultivated Garden of Eden.

Heaven is the lost Motherland in the memory of all humans. When a large and fully cultivated continent disappears in a natural catastrophe, the whole world population is remembering it as a spiritual Heaven. The deceased superior Motherland council is remembered as the many Gods in the world.

Hell on earth started in the time after the Motherland was destroyed. Without the superior leadership of the Motherland council the chaos of wars and conflicts started, and never stopped.

Life on earth is a living Hell for a majority of the world population and has been for some twelve thousand years. All it takes to restore paradise on earth is to remove the three factors of the Original Sin from the common world of thoughts. Remember to do it with only peaceful means, using only the knowledge about the lost Motherland as derived from the Diagram Star.

The tree factors of the Original Sin are the enemy world of thoughts that the whole world population is fighting against. The Hebrew word for enemy is the Devil, and according to the known history the Devil has been in charge of human thinking for the last twelve thousand years.

Adam and Eve, in the Hebrew language, mean the whole world population. They left a paradise world, and the new world that is described in the Bible, under the camouflage of religion, is the paradise that can be built for our children and their descendants.

The Diagram Star

This is the Diagram Star. It is found chiseled on a stone tablet dated to be more than thirty-five thousand years old. The Diagram Star is however much, much older. The star shaped diagram is the first book known to mankind and has, as confirmed in the Bible, been with humans on earth from before the beginning of time and will be with humans until after the end of time.

The Diagram Star has always been known as the Zodiac, with the sun and the moon in the centre and the twelve star signs in the sections around. The many stories connected to the star signs were about the qualities and deeds of the twelve members of the superior Motherland council. They were the government leading the world. All the councils, Masters and other leaders all over the world had to answer to them.

When the Zodiac is drawn on a paper or chiseled in to a stone tablet it becomes the Diagram Star, and it is a mental bridge going back to the time when all humans knew the whole world history and why they lived on planet earth. With the Diagram Star as a common source of knowledge and book of law, the whole world population lived with lasting peace.

As a consequence of the natural catastrophe that destroyed the Motherland the three factors of the Original Sin started. It all developed in to the many severely different public opinions that at present time is about to destroy the world. The three factors of the Original Sin are by definition all the national states, the global capitalistic system and all the religions in the world. It is only knowledge from the Diagram Star that can remove the Original Sin from the common world of thoughts and create lasting peace in the whole world.

It is the Diagram Star itself, chiseled in two stone tablets that are the symbolical content of the Ark of the Covenant described in the Bible. The Ark of the Covenant is a fictitious camouflage over important world history that is hidden in the Bible. The gold that covers the Ark of the Covenant both on the outside and inside, the two angels and other decorations, symbolizes the camouflage of religion that is covering all the stories in the Bible. Under the camouflage of gold and glitter the Ark of the Covenant is protecting, preserving and passing on the knowledge of the Diagram Star to coming generations.

The Bible is the Ark of the Covenant. It is not in enemy hands; it is only covered by wrong thoughts and believes. All you have to do in order to take the lid of is to remove the camouflage of religion from your thoughts. You truly need to activate dormant brain cells and perhaps grow new ones in order to understand it all. You, together with the whole world population, will find the Diagram Star and the natural laws and rules of the Motherland in the Bible.

Read also about the temple that Salomon built in Jerusalem. Cedrus wood and gold covered the temple both outside and inside. Artists and craftsmen created a magnificent building. The priests came with the Ark of the Covenant and placed it in a special room inside the temple. The story describes clearly how the full history of the lost Motherland is preserved and passed on to new generations, camouflaged inside a holy glorified religion. It had to be done, and by looking at the world around you, you understand why.

The description of the Ark of the Covenant and the temple in Jerusalem is a valid description of the religion Christianity and all other religions in the world. They all cover up very important historical knowledge. If all the gold and glitter are removed, there is nothing left to hold up the many religions that so many humans live with as a part of their life. Like the city walls of Jericho, the belief in the religious camouflage will crumble and fall.

The laws and rules for living used before the Motherland was destroyed, called the Commandments, are in our present time placed inside the religions of the world. They are modified by the laws and rules of the national states and are completely overruled by the three factors of the Original Sin.

The Zodiac

The Zodiac is the model for the Diagram Star. Place the sun and the moon in the centre and the twelve cosmic signs in the sections around. Then you will learn all about the world history and the thoughts of the superior Motherland council, and you will be on the way towards a profound knowledge that explains the origin of all the religions, tales, myths and legends in the world.

It is from all the seven sciences of the past that the Masters of old got their formula for writing the many camouflaged stories that became the Bible and the foundation for all the religions in the world. Place the twelve star signs in the sections of the Diagram Star and place the sun in the centre. In groups of three the star signs are connected to <u>the four elements</u> that are <u>fire</u> (ram, lion, the archer) <u>earth</u> (bull, virgin, Capricorn), <u>air</u> (twin, weight, Aquarius), <u>water</u> (cancer, scorpion and fish).

In order to be able to read the Diagram Star like an open book, you need to know the formula or code that was made by the Masters of the past. The diagram made with the Zodiac as model is found camouflaged many places where you live today, and in the Bible.

One is Jacob and his twelve sons in the Old Testament. Another is Jesus and his twelve disciples. Also the Bethlehem Star is a camouflaged Diagram Star and the three wise men are symbolizing the three kingdoms of the lost Motherland. As wise men they are symbols for the group of Masters who had as mission in their life to preserve and pass on the history of the Motherland to the generations to come. Some two thousand years ago the Motherland history was born again, camouflaged as Baby Jesus.

Outside the Bible there are copies of the Diagram Star all over the world and the most distinct one is Stonehenge in England. Stone circles all over the world are copies of the Diagram Star, with the mission of preserving and passing on history to coming generations. All Stone circles are ambiguous and was used to remember the history of the local tribes, their heroes, chiefs and population. Back then the Diagram Star was known and remembered as the Zodiac and celebrated with ceremonies a number of times every year.

The Masters of the past is to be praised, as they managed to hide all their knowledge so masterly in all the camouflaged stories in the Bible.

Many of the people of the past are known to have made a copy of the Diagram Star with the sun as model. The Maya people of Yucatan, Naga-Maya people of India, the Babylonians,

Assyrians, Egyptians and the Pueblo Indians in the south-west of North-America are the best known.

In the time after the Motherland was destroyed in a natural catastrophe, almost all peoples started filling the Diagram Star with signs and invented dogmas about how it happened. This was not the right thing to do, because the signs and drawings, the legends and myths and the assumptions and dogmas covered the Diagram Star and made it impossible to understand for the generations to come.

The Diagram Star is the carrier of the whole world history. The Masters who wrote the many camouflaged stories of the Bible kept the diagram clean and chiseled it in to stone tablets to make sure it would be found and understood at a later time. But out among the warrior kings and priesthoods the Diagram Star was filled with signs and symbols they used to control the population. The greedy and merciless Egyptian priesthoods was among the first, and when other tribal leaders learned about the effect the dogmas and assumptions had on humans that had lived for many generation without a formal education, they started doing the same.

In our present time all the religions and sects in the world are a good proof for how wrong life for all humans can be when an elite of warrior kings and religious leaders forces the population to believe in a long line of meaningless dogmas and assumptions. People are allowed to believe or not believe, while removing religion all together is somehow unthinkable. Now you know it can be done. Religion is an important part of the three factors of the Original Sin and they have to be removed from the common world of thoughts.

The colony on the Nile delta was founded some 16 thousand years ago, and it was an obedient kingdom all the time up until the Motherland was destroyed. The Motherland was warned about the coming destruction by volcanic activity and severe earthquakes, and the superior Motherland council decided to move and build a new Motherland in old Egypt on the Nile delta. For a long time, perhaps 400 years, the kings in Egypt were obedient to the laws and rules of the Motherland, but at one point in history the Pharaoh of Egypt started exploiting the population, stealing all their riches and forcing them in to a life as working slaves, soldiers and servants.

The Masters, the protectors of the history of the lost Motherland, used Egypt and the land called the Middle East as a background when they wrote the camouflaged stories that became the Bible. The story about Jacob and his twelve sons is clearly symbolic and describes how the whole world was populated from the Motherland. Jacob was given the name Israel by the Master writing the story, and the Israelites in the Bible are symbolizing the whole world population living in present time.

The lost Motherland

The geographical position of the Motherland was in the Pacific Ocean, and among the many islands Easter Island was a part of the large continent that went under in an inferno of burning gasses and boiling water. The catastrophe itself lasted less than one day and a night, but it marks the beginning of a new era with the three factors of the Original Sin. Under the camouflage of religion it marks the beginning of a crime against mankind that still goes on. Life turned suddenly from living in a peaceful Garden of Eden to a living Hell.

No you all know that the Diagram Star is to be studied as it originated from the Motherland before the catastrophe. The study will take your back in time some twelve thousand years and you will see what was right and what is wrong in the world. In order to be able to remove the three factors of the Original Sin from your world of thoughts, begin to read the following explanation of all the camouflaged stories in the Bible. It is vital for a quick revival of dormant brain cells that you are able to understand that everything humans have thought since the beginning of time is embedded in the spiritual signs of the Zodiac, known as the great spirit of the world, which is the common world of thoughts. The twelve star signs are taken down from the night sky and their history is made available for the whole world population in the Diagram Star.

The Old Testament

God creates everything

Moses 1, 1-19

Long, long ago there was nothing but darkness. It is difficult to imagine how it was with only darkness and nothing else, except God.

Then God created light. Then it became day and night instead of only darkness. Thereafter God created the earth and divided it in to oceans, seas and large land areas. God created plants and trees and they grew up everywhere.

God also created the stars and planets. The sun should shine in the day and the moon at night.

The creation of the whole universe, the solar system and planet Earth with all earth life, as it is explained in the Bible, is a result of wrong translation of the Egyptian hieroglyphs. Under the camouflage of religion is the true story about how everything in the universe and on earth came to be as a force of the nature.

Everything that humans know as the common thoughts of mankind was created by the forces of the universe, commonly known as Mother Nature. The creation of the universe and of the earth and all earth life is outside the human field of understanding, for the time being. By looking at the Diagram Star you will see how everything came to be. The knowledge mankind needs in order to understand it all is hidden under the camouflage of religion. Right now saving planet earth from total destruction is more important than knowing how it all came to be.

The Bible is the Ark of the Covenant and the lid that hereby is removed is all the religions in the world. Religion is defined as believing in dogmas and assumptions based on not knowing. When the religion is removed knowledge becomes visible for everyone to see.

This explanation of the Old Testament is taking you back in time some twelve thousand years, and tells you the whole history of the Motherland that were destroyed in a natural catastrophe. You are told how the forces of evil came to be as dominant as they are in our present time. The New Testament about Jesus and his apostles is telling you and the whole world population how to build a new Motherland and how to elect a new superior Motherland council.

You need to know the lost world history in order to be able to know what is right and wrong in the world you live in and what needs to be done in order to create lasting peace for our children and their descendants.

The God of all creation is defined as the powerful force of Mother Nature. The nature of life is the earth's atmosphere and it is the force of movement in all earth life. The force of Mother Nature is the aura of life around your body and in your body; call it your soul or your spirit of life if you like.

The strong force of Mother Nature's laws and rules for living was made known to all humans by the common and natural knowledge derived from the twelve star signs of the Zodiac. Everything about the Zodiac is thoughts decided to be natural right by all humans. The thoughts are for all times embedded in the Diagram Star, which is the official emblem of the superior Motherland council.

The words spoken by God in the Bible are all the thoughts imbedded in to the Diagram Star, spoken by the superior Motherland council. Everything that is natural right in the Bible is the common laws and living rules of the Motherland, while everything considered wrong and evil came to be after the Motherland went under, and is the three factors of the Original Sin.

For the last twelve thousand years humans have lived in the darkness of oblivion that comes from the lack of common knowledge of the past. Everything that is wrong in the world is enforced on the population by greedy and despotic warrior kings and priesthoods with the use of warfare and brutal force.

The important role of the Diagram Star as a guide for lasting peace got lost in the chaos of wars and conflicts that started after the Motherland was destroyed in a natural catastrophe. All it takes to remove the darkness of oblivion is to bring the strong light from the Diagram Star back in to the common world of thoughts. The bright light of knowledge is hidden in the camouflaged stories in the Bible.

Everything was looking good

Moses 1, 20-26; 2, 3-6

When God did see all the water on earth, he created big and small fishes. Some was so small that it was impossible to see them. In the air he created big and small birds in all colures. It was light blue, brown, black and white.

When God looked out over the planet earth, the fruit was plentiful in the trees and the wind sighted through the grass. He knew that this was a good place for animals. He created small bees and large elephants, crocodiles, sheep's and lions, all kind of animals.

But they did not have names yet. All the animals found their places to live in the nature, and there was not too many of them either. They all had enough food and water.

God as a creator of all earth life is defined to be Mother Nature. In the time before the Motherland went under the whole world population lived together on the planet with lasting peace. The true definition of God is the twelve members of the superior Motherland council. The council enforced the laws and rules for living given by the nature and the whole world population lived with long lasting peace.

God as described in the Bible is a camouflage for the superior Motherland council, and the enormous amount of knowledge they made available for the whole world population. They did not create the universe and everything in it, but they knew how it happened. Through common education absolutely everybody knew how to live right. If one person did wrong, the whole village knew and he or she lost pride, trust and happiness for the rest of their life.

The beginning of all earth life on planet earth started like this, that at one time a long time ago, in the time after the young planet earth had become green and fertile, it was fertilized by one or several cosmic eggs that came from the open and still unknown universe.

Cosmic eggs like that are in present time called spaceships, and if the development continues as it should, many cosmic eggs will be built by humans and sent off in to the unknown universe. The cosmic eggs will be loaded with all existing earth life in one form or another, and when it at the end of the journey land on a distant planet, the atmospheric qualities on the new planet will decide if the cosmic egg will hatch or die.

Like this it is possible to see the whole lifespan of the planet we live on, from before the beginning of time and until after the end of time. The meaning of all earth life is natural cell division. Planet Earth is a living unit and normally a living planet will fertilize many new planets before its lifespan comes to an end.

The meaning of life and the nature's task for humans on planet earth is to use their knowledge and the physical abilities of the body to build cosmic eggs. Therefore the whole world population has to be organized from a new Motherland and learn to do the work together.

Everything was really looking good on the whole planet and the natural evolution were developing as it was meant to be. Many things were different from the world of today and both technological and mentally the humans were more advanced than we can imagine.

Then the Motherland itself was destroyed in an inferno of burning gasses and boiling water. It happened some twelve thousand years ago. A whole continent collapsed and disappeared in to the ocean in just a short time. The continent was built on many very large gas pockets that broke, due to an increase in the oceans water level, severe volcanic activity and movement of the crust of the earth.

All communication between the many colonies and civilizations in the world came to an end. Many tribal people are still waiting for the traditional yearly visit from the Motherland, and keep the memory alive with yearly festivities, like in songs, dances and other ceremonial activities.

Also the symbols and emblems of the Motherland lives on, and the most important and commonly used in education was the Diagram Star. The diagram derived from the twelve Zodiac signs was remembered by every single human on planet earth.

All the crosses in the world are a copy of the Diagram Star. The cross Jesus was nailed to was a religious camouflage over the official emblem of the Motherland. Jesus is the born again history of the Motherland and the cross is the Motherland emblem. When the camouflage of religion is removed Jesus and the cross is the key to the world history that has been lost for some twelve thousand years.

The first man and woman

Moses 1, 26-31; 2, 1-7, 18-23

At this time there were no humans on earth. God wanted to create someone like himself. Then he grabbed a handful of dust, blows on it and created the first man.

God was leading all kind of animals to Adam. "You can call them what you want," said God. One creature Adam called hippo, another butterfly. When Adam was finished naming all the animals, God saw that none of them could be Adams special helper.

While Adam was sleeping God took a rib from him and from it he created a human that was like him, but still different. She became the first woman. When Adam woke, he became very happy. "Now I have one that can be my friend," he said. But she had no name.

After God had created Adam and the woman, he was pleased. He decided to rest one day. Everything that he had created, he blessed.

Adam and Eve is, under the camouflage of religion, a symbol for the whole world population. Now think of God as Mother Nature. It is the strict laws and rules of Mother Nature the superior Motherland council was elected to enforce on to the whole world population. All earth life, included the human beings, had to fit in to the conditions of the earth's nature, in order to survive as a life form.

Planet earth is a living organism and humans are only one life form of many. You know that the humans are the only living creature on earth with the ability to build starships that can travel through the universe. The building of cosmic eggs in order to populate the universe is the meaning of life.

The knowledge destroyed during the time that have passed since the Motherland went under, is immense. When you are told that planet earth is one of many planets that have been populated, it is simply beyond your imagination.

If the earth population should be unable to populate a new earth planet before this planet dies of old age, the reason is that the three factors of the Original Sin have destroyed the knowledge that should be in the common world of thoughts, in the Spirit World. You and the whole world population have been living with the three factors of the Original Sin for some twelve thousand years, and it is because of this that your dormant brain cells have to be activated.

Do you begin to understand that you and the whole world population truly are living with your thoughts outside the natural order of Mother Nature? You are destroying planet earth with human activity that wasn't meant to be. You were created as a being able to survive and develop according to the laws and rules of the nature on planet earth. The way you and the whole world population are living now and have been living for the last some twelve thousand years, is totally against the laws and living rules of Mother Nature.

In the time before the Motherland was destroyed, education was the main activity for all humans, and they lived with lasting peace in a world that truly was a paradise for everyone.

The Motherland was destroyed and sank into the ocean making many enormous flood waves. After the catastrophe the three factors of the Original Sin started. You and the whole world population are living your daily life with the inheritance that really is an ongoing crime against mankind. The merciless building of national states by use of warfare and brutal force started back then, and just never stopped.

The humans living on planet earth some twelve thousand years ago were forced to leave their peaceful paradise were everything was good and begin living in a world where the force of evil took control over all humans.

The right of the strongest grew forth, and the laws and rules of the lost Motherland were overruled by the laws and rules that were made by self elected warrior kings and priesthoods. Humans had to learn to do as told by their rulers, or die. The three factors of the Original sin became mental walls between religious belief and common knowledge. Like cancer the forces of evil grew strong all over the world and the forces of good that had ruled before the Motherland went under, had to fight against ruthless and greedy warrior kings and priesthoods and their armed forces. The forces of evil did win and have ruled the earth ever since.

In the beginning the strongest tribal people built their own armies of warriors, first in order to defend them self against ruthless enemies who wanted to steal their land and force the population in to a life as an obedient working slaves, soldiers and servants. In order to be able to pay for the building of defense, the tribal leaders had to steal riches in form of gold and precious tings. This they did by taking their army of soldiers on regular crusades against the enemy tribes where they killed and robbed.

Brothers were killing brothers, because they no longer had the superior Motherland council to control them. The self elected warrior kings got greedy because of what they could do with a strong army of soldiers. Already back then the soldiers had to fight for his king, or be killed as a traitor and a coward.

In the course of a few hundred years planet earth turned from being a paradise in to the earthly living Hell that the world has been for the last some twelve thousand years.

The Garden of Eden

Moses 2, 8-17, 17, 24-25

God choose the most beautiful place on earth for Adam and Eve to live on. It was a garden called Eden. In Eden all the animals lived in peace with each other. No one was afraid. Adam and the woman were very fond of God. They had no cloth on, wandering around in the garden. They had no reason to be ashamed. For them there were something else that were more precious than all the beautiful flowers, the tall trees and the lovely scents in Eden.

It was the certainty that God loved them. God said to Adam and the woman that they could do what they wanted. There was only one commandment for them to follow. God said: "You can eat fruit of all the trees in the garden, except for one. It is the tree with the knowledge of good and evil." The two humans understood what he meant.

Knowledge about the difference between good and evil in our present time is deduced from the three factors of the Original Sin alone. Everything humans of present time know as evil was really forbidden and almost an unthinkable knowledge in the time before the Motherland was destroyed. The whole world population lived with the forces of natural good in a paradise garden of Eden, totally without knowledge of evil.

The whole world population lived without national state borders and without the many national armed forces. They lived without the global system of capitalism that is a strong wall of money between the rich and the poor. And people lived totally without the many religions in the world. They were not captives of a dictating nation, but members of a tribal people.

The whole world population lived in self supported villages with lasting peace under a common set of laws and rules for living. They lived with the same knowledge and spoke the same language.

Just imagine the world without the constant fight between good and evil. And imagine a world with only love and without the opposite hate. Without all the other opposites that came to be with the imposing of the Original Sin, people all over the world lived without hope for a better life, because life was as good as good can be.

The three factors of the Original Sin is the whole motivation for the fight between good and evil. In a world without the three factors the concept of good would find back to the original meaning and planet earth would ones again be a paradise for all mankind.

The lost Motherland really was the most beautiful place on earth. The people who lived there had survived the last large ice-age. The difference between the people whom lived in the Motherland and the many aborigines, who had survived elsewhere in the world, was the education and the use of a fully developed technology. The technology and the common high degree of knowledge gave the people in the Motherland an advanced ability, and the aborigines looked up to them as leaders and wanted to be like them.

After the large ice-age whole tribes started migrating from the Motherland to places all over the world. They continued to emigrate and immigrate and everyone lived organized and peacefully together all the time until the Motherland was destroyed some twelve thousand years ago.

It was the superior Motherland council that supervised everything that happened in the world, and their major tool for keeping the peace was the consistent use of the Diagram Star in common education. Because of their long history it was the superior Motherland council that was remembered as gods after the Motherland was destroyed. The council members were ordinary humans that lived and died, while it was their title that lived on all through the long and peaceful history. Their history was forever imbedded and updated in the Diagram Star.

When the Motherland was destroyed, the large continent was remembered by the whole world population as a spiritual Heaven on the night sky. The twelve council members were remembered as gods in the spirit world. It was not ever a religion, but memorized knowledge about a time that had been the best of the best for all humans.

Religion developed as a camouflage over the knowledge about the Motherland and its history. While the warrior kings and priesthoods did their best to erase the knowledge about the global system of government that would take away their luxury life as elite, a group of Masters started preserving and passing on the whole history of the Motherland, camouflaged in the stories that later became the Bible and the foundation for all the large religions in the world.

The Motherland is the Garden of Eden, and before it went under, during the long and peaceful history, the continent was cultivated in to a fertile and beautiful garden landscape. The number of people living there was strictly controlled and kept on a level that made living well for everyone.

The history tells that 64 million people lived on the continent in the time it was destroyed. The continent was divided in three kingdoms by natural water channels. It was destroyed in a catastrophe that lasted one day and one night.

Not long after the catastrophe the three factors of the Original Sin were imposed on people and the chaos of wars and conflicts started and never stopped.

It is common knowledge that the ongoing crime against mankind is killing thousands of humans every single day. The horrible truth is that thousands of humans have died for the same wrong reason, every day for many thousand years. You can help stop the madness and begin build a peaceful world for our children and their descendants. The only possible way to do it is to build a new Motherland and elect a new superior Motherland council with the use of only peaceful means.

The lost Motherland had a complete net of paved roads. The roads looked like a spider's web from above and the stones were laid so tight that not even grass could grow between them. The roads that the Romans built many places in Europe, and still exist were built with knowledge from the Motherland.

The Motherland and the civilizations around the world had flying vessels were they were needed. They were used mainly to transport selected students to and from the regions centers for higher education and to bring aid to people in need after a natural catastrophe.

There were seven centers for higher education on the continent of the Motherland. The best students came from all over the world to be educated as Masters of all the seven sciences. Some of them were elected to be council members in the Motherland, while most of them returned home to be teachers, philosophers, and doctors and placed in other leading positions.

The people lived with knowledge of the spirit world and they held the force of Mother Nature as the highest form for being. The superior Motherland council gave them the laws and rules to live by. It was by living the way the nature intended that gave humans everything they needed to live their lives with lasting peace in a safe environment. They lived pact with nature and held common education as their main activity. Mother Nature is grand and includes the whole universe, everything that is visible and invisible for the human eye. Have a look at the Diagram Star, and you will see that it foremost is a diagram explaining the Zodiac and cosmos.

The most important book in a world without written language and textbooks was and still is the Diagram Star. From it the students could learn everything they wanted and remember is as long as they lived. This means that the whole world population lived with a fully developed knowledge in the time before the Motherland went under. Knowledge has a cycle similar to water. It is always a part of earth life, and all humans have to do is to learn everything their personal spirit is capable of. The knowledge was common for the whole world population.

Like this it shall be again, soon, all over the world. You have to remove the enforced religious belief from your world of thoughts and replace them with knowledge from the Diagram Star. The serpent in the tree is a symbol for the three factors of the Original Sin, which you all are living with as an important and demanding part of your everyday life. Stop listening to the words of the serpent and start listening to your own inner voice and do what you think is right. With your inner eye you can see what's natural right and what's unnatural wrong in the world.

It is only with knowledge from the Diagram Star, and only with peaceful means, a world with lasting peace can be built. The world population of today is living like blinded by religion, either they are religious or not religious. You are all living your lives on planet earth like you are living dead. Right now is a good time to wake up and do the right thing.

The future of all mankind is in danger of been dramatically changed for the worst if you do nothing at all, but there is still time to build the world in too a true paradise for our children and their descendants.

The serpent in the Garden

Moses 3, 1.19

There was one animal in the Garden of Eden that were smarter than all others. It was the serpent. One day it came to the woman and started tempting her. "You don't have to listen to everything God is saying," it said. "You can just go ahead and eat from the tree in the centre of the garden. You will not die. If you do your eyes will be opened and you will know the good from evil."

The woman walked to the tree. At first she did not know what to do. But then she decided. She took a fruit and took a bite from it. Then she went to Adam and asked him to taste him to. Just after they had eaten of the fruit, there came like a dark cloud on the sky. Suddenly it felt cold in the garden. For the first time they were afraid.

They had done something wrong. God was distressed because he had to punish them. They were his children and he loved them dearly. He wanted Adam and the woman to know that they made the choice them self. Some choices would lead to the good and some to something that were evil.

When reading the many camouflaged stories in the Bible you can easily separate the good from evil. The building of kingdoms in the world with the use of warfare and brutal force was wrong and evil from the beginning, and still is. It was the warrior kings who forced the population in to a life as working slaves, soldiers and servants. The priesthoods made up the dogmas and assumptions and told the population what would happen to them if they spoke against their leaders.

Now imagine a world were only the good forces is ruling the common world of thoughts; a world where people didn't know about the forces of evil. They lived in small tribal communities were everyone knew each other. If one person did something wrong, the deed would follow him his whole life. To live a life without the honor and respect of his own tribe was the worst thing that could happen to a human.

If all humans on earth lived according to the laws and rules given by the superior Motherland council, as taught from the Diagram Star, nothing evil could happen, at least not in an unnatural large scale.

The tree of knowledge is a symbol for the Diagram Star and is the holder of all knowledge present on planet earth. The fruit is just a fruit. The serpent is the force of evil entering the world, and eating the fruit is a symbol for the first violation of the law, the first simple deed of following the temptation and doing wrong against the laws and ruled given by the superior Motherland council. The act was the birth of evil in the world.

After the Motherland was gone and the superior Motherland council had died several hundred years went by before the humans discovered that they would not be punished for doing wrong and evil deeds. Both the Motherland and the superior Motherland council had become spiritual and existed only in the thoughts of all humans. They lived on in the memory of the whole world population, but they had no physical power to stop evil from entering the common world of thoughts.

In the time after the Motherland went under, the superior leadership of the council and all communication and common education stopped, and the tribal peoples had to make it on their own. For some time they continued to live in peace with each other, perhaps a generation or more. Then someone started using warfare and brutal force to take control of the most fertile land for their own use and soon after humans everywhere started killing each other because of the greed and the lust for personal power and riches. The strongest tribal leaders started making borders around their land and implemented their own laws and rules for living. The three factors of the Original Sin had started.

With the Original Sin the common education for the whole world population came to an end. Teaching with the Diagram Star became forbidden by the warrior kings and the priesthoods and the knowledge about the lost Motherland was gradually forgotten in the chaos of wars and conflicts that you know so well.

The first stories in the Bible are important and it is better to tell you too much than too little. Many of you will understand faster than others, but everyone will understand the importance of doing the right thing from now on. If you do nothing you will be sitting in front of your TV-set and watch the destruction of the world continues until the end.

The story about the woman that is tempted to eat the forbidden fruit from the tree of knowledge is a good example for the fact that under given circumstances humans can feel tempted to do short sighted good deeds that in the long run is bad for the whole world population.

The thing that happened after the Motherland was destroyed was that some humans with the right personal abilities started using the misfortune of all other humans to their own benefit. The plows, pickaxes and other tools for agriculture was melted in to weapons of war, and the first wars and conflicts between tribal people started, and never stopped.

Cain and Abel are symbols for the fighting that broke out between tribal people, as a consequence of the lack of a superior leadership from the Motherland and the new knowledge about good and evil.

From the time the three factors of the Original Sin started, humans have broken the laws and living rules of the Motherland, first by attacking neighboring tribes, stealing their land and everything they owned. Those who fought against the new rulers were killed and all others had to submit and start a life as working slaves, soldiers and servants.

It was the natural way of life in an earthly paradise world that was destroyed. The whole world developed in to a living hell for all humans. Warrior kings and priesthoods created the many national states by use of armed forces, and the tribal people living inside the borders had to be obedient to the rulers in charge if they wanted to live. Those who could leave left in order to find new land to live on, but found nowhere they could live as they wanted to.

The rulers invented a rewarding system that gave all those who submitted to them good land and protection. In return people had to pay taxes that were meant to keep them poor and depending on having to work hard in order to survive. Like this the mental wall between the rich and the poor was made and it still exists.

Just like today the population of a national state was educated to serve their ruler. After a few generations with wars and conflicts the feeling of national belonging grew fort as a pride over being fighting on the side of a strong warrior king. The tribes were divided and the feeling of tribal belonging was shifted to belonging only to a smaller family, easier for the rulers to control. They were forced to admire their king's ability as a national leader and his life in luxury and to respect and honor the holiness of the priesthoods and the religion. They were forced to live and obey the laws and living rules of the nation.

The opposition against the new system of government was strong in the beginning, and a group of Masters founded an underground resistance that had as a life mission to preserve and pass on the knowledge about the history of the lost Motherland from generation to generation.

What humans of today has to do, is to recover the knowledge of and from the Diagram Star and implement the global government system with common laws and living rules for the whole world population. The Masters of the past did what they could and they did it well.

What will happen when the whole world population gets to know that their many religions are a simple camouflage over the world history from the time before the Motherland was destroyed?

Will you be brave enough obey the fact that a new world with lasting peace only can be built with peaceful means and with the participation of the whole world population?

Away from Eden

Moses 3, 20-24

God said to Adam and the woman that they had to leave the Garden of Eden. Or else, he said, they would be disobedient again and eat from another forbidden tree, the tree of life.

Adam and the woman looked at each other. They had each other, but still they were afraid for the future. After they left Eden they had to work hard to find enough food.

Adam gave the woman a name. He named her Eve, which meant "alive".

Adam and Eve bent their head. They were sad, even if they knew that God still would show them his love. The worst punishment was that they never came to be as near God as they had been before they were disobedient to him.

Because the Motherland was destroyed and the whole world population was facing a growing chaos of wars and conflicts, the life of humans that survived the catastrophe changed from a life in a global paradise and in to an infernal Hell. The lost Motherland became the spiritual Heaven and the dead superior Motherland council became the many spiritual Gods in the world. The strong and natural superior leadership was suddenly gone, and the whole world population had to make it on their own. The physical Devil on earth is not the descendants of the warrior kings and the priesthoods, but the three dominating factors of the Original Sin that they created.

The natural catastrophe destroyed the Motherland and it was the fight to survive without a superior leadership that changed the living conditions so dramatically for all humans. Humans experienced being afraid for each other for the first time, and the brutal force from the self appointed warrior kings and priesthoods took away all their safety and happiness.

The strong family ties and tribal belonging were brutally broken down, often by use of regular warfare and brutal separation of family members. View the world around you and see if things have improved through some twelve thousand years of history. Still all humans are born in to a mental national prison presented as the nation's despotic laws and rules for living. Everyone gets a name and a number and are raised and educated in to a lifetime of enforced labor for the nation. When the working ability comes to an end elderly people are for pure economical reasons separated from their family and placed in a home for old people. Many live there for many years before death comes as liberation.

A natural life for humans was not meant to be like this. Thousands of humans live to see their own family destroyed because they don't have the kind of tribal connection that creates natural safety and happiness.

Humans who doesn't submit and willingly give their life to work for the nation and for the common good, will automatically find themselves on the sideline of the community, without the possibility to live a normal life. The democracy derived from the three factors of the Original Sin, are plain and straight forward dictatorship over people without a will of their own. The reason for the lifelong submission and national obedient is that no one knows about the peaceful global government from before the Motherland went under.

In order for humans of present time to find back to their own tribe, or contribute in building new self supported tribal communities, it is necessary to remove the three factors of the Original Sin from the common thoughts of mankind. Read the definition of the Original Sin and remember it.

It is you, everyone that lives in present time, who is Adam and Eve. In order to be able to rebuild a Motherland and a world with lasting peace, you have to study the Diagram Star, and understand that the knowledge it gives to you will enable you to remove the three factors of the Original Sin from your world of thoughts. Without the force of evil present in the common world of thoughts, the force of good will restore lasting peace in the world.

You have to learn what went wrong back then, before you can start the work to do things right. Symbolical, before Eve eats from the fruit and learns about good and evil, the humans had no knowledge of evil, and natural good was alone ruling the world. If you have the power to break the circle of evil, the constant fight between good and evil will come to an end. You can do that by eating the fruit form the tree of life, and start living again. You will discover the reason for living and find back the true common laws and living given by the superior Motherland council.

For the same reason as a community of bees needs a queen bee in order to function right, the humans of present time needs a new Motherland and one set of laws and rules for living for the whole world population. Think thorough through what all humans truly needs in order to live a life with safety, belonging, happiness and love, in a world without the three factors of the Original Sin.

Cain and Abel

Moses 4, 1-2

Soon after Adam and Eve left the Garden of Eden, they had a child. It was a boy they called Cain. Later they had another boy. Him they called Abel.

Cain and Abel grew up outside Eden. They helped their parents, and they had to work hard to get enough to eat.

Cain helped his parents to till the land. He was glad when the rain came, to water the plants. The corn he harvested could be grinded to flour, and from it they baked bread. He harvested also vegetables and fruit.

Abel had sheep's and goats. He milked the goats, and from time to time he slaughtered one animal so they had meat.

This story first of all tells the humans in present time about how good and evil slowly came to be a strong factor controlling and destroying family life. And it is also a story about how tribal people from living together in peace started envy each other's land, riches and personal fame and fortune. Those who do right according to the laws and rules of the Diagram Star are prospering and do well in life. Those who do wrong will never be truly happy ever again in their lifetime, because wrong will follow wrong in the circle of evil.

This first part of the story about Cain and Adam is about how life could have developed with lasting peace, if all humans had continued to work hard together as brothers should. But the camouflaged story, written by the Masters of the past, tells the story about how the force evil developed in the time after the leadership of the superior Motherland council was gone.

You will find, through all the camouflaged stories in the Bible, that there always are one good man, doing only right in a world controlled by the forces of evil. Like present time the humans carrying the force of good is always second in command. They are the humans revealing the history and the laws and living rules of the lost Motherland. In the story about Cain and Abel, the brother who is doing right is brutally murdered. The brothers are symbols for the whole world population. The forces of evil have ruled over the forces of good ever since the Motherland was lost.

The situation in the world of today is that thousands of humans dies every single day after a lifelong battle just to provide food and housing for the family. It is like this because there are a strong visible mental wall between the rich and the poor countries and likewise between the rich and the poor people within the nation's borders. Only a few humans have the personal strength and ability to cross over the wall from being poor in to being rich. Many fail when trying, but the large majority of poor people and nations stay poor, always.

It is like this because all humans are denied the possibility to live like humans lived in the time before the Motherland was destroyed. They have to spend all their life fighting hard to fill the demands from the three factors of the Original Sin. The definition of the Original Sin is as you now should know a true crime against mankind.

The first murder

Moses 4, 3-16

One day Cain gathered some of his harvest and offered it in thanks to God. Abel did the same, but he choose the best and the fattest among his lambs.

God looked on the gifts that the two boys brought with them. God was pleased with Abel and his offering but with Cain he was not content. Cain was angry. He thought that God wasn't just. God said to him that he now had the choice to do the good or do the evil. Cain chooses the evil. He was angry at his brother.

Cain thought out a plan. One day he was alone with Abel in the field, he did something terrible wrong. He killed Abel.

God called to him: "Where is your brother Abel? Cain only shook his head.

"You have done wrong," said God. "The punishment shall be that you no longer are able to till the land. I will send you away to another place, far from here." Then Cain had to live in the land of Nod, which means "wandering."

Burnt sacrifice of all kind was an act of goodness in the time before the Motherland was destroyed some twelve thousand years ago. It was done in order to honor and remember the dead. The act was a vital part of their history. After the Motherland was destroyed in a catastrophe where millions of people died, people started making altars and burning sacrifice in order to remember the superior Motherland council. It was a sacred act to remember the lost Motherland. Every time you light a candle, you feel something real deep inside.

The offering of animals and telling stories about the lost Motherland made the event in to a ceremony that was repeated ones a year. Many places in the world the catastrophe was illustrated by the sound of drums and dancing around the fire.

As time went by it was the power of evil and greedy priesthoods who started forcing people to bring sacrifices to the temples. Those who refused were severely punished. Rich people had to pay redemption for their sins and the priesthoods got very rich and powerful. Stories were made up based on the wrong translation from Egyptian Hieroglyphs and hieratic characters, and the camouflage of religious belief came to be.

Under the camouflage of religion this story tells about some of the many opposites that came into being after the catastrophe. The long lasting world peace was broken by the first wars and conflicts. The forces of good were attacked by the forces of evil. Many tribal people went to war against their neighboring tribes in order to take their fertile land as their own property. Those who defended them self and their family were killed and the others were forced in to a life as slaves, soldiers and servants.

Everyone knew that this was wrong, very wrong, but without the almighty superior leadership from the superior Motherland council, the tribal leaders chose to do wrong. The reason was always the false pride of being a winner of battles, fame and fortune being a rich and successful warrior king gave them. With a group of self appointed priests they started making their own dogmas and assumptions about the lost Motherland and dictated the people living on the land to submit to the new local regime. The tribes started building large armies, mostly for defense at first, but the quest for new land, more slaves, more personal power and riches grew stronger, generation after generation.

This story tells the beginning of the chaos of wars and conflicts that still goes on in the world; the beginning of the Original Sin. It was and is a brutal crime against mankind, and was by nature never meant to be.

You all have to seek knowledge from the Diagram Star and break the circle of evil in the world. Life is truly a living hell for all humans and has been since the Motherland went under. You do live without the knowledge that comes from proper education and are therefore without guilt. If you can forgive yourself, you can also forgive all other humans.

A religious belief in what had happened with the lost Motherland and why, was enforced on the population. Cain is a symbol for the tribal people that based their way of life on the dogmas and assumptions made up by unscrupulous and often self elected priesthoods and warrior kings. Abel is a symbol for all good and right in the world. It was back then, not long after the Motherland went under, that Cain killed Abel. The story tells that the forces of evil took control over the whole world population.

If the Egyptian hieroglyph is translated correctly, it plainly tells the humans living in present time that they have done wrong ever since the Motherland was lost some twelve thousand years ago. You and the whole world population are descending from Cain, and you are still living in the symbolic land of Nod, wandering aimlessly in a mental desert without the knowledge about the lost Motherland. Only by recovering the knowledge about the lost Motherland the people living in the world will be able to build a new world with lasting peace.

Try comparing the whole planet Earth with a burning candle. After the Motherland was lost in the catastrophe, it was like the fire was gone out. Adam and Eve are symbolizing the whole world population. The son that replaced Abel, named Seth, had many other brothers and sisters and they are together a symbol for the whole world population in the time after the catastrophe. Most of them lived like before and respected the laws and living rules given by the superior Motherland council. Cain is a symbol for the forces of evil that spread all over the world. The self elected warrior kings and priesthoods started attacking peaceful villages, killing all resistant, stealing all the valuables and claiming the ownership to the land. The story tells us that the forces of good survived symbolized by Seth.

Planet earth is one complete body and all the people need only one superior Motherland council to make them live together as brothers and friends again.

What the Master writing this story wishes to tell to people living in present time, is that in a world with a new Motherland and a new superior Motherland council, the fight between good and evil will disappear for never again to return.

What people living in present time are fighting for is a good life for all humans, with enough of everything they need to live a good life on earth. Everyone wants to live in peace with safety, friendliness and happiness as well as enough food and housing for everyone in a world with ever lasting peace. But fighting for the right reason without knowing what the right reason is makes the fighting impossible and everlasting. By reading this you will know enough to leave the mental desert of oblivion, cross the river of knowledge about the lost Motherland and begin building a new world with lasting peace.

Noah and the Ark

Moses 6, 5-22

Many years went by. The population on earth had stopped thinking about God. They did not teach their children that they should say thanks to God. They lied, they hurt each other and they did wrong in all their doing.

God was very sad when he saw all the evil humans did to each other. He wished that he not had created humans together with the animals and decided that he would remove all earth life, everything that he had created.

In this period of time, when everyone was evil, there was a man who was different. His name was Noah. Noah had often prayed to God for help. He listened to everything God said, and did it. This God liked.

God said to Noah: "I have decided to destroy all earth life. I shall bring upon earth a great flood, and every living thing shall drown in it. But I will spare you and everyone you love. Build a large boat, and make it like I tell you. Of every living creature upon the earth you shall bring into the boat two of each sort and keep them alive. They shall be male and female. Then fill it with food. On it you will be safe."

Noah trusted God. He got the drawings for the boat, which he called the Ark.

The Bible tells that nine generations past by before the time of Noah. But the story is written for the humans living in present time. God is defined to be the superior Motherland council, now in the Spirit World. The Spirit World is the common world of thoughts and without formal education people had to begin living by the laws and rules imposed by the warrior kings and the priesthoods. People forgot more and more about the peaceful paradise world that had been. But they all had dreams about the lost Motherland and knew that their elite of leaders were wrong, terribly wrong.

This camouflaged story was written a very long time ago, but it is all about you and the whole world population living in present time. It is you who denies that the lost Motherland ever existed and has forgotten all about the superior Motherland council that used to rule the whole world with lasting peace. The three factors of the Original Sin have taken full control over your world of thoughts and the common world of thoughts.

This story is all about how the forces of evil thoughts can be completely removed from the common world of thoughts, from your world of thoughts. Noah and his family is a symbol for the forces of good thoughts in the whole world population. The Egyptian hieroglyph is clearly stating that this is about good and evil thoughts, and not about human beings. It is only knowledge about the lost Motherland that can restore lasting peace in the whole world. Lasting peace on earth is wholly based on good thoughts and therefore the common world of thoughts has to be thoroughly cleansed.

The formula for doing that is crystal clear in the camouflaged story about Noah and the Ark. Water, Earth, Air and Fire = Knowledge. The whole planet Earth is going to be flooded with knowledge. The knowledge that are hidden under the camouflage of religion, will first of all remove all the religions from the common world of thoughts. All the national states and their armed forces will be the next to go and then the destructive physical wall of money between the rich and the poor, as in the global system of capitalism, will be taken down. No one needs the three factors of the Original Sin to live a good life anywhere on the planet.

Humans living in present time have forgotten what God is under the camouflage of religion. God is the spiritual human beings of the superior Motherland council. The reason people forgot about the lost Motherland and the common leadership was the lack of common education. The knowledge was covered up by the many myths, legends and the dogmas and assumptions that were imposed on the population by warrior kings and priesthoods.

The parent could not tell their children about the lost Motherland that was destroyed in the natural catastrophe, because they did not know. The Masters who knew the whole story had to live in hiding for warrior kings and priesthoods. As an opposition to the elite they were often wrongly accused and killed, but they still managed to write the many camouflaged stories that later became the Bible.

Noah and his family symbolize the good thoughts left in the world while the evil thoughts are symbolized with the majority of the word population. The Master who wrote this story had the power of knowing that the common world of thoughts in the world was all good in the time before the Motherland went under. Everything people thought back then was right and good. The wrong and evil thoughts imposed by the despotic warrior kings and priesthoods are still dominating the common world of thoughts. The Master had to think out a valid camouflage for everything they knew, and write the stories so well that they became popular and were remembered by many.

This camouflaged story is all about cleansing the common world of thoughts, meaning your thoughts of and the thoughts of the whole world population, by flooding the whole world with knowledge about the lost Motherland. Not one human is going to die in the process. It is only the wrong and evil thoughts derived from the three factors of the Original Sin that will that will gone for good.

With the story about Noah and the Ark the Masters are speaking directly to you and the whole world population in present time, saying that the knowledge have survived for thousands of years under the camouflage of religion, in legends, tales and myths. Now time has come to flood the whole planet earth with knowledge and drown all the religions, myths and legends.

The world needs a new Motherland with a new superior Motherland council with representatives from all the people in the world. A global system of government with common laws and rules for living has to be implemented by use of only peaceful means.

The day an understanding of this finds its way back in to the common thoughts of people, the first step towards a world with lasting peace is taken. It will be a world were all humans live self supported communities and have a technology that makes communication and working together possible. Education will again become the most important activity in a world where everyone have all they need to live a good life.

Noah is a fictive person and the Ark is still on the drawing board. The Master who wrote the story is telling the whole world population that it is only the knowledge derived from the Diagram Star that can make humans able to build a world with lasting peace. The great flood is a mental fight between good and evil that will take place first in your own world of thoughts. It is a spiritual fight you have to win in order to liberate your mind from the long occupation of the Original Sin. To live when the planning of the building of a new world with lasting peace begins will be your reward.

The Great Flood

Moses 7, 1-16

When the Ark was finished, Noah and his family went inside. They left the door open. Soon animals, birds and all kind of insects started finding their way to Noah's Ark. It sure was a sight! There was so much noise that Noah's neighbors came to see what the strange man was doing. They shook their heads resigned.

It was lions that roared, donkeys that bragged, dogs that barked, birds singing and sheep's that bleated. Couple after couple went inside the Ark, all kind of animals in all sizes. Small worms wriggled, horses whinnied and hares hopped.

After all the animals were inside, God closed the door, so no one could get out. Then it started to rain. It rained and rained and rained.

This camouflaged history is a lot more than an unbelievable historical tale. It constitute the recipe on what a cosmic egg of the future, also called space ships, will have as cargo when they start of on a journey out in to the universe to populate a new planet with earth life. A planet is a living organic unit and has to be fertilized before earth life can multiply normally. But it is also a story about how this planet earth was populated a long, long time ago. In the time before the Motherland was destroyed all humans knew this, and more. It was their world history, and now it will be yours.

Look up at the sky and think about what you really see and what you know is right. You see the sun in the daytime and the moon and the stars at night. You know that the humans living in the past made the stars in to the twelve Zodiac signs. With their own hands they chiseled the Zodiac in to a stone tablet and called it the Diagram Star. Every village all over the world had a copy of the Diagram Star and qualified teachers to tell them the many aspects of the diagram and what they could achieve in life if they lived right thinking only good thoughts. The whole world really was a paradise in the time before the Motherland went under.

In the time after the Motherland was destroyed in the catastrophe, the event was remembered by everyone, and the Masters who wrote the story many years later, used the catastrophe itself as a camouflage in order for the story to be remembered for all future. But under the camouflage is the true story about what needs to be done in present time in order to restore the knowledge humans need in order to be able to build a new world.

The Masters, a small group of vise men, had as their life mission to preserve and pass on the history of the lost Motherland from generation to generation. The mission was to let you, the people living in present time, know what you all had to do before a new Motherland could be built and the global governing system could be restored on earth. The Masters are telling you and the whole world population how the future humans can succeed in exploring the universe, if they work together under the guidance of one superior Motherland council.

The journey with the Ark of Noah tells us, under the camouflage, what will happen on planet earth as soon as the knowledge from the Diagram Star is spread to the whole world population by use of Internet and modern technology. It will "rain" knowledge all over the world.

The Rescue

Moses 7, 7-8, 1

> *It rained and rained. The water poured down from the clouds. In forty days and forty nights the rain fell heavy. The Ark of Noah ascended higher and higher. The water lifted it up over the mountains.*

> *When water covered the whole planet earth, all life was gone. People and birds died. There was not a single dry place to live. Everywhere was water.*

> *Days became weeks. Noah and his family stayed inside the Ark. Outside were dark and sad, since the clouds heavy with rain stopped the sun from shining.*

> *God did not forget his promise to Noah. After forty days he sent wind over the earth.*

The specific knowledge that can break down the strong mental walls of religious belief is clear and easy to understand: The stories in the Bible is not what you read, they are hiding the lost world history from the time before the Motherland was destroyed in a natural catastrophe.

A small example of the knowledge all humans needs to restore, are that you "have to be conscious of your own thoughts" and know that you yourself decides what's right and what's wrong in the world you live in. In present time you live your whole life believing that everything you are taught is right really is right. With the imposed thoughts of religion you are not present in the world with thoughts of your own.

The wrong and evil thoughts came to you through your senses, your eyes and ears, and it is air, your breath, that brings the thoughts to your brain. Your soul, also called your spirit of life, which you know to be your breath, is transporting the thoughts that make you decide what you do. It is very important for you to be able to distinguish between the wrong thoughts that are enforced on you from the world you live in and the good thoughts that come to your soul from the spirit world.

The knowledge about the lost Motherland and the global government system with common laws and living rules is to be found in the water and blood in the human body. All humans are born with thoughts that by nature make you do the right, but in a world where the common world of thoughts is ruled by the three factors of the Original Sin, the basic good and right thoughts are overruled by the evil and wrong thoughts. All humans have a solid base of good and right thoughts, and it is foremost the traditions, the laws and rules of the nations that imposes wrong and evil thoughts and creates the desperate quest for riches and personal power.

It is the enforced dogmatic teaching that started after the Motherland was destroyed that is wrong as wrong can be. Warrior kings and priesthoods enforced their despotic ruling and their invented religion on the people for thousands of years, in order to make everybody forget about the lost Motherland and the global system of government. Your soul, your spirit of life, your aura, and your breath is fully occupied by the evil forces of the Original Sin. You breed in the pride you feel for your national state, with an enforced national religion and are totally bound to the use of money. Yours and the common world of thoughts from the time before the Motherland went under are covered with a lid made of the darkness of oblivion.

In the long line of history all the religions of the world have had time to plant roots in the common world of thoughts, which you are a part of. The national priesthoods, with the blessing of the national political leaders, uses every Sunday, every holyday and any given opportunity, to tell the population about the camouflaged stories in the Bible, and explain to them as good as they can the symbolism of the unbelievable religion.

Now you know that all the religions in the world are a simple camouflage over the full history of the Motherland and the knowledge from the Diagram Star. The religious belief is wrong and it is also wrong to stand back and disregard religion. You have to make your way in to the many camouflaged biblical stories and discover the lost world history. It is the only way to cleanse your world of thoughts.

The stories in the Bible are a lot more than what they seem to be. They carry with them knowledge about the history of the world from before the Motherland was destroyed some twelve thousand years ago. In our present time, the world leaders are deeply worried about global warming, the never ending wars and conflicts and catastrophes caused by the forces of nature. They just don't know what to do.

Time has come to inform the whole world population that they still are working slaves, soldiers and servants to a government system that started thousands of years ago, in old Egypt. Most likely, like Pharaoh in old Egypt, the world leaders and the priesthoods of present time will wait until their own family is threatened before they start thinking about returning to the global system of government under the superior rule of a new Motherland.

The Master is in this story saying that even if knowledge about the lost Motherland is "raining" down on the whole world population for forty days and forty nights, the world leaders will still have difficulties understanding how life on earth will be like, without the three factors of the Original Sin.

The cleansing of thoughts and the waking of dormant brain cells will take place on a mental level for every living person on the planet, and even if it takes forty years or more, no one can stop the rain of knowledge from flooding your mind.

The Ark comes to rest

Moses 8, 2-9, 17

Noah woke up in the dark. What had happened? In a flash he realized that the rain had stopped. Noah could hear the waves against the shipside. Always before had the sound of rain made it impossible for him to hear the waves. At last the rain had stopped!

Noah went to wake up everyone. "It is over! The great flood is over! Let us thank God for ending the bad weather!"

But it took several months before the earth was dry enough for him to let out the animals. They made even more noise than when they had entered the Ark. They whinnied, roared, meowed and yelped, while going down the gangway, two by two, and disappeared out all over the earth.

Noah and his family said tank you to God for taking care of them. When God heard that they thanked him, he promised that he never again should eliminate all living creatures. He saw all the colors and created the first rainbow. "As a token of the covenant between me and the earth I set the rainbow in the cloud for all to see that I shall never let another great flood destroy all earth life again.

Every human knows that Mother Nature always is the driving force in everything that happens on planet earth. Mother Nature is the earth's spirit of life and is the driving force of all human activity. Some twelve thousand years ago the humans living on planet earth suddenly lost their superior leadership in a natural catastrophe. Human beings started fighting each other because the tribal leaders wanted to protect their own family and tribe from starving to death.

Many tribes were on the move to find new fertile land to live on, and when they discovered that all the good land was occupied and that no one would help them, they started attacking other tribes in order to stay alive. The superior leadership from the Motherland council was gone and it was the laws and rules of the strongest that always survived.

It was the law of the nature that made humans do wrong and evil deeds, and when they succeeded the newly self elected warrior kings had to continue to fight to protect their family and tribe. A leader just had to be strong and evil against all enemies in order to be a good leader for his own people. It was like the forces of evil grew as an act of the nature. Without the leadership of the superior Motherland council the whole world population, every tribal people, had to make it on their own and the laws and the rules of the strongest was used against all enemies.

Like this the nations was built and the nations still fight each other in order to be the strongest and richest nation in the world. It is wrong as wrong can be, and the only way to make it right is to build a new world with a new Motherland and a new superior Motherland council. Only then the Ark of Noah will come to rest.

The Diagram Star has been dark for long time. Humans are living without the enlightening that comes from knowing the Diagram Star through common education. The knowledge humans need in order to be able to build a new world with lasting peace is only found in the light from the Diagram Star.

The rainbow is a symbol for the Diagram Star. For twelve thousand years the light has been out, covered with the dark clouds of the Original Sin. Study the old paintings in this book. Many of them are painted by Masters and have a hidden and long forgotten meaning.

The dove with a twig in the beak is waiting to build a new nest. It is a true symbol for the new peaceful earth humans are waiting to build as soon as they know how. Now you know what water is symbolizing. The Ark is a symbol for the whole earth and Noah and his family is symbolizing the whole world population after the knowledge about the lost Motherland is recovered.

Remember that no humans are going to die when the world is flooded with knowledge about the lost Motherland. It is the three factors of the Original Sin that are to be detached from the thoughts of every human being living in present time. The religious belief will be replaced with common knowledge that will enable the whole earth population to build a new world with lasting peace.

A city is built

Moses 10, 1-11, 4

The sons of Noah had many children, and in time they also had many children, and like that it continued. The families spread all over the world. They learned to till the land, keep farm animals and build large cities.

Because they all came from the same family, they spoke together in the same language. When a stranger came from far away, everyone could understand what he said.

Some tribes got together and said to each other: "Let us build the largest and best city that ever have been, so we all can be famous. Then we don't have to wander around and live in tents any more. We get a homestead were we can live always."

They were clever people. Instead of stone they used bricks made from clay and slime for mortar. Walls like that no one had seen before, strong and tall as they were. People were proud of their buildings. They did not thank God.

"Truly we are clever", they said.

This camouflaged story has many aspects. We get to know that the descendants of Noah multiplied and populated the whole planet. They started building cities with walls around and houses of clay bricks. They did not say thank you to God.

First of all it is a story about the descendents of the first tribes who emigrated from the Motherland and populated the whole world. This story takes place sometime after the Motherland was destroyed in a natural catastrophe.

God is a camouflage over the superior Motherland council, and at one point in time some of the tribal people stopped following the common laws and rules that had been mandatory for all the whole world population. They broke the common law when they started building large cities with protecting walls around.

The underlying meaning is that they wanted to be proud and famous. They misused their knowledge and started working against the strong laws given by the superior Motherland council. They did not build what they by nature needed to live a good life together. Their activity created pride, envy, greed, hate and enemies that wanted to attack them steal all their property and make them all in to slaves, soldiers and servants. They built the cities with walls around in order to protect them self from enemy attacks.

They all knew that they broke the common laws and rules for living, and they themselves were an evil enemy in the eyes of all the tribal people they had attacked and concurred. The building of cities with walls around was the start of the Original Sin. Their activity created thoughts made it impossible to live together as brothers and friends.

One of the important laws of the lost Motherland is that no one in the world is greater than others. All humans are equal. The quest for riches and personal power through the entire world history is wrong as wrong can be.

The thing that grew in pace with the tall and strong walls around the cities was the human egoism. The leaders wanted to rule over as much land they could take by use of warfare and brutal force. This was, one can say, a natural development in a world that had lost the supreme leadership of a Motherland. Many different warrior kings and priesthoods have tried to be the strongest, richest and most famous leader in the world. When they had strong and tall walls built around their cities and castles, it was for their own protection. It wasn't right then and it isn't right in our present time.

The Diagram Star is the ground drawing for how a natural building of a whole new world with lasting peace will be. Self supported villages and communities built with the same ground drawing shall ones again cower the earth and people shall ones again live under one common set of laws and rules for living. All the houses will be without locks on the door. Education will be the most important activity for all humans, and the best students will become Masters of the future.

The Biblical concept God is the strict laws and living rules of Mother Nature, supervised by one new superior Motherland council. The whole world population will be educated in the light of the Diagram Star.

The many religions in the world came to be because of the warrior kings and priesthoods and their devoted helpers. The lack of formal education and wrongful teaching created the many legends, tales and myths. Now you know that all the Gods in the world have their origin in the superior Motherland council. They were the maker of the common laws and rules in the time before the Motherland went under.

In order to stay in power as elite, warrior kings and the priesthoods made up stories based on dogmas and assumptions and forced the population to believe in them. With the use of warfare and brutal force over a period of many generations, all the knowledge about the lost Motherland

and the global system of government was wiped out from the common memory. All people had in their common world of thoughts were the enforced belief in the invented fictive stories made up by the priesthoods and approved by the warrior kings and their helpers.

The emigration and migration of humans and population the whole world is a result of natural cell division. The humans started building cities with walls around in order to protect them self. Note that in this story the humans have no specific named common leader. The world population in present time still does not have a common leading force, telling them to do the right thing.

The world needs a new superior Motherland council to supervise the building of a new world with lasting peace, and the time is now. Without a common set of laws and rules for living, the chaos with wars and conflicts will continue.

The tower of Babel

Moses 11, 5-9

In the city the descendants of Noah started building an enormous tower. People thought they were so clever and able that they could build a tower up over the clouds to heaven.

When God saw what people tried to do, he knew he had to stop them. Or else they would soon start believing about them self that they were gods and not humans. They would be far too proud, and that is not healthy. Therefore he confused them in a way that they no longer could understand each other's language.

People did not speak the same language any more. There were many languages. When people greeted one another and said something, the other person did not know what to answer. It was difficult to get things done, and the large tower in the city was never completed.

The town that never was finished was named Babel. It means confusion, and the name was given to the city because it was here that God confused the language of humans.

The symbolism is clear. Before the Motherland was destroyed and for some time after, the whole world population spoke the same language and were in regular contact with each other. They were living together like a global family with long lasting peace.

After the Motherland was destroyed all communications between the many tribal communities stopped. All common education stopped and over a long period of time the languages changed for natural reasons. But there is still a common spiritual understanding above all languages. People speak, in general, the same language using different words and pronunciations.

The building of the tower is a symbol for the time when the world population stopped working together for the common good. People started working for personal power and fame. The tower they started building back then is based on the three factors of the Original Sin. It is a very good symbol for the building of the global capitalistic system. The monetary system is living through a severe setback in our present time, and living is getting more and more difficult for the majority of poor people living in the shadow of the tower.

The descendants of Noah started building the tower in cities all over the world and the humans living in present time is still at it, building their world based on the chaos of wars and conflicts, on a global capitalistic system and all the religions in the world.

Everybody can see that it is wrong to continue to build the world as it is done in our present time. It has been wrong since the building started. Because the physical superior Motherland council died and became spiritual, there is no organized power strong enough to stop the building. Only Mother Nature is strong enough to take action and protest against the destructive human activity that are slowly destroying planet Earth.

And then there are you. You can take action along with the whole world population. First of all you can spread the knowledge that is found under the camouflage of religion to as many humans you possibly can reach with the use of Internet and modern technology. Then the building of the new world can begin.

Look around you and see the national leaders struggling to build their national tower higher and bigger than any other national state in the world. The constructors are a symbol for the many rich national states and the many national and multinational companies that uses all possible means to build global towers everywhere in the world where there is money to make. It is wrong and has been wrong since the building started. The working slaves, the soldiers and servants doing the physical work, are you, and only the richest of the rich get to live in luxury. The tower you all participate in building is the global capitalistic development that are about to destroy the earth completely.

All the national states have borders that are guarded day and night, and they are organized like regular prison camps. You are given a name and a number when you are born. You are educated to work hard for the nation all your life. The laws and living rules of the national state are to be followed no matter what. The world leader and many of the richest humans are building their homes like regular prisons, protected by personal guards, alarms and code locks. In reality all homes are regular prisons and humans are not meant to live like that.

Humans are meant to live in open self supported tribal villages in large borderless civilizations. That kind of freedom is only possible in a world were all people speak the same language and are working for the common good in a world with lasting peace. Humans are not meant to live with hope. The meaning of life on earth is to live with everything you hope for.

The world is not meant to be controlled by the three factors of the Original Sin, and you know that. A Biblical description of the world as it is supposed to be is described in detail in the story were Jesus and the twelve disciples are eating the last supper. Look up the Diagram Star and place Jesus in the centre of the star and the twelve disciples in the twelve sectors around. Jesus is a symbol for the born again Motherland history and the twelve disciples is a symbol for the twelve new members of a new superior Motherland council.

The whole world is meant to be like the last supper all the time, with one superior Motherland council representing and leading the whole world population. Make sure you understand that Jesus is the spiritual born again Motherland history, and the new superior Motherland council has to learn everything about the lost Motherland before they can be the leaders of the whole world population. All humans are meant to live together as brothers and friends in a world with lasting peace.

The tower is a symbol for the effect the three factors of the Original Sin have had for the development all over the world since the Motherland went under. The building of the tower in the city of Babel is still going on in an escalating tempo. Humans are fighting like desperate in order to active the fame and power that only money can give. And it is all for nothing, because Mother Nature is about to make the tower fall.

The tower of Babel has to be built down by use of only peaceful means, in order to avoid a free fall that will take many human lives. Seems like impossible now, but go for it. Your descendants will be proud of you. If you do nothing, there might not be any descendants at all.

Remember that the development of today has been going on for some twelve thousand years. The Masters of all times are telling you that you and the world population of present time are not to blame, because you did not know about the lost Motherland and the previous world history with lasting peace. The reason that no one knows about the lost Motherland is the camouflage of religion.

The humans of present time are living with a development that is not natural as a part of their daily life. Everything that is not natural will have to be removed before the development for the future can be natural and right.

Give your thoughts time to develop. Listen to the Diagram Star. Let it speak to you as it has spoken to Masters always though the ages, and you will know how life on earth can be lived right. Only a new physical superior Motherland council can be omnipotent, omniscient and omnipresent, able to lead the whole world population.

God chooses Abram

Moses 12, 1-9

Many, many years later there lived a man called Abram. He was married to a woman called Sarai. They were happy, except for one thing. They didn't have any children. The years went by, and it seems like they shouldn't have any.

One night Abram heard that God spoke to him: "Abram, you shall have a very large family. All humans everywhere shall be blessed because of you."

The Lord told Abram to leave his country. Abram did not know where the Lord would lead him, but he did as God said. He told Sarai what had happened, and she too believed in God. She asked her servant to pack the tents and load them on the camels.

"Where shall we go?" they asked.

"That I do not know," she answered and smiled. If Abram could wait for God to tell them were to go, then could she.

Let us assume that the camouflaged story about Abram and Sarai was written a couple of thousand years after the Motherland was destroyed in a natural catastrophe, and that people all over the world had continued to develop under more or less chaotic conditions without any kind of communication and common education.

Adam and Sarai is a symbol for the part of world population that wanted to continue to live their lives just like they had done before the Motherland went under. They wanted to think right and live right with the common knowledge and the laws and rules that ensured lasting peace on earth. But many tribes started violating the common laws and rules for living by using the force of warfare and brutality. The peace loving people had no choice. They had to leave their homestead and go searching for new land to live on.

Under the camouflage of God speaking to people or visiting them in dreams is the Diagram Star. The official emblem of the superior Motherland council is still speaking directly to the whole world population. The diagram is symbolical speaking to Abram like it has spoken to humans always and will speak to you when you search for the right thing to do in your life. With knowledge of the Diagram Star the thoughts that comes to you from the spirit world becomes understandable.

The Masters and their students lived in small and isolated groups, mostly in tents and caves. Some of them were scholars and scribes working undercover as teachers and advisors for the elite. Many died protecting what they knew about the lost Motherland.

In the same moment a village was attacked by the warrior kings and the priesthoods, the long history of the village and the population was wiped out for all times. Imagine people had a history from the beginning of time, remembered by traditional yearly ceremonies and in their many beautiful old and valuable ornaments of gold, silver and precious stones. Many Masters, often working as teaches in the villages, were systematically killed for their knowledge and teaching of the Motherland history. The surviving Masters wrote the stories about the many villages that were looted for all valuables and burnt to the ground. The surviving village populations were forced in to a life as slaves, soldiers and servants for the new ruler of the land.

In present time the property of the very rich national states and very rich people in the world is in one way or another originating from organized criminal warfare like described above. It started long ago in old Egypt, and is explaining the enormous riches in gold, silver and precious stones that the Pharaohs are known for.

The Master wrote the camouflaged story about Abram and Sarai in to their time of history. All the camouflages stories in the Bible is written in to the time the writers lived in, and now it is done again, perhaps in vain, because of the mental blindness of the whole world population. The Masters of the past is telling the humans living in present time what they have to do in order to break the long lasting spell of evil thoughts. The knowledge about the lost Motherland is found in the Bible, under the camouflage of religion. The Diagram Star has to return soon to the common world of thoughts and make the building of the new world, the Promised Land, possible.

Abram and Sarai is a symbol for what the whole world population has to do in present time. Not to leave their homestead, but to leave the world of thoughts that is enforced on people for

37

some twelve thousand years. See the wrong and evil in the world and dispose of it. Then the knowledge from the Diagram Star will remove all religious belief and the whole world will ones again be a paradise for all humans.

It is the building of a new world that is the mission that awaits you all. Like Abram and Sarai you have to leave your well known common daily world of thoughts that are derived from the Original Sin and start searching for the world of thoughts that were common in the time before the Motherland went under. Every human that are searching for a way to build a safe world with ever lasting peace for our children and their descendants, have to follow their inner voice and start working right now. A new understanding of the world you live in will tell you were to go in order to set a totally new course for mankind. It is a course that after some time will lead the whole world population back to the peaceful paradise world of the past. It will be a world without the opposites like good and evil, richness and poverty, love and hate, and more.

Please read the following sentences. If they are hard to understand read them again and again.

Knowing that the talking biblical God is the Diagram Star, carrying the whole world history and the laws and rules given to the whole world population by the superior Motherland council, the mental journey towards a new world with lasting peace can begin. The Master who wrote this camouflaged story several thousand years ago had the whole world in mind and the Promised Land is truly the whole planet earth.

No Master had thoughts about anything other than that the three factors of the Original Sin sooner or later would be removed from the face of the earth. With the force of evil totally removed, the force of good would find its way back to what good is meant to be for all humans. Very important to the Masters of the past was that the humans who finally managed to build a new world would have the knowledge about the past they needed to build lasting peace with the use of only peaceful means.

Perhaps it is too late, so that the tower of Babel is built in a manner that it cannot be dismantled peacefully stone by stone even if the whole world population works together. The tower is built, founded on all the national states, the global capitalistic system and all the religions in the world. It is never too late for you to start doing the right thing. If the tower built inn to the clouds should fall by the strong force of Mother Nature, the few surviving humans would need the knowledge about the lost Motherland and the Diagram Star in order to be able to start building a new world with lasting peace.

All the religions in the world have to be removed with the use of the knowledge that the religions are a camouflage over. If the beliefs in all the religions are allowed to continue in to the future, the camouflage will continue to cover the knowledge about the lost Motherland. And the chaos of wars and conflicts will continue.

Abram is a symbol for a leader that does everything right in a world were all others do wrong according to the laws and living rules of the nature. If you follow the red line of people doing right through the whole Bible and remove everything that is wrong, you will find the receipt for building a new Motherland and a whole new world with lasting peace. The promise is still valid.

Gods promise

Moses 13, 14-18; 15, 1-21; 17, 1-27

God was leading Abram and Sarai with all their camels, sheep's, goats and servants to the land of Canaan, where he said: "This is the land that I want to give to your children." But God did not want Abram to stop in Canaan. Not yet.

Abram and Sarai moved their tents to Mamre in Hebron. The years went by. All the time they wanted to have children. But then Sarai got too old to have children.

One night Abram heard God say: "Look up at the sky and count the stars." Abram saw that the stars blinked all over. "One day your family will count as many as there are stars on the sky," said God.

Then God gave Abram and Sarai new names. Abram became Abraham, meaning "the father of many" and Sarai became Sara, which means "princess."

Abraham and Sarah is a symbol for the humans who lived in the time after the Motherland was destroyed. They are a symbol for the whole world population in our present time; living as right as they can while waiting for lasting peace in the world, peace from all wars and conflicts. You are all waiting for an end to all evil and an end to all poverty and human need. It looks like it is never going to happen, and humans all over the world are in the process of giving up hope. Abraham and Sarah is a symbol for the humans that never will give up hoping for a world without evil.

You do know that all children are born good and innocent. But they are born in to a world where the three factors of the Original Sin are dominating the common world of thoughts completely. Abraham and Sara are symbolizing the lost Motherland, the paradise world with lasting peace, where all humans lived in the light of the Diagram Star. The child they are hoping to give birth to is a new Motherland and a new superior Motherland council.

It is the fight between good and evil in present time the Master is describing in this story. The good and peaceful people in the world are about to give up hope. It seems like there is no end to all the evil in the world. Praying for help from a spiritual God based on religious belief is wrong. Only by removing the camouflage of religion and finding the hidden knowledge about a lost Motherland will make the building of a new world possible. The knowledge is spiritual and only you and the whole world population working together can make the building of the new world real.

The three factors of the Original Sin have to be removed with only peaceful means. Lasting world peace can never be achieved by the use of warfare and brutal force. And it is only after all the wrong and evil thoughts is removed from all human thinking, that the good people on earth under the rule of a new superior Motherland council, will be as many as the stars on the sky.

All the national state leaders in the world are doing what they think is right, making strong and visible walls keeping the population inside the national borders and unwanted strangers out. Everyone is free to leave the country, but on the other side there is another national state, and your nationality follows you wherever you go.

It was the building of national states with the use of warfare and brutal force that was wrong. They were all built with the forces of the three factors of the Original Sin. Inside every nation there are people who are longing to build a new world without the forces of evil, but they don't know how it can be done with the use of only peaceful means. If the good people in the world were given the chance they would build a new world with the knowledge derived from the Diagram Star.

It is still possible to think about the whole world population as one great family descending from Abraham and Sarah. A new Motherland can and will be built with their good qualities, symbolized with their son Isaac. It is the thousands of years from the Motherland were lost and until today that are their old age. Now the time has come to make the world history of the lost Motherland be born again.

With representatives from all the people in the world elected in to a new global Parliament; peace will last until after the end of time. The common laws and rules for living will prevent the existents of warrior kings and priesthoods and all the fighting between good and evil will stop forever. All the national states, all kind of global capitalistic force and all the religions in the world, will just disappear from the human world of thoughts.

Abraham and Sarah are symbolizing the good thoughts in the common world of thoughts and in your world of thoughts. The whole world population has to live like them, with only the forces of natural good thoughts, if there again shall be lasting peace on planet earth. The symbolism is so outstanding clear and real. Their son Isaac is born to symbolize that the history about the lost Motherland lives on as a read thread through all the camouflaged stories in the Bible.

If the world population does not, by use of peaceful means only, unite and become a complete united world population very soon, the symbolic darkness of oblivion will rule the world until after the end of time. Just imagine the whole world population, multiplying and dying as captives of their national state, without knowing why you ever lived.

The promise of God is the strong and uncompromising laws and living rules of Mother Nature. And if humans fail to act, the force of Mother Nature will take action and lower the final curtain over a long and troublesome period of time. Any one of you can be a prophet and speak on behalf of the nature. You see Mother Nature talking to the leaders of the world every day, but they just don't know what to do. The many world leaders really do need a common omnipotent, omniscient and omnipresent leadership from a superior Motherland council.

Humans are facing and epoch that will be extreme to live with, with global warming, escalating wars and conflicts, global famine and thousands of humans dying just because they are poor, if the Original Sin is allowed to continue to dominate the common world of thoughts.

On the way to Sodom

Moses 18, 1-33

Not long after God spoke to Abraham, three shepherds came to visit. He knew that one of them was the Lord. Abraham walked up on a hill with them, from where they could look down on the city of Sodom.

The Lord said: "I have heard how much evil there is among people in Sodom. Now I want to destroy the city."

The two men traveling with the Lord was angels in disguise. They went to Sodom.

Abraham wanted very much to ask the Lord a question, but did he dare? He knew that even if God was his friend, he was also God. He asked: "Lord, what if there are fifty good humans in Sodom? What will happen to them?

God said: "I will not destroy the city if there are fifty good humans there."

Abraham continued to ask, time after time, and for every time he used smaller numbers. Would God save the city if there were forty-five good humans there, forty, twenty, or only ten?

Every time the Lord answered yes.

Abrahams nephew Lot had chosen to settle near the city of Sodom, were the land were fertile.

Under the camouflage of religion the Master writing this story is speaking about the world he lived in, and also about the world you live in at present time. Now you live in the present world, and even you, a normal intelligent human, can see that Mother Earth itself slowly is about to destroy planet earth, because of destructive human activity.

The destructive activity is all caused by the three factors of the Original Sin. The whole world population is for that reason forced to be evil, even if all of them really do want to live their lives doing only good. But doing well in a world where the forces of evil are in command, becomes an endless fight between good and evil. The only way to end the fight is to find knowledge about the past and tell the whole world population. Because nobody knows about the Motherland that were destroyed some twelve thousand years ago and the global system of government, people have to live with the force of evil and work for a better world without braking the laws and rules of the nation. The world leaders know that it cannot continue much longer.

Sodom is a symbol for the whole world. In the biblical story only a few people survived. If you decide to do your best to make the world a better place by telling as many people as possible about the lost Motherland, there is no going back. There is still time, and if the knowledge is spread to the whole world population in time, nobody have to die except for natural causes.

It is important to understand that "the force of evil" is thoughts imposed on the whole world population as being right because your national state government says it is. The three factors of the Original Sin are occupying your mind and you don't know that the present ruling system with the many national governments in charge is wrong. You believe you are doing the right thing when you follow the laws and living rules as you are taught to do.

Very few humans, if anyone at all, know about the global system of government from the time before the Motherland was destroyed some twelve thousand years ago. You can find the knowledge under the camouflage of religion and in the myths, tales and legends of the past.

The message hidden in the Bible is meant for humans living in present time. If it is difficult to understand you have to use the formula of the Masters and use all the time you need to study. If you accept the definition of the three factors of the Original Sin and understand that all the camouflaged stories in the Bible have a hidden meaning, then you are symbolical on the way out of the city of Sodom.

It is also important to understand that the coming struggle to remove all evil from the thoughts of mankind will take place in the minds of people. It is a spiritual and intellectual fight that only can be won with the knowledge hidden in the Bible. The Bible truly is the Ark of the Covenant.

Lot is saved

Moses 19, 11-29

There were not ten good people in the city of Sodom, only four. The only bright spot in the evil city of Sodom was a man named Lot. Abraham was his uncle. Lot lived in Sodom with his wife and their two daughters.

Lot met with the angels that were disguised as humans. "Come in to my house," he said. "It is not safe to be in the street in this city."

The inhabitants of Sodom still tried to take the angels. The angels said to Lot: "It is best if you come with us. The Lord will not put up with this evil place any longer. He is going to destroy the city! We shall help you and your family to get away, but you must not look back!"

Only a few hours later the Lord let a rain of fire and sulphur fall upon the city of Sodom. Lot and his family were safe, but his wife looked back and she immediately turned in to a pillar of salt!

God kept his promise to Abraham and saved all the good people in the city of Sodom.

The Master who wrote this story knew the world history from before the destruction of the Motherland and up until his present time. We all know the world history from the time the Bible was written and until our present time. It is easy to predict the future when you know the past. It is only knowledge about the lost Motherland and the global system of government that make it possible for humans to tell difference between the good system of government of the past and the evil system of government of present time.

So, what does it take to convince you to symbolical leave the city of Sodom? Remember that the cleansing of thoughts will take time and there are no turning back ones you have started, because the world as you know it will no longer exist.

The Master already knew, some two thousand years ago, that only a total change of human thinking and a return to the global system of government from before the Motherland went under, can remove the three factors of the Original Sin and recreate a lasting peace in the world.

The planet earth has to be organized as one whole unit. Before the Motherland went under the whole world was organized like for example a beehive, with one superior leader, the queen bee. If the queen bee dies there is a natural outbreak of chaos in the beehive. When the Motherland was destroyed in a natural catastrophe some twelve thousand years ago, the chaos of wars and conflicts started and just never stopped.

If the world is described like a bicycle wheel it is the hub that is missing in our present time. If you look at the Diagram Star as the present world, it is a star without light. All humans are living in the darkness of oblivion. The whole world is without the bright light of knowledge. The bright starlight is covered with the camouflage of religion.

The reason the Diagram Star is still dark is that the warrior kings and priesthoods wanted to keep their position as superior elite, with the luxury, riches and personal power they inherited from those who started using the three factors of the Original Sin to control their population. The world leaders still do inherit evil, not knowing that the political system that allows them to do so is totally against the strict laws and living rules given by the superior Motherland council, as chiseled in to the Diagram Star.

Do the people living in present time have to live through a real burning Sodom before they understand that the world really needs a new common leadership? A new superior Motherland council can only be elected from a democratically elected global Parliament. They will lead the whole world from a new Motherland.

Abraham live, thinks and acts in a way that all humans should do. Everything he does is right in the light of the Diagram Star. He is the kind of human that protects and passes on the forces of good in a world that is totally taken over by the forces of evil. The leading persons in the Bible stories are shifting with the generations, but they always do the right thing under the circumstances they live with. The power of evil is always in command and will endure until it collapses under the strong force of knowledge about the lost Motherland. You know that all the people in the world have the power of good in their spirit of life. Everyone want to be only good and after the power of evil is gone for good, knowledge about the lost Motherland will help them build a world with lasting peace together.

Remember that Abraham and Sarah is fictive symbolic persons, and that it is the Masters of the past who in this manner are preserving and passing on the knowledge of the lost world history to people living in present time.

Can you imagine how the power of good shifted from physical to spiritual when the Motherland was destroyed? Only the power of knowledge about the lost Motherland can restore the physical power all over the world.

Isaac is born

Moses 21, 1-6

God had promised Sarah and Abraham one child and Sarah had no reason to worry. When the three guests visited them, the Lord had promised that they should have a child within one year.

And really, less than a year after the impossible happened. Sarah, who was far too old to have children, gave birth to a son. Abraham was one hundred years when Sarah's child was born. He and Sarah were happy, so grateful to God for finally answering their prayer, and they cried of happiness.

Every time Abraham saw the boy, he smiled. And Sarah smiled all day long. The child made them very glad, and often they laughed together. They called the boy Isaac, which means "he laughs" and just seeing the boy made them happy.

This camouflaged story has a true historical importance. The Master is telling people living in present time that the memory of the superior Motherland council lives in Abraham and Sarah.

Their son Isaac symbolizes that the knowledge about the lost Motherland is preserved and passed on in to the future.

Just imagine what would have happened to the whole world population if the knowledge about the lost Motherland had died completely a few thousand years ago. The chaos of wars and conflicts would have continued until the whole world was completely destroyed by the evil forces of the three factors of the Original Sin. Don't you let the knowledge die now. Don't deny the existence of the lost Motherland, as your forefathers did a long time ago.

Abraham and Sarah is still a symbol for the whole world population. In the chaos that followed the first couple of thousand years after the Motherland went under, the knowledge of the Diagram Star and the world history as a whole was about to be completely lost. It is described as almost impossible, but, still the knowledge survived as the only right way to live for all humans beings.

The whole Bible is telling stories about how the force of good survived in a world with the force of evil in command. The stories is clear on the point that the force of evil, meaning the three factors of the Original Sin, is an intruding force that mankind can do without.

When the knowledge from the Diagram Star again is made known to the whole world population, a tremendous gladness and laughter will sound from people all over the planet. Isaac is a symbol for the whole world population, which in our present time symbolically has a knife at the throat and the world leaders are not happy about the how world develops. They keep washing their hands while watching thousands of humans die every single day all over the world. Think about the happiness that will be really true for all humans the day the knife is removed.

Abraham and Isaac

Moses 22, 1-2

"Abraham!" It was God speaking. "Take your son, your only son, Isaac. I know you love him, and therefore I ask you to do this that is so difficult. I want you to give Isaac back to me!"

Abraham did not reply. The God he knew would never ask him to kill his own son. This Abraham knew. God had promised that Isaac should have many children. How could he do that if Isaac was to die as an offering to God?

It was like holding a friend in the hand when you don't know where you are going. Your friend has said that there is a large hole in the ground in front of you, and you can fall down in it. But you are holding your friend in the hand, because he is the only one that you can trust. Your friend will never let you down. Step by step you follow him.

Abraham knew that he could say no to God if he wanted. He could refuse, he could escape his way and try to hide, but who can hide for God?

Or else he could choose to trust him. Perhaps there were more in God's plan than it seemed.

The Master writing this camouflaged story is asking you to look at this story as a symbol. That you can do with all the stories in the Bible, when you know them well. When you find the hidden message, you know that the Master is speaking directly to you, and you will remember the story as long as you live.

Not you nor the whole world population can say no to the strong forces of Mother Nature. Under the camouflage of religion is the message from the Master that mankind is facing extinction if people continue to live as they do. Your son is on the altar of evil and you are holding the knife on his throat. Only just before the kill you finally do understand the message from the Spirit World. You and your son is a symbol for all the fathers in the world. If all the children in the world die it will be the beginning of the end for mankind. The angel taking to Abraham is the spirit world talking to you.

Most, if not all of the camouflaged stories in the Bible is translated wrong from hieroglyphs and in to the Hebrew language.

The only way to save the world is to elect a new superior Motherland council to enforce the common laws and rules of Mother Nature again. They are all found in the Diagram Star.

No one can hide from the light of knowledge that comes from the Diagram Star, but with the imposed religious belief, the knowledge in the Bible has to be shown to you.

The Diagram Star is always casting the light of knowledge out across the whole planet earth. But the light of knowledge is never reaching the people because they all are living in the darkness of oblivion. People don't have the common education that makes them understand what the knowledge hidden in the Bible can do for the whole world population. Knowledge has a cycle just like the water, and every child that is born have to be educated in order to know.

Ever since the Motherland went under, common education has been absent for many reasons, but mostly because of the wrongful enforced teaching by the warrior kings and priesthoods. And the utterly wrong teaching of the religious dogmas and assumptions is still going on as common inheritance. Because of the so called holiness the knowledge is kept hidden under the lid of camouflage religion. The Bible is the Ark of the Covenant and the religious holiness is the lid.

Humans don't see the light of knowledge and they don't know that their daily activities in an inherited quest for making money, is about to make planet earth uninhabitable. Sooner or later the earth will be desolate, perhaps totally without earth life. It is the sons of the people living in present time that has the knife of extinction on their throat, and the thousands of humans who die every day, dies without knowing why they have ever lived.

Twelve thousand years is a very short time in the history of mankind. Are the ongoing destructions just going to continue because of human ignorance and because of you being loyal to the laws and living rules of your nation?

Planet Earth is one unit, a single living organism that originally was meant to be ruled by the forces of Mother Nature alone. Mankind, without the three factors of the Original Sin, is an important part of all earth life. All the peoples in the world descend from the Motherland in the beginning, and populated the whole planet. The Motherland really existed and the superior Motherland council was omnipotent, omniscient and omnipresent.

With one common set of laws and rules for living taught to the whole world population with the use of the Diagram Star, a lasting world peace was secured. The whole world was a peaceful paradise with the Motherland as the Garden of Eden. Then the Motherland itself was destroyed in a natural catastrophe some twelve thousand years ago.

In the chaos that followed the catastrophe the surviving peoples did learn about the forces of evil, and the planet have been a living Hell for all humans ever since. Wars and conflicts has been the outlining of earth history for the last twelve thousand years. The Motherland is been remembered by the whole world population as a Heaven in the Spirit World, in the common world of thoughts. Under the camouflage of religion, Heaven is the Spirit World, from where God is speaking. God is the late superior Motherland council, and is far from omnipotent any longer. But they are omnipresent and omniscient in the world, talking directly to you from the spirit world. The dominating forces of evil, the three factors of the Original Sin, have occupied your world of thoughts from the day you were born.

It is a fact that only a total change in the present way of thinking can save planet earth from total destruction. The electing of a new superior Motherland council can never happen with the present system of ruling the world, with many individual national states desperately clinging to their religion and global capitalistic system.

People ask me how the world we all live in can function without the many national states and their armies, without the global capitalistic system and without all the religions in the world. My answer is that the world population really does have a knife at their throat, and the only way planet earth can be saved from further destruction is to remove the three factors of the Original Sin from the common world of thoughts.

Think trough what you and your family needs to survive and to live a good life on your land. Will you sacrifice the whole planet and all earth life, just to continue to live the meaningless life you have lived up until now?

In a future world, like God promised Abraham, education will again be the most important activity of all humans. Knowledge from the Diagram Star will give you and the whole world population a true meaning with life.

Also the technological revolution will after some time get back on a track that is natural, and the building of cosmic eggs can commence. In a world without the desperate quest for riches and personal power all kind of polluting human activity will stop.

The Masters plan with this camouflaged story is to make humans living in present time the true message and ask them to spread it to the whole world population by use of modern technology and Internet.

Call the Spirit World for Heaven if you like. Your world of thoughts is anyway a part of the Spirit World, and without the three factors of the Original Sin as an evil occupation forces in your mind, your thoughts will return to be in contact with the Spirit World on a permanent base.

All humans are connected to the common world of thoughts, and the camouflaged story about Abraham and Isaac is telling you just how important it to think the right thoughts and do the right things. Your thoughts and your actions are following you all the way through your lifespan, no matter what. You know that good deeds always follow good thoughts and make your life a happy life, while evil deeds comes from evil thoughts and unhappiness will be a heavy burden to carry through a lifetime on earth.

Testing faith

Moses 22, 3-8

Early next morning Abraham woke his son: "Come, Isaac, we are going on a journey."

Since Isaac was a young man now, he was asked to carry the wood. Abraham said to him that they were going to give an offering to God. Abraham carried the knife.

"Father," said Isaac.

"Yes, my son?"

"I have the wood," said Isaac, "but where is the lam that we use to offer?

Abraham replied: "God will provide the offering."

After three days Abraham said that they had come far enough. He asked Isaac to lie down on the altar he built.

This is a totally unbelievable story, camouflaged by a Master. Abraham is taking his only son out on a journey, to give him as an offering to God, because God have asked him to do so.

You know the definition of God. Abraham is a symbol for the knowledge about the lost Motherland and if his son Isaac dies, the history is lost for good. The knowledge about the lost Motherland has been lost until it now is told to the whole world population. It is really you, the humans living in present time that are holding the knife at the throat of your children and their descendants.

Under the camouflage of religion, the Master is describing the world he lived in, and from what he knows from the past world history, he can tell what the future will be like, if humans living in present time don't listen to what the Diagram Star and Mother Nature so clearly is saying.

The whole world population has been on a journey for a very long time, and in our present time of history the symbolic altar is ready built and all the young children in the world is already on the altar, ready to be sacrificed because of the three factors of the Original Sin. Isaac is a symbol for all our children and their descendants.

This is the true image: The whole world population is walking towards a bottomless abyss, holding hand with the forces of evil. You are all powerless under the laws and rules of your nation, the global capitalistic system and all the religions in the world.

Mankind are already well in to the process of making themselves extinct, and the reason is ignorance, lack of knowledge about the past history, and religious belief enforced on them for many, many generations.

This story is describing two kinds of offerings, the one that is good and the one that is evil. You know which is which. You know that when you light a candle for someone who is dead, it is an act of goodness and feels so right. And it is.

The origin of making and altar and burning sacrifice started off in the time after the Motherland had been destroyed in a natural catastrophe. It was an act of goodness remembering something they knew had happened. Whole villages made an altar and built a fire of wood in order to remember the lost Motherland. The sacrifice of animals was a symbol for all the humans and all kind of earth life that died in the catastrophe that are described as a burning inferno of gasses and boiling water. People were organizing yearly ceremonial festivities in order to remember the lost Motherland and the late superior Motherland council, and they continued to live according to the laws and rules of the Motherland for a long time after the catastrophe. The offerings were not religious, because they knew that a whole continent had disappeared and all the people living on it had died. They knew that the souls of the dead were in the spirit world, and burning a fire symbolizes knowledge and contact with the spirit world. Fire = Knowledge, says the formula.

The lost Motherland became a spiritual Heaven and the superior Motherland council became the many spiritual Gods all over the world. As spiritual beings they had lost all their power. Therefore a new Motherland has to be built and a new superior Motherland council elected in order to restore lasting peace in the whole world.

After many years, perhaps a few generations, the ceremonial festivities turned evil. The lack of common education made it possible for greedy and selfish priesthoods to take charge over the whole population. Everyone who dared to protest was accused of terrible evil abilities and killed. For the first time ever people lost their happiness and got scared for each other. They could all see that the priesthoods were wrong and that the people they sacrificed on the altars were good people. The whole population was forced to believe in the stories the evil priesthoods made up. It was the wrong doings of the priesthoods who made up the dogmas and assumptions and forced people to believe in them. It was, and it still is the priesthoods who elect their favored soldier to be a warrior king. In this way the era of a living Hell started on planet earth. It has lasted for some twelve thousand years. Thousands of humans die every day, sacrificed on the altar of evil.

Now the moment is approaching rapidly, were the destructive and evil human activities create a situation where Mother Nature itself is holding the symbolic knife against the throat of mankind.

Saved in time

Moses 22, 9-18

Isaac looked at his father. In his eyes he could read love. Isaac chooses to trust his father. When he lay down on the altar he prayed to God for protection.

Abraham stood over Isaac with lifted knife. Then he heard an angel saying: "Abraham, Abraham."

Abraham lowered the knife. "Don't harm the boy. You have shown that you trust in God, also when it comes to your only son, Isaac."

Abraham looked up and saw a sheep stuck in a bush nearby. God had provided the offer.

The angel called from heaven again: "Abraham, God is saying that because you believed in him, he will make your family as numerous as there are stars on the night sky. The whole world population is to be blessed through you."

Isaac and his father embraced each other. Both father and son were happy because they could be together.

To be blessed means to be safe and secure in the light of the Diagram Star. It is a blessing that you are given in inheritance from your parent and their forefathers when living in a world with lasting peace. Being blessed is to have the family and the history as a base for your life on earth.

Look you around and read the clear words the nature is calling out to the whole world population. The nature is a necessity for all earth life; it preserves life and passes it on like nature is meant to do, always. Look nature in the eye and feel the love it shows to all earth life. Mother Nature is the natural love that makes you feel a profound happiness when you are living and feeling happy with your family. The true feeling of being blessed stopped some twelve thousand years ago, when the force of evil took control and made people afraid for each other.

Do you feel safe and secure in a world where thousands of humans dies every day, caused by the chaos of wars and conflicts, the poverty and the enforced believe in religion?

It is the three factors of the Original Sin that are in the process of destroying the whole world, symbolized with this story about Isaac on the altar with the knife at his throat. The symbolism is right, because who other than the fathers and their forefathers are holding the knife? Will they hear the call from the Spirit World in time? Will they understand and do the right thing?

It seems like the world leaders are willing to sacrifice everything that by nature is good because of an unnatural and destructive life form that are serving only the richest of the rich humans in the world.

The whole world population is truly working slaves, soldiers and servants of the laws and living rules of their respective national state. Will the world leaders continue the destructive life form and make the planet impossible to live on for our children and their ancestors?

You and the whole world population have to tell the world leaders what you think is right. Remember that the world leaders are simple human beings, just like you. Everyone must start working to stop the destructive human activity by use of only the natural force that comes with knowledge about the lost Motherland.

First every human being must fight the battle in their world of thoughts and really divide everything that is wrong and evil from everything that is right and good. It is the right thoughts of many humans together that can make a difference in the common world of thoughts.

The three factors of the Original Sin have occupied the common world of thoughts for some twelve thousand years, and the world leaders have learned to use the natural and the good as opposites that justifies the act of unnatural and evil activity. War and peace are opposites were war is evil and peace is good. The two have to be separated and the use of war and evil is to be removed completely from the common world of thoughts. When it is done the right and the good will rule the world alone. Symbolically the knife will be removed and our sons and their ancestors will be able to finally build a world with lasting peace.

It is only when the whole world population lives together like a family, think the same thoughts and live by the same set of laws and rules for living, that a world with lasting peace can be built.

If the Original Sin is seen at as a deadly tumor for the whole world population, too far gone to heal, the nature will take its course until death is a fact for all earth life.

The humans really need to be spoken to in a high voice, by an angels speaking on behalf of Mother Nature. People all over the world are really in the process of destroying the future for our children and their descendants. The angel is best defined as you own inner voice. Only by listening to your inner voice you will be able to find an understanding of what is right to do, for you.

No matter what you do, planet Earth is desecrated and misused through some twelve thousand years, and the angel in this camouflaged story is calling you to start doing the right thing, hopefully in time to stop destroying planet earth completely.

How the camouflaged stories in the Bible came to be. Try again to look at the camouflaged stories in the Bible as images, as hieroglyphs, as holy carvings. Now, after many years of work, the Egyptian hieroglyphs become visible as the true story about the lost Motherland. The translation in to the Hebrew language was done by priests, scholars and scribes who did the best they could. The warrior kings and the priesthoods of the time wanted the history about the lost Motherland to be completely forgotten because they wanted to continue to live in luxury with total control over the population.

Only a living human being can be the messenger who tells the whole world population that all the religions in the world are camouflage over lost world history. The knowledge humans need in order to be able to build a new world with lasting peace have to be told by many human beings working together. The first Christians and the twelve apostles died because they knew the story about the lost Motherland. Now think about everyone else who have died and dies every day because of religious nonsense that is the inheritance imposed on you and your children. Be brave and use Internet and modern technology.

Moses is not a person. He is a camouflage over the superior Motherland council, who gave the laws and rules for living to the whole world population.

A difficult mission

Moses 24, 1-61

Many years later Abraham said to his servant: "Travel back to my homeland and find a wife for Isaac." It was a difficult mission, for there were so many women!

The servant prayed to Abrahams God during the whole journey. He came to a well in the land were Abraham ones had lived. He prayed: "Lord, you, the God of Abraham must choose the women you mean are the right for Isaac. If I ask her for water and she replays: "Drink, and I will water your camels as well, then I know it is her."

Soon the servant saw a flock of young women who came to the well. He asked one of them if he could drink some water from her jar. This was the test. What would she replay?

She said: "Drink and I will water your camels to." The servant was glad. Not long after he had explained why he had come to this land. He found out that her name was Rebecca. Soon she should be Isaacs's wife.

Abrahams God is a symbol for people living by the laws and rules given by the spiritual superior Motherland council. A well full of water is a clear biblical symbol for their official emblem, the bright shining Diagram Star. Everything that happens at a well full of water is natural and right.

Like everything else in nature humans multiply by cell division. In order to have children that can pass on human life on earth it is a law of nature that a man and a woman represent a whole natural unit. Symbolical man and woman are one when together in a marriage. They are in the centre of the Diagram Star, and the cell division they do together produces their sons and daughters that can be symbolical placed in the sections around the centre. The Diagram Stars tells how the whole world was populated.

Abraham and Sara had one child, Isaac, and they find a wife for Isaac when time is right. Rebecca is brought in to the camouflaged story beside a well full of water, and the Master writing the story is telling you that Rebecca is born by knowledge and goodness and that she is the right woman for Isaac.

Rebecca

Moses 24, 62-67

The day Rebecca and the servant came; Isaac was out in the field. He were waking and thinking when he looked up and saw the camels coming in his direction. "Who is that beautiful woman?" he thought.

In the same moment Rebecca saw Isaac. "Who is that handsome man?" she asked Abrahams servant.

"It is Isaac." When she heard, she hurried covering her face with her veil. But her eyes sparkled when Isaac stopped her camel. It was love at first sight. God had provided the right person for Isaac – and for Rebecca.

Everything that happens in this story is by nature right. Every man needs a woman by his side in order for them to be a whole productive unit together. It is always a mother and father that is the centre in all families and the family lines back in history are very long, longer than you think. The children get older and soon become the centre in their own families and like that the life of humans on earth moves on in to a future that always is there, in front of present time.

A tribal people consist of many different families, and all young men and women had to have permission from their parent and the tribal council in order to get married.

In our present time, in the so called rich and modern part of the world, it is only horses, dogs and other domestic animals that are bred. Humans are mostly a hybrid race were the reproduction of children is more by change than by nature. The natural feeling of tribal belonging is long gone and replaced with an enforced national belonging based on the history of war and conflicts.

Marriages without the family pride and tribal belonging are left to change and most of them fall apart. When the dance around the golden calf becomes the most important activity of the majority of people and inherited riches and power based is the main motivation for a marriage, live suddenly turns meaningless.

All the members of a tribal council are teachers, scholars and wise men, and when the time comes that the tribe gets too big to feed properly of the land, a part of the tribe is selected to leave and find new land to settle on. Like that the tribe is divided by regular cell division, and like that the whole world was populated.

All tribal people in present time that are called aborigines have their origin from earlier Motherlands in other parts of the world. Most of them struggle hard to continue to live like they always have done, because they know that their life form is the only one that will survive the next large is-age. It is only people living in self supported villages that will survive.

The twin brothers

Moses 25, 22-26

Isaac and Rebecca were married and lived happily together. But the years went by and they did not have any children. Rebecca and Isaac waited and waited, until Isaac prayed to God that he had to make it happen that Rebecca had children.

Shortly after God answered Isaacs prayer, but not the way he expected. Rebecca was not going to have one child, but two! Twins!

The children grew in her womb. Rebecca often felt them kicking. One night she woke suddenly. The children had kicked each other so hard that she felt it hurting. She prayed to God: "Lord, is there anything wrong with my children? If it hurts in me when they kick like that, it must hurt them as well. What is happening?

God answered her: "The two boys you are carrying shall be fathers to great tribal nations. One nation will be stronger than the other, and the oldest will do as the youngest asks him to do."

The time came for Rebecca to have her children. The oldest was red. The whole of the little body was covered with hair. He was named Esau, which means "hairy."

A few minutes later the brother was born. He held on to Esau's foot with a little hand, and the parents named him Jacob, which means "Him who holds the heel."

The camouflaged story about the twin brothers Esau and Jacob, fighting already in their mother's womb, is a symbol for nations fighting each other in present time. Rebecca is a symbol for Mother Earth and the twin brothers is not just brothers fighting for the right of the first born to their father's position as a chief; they are fighting for the best agriculture land and for the riches and personal power that comes with being the strongest.

The twin brothers symbolizes national states and tribal people that up through the known world history have fought for the same thing; the best land, being the richest and strongest nation and the world.

The camouflaged story is about individual humans, families and the whole world population, which constantly are breaking the common laws and rules for living as given by the superior Motherland council. Everything changed for the worst after the Motherland went under.

In our present time there are an ongoing chaos of wars and conflict between peoples that truly are brothers. They fight to be the largest, richest and strongest nation, and it is a fight that leads towards a total destruction of Mother Earth. Very soon the Mother Earth has to take action and tell the world leaders living by the laws and rules derived from the three factors of the Original Sin is wrong. When living right the best leader is always democratically elected from the whole village population.

An expensive meal

Moses 25, 27-34

Many years went by and the boys grew up. They were clever and skilled in a different way. Jacob was a quiet boy. Often he helped at home and he spoke a lot with his parents. Esau was fond of hunting and it happened that he shot wild animals.

One day Jacob was making a meal, Esau came home from hunting. He was very hungry, after not eaten anything the whole day.

"Please! Let me have some of what you are cooking!" he said to Jacob and sat down by the fire with him. He was very impatient while waiting for the meal to get ready, so he could eat.

Jacob heard the elder brother talk about how hungry he was and he started thinking out a plan. Esau had something Jacob wanted to have. It was the right of the first born. Jacob therefore made an agreement with Esau and said: "If you are as hungry as you say, you can sell me the right of the first born, and I will give you food."

Esau did not listen to what his brother said. He was so hungry that he thought he was going to die. Therefore he did not care about anything else. "I agree to anything, if I only get food!"

"Swear on that," said Jacob.

Esau did swear. He sold his right as a first born to Jacob.

The time before the Motherland went under really was a paradise for the whole world population. The whole world was living with one set of laws and rules. The Motherland Parliament had twelve democratically elected members from all tribal peoples in the world. It was a world without national borders, without the global capitalistic system and without all the religions in the world.

It is this paradise world with lasting peace that is the birthright for the whole world population. The birthright was taken away because people all over the world suffered from a severe famine in the time after the Motherland was destroyed. Therefore you and the whole world population have lived in the land of Nod for several thousand years, aimlessly wandering and not knowing that your forefathers sold your birthright for food.

All this happened because the Egyptian hieroglyphs telling the full story about the lost Motherland was translated wrong in to the Hebrew language by incompetent people. Time has come to claim your birthright back. Your birthright is to live in a world with lasting world peace, a world where no one is afraid, hungry, cold or homeless. The world needs a new Motherland and a new superior Motherland council, and you can make it come true.

This is a valid example of the cruel and merciless trade activity that went on and still goes on between the rich and the poor nations in the world. There are national state armed forces behind all kind of trade, and the rich countries work closely together in order to exploit the many poor countries to the maximum. The aid the rich nations give back to the poor nation to help them survive as a nation is the modern way to make the poor nations in to new colonies, totally dependent on financial aid from the rich nations in order to survive.

In the poor nations thousands of humans dies every day because of reasons caused by poverty. The poor nations in the world are selling their birthright to the rich nations in order to avoid people from starving to death. It is a poverty imposed on them by the imperial colony builders of the past.

The empire builders in our known world history are to look at as merciless murders and criminals, every single one of them. They lived with the three factors of the Original Sin and passed it on to new generation by use of an illegal law of birthright. The empire builders of present time are, with the same merciless and cruelty, building their existence on the three factors of the Original Sin. They keep on building the tower reaching for the sky, and they are proudly calling out to the world how great they are as a nation.

Shall the tower be taken down by use of only peaceful means while it still can be done, or is it going to fall by the strong forces of Mother Nature in an infernal ocean of fire? No matter what, the tower has to come down before a new world can be built for the coming generations.

It is the world you live in that is the land of Nod. Mankind sold their birthright a long time ago, because of a severe global famine. Soon the forces of evil took control of every single human being. Your forefathers choose to settle on new fertile land and live like slaves, soldiers and servants. Now you inherit their wrong choice, not knowing how life was back then in a world with lasting world peace. You don't know your rightful heritage because the history about the lost Motherland was denied and made in to a religion.

Rebecca is clever

Moses 27, 1-40

When the brothers became older, is becomes clear that Rebecca was most fond of Jacob. She loved Esau to, but she wanted Jacob to have the best of everything.

When Isaac got very old, he lost his eyesight. One day he said to Esau: "My son, since you are the oldest, I will give you my blessing. But first I want you to shot a wild animal and make me a good meal. Thereafter I will give you my blessing."

Rebecca heard what he said. When Esau was gone, she said to Jacob: "Your father is going to give Esau the blessing, but I want you to have it. Go home and slaughter a couple of your best kid goats. I shall cook them like Isaac likes the meat. Then you can go to him with it, and you get the blessing instead of your brother.

Jacob did as she said. When the meal was ready, Rebecca tied goat fur around Jacobs's neck and arms, to make him look like Esau. Jacob went to his father.

"How could you find it so quickly, my son," Isaac asked.

"The Lord helped me."

"But you sound like Jacob? Come here," said Isaac. He felt on him with his hands. "You feel like Esau."

Isaac tasted the food Jacob gave to him. He liked it. "Now you shall have the blessing," he said.

A blessing is something special. Isaac knew that God was listening. He asked him to make his son a rich man and that other tribal people, among them his own brother, should serve him. He asked God to bless all people that were good to him and course everyone that wanted to harm him. When Isaac finished praying, Jacob left him.

As soon as Jacob had gone, Esau came home from the hunting trip! He ran in to his father, but Isaac said: "Why do you come back again?"

"I have not been here before," Esau protested.

Isaac sighted. "Then it must have been Jacob, Esau. Your brother has stolen your blessing.

Esau became furious with his brother and wanted to kill him.

The symbolism in this story is that Rebecca, as a symbol for Mother Earth, uses natural selection, instead of following a law that is truly unnatural and made up by the warrior kings and priesthoods. The Master writing this camouflaged story knew that Rebecca did the right thing. Even in a world with a brutal and merciless fight for personal power and riches, it is the forces of Mother Nature that gives the victory to the person with the best personal abilities and the strongest spiritual strength.

Think through the never stopping fight between good and evil once more. Without the evil present in the common world of thoughts, represented by the three factors of the Original Sin, the forces of good, represented by the Diagram Star, would get back its original and natural meaning.

According to the laws and rules given by the superior Motherland council the election of a tribal leader is done by all the tribal members in agreement with the village council. Even if a good leader has many sons, there is no guarantee that any of them is the best suitable leader.

A divided family

Moses 27, 41-46

Esau could almost not believe that his brother had swindled him a second time. First Jacob had taken from him his right as the first born, all the riches that Isaac should leave when he died. And now he had taken the blessing, Gods protection for the future. Esau became so angry at his brother that he decided to kill him.

Rebecca discovered what Esau was thinking, so she warned Jacob. "You have to travel far away. Go to your family," she said. Jacob packed his tings quickly; said god by and disappeared in to the desert.

When Esau heard about it, Jacob was already long gone. Esau understood that it was no use in tracking him. Therefore he stayed with his parent and took good care of them, old as they were.

Esau did not get his father's blessing, and he was stupid enough to sell his birthright for a meal, but he understood that it was an honor to take care of the parents in their old age. He wanted to take care of the family until Jacob returned home.

The Diagram Star is among many other things speaking about natural selection and cell division. The nature always make the right selection out from the best genetic abilities, while humans in present time always make their choices out from their egotistic and self written unnatural laws and rules for living.

The humans, who survived the catastrophe that destroyed the Motherland some twelve thousand years ago, were forced to continue their lives without the common laws and rules for living that were natural and right. They had to think for them self and make choices to protect their own family and tribe. The decisions they had to make were often very difficult because those who made them knew they were wrong.

This is the camouflaged story where Mother Nature herself is selecting the best person to be the forefather for the whole world population. The descendants after Jacob is a symbol for the whole world population and the Master writing the story is telling you that your forefather Jacob did not have the best personal qualities and personal strength. He followed his mother's advice, swindled his brother for his birthright and escaped like a coward in to the desert. Just remember it is a camouflaged story that had to be acceptable for the enemy at the time it was written in to the Bible, the Roman emperors. The story is fictive, explaining how the whole world population had to accept that the forces of evil were in charge over the forces of good.

With the camouflage the whole Bible is describing how the chaos of wars and conflicts developed from brothers fighting brothers to the warrior kings and priesthoods who are controlling the whole world population in present time.

Wrestling and Jacobs's new name

Moses 32, 1-31

After twenty years in the land of his mother the day came when Jacob wanted to go back home. He had two wives, many children and hundreds of sheep's and goats.

When Jacob came near to his home, he became more and more nervous for the meeting with Esau. Was his brother still angry at him?

The night before they should meet, he felt small. It was a night full of surprises, a night that Jacob never would forget. While he stood alone under the stars and prayed, a man came out from the desert. It was dark, and Jacob could not see who it was. It was not Esau. No matter who it was, it was a strong man, and he started to fight with Jacob.

The whole night they fought. They rolled around in the sand. Jacob was breading hard. But it looked like neither of them should get the upper hand. They were equally strong. Then the stranger touched Jacobs's hip joint and it game out of joint. It caused him a terrible pain.

The strange man said: "Let me go, because the sun is soon to rise."

Then Jacob understood who it was. "He is not a human," he thought by himself. "Either it is an angel, or…. Could it be true? Is it God the Lord himself?"

"What is your name?" asked the stranger.

"Jacob."

"Your name shall no longer be Jacob. Your new name is Israel, because you have fought with God and with man and won," said the stranger.

"And what is your name?" Jacob asked.

The stranger did not replay. He blessed Jacob. Suddenly he was gone, and Jacob understood that he had been face to face with God.

The sky was shining in pink and gold when Jacob returned to camp.

Jacob, who got the name Israel in contact with God, is symbolizing the ancestor of all humans, the father of the symbolic twelve tribes that emigrated from the Motherland in order to populate the whole world. Most of the tribes are in our time so mixed together that it is difficult to tell them apart. The tribal people that are descending from the son of Jacob called Juda and are calling themselves Jews have kept together by use of their old traditions. Jacob, who got the name Israel, is the symbolic forefather for the whole world population.

The Jews have only one part of the Diagram Star in their flag. It is an empty star, without the double circle symbolizing the sun and the moon in the centre and without the twelve sections around, symbolizing the superior Motherland council and the whole world population. They call it the star of King David. Do the Jews know that the whole story about King David is fictive, explaining the building of a new Motherland and the election of a new superior Motherland council? Do the Jews know anything at all about the lost Motherland?

It was the whole world population, including the Jews, who made the choice of hiding the Diagram Star in the Ark of the Covenant and start the dance around the Golden Calf. The strong light that was looked in to the gold plated chest was the knowledge about the lost Motherland symbolized by the Diagram Star. The diagram is the official emblem of the superior Motherland council, a symbol for the sun, the moon and the twelve star signs of the Zodiac. Back then the people made the choice to forget about the lost Motherland and continue the dancing around the Golden Calf. Remember now that this camouflaged story was translated in to the Hebrew language from Egyptian hieroglyphs. The translation was far from correct.

Then eight hundred years passed before the story was written again, camouflaged in to a religion by people who wanted to preserve and pass on the history about the lost Motherland to coming generations. The first Christians knew the history and how people lived with freedom in the lost Motherland, and they were killed for what they knew. The twelve apostles were Masters and teachers and they were also brutally killed for what they knew.

Without the common teaching in the symbolic light of the Diagram Star, the knowledge about the lost Motherland and its superior council faded and was remembered only in the many legends, myths and tales. The new generation had to hold on to the all the stories as a hope for the coming of a new world with lasting peace. The camouflaged stories grew in to the strong belief in the many religions in the world. The religious believers don't know that religions are the third part of the Original Sin.

The dancing around the Golden Calf still goes on, and the religious leaders are dancing in the inner circle with the rich and the powerful. More and more people are dying in the outer circles because no one knows how to stop the dance. But the hope for a new world under the laws and rules that are given by a new Motherland council still lives on.

The Diagram Star, without its complete form, is meaningless. It is found used by people all over the world in one shape or another. From ancient times all stone settings are the history book of the local population as well as a copy of the Diagram Star. One copy as the one used in this book was found in a Maya temple in Yucatan.

Women and men who lived with the knowledge about the origin of the Diagram Star and the global government system that kept lasting peace in the world before the Motherland went under, was systematically killed, wrongly accused as witches and wizards, while the meaningless camouflage religion was imposed on the population by use of warfare and merciless force.

It is important to know that the wizards and witches of our resent history were the last humans living with the knowledge hereby told to you. They were the last good people with knowledge about the lost Motherland, while the warrior kings and priesthoods were living in luxury using the three forces of the Original Sin to control the population completely. Therefore it is natural if the knowledge presented here is turning your world of thoughts upside down. The total change that happened to Paul on the road to Damascus is a good description of what will happen to your world of thoughts.

There will shine a light for you to, when you realize that all the camouflaged biblical stories have been written in order to preserve and pass on the knowledge about a global system of government. It is truly the only political system that can restore lasting peace on planet Earth.

Knowledge about the Motherland, the Diagram Star and the common set of laws and rules for living, was systematically wiped out by the warrior kings and priesthoods. Only the group of people calling them self the Masters used their life to preserve and pass on the history about the Motherland.

Jacob got the name Israel from the Master who wrote this camouflaged story, and he is telling you and the whole world population that all the tribal people that descend from the symbolic twelve sons of Jacob are the biblical Israelites.

It is clear that all the descendants of Jacob are a symbol for the whole world population, and therefore you all are the rightful biblical Israelites. The so called modern populations in the industrialized part of the world are slowly destroying all earth life. Every one of you descends from the biblical Israelites, who symbolical made the first choice and settled in old Egypt. There they became slaves, soldiers and servants for Pharaoh, the force of evil, as you all still are.

The God that Jacob fought with is the spiritual force of the superior Motherland council that the Diagram Star is telling about. Jacob became Israel, the forefather of the whole world population. The fight was mental and took place in Jacobs's world of thoughts.

In a sense it was a fight between the light of knowledge and the darkness of oblivion. It is the mental fight that you and the whole world population have to fight in your own world of thoughts and win. The knowledge has to be won back, in order to know how to build a new world with lasting peace.

If the camouflaged stories like this not had been preserved and passed on from one generation to another, the knowledge from the Diagram Star would have been lost for all times. The Masters of old never gave up, because knowledge is the spiritual sword that can demolish all religious belief in the world.

Trouble in the tent

Moses 37, 1-4

Finely Jacob came home, and he learned that Esau had forgiven him. Jacob came home just before his father died. After that Esau left home in order to create a home of his own.

On the long journey home Jacobs favored wife, Rachel, died. She left to sons, Joseph and Benjamin. Jacob had ten sons more.

Jacob settled in the parents' home, were he raised his twelve sons. He was particularly fond of Joseph and Benjamin, because they were Rachel's children. This his other sons did not like.

One day Jacob gave to Joseph a very nice coat. He sent for his son and said: "Here, my son, this is for you."

Joseph was surprised. It was great fun to get a new coat, and the like of this he had never seen before. "I do not deserve something that nice," he said.

"Don't be foolish, Joseph. It is a gift. I give it to you because I want you to have it."

Joseph accepted the gift. But when his brothers saw him with the new coat on, they became even angrier with him then before. "Why don't we get gifts like that?" they mumbled.

The symbolism in this story is also clearly visible for everyone with knowledge of the Diagram Star and the Masters formula: Water = Knowledge.

Rachel came in to the story for the first time at a well full of water. This means that her two children are conceived right according to the laws given by the superior Motherland council. They are in a class of their own, thinking only right in a world where envy, greed and wrong thinking was developing. The two brothers are a part of the red line of good people in all the camouflaged stories that is preserving and passing on the knowledge about the lost Motherland.

A well full of water is a symbol for knowledge and good and an empty well is a symbol for ignorance and evil. The ten other sons of Joseph were born by Rachel's older sister Leah, a wife Jacob was tricked to get married to.

For all the Masters the underlying story was easy to understand. They had grown up being educated to read the stories like symbols, and to hide their knowledge from the ruling elite. Most Masters lived under cover hiding for warrior kings and priesthoods. Even if the last Masters died long ago, they were an underground movement that still exists in the common world of thoughts. Every one of you has the ability to think their thoughts, but how many of you are brave enough to oppose the laws and rules of your national state and the world.

59

It is a fact that the knowledge the Masters protected and passed on to coming generation, still is strongly opposed by religious leaders that hold on to their wrongful belief in dogmas and assumptions. Now the lost knowledge truly is approaching the light, and it will finally put a stop to the chaos of wars and conflicts in the world.

The beautiful coat that Joseph gets from his father has the same meaning as a fathers blessing of the son who is to preserve and pass on the knowledge of the lost Motherland. The Master writing this camouflaged story has to describe Joseph as a person doing everything right no matter what.

Before the Motherland was destroyed the whole world population lived doing only right. The belonging to a tribe and living with the respect and pride coming from doing only right was very important. The very few who did wrong was severely punished by disrespect from everyone and perhaps expelled from the tribe for life.

Therefore it is important to see the red line of people struggling to do right in a world where the forces of evil always have the upper hand. The people doing only right and good in the Bible are describing how living was like in the time before the Motherland went under. The general idea is that the global government system of the lost Motherland will return soon, very soon.

Josephs dream

Moses 37, 5-11

On morning Joseph woke up quickly. He had dreamt something strange. It was so unreal that he felt he had to tell somebody.

He went to his brothers. "You cannot guess what I dreamt tonight," he said when he found them. The brothers did not seem enthusiastic to see him, but Joseph was so preoccupied with his dream that he did not notice. He said: "I had a strange dream. We were all together out in the field binding sheaf of corn. Suddenly my sheaf of corn stood up, while yours sheaf of corn was standing in a circle around mine and bowing for it."

The brothers got angry. "Who do you think you are? You are not a king! We will never bow to you!"

A few nights later Joseph had another dream. And he told it to his brothers. "Listen," he said, "This time I dreamt that the sun and the moon and eleven stars bowed to me." It made the brothers even angrier.

When Joseph told his father, Jacob became angry to. "You must never be proud, Joseph," he said.

With this camouflaged story the Master is outlining the whole following story about Joseph. The story is simply about how the three factors of the Original Sin was formed and put in to the system of government rule. Joseph's dreams are told in the beginning, so they in the following stories can come true.

The dream, with the camouflage removed, means that the twelve tribal people that have their origin as the sons of Jacob, are the symbolic twelve tribes that emigrated from the Motherland and populated the whole world.

This is a good example of how the hieroglyphs writings about the lost Motherland were wrongly translated in to the Hebrew literary language. In the dream Rebecca is a symbol for the lost Motherland and Jacob is a symbol for the superior Motherland council. Put them in the centre of the Diagram Star and the twelve sons in the sections around.

Joseph is a symbol for the new Motherland that was planned to be built in old Egypt before the forces of evil took command. In the dream he becomes the superior Motherland council and his brothers are symbolizing the whole world population. The evil Pharaoh and his armed forces put a stop to the plan to build a new Motherland. The force of good was and still is second in command.

The dream about the sun, the moon and the eleven stars is about the Diagram Star, the official emblem of the superior Motherland council. It is a fundamental fact that all the people in the world have to elect a new superior Motherland council among them self, and obey them in all matters of life.

The camouflaged story about the biblical Israelites is telling you, their descendants living in present time, about the process were the whole world population became working slaves, soldiers and servants under the laws and rules of the superior elite of self appointed warrior kings and priesthoods.

The underlying message is that the whole world population still is governed by the same despotic government system that first was imposed in old Egypt. It is a global government system with many national states, a global capitalistic system and all the religions in the world, still controlling the common world of human thoughts.

It is the rule of the many national states that the world leaders have great difficulties letting go, possibly because they don't know about the hidden message in the Bible. They will have to remove the three factors of the Original Sin, in order to save mankind from making them self extinct.

In present time the whole world population is still submissive slaves, soldiers and servants, and does willingly let their lives be controlled by the three factors of the Original Sin. In order to demand full freedom from organized legalized slavery, all humans have to find the knowledge about the lost Motherland and learn to read the Diagram Star as an open book. It is the only way to build a new world with lasting peace.

The building of national states all over the world, the capitalistic system and all the religions in the world are truly a severe crime against mankind, and the people living in present time are preserving and passing on the inheritance of their forefathers, believing it is the only right thing to do.

Joseph is thrown into the well

Moses 37, 12.24

One day Joseph played with Benjamin, Jacob said to him: "Joseph, I want you to go to your brothers, were they are with the sheep. Se that everything is in order with them all and then come back to me and tell me how they are.

Joseph was glad and went away. He thought it was a nice day for a mission like that. He walked far, but finally he saw the brother's camp in a distance.

When the brothers saw him coming, they immediately started planning. "There is the stupid dreamer Joseph coming," they said. "Now we know how to get rid of him ones and for all. Let us throw him in one of the dry wells here, and we can say the he was killed by a wild animal. Ha! If he dies, then his dreams will certainly not come true.

"No, wait!" the oldest brother said. His name was Ruben. "Throw him in the well, but don't kill him, at least not yet." This he said because he knew if he managed to get Joseph out of the well and save his life, his father Jacob would look at him as a hero.

Joseph hurried up the last little hillside and smiled to his brothers. At last he had found them. But when he saw how they were looking at him, his smile disappeared.

The brothers formed a ring around him. Wherever he saw, he saw hostile faces. Before he knew what was coming, they jumped at him. They tore of his nice coat and threw him in to the dark and dry well.

Joseph called out his fright, but it did not help. He landed on the bottom of the well and looked up. All he could see was the laughing faces of his brothers. They poured sand over him. Joseph covered his face with his hands and stood against the wall. When the brothers went away, he started crying. He wished that he was back with his father and brother again.

The superior Motherland council is powerless as spiritual human beings. They cannot prevent the power of evil for taking control over the power of good. But the power of good grows strong and gets to be second in command. By now you should be able to see how the force of evil uses the force of good to control people.

Everything that happens at well without water is a symbol for wrong doing. What the brothers did was because of their envy. It is about the law of inheritance and succession and the strong wish for personal riches and power. The story is also about obtaining respect as a good person on false premises. True respect can only be obtained by doing right.

Look at the twelve brothers as the whole world population. Is there tribal people and nations that are treated in this way by the many stronger nations in the world? A long time ago, everyone who always did right and knew all about the common laws and rules for living from before the Motherland was destroyed, was symbolical thrown in to a dry well, and is still there waiting to get up.

In our present time it is the evil doing of the descendants of the ten brothers that dictates the evolution of the world. The time has come to make a mends and let the forces of only good return to the world.

If you look back in history, it is situations like this that the Masters and their followers had to live with when they were working to preserve and pass on the knowledge about the global system of government the lost Motherland. One Master often stood alone against a warrior king thinking only about his own personal power and riches. A Master had only his superior spiritual strength to rely on. A solid prove that the forces of evil did win over the forces of good is the chaos of wars and conflicts that still goes on in the world.

A dry well is a symbol for a Diagram Star without knowledge. Water = Knowledge. The eleven brothers were thinking evil thoughts and did an act of evil. All they need to stop thinking evil thoughts and do evil deeds are a symbolic return of water to the well. That will happen when they understand that their thoughts and deeds are wrong and evil. The whole world population cannot be punished for doing wrong, when the common laws and rules of the national state says that they are doing things right.

On the way to Egypt

Moses 37, 22-35

Later the same day one of Joseph's brothers got a terrible idea. Juda pointed at a caravan. "Do you see the slave traders over there? Let us sell him to them." Ruben was not there, so he could not save Joseph. He was out looking after the sheep.

When the slave traders got closer, the brothers pulled Joseph up from the well. The traders paid twenty silver coins for him, but him on a donkey and continued their journey in to the desert.

When Ruben came back to the camp, he went straight to the well. "Joseph," he whispered. "Are you ok? I will get you up tomorrow." He was still trying to be a hero in the eyes of their father. But he got no answer. "Joseph!" he called. Still he did not get a reply.

"Why do you speak to an empty well?" Juda laughed.

"But where is he?" asked Ruben. "What have you done to our brother?" He took hold in Juda and shook him.

"Relax," said Juda. "Here is your part." He gave him two silver coins.

"Have you sold him as slave?"

"Yes, our spoiled brother is now on the way to Egypt," Juda laughed.

Ruben knew how much Joseph meant to their father. This news would break Jacobs's heart.

The next day the brothers slaughtered a goat and dipped Josephs coat in the blood. Then they went home and showed it to Jacob.

Jacob cried out loud: "That is my son's coat! A wild animal have killed him. Joseph is dead!"

This is also in the beginning of the Original Sin. The difference between the good and the evil is put in motion. The twelve brothers are together a symbol for the twelve tribes that in the time after the Motherland was destroyed symbolized the living conditions for the whole world population.

This is also a hieroglyph wrongly translated. The ten brothers did something evil against their brother Joseph, but as the story shows their evil deed lead to first something good and then something bad for the biblical Israelites. They survived a severe famine and prospered in old Egypt for some four hundred years. Then they discovered that they were nothing but slaves, soldiers and servants.

Joseph is in this camouflaged story sold as a slave. He continues to do right in a world where the forces of good always are second in command. He and ends up ruling all of Egypt, with only the laws and rules of Pharaoh over him. The story tells us that the good forces, with Joseph as a superior leader, invite his father Jacob and all his brothers to settle in Egypt. The good Pharaoh gives them the best land.

This is just what the superior Motherland council would have done in the time before the Motherland was destroyed. The kindness and wisdom of Pharaoh proves that he was in the last group of people who arrived directly from the Motherland before it went under. For a long period of time Pharaoh was a council of twelve members and tried to rule the world with only the forces of good. Then the Pharaoh turned evil and forced the biblical Israelites, the whole world population, in to obedient slaves, soldiers and servants.

Joseph is a symbol for the new superior Motherland council, trying to do build a new Motherland in old Egypt and be as good as possible in a world where all humans on planet earth are missing the firm and physical leadership of the lost Motherland. It was the good leadership of Joseph that helped the Israelites to survive during a severe and long lasting famine.

The ten evil brothers of Joseph are a symbol for the whole world population. They did regret all their evil deeds and became good people when the living got difficult for everyone. The leadership of Joseph is a symbol for what the superior Motherland council always would do for people in need anywhere in the world, in the time before it was destroyed. The Egyptian hieroglyph this story was translated from is simply telling the true Motherland history, how it was and how it can be if you all learn to read the Diagram Star as an open book.

Pharaoh of Egypt later became a tyrannical governing system that in our present time still is used by national states all over the world. All humans, including the world leaders, are all born in to the evil government system with many national states, with a global capitalistic system and all the religions in the world.

If only all humans in the world could get to see the Egyptian Hieroglyphs and learn to understand them correctly, you would all know the lost world history, the world history mankind needs in order to be able to build a new world with lasting peace.

It is impossible for the national leaders in present time to even imagine a global government system without the tree factors of the Original Sin. The inherited laws and rules they live by and obey to the letter; is Pharaoh after he became an evil dictator. Even if the slaves, soldiers and servants in the rich counties are well paid they are still submissive slaves, soldiers and servants under an evil ruling system they have inherited.

In the time before the Motherland went under people lived with a strong sense of belonging to their tribe. Jacob and his twelve sons are explaining how all the people in the world were living as brothers and friends until the three factors of the Original Sin drove them apart. The tribal people were used to live with long lasting peace. They were all living in self supported villages; and they were all rich in gold, silver and precious stones.

The enormous riches of the Egyptian Pharaoh came from demanding a high prize for food in times of hunger. Because of their greed and quest for personal power, all the rich and self supported tribal people were systematical attacked and robbed for everything of value. The many different tribes living in villages or in tents as nomads were forced in to a life as a slave worker for the small elite around Pharaoh. With the stolen riches and the large workforce they started building the many large monuments.

The Pharaoh elite were the last of the people who came from the Motherland before it went under for good. They lived with the advanced knowledge and obeyed the common laws and rules for living for a long time, before they got greedy for riches and personal power and stated making laws and living rules of they own.

What Pharaoh did is a symbol for what happened all over the world in the time after the Motherland was destroyed. Self elected warrior kings and priesthoods started to attack tribal people, stealing all their valuables and forcing them in to a life as obedient slave workers, soldiers and servants. The many brave humans fighting against the new ruler was brutally killed.

It is the descendants of the slaves, soldiers and servants that are the whole world population in our present time. The knowledge of the Motherland and the global system of government with common laws and rules for living, were forgotten up until present time. By use of modern technology and Internet it is possible to spread the knowledge to the whole world population.

Egypt and the land around the delta Nile is a background symbolizing the whole world, like a theatrical stage. Jacob and his twelve sons are symbolizing the whole world population. All the camouflaged stories in the Bible are always told to people living in present time. The Masters is describing the world as it was and still is, and it will stay that way as long as the tree factors of the Original Sin are allowed to occupy your world of thoughts.

Joseph in Potiphars house

Moses 37, 36-39

Joseph traveled a long time with the slave traders and it was very hot in the desert. "Lord God," he whispered. "I don't know how life will be in Egypt. Maybe I have to drag stones to their pyramids. But, Master. Look after my brother Benjamin, and let me see my father again."

After many days journey the caravan came to a large city. Joseph was sold on the slave market. When he saw his new master, he knew at ones that God would help him.

The man who bought Joseph was named Potiphar. He was rich, but there was something that was more important. He was a good man. Joseph did not have to drag stones to the pyramids. He became a servant in Potiphars house.

Joseph worked eagerly for Potiphar. All the time he tried to find something that had to be done. Every time he was asked to do something, he wanted to do it properly, in order to make God pleased with him.

First and foremost he kept the house clean. Then he supervised everything that was done in the fields, and he also had an eye on preparing of food. Soon Potiphar put him in charge over everything he owned. The only thing Potiphar had to do was to decide what he himself was going to have for dinner every day.

The Master writing the story is telling the people living in present time that the way Joseph lives, thinks and acts is the only way to live under all circumstances. If he had done different, he would be just another submissive slave. By following his own conviction about doing everything right in the light of the Diagram Star and by using his spiritual strength and abilities, his personality is making him a leader wherever and whenever he lives.

The hieroglyph is describing how life was for the whole world population before the Motherland was destroyed in a natural catastrophe.

People lived with the forces of good totally without knowing the forces of evil. They were all living in self supported villages and had all they needed to live a good life on planet earth. Imagine the difference and what effect the removal of the three factors of the Original Sin would have for our children and their descendants.

Joseph is the red line of rightfulness that is found in all the camouflaged stories in the Bible. All the religions in the world, as well as the many myths, tales and legends came in to the common world of thoughts after the Motherland was destroyed. In the light of the Diagram Star it is possible for every one of you to travel back in time and see for yourself what it is like to live in a world where everyone lives with democratically elected leaders like Joseph.

All you have to do to understand the global system of government of the lost Motherland is to wake up some of your dormant brain cells and perhaps build some new ones. One good example in our present time is that not one of the royal families in the world is really needed. They are just taking up space while preserving and passing on the three factors of the Original Sin.

How Heaven and Hell came to be have a natural explanation. You know that when someone in your family dies, you remember them and imagine their spirit has gone to a spiritual world, and as thoughts they live on in your mind as long as you live. When the Motherland was destroyed some twelve thousand years ago, 64 million humans died in the catastrophe. Among them was the superior Motherland council, known to the whole world because every tribe had a representative as a regular Motherland council member.

Therefore you can think and decide for yourself how the superior Motherland council would be remembered by the whole world population. The whole Motherland was remembered as a spiritual Heaven, and the twelve members of the superior council were remembered as the omnipotent, omniscient and omnipresent God, still representing the good forces of nature in the world. But as spiritual beings they had lost their physical power. Gradually and unstoppable the forces of evil took control over the common world of thoughts.

Hell was the name for the forces of evil that took control over all humans. The three factors of the Original Sin made life on earth in to a living Hell for the whole world population. The self elected warrior kings and priesthoods started exploiting the population everywhere, forcing them in to a life as a willing working slaves, soldiers and servants. You are still living in Hell, but now you can do something about it. Start planning how you want the Promised Land, meaning a new world with lasting peace, to be built. The whole world population has to build a peaceful future together, actively with the use of only peaceful means. The waiting for Jesus to come back as a person is ridiculous. The Egyptian hieroglyph clearly states that Jesus is the born again Motherland history. Only the history about the lost Motherland can tell mankind how the new world with lasting peace can be built.

There is nothing holy in the world as decided by the religious leaders. The word Holy is derived from the wholeness in nature, the wholeness that no humans are allowed to alter. Humans have changed the wholeness of nature for some twelve thousand years, and the result is the world you see around you. If the destructive human activity continues in to the future, there will be no future for our children and their descendants.

Learn to understand the Diagram Star fully. It will open a whole new world of thoughts for you, and give you a true meaning with your life on planet earth. All humans have their own Diagram Star as a base for their thoughts. All you have to do is find it and learn to understand it. With the knowledge you are given the natural gift of being able to divide right from wrong in all matters of life.

In prison

Moses 39, 7-20

Joseph grew in the time he was with Potiphar. He became a young man. Everything he started to do was successful for him.

On day Potiphars wife looked out the window, she thought: "This Joseph is truly a handsome young man. My husband is away for some days. Perhaps I can get Joseph for myself." She asked Joseph to come in to her bedroom.

When Joseph came, she said: "Come in to the bed with me, Joseph. You are handsome and strong. Kiss me!"

He shook his head. "You are very beautiful," he said, "but it would not be right."

Potiphars wife felt insulted by a slave saying no to her, so she tried to force him to kiss her, but he pushed her away and ran out. She got a hold of his coat and tore it of him.

When Potiphar came home, she showed Josephs coat to him, and then she lied: "Joseph assaulted me! You thought you could trust him, but you were so wrong. It is a terrible man you have in the house!"

Potiphar believed what she said. He sent for the guard and told them to put Joseph in prison. "Throw away the key," he shouted when the guards pulled Joseph with them.

Thou shall not covet thy neighbor's wife. You shall not be unfaithful. You shall not lie. All the Ten Commandments are to be lived by, and there are no exceptions. But in a world with the three factors of the Original Sin in command you have to obey the evil laws and rules that are added to the commandments by your national leaders and priesthoods.

Through all the camouflaged stories in the Bible there are events that clearly describes people doing things wrong and people doing things right. Separate right from wrong in your own world of thoughts.

If Joseph had given in and done what Potiphars wife wanted, he would have been just another obedient slave. He would have lost his spiritual greatness as one of the pillars in the Bible and become one of the many humans that seek to live as egotistic as possible all the time.

What about you? Don't think about what you have been, but what you can be in a world where long lasting peace is secured with the force of everybody doing the right thing, as a rule.

The personal strength and greatness of Joseph, described in this story, is not found with any of the so called great emperors and warrior kings in our known history. Every single one of them, from Djengis Kahn to the present leaders of the world, is without the spiritual strength that Joseph is an example for. They are committing crimes against mankind, every one of them.

But the world leaders are living without knowledge about the lost Motherland and the Diagram Star and they all do the best they can under the circumstances they were born in to. What colossal natural catastrophes do they have to live through, before they understand that what they are doing is as wrong as wrong can be?

In order to grow as a human being it is often necessary to break with an otherwise perfect life situation. The Master who wrote the camouflaged story had plans for Joseph.

Another thought for you. No matter who you are and where you live in the world, you have the personal qualities of Joseph in you and know them well. But in a world with the forces of evil in command you would do as you were told.

Two men have dreams

Moses 40, 1-23

Joseph was in prison for a long time. One morning two prisoners came to him. They had a problem. "We dreamt something terrible tonight," they said. "Can you tell us what they mean?"

"No," Joseph answered. "I cannot help you, but God can."

One of the prisoners had been the butler for Pharaoh. He said: "In my dream I saw a tree of grapes with three branches. As soon as the flowers blossomed, they turned in to grapes. I held the cup of Pharaoh in my hand and I crushed the grapes in to the cup and gave it to him."

Joseph quietly prayed to God for help. The answer came at ones. "I know what your dream means," he said. "The three branches mean three days. After three days Pharaoh will set you free. Be so kind to ask Pharaoh to let me out of this prison!"

The other prisoner had been the chief baker for Pharaoh. He said: "In my dream there were three baskets of bread. I carried them on my head. In the top basket there was bread for Pharaoh. But a whole lot of birds came, and they did eat all the bread."

Joseph took a heavy breathe. God had shown him what the dream meant. It was not easy to say it. "The three baskets mean three days. After three days Pharaoh will take you life, and birds shall eat your body."

Three days later it happened just like Joseph said.

Not Joseph, but God can help. This means that only a new superior Motherland council can help your dreams to come true in present time.

By use of the Masters formula Joseph is a symbol for knowledge about the lost Motherland. He is in the centre of the Diagram Star and his integrity is unshakeable. I cannot, but God can, he says. This he can do because he lives with the Diagram Star in his thoughts all the time. The diagram shaped like a star is his mental access to the spirit world, where the late superior Motherland council is. The twelve members are his spiritual guide. While in the prison, Joseph helps everyone and are never tempted to do anything wrong. The Master writing the story makes things happen this way for a reason. You are living your life in a mental prison made by the laws and rules of your country. Only the building of a new Motherland and electing a new superior Motherland council can set you free.

Potiphar uses Joseph's knowledge and personal skills because he sees them as right. Joseph is a fictive person used by the Master writing the story in order to make this camouflaged story remembered and passed on in to the future generations.

The stories had to be accepted by the local warrior kings, the roman rulers and the priesthoods, so the parents could tell the stories to the children without risking been punished for it. The camouflaged stories was protected and passed on as more important than human lives, because only the camouflaged Motherland history and the global system of government could set the humans free from being slaves, soldiers and servants under the ruling elite. Before the camouflaged stories became an enforced religion most humans knew their hidden meaning. Joseph was an example human for the whole world population.

The Master who wrote this story knew that understanding the Diagram Star was the only way to set the whole world population free from their mental prison enforced by the three factors of the Original Sin. It was only because Joseph acted the way he did he was thrown in prison, and in prison people came to him for help.

It is the knowledge from the Diagram Star that gives him the ability to tell the two prisoners what their dream means. Helping the two prisoners is access to tell Pharaoh what his dreams means. Thinking and living right in all situations helps him out from the prison and in to the position as the ruler of Egypt with only Pharaoh over him. The story shows you that the forces of good really can rule the whole world without the forces of evil.

This is an important symbol. In our present time Joseph is still in prison and his knowledge about the lost Motherland is cowered up with the many religions in the world. He symbolizes the whole world population, still dreaming about a peaceful world and waiting to be set free. The knowledge of and from the Diagram Star never can be destroyed completely from the common world of thoughts, even if it is kept hidden in the global darkness of oblivion.

Joseph is trying hard to get out of prison, just like the lost history of the Motherland is trying to get out from under the camouflage in the Bible. Look at the bright shining Diagram Star as hidden inside the Ark of the Covenant. It is time to remove the lid and let the whole world population know the world history that is hidden from them.

Think again about a whole world filled with people living like Joseph. It is living with only the forces of good, while you are living in a world where the forces of evil are occupying your world of thoughts. It is a world of difference.

Pharaoh's dreams

Moses 41, 1-8

Two long years went by. Joseph did not hear from Pharaohs butler. He was busy taking care of other prisoners. He gave them some of his food and cleaned their cell. Day after day he looked to the small windows on the wall, where the sunshine gave light. He asked God for help, so he could be set free from prison.

One morning Pharaoh woke and called out: "I dreamt so horrible tonight! It was so real, and I am sure it meant something special." He looked at his servants. "You must not just stand there! Find someone who can interpret my dreams!" he shouted. The servants ran off in fear.

All the wizards, fortune tellers and wise men came. They listened to Pharaoh while he told them the two dreams. They pulled out pictures from their rolls and shook their heads. No, they could not interpret the dreams.

You should know by now that Joseph is a symbol for the knowledge about the lost Motherland. The Master writing the story knows the full story. The small windows in the prison are a good symbol for the star diagram that keeps the history about the lost Motherland alive in present time. Even if it is hidden under the camouflage of religion, knowledge about the lost Motherland will always be there. Knowledge has a cycle just like water, it is a vital part of human thoughts and all humans are now searching for a meaning with life on earth. Break down the mental dark prison wall and let the sunshine in to your world of thoughts.

Do not shake your head and think it cannot be done, because it can. The knowledge from the Diagram Star will rock the world, and that's what's needed in order to let your dreams come true. All the time since the Motherland went under some twelve thousand years ago, the knowledge of and from the Diagram Star have been looked in and forgotten in the Ark of the Covenant, in a symbolic prison. Now the world leaders, living with their shattered religious faith and totally without knowledge about the lost Motherland, are facing global warming and escalating natural catastrophes. They must be told, not what to do, but what will happen no matter what they do.

Pharaoh is a symbol for all the world leaders, political, religious and military. Soon they have to realize that all the three factors of the Original Sin have to be removed all together in order to save the world. All the leaders will be replaced with council of twelve, with the new superior Motherland council in command.

You know that the three factors of evil are: the many national states, the global capitalistic system and all the religions in the world. Only you and the whole world population working together can save the earth and build a world with lasting peace for your children and their descendants. Stop waiting. It is time to put the good force of knowledge in to action with the use of only peaceful means.

Notice that Joseph always knows what he is doing, he knows. Also notice that he always is positive, friendly and helpful, no matter what. He is a symbol for the knowledge that represents only the good in the world, only the good like it was before humans learned about evil.

Knowledge about the lost Motherland is accessible for absolutely all humans in the world. You know what's wrong and what's right in the world, but after been brainwashed to the extent that you believe that religion is right and important, you obey the laws and living rules of your nation without a second thought. How can it be? While thousands of people dies every day, caused by the three factors of the Original Sin. How can it be?

Fat and thin cows

Moses 41, 9-32

The royal butler stood beside Pharaoh. He should see that Pharaohs cup always was full of vine. It was not easy when Pharaoh was so angry.

Then he remembered what he had promised the prisoner. He felt shameful because he had forgotten Joseph completely.

"Pharaoh," said the butler. "While I was in prison, I gave a promise to a Hebrew slave. He told me what my dream meant, and he wanted that I should speak to you on his behalf. I am sure he can be of help now."

Pharaoh nodded. "Go and get the prisoner," he said, and two guards left to do that.

Joseph shaved and dressed in clean cloths, and then he walked to meet Pharaoh. He told Joseph that he had dreamt, and that nobody could tell him what the dreams meant. "Can you tell me that?"

"No, I cannot, but God can," Joseph replayed.

"In my dream I stood by the river Nile," said Pharaoh. "Then seven fat cows came out from the river. After them came seven skinny and ugly cows. Then the seven skinny cows ate the seven fat cows, but when it was done there was just as many skinny as before."

"But I dreamt more. I dreamt about seven good spikes of corn. They grew on one straw. After them grew seven spikes of corn up that were dry, thin and burnt by the eastern wind. The thin spikes swallowed the seven good spikes. All this I told the fortune tellers and wise men, but no one could tell me what it means."

Pharaoh looked at Joseph.

Joseph started praying: "Dear God, what does all this mean?" Suddenly he knew. God opened his mind and he understood what the two dreams meant.

"Pharaoh, the dreams means the same. There will be seven good years with large crop from the fields, but after them there will be seven bad years with almost no crop at all from the field. There will be famine that will be severe for everyone. God sent the dream twice because it is of great importance and God will make it happen soon."

Joseph told Pharaoh about other things that were going to happen.

The Masters selected the history of the Hebrew tribe and camouflaged it by use of the formula, in order to make the camouflaged stories remembered for a long time. Certainly there have been periods with good and bad crops in Egypt, but this story was written much later in the time of the Romans. The priesthoods and scholars who translated all the camouflaged stories from Egyptian Hieroglyphs and hieratic characters in to the Hebrew language made some serious mistakes for reasons not known. The translations from the Hebrew language in to modern written language were equally wrong. The translators had no knowledge of the formula, and wrote the stories down with the camouflage intact.

Like this all the religions in the world was created with a lot of dogmas and assumptions. The world leaders in present time can ask the all the scientists, scholars and religious leaders in the world what to do to create lasting peace in the world, but they will have no answer. The answers the world leaders need are only found in the Diagram Star. They are found beyond twelve thousand years of wars and conflicts, in the history of the lost Motherland. The lost world history has to be taken out from the darkness of oblivion.

Water = Knowledge, say the Masters formula.

River Nile is in this story a symbol for knowledge from the Diagram Star. The cows are coming out from the river. This means that the story came as a dream from the spirit world. The dream was a warning to Pharaoh, and Joseph tells him what the dream means.

The famine on planet earth is increasing rapidly in our present time, caused by the global capitalistic system and the two other parts of the Original Sin. Thousand of humans are dying every day, because of poverty, wars and conflicts and because of imposed religious belief. It is the present time and the future that is important for mankind, but the world leaders have to know the history about the lost Motherland in order to be able to build a new world.

In the time before the Motherland was destroyed the whole world population lived with lasting peace, obeying the common laws and rules of the Diagram Star. Everyone lived in strong houses, had enough to eat and lived together as brothers and friends. They had no knowledge about the evil force of the three factors of the Original Sin that are causing all the problems the whole world population is facing, namely the many national states, the global capitalistic system and all the religions in the world.

Joseph helps Pharaoh

Moses 41, 33-42

Joseph stood in front of Pharaoh. He took a deep breath. "Pharaoh should appoint one man to be responsible for all the food in Egypt," he said. "Large storage houses are needed, so people can get food in the seven years of famine. Then people don't have to starve."

Pharaoh called his advisors. They mumbled and nodded, and then they mumbled more. They stood back when Pharaoh said to Joseph: "Your God is with you in a special way. He helps you, so you can see were others are blind. I feel I can trust you. You are the right man for a job like that. You are to rule over my house, my people and all the storages of food in the land. There shall be no one over you in whole of Egypt, except myself."

Joseph stood back in surprise. The very same morning he had been a prisoner. Now Pharaoh himself gave him a new Egyptian name, Zaphnathpaaneah. The name meant "God speaks. He lives." Pharaoh understood that God spoke through Joseph. And Pharaoh gave him for his wife Asenath, the daughter of Potipherah, priest of On.

It all happened just like Joseph had said. Seven good years came and Joseph filled all the storage building and built many new that also were filled.

When the seven years of famine came, Egypt was the only country that had enough food. People came from all the other countries to get something to eat.

The famine, as it was called, stretched all the ways to Canaan were Joseph's father and his brothers lived.

They had become rich in the seven years of plenty. But when the seven years of famine came, they had very little food. The oldest of Jacobs's sons were adults with families of their own. They were all hungry.

The brothers wondered what they should do. Where could they get food for the families? Jacob knew that there was food in Egypt. That he had heard from a merchant. He said to his sons: "If you don't want to starve to death, you should go to Egypt. Bring enough money and buy corn for all of us."

Joseph is a symbol for the superior Motherland council and represents everything good under the rule of evil. Pharaoh is a symbol for the evil governing system with many national states. As long as the evil system is ruling the world, all the leaders in the world have to do their best for the population they rule over.

In this story Egypt and all the countries around are a theatrical stage for the whole world in present time. Everything that has happened in the history of mankind did happen in present time. Present time for the world population is always now. Ever since the Motherland went under, the whole world have been ruled by a system that is as wrong as wrong can be. It is called the three factors of the Original Sin.

Where are the large storage rooms in present time? How can the poor people with no money buy food? The poor nations in the world have not had seven years of plenty, not ever, and in present time thousands are dying every day because of famine caused by poverty that again is caused by the three factors of the Original Sin.

Some twelve thousand years with little or nothing of everything, is the history of the poor people in the world. There is a very high and strong wall of ignorance between the rich and the poor, and very few nations manages to clime the wall and get over to the side of the rich. The poor nations have to submit to the dictating rich nation before they are given any help at all. The wall between the rich and the poor people are the global capitalistic system.

This story tells about Pharaoh, a true symbol for the world leaders in present time, being warned about a coming famine that will last seven years. Joseph, a symbol for the knowledge derived from the Diagram Star and the lost world history, is set free from prison and put in charge over all of Egypt in order to save people from dying of starvation.

Therefore it is the knowledge lost Motherland and the Diagram Star that can do the right thing in present time and save millions of human lives from starvation alone. A new superior Motherland council, with the Diagram Star as their official emblem, will also put a stop to all the wars and conflicts and remove all religious beliefs in the world.

The Egyptian hieroglyph is clearly describing how the whole world population lived in the time before the Motherland went under. Remove the forces of evil from this camouflaged story and it is all about how the superior Motherland council would take control, give the solution directly to the local councils and save people anywhere in the world from famine due to natural catastrophes. It would be done for free in a world without the use of money.

In old Egypt the evil power of Pharaoh did help everyone who could pay. If a tribe had used all their valuable items and could not pay for the food, they had to submit and work as slaves, soldiers and servants for the rest of their lives in order to feed their families. The life on earth changed from a living paradise to a living hell during a short period of time, and it never changed back.

The Master is telling you, living in present time, that all the people in the world have the freedom to choose their own leaders, but when everyone is trapped inside the national state borders with national laws and rules for living, the freedom is totally controlled. You are all slaves, soldiers and servants, still.

The meaningless life for all mankind is justified by a religion that builds on camouflaged stories, written by Masters living in hiding or working under cover for the warrior kings and priesthoods. It was the roman emperor Constantine that started using the camouflaged stories as a tool to better control the many different people the Romans ruled over. The religion was enforced on to the population with use of warfare and brutality, without exceptions. Those who refused to be baptized were killed. Over the years the religion Christianity grew in to something it wasn't meant to be. But it is truly a camouflage over important knowledge.

God, who speaks through Joseph, is the spiritual superior Motherland council speaking through the Diagram Star. It is disclosing the timeless laws and rules for living that always will be right for all humans. The Diagram Star is like a book carrying all the eternal truth in the world. The model for the Diagram Star is the Zodiac, the twelve star signs with the sun and the moon in the centre. The evening sky had a deep and profound meaning for the people living before the Motherland went under.

It is the Diagram Star that is placed on the top of every Christmas tree every year. The Stonehenge in England is a copy of the Diagram Star. All the stone settings in the world are to look at as history books of the past. They all speak to the population living on the land, but the chaos of wars and conflicts in the time after the Motherland went under, have erased the original knowledge from the common world of thoughts and replaced it with religions, legends and myths.

Listen to your inner voice! Decide for yourself what's right and what's wrong in the world you live in. Claim the lost world history back in your life and find the true meaning with life on planet earth.

Don't wait until the famine reaches you and your people.

Joseph and his eleven brothers are symbols for the twelve tribal people who emigrated from the Motherland and populated the whole world. This story describes in detail how the whole world population was forced to live as working slaves, soldiers and servants for a self appointed elite.

The brothers learns a lesson

Moses 42, 4-38

The brothers brought with them many camels and mules and set off for Egypt. But not all the brothers left. Benjamin stayed at home.

Benjamin was the son the Jacob loved the most. After he had lost Joseph, he never let Rachel's youngest son out of sight. Jacob was still mourning over Joseph and missed him strongly. But Benjamin could make his father laugh and smile. No, Benjamin was not going to Egypt. What should he do if he lost Rachel's second child to?

Benjamin and Jacob waved to those who left for Egypt. Soon they could see only a cloud of dust after them. Jacob took the hand of his son and they started praying. They prayed for the ten brothers, that God should protect them and lead them safe back home again.

When the brothers arrived to Egypt, they went straight to the man who was in charge of the sale of grain. It was Joseph, but they did not recognize him. He looked like and Egyptian now. But Joseph recognized them, but he did not reveal it. Instead he called them spies.

"No, we are not spies," they protested. "We are ten brothers. We were twelve, but one is dead and the youngest is at home with his father."

"I don't believe you," said Joseph. "If you not are spies, you can go home and bring your youngest brother. In the meantime I will keep one of you as prisoner." Joseph pointed at his brother Simeon.

The brothers were utterly surprised. Joseph continued: "But before you go you must spend three days in prison."

When the three days were gone, the nine brothers left for home with grain they had bought. On the road they discovered that the money they had paid was put back in the sacks. "No, no," they said in despair. "The Egyptian will think we have stolen the grain!"

When they got back home, they told Jacob what had happened. They asked to take Benjamin with them to Egypt.

"No, that will never happen! No one shall take my Benjamin from me. No! Benjamin stays here." Jacob would not listen to his sons. He thought it was bad enough that Joseph was dead and Simeon was left in Egypt. No one should take Benjamin from him.

Famine because of natural catastrophes is a historical fact. This camouflaged story is very old and is about the time after the Motherland went under. Pharaoh is described as a wise and ruthless dictator. Tribal people from the whole region could buy grain from his storage houses, and Pharaoh got richer and richer.

The history about Jacob, his two wives and his twelve sons is preserved and passed on by the Hebrew people trough several thousand years before it was written down as it appears in the Bible. The story came to Egypt and a few other places in the world from the Motherland in time before it was destroyed. The translation from Egyptian hieroglyphs to the Hebrew language was done with many assumptions and misunderstandings, and the Masters, who knew the complete and correct history about the lost Motherland, used the many stories as they were, while they protected and passed on formula or code that fully explained the specific mistakes that were made in the translation. An educated Master did not have to translate the hieroglyphs at all, because they knew the full history about the lost Motherland from their own teachers. The Diagram Star was their history book.

Because the full history about the lost Motherland now is known, the details about how the many camouflaged Biblical stories came to be are not important. The history about the lost Motherland and the global system of government had to be protected from a long line of warrior kings and priesthoods and for the roman emperors at the time the Bible was written.

Moses is a fictive person. The hieroglyph tells us that he is a symbol for the spiritual superior Motherland council. The stories in the beginning of the Bible is describing the lost Motherland and how people lived there and all over the world before the large continent was destroyed in a natural catastrophe. If you remove all evil from the stories you find the world history from before the catastrophe. The stories with the forces of evil are the world history after the catastrophe.

Egypt and the region around is the background, a theatrical stage for the whole world and a famine makes the perfect drama for all ages. The severe famine was used as camouflage in the same way as the so called Great Flood was used. It is stores with underlying historical factors, but they are all together fictive and a camouflage over the history of the Motherland.

The Masters wrote the camouflaged stories in order to preserve and pass on knowledge about the only global government system that could bring back lasting peace to planet earth.

A famine can and will drive humans to do things they really don't want to do. It has to do with protecting the family and tribe. Unjust treatment that builds on lies, fraud, envy and hate has among other negative outcome their origin from the three factors of Original Sin. The life under the rule of Pharaoh is all in sharp contrast with the life before the Motherland was destroyed, when the forces of evil did not exist. In a world without the three factors of the Original Sin, people all over the world would help each other without even thinking of being paid.

Joseph is giving his brothers a punishment that can seem strict and unjust to them, but he gives them grain for free to take home. He is holding one of the brothers back as a prisoner and tells them to bring their youngest brother to Egypt. It is a punishment that ensures Joseph that his brothers will come back.

Benjamin goes to Egypt

Moses 43, 1-34

The grain from Egypt was running short. Soon there was almost nothing left and the famine continued. And the time came when Jacob and his sons, their wives and children, had eaten up the grain which they had brought from Egypt. They had to cut down from three meals a day till two. Soon they could only eat one meal a day.

Time and time again the brothers asked their father if they could go to Egypt again. After all Simeon was still left there. But Jacob always answered no. He knew it was the same as maybe never see Benjamin again.

But in the end he had no choice. Jacob had to think of his large family. Therefore he said yes. Juda, who ones had sold Joseph as slave, said he should guard Benjamin well. "Nothing will happen to him," he promised.

"Just to be on the safe side you should bring double as much money this time," said Jacob. "Then you can pay the Egyptian back for the grain you bought last time. You shall also bring gifts to him, honey, perfume, nuts and more."

When they got to Egypt they went straight to see Joseph. He looked at Benjamin, who had become a good-looking young man.

"Come with me," said Joseph, "and we will eat together." Simeon came from the prison. When the brothers came to Joseph's house, they told a servant about the money they had found in the sacks on the way home last time. He said everything was in order, and went inside.

"How is your father?" Joseph asked, while holding his breath.

"He is in good health," they answered.

Joseph looked at Benjamin again. He laid his hand on Benjamin's head. "My God be with you, my son," he said. Suddenly he had to turn away. The brothers bent for him, just as in the dream a long time ago.

It was too much for Joseph. He ran out of the room. When he was alone, he cried. "God," he prayed, "you have leaded us together again. I love them all."

Joseph dried his tears and went back to his brothers. They arranged for a great feast, and it lasted all night. But Joseph did not reveal who he was.

Can it possibly happen in our present time that all the people in the world get together again and start living like brothers and friends? It can happen, but only if the three factors of the Original Sin are removed from the common world of thoughts with the use of only peaceful means. Right now Mother Nature is helping to make the world leaders decide to do the right thing.

Jacob and his twelve sons are still a symbol for the whole world population in present time, and when a severe famine spreads to the rich nations, brother will fight brother over one piece of bread. Therefore the knowledge found in the Bible has to be spread to all the people all over the world, before it is too late. Only by working together like brothers and friends, the world can be saved for our children and their descendants.

Without knowledge of the Diagram Star and the global system of government, and with a escalating struggle nation against nation with the Original Sin as the foundation for doing right, future look darker now than ever.

Knowledge and true love between all humans must get back in the light of the Diagram Star again. In the time before the Motherland went under all the humans living in a region that was struck by a famine, would have been helped according to their need, without paying for it.

It is in our present time difficult for humans to comprehend how life would be like for the whole world population, without the many armed national states, without the global capitalistic system and without all the religions.

Think about what the basic needs are for yourself and your life as a human being. Neither you nor others need more than an education that gives an abundance of knowledge, enough food and a home for you and your family. To live together as a family and a tribe of several families are the way of living that is natural for all humans. In that way the humans in present time will find back to the true happiness and safety that is destroyed by warrior kings and priesthoods, and long forgotten. It is a love; a happiness and a safety that are impossible to find in a world where humans spend all their time building the tower of capitalism higher all the time, while they protect them self with armed forces and claim that the God of their religion always is right.

Shall the whole planet Earth be destroyed because only a few rich and powerful humans want to get richer and more powerful? What does it take to wake up the whole world population and make them understand what's going on? Perhaps a trap must be made, that proves that the richness and personal power that everyone is struggling to achieve, is derived directly from the three factors of the Original Sin.

All the inhabitants in a tribal community will live together as whole unit were personal pride and the respect of each other is important. If one member of the tribe does one wrong thing, it will be remembered for all his life, with loss of personal pride and the respect of family and tribe as a result.

In our present time the family and tribal pride and belonging is completely broken down and erased by an enforced and meaningless national pride and belonging.

The silver cup that were stolen

Moses 44, 1-34

Next morning the brothers started thinking about going home. They were all very pleased. They had Simeon with them and had bought grain for the family, and they even had dinner with a famous man. Best of all was that Benjamin was safe.

They had no idea that Joseph had a plan. He had ordered a servant to put his silver cub in Benjamin's sack. Soldier from the castle came galloping after them. They went straight to the brothers.

"Get down from the camels and mules!" they shouted.

"We have done nothing wrong!" Ruben protested.

"One of you has stolen the masters silver cup!"

"Why should we do that?" the brother shouted surprised.

The soldiers went from camel to camel, from the oldest brother to the youngest. They ended with Benjamin. When they opened his sack, the soldier shouted loud. The brothers tried to protest, but for no use. They looked at Benjamin. "What have you done?"

Benjamin was so surprised he could only shake his head and say: "I have not taken it!"

The soldiers ordered everybody back to Joseph's castle. The brothers told him that they never meant to take his silver cup. He had to forgive them.

"You can go," said Joseph. "But the thief must remain here."

Then Juda intervened. "Our father will die if we return without Benjamin," he said. "He has already lost one son. He could not cope with the loss of one more. Please let me take his place. If Benjamin shall remain here, not one of us will return home."

Juda fell on his knees.

This camouflaged story shows that humans can change from evil to good. It is all depending if the event in question is of personal selfish reasons or for reasons concerning family and tribe. In other words the act of evil when Joseph was sold as a slave was an action derived from the Original Sin and the fight for Benjamin is an act derived from the Diagram Star.

This means that both Juda and his brothers have changed for the better and that they deeply regret what they did to Joseph.

A change like that in character and common thinking have to happen to the whole world population before the ongoing destruction of planet earth can stop. It is only possible if you and the whole world population recognize the Diagram Star and learn to live life like humans are supposed to live.

People living in present time are breaking the strict laws and living rules of Mother Nature because they have learned it from parents and earlier generations. There seems to be no way out of the circle of evil doing people was forced in to a long time ago.

In our present time we see and feel the result of some twelve thousand years of building cities with walls around and the symbolic towers made of a global capitalistic system and with religion as a mental wall preserving and passing on the evil destructive activity to coming generations.

All the many different national populations in the world are truly a like flock of sheep's doing what they are told to do, just like their forefathers in Egypt did. Nobody gets to know that the building of national states was totally against the strict laws and living rules given by the superior Motherland council. Humans born in to a nation is given a name and a number and has to obey to the laws and living rules of the nation. People can think and believe what they want, but the thought of removing all religions from the common world of thoughts seems to be unthinkable for the world leaders.

The strong and merciless wall between the rich and the poor is based on crimes of the past. It is crimes against mankind that is passed on as inheritance from generation to generation. Now the few rich nations in the world are working together in order to plunder the poor nations systematically by giving them financial aid.

Columbus started genocide on the American continent that went on for some four hundred years, in the name of a God that is a meaningless camouflage over a powerful and peaceful global government system. From then on most of the world have been occupied and stolen from the aborigines by use of warfare and brutal force. The thieves are all descendants from the twelve sons of Jacob.

It is just possible that the true world history is too heavy a burden for most humans living in present time. But Mother Nature is rocking the tower of global capitalism and the people living on the top doing the destructive building is getting nervous about a highly possible collapse. Perhaps they will realize too late that what they are doing is totally against the strict laws of Mother Nature.

The whole world population can start working together and prove their wish to live together like brothers and friends, by starting to build a new global government system with one set of laws and living rules for all. The work has to be done by use of only peaceful means. Therefore it is of great importance that the global system of government that the Bible is hiding under the camouflage is made known and passed on to coming generations.

When the cosmic diagram was to be made to preserve and pass on all the knowledge in the world all through the time of history, the choice was the Diagram Star. The Diagram Star has been with mankind from before the beginning of time and will be with mankind until after the end of time.

The Zodiac has been on the night sky always and is the model for the Diagram Star. The superior Motherland council had the Diagram Star as their official emblem, one star sign to each of the twelve members, and when a proud father is lifting his newborn child up over his head towards the stars on the night sky, he is praising the spirits of the council saying thank you for life.

The Masters of old are to be praised and saluted for their work for restoring lasting world peace. They preserved and passed on the knowledge of the Diagram Star in the many camouflaged stories in the Bible. The sun, the moon and the zodiac signs are model for the Diagram Star, and neither Pharaoh, nor the Maya-people or any other aborigine people, worshipped the sun. The sun was the reason for earth life and the carrier of knowledge. The Diagram Star is an everlasting source of world history that normally were preserved and passed on by use of common education.

Try now to understand the important difference between the two brothers Joseph and Benjamin and the ten other sons of Jacob. In all living nature there are always a few cells that are of better quality than others. Also humans are born with different qualities, some better than others. It is the nature's way of ensuring the best of the best to be recognized and chosen as leader. It is not personal riches and power from armed forces that is marking the greatest leaders in the world. It is their personal qualities and their spiritual strength. With the present system of global governing with many national states and all with their own laws and rules for living, it is a true fact that many great leaders with an ocean of spiritual strength are born, lives and dies without been recognized.

Joseph reveals who he is

Moses 45, 1-24

Joseph looked at Juda, on the knees at his feet. He saw too how afraid Benjamin was. So he asked the servants to leave them. "I want to be alone with these men," he said.

When the servants had left them, Joseph said: "I am Joseph, your brother." They did not believe him. They were so frightened that they didn't even heard what he said. "Don't be afraid," said Joseph and walked closer. "I am Joseph, he that you sold as slave to Egypt."

The brothers looked at him wondering. Now they became even more frightened. If the man really was Joseph, he could kill them for what they did to him.

"No, no, you don't have to be afraid, my brothers. God sent me here to make sure there is enough food for the family."

The brothers looked at him with eyes wide open.

"Don't you see?" he asked. "It was not you who sent me to Egypt, it was God. God made me ruler over Egypt. I have no other than Pharaoh over me. All this is a part of Gods plan for our family. Hurry back to my father and tell him to bring the whole family to Egypt. I will see that you have enough to eat."

Joseph embraced Benjamin and gave him a hug. Then he started to cry. He was so happy to see them again.

When Pharaoh heard about what had happened, he gave the brothers many wagons, so they could get their families and bring all they owned and settle in Egypt. Pharaoh and Joseph were happy together.

Before they went, Joseph sent with them many animals and precious gifts. "This is for my father," he said.

This is the way the early dynasties of Pharaoh was ruling the many different peoples in Egypt. With a strict hand and as good leadership they were thinking of the future. A larger population would give more income to the state in form of taxes and fees. Pharaoh knew that Jacob and his sons were rich with gold, silver and precious stones and they had to pay for grain just as anyone else as long as the famine lasted.

The early dynasties of Pharaoh were the last tribal people to emigrate from the Motherland before it was destroyed in a natural catastrophe. They were few in numbers, but as descendants directly from some of the members of the superior Motherland council they had a great advantage as rulers. But as we know from their history, they became greedy and ruthless dictators after a few generations and held their knowledge of the lost Motherland to them self in esoteric writings.

The Masters who preserved and passed on the knowledge of the global system of governing were few and it was not until they and their knowledge became a threat to the Pharaohs and their system of ruling, the persecution of them started, and never stopped.

Try now, again to place Jacob, who was given the name Israel, and his two wives, in the centre of the Diagram Star and their twelve sons in the sections around. The diagram is telling you how the whole world was populated and also the lost world history from before the Motherland went under. Jacob is a symbol for the superior Motherland council and his two wives are a symbol for the fertile Motherland and the twelve sons are symbols for the whole world population.

This is the end of the Book one of Moses, and it is in its place to say a few words about the spiritual aspect of life. All human spiritual activity is thoughts. Without the spirit of thoughts and physical movement there would not be any earth life at all. Your soul is the aura that is like a bobble around your body, and your soul is the carrier of your thoughts. The thoughts are transported to your brain through your senses, your breath and your blood.

It is in the aura that encircles your body that all you thoughts are to be found. All humans are affected by and learn from thoughts that come from the aura of other people, both living and dead. The human brain is a receiver of thoughts that comes through all your senses, via your breath to your lungs and from your lungs via your blood to your brain.

It is the person's degree of spiritual strength and understanding that decides the content of the thoughts. When a human dies, it is only the invisible thoughts in the person's aura that lives on eternally as a part of the spirit world.

The knowledge of the past is thoughts that live on in the air that all humans breathe. There is neither heaven nor hell in other places than in the human brain and it is the thoughts that are enforced on the population by the ignorant and greedy spiritual leaders that are making a living hell for all humans. Heaven is the world as it is remembered to be before the Motherland went under. The only spiritual world that exists and is common for all humans and all earth life is the air around us all, which is the Great Spirit World.

The Great Spiritual World covering the whole planet earth and is around our bodies at all times. All the thoughts in the spirit world are accessible for every human being. Thoughts about how a new world with lasting peace can be built for our children and their descendants are recovered from the spirit world, the common world of thoughts. It is my contact with the spirit world that makes it possible for me to tell you about the Diagram Star and the history of the lost Motherland.

Moses in the bulrushes

2 Moses 1, 2-4, 6-20

Joseph's family moved to Egypt. Here they lived for four hundred years. They grew in number and were called Israelites or Hebrews.

Four hundred years after Joseph had brought his family to Egypt; there was an evil Pharaoh on the throne. He did not like the Israelites and made them in to slaves. They had become so many that they were a threat to him and his kingdom. Therefore he ordered all the new born boys to be killed!

The mother of a little boy did all she could so that her boy should not die. He was a beautiful child with large, dark eyes. For three months she managed to hide him, but she realized she could not continue for long.

"There must be something we can do to save him," she said to her husband. Night after night they prayed for help. They had two other children, Aaron and Miriam, and they prayed together with them.

One day they got an idea. The Mother made a basket of bulrushes. It became a little boat. They put the little boy in it after wrapping him in a soft blanket.

Miriam and the mother went to the river with the basket and the boy. They put it gently on the water. "Watch out for your brother, Miriam," the mother said.

Remember that under the camouflage the whole of Egypt and the surrounding land is a theatrical stage symbolizing the whole world in present time. The twelve sons of Jacob are symbolizing the first tribes that emigrated from the Motherland and populated the whole world. The story is brought in to our present time, and you and the whole world population are all biblical Israelites with Jacob, named Israel, as the symbolic forefather.

Symbolical and mental the whole world population still is in Egypt, working as slaves, soldiers and servants to the ruling system the evil Pharaoh started. The following camouflaged biblical stories are a description about how the three factors of the Original Sin developed in the world, getting stronger all the time. But if you remove evil from the many stories and keep the good, you find the history about the lost Motherland.

With knowledge of the Diagram Star and the Masters formula, it is not difficult to separate the history of the lost Motherland and the global system of government from the forces of evil.

During the course of four hundred years the symbolic twelve tribal families grew in number became to dominating for the Egyptian elite. The order to kill all Hebrew new born boys and save all the new born girls have certainly happened before in the course of history, and are used by the Masters writing this story in order to make it remembered.

River Nile is water, and by now you know that Water = Knowledge and that the spirit world is the common world of thoughts. Moses was born by water and spirit, namely thoughts and knowledge. He is a fictive person written in to the history of the Hebrew people. Moses is the spiritual superior Motherland council.

The Masters writing this story already knew what humans in present time have to do in order to be set free from the dictating rule of the national state laws and rules for living, but they never estimated the three factors of the Original Sin to last as long as they did.

The Promised Land, meaning a new world, was promised you by the Masters of the past, and they sincerely meant the whole world. A world with lasting peace can only be built by the whole world population working together with knowledge from the Diagram Star. To make sure that the lost Motherland history wasn't forgotten, they wrote the many camouflaged stories. The Masters knew that the camouflage would be removed before it is too late.

Only by understanding that Adam and Eve are symbols for the whole world population and the whole planet earth really was a paradise before the Motherland was destroyed, you can understand the true message of peace that the Books of Moses is preserving and passing on though the history.

It is a milestone for your thoughts that you have to read and study the Bible to find the message from the past, a message that under the camouflage of religion speaks of a global government system with common laws and living rules for the whole world population.

Think of war and peace as two opposites like it is in our present time, when all wars and conflicts is an activity that is deduced from the three factors of the Original Sin. If the Original Sin is removed, not only from the face of the earth, but from the common world of thoughts, all the evil and destructive activity will stop. The whole world population will again live with peace without the opposite wars and conflicts. Peace on earth will then return to its original and natural meaning.

Saved by a princess

2 Moses 2, 5-9

God had heard the prayers that this family had sent up to him and he had big plans for this boy. The basket drifted down the river. In this moment one of Pharaohs daughters had decided to have a bath in the river by the castle.

The princess stood out in the water. She laughed to her maid servants. The sun was shining bright and the birds sang for her. The princess splashed exited in the water and her maid servants laughed and had fun.

Suddenly one of them saw the basket. "Princess, come and see what the river gives to us," she shouted. She carried the basket to the shore and put it down.

"Oh!" sighted the maid servants. In the basket lied a beautiful baby boy. He had kicked of his blanket and cried.

"It must be a Hebrew child," said the princess. She knew that her father had commanded that all Hebrew boy children should be killed. It made this little boy even more precious. "He is hungry. Is there something we can give him?"

Miriam had followed the event all the time and she had prayed to God. She wanted very much that the princess should save her little brother. Now she ran to her. "I know a Hebrew woman who can give him food," she said. "Do you want me to fetch her?"

"You can bring him with you, but when he gets so big he can eat by himself, I want to see him again."

Then Miriam took the boy with her. Her parent became very happy, and the family took good care of him. They tanked God for answering their prayers.

Moses is a symbol for the superior Motherland council. The twelve members gave the whole world the common laws and rules for living. Place Moses in the centre of the Diagram Star, and the twelve tribes called the Israelites in the sections around.

The whole history about Moses is a camouflaged historical tale. Under the camouflage the story tells the people living in present time how to build a new world with lasting peace. Knowledge about how to do it is coming from the river Nile camouflaged in the body of a little child called Moses, as a gift to mankind. The story is written by an unknown Master, using the formula: Water, Earth, Air and Fire = Knowledge about the lost Motherland. The formula is derived from the Zodiac, the twelve star signs, the sun and the moon. The Diagram Star is the official emblem of the superior Motherland council.

The story also tells how the Spirit World always helps people that are suppressed as slaves, soldiers and servants to self appointed ruling elite. In our present time the rich elite is living more or less in hiding, not responsible for what the world leaders do. The rich elite is a small superior group of humans that also are suppressed under a set of national laws and rules for living, and a majority of them have inherited their riches, while only a few, if any, have the personal ability and spiritual strength to manage the riches wisely.

There are a strong mental wall between the rich and the poor, and very few poor humans have managed to climb over the wall and become rich. The same goes for the many national states that all the time are trying to build their capitalistic tower high enough to be named among the few rich nations in the world.

All the national leaders are like blindfolded being guided in their work by their own national laws and rules for living. It is the laws and living rules that have been forced on them through tradition and an unbroken line of wars and conflicts. And it is still the national leaders with the strongest war power who decides who shall live or die. The present world population is truly living like living dead and blind, and will because of a forced on and trained willingness fight to death for the national state they are born in to. Nobody, not the very rich, not the world leaders and not the population, knows that the chaos of wars and conflicts are derived from the three factors of the Original Sin and can be removed by a common act of willpower.

The message the Master who writes about Moses brings to all of you, is that the present warrior kings and priesthoods have no other than a self appointed right to lead the world the way they do. Therefore challenge them together and tell them to stop. It is time to start all over again, without the armed forces, without the global capitalistic system and without all the religions in the world.

All over the world people are dying by the thousand because of merciless exploitation that creates poverty. It is of the outmost importance that as many humans as possible gets to see the Diagram Star and learn to understand that it is a diagram that can be read like an open book.

Moses fights for freedom

2 Moses 2, 10-14

> *When the boy was three years of age, the family took him to the princess. She smiled to him. "This boy shall be my son," she said.*

> *As Moses grew older, he was told that he was a Hebrew, not Egyptian. When he saw how his people were treated as slaves, he got angry. "It is not right," he said to the princess.*

> *"We cannot oppose what Pharaoh sais," she replayed. "He is king."*

> *The years went by, and Moses became an adult man. One day when he was out walking he saw an Egyptian hit a Hebrew slave.*

> *"Stop that!" he shouted and hit the Egyptian so hard that he fell against a stone wall and died.*

> *The next day he saw two Hebrew slaves fighting. "You must not behave like that," he said to one of them. "Why do you hit him?"*

> *The two Hebrews looked at Moses and his fine cloth. They laughed. "You are the right to tell us not to fight," they said. "Was it not you who killed an Egyptian yesterday?" They knew that as soon as Pharaoh was told what Moses had done, he would be killed.*

> *Moses was frightened. "If these two slaves know that I killed the Egyptian, many others must know as well," he said to himself. "I must get out of Egypt as fast as I can!"*

This shows how utterly wrong an Egyptian hieroglyph can be translated. This is a fictive story written to make the life story of Moses as a Hebrew leader complete. Look at the story as a parable and see Moses as the lost superior Motherland council and his mother as the lost Motherland history. Pharaoh is a symbol for all evil in the world. When the laws and rules given by the superior Motherland council are introduced in Egypt, they are regarded as a strong threat against the despotic rule of Pharaoh.

The story tells that Pharaoh could not remove the threat by killing all the new born Hebrew boys. Moses, as the spiritual superior Motherland council, survived within the inner circle of Egyptian elite. The history of the lost Motherland was written by their forefathers. This clearly states the fact that the history of the lost Motherland wasn't destroyed, but was preserved in the Egyptian temple library. When Pharaoh found out and wanted to destroy the writings on the clay tablets and papyrus, they were rescued and sent out to a safe place in the desert.

The knowledge the world population needs in order to build a new world with lasting peace is symbolical still hidden in a well full of water in the desert. Only a few humans have known about the well. They don't have to go in to the desert and find the well, because they have the Diagram Star as a foundation for all their thoughts. They know all there is to know about the lost world history. The knowledge about the global government system from the lost Motherland has to be made known to the whole world population. It will not be easy, and it has to be done with use of only peaceful means.

This incident marks what Moses thinks about Pharaoh as a regime and the wrong that is done to the Israelites. Under the camouflage it is you and the whole world population that are treated like slaves, soldiers and servants. As said before the biblical Israelites descend from Jacob and his twelve sons. They are a symbol for the whole world population and are still been held captives inside their national states borders. Pharaoh is a symbol for the regime, the national state laws and rules that keep you all as captives. The time has come to lead the history about the lost Motherland out from the dry and deserted mental desert where it has been hidden for so long.

All humans' gets a name and a number when they are born and are forced to educate themselves and work for the best of the nation as long as they live. They have so follow the laws and living rules of the nation, if they want to be respected and included as willing working slaves, soldiers and servants. It is a meaningless life for all humans. You are all living like dead and blind people in the darkness of oblivion.

Just like in the time Pharaoh ruled, the elite have their elected government servants inside every large and small corners of the country, taking taxes and fees for every little thing. The whole population feels all the time that something is terribly wrong, but no one dare to oppose the government and the laws and living rules of the nation. Many try to oppose the wrong where they live within legal terms, but without knowledge of the lost Motherland history, they could not succeed.

Only with knowledge from the Diagram Star as a double-edged spiritual sword, the common willpower of humans can win over the three factors of the Original Sin. Remember that the whole world population is living with the three factors of the Original Sin as a dominating part of their world of thoughts. The coming and decisive battle for freedom and ever lasting peace will have to take place in the common world of thoughts and in the thoughts of every living human being.

The solution to liberate the whole world is given to you in the Bible. A new Motherland has to be built, with a superior Motherland council with representatives from all tribal peoples in the world. The whole world population has to be divided in too many tribal people after all the national borders have been wiped out. Likewise the global capitalistic system and all the religions in the world have to be removed for all times. People are to again live in self supported villages and work for the family and the tribe.

The thorn bush on fire

2 Moses 2, 15-3

Pharaoh was told that Moses had killed the Egyptian. The guards pursued him out in the desert, but they did not find him. In the desert Moses met a wise man called Jetro, and he married one of his daughters. During the next forty years he lived with his family in the desert.

One day Moses herded Jetro sheep's, he saw something strange. At the foot of a mountain he saw a bush on fire, but the fire did not spread to other bushes and the bush on fire did not burn up!

Then he heard a voice that said: "Moses, Moses!"

"Here I am!"

"Don't come any closer," said the voice. "Take the shoes of your feet. You are on holy ground. I am your fathers God, Abrahams God, Isaacs God and Jacobs God."

When Moses heard that, he covered his face. He was afraid to look at God.

The Lord said: "I have seen how bad the Egyptians are treating my people. Time has come for me to set them free. I will lead them back to the land that I promised Abraham and Isaac long ago. It is a wonderful land, with god possibilities to till the land. Go no, Moses. I am sending you to Pharaoh because you shall lead my people, the Israelites, out from Egypt.

Fire = Knowledge, the Masters formula says. A burning bush talking is a camouflaged Diagram Star. It is only knowledge about the lost Motherland and willpower that can liberate the biblical Israelites and help them to build the Promised Land. Under the camouflage of religion the Israelites is every one of you and the Promised Land is lasting peace on the whole planet earth.

The Israelites are a symbol for the whole world population. Egypt and the surrounding land is a symbol for the whole planet earth and Pharaoh is a symbol for the present global government system with the many national states that are holding their population captives as working slaves, soldiers and servants.

It is now clear that the history of the lost Motherland is a real threat to the existing governing of the world, with many national states, a global capitalistic system and all the religions in the world. But just like Pharaoh had to give in to Moses and the ten plaques, the world leaders have to give in to the increasing chaos of wars and conflicts and the growing number of natural catastrophes.

It is you, your children and their descendants who shall live to find out how a global government with common laws and living rules for all people will function. But first the three factors of the Original Sin must be removed completely with only peaceful means. With strong and fundamental help from the history of the lost Motherland the freedom seekers will succeed.

As the story goes and history clearly shows, Moses did not succeed back then. The camouflaged story is a recipe that tells you how to do it, with help from modern technology and Internet.

Moses met his wife at a well full of water in the desert. A well full of water symbolizes a bright shining Diagram Star and everything that happens at a well is right. The light from the bright shining star is always shining light out over the whole world population. It is because the people are without the necessary knowledge that they don't understand what the Diagram Star is saying.

Now it is all up to you to save the world. By use of Internet and modern technology you can create a strong movement by gathering the whole world population and work together. Moses is a symbol for the laws and living rules that all humans have to live by, always. Not an easy task, but together you can do it. There are no God talking to you, but there is a talking Diagram Star.

The world leaders do not have a clue of what to do regarding the global warming and what it may bring of natural catastrophes. You and the whole world population have to work together to first liberate your selves by cleansing the common world of thoughts. It is only the thoughts that was imposed on your ancestors and still are imposed on to you that are the enemy of a world with lasting peace.

Many excuses

2 Moses 3, 11-4, 9

Moses said: "Who am I? I am not great enough to tell Pharaoh to let your people leave Egypt."

Gods answer was simple: "I will be with you."

Moses said: "But no one will believe me if I speak in your name. How shall I show my people who you are?"

God said to Moses: I AM. That is my name. That you can tell to the people. Tell them that the God that chose them as their special people, have sent you."

Moses was still not ready to do what God asked him to do. He came with one excuse after the other. "When I tell them who you are, they will not believe me," he said.

"The oldest in the tribes, the leaders, will believe you," said God. "You can ask Pharaoh if you can take the people on a three day journey in the desert. Ask him for three days when the people can worship me. When Pharaoh refuses that, I will make wonders and signs among the Egyptians.

"But just suppose that they still don't believe me," Moses said.

"What have you in your hand?" asked God.

"My rod," said Moses.

"Throw it on the ground," said God.

When Moses did that, the rod turned in to a serpent and he stepped back from it. God commanded him to pick it up, and when he did the serpent became the old rod again.

The Diagram Star is the key to the knowledge humans have searched for as long back as history is recorded. What happens when one single human break the spell and remember the paradise world from before the Motherland went under?

After many years of work I have found that no one believes what I am saying. A lost Motherland is denied to have existed by world leaders. They don't even look at my work. They are busy giving money to the poor nations in the world, while watching the world collapsing around them. But my work goes on; hoping that one day one reader with the needed authority will understand how important my work is for the existence of mankind.

My definition of God the father, the Son and the Holy Spirit is that they are the spirit of twelve members of the superior Motherland council. They died when the Motherland was destroyed in a natural catastrophe some twelve thousand years ago and were remembered by the whole world population.

Before the Motherland went under the laws and rules for living were given by the physical superior Motherland council, by the twelve democratically elected human beings. The Diagram Star is official emblem of the Motherland council; the visible book used in common education by the whole world population. The Diagram Star truly speaks to all humans who knew it existed. In this story the bright shining star in the centre of the diagram was displayed as a talking bush on fire. The burning bush symbolizes that the history of the lost Motherland is knowledge that is impossible to destroy.

Humans are supposed to live under the strict natural laws and living rules given by the superior Motherland council. Said with a few words it means a life without the three factors of the Original Sin. The whole world is slowly being destroyed by the destructive human activity that nobody needs in order to live a good life. They can continue to do that because the power of the superior Motherland council is spiritual. As this story shows, God have no power over Pharaoh and his soldiers. Only the power of Mother Nature is stronger than Pharaoh in the end. How long will the world leaders of present time wait before they let the whole world population free from their long lasting captivity?

The Masters who wrote the camouflaged bible stories knew this, and they could foresee that the forces of Mother Nature would stop the negative activity. But will it be too late? Will the humans who survive know how to build a new world with lasting peace together, or will they fight each other like Cain and Abel did?

The Diagram Star is the burning bush and it speaks to you. The bright shining star can enlighten you and tell you what to do, but in order to understand you need to listen and learn. You have to wake up and study the hidden message in the Bible for yourself, in order to discover what really is hidden under the camouflage of religion. Only then, you and the whole world population can begin the difficult process of making the world leaders understand that the world has to change back to what it was before the Motherland went under.

You need to learn everything the Diagram Star is saying. It will tell you the whole world history, all the laws and rules for living given by the superior Motherland council, the seven free sciences and a lot more. The lost Motherland was a large continent that now is a spiritual and invisible heaven, but truly accessible for all humans who wants to understand its history. The study will take you inn to a common world of thoughts that are natural right.

If you don't listen and learn, Mother Nature is going to continue to tell you and the whole world population what must be done to save the world, until you all understand that there is no other way.

The Books of Moses is a camouflaged recipe for what the world leaders together with the whole world population have to do together to save the world. All the weapons of war have to be melted down and made inn to pickaxes, spades and other tools for tilling the land. The long walk in the desert is still going on. Your forefathers were given the choice as you are given the choice now. Do you want to begin building a new Motherland and elect a new superior Motherland council, or do you want to continue the dance around the Golden Calf?

Pharaoh says no

2 Moses 4, 10-5, 2

> Moses came with all the excuses he could think of. When he said to God that he wasn't any good to speak, the Lord said that his brother Aaron should speak for him. At the end Moses had no more excuses. He bent his head. Moses was the man God had chosen for this mission.

> After the bush had stopped burning, Moses said god by to his family and went to Egypt. On the road he met his brother, Aaron.

> When Moses and Aaron arrived in Egypt, they went straight to Pharaoh and said: "The Lord, the God of Israel says: Let my people go, so they can worship me for three days."

> Pharaoh said no. "Why should I obey your God?" he said. "I will not allow something like that!"

The leaders of the world in our present time do not obey the laws and rules given by the superior Motherland council. The disobedience started in the time after the Motherland went under some twelve thousand years ago and has continued ever since.

There have to be a Moses, meaning a complete history of the lost Motherland and an Aaron, a human being with the authority to speak to the world leaders. Aaron of present time is in short the international press, the reporters and editors of the modern media. Together they have to take a stand and know that there is no turning back.

The Master who wrote this camouflaged story is describing how difficult it will be in our present time to persuade the world leaders to give up their despotic government system and let the population build and live on the land in self supported villages and tribal communities. The national states will vanish with a full stop in the collecting of taxes and fees. The national laws and rules for living will disappear and become replaced with one common set of laws and living rules for the whole world population. Knowledge will replace religious belief and the global capitalistic system will simply disappear.

All political parties will be removed completely and replaced with councils were the council members are democratically elected for life.

The richest of the rich will protest against this change when they understand that they have to say goodbye to their life in luxury, and most of the politicians will join them in their protest, until the knowledge from the Diagram Star is fully understood by everyone. The total changes in the way of living will take time, and even if it takes forty years or more, it is the only way to lasting peace.

All humans in the world will have all they need to live good and natural lives on planet earth. The wall between the rich and the poor will simply disappear with the global capitalistic system. It is completely insane to base the life and death of all humans on a system where only the rich have safe homes and enough food to eat.

The future logistic and transport system will be flying vessels of many sizes, for use in rescue operations in areas with famine and all kind of natural catastrophes. The flying vessels will be placed on strategic places all over the world and used for example when the best students are to be moved back and forth to the education centers every year.

In the world at present time, Pharaoh is the ruling system based on the three factors of the Original Sin and the biblical Israelites are the whole world population. In order to change the government system back to what it was before the Motherland was destroyed, the world population first of all needs to know what to do.

Mother Nature has to hit hard in the rich part of the world in order to make the world leaders change their thoughts and do the right thing in order to stop destroying the earth because of personal greed for riches. The power that keeps the three factors of the Original Sin strong all over the world comes from armed forces and self made laws and rules for living.

God promises to intervene

2 Moses 5, 22-7, 16

After Moses had met Pharaoh, he prayed to the Lord: "God, I am so confused. What shall I do?"

God answered: "Seeing that Pharaoh will not let the Hebrews go, I will do great things in Egypt. They shall feel that I am God."

Pharaoh had said that he did not know the Lord when Moses first met him. But soon he should learn to know him. All this was a part of Gods plan.

"Go back to Pharaoh again and ask him ones more for permission to let the people leave the land," said God to Moses.

But Moses had objections to that. "Why should Pharaoh listen to me?" he said.

God said to him that is wasn't him that should speak. Aaron should do that. He said if Pharaoh did not want to listen, he would intervene.

Moses and Aaron went back to Pharaoh. To prove that they really spoke on behalf of God, they throw Moses rod on the ground. It became a serpent. Pharaoh then sent for his wizards. When they throw their rods on the ground, they all became serpents. But then Moses serpent ate all of their serpents. Still Pharaoh would not do as Moses asked. The Lord said to Moses: "Seeing that Pharaoh doesn't want to listen, time has come to show him the true power of God."

The true power of God is in the power of the superior Motherland council before they died in the catastrophe some twelve thousand years ago. The power of the superior Motherland council was truly omnipotent, omniscient and omnipresent in the time before the Motherland was destroyed.

The power was preserved and passed on by the Motherland global parliament. Every people in the world had selected twelve of their best leaders and sent them off to live in the Motherland with their family. They were elected to the global parliament for life, and when one of the representatives died, a new one was democratically elected from the homeland. Every little self supported village had their representatives in the Motherland and the whole world population lived and obeyed the same common laws and rules, as found in the Diagram Star.

From the many highly educated and qualified representatives the twelve members of the superior Motherland council was elected. As long as they lived they had the power to preserve lasting peace in the whole world. After they died and became spiritual beings, the power was lost. The warrior kings and priesthoods added some laws and rules of their own, and the quest for riches and personal power took control over the whole world population.

This story is all about what the whole world population has to do in present time, in order to be set free from being slaves, soldiers and servants. You have to build a new world with lasting peace, together. Only a new superior Motherland council will have the power to remove the three factors of the Original Sin from the common world of thoughts.

The prophets back then had the knowledge, but they did not have Internet and modern technology. They had only the sword of knowledge to fight with, and they lost against the armed forces of the dictating warrior kings and priesthoods.

Now time has come for the whole world population to use its power to stop the destructive and not necessary human activity. The global capitalistic system has made it possible for completely empty minded humans to build a few rich nations, based on the sins of their forefathers. The quest to become the richest with the strongest armies is an ongoing struggle that never will end, at least not before Mother Nature intervene and squeeze them to the ground. But the force of nature is not enough. The whole world population has to demand freedom together and the power of knowing the full history of the lost Motherland will be enough.

What will the empty minded and otherwise clever humans do the day the tower of capitalism collapses all over the world? What does the world leaders do the day a global famine is a fact? Will they then listen and set the people free?

Terrible plagues

2 Moses 7, 17-10, 20

When Pharaoh refused, God punished the Egyptians because they did not let the people go. God sent ten plagues over Egypt. It was large natural catastrophes that came suddenly. Pharaoh sent out wizards and vise men to end the plagues, but it was God who stopped them, after Moses asked for it.

In the first plague the water in all of Egypt became red as blood. When Moses stretched his rod out over the river Nile, the water turned to blood. The same thing happened in all the channels and creeks, dams and lakes. The fish died and the river stank.

One week later God asked Moses to ones again go to Pharaoh with a prayer that the Hebrew people should be allowed to go out in to the desert. He asked Moses to warn him that if he didn't do as they asked, God would fill the river Nile with frogs.

When Pharaoh refused, frogs came by the thousands. They crawled up from the river and from creeks and canals, and covered all of Egypt. People woke up to the croak from frogs everywhere.

Pharaoh asked Moses to make the frogs disappear. Moses prayed to God and the frogs died, but still Pharaoh did not believe in God. He did not want to let Gods chosen people go, because they were good and willing hardworking slaves and servants.

God sent lice, which were very annoying. The lice were everywhere. The Egyptians had to cover their mouth when they should speak. Otherwise the small insects got stock in their throat. After that God sent a plague of larger flies.

God sent diseases on the cattle, and both humans and animals got itching on the skin.

God sent hail and thunderstorm. The wind was strong and grasshoppers came in great multitude over the land. They ate everything green they found. Soon there were only dry branches and sun burnt fields left in all of Egypt.

God also let the sun be gone for three days. Instead of the night turned in to daytime, there was only night for three days.

God gave Pharaoh one change after the other, but he did not want to change and let the people go. Still he did not want to let the people who descended from Jacob and his twelve sons, who were Hebrews and called them self Israelites, depart from Egypt. After God had made the sun be gone for three days, Pharaoh became so angry that he shouted to Moses: "Go away! I do not want to see you here again!"

This is nine of the ten plagues that people all over the world know well and have lived with for some twelve thousand years. The Masters who wrote the camouflaged story used the worst plagues he could think of as examples. He knew that they would not be the same all the time, and the specific plagues for the next generations could not be predicted.

Pharaoh is a symbol for the present system of governing the world, with many nations, a global capitalistic system and all the religions in the world. He is a symbol for the ruling system that was built by warrior kings and priesthoods not so long ago. The population in most of the rich countries is still willing working slaves and servants, not to any persons, but to a national political system of inherited laws and rules for living.

All the populations inside the national state borders are truly to be compared with wells totally empty for water. Nobody knew. The whole world population still lives without knowledge about the lost Motherland and its history. It is a knowledge that is needed in order to be able to build a world with lasting peace for our children and their descendants.

All the world leaders are servants to the present ruling system. They preserve and pass on a ruling system they inherited, first used by Pharaoh in old Egypt a few thousand years ago. They are preserving and passing on the three factors of the Original Sin, without knowledge that the common thoughts of mankind have been occupied for some twelve thousand years.

How many more plagues will it take before the world leaders of present time, let the world population free from the mental occupation and restore the knowledge of the past?

Around all over the world and especially in the poor nations, the population lives through the biblical ten plagues every day. Thousands of people struggle for the daily bread for them self and the families. Life is without mercy and the help given from the rich nations means little or nothing. The brutal exploitation of the population in all countries as a workforce is nothing but modern legalized slavery. Stealing the natural recourses from the poor nations continues with increasing force, and the only reason is the make the rich nations even richer.

Now think for a moment of the paradise the whole world was before the Motherland went under. It was a true paradise, and with the knowledge from the Diagram Star, it can be built for our children and their descendants.

When the time comes that the three factors of the Original Sin is completely removed from the common world of thoughts, all the negative opposites of today will disappear. Rich and poor are opposites that both will disappear and be replaced with a common public richness that hasn't anything to do with money. War as an opposite of peace will disappear and the word peace will get its natural meaning back. Hate will be gone as an opposite of love and love will get back its natural and deeper meaning. Think about more negative opposites yourself.

The world of present time is still in a chaos of wars and conflicts and the whole world population is still working slaves, soldiers and servants. Now time has come to break the spell of evil. The walk in the desert will be mental and a total change of the common world of thoughts. You yourself have to make the long desert walk in your mind, if your children and their descendants shall think of you with honor and pride.

The last plague

2 Moses 11, 1-10

Pharaoh did not do as God said. Now he was warned though Moses that there would come a last plague. And after the tent plague would Pharaoh finally let the Hebrew people leave Egypt.

"The eldest son in all Egyptian families, either they are slaves or free, shall die," said Moses to Pharaoh. "The first born of all animals will die to. But the children of the Hebrew families will be safe. This will show that there is a difference between Gods people and yours."

Pharaoh did not believe that something like that could happen. It meant that also his first born son also should die. They would lose all the new calves, lambs and young goats to. Pharaoh trembled by rage. How dared the Hebrew threaten him this way!

Pharaoh decided to not believe in the power of God. He said to himself: "This cannot happen."

"Get out! Out from here!" he shouted to Moses, and Moses left Pharaoh.

Certainly this has never happened. Not yet. This is a true symbol for the fight between the good and the evil in the world at present time. The fight between good and evil have to be settled first of all in your own world of thoughts and in the common world of thoughts. This camouflaged story illustrates how difficult it will be for humans to even begin to think that their way of life is destroying planet earth.

Will the worlds national leaders really wait until people and animals die on their doorstep; before they let their people go?

Remember that there is only one world population and one common world of thoughts. The building of nations have divided a common world of thoughts in too many different believes and thoughts. In order to create lasting world peace all the many people in the world have to be united again.

Consider the fact that both the Hebrew and the Egyptian people are in your thoughts all the time with Pharaoh in command. Therefore, in order to be set free from the slavery, the rule that Pharaoh started using and you know so well, have to be recognized as wrong in your mind. It is easily done by learning to know the Diagram Star. Only knowledge about the lost Motherland can remove the imposed belief from your world of thoughts.

Only after you and the whole world population knows that the present ruling system, with many nations, a global capitalistic system and all the religions, slowly but surely are destroying the world, the global system of ruling as presented in the Bible can be restored.

The world leaders have to get together and start working together towards a total change of thinking, and plan to remove the three factors of the Original Sin as soon as possible. When the common thoughts in the world are recognized as wrong, they will not be used any longer.

Will the world leaders wait until the long lasting famine in the world reaches also the rich countries in the world and their own people starts dying by the thousands every day? Will they wait until brother kills brother over one piece of bread? Will they wait until there is no food at all left to buy, even for the richest of the rich? Will they then know what to do?

Perhaps they in time will discover that only the people living together as tribal people in self supported villages will survive in to the future, as they have done before. In our present time it is still possible to build modern villages with the technology and communications systems intact, just as they had before the Motherland was destroyed in a natural catastrophe some twelve thousand years ago.

The change will take time. Don't wait too long.

The night of the Passover

2 Moses 12, 1-42

The Hebrew people were frightened. When they heard what God intended to do, they wondered what would happen to them. Were they safe?

Moses said the God had told them what to do. Everyone who did like God said had nothing to be afraid of.

The night the last plague came over Egypt, is called the night of the Passover. It means passing over, and the name reminds that God passed over the people who descended from the twelve sons of Jacob. He protected them. Moses said that they always should remember the night of the Passover. They were to tell everything that happened to their children, and they should tell their children again, in to the future.

The Easter night the Hebrew people had meat from lamb and bread to eat. Before the meal they had painted blood from the lamb on the top and the two side posts of the door were they lived. When God passed by, he would see what homes to spare. He knew were the Israelites lived.

Soon the wailing and weeping could be heard all over Egypt. All Egyptian parents wept that night. The Israelites waited. They knew they were safe because they were Gods chosen people.

When Pharaoh saw that his oldest son died in bed, he knew that it was his fault. Nothing of this would have happened if he had listened to Moses and Aaron.

Pharaoh gave order that Moses and Aaron should come to him that night. "Leave Egypt with the Hebrew people and all your animals!" he said.

That night every door of the Israelites was knocked on that night. "Time has come." They brought with them everything they owned. With all their animals they left Egypt. They were on the way to the Promised Land that God had promised them.

The Promised Land is the whole planet earth. The only way the spiritual superior Motherland council can keep the promise is by making the whole world population work together. A new Motherland has to be built, a new global parliament has to be democratically elected and a new superior Motherland council has to be elected.

It will take time to melt all weapons of war in to pickaxes, plows and other tools for tilling the land. All the national states have to be built down and all the religions in the world will vanish to. Then the new world will be right where you live. The best of all will be a whole new common world of thoughts and the whole world population will live together as brothers and friends.

Jacob got the name Israel in order to make it easier for people living in present time to understand that the sons of Israel is a symbol for the twelve tribes that emigrated from the Motherland and populated the whole world. The biblical Israelites are a symbol for the whole world population in all the camouflaged biblical stories. Every one of you has a direct line back to the Hebrew tribe.

The Jews are only one of the tribes. The many tribal peoples that emigrated from the Motherland to populate the world are real, but they were a lot more than twelve.

The biblical Israelites in our present time is all of you, and you are truly frightened for the reactions Mother Nature can come up with, if the destructive human activities based on the three factors of the Original Sin are allowed to continue. There are no human enemies in the world, only good and evil thoughts.

Pharaoh is a symbol for the driving force that all the world leaders are in present time, and they will all refuse to make the change that will take away their riches and personal power. The world leaders knows that without their willing working slaves, soldiers and servants, without all the national traditions and all the political leaders, everything they have worked for will crumble and fall to pieces.

If it doesn't happen soon and only by use of peaceful means, a long line of global natural catastrophes will destroy planet earth completely.

The global warming that the earth is living through in our present time is only one aspect created by the three factors of the Original Sin. How long will it take and how many of the sons of the world leaders have to die before all production of products made by oil comes to a complete stop?

All human activity that has to do with capitalistic gain has to stop. This means that all of you and the whole world population, sooner before later, have to begin the desert walk to cleanse your world of thoughts and make a mental change that possibly will take more than forty years. You are not to leave the place you live. The walk in the desert will take place in your mind, and you have to learn to live like nature intended. Only then you can mentally enter the new world, happy and certain that life is back on the right track. It will be relatively simple if you learn to let the knowledge from the Diagram Star guide you.

If nothing is done soon the wailing and weeping that you all can hear from the dying people all over the world in our present time, spread to the rich part of the world. For what is money good for, if there is neither food nor shelter for sale any longer? My prophetic advice is to begin living in self supported tribal villages again, before it is too late.

Imagine a farm producing food for four hundred human beings living in the region. They are depending on work for money so they can buy the food they need. If the four hundred humans went to live and work on the farm, they would be self supported with everything they need to live a good life.

Time has come for all of you to change from your way of life as a willing working slave, soldier and servant for your national state and find your way back to your own tribe and a natural tribal belonging. In our present time all the national states in the world are like prison camps to look at. You are your own prison guard. Think for yourself. Think about the meaningless lifespan you and your family lives, and if you really want to pass it on to your children and their descendants.

With God in the lead

2 Moses 13, 17-14

The whole people of Israel gathered at the edge of the wilderness. God was in front of them as a pillar of cloud in the day. At night they followed a pillar of fire to give them light. Like this they could travel both day and night and they always knew were to go.

God guided them along the desert road to the Red sea. It was many Israelites. They walked on both sides of the road with all their animals, and the dust was around them like a cloud of sand.

In Egypt Pharaoh had changed his mind. "Who shall now build, and who shall make the clay bricks?" he asked himself. He took six hundred of his best chariots, with his best soldiers from his army, and they went after the people of Israel to bring them back.

"Make camp at the banks of the Red sea," said God to Moses. "Pharaoh will believe that you are caught between him and the sea. But this will be a new opportunity for me to make a wonder. The Egyptians shall understand that I am God."

The Israelites camped were Moses asked them to do so. But it did not last long before they became restless. Those who were in the outskirts of the camp could hear that someone was coming. When they looked they saw a large cloud of dust rising from the desert far away, and it came steady closer. The Israelites cried out in fear. It was Pharaoh who came! They had no chance to get away. In front of them was the sea. "We are trapped!" they screamed.

The shouted to Moses: "What have you done? Have you lead us out of Egypt only to be killed in the desert? It would have been much better if we had continued as slaves! Then we would at least have lived!"

Moses was calm. "There is no danger," he said. "God will fight for you. Only be still. Believe in him."

The people did not believe him. They panicked and ran from one side of the camp to the other. They walked restless up and down the seashore like animals in a cage. The children started crying and running around. The women looked at the chariots coming closer all the time. It would not be long before Pharaoh and his six hundred warrior chariots would be right in front of them!

This will also happen in our present time. It is going to be extremely difficult for the whole world population to give up the life as obedient working slaves, soldiers and servants and break the nation's laws and rules for living. But the process of fighting for freedom from the three factors of the Original Sin has to be completed. There is no time to hesitate or even think of going back if planet Earth is to be the home for future generations of human beings.

The Diagram Star is the bright light spoken of so often in the Bible. The people living in our present time live in the darkness of oblivion, because their life is a constant quest for riches and personal power. You have to remove the camouflage of religion in order to see the light and understand the words spoken by the Diagram Star. Then the mental walk in the desert can begin. You have to do the walk alone, with only the symbolic bright shining star to lead you.

The Masters formula says that the four elements: Water, Fire, Air and Earth = Knowledge about the lost Motherland. The mental walk in the desert will give you the knowledge that humans have searched for so long. Moses was born from the river Nile. It means that Moses is born by knowledge and thoughts. He is a spiritual being representing the superior Motherland council, who is in the spirit world. Moses speaks for them. He is the voice talking to you. Aaron is a real human being, talking for Moses. The message from the spirit world is meant for you. Soon you will feel that thoughts are coming to you from the spirit world. Call them angels if you want.

You need to understand that you and the whole world population are in the desert aimlessly walking and have been there for some twelve thousand years. The building of a new world lies ahead. The building of a new world has to start before it is too late.

Remember now that this escape from old Egypt never happened. Pharaoh and old Egypt is the historical background, a theatrical stage set for this camouflaged story. The story is a true recipe for what the whole world population has to do in present time, in order to be free and begin living the life as nature intended, like brothers and friends with one set of laws and rules for living.

A wall of water

2 Moses 14, 14-31

Moses tried to calm the people of Israel. "Don't be afraid," he said. "To day you shall see what God will do." But the people were so anxious that they almost didn't hear what he said.

Now God spoke: "Why are you calling me, Moses? Lift your rod, and the sea will divide. There shall be a wall of water on both sides. You shall not even become wet. Walk through the sea with all the people. I will protect you. When the Egyptians try to follow you, the walls of water will fall and they will drown every one of them."

Moses lifted his rod. It started to blow a strong wind from east, and soon the water stood like a colossal wall. There was a passageway between the two walls of water! In the dark the Israelites and all their animals started to walk through the sea. They could almost not believe what happened.

In the morning they were safe on the other side. When Pharaoh woke, he shouted: "If they can cross the sea on dry ground, so can I."

Pharaoh and his soldiers hurried after them along the passageway in the sea. When they were about half way across God asked Moses to lift his rod again. He did, and suddenly the walls of water fell back on place.

Pharaoh and his six hundred soldiers, all the chariots of war, the horses and everything they had with them, were washed away by the water. The Israelites saw everything that happened, from where they stood on the other side.

The descendants of Israel saw the power of God, and they said: "God shall be our chief!" The long journey they had to look forward to, did not seem so frightening any longer.

The Red sea is a symbol for the ocean of knowledge that will open up for you and the whole world population as soon as you decide to let the Diagram Star guide you on a mental walk in to a symbolic desert. Perhaps you have to stay in a real desert for some thirty days so you as a living human being can think through what you really need in order to live a good life on planet earth.

Remember that you are a part of the common world of thoughts that controls and manage all human activity on planet earth. Every single human being is to be guided personally by the common knowledge from the Diagram Star.

The first thing you will do after you have reached a sufficient level of understanding the Diagram Star, is to remove all the weapons of war from the face of the earth. Like many Masters have said before me, is that all the weapons of war have to be melted and made in to plows, pickaxes and other farmers tools. It is my vision and my hope. In a future world built with knowledge in the light of the Diagram Star, all humans in the world will live with everything they hope for, always.

Remember the symbiosis that the Israelites and the Egyptians together is the whole world population. The Egyptians does what they are told to do and the Israelites does what they know is right. Your inheritance is to do what you are told are right even if you think it is wrong. It is the thinking derived from the three factors of the Original Sin that are wrong and have to be removed from the common world of thoughts. The thinking derived from the Diagram Star is right and when the whole world population thinks the same, peace will last forever.

The water of the Red sea is symbolizing that the present government rule with many national states, with their armies and borders, will be washed away from the common world of thoughts when people gets to know about the lost Motherland history.

The power of knowing the history of the past is one of the greatest powers humans can possess. Knowledge about planet earth has a cycle just as water, and cannot ever be destroyed. But the active learning is necessary for humans. Therefore it will take time for you to fully understand what knowledge about the lost Motherland history can do for all humans on earth.

Without water

2 Moses 15, 1-27

After Pharaoh and his soldiers drowned, the Israelites started singing and dancing. They were so happy they were saved.

Miriam, Moses elder sister, was leading on in the dance. They danced between the campfires. She was playing tambourine, dancing in front of all the women.

Moses sang a song about Gods mighty force and power. He thanked God for saving his people and leaded them out of Egypt.

Soon came the day they had to be on their way again. They followed Gods pillar of clouds. For three days they walked through the desert. They could not find water anywhere. Finely they stopped at a well with bitter water. If they drank from it they would get sick. It was terrible to see water without being allowed to drink. People got even thirstier.

Two million thirsty human beings started to grumble. They shouted to Moses: "What have you done with us? Here we are in the middle of the desert almost dying of thirst. We could have stayed at home in Egypt were it was safe and good. We had water and fruit and fish. Here we have nothing!" They had already forgotten Gods promise to take care of them.

Moses called to God and the Lord showed him a tree. He throws the tree in the well and the water became fresh and good. People ran to the well. They drank all the water they could and laughed from happiness.

"You must never forget that God is taking care of us," said Moses to the people. To prove that, God leaded them to a place where there were twelve wells with water and palm trees that gave them shade for the tents. It was an excellent place to camp. The Lord had truly shown that he took good care of them.

After all the national states and their form of despotic rule with armed forces are gone, there will come a time with tremendous joy and happiness for the whole world population. But a complete change of ruling system will not be a dance on roses for anyone. Many humans will, because of lacking information and knowledge, feel completely lost and without safety for what the new global ruling system will bring.

But you do know for certain that the present ruling system where all humans are separated and forced to live inside guarded national borders, is totally unnatural and against all the strict laws of nature. Also you know that the natural and original system of ruling is the whole world population living like brothers and friends in borderless tribal communities, with one set of common laws and rules for living.

A pond with bitter water is a symbol for the uncertainty and misunderstandings that will come to be all over the world after the some twelve thousand years of slavery has come to an end. But most humans will know the Diagram Star well even before the transformation begins.

The Diagram Star is telling you all clearly and in detail how to build a new world with lasting peace. Begin with the new centre and build a new Motherland first. Then you call on twelve men from every tribal population in the world to assemble in the new Motherland. From them, the best of the best, the twelve members of a new superior Motherland council is to be elected. They will be omnipotent, omniscient and omnipresent.

Then the building of the many self supported villages will start and continue over time until every single human being is belonging to a tribe. The most important human activity will be education in the light of the Diagram Star. The evil times will be gone and only good times will rule the whole world.

The place with twelve wells of pure and fresh water is a symbol that truly is a promise that all the twelve tribe's descending from Jacob, who was named Israel, will find knowledge, prosperity and lasting peace.

Remember what the Bible is saying: "The Diagram Star have been with humans from before the beginning of time, and will be with humans until after the end of time."

Give yourself time to understand the ocean of knowledge that is hidden in the Bible. The stories are often about the same, the fight between good and evil, and even if good is always losing ground to evil, good will always prevail. You all have to learn how to remove evil from the world for all times, and never let it return. The camouflaged stories in the Bible are telling you what to do. You are all forgiven, because you didn't know. Now you know.

Remember that human's with knowledge is like wells filled with good water.

Without food

2 Moses 16, 1-36

Soon came the time to break camp and move on. It did not last long before people started complaining again. They did not like the hot sun and they complained about the shortage of food and water. The children cried, the women complained and the men murmured.

When they had been in the desert for about two months, they did not have any more food. The Israelites shouted to Moses: "What have you done? Here there is no food. Now we are all going to die. It is your fault, everything!"

"God will provide for us all," Moses replayed. "Just trust in him!" But they did not want to listen to him. They were angry and felt sorry for them self.

Then the Lord said to Moses: "I shall give my people bread in the morning and meat in the evening. They can really trust me for all they need. They shall learn to believe in me."

The next morning the ground was white with small drops of dew. The sun dried the dew and people could see the small white flake there. It was bread they could eat.

In the evening a large flock of quails landed around the camp. People could catch as many as they wanted. They grilled the birds and ate the meat. With the will of God the Israelites should have enough food for their long walk in the desert.

The new Motherland superior council will provide by means of careful long term planning. The gathering of tribes in villages will have to be with a surrounding land area large enough to feed the people living there. The getting use to the new way of living will take perhaps a generation or two. There is no going back.

Manna from heaven is a symbol for the thoughts that comes directly to you from the Spirit World. It will take care of the human hunger for knowledge.

The lack of food and water is the camouflage in this story. The Israelites are the whole world population and the symbolic mental walk in the desert has not yet begun. But soon after you all have started the process of changing from the present system of ruling to a global system of ruling with a common set of laws and rules for living for everyone, there will be a natural need to ensure the people that everything will be better and everyone will have all they need to live a good life on planet earth.

Going back to the global system of ruling with one Motherland for all the many different populations in the world, means that the original and only democratic system of ruling will be restored. If nothing is done the present ruling system will fall by its own force.

Manna from heaven is insurance to your thoughts that even if the complete change of ruling system will be very difficult for you and your family, it will be a paradise for your children and their descendants in near future.

The people will need to be told all the time, that even if the mental walk in the desert will take forty years or more, your children will be proud of you for taking a stand, for saving the world.

In the Spirit World are the thoughts of all humans that have lived on planet earth ever. One can think the Great Spirit World as a common databank full of thoughts that are natural and necessary for humans in order to survive and live full and good lives on the planet. The thoughts are the same for all humans. It is the spiritual strength and physical abilities that with the environment are the foundation for every human being.

The thoughts are the same and equally important for all earth life in the process of reproduction and natural evolution. It is the natural and right thoughts about all aspects of life that are gathered in the Diagram Star. The Diagram Star is like a keyhole and Moses is the key that leads the common world of thoughts back on the right track. Moses is the lost world history.

All through the lifespan on planet earth it is the thoughts that are the foundation for spiritual strength and makes it possible to transfer thoughts in to words and physical activity. When the human body dies it is only the thought that lives on in the Spirit World. The air around the world and the air around your body is the Spirit World, and it is the air, the earth, the sun and the water that makes the physical earth life possible.

The whole world population lives inside the spirit world and is totally depending on it. The Great Spirit World is full of thoughts that all humans living in present time desperately want access to. Most important it is to get access to the lost Motherland history and how the whole world again can be a paradise for the whole world population. Then it is so terrible wrong that the three factors of the Original Sin is blocking the access to the knowledge about the lost world history from the time before the Motherland went under. The tree factors of the Original Sin are the lid on the Ark of the Covenant. The whole world population is truly blinded by the man made force of evil and is living their lives like living dead. Life without access to the common world of right thoughts is no life at all.

The three factors, the national states, the global capitalistic system and all the religions in the world have occupied the common world of thoughts from the time the Motherland was destroyed some twelve thousand years ago. How all the children of Israel was cut off from common education and made in to willing working slaves, soldiers and servants, is very well described in the camouflaged story about everything that happened with Jacob and his twelve sons in Egypt. The story is explaining how your world of thoughts came to be.

In our present time the situation is that the whole world population, with few exceptions, still is living like slaves, soldiers and servants of a despotic ruling system with many national states and a global chaos of laws and living rules that are totally against the human nature.

Manna from heaven is the liberation of thoughts that every human being will experience like a revelation. It is a new and meaningful world of thoughts that will open the mind of all humans.

Thousands of humans die every day all over the world, by starvation, for reasons that come from poverty, from imposed religion and imposed feeling of national belonging. If nothing is done to enlighten the whole world population with knowledge that is found in the Bible and in the many legends, tales and myths, it is possible that mankind will perish because of yours inherited belief in being right in the way you live your life.

Therefore start the mental walk towards a total change of government systems in the whole world now. Search the Bible and take back the lost history and the knowledge hidden there. The use of modern technology and Internet will make it possible to coordinate the whole world population in a common movement and create a lasting world peace for our children and their descendants.

God on the mountain

2 Moses 19, 1-25

The Israelites wandered through the desert for three months. When they came to a mountain called Sinai, they camped there. The women were happy for the rest. They took care of the children. The men tended to the animals and mounted the tents. Soon the smell of food was all over the camp.

In the evening Moses walked around amongst the families. When the children came running to him, he touched their heads. After Moses had seen the people he walked back to the mountain. He knew that God would meet him there, and the time was now.

As Moses climbed up the mountain, he could hear God calling him: "Tell the people that if they obey me, they shall be my chosen people." He walked down again and gathered all the leaders and told them what God had said. The men stood with torches in their hands while Moses spoke to them. "God the Lord have chosen you. Will you obey him?"

"We will do as the Lord sais!" they answered loudly.

Some days later Moses and Aaron walked up on the mountain. Now it was covered by smoke. Then they all heard the sound of a large bassoon. The people heard the sound, but could not tell where it came from. They trembled with fear. This was a great moment for the Israelites. God had come to meet them.

It is truly sad to see how wrong the Egyptian hieroglyphs have been translated and how stories are made up and written almost like complete nonsense. It is totally outrageous that otherwise clever human beings by national traditions are forced to believe that the stories are true and really happened.

It will truly be a great moment for the whole world population by the time everyone realizes that the God of all religions is the twelve elected members of the superior Motherland council. They all died some twelve thousand years ago.

Think of the mountain as a symbol for the lost Motherland and God as the superior Motherland council.

The day that you all understand that the whole planet earth is meant to be ruled from one Motherland by one superior Motherland council; that day you will really get your eyes opened for the fact that it really is possible to build the Promised Land, meaning a whole new world with lasting peace.

The Masters formula is easy to understand. It builds on the four elements: Water, Air, Earth and Fire. All the biblical events that takes place for example by a river, a sea, a well full of water, by a burning bush, on a mountain and from the air, is a place where the natural forces of good wins over the forces of evil.

Now think through what really happens on and at Mount Sinai. The Hebrew people have recently left their life as slaves, soldiers and servants in Egypt and this is when they have to make a choice for how they want to live their lives. The people living back then did not have a choice. It is in fact the choice that you and the whole world population have to make, now that you know the two choices you have before you. Will you continue to dance around the Golden Calf and watch the world fall apart around you, or will you choose to build a new Motherland and elect a new global parliament and a new superior Motherland council.

The last some twelve thousand years all humans in the world have lived in a mental desert, with a never ending chaos of wars and conflicts. Your forefathers had the knowledge and could choose, but if they even spoke about the lost Motherland, they were killed by the warrior kings and the priesthoods. Now you know about the global system of government from before the Motherland was destroyed. You can choose to build a new Motherland and restore the paradise world of the past, or you can continue to live like you do and watch the world being destroyed all around you.

The spiritual superior Motherland council is giving you the choice from the spirit world. They have no power to force you, but they have the power to inform you about the history about the lost Motherland and show you the power that they used to have over the whole world population. Only a new and physical superior Motherland council can restore that power.

Notice the first letter in all the biblical names. They all have a meaning and all names starting with M is derived from the Motherland, the lost continent of Mu that was situated in the Pacific Ocean. The whole continent was divided in three by natural channels and lakes. It was founded on some very large gas pockets in the ground. They all collapsed together because of volcanic activity and movement in the earth's surface. A prove for this is Easter Island. Some twelve thousand years ago all vegetation was washed of the island by one or several large flood waves. A lot of the soil was moved about and many of the large statues was tilted or half buried by the soil.

In the meeting with God on the mountain, which is a camouflaged story written by a Master several thousand years later, the meeting and the important choices you all have to make, is described.

My prediction is that you all have to live trough a few days in your life where you truly realize that the life you live have to change dramatically very soon if your children and their descendants shall have a planet earth they can live on. You have to start learning to live in a world without the three factors of the Original Sin. The day you do that mentally will be a great moment in your life, the first day of a new meaningful life in a new world.

The first Ten Commandments

2 Moses 20, 1-21

When Moses and Aaron arrived on the top of the mountain, God came to meet them. He came on a cloud of smoke and fire. He wanted to give his chosen people laws, or commandments. The meaning was that they should learn them and live by them. Then they would know the different between right and wrong.

God gave Moses the Ten Commandments: "Tell the people," he said, "that I am the Lord your God. It was I who lead you out of Egypt, where you were slave. You must not worship any other than me. I will be your only God. Make no statues to worship.

You must not swear, and you must not use my name in a superficial manner. You must only use my name when you pray.

The seventh day of the week shall be a day of rest. You must not work on the Sabbath.

Listen to your mother and father. Show them respect and honor. You shall never mock them.

You shall not kill. You shall not commit adultery. You shall not steal. You shall not wrongly accuse your neighbor. You shall not envy your neighbor, nor desire his house, his wife, his servants, his animals, nor anything that is his."

When God finished speaking, all the people saw the thunder and lightning and heard the noise of strong bassoons.

Every nation in the world is breaking all the Ten Commandments all the time, because they preserve and pass on the three factors of the Original Sin from generation to generation. The never ending breaking of the natural laws and rules given by the superior Motherland council is creating the chaos of wars and conflicts that all humans know so well.

No one will come to liberate you and your fellow humans from the life that was imposed on to your forefathers many thousand years ago. The whole world population is still working slaves, soldiers and servants, breaking the strict laws given by the superior Motherland council. You break them every day while just doing what you believe is right.

It is only the knowledge about the lost Motherland history that can set your world of thoughts free and tell you what to do to save the world from being completely destroyed by the humans that are leading the destructive activity.

It is the Diagram Star that preserves and carries the right laws and living rules trough the ages. They cannot be destroyed, not ever, because they are natural, telling humans to live like nature intended. You must begin your own mental walk in the desert and find the full understanding of what's right and what's wrong in your life.

It takes a good deal of mental activity to learn to know the Diagram Star well. You must do it yourself and the time to start is now, if you haven't started already. By now you know that the Diagram Star is telling you everything the superior council of the lost Motherland knew about governing the whole world population with only peaceful means. Think of them as spiritual beings in the Great Spirit World.

The Diagram Star was and still is the emblem of the superior Motherland council and it was used in common education all over the world. The whole world population is hereby given the Diagram Star and all the commandments in their hand. It is your choice to start doing the right thing and build a new Motherland. Your choice can save the world.

The Ten Commandments was not carved in to a stone tablet with letters and words. Every Master had the ability to carve the Diagram Star in to a stone tablet, as it has been done time and time again in the history of mankind. By now you should know that the bright shining diagram is a book containing the full history of the world from before the Motherland was destroyed. Now the diagram is shown to you. In the Bible you can read about the Morning Star, which have been with humans from before the beginning of time and will be with humans until after the end of time.

You can also read in the Bible that many thousands of years ago, the warrior kings and priesthoods choose to live without the knowledge from the Diagram Star. The population was forced to obey the despotic and evil leaders and forget everything they knew about the lost Motherland. It was done by ending the common education and forcing the people to obey their new laws and rules for living.

Wiping out the history about the lost Motherland from the common world of thoughts was an unforgivable crime against mankind, and it is the inheritance from them that are slowly destroying planet earth right now. Not to mention the millions of human lives that are lost under the rule of the three factors of the Original Sin.

The meeting on Mount Sinai is taking place right now, and you and the whole world population is given the last change to make the right choice. The Ark of the Covenant is open and you know the content. Be brave and make the right choice. The destiny of mankind is in your hands.

It is only the Diagram Star that can restore the knowledge that all humans need to liberate them self from the prison of their national state and build a new world with a natural freedom.

God cares for his people

2 Moses 20, 22-31, 18

Moses stood face to face with God. God and man were together. God was very fond of Moses and he wanted very much that his people should understand that he cared for them.

God said: "I shall preserve you, so you always are healthy. You shall have many children, so that you are strong when you reach the Promised Land."

Moses had been deep into the dark cloud. There he spoke with God for a long time. Sometimes he came out and looked down on the people below. When God said that he would give Moses the Ten Commandments written on two stone tablets, he stayed on the mountain.

Moses stayed on the mountain for forty days and forty nights. People waited and waited for him.

When God was finished talking to Moses about all this, he gave him two flat stone tablets. On them God himself had written the commandments.

Study an anthill or a community of bees and learn what natural laws and rules for living that applies for them. It is the same natural laws and rules for living that applies for all life forms on planet earth, including human beings.

Human beings are no exception, except for the fact that they have as a main mission to preserve and care for all earth life. In a world without the three factors of the Original Sin, the main mission for humans would be to build cosmic eggs and transfer all kind of earth life to new earth like planets. Planet Earth is a living organism and has a lifespan that will come to an end, and it is of course the laws of the nature and the meaning with the human ability to build space ships that all earth life is to reproduce to new planets.

It is a law of nature that the transfer of earth life to new planets has to be done while this planet earth still is productive. Think of planet earth as a three in the forest reproducing with the use of pollen as seed. One thing is for sure, the transfer of earth life to new earth like planets cannot be done as long as the three factors of the Original Sin are occupying the common world of human thoughts.

The chaos of wars and conflicts that started after the Motherland went under did put a stop to the natural evolution that humans are the only beings capable to do. Instead of building cosmic eggs and sending them out in to the universe as pollen from a tree, the humans are using all their ability to preserve and pass on the three factors of the Original Sin from generation to generation. It is more than a sin; it is a gruesome crime against mankind.

Motivated by inherited and enforced national and personal egoism the whole world population is working like desperate in the quest to be the richest and the strongest nation in the world. While the rich nations in the world get richer all the time, the many poor nations in the world are getting even poorer.

There is a high and strong wall between the rich and the poor people in the world that are getting more and more difficult to cross. It is all about the tower people are building in to the sky. The tower walls are trembling as we speak, and when they fall there will be no one to turn to for help.

With a controlled change to the global ruling system from before the Motherland was destroyed, millions of human lives can be saved. A new superior Motherland council and the common laws and rules for living that are found in the Diagram Star, will take care of you all in the best possible way.

It is the Diagram Star that Moses is carrying down from Mount Sinai. The light from the Diagram Star is to be found in the Ark of the Covenant and the Bible is the Ark of the Covenant. There is no other information that can bring the common world of human thoughts back on the right track.

Humans in present time have the choice between taking the laws and living rules of the lost Motherland in use again, or continue their dance around the Golden Calf until the people closest to the centre, the richest of the rich, starts to die from reasons that are to blame on their unlawful inheritance, the selfish greed of the first self elected warrior kings and priesthoods.

The Golden Calf

2 Moses 32, 1-35

When Moses turned to leave, God said suddenly: "Something terrible have happened! The people have already forgotten their promise. They worship a golden calf."

People waited patiently for Moses to come down from the Mountain. When he did not come, they thought he was dead. They did not trust in God, and asked Aaron, Moses brother, to make another god for them.

The people gave Aaron their gold rings, and after melted them he made a golden calf from it.

God became angry. He said to Moses: "I will wipe out all of them. Then I will start all over with a new selected people."

But Moses begged him to not kill them. He walked down from the mountain with the stone tablets that God had given him. The closer he came, the stronger was the sound from the camp.

Then he saw the golden calf glitter in the bright sunlight. "You have done a terrible sin!" he shouted. The music stopped and the people waited in silence.

"How could you do this after everything the Lord have done for you!?" he shouted. In anger he throws the two stone tablets with Gods writing to the ground. They broke in to thousand pieces.

Moses punished the Israelites. Then he went back up on the mountain. God told him he was very disappointed with the children of Israel.

The story of the lost Motherland was told and told again at campfires all over the world, before this camouflaged story was written down as an important part of the Bible.

This story is about a crossroad where the whole world population has to make the right choice. Do you want to live in a paradise world with lasting peace under the light of the Diagram Star, or do you want to continue to live like you do, as an obedient bystander, watching the never ending wars and conflicts in the world and see people die from reasons that comes from poverty and religion?

The dancing around the Colden Calf is symbolic and started a long time ago, and it is still going on. Only when these words are truly understood, Moses will come down from Mount Sinai. Moses is the full history about the lost Motherland. Only if you and the whole world population act correctly and start living according to the commandments given by a new superior Motherland council, the new world can be built.

The biblical Israelites are a symbol for the whole world population in our present time. With the use of warfare and brutal force and under the cover of a false religion the people descending from Jacob and his twelve sons have populated the whole world, while dancing around the Colden Calf. Everywhere they came; they stole the land and made the population who lived there in to slaves. In fact our forefathers made the whole world population in to slaves of the three factors of the Original Sin.

Everyone who protested and refused to submit to the warrior kings and the priesthoods was killed. Many places in the world regular genocide were committed. It happened in our resent history when the whole American continent, from north to south, was invaded, occupied and populated. Those who had their homeland there were still living under the laws and rules of the Motherland. Totally defenseless the many aborigine peoples were slaughtered or moved from their homeland.

In our present time the merciless exploitation is taking a new course on the African continent and many other places in the world. Under the cover of the global capitalistic system of economical aid, the modern colonization of the poor countries continues. In addition to the many religions in the world, the global capitalistic system is the most merciless weapon, because thousands of humans die every day of reasons caused by poverty.

It is a shame for the populations in the poor countries to accept all kind of aid from the rich countries. They see with their own eyes that people die all around them every day, and they see the so called leaders wading in personal luxury. The strong mental wall between the rich and poor are the same all over the world and are becoming more and more visible all the time.

The three factors of the Original Sin are spreading like evil cancer all over the globe. One may ask if a change of ruling system will come too late. Well, then a new superior Motherland council have to start building a new world all over again. The threat from the nature is real. The global warming is a normal part of a cycle, triggered by human's activity. And it is already predicted that it will be followed by many natural catastrophes that will take perhaps millions of human lives.

What aid can the national states give you, when there is nothing left to give? Any one of you can find yourself standing inside a supermarket with a sack full of money, with no food to buy.

Therefore the time has come to stop the ongoing dance around the Golden Calf. Twelve thousand years is a short time in the history of mankind. Think about the world you want to leave to your children and their descendants.

The Master who wrote this camouflaged story lived in the time of the Roman Empire and their elite of rulers. The Romans killed everyone who spoke against their despotic system of ruling. The Master knew that the dance around the Golden Calf would continue in to the future, until Mother Nature as the only capable force would interfere and threaten to kill all humans living on the planet.

It truly is Mother Nature that reacts against the humans living in present time. There is no God or gods that can do anything as said in the Bible. The dance around the Golden Calf is the daily struggle humans use in the desperate quest for riches and personal power. They are not many, the humans who dances. Most of the world population is poor and hungry and are standing all their lives in the outskirts of the dance watching and waiting for the laws and living rules of the lost Motherland to return.

The Ten Commandments are written again

2 Moses 33, 1-34, 35

Moses asked God to forgive the Israelites, and God said because he prayed, he would do that. God and Moses were friends and God remembered the promises he had given the people.

Since Moses was a good friend of God, he prayed: "Show me your way!" God said that Moses would die if God let him see and learn everything about him. It would be too much for him.

But God said that Moses could come back to the Sinai mountain top. There God would walk past Moses, so he could see more of him. It was the closest anyone had been God ever!

Moses climbed up on the mountain again and the Lord came down from the cloud to be with him. Moses fell to the ground with his face down. The glory of God was too much for him. Moses closed his eyes and said again and again that God was great. Again he asked God to forgive the people and let them be his chosen children still.

God went along with that. He gave yet another promise. For the second time he spoke the words of the law and living rules to Moses, so he could give it to the people. God said that he would lead the Israelites to the land he had promised Abraham to give to his children.

God gave his ten commandments for the second time. Moses stayed on the mountain for forty days just like the last time.

After forty days Moses walked down from the mountain and back to the camp. This time the Israelites had kept their promise. They waited for him. They had behaved well.

Do you really think that Mother Nature will forgive you all the destructive activities you have participated in? Forgive not only you, but the forefathers of all humans all the way back to the first sinful activities that started the reign of the three factors of the Original Sin some twelve thousand years ago? You should know that forgive and not forgive is not an issue for Mother Nature. If you stop destroying planet earth, the normal natural development will repair the destructions. Human beings have to live in natural coexistence and what humans destroy while doing wrong deeds towards fellow human beings; humans have to mend themselves, if possible.

For the last some twelve thousand years humans have not behaved well at all, and mending human relations will be very difficult.

Are you ready to receive the laws and living rules of the Motherland one more time? Moses is coming down from the mountain with the commandments to give them to you and the whole world population. You know very well that the dance around the golden calf is still going on, and Mother Nature is very angry shaking the ground.

You should by now know the consequences of continuing the negative activity with the only motive to make more money. And you should also know that if the three factors of the Original Sin are removed completely, you and the whole world population will be able to continue to live a natural and good life with everything you need. It will be a good life completely without the opposition of evil.

You have to choose right now. What do you need to live a good life? What is it every human really needs to live a good life on planet earth?

The answer is a complete common education, a home on a homeland and enough food. This you will all have when living in self supported villages of different sizes. All the tribal communities will have room for a certain number of large families, living together and working for each other. There will be no taxes and fees to pay in a world without the global capitalistic system. There will be no wars and conflicts in a world without the armies of all the national states. There will be no religions and sects in a world where all humans know their origin and their future. A world like this will give you back a strong sense of tribal belonging, and whatever your work will be, you will be highly respected and cared for; and be forever happy and content.

With a common world of thoughts that have been occupied for some twelve thousand years by the three factors of the Original Sin, it can be a problem for most people to ask the Spirit World for help. It is all about logic thinking. In order to find back to the laws and living rules from before the Motherland went under, you have to make the journey back in time and see for yourself.

You are not to ask for this information; you have to decide totally on your own what is right and what is wrong in your world of thoughts. You yourself are a strong spirit in a living body and you are always in contact with the Spirit World. You know that it is only the right choices in your life that gives you lasting happiness.

You can easily imagine what happened all over the world in the time after the Motherland went under in an inferno of burning gasses and boiling water. Legend tells that 64 million humans died, and among them was the superior Motherland council. It was an act of nature that the chaos of wars and conflicts broke out and just never stopped.

Therefore it is the twelve members of Motherland council that became the biblical God and his Heaven is camouflage for the lost Motherland. The whole Motherland and all its inhabitants are spiritual beings in the Spirit World. All the religions, tales, legends and myths in the world have their origin from the Motherland.

All the camouflaged stories in the Bible are telling you all you need to know in order to start thinking about how the world was put together before the Motherland went under and then you strait away can outline how the new world can be built, before it is too late. The Promised Land is the whole planet earth and includes the whole world population.

The terrible guilt that mankind carries with them from one generation to the next was created by the warrior kings and priesthoods several thousand years ago and are imbedded in your thoughts with the traditions that comes with imposed belief in the religion of your national state. Not one of the descendants of the twelve sons of Jacob, named Israel, is without guilt, but it is a guilt that the generations of the future will forgive you, if you all work together and removes the three factors of the Original Sin completely from the common thoughts of mankind.

If you do nothing now, now that you know what you are doing wrong and how to make it right, the future generations, your children and their descendants, will never forgive you. You have the power to win back the control of your own world of thoughts, and with the use of modern technology and Internet, you can make many humans around the globe able to find the clue they need to do the same. Remember that you do it for your children and the whole world population. The worst scenario that can happen if nothing is done; the evolution of man has to start all over again, with only a few survivors.

Everything the world leaders do in our present time to stop the global warming is an insult to mankind. The crime against mankind that the three factors of Original Sin are is preserved and passed on with an escalating destructive force. What is the opposite of this infernal greed for riches and personal power that no one really needs?

Who is Moses in our present time? By learning to understand the Spirit World it is possible for every one of you to find the right understanding, and through your own world of thoughts travel far back in the history of mankind. Only totally free for religious dogmas and assumptions is it possible to gather thoughts that are more than twelve thousand years of age. Moses is the history of the lost Motherland.

All humans who find understanding in the Diagram Star and the knowledge about the lost Motherland it preserves and passes on will be a teacher in our present time. Moses is a symbolic spiritual contact between the Spirit World and the whole world population. In the Spirit World the Motherland history are with and an ocean of thoughts that will give all humans a new meaning for living. And when a new Motherland is built the contact with all the people in the world will be spiritual, coming to you through the physical Diagram Star. Then the new superior Motherland council will be physical present for everyone, and breaking the laws and rules for living will not be an option.

The biblical Israelites, meaning you and the whole world population, are still dancing around the Golden Calf. Or perhaps you are doing like the majority, just watching the richest of the rich people dance. You are behaving well, you know something is terribly wrong, but until now you didn't know what.

The Ark of the Covenant was made at the mountains foot. It was a container for the Ten Commandments, the camouflaged story tells us. Now you know it was the Diagram Star that symbolical was put in a container.

From then on the world population lived in the darkness of ignorance and all public and common education about the history from before the Motherland went under stopped. Only the high priest and the priesthood knew, and told the warrior kings only what they needed to know. It was impossible to destroy knowledge for all times, so it was covered up with religious dogmas and assumptions.

The Masters who knew about the Motherland and the global system of government gave the story to the whole world population, but the warrior kings and the priesthoods had other plans. They would not give up their life in luxury with loads of riches and personal power, and they still rule the world with their religious nonsense, armed forces and a global system of capitalism.

Then the Masters wrote down the history of the Motherland and the global system of government in their many camouflaged stories that later became the Bible and other religious books. The Bible is the Ark of the Covenant and the lid is the camouflage of religion.

The many camouflaged histories written by Masters was remembered, preserved and passed on from one generation to the next. Most people knew about the camouflage for a long time, but even to speak about it was dangerous and against the laws and living rules of the warrior kings and priesthoods of the time.

Remember the formula: The four elements = Knowledge about the lost Motherland history. Everything that happens on a mountain is right. God comes on a cloud of fire and every world he says is directed to you, living in present time. The Ark of the Covenant was built at the food of the mountain. The action was right under the circumstances because the knowledge of the Motherland and the Diagram Star was preserved and passed on through the history. The building of the Golden Calf and the dancing was wrong, and the dancing is still going on, while the lost Motherland history just has been discovered.

Even how the Ark of the Covenant was built is a symbolism that is clear as crystal. If the gold is removed from the outside and inside, it is just an ordinary wooden box. The symbolism is also used in the building of the temple in Jerusalem. If the gold and glitter is removed, the religion is gone and it is just another public house. And the symbolism is used in the camouflaged stories in the Bible. If the holiness and glory of religion is removed from the Bible, the stories are the full history about the lost Motherland.

As it is you and the whole world population is still wandering aimlessly around in a mental desert. You, living in present time, are still carrying the Ark of the Covenant with you as a load in the form of a holy Bible. In your desperate search for knowledge that will give life a meaning, you are hereby told that the knowledge you are searching for is to be found in the Bible.

You have to tear yourself loose from the mental occupation that has been with humanity for several thousand years. The whole world population has to walk together through the ocean of knowledge from the Diagram Star. The religion controlling your life isn't sacred any more.

At the border of the Promised Land

4 Moses 13, 1-30

The Israelites traveled for many months through the desert. One day God said to Moses: "Send scouts in to Canaan, the land I promised to give to you. Ask them to find out about the land and the people who live there."

Moses did as God said. He chose one man from each of the twelve tribes of Israel. Before they left the camp, Moses lifted his hand and blessed them.

After many days the twelve men came back. One of them was Kaleb, and another was Joshua, who was a general. Kaleb and Joshua said to Moses: "You should have seen the land! It was so beautiful! There were big trees, soft meadows and hills. We saw flowers everywhere and rich crops. The land is just like God promised us. It is indeed flowing with milk and honey."

There was only one problem. The people who lived in the land were strong warriors. Joshua and Kaleb knew that they could take the land with the help of God.

But not everyone agreed with them. Some of the other scouts made the people doubtful and it lead to the journey were stopped for everyone that day.

Are you able to see under the camouflage of religion and understand that this story is all about you, you and the whole world population? The border in question is between two different worlds. The border you are living with is the laws and rules of your national state and all the religions in the world. The wall around the city of Jericho is symbolizing the mental border that you all have to cross. Now you are told that the Promised Land is the history about the lost Motherland and the paradise world that Adam and Eva left long ago. With the knowledge about the lost Motherland you and the whole world population will be able to build a new world with lasting peace. You must be brave enough to cross the border, and you must tell the whole world population about your discoveries.

You are all standing at the borders of the Promised Land, where you have been for several thousand years. Only with the knowledge from the Diagram Star you will be able to build a new world with lasting peace. Some of you know this, but most of the world population is living with fear for the many national states and their self written laws and rules and their strong armies.

You are all afraid to oppose the world you live in and know so well, because you don't know how easy the imposed religious belief will evaporate from the common world of thoughts, when the religious belief is fronted with knowledge from the Diagram Star. The strong warriors in Canaan are the three factors of the Original Sin, and they have to be removed before the whole world population can build a new world with lasting peace.

Sadly the three factors of the Original Sin are still ruling the common world of thoughts. Most of you have difficulties to even imagine how to live in a world without the force of evil. That means that you are still working slaves, soldiers and servants to a regime that started with Pharaoh in old Egypt.

The knowledge you need in order to build a new world with lasting peace has been lost for a long time. The educational enlightening from the bright shining Diagram Star has been covered with the veil of religion for some twelve thousand years. If you want your children and their descendants to live in a land that symbolically are flowing with milk and honey, you have to start the mental process right now, and remove the camouflage of religion from your own world of thoughts.

Do you now understand that the camouflaged stories in the Bible are timeless, in the sense that they are written for the people living in present time? Do you now understand that it is you yourself and the whole world population that are at the border of the Promised Land and that you have been there for several thousand years? There is no one else living on planet earth. It is you, all of you that are slowly destroying the world we live in, while living without the knowledge from the Diagram Star.

It is the common world of thoughts that have been occupied by the three factors of the Original Sin for some twelve thousand years. The only action that is strong enough to set you mind free is to open the Arc of the Covenant and let you self be enlightened with knowledge. Knowledge will be like a mental sword against all religious belief.

What will happen to your religious belief when knowledge enters your mind? You will discover that you already live in the Promised Land. It is occupied by the three factors of the Original Sin. The discovery will take you out from a meaningless life as blinded and living dead and inn to a life that gives you a natural meaning that you fully understand.

Now the request from the Spirit World to all of you is that you become a scout and take a mental journey inn to the Promised Land. It means quite simply that every one of you is asked to carefully think through how life on earth will be like for humans all over the world, without the three factors of the Original Sin and with knowledge about the lost Motherland and the Diagram Star. As scouts you are the first to know. With the use of Internet and modern technology you can tell the whole world population of your findings.

Then leaders can be elected from all the many different people in the world, leaders that have a high degree of spiritual strength and live with a strong wish to start planning the building of a united world with lasting peace. They will be the new Motherland parliament. From them the new superior Motherland council will be elected.

This time the scouts and the world leaders will agree to start building the new world with lasting peace, because they all know what the whole world population have been through, and because there is no other way to save the world. Why not choose Africa as a new Motherland and start building self supported villages with only peaceful means.

We are too weak

4 Moses 13, 31; 5 Moses 1, 19-33

The other scouts did not agree with Joshua and Kaleb. They did not trust on God to help them to victory. They meant that the Israelites were too weak to fight against the tribal people of Canaan.

The Israelites believed in the other scouts instead of counting on Gods promises. "O, Moses," they said. "What have you done?"

Moses sighted deep. Now the people started complaining again! "Moses, we want to go back to Egypt!"

"Moses, it was your idea that we should leave Egypt. We should not have listened to you. Now we all are going to die. What have we gained from all the hardship then?

Moses and Aaron fell to their knees. They begged the people intensely to believe in God. Joshua and Kaleb tore their clothes to pieces. They shouted that the Promised Land was a good place to live for all of them. But the people did not change. In addition they felt very sorry for them self.

When writing this explanation of the Bible, I do stand alone against the whole world population, at least for the time being. There is as far as I know no one else who has found the connection between the Zodiac signs, the Diagram Star and all the camouflaged stories in the Bible. The Bethlehem Star is a camouflage over the Diagram Star, and it symbolism speaks to me as it have spoken to the wise men of the past. And I am telling all of you about the history of the lost Motherland and the global government system that is the only world management that can create lasting peace on planet Earth.

Joshua and Kaleb of present time will also experience a strong opposition against even starting the process of changing the thinking of the many national states in the world and their respective populations. People don't even realize that they are working slaves, soldiers and servants to the regime that started in Egypt and just never have ended. Mentally your mind is occupied and you are all symbolical still in Egypt.

It is not like you have a choice in our present time. If the mental walk in the desert doesn't start very soon, it will be too late to do it in organized form with only peaceful means, and the worst scenario is that a majority of the world population is wiped out in a chaos of escalating wars and conflicts. This will happen only because all of you in the rich part of the world choose to live like you always have done, and are afraid for the change.

It will be a true inferno if the population in the poor countries gather their forces and start a real desert walk in to the so called rich countries, were they will be met by a strong military force and the belief that God is on their side. Joshua and Caleb of our present time will also have a good reason to tear their clothes to pieces in despair, because they know it can happen any day now.

Thousands of humans are already dying every day within the borders of their national states. The border that has to be removed is between two different systems for governing the world. You live with the wrong and evil system that you don't dare to question. The good and right system of governing the world is explained in the history about the lost Motherland. The crossing of the border in to the Promised Land have been tried several times in the past and failed. Now you can do it and succeed.

What I am asking you to do, is to believe in the information the Diagram Star can give you and the whole world population. The Masters who wrote all the camouflaged stories in the Bible did not have Internet and modern technology. You have. Spread the message hidden in the Bible before it is too late. Knowledge makes you strong.

Forty years punishment

4 Moses 14, 13-45; 5 Moses 1, 34-46

Again God forgave the Israelites. But they had to pay for their sin. Too often they had refused to believe in God and trust him. Therefore God said that they would not be let in to the Promised Land.

"These humans shall wander around in the desert," said God. "They shall use the rest of their life's doing that, all of them, except Joshua and Caleb, who believed in me. I could have leaded the people in to the Promised Land within one year. Instead the Israelites shall wander around in the desert for forty years. All those who did not believe in me will die in the desert. That is the punishment for their disbelief. But their children shall settle down in the land with milk and honey."

When the people heard this they cried out their grief, but it was too late. God had given his verdict over them.

In spite of Gods punishment, the people decided, because they were so close, they would go in to the land of Canaan and fight with the people who lived there. The Israelites had forgotten that God had told them it wasn't them who should fight against the tribes who lived there and drive them away. It was their children who should do that.

The Israelites went to war, but were defeated. Many men died in the battle. God was not with them.

The next forty years the Israelites wandered from place to place. The Lord did not stop to lead them, but he did not take them to the Promised Land. The punishment was real. They had to spend the rest of their life wandering in circles. They were close to Canaan, but they did not get inn to the land.

You know what mankind has done for the last several thousand years. Symbolical you all are still in Egypt. The many tribal people that left and populated the whole world took the ruling system of the Pharaoh with them and have lived against the laws and living rules given by the superior Motherland council all the time. The laws and rules of the lost Motherland are hidden in the Ark of the Covenant, and they are found in the Bible, under the camouflage of religion.

It is not too late to put the governing system with many national states to a complete stop and start building a new world with one Motherland and one set of laws and rules for the whole world population. If a majority of the world population is in favor of the change, there is time enough to do it.

Is it too late for Mother Nature to forgive? Not if the change of living is done in time and the laws and rules of the superior Motherland council is understood and followed to the letter.

It is time to widen the definition of God for you. God is the superior Motherland council. The twelve democratically elected council members hold the title for the duration of life. Their official emblem was the Diagram Star. The sun, the moon and the twelve star signs of the Zodiac is the model for the Diagram Star and the members of the council had one star sign as their personal emblem. When one member died the title was passed on to a young and democratically elected Master. You can imagine that the titles of the council have been uses for at least two hundred thousand years, and it is the titles that hold the power of superior long lasting leadership. When the whole Motherland continent went under in an inferno of burning gasses and boiling water, the whole superior Motherland council died and was remembered by the whole world population.

The reason the biblical God has no power to control the Israelites is because the superior council is dead and gone with the whole Motherland continent. The Israelites have lost their superior leadership and soon learn that they can break the laws without being punished. But the last twelve thousand year has been a long and gruesome punishment for humanity. The many humans who have died, not knowing why they lived, is numerous as the stars in the universe.

The Motherland had three kingdoms and was named the Empire of the Sun. The many tribes that immigrated and populated the world settled on land that was given the name Son of the Empire of the Sun. The tribes developed from colonies, to kingdoms and empires. The titles were always connected to the land they developed and lived on, and the title king was given to a man chosen by the council. The title was not passed on as inheritance back then. Humans living without the three factors of the Original Sin did certainly think differently and used their natural abilities in a more sophisticated manner.

Make a note that this is prove for wrongly translated Egyptian hieroglyphs. In the New Testament Virgin Mary is the lost Motherland, named the Empire of the Sun and Jesus is the Son of the Empire of the Sun.

Now think of what humanity have lost during the twelve thousand years since the Motherland went under. The Bible is telling two stories. The camouflage is telling you how warrior kings and priesthoods took control over the population and made them in to willing working slaves, soldiers and servants. Under the camouflage is the story that tells people living in present time the story about the lost Motherland and how build a new world with lasting peace.

Moses is the Motherland history in the centre of the Diagram Star, and the symbolic twelve tribes descending from Jacob, named Israel, in the sections around the star. Moses, as the story, dies in the desert, and the biblical Israelites go to war. The whole world population is still fighting and the Motherland history is still forgotten.

The choice between life and death

5 Moses 29, 1-30, 20; 31, 2

Moses was more than one hundred years. For the last time he called the people together. With a strong voice he said: "You have to choose! Everyone who wants to live can raise their hands!"

People mumbled among them self and asked each other what he meant.

"Of course we all want to live!"

"Yes! Yes!" they shouted and lifted their hands.

"Now all of you who want to die, can raise their hands," Moses shouted to them. Quickly the hands came down. The people became silent and everyone waited. Only one little child was crying.

"To day," Moses shouted to make everyone pay attention. "To day you all have said that you choose life and not death. God promises to give you food and water, a good land and large livestock's. This is life. He will give it all to you, if you obey his commandments.

But if you follow your own heart and become proud, if you forget how God let you out of Egypt, life will be very bad for you! Do you believe me?" Moses made a pause.

"Yes, Moses, we will obey God!" Moses bent his head and prayed that they all would do that. He was very fond of his people, even if they had given him many difficult times.

It may seem like you and the whole world population has an abundance of time before you have to change your way of living, but you don't. If the chaos of wars and conflicts in the world continues, the number of people who dies every day will escalate rapidly and the future for your children is grim.

If you and the whole world population do change your way of life and begin to build a new Motherland and elect a new superior Motherland council, then your children and their descendents will have a bright future with lasting peace.

Look at Moses as a great spiritual leader. Think of him as a spokesman for the superior Motherland council of twelve. Moses could be the spiritual leader of a new global parliament with members from every nation in the world. The only book of laws and rules for the whole world population would be the Diagram Star and the superior Motherland council would be omnipotent, omnipresent and omniscient like before.

The whole world population in our present time really does have a choice, and that is to continue to break the laws and rules of the lost Motherland and die when the world is completely destroyed, or return to the laws and rules of the lost Motherland and live.

Do you all, the people living in present time, understand that you still have time to choose if you want to live or die. You see thousands of people starving to death every day in the poor countries all over the world. The global warming will gradually turn most of the fertile land in to dry desert land. When the time comes that there is no food left in the so called rich part of the world, the people living there will go to war against each other and take fertile land where they can. Brother will kill brother for food. But victory will only postpone death. Your forefathers made the wrong choice back then, and the whole world population is slowly dying, not knowing why they ever lived.

If you choose to continue to live with the present system of government of many national states, with one global system of capitalism and all the religions in the world, you will all die before time, in a mental desert, after having lived a totally meaningless life. Mother Nature is calling out loud to the people: Make your choice now. It is now or never!

If you all choose life this time, the change you all have to go through is dramatic, a change of ways that only can be done with peaceful means over a relative long period of time. The right choice will take you out of the desert and inn to a world that is flooded with milk and honey.

You will have to stop using things made from oil, things that you don't really need. The ongoing fight for global economic growth must stop completely. The making of products that nobody needs have to stop and the same goes for all use of money, the buying and selling in order to make a profit.

It is easier to tell you that the life you are living right now have to stop. The life as mentally blind and living dead on an aimless desert walk has to stop. Only then the life in the light of the Diagram Star can begin. If you choose to change; choose life, the whole world population will do the same. If you do it alone, you will at least know why you live. The truth will set your thoughts free.

Moses song and his last days

5 Moses 31, 1-34, 7

Before Moses died, he wrote a beautiful song to the people. He knew that he was going to another Promised Land than Canaan. He was going to his best friend, God.

Moses song was about the love of God. He sang about Gods faithfulness through the years, his force and his power.

When Moses was finished singing, he felt very tired. He wanted very much to see the Promised Land. Now he asked God if his last hour had come.

"Yes," answered the Lord. "You shall see the Promised Land, but you shall not enter it. Walk now up on the Nebo Mountain. From there you can see the land of Canaan." When Moses got to the top, he could see across the river Jordan. There was the Promised Land.

Moses stood there for several hours. He gazed at the land he longed for so much. It was like his eyes never got tired of looking at the land God had promised to the Hebrew people, now called the Israelites. Wild flowers colored the hills and tall trees were moving softly in the wind.

"Thank you, Lord," said Moses. It was enough for him to just see the land. While Moses gazed at the land that soon should belong to his people, he died. He died as a strong man. Still he was able to see and think clear. God buried Moses in the valley close to the mountain. Moses was Gods friend.

You should be able to see the similarity in the story about Moses and the story about Jesus. Both stories have the same origin from the Egyptian hieroglyphs. If you ask why they were so incorrectly translated, it has to do with the importance of preserving the history about the lost Motherland and passing it on to coming generations. The Masters of the past truly succeeded.

Moses is the history of the lost Motherland and because of the choice people made at Mount Sinai the history is returning to the spirit world, where it was before it was born from the River Nile. It is back where the spiritual superior Motherland council is, hidden under the camouflage of religion. Now the history about the lost Motherland is shown to you. With the knowledge about the past the new world can be built. Even if you don't get to live in the new world, you can make sure you children can begin living in a world where there is no evil.

If you read the whole song in the Bible, you will soon understand that the song is about you, the people living in present time. The whole world population is a wayward generation, children in whom there is no fait. You must understand that the land Moses is gazing at from a mountain top is the new planet earth that the whole world population have to build together in order to create lasting peace.

After the camouflage is removed you are the last in a long line of generations that are totally under the control of the three factors of the Original Sin. You all have inherited a system of government with many national states and the laws and rules of the forefathers that are totally wrong. You didn't know and therefore you are without guilt.

Just as Moses you can all see the new world that you can build with the knowledge from the Diagram Star, meaning you can see and know what is so terribly wrong in the world where you live. Before reading this you didn't have the knowledge about the lost Motherland. The reason for not knowing is that after the wrong choice was made back then, symbolized by what happened at Mount Sinai, the knowledge was hidden under a camouflage of religion. The knowledge humans needed to build a new world, was hidden in the Ark of the Covenant. It was and is the only way the knowledge could be preserved and passed on from generation to generation and on to you. Are you brave enough to oppose the leaders of the world and tell them what you know?

Now you know the formula saying: Water, Earth, Air and Fire = Knowledge. This means the sun; the moon and the twelve Zodiac star signs are giving the humans knowledge. The Diagram Star is the Zodiac down on earth, in your hands, carrying the knowledge about the lost Motherland through the history, and now the lost world history is told to you and the whole world population. All you have to do is to mentally follow Joshua across the river Jordan. The story is telling you how to break the spell and destroy the three factors of the Original Sin. The crossing of the river never happened. It is a recipe telling you how to do it.

Most adult humans living today will not live long enough to settle down and live under a global system of government with common laws and rules for the whole world population. It is your children and their descendants that will live to experience a new world with lasting peace.

Several thousand years ago the Masters truly meant that there had to be a natural catastrophe of global dimensions to get you to understand that the foundation for your life is wrong. The religious Doomsday is only camouflage, but with a true meaning underneath. You will have to judge yourself and forgive. If you can forgive yourself, you can forgive the leaders of the world. There are no enemy humans, only imposed enemy thoughts.

The Masters of the past did not have Internet and modern technology, like you have in our present time. You can make the whole world population know that the whole planet earth ones again can be a paradise for absolutely all humans, with no exceptions.

The Bible continues to speak about a development where the three factors of the Original Sin are growing as the ruling force of the world. The chaos of wars and conflicts develops up through the Old Testament, and the fight for the daily bread gets harder all the time. Millions of humans have died and many more will.

But the stories are hiding the full story about the lost Motherland and a paradise world where only the force of good was known.

Joshua sends spies

Joshua 2, 1-3

When Moses died, Joshua was appointed leader by Gods chosen people. Just after they all had camped at the bank of the river Jordan, Joshua called on two of his best men. They were brave and competent soldiers. "I will send you out on a secret mission," he said.

The two men did like exciting challenges.

"I want you to investigate the land on the other side of the river. Sneak in to the city of Jericho and find out how strong it is. Find out if the people are getting prepared for battle, and how many soldiers they have. See what weapons they use. Are they made of bronze or iron? When you have investigated all this, you come back and tell me what you found. After we have crossed Jordan, we will attack Jericho."

The men nodded. The same afternoon they walked inn to the city. It was surrounded by high and thick walls. On top of the wall were guards.

The two men passed some guards. One of them turned and shouted: "Who is the two strangers over there?

"They look like Israelites!"

"Stop them! Spies! These men are spies! Stop them!"

The two med heard that the guards came after them. They ran first in one direction and then in another. They ran fast through the narrow streets and tried to find a place to hide.

"Come here!" they heard a voice. The men stopped and looked up. They saw a women hanging out a window over them. "Hurry up!" She pointed at a door. Joshua's two spies went quickly inside.

As said before, also you will send spies out to find out how strong the religion is in your part of the world. You will have to consider addressing all three factors of the Original Sin at the same time, because if one of them falls, the other two will follow. Will the many religious congregations around the world welcome your answer to all their questions, or will they refuse to believe you and fight for their self made human rights?

I am telling you that your only weapon will be the strong double-edged sword of knowledge about the lost Motherland, and you will eventually win over all religious belief. The walls of Jericho are a symbol for all the religions in the world. Religion is one thing. Imposed nationalism and the feeling of national belonging is another. The third factor is the global system of capitalism. You cannot take out one without taking out the two others, but give it time and they will truly fall.

Persons with knowledge of and from the lost motherland will possibly not be welcomed within the mental walls of religion anywhere in the world. They will be recognized, not on their cloths, but in their free and not afraid approach. How they will be welcomed is very much depending of what country they live in.

But in all the nations of the world there are people who will fight with all possible peaceful means to tell others what they know about the lost Motherland and a global system of government with one set of laws and rules for living for the whole world population. And most of the people do really seek and want a peaceful change to a government that really can create lasting peace in the whole world. What you all need is knowledge about the lost world history that the Masters of the past wrote down, hidden under a camouflage of religion.

The Masters of the past did not know that their camouflaged histories would be taken in use by their sworn enemies, first the roman emperor Konstantin, and from then on the warrior kings and priesthoods, to be used as a tool to control the population. The religion was imposed on people all over the world with the use of warfare and brutal force, with the camouflage intact. The religion was used as an excuse for the brutal forming of national states and for making the population within the borders in to obedient working slaves, soldiers and servants, in the name of nameless and powerless God. Their only force was in armed soldiers.

It will be difficult to accept for everyone, but special for the national states leaders, their priesthoods and the richest of the rich, when they learn that they truly are preserving and passing on the three factors of the Original Sin.

The spies escape

Joshua 2, 3-14

The Israelite spies looked around and saw a woman on the other side of the room. "I will hide you," she said. "Just follow me."

The woman from Jericho led them up on the roof top. There she showed them were they could hide. The spies were there until it got dark in the evening.

When the king of Jericho heard about the Israelite spies, he ordered the soldiers to search the whole city. Soon they came to the house where they were in hiding.

The soldiers went in to the woman's house. When they asked her, she answered: "Yes, they were here, but they disappeared. If you hurry, you can catch them." The soldiers got out of the house in a hurry. They ran out the city gate before it closed for the night. Now they could not get back until the next morning.

"Hurry up," the woman said to the Israelites. "Now you have the change. Get out away from here while the soldiers are gone."

The two men came out from their hiding place. "I know your people, the Israelites," she said. "God is with you. He is blessing everything you do. Everybody here in Jericho is afraid to battle with you. If I help you to escape, will you then remember me and not harm me and my family when you attack Jericho?"

"You saved our lives, and we shall save yours," said the men. "Yes, we shall save you and your family, if you help us to escape from here." The woman nodded. She walked in front of them up a ladder.

A promise shall always be kept, no matter what. If you break a promise, the deed will follow you for the rest of your life as a burden of shame.

Who is the woman in this camouflaged story? Imagine the city of Jericho as the common world of thoughts for the whole world. Then the woman is a symbol for the thoughts that you carry deep inside you. It is the thoughts that make you know that the thoughts that controls your life from birth to death, is wrong. The woman knows that she does the right thing when breaking the laws and rules of her king. Are you brave enough to do what you know is right, even if you have to break the laws and rules of your national state?

Only by removing all the evil and wrong thoughts in the world the good and the right thoughts will get their natural power back. There are no human enemies anywhere in the world and warfare against the forces of evil is not an option. The wrongly imposed thoughts have to be removed from the common world of thoughts with the use of only peaceful means.

The woman is a symbol for one single thought in your mind, that tells you that the chaos of wars and conflicts are wrong, that the global system of capitalism are wrong and that all the religions in the world are wrong. The single but true thought is enough for you, given the right circumstances, to break the laws and rules of your national state and work for the good forces who wants to build a new world with lasting peace.

The thoughts about all the wrong and evil there is in the world is inherited from parents and forefathers through thousands of years, and the laws and the living rules of your nation tells you that you will be severely punished if you even think that the leaders of your nation and the whole population is wrong and you alone is right.

But the single thought in your mind is truly right and you are not alone carrying a single thought of what's natural and right in your mind. You have always learned that you shall not betray your national state. In this case you have to do as the woman in this story; you have to betray your own people because of what you know and they don't.

Think of yourself, your family and your people as working slaves, soldiers and servants of a government system that is wrong and have been wrong for thousands of years. It is wrong to live inside your national borders protected by soldiers. You know that one good thought of knowledge can win over the whole world of common thoughts that are derived from evil, meaning the three factors of the Original Sin. You have to be brave and break the circle of evil, no matter what. It is the only way towards lasting world peace. The city wall of Jericho is a symbol for all that is evil in the whole world.

Now think of the twelve tribes called the Israelites as the whole world population. Your single thought of right is from the biblical Israelites and what they do to spread the good thoughts all over the world is a recipe to follow. It is the right imbedded in the Diagram Star that are about to be spread out to the whole world population, not by use of bassoons, but by use of Internet and modern technology.

The double-edged sword of knowledge is a million times stronger than religious belief. Remember now that there are no human enemies in the world. The enemies are the thoughts of the three factors of the Original Sin, and you have to remove from your own world of thoughts first. If you can forgive yourself, you can forgive all your fellow humans beings.

Every human being in the world have to be their own spy and mentally enter all the camouflaged stories in the Bible and remove the religious belief by use of the single thought of knowing what's natural right. If you know the full history about the lost Motherland, you know the right and natural way to govern the whole world. The single thought of right will break down the enormous walls of wrong doing and then the single thought of being right will grow and grow and grow until it have reached the whole world population.

The new common world of thoughts will give you and the whole world population a true and natural meaning with life.

Remember that the biblical Israelites symbolically are carrying with them the Ark of the Covenant on their long walk in the desert. The contents are the Diagram Star. The Ark of the Covenant is the container of all the knowledge you need to be fully enlightened. Your single thought of being right is a seed of knowledge that will grow in your mind and become the symbolical tree of life.

You can now imagine the pact that was made on behalf of the whole world population back in the far past. The Diagram Star was hidden in the Ark of the Covenant and protected by the high priests. Common education in the light of the Diagram Star stopped, but the knowledge was never completely forgotten. Over time it became the little single thought that is natural right and is like a seed in your world of thoughts. Give the seed nourishment and feel it grow.

Now we can all say thank you to the many generations of Masters that have carried the full history of the Motherland and the global system of government up through the whole history, under the camouflage of religion.

Time has come to stop the circle of evil and demand that the ongoing destructions caused by the three factors of the Original Sin shall come to a complete stop. A good start is to start spreading the message from the Bible all over the world.

The red string

Joshua 2, 15-22

The two men climbed up the ladder and came to a little room. "Now I shall explain how you shall get out of here," said the woman. She pointed at a little window. This part of the house was in fact a part of the city wall around Jericho. The woman gave them a rope. "If you climb out here, you are outside the city. Go up in to the hills and stay there for three days."

The men took the rope. "What is your name?"

"My name is Rahab."

"When the Israelites attack, Rahab, you shall fasten this red string to the window. No one that lives here will be harmed when we attack Jericho."

The other spy added: "But if you betray us for anyone, and we are caught, our soldiers will show you no mercy."

She nodded. The men opened the window and fastened the rope to a pillar. Slowly they lowered them self's down outside the house and down the city wall. They reached the ground without being discovered and disappeared in the dark. Rahab pulled up the rope. She knew that this was her ticket to be saved.

You are on one the desert side of the river and you know nothing about what life will be like on the other side. You were born in the mental desert as your parent and ancestors before you for many generations. Perhaps it is pure coincidence that will make you will feel happiness and longing to get to the other side as soon as you take the first step in to the symbolical river Jordan.

In the real world you need to know the history, know the world you are leaving and the world you are walking in to. There is only one way to know what life in the new world will be like, and that way is to know the history about the lost Motherland. Hidden in the Bible, under the camouflage of religion, you will find knowledge in abundance and you will know how to build a new world with lasting peace. The river Jordan is symbolizing knowledge and you know that when you find knowledge there is no return in to the darkness of oblivion and belief. You will straight away know that everything you are doing are right, even if it is in direct opposition to the present established world of common thoughts.

You will start the siege and make the whole world know that you are there and that you are going to destroy all that is wrong in the world and make things right, ones and for all.

But it is truly not coincidences that will help you, even if it seems like that. You must trust in the spirit world to help you, in the form of inspired thoughts coming directly to you or as good advises. You will be able to divide the right from wrong without hesitation.

You know a lot about the many dominating religions in the world already. They are all an important part of the three parts of the Original Sin and a tool for all the leaders of the national states and their priesthoods to control and manipulate the population in to an unconditional obedience.

You know by now that all the religions in the world are camouflage over knowledge about the lost Motherland. All it takes for the walls of religions to crumble and fall is to fill your mind with the answers to all your questions. The imposed religious belief will quickly change to knowledge as derived from the Diagram Star.

On the border of the Promised Land

Joshua 2, 23-3, 13

The Israelite spies hide in the hills for three days. Then they understood that there no longer was any danger to them and hurried back to the camp and reported to Joshua.

"It is almost too good to be true," they said. "The woman, who helped us, said that everyone in Jericho is afraid for us. The city is ours."

Together with Joshua the three men bent their heads and thanked God. When Joshua was finished with his prayer, he looked at the two spies. "We move on Jericho in a couple of days. The day we have waited for so long, is here." They did not understand what he meant at first, but Joshua smiled and said: "The day God is going to lead us in to the Promised Land have come."

The two men understood that he wanted them to spread the good news, and they ran off and told everyone in the camp. Soon everyone knew. "The day has come!"

People were exited and very happy. They had waited eagerly for this to happen and actually counted the days. Forty years of wandering was over!

The book about Joshua is all about the long desert walk coming to an end. The whole world population has been aimlessly walking in a mental desert for some twelve thousand years. The desert is your state of mind. You are living in the darkness of oblivion, with your world of thoughts occupied by the three factors of the Original Sin. The circle of evil has to be broken.

Now you know the full history of the lost Motherland, and the knowledge makes it possible for you to know the world you will find when you decide to leave the world you live in. The symbolical attack on the city of Jericho is telling you how the strong walls of religious belief in the world will crumble and fall. Only then the building of the new world with lasting peace can begin. The attack never happened back. You are all still on the wrong side of the river of knowledge, wandering aimlessly in the desert.

You should know that the word Hebrew means "one from the other side of the river", meaning one who doesn't know. Now the time has come to enter the new world, a world of common, natural knowledge. It is truly the walls of religious belief that will crumble and fall after all this time.

The Diagram Star is hidden in the Ark of the Covenant, and by now you know that the Bible is the Ark of the Covenant. The knowledge hidden under the camouflage of religion has traveled through the world history, preserved by the veil of dogmas and assumptions you know so well.

The deception makes humans wait for a superior power to help them make the crossing. By now you should know that the superior power from a Motherland council was lost some twelve thousand years ago. They became spiritual and the dogmas and assumptions made them in to a nameless and powerless God. The meaningless waiting has to stop right now. Only you, the humans living in present time, can cross the symbolic river Jordan and begin building a new world with lasting peace. Only the whole world population can elect a new Motherland parliament and a new superior Motherland council. The spiritual help that you need to complete the symbolic crossing is found in the Bible, in the Ark of the Covenant, in the Diagram Star.

The stone tablet with the Diagram Star is symbolical hidden under the holy golden lid of religion. Is this clearly understood? If the walk towards full understanding takes a long time, the excitement and happiness will be great the day that you and the whole world population really know that the three factors of the Original Sin is under siege and are about to fall. You know how to do it and with the help from the spirit world you will do it right. There is no going back.

Remember that there are no humans telling you to do this, no national leaders and the priesthoods. This you do for you, your family, your tribe and most of all for your own children and their descendants. The whole world population has to do exactly the same, together as brothers, as one people. The tribal leaders and al the many democratically elected councils in the world, will all have the same orders and knows what to do. There is no disagreement between any people, even if it feels like a strange thing to do.

The aimless wandering ends when the river is crossed. It will be a mental journey inn to a new world of common thoughts, a true liberation from the three factors of the Original Sin. It means a total change in the way humans lives on planet earth. Everybody will know the difference between right and wrong. It will be very difficult to make the change in living for you and perhaps also for your children, but the future generations will be born in to the global system of government, with lasting world peace and with a new superior Motherland council to supervise it all.

It is the end of some twelve thousand years as working slaves, soldiers and servants that are about to happen in this camouflaged story. Children will no longer be born inside the borders of a national state as already captivated prisoners. All the national states will stop to exist. Education will be the main activity besides the daily work in the self supported village.

You will all be working for your family and your tribal community and in return you will be provided with everything you need to live a good life on planet earth. Living like this, together in a community where everybody knows everybody, will make the strong feeling of tribal belonging grow back. Think of the difference.

Do you feel that these words are correct? Think about what the world will be like without the three factors of the Original Sin controlling every moment of your life.

And think for a moment about the life a majority of humans live in our present time. What will you do the day that there are now food for anyone, the day soldiers are guarding every field, with orders to kill those who tries to steel food for them self, their children and the family.

It is already happening in many places all over the world. People die by the thousands every day, caused by the three factors of the Original Sin.

You know the definition of the Original Sin by now. Think through your world and the future your children have to look forward to. Think through and understand the message from the past, the history of the Motherland that the Masters so masterly have preserved and passed on from generation to generation and now have passed on to you.

The mental walk across the river Jordan has to start now. It is not too late, and you do it for your children and their descendants. I can assure you, not one of you will miss the world you know so well, the world with an escalating chaos of wars and conflicts, a never ending personal quest for riches and personal power.

Crossing the river Jordan

Joshua 3, 14-4, 24

Joshua ordered the priests to carry the Ark of the Covenant across the river Jordan. When the priests touched the water with their toes, the water withdraws and became a high wall. There was a dry path in front of the priests.

They walked out in the middle of the river. Not a drop of water fell on them. They were completely dry! The Joshua ordered the people to follow. One family after the other, camels, donkeys, people and animals, crossed river Jordan that day. They walked past the priest that carried the Ark of the Covenant.

The whole day went by before all the Israelites had reached the other side of the river. This was their new land. When everyone had crossed the river, Joshua looked down from the hill where he had been standing and remembered the promise God had given Abraham.

God had said: "I will make you in to a great people. You shall be more numerous than the stars on the night sky. The land of Canaan shall belong to you."

Joshua asked the priests to come up on the river bank. In the same moment they were up, God made the water run back in place again. After nearly four hundred years the children of Abraham had arrived home in the Promised Land.

Remember now that the Promised Land is the whole planet earth, the new world with lasting peace. The biblical Israelites are the whole world population. Four hundred years was an educated guess made by the Masters who wrote the many camouflaged biblical stories.

The walk in the desert is a symbolic passage between the darkness of the slavery and the bright light of freedom. You are all still living in the dark shadow of the three factors of the Original Sin, still blinded, without willpower, you let you self be used to participate in activities that are against the strict laws given by the superior Motherland council. You know that the building of national states with the use of warfare and brutal force was wrong. You know that all the religions in the world are camouflage over lost world history and you know that the global capitalistic system is wrong. What is there in the inheritance you give to your children that you can be proud of? Will your children continue to be proud of you and the nation after the world is completely destroyed?

The whole world population is truly at a crossroad in our present time. With the knowledge that you all need in order to break down the strong walls of the three factors of the Original Sin, you should be ready to begin right now.

To recreate the whole world in to a peaceful paradise, the process described in the camouflaged Bible stories have to be followed to the letter. If you choose to do nothing and continue to live by the laws and rules for living in your national state, you will be sitting on the fence, watching the world being destroyed all around you. How many of your family have to die, before you begin to act?

The Masters formula is the key to understanding the world you can begin to build in your world of thoughts. The whole population of the world has to learn to know the Diagram Star and find the full knowledge about the lost Motherland, before the camouflage all the religions in the world can be removed from the common world of thoughts.

This you can do by opening the Ark of the Covenant and let the Diagram Star enlighten the whole world population. Only then you can all symbolically walk across the river Jordan in to a real world with lasting peace. The knowledge will do wonders for the common world of thoughts, and a new world with lasting peace will come true for every one of you.

The kings and their priesthoods were always frightened by the stories about the lost Motherland and a global system of government that would take away their prominent positions and their life in luxury. The fact that the religion was a camouflage over knowledge could easily be discovered by anyone given the time and opportunity to do so. Over time the walls of the religions in the world became higher and stronger, protected by armed soldiers and the despotic laws and rules for living given by the warrior kings and their priesthoods.

It was because the kings and the priesthoods denied the truth to be commonly known, the persecution and killing of the so called witches and all kind of opposition started. The few who knew the full story about the lost Motherland were intelligent human beings, and they were killed because of what they knew. It is not certain what all the witches and wizards knew everything, but certainly they knew that the religion that were imposed on them were pure nonsense.

As it seems in our present time, all the national states have to put down their weapon of war first of all, and melt them in to pickaxes, plows and other tools for farming the land. Then it is the mentally strong walls of religion that have to come down, with the use of only peaceful means.

After the whole world population is settled in self supported villages, the global system of capitalism will be gone for good. Just imagine a whole world were absolutely all humans have all they need to live a good life.

It is not natural, like it is today and has been for thousands of years; that parents have to watch their children die, because they have no money to buy food.

The walls of Jericho fall

Joshua 5, 13-6, 27

Joshua knew that he soon had to attack Jericho. He prayed for the Lord to help. Then God showed him a really peculiar plan.

Joshua said to his soldiers: "We are going out marching!"

None of Joshua's soldiers had been in a war like that before. Marching was not war! But they listened to Joshua and the plan that God had given him.

"We will do as God told you," they said.

The next day all the soldiers lined up. It looked like a parade. First the priests walked carrying the Ark of the Covenant on their shoulders. Then Joshua walked in front of all his soldiers.

The people in Jericho saw the Israelites coming, and they shivered with fear. "This will be a terrible battle," they said. "We are all going to die, because God is on their side."

But the Israelites surprised them. They did not attack. Instead they walked around the city, outside the tall walls that surrounded it. While they walked they were completely silent. Joshua had said that there should not be made a sound. There were no battle shouting, just hundreds of hundreds of soldiers that were completely silent. The only sound that was heard was seven priests blowing their bassoons.

The army of the Israelites marched around Jericho. Then they went back to the camp and rested.

The next day the same thing happened. For six days they marched around Jericho. All the time it was completely quiet, except for the bassoons.

Then, the seventh day Joshua commanded the army to walk seven times around the city of Jericho. After the seventh time, still with the sounds of the bassoons, the soldiers started shouting the calls of battle. They yelled as loud as they could.

And in this moment, the walls of Jericho fell with an enormous crash! God had done a new wonder. The Israelites walked in to the city. Only one family survived. It was the woman Rahab and her family.

This is the way that you and the whole world population have to go to war against wrongful imposed thinking. You have to be able to separate all that is evil and wrong from all that is good and right first in your own mind. Then you will know what the spiritual superior Motherland council want you to do. Your weapon is the knowledge about the lost Motherland history and the bassoons are a symbol for the Internet and modern technology.

The number seven stand for the seven original sciences that can be derived from the Diagram Star. You know by now that all knowledge is in a cycle, just like water. Just like the water has to fall from the sky, again and again, the knowledge about the history of the world has to be taught to students, again and again.

The walls of Jericho are a symbol for all the religions in the world, which are used by all the national leaders as a tool to control the population. Without the false greatness of the gold and glitter, the large castles, churches and cathedrals, and without their traditional ceremonial dress code, the warrior kings and their priesthoods are regular human beings, not greater than you in any aspects of life.

Regular humans are blinded by religion whether they are religious believers or not believers. The reason is that there are always a national army behind the religions and the global capitalistic system. If you distance yourself from both religious belief and religious not belief, you will find no answers. You have to begin studying the Bible and remove the camouflage of religion and you will find the hidden message.

When all the religions in the world crumble and fall inside your world of thoughts and the common world of thoughts, the knowledge from the Diagram Star will find its way back like a force of nature. You will find a deep and profound understanding of the global system of government, which are the only natural way to rule in a world with lasting peace.

If I have told you before I will tell you again and again, that you must open the Ark of the Covenant and learn to know the Diagram Star. By use of Internet and modern technology you must shout out the message hidden in the bible to the whole world population. It is the message of lasting world peace.

The symbolic help Joshua got from God was a spiritual sword that carries the power of knowledge about the lost Motherland. You are the carrier of the spiritual sword in our present time; you who want to build a world with lasting peace for our children and their descendants.

Remember now that the definition of God is the superior Motherland council members who died some twelve thousand years ago, before the chaos of wars and conflicts started. After the knowledge is restored a new Motherland has to be built and a new superior Motherland council shall bring back lasting peace for the whole world population.

The wise woman under the palm tree

Judges 4, 1-16

Many years later the Israelites had forgotten everything they had promised Moses and God. They worshipped other gods. Therefore the Lord let the enemy, king Jabin and his general Sisera, win over them.

On that time the Lord had raised a woman named Deborah to be judge for the Israelites. God had blessed her with wisdom. She loved the Lord. Frequently she asked the people to listen to God and obey him, but most of them only laughed at her.

As judge Deborah listened to people's problems. When she judged, she sat under a palm tree. People stood in line waiting to talk with her.

One day Deborah sent for Barak, an Israelite soldier. "Take ten thousand men with you to the mountain Tabor, she said. "When general Sisera find out you are there, he will come with his soldiers and chariots. We are going to war and we are going to win over him on the river bank."

Barak said: "I will go if you accompany me, but not otherwise."

Deborah smiled to him. "Have you less faith in God then in me?" she asked. "Well, well, since you don't trust in God, he will see that a woman wins victory and not you."

When the day of the battle came, Barak was leading his soldiers. Deborah lifted her hands and prayed from the mountain top. God made many things go wrong for general Sisera, and not before long Barak and his soldiers had won the battle. Sisera himself got down from his chariot and fled on foot.

This story is story about how the forces of good are going to win over the forces of evil. Under the camouflage there is a true story that has to be written in to our present time. The Israelites is still a symbol for the whole world population.

The story is telling people living in present time, that wars and conflicts developed, with warrior kings and priesthoods in charge. Concentrate and try to look at both armies as human thoughts, as the common world of thoughts. Both sides have forgotten all about the common laws and rules of the Motherland. On both sides the soldiers fight for their kings and priesthoods because if they refuse they will automatically be called traitors and killed by their own leader. It is the imposed thoughts about being faithful to your national state laws and rules that occupy the soldiers of all the armies in the world at present time.

They all fight because that is what all the national armies do. According to the laws and rules from before the Motherland was lost, there were no national states with armies anywhere in the world, and wars and conflicts was unheard of.

Deborah, the wise woman under the palm tree, knows about the Motherland and the global system of government. When she asks the people to believe in God and obey him, she is talking openly about the Diagram Star and the laws and living rules from the time before the Motherland went under. Most people laughs at her when she talks about a world with lasting peace; a world where there is no wars and conflicts at all.

She is a symbol for the thoughts that are right in the world. The battle to remove all that is wrong in the world will take place in the common world of thoughts.

The Master who is writing this story is talking about the dreams and wishes of the whole world population for the last twelve thousand years. He describes the return of the knowledge of the lost Motherland history and the Diagram Star, and how one true thought of knowledge even from a woman can win over all the thoughts that is derived from the three factors of the Original Sin.

The return of the belief in God is under the camouflage of religion the return of knowledge about the lost Motherland and a global system of government that truly can remove the three factors of the Original Sin from the face of the earth, for all time.

Remember that the mountain and the river are Earth and Water and are according to the Masters formula a symbol for the knowledge humans needs in order to be able to build a world with lasting peace.

The battle spoken of here never happened. Historical correct it is to say that the forces of good kept fighting all the time, and if the good forces occasionally did win, the winner had to become evil in order to survive as a warrior king. The proof that evil always won is that you all still are working slaves, soldiers and servants of a system of government that symbolical started in old Egypt. What the whole world population still is fighting for is a world with lasting peace. It is a battle that only can be won with peaceful means in the common world of thoughts.

Think about the coming battle as the sword of knowledge fighting against the religious belief that still is enforced on people with warfare and brutal force. Knowledge about the lost Motherland can easily win over all religious beliefs in the world, but as long as the religious belief still is an important tool for the national states to control their population, it will not be an easy battle.

Who will kill Sisera?

Judges 4, 17-22; 5, 1-31

When general Sisera saw that he had lost the battle, he fled. He searched for a place he could hide. Then he saw the tent of a friend of king Jabin. "Aha," he said to himself. "They will hide me."

A woman met him. Her name was Jael. "Come in," she said. Sisera had no idea that she hated him and his whole army. Jael gave him milk to drink, and then she covered him with a blanket.

General Sisera soon fell asleep. Then Jael walked softly to him and killed him with a hammer and a tent peg.

In the meantime Barak was looking for Sisera. When he came to the tent of Jael, she walked to meet him and told him what she had done.

Barak brought her to Deborah and the soldiers. There was a loud rejoicing from the Israelites when they heard about the victory. They asked who had killed Sisera.

Barak looked at Deborah. He had to give the honor of the victory to a woman. Therefore he lifted the hand of Jael, so everyone could see her. "This woman, Jael killed Sisera!"

All the Israelites rejoiced for Jael. But Deborah and Barak told them that it really was the Lord that had won the battle for them. Then they sang the song of rejoicing.

The twelve tribes of Israel concurred Jabin, king of Canaan, and the land had peace for forty years.

A woman named Jael killed general Sisera. It is possible that something like this really happen in the past. The Masters were good at using historical strongholds in their camouflaged stories. They knew the full history about the lost Motherland and knew that the translation from Hieroglyphs to the Hebrew language was wrong. They also knew that the Hebrew language have many words with several meanings. They succeeded in preserving and passing the camouflaged stories though the history and now the stories enter inn to your world of thoughts with the correct meaning. One good example is Adam and Eve. The two names mean the whole world population.

So, who of you are brave enough to use you knowledge about the lost Motherland actively and go up against what may seems like the whole world population and win over the evil thoughts of the three factors of the Original Sin?

The Lord God is defined to be the superior Motherland council. The twelve members are in the spirit world in the form of spiritual beings, as thoughts that always will be accessible for all human beings. The laws and living rules given by the superior Motherland council is carried through the history by the Diagram Star. Everything a human can read from the diagram shaped like a bright shining star is spiritual.

Before the Motherland went under it was the superior Motherland council who were in charge of the evolution on planet earth. After the Motherland went under and millions of humans died, the lost continent was remembered as a heaven in the spirit world.

It is only the true story about the lost Motherland that can win over all the beliefs that has grown in to the many religions, myths and legends in the world. Removing the three factors of the Original Sin from the common world of thoughts is the victory wanted by all the descendants of the twelve tribes of Israel.

The knowledge of the lost Motherland history and the Diagram Star is still preserved and passed on by a small group of humans called Masters. This attempt to make the lost world history known by all humans is done by one person in direct contact with the spirit world. No matter what outcome, the knowledge about the lost Motherland will always be preserved and passed on to coming generations.

Because it is a fact that it still is the three factors of the Original Sin that controls and rules over all the choices a human makes in life. The world leaders are strong and intelligent humans that really do believe that they and everybody else in position to make a difference are doing the right thing all the time. Will you wait until your first born son dies before you have a change of thoughts?

The world leaders in present time do not know anything about the Diagram Star and the global system of government that was the foundation for lasting peace in the time before the Motherland went under. They denied and still deny that the Motherland ever existed and are following the long tradition of warrior kings and priesthoods of the past. They all continue to work hard to be rich and powerful, and with their religious belief or not belief they all continue the dance around the Colden Calf.

Remember now that all the three factors of the Original Sin are occupying the thoughts of all humans, while the thoughts about the Diagram Star still are few. The thoughts that can create lasting peace in the whole world is in the common world of thoughts and the battle against evil with the use of only peaceful means will take place. The few humans with knowledge about the lost Motherland history will win over the many humans that still are under the strict control of the Original Sin.

Will you choose to live with the three factors of the Original Sin, now that you know it is inherited from the self elected warrior kings and priesthoods of the past? Will you continue to watch the world you live in being destroyed before your eyes, or will you use your change to move from belief to knowledge and face the battle with all your mental force?

Gideon starts his service

Judges 6, 1-40

It didn't last long before the Israelites forgot their promises again and went back to their evil ways. Because they worshipped other gods, God could not make them strong. A warrior tribe called the midianites won over them. The midianites ravaged the land of Canaan and the children of Israel were obliged to live in dens in the mountains and in caves and fortified places.

God now choose a man named Gideon as savior for his people. He sent an angel to Gideon, and he said that he had to tear down the altar of Baal and the statues of all the other gods that the Israelites worshipped on hilltops.

Gideon knew that the other men in the village could kill him if he did something like that, but he still went ahead and did it, because God asked him to do it.

Gideon and ten of his servants walked up on the hill. It was here the strange gods were worshipped. They broke an altar and all the statues. Then they in silence built another altar. They slaughtered one bull they had brought with them, and sacrificed it on the new altar. Then they prayed to God: "Dear God, protect us all."

The next morning, when the men in the village found the broken altar, they asked: "Who have done this? We shall kill him!"

But Joash, Gideon's father, said: "If their god really is God, so let him punish him who did this." The men agreed with him. Therefore Gideon was safe and the Lords altar remained standing.

Soon after started rumors that the midianites had plans to attack the Israelites again. Gideon then said to God: "Lord, if you really have thought of helping the Israelites to victory, then show it to me. I am putting a fleece of wool on the ground tonight. If it is wet by the dew and the earth beside is dry, I shall know that you mean that we shall go to war against them."

The next morning the fleece was wet and the ground was dry. But Gideon was still in doubt had had to be absolutely certain. "Lord, forgive me," he said, "but grant me one more sign. Let the fleece be dry and let the ground all around be wet by dew."

The Lord did so. Now Gideon was certain that he did what God wanted him to do.

You have to know that people who are locked inside their national states are weak and the enforced belief in religion is covering up the knowledge about the lost Motherland. All the national states in the world and everything the population does are in pursuit of money, of riches and personal power. You are doing what you think is right according to the laws and rules of your nation, but it is wrong as wrong can be.

The laws and the rules given by the superior Motherland council as in the commandments are completely ignored by all the national leaders in the world. They lead the people according to the three factors of the Original Sin, and the camouflage of religion is one of them. Not one of them knows that the God of Gideon is the superior Motherland council and the alter they built was to remember them.

Remember now that no nation or national coalition will be strong enough to lead the whole world with lasting peace. Only a new global Motherland parliament and a new superior Motherland council will have the power that is omnipotent, omniscient and omnipresent.

Gideon was certain that he did what the superior Motherland council wanted him to do, and so do I. Knowing the history of the lost Motherland is a call from the spirit world that just can't be ignored.

This story is telling you that it was the building of national states that were wrong. The imposed laws and rules of the nation are the force of evil and keep the population obedient as working slaves, soldiers and servants.

If you do wrong in our present time, you can only be punished according to the laws and rules of you nation. Under the camouflage God is the superior Motherland council, and it is the laws and rules from the time before the Motherland went under, that Gideon is acting on. He is trying to help the whole world population back on the right track of life.

Even after the superior Motherland council had died and the whole continent was gone, the laws and rules for living had to be followed in order to live right and do the right thing. But without the physical possibility to punish people who did wrong, the three factors of the Original Sin soon spread to people all over the world. Evil and wrong doing took control of the common world of thoughts, and everyone who tried to make people return to a way of living that was right according to the laws and rules of Mother Nature, was often killed.

In order to understand what this story is hiding, it is necessary to know the laws and the rules for living from before the Motherland went under. The essence is that the spirit world wants you to make the history of the Motherland known to the whole world population. No matter how unbelievable it may sound, it has to be done. Then the whole world population will live together like brothers and friends, with lasting peace.

Whit the knowledge about the lost Motherland you have to choose what to do. If you choose to do like Gideon and fight for a new world with lasting peace, the mental war you are going to launch is aimed directly at the common world of thoughts, and the sword of knowledge is your only weapon.

It is necessary to understand that everything humans think about God and goods, religions, legends, tales and myths, has its origin from the Motherland. Before the Motherland went under the whole world population lived with knowledge and one common set of laws and rules.

After the Motherland went under, the dogmas and assumptions were invented by greedy and selfish warrior kings and priesthoods. What really had happened with the Motherland was soon more or less forgotten and was remembered as legends, tales and myths. The history was written in Egyptian hieroglyphs and hieratic signs that only a few Masters could understand. Therefore the conclusion is that all the religions humans believe in, is wrong as wrong can be.

The Masters who wrote the camouflaged stories knew for a fact that intelligent and spiritually strong people easily could separate right from wrong and see the true story underneath the camouflage.

But they could not know that all the intelligent and spiritually strong humans, who figured out the whole story about the lost Motherland and the global system of government, should be brutally killed by the warrior kings and their priesthoods, after being called witches and heretics.

Do you now begin to know the horrible foundation your national state is built on? The new altars that you build in remembrance of the superior Motherland council will be an act of goodness. You have to start building a new world with lasting peace with one set of laws and rules for the whole world population. The only way to do that is to remove the camouflage of religion from all the Biblical stories.

In a true democracy the leaders of the world, the new global parliament in a new Motherland, is to be democratically elected from every tribal people in the world. It is the best students of the whole world population that are to be educated in to a degree of Master, and from the best Masters in the global parliament the council members are elected from. It was done like that before the Motherland went under some twelve thousand years ago, and it can be like that again, if you make an effort. Just start with the cleansing of your own world of thoughts.

In our present time it is truly the three factors of the Original Sin that are the evil gods that most people worship, because they don't have the knowledge to think differently. It is the dance around the Golden Calf that still goes on.

So what will happen if you in partnership with a lot of people start to mentally tear down the churches and cathedrals, the global capitalistic system and all the national states, and start to melt all the weapons of war in to pickaxes, plows and other farming tools?

Will you be killed, like the first Christians, the twelve apostles, the withes and the heretics? No, certainly not. The world leaders are searching desperately for a permanent solution to put a stop to the long history of wars and conflicts all over the world. They will, in order to be remembered as good people, start using all the power they have to make the change of government with only peaceful means.

To many to win a victory

Judges 7, 1-8

Many men followed Gideon. Everybody was eager to fight the midianites. Gideon leaded them down to a river. On the other side was the army of the midianites.

But the Lord said: "Gideon, you have too many soldiers with you. If you win the people will be proud. They will believe that they won the battle all on their own. I will teach them to trust me and believe in me. Tell everyone who is a little fearful and afraid to return home."

Gideon did so and about half of the men went home.

"Still they are too many," said God. "Lead them down to the river. Those who kneel when they drink can go home, while those who lap the water with their tongues like dogs when they drink can go with you in the battle."

Gideon did as God said. He pointed at those who kneeled. "You can go home," he said.

After they had gone, Gideon counted the men he had left. They were only three hundred. "God will fight for us," said Gideon.

137

When this camouflaged story is written in to our present time, it is all about the battle that will take place in the common world of thoughts. And to win the battle a relative small number of able bodies are needed.

It is not trained soldiers that are needed, and certainly not a large number of people that are not qualified for the important mission this is. Let us say that it is people with a strong spirit and ability to spread the knowledge about the lost Motherland history to many people all over the world, which is needed to the battle in our present time.

It is a mental war that is about to happen, and the sword Gideon is carrying is his knowledge about the lost Motherland. The battle will be between the three factors of the Original Sin and the knowledge from the Diagram Star. Only the wisest among you will be chosen to lead the battle. And the battle will be fought by simply spreading a drawing of the Diagram Star and a short explanation. After it is done, the whole world population will begin thinking new thoughts. Everyone will know the history about the lost Motherland and nobody will believe in religion.

Thoughts about this are like seed, and it needs to fall in good ground in order to grow, and soon the seed will grow in to the thoughts of the whole world population.

A voice in the night

Judges 7, 9-15

> *The same night the God told Gideon to cross the river and spy on the midianites. In the dark, Gideon and his servant crawled close to the camp of the midianites. There were thousands of them, and there were more camels than people. Everywhere there were camels.*

> *God had said to Gideon that when he spied on the midianites, he would hear something that would help him win the battle. Inside the camp Gideon waited behind a tent. He heard voices from inside.*

> *"I have just had a strange dream," said one midianitt soldier to another. "Down the hillside bread came rolling in to our camp. The bread hit our tent, and it fell."*

> *"I know what it means," said the other soldier. "Gideon and his army will win the battle tomorrow. That is because the only true God is leading them."*

> *Gideon thought for himself: "Even the midianites is afraid. They know that God is on our side."*

Like the midianites, the humans who are fighting to keep the present system of government with many national states, the global system of capitalism and the many religions in the world, will know that they are going to lose the battle. Everyone knows that knowledge will win over religious belief.

The opposition will have a change of opinion, and soon the whole world population will be building a new world together.

Trumpets and light

Judges 7, 15; 8, 21

Gideon thought that if the enemy really was that afraid, he had almost won the battle already. He bent his head and thanked God. Then he hurried back to the camp of the Israelites. He woke the soldiers and told them what he had heard.

"We have practically already won the battle," he said." If we attack at ones, we will surprise them. Let us make a lot of noise, and they will think that we are far more than three hundred. Tonight you will see how great the Lord is."

He divided the men in to three companies, and he put a trumpet in to every man's hand, and gave them empty pitchers with light inside them.

"Watch me and do likewise," Gideon said to them. "And see that when I come to the outskirts of the camp, you do whatever I do. When I and those who are with me blow on our trumpets, you blow on your trumpets to, on every side of the camp, and shout: The sword of the Lord and of Gideon."

They surrounded the camp of the midianites. Not even the camels noticed that Gideon's soldiers were there.

Suddenly Gideon gave the signal. The men blew in their trumpets. They shouted and broke open the pitchers that had light inside. The noise was terrible. The midianites woke frightened and thought that a large army had attacked them. Therefore they ran as fast as they could. But because the sound and the lights were all around the camp, they did not know where to run. Gideon won a great victory.

They drove away every midianitt. Only a few got away, but they were not safe. Gideon and his men chased the enemy far away.

"The Lord helped us to victory today," said Gideon to the Israelites, and the whole people bent down to thank God. The Israelites lived in peace for forty years, during the life of Gideon.

All the camouflaged stories used in this book are from a children's bible, and even a child will understand that this stories is about something other than a war between enemies were whole armies get killed. The battle is about removing all evil thoughts in the world and bring the force of good thoughts back as being the ruler of your world of thoughts.

What does it take to chase the thoughts that are totally wrong and evil from your world of thoughts and let them be replaced with thoughts that are completely right and always good? All it takes is the sound of knowledge and the light from the Diagram Star.

God is the superior Motherland council speaking to you directly from the spirit world, telling you to always do right. The superior Motherland council, who is in the spirit world, speaks to you as thoughts and visions. When you think you see things with your inner eye and knows the difference between right and wrong. The biblical Israelites are the whole world population and the midianites are symbols for all the wrong thoughts in the world at present time.

It is the men with good and right thoughts that attack the men with evil and wrong thoughts in this battle. Gideon is fighting with the sword of knowledge symbolized by the loud sound and the light from the pitchers.

Now look at the world around you and analyze your own world of thoughts. Do you want to continue to see the world falling apart because of the wrong and evil thoughts in the world, or do you want to fight for a totally new world with only right and good thoughts for your children and their descendants.

The children of Israel are the descendants from Jacob and his twelve sons. The Israelites are a symbol for the whole world population.

Again the knowledge from the Diagram Star is to be spread all over the world, by use of Internet and modern technology. The believers will cling to their imposed religious belief, but they will all be frightened. When confronted with the knowledge about the history of the lost Motherland and the light from the Diagram Star from all corners of the world, they will surrender and possibly have a thorough cleansing of their common thoughts. The religious belief will over time lose the battle and be gone for all time to come. Back then, the Israelites symbolically lived in peace for forty years after the history about the lost Motherland was made known. Forty years symbolizes a number of years not known.

The battle between good and evil will continue until the evil is totally removed from the face of the earth. It can only be done by removing the three factors of the Original Sin from the common world of thoughts. And remember that the battle can only be fought with peaceful means, symbolized with enlightening knowledge from the Diagram Star.

In battle with a lion

Judges 13, 1-14

Many years' later Gods people had started worshipping false gods again. Now it was the Philistines that were their great enemy. On this time there was a man called Manoah of the family of the Danites, and he had no children. The angel of the Lord appeared to his wife and told her she was going to have a son. They were told to not cut the sons hair, because it should be a sign that God had great plans for him.

And in due time they had a son whom they called Samson. When Samson got older, the Lord sent his Holy Spirit to him and made him incredible strong. This God did every time he wanted to teach Samson something special.

Samson was in love with a girl who was philistine and he wanted to make her his wife. Therefore he went with his parents to the girl's village to make plans for the wedding. On the road Samson walked alone a couple of hours behind his parents. When he walked across a field he suddenly heard a strange sound. What could it be?

Then a large lion came towards him. It roared and showed the long teeth. Samson had no weapons, but the Holy Spirit came over him. He became stronger than any other human. When the lion attacked, he forced it down and killed it!

God's people, the whole world population, started worshipping false gods only ones. It all began some twelve thousand years ago. The many biblical stories are all about how the forces of good can win over the forces of evil. They are written by different Masters with many years in between.

Think for yourself! This is one of the many camouflaged biblical stories that the whole world population have been forced to believe in. You know what's wrong and what's right in this story. It is a tale with an important hidden meaning.

This camouflaged story is very complete and important with a message much as the other stories, speaking of the force of God as the good force that can break down the force of evil and remove it from the common world of thoughts ones and for all.

The force of God is the power of knowledge, of knowing the history about the lost Motherland. A few humans with knowledge could not win over the physical force of armed soldiers and the self made laws and rules imposed on the population by worrier kings and priesthoods. Back then they only had their voice to use when spreading the knowledge to as many people as possible. You have Internet and modern technology.

The story begins with telling the reader that Gods people again had started to worship false goods. Under the camouflage Gods people are the whole world population. God is the spiritual superior Motherland council. Only the physical power of a new superior Motherland council can win over the three factors of the original Sin and create lasting peace in the whole world. Israelites and Philistines have the same origin; they are just born with a different way of thinking.

With the forces of evil in command, the tribes fighting each other had to find different names and also live with different laws and rules for living, and in all the known history of the world, some twelve thousand years; the forces of evil have played the many tribal people against each other in the quest for riches and personal power.

The forces of evil have all this time been fighting the good forces that come from knowledge about the lost Motherland and knowing the Diagram Star, and the good forces have always lost. But the force of evil does need the force of good in order to build the so called democracy inside their national borders. All humans who dare to oppose the national state and the priesthoods are still treated as an enemy. You have to understand that it is the laws and rules of your nation that are the enemy of the only way to create lasting peace in the whole world.

This camouflaged story is meant to preserve and pass on the knowledge about the lost Motherland to coming generations in clear words and give them back hope that one day the knowledge will find its way in to the common world of thoughts and break down the religious belief forever.

The democracy in our present time is a sham, giving all the working slaves, soldiers and servants the right to choose their own leaders. The laws and the rules for living are dictated within every national state. People think they are free, but they are living like in a prison camp and don't know anything about the paradise world of the past. This is why otherwise clever humans are called blind and truly live their lives as living dead.

Samson is a symbol for the small part of right and good thoughts preserved by nature in every single human being and their persistent and useless struggle to build a new world with lasting peace. It is only the knowledge about the lost Motherland that can give the whole world population the spiritual strength that Samson got from God.

Under the camouflage the strength of Samson is spiritual. It is strength that the whole world population will need the day that the three factors of the Original Sin is removed from the common world of thoughts and replaced with knowledge derived from the Diagram Star.

The Master who wrote this story is telling the people living in present time to forget all the unbelievable stories they still are forced to believe in, and start to think for them self. Not by dismissing the many unbelievable stories in the Bible as pure nonsense, but by removing the camouflage of religion from them and reveal the hidden message. All humans have an ability given by nature to separate everything that is wrong from everything that is right.

Samson's riddle

Judges 14, 8-15, 20

Later, a few days before the wedding, Samson came by the field where he had killed the lion. He walked up to it and found it with a swarm of bees and honey inside. He tasted the honey. It was very sweet.

The same evening he spoke with some of the men in the girl's village. "I have a riddle," said Samson. "Is there anyone of you who will make a bet with me that he can solve the riddle?"

"Yes sure!" All the men were in on it. Samson did bet thirty fine shirts and thirty fine suits. The men had to solve the riddle before the eight day of the wedding.

"Here is the riddle," said Samson. "Out of the ether came forth meat, and out of the strong came forth sweetness."

No one knew the answer. The wedding was on and three days passed. The thirty philistines could not think of an answer. Therefore they went to Samson's bride: "Get him to tell you the answer to the riddle. If you don't, we will burn your father's house and kill you and Samson."

The girl was frightened. She asked Samson to tell her the riddle. Day after day she nagged and nagged. She cried and asked, and finally on the seventh day he gave in and told her the answer. This she told the philistines.

Samson was mad because they had frightened his bride. He therefore went to another philistine village and killed thirty men. Then he gave their clots to those who had won the bet. The Philistines took revenge by marrying his bride to another philistine. They would not let him in to their village any more. Samson and the philistines did hurt each other all they could.

When the philistines started killing other Israelites, Samson let himself be captured by the enemy. Then the Holy Spirit of the Lord came over him and he broke loose from the ropes that they had tied him up with. Again he became frightfully strong, just as when he killed the lion. Samson killed many philistines that day that he freed himself from the ropes.

This is a completely unbelievable and unnatural story that shows the long lasting struggle to avoid that the knowledge of the lost Motherland was completely forgotten. The camouflage is taken out from the real world at the time the history was written. It is a tale, meant to be told by campfires and never forgotten.

Samson is a symbol for the whole world population that one's again is getting the strength of knowledge given to them from the spirit world. The story shows how difficult knowledge about the lost Motherland had to survive in a world full of enemies who wanted to continue to live with the three factors of the Original Sin. In the same time the story shows how strong the knowledge about the lost Motherland is rooted in the people. When the story is told the listeners nourished their hope to ones again live like free people, free of the dictating and ruthless control by the warrior kings and the priesthoods. Back then people knew that the story underneath the camouflage of religion could get them killed. In our present time people believe in the camouflage story and know nothing of the message from the spirit world.

The philistines are a symbol for the large majority of people who broke the laws and living rules given in the Ten Commandments and made up their own laws and rules for living. Samson is a good symbol for the people who were fighting against the three factors of the Original Sin. He let himself be captured and with the spiritual strength given him with his knowledge about the lost Motherland, he fought and freed himself. That's what you have to do. You have to get in to the common world of thoughts with your knowledge about the lost Motherland and fight for freedom for the whole world population.

Remember that in our present time the fight will be between the two systems of ruling the world and the battle have to take please in the common world of thoughts, were the only weapon is the sword of knowledge. Only a common wish for peace and knowing how to make it come true can build lasting peace in the world.

You are all living with the system of government with many national states, all the religions and the global system of capitalism. People die by the thousands every day. Billions of humans are living below the so called poverty line of one dollar a day.

I am telling you about the global system of government from before the Motherland went under; when every single human had all they needed to live a good life, with the good and secure feeling of belonging to a tribe. The whole world population lived with lasting peace for many thousand years. It is the knowledge about the lost Motherland that is betrayed and looses the battle in the end. But the story goes on and describes how the knowledge derived from the Diagram Star regains power and destroys all the three factors of the Original Sin. You and the whole world population working together can make it happen.

Samson and Delilah

Judges 16, 1-20

For twenty years the enemy left Samson in peace. He became judge for the Israelites and told the people how to follow the law of God. On that time the spirit of the Lord had given Samson extremely strength. He was famous for his strength. With the help of the Lord he could do anything.

The philistines were still interested in capturing Samson. One day, after many years, Samson fell in love again. The woman he loved was named Delilah. She was a bad woman. She made a deal with the philistines. She should lure Samson and then surrender him to the enemy. They promised to pay her well for it.

Time and time again she nagged on him: "How come you are so strong, Samson? What is the secret of your strength?"

Samson did not like her nagging at all. It reminded him how he had lost the woman he ones married. "Please, Samson! Tell me why you are so strong!" Delilah begged him to tell her the secret, every morning, midday and evening she begged. She didn't give up. She was too fond of money to do that.

One day he could not take it anymore. "Well, well, woman!" he shouted out. "Now the nagging has to stop! The secret of my strength is God. He makes me strong as long as my hair isn't cut. Ever since I was little my parents have understood that God has a plan for me."

That night Delilah sent for the philistines again. She made Samson fell asleep with his head on her knees and saw that he didn't wake up when the philistines came in to the room. One man cut of his hair, and when Samson woke up it was too late. Samson was too weak to fight the philistines. They captured him and gave Delilah the money.

There is a lot to learn from this camouflaged story. It is a tale about how Samson with his strength is killing many philistines and he is telling Delilah several lies about his strength before he finally tells her the true secret; the strength is in the seven locks of his hair. He was meant to tell her. Telling her was the plan. Remember now that the story is written by a Master and that God is the superior Motherland council. The story has a hidden meaning.

The number seven symbolizes knowledge about the seven sciences derived from the Diagram Star. Knowledge is a spiritual strength that by nature comes from the spirit world. All humans know that killing people is against the law given by the superior Motherland council. The same goes for lying and stealing.

In order to destroy the three factors of evil the force of good have to get inside the common world of thoughts and grow strong. The Master is explaining how it can be done. The enemy is willing to pay for the knowledge that makes Samson so clever, brave and strong. The knowledge about the lost Motherland is derived from the Diagram Star, and knowledge will by nature win over religious belief. If you read the story knowing the symbolism, you will remember it like you remember a symbol.

Think of the statement that God has a plan for Samson. The Master writing the story is telling the people living in present time how the knowledge from the Diagram Star will win over the three factors of the Original Sin. The knowledge has to be captured and taken in to the enemy camp by the enemy, who desperately want to know, and then the knowledge about the lost Motherland will break loose and win over all the three factors of the Original Sin.

There is more to this story. The global capitalistic system is one third of the Original Sin. Samson is a symbol for all the knowledge that the Diagram Star is carrying through the ages. It was the knowledge of the superior Motherland council and was called omniscient. The seven fundamental sciences can never be destroyed or completely forgotten. Delilah is a symbol for the cunning, greed, betrayal and evilness that all humans use in order to get what they want no matter what means they use.

Apparently she has the same mission as Juda in the story of Jesus Christ. The philistines want to destroy the power of Samson ones and for all, they capture him, blinded him and throws him in prison. In the process they destroy his knowledge all together by cutting his hair. But knowledge will grow again and soon be covering the whole planet earth, just like Samson's hair. The roots of knowledge cannot be destroyed, because they are rooted in the spirit world.

Now think about how the camouflaged story about Jesus Christ was taken by the roman emperor Constantine and made in to a tool, a third part of the Original Sin. The betrayal of Juda and the money paid to him have precise similarities. Therefore the whole camouflaged story about Samson has the same true story hidden under the camouflage. The knowledge about the lost Motherland is inside the enemy camp, written in the Bible, hidden under the camouflage of religion. As a captured story just waiting to be taken out in to the common world of thoughts and told to the whole world population. The outcome will be that the knowledge derived from the Diagram Star breaks loose and destroys the religious belief and the two other factors of the Original Sin. Only then a world with lasting peace can be built.

Samson's revenge

Judges 16, 21-31

The philistines were very enthusiastic when they left with Samson. After twenty years they finally succeeded in capturing him. "All we had to do was to cut off your hair! Now you are weak as a child!"

The philistines were nasty to him. They blinded him and throw him in jail. Poor Samson, he could no longer count on getting out, ever again. But after some time the hair started grow long again. A little by little he felt that the Lord gave him back the strength he use to have. He would never see again. Now he asked God that he should get revenge for what the philistines had done to him.

"Lord!" he called out loud. "Give me back my strength!"

The months past, and Samson got stronger and stronger. On day the philistines should have a large festivity in a great hall. There were more than three thousand people there.

"Let us get Samson," they said. "Yes, we can have some fun with him."

The prison guard came with Samson. When he entered the room, he heard the people mocking him. He asked the boy who guided him to take him to the two pillars in the centre of the hall. It was the two pillars that were holding the large house standing.

When Samson had found a good place between the two pillars with his hands on them, he called out: "Lord God Almighty, give me back my strength! Let me this one time beat the philistines, and let me die with them! Help me to set your people free!"

The Lord heard Samson. His Holy Spirit filled Samson with strength and he pulled the pillars so they fell. "Let me die with the philistines!" Samson shouted. The roof and the whole house fell and everyone inside were killed.

Do you begin to understand the magnitude of this story? All three factors of the Original Sin are at the present time occupying the common world of thoughts completely. The whole world population truly is captives inside a strong mental wall of belief. The large hall is a symbol for the whole world and the philistines is a symbol for the whole world population. Samson is the spiritual force of good that comes with knowing the full history about the lost Motherland.

The knowledge derived from the Diagram Star is here now, always among you and everywhere in the world. You just don't know, because your world of thoughts is occupied by religious belief and the two other factors of the Original Sin. The knowledge about the lost Motherland was captivated by the enemy, first by the roman ruler Constantine, and is from then on it became all the religions in the world. Now you know where the knowledge is hidden and all you have to do to set yourself free is to tell the secret to the whole world population.

"Lord almighty, give me back my strength. Let me beat the Palestine's." The strength in question is the omnipotent force of the superior Motherland council in the time before the Motherland was destroyed. When a new Motherland council is elected and a new Motherland is built, the strength will again be physical and real. The new superior Motherland council will have representatives in the councils in every little village all over the world, and their strength will be strong enough to remove all the three factors of the Original Sin from the common world of thoughts. It has to be done with only peaceful means.

The biblical Palestine's is a symbol for the evil enemy which still rules planet earth, the enemy being the governing system with many national states and the chaos of wars and conflicts that started in the time after the Motherland was destroyed by a natural catastrophe.

The philistines are still in power, mocking the knowledge given to you now, directly from the spirit world. It is up to you and the whole world population to accept the knowledge and use the power right. The philistines are the evil thoughts that occupy the common world of thoughts, and you believe they are right. You are all blinded and live your lives as living dead. Give your life a meaning and break the spell of evil now. You are symbolically standing with your hands on the two pillars.

Ruth, the faithful daughter in law

Ruth, 1, 1-13

It happened, in the old days when the judges ruled over the Israelites, that there was a famine in the land. A woman named Naomi was one of the few who prayed to God. When she married, she moved from her homeland to live with her husband. She had two sons, and she loved them very much. Then her husband died.

Naomi had thought her sons to believe in the Lord. When they grew up, they married girls from Moab, the land where they lived. The Moabites had been the enemies of the Israelites for many years, but Naomi did not care at all about that. She loved the girls just like they should have been her own daughters.

The two sons died to, and Naomi and the two widows were suddenly all alone. It was terribly sad for the three women. The two young ones were named Orpah and Ruth. They lived with Naomi and helped her best they could. But there was little food in the land. The three women did not find enough food to eat.

"My daughters," said Naomi. "I have heard that there is food in the land of Judah where I grew up. It is far from here. My people are one of the twelve tribes of Israel. I have decided to go there now, but it is better for you to go back to your parents. They will take care of you. Maybe you find new husbands there."

The young women answered: "No, we want to come with you."

But Naomi shook her head: "What shall you do? I am too old to get married again. Don't be foolish. Go home."

Naomi loved her daughters in law and wanted most of all that they stayed with her, but in the same time she thought of what was best for them.

It is in times with famine and severe difficulties that humans with real thoughts for others well being comes in to light and shows the world around which good people they are. Naomi is a symbol for humans who think and acts right with a visible and strong spirit. She is the best of the best and does everything right all the time.

The Master who wrote this camouflaged story is portraying a woman who is going to be the grandmother of a king. She is Ruth, the faithful daughter in law. The story is fictive, and if you remove the forces of evil you can clearly see the description of a totally good person. Ruth is the carrier of the knowledge about the lost Motherland, and with a new Motherland the whole world population would live like she does.

Naomi is one of the few praying to God. Under the camouflage she is a carrier of knowledge about the lost Motherland and the global system of government. Her way of doing things is equal to everyone who lived in the time before the Motherland went under. Doing things right all the time is something she does for herself, for her own peace of mind. She is living in the light of the Diagram Star; living like all humans should live all the time. By doing that she is passing her knowledge on to her daughter in law. Humans who are all good, stays good. They are the carriers of good thoughts in a world of evil.

In our present time it is humans like Naomi who suffers the most. They know that the world history ever since the Motherland went under, have been utterly wrong and a living hell for the whole world population, and they know that the whole world used to be a paradise, without the three factors of the Original Sin.

The tribal belonging was strong in the time before Christianity was made a state religion, before the feeling of national belonging was forced upon people by warfare and brutal force. This story about Naomi is also projecting the fact that all tribes were equal in the light of the Diagram Star. The tribes of Israel are the tribes descending from Jacob and his twelve sons. Jacob got the name Israel and is a symbolic forefather for the whole world population.

A faithful woman

Ruth 1, 14-22

Orpah went to Naomi and said: "I will do as you say," she said. "I will go back to my parents." The elder woman embraced her. They cried together, because they knew that they would never see each other again. Then Orpah packed her tings and left.

But Ruth did not want to leave her mother in law. She put her hand on Naomi's shoulder and said that she wanted to stay, no matter what happened. In her heart Naomi was glad that Ruth stayed with her. She knew that if she didn't get help, she would end as an old begging woman. But in the same time she wanted the best for Ruth, so she said: "No, you must leave to, Ruth."

But Ruth had made her mind up. "No, it is you that are my mother now. Let me stay with you, Naomi. Your people shall be my people and your God shall be my God." Ruth had heard about the one true God. Her husband had talked about him, and she believed in God. "Please, Naomi," Ruth said. "I will never leave you. God will look after us."

Finely Naomi said yes. The two woman went to Bethlehem were Naomi had grown up. When they arrived, many of the older people remembered her. "Is it really you?" they asked. "Naomi, have you have returned to us? It was nice to see you again."

Old friend embraced her and the rumor spread. "Naomi has come home! Her daughter in law has come with her."

Humans that are faithful and good are welcome everywhere in the world. A good reputation is important in any case, and getting one is done by being honest and true to the person you are, always seeking to do everything right no matter what the consequences are. Both Naomi and Ruth do what is right for them under the circumstances and they are both welcomed back in the Naomi's home town Bethlehem.

One thing is certain, and that is that humans who manages to mentally remove the religious camouflage from the stories in the Bible and finds the hidden knowledge, will never return to the meaningless religious belief in dogmas and assumptions. The three factors of the Original Sin is the true evil force in the world, and the understanding how destructive the three factors are you find by looking at the world you live in.

The whole known world history is a solid prove that the wrong doings is making the world in to a living hell for the whole world population.

In a future world with one new Motherland and a new superior Motherland council, everybody will help each other and work together to provide enough food for absolutely everybody. Living in self supported villages and tribal communities; everybody will have everything they need to live a good life on planet earth. Humans are not supposed to live with hope; they are by nature meant to live with everything they need and therefore nothing to hope for.

Ruth goes to work

Ruth 1, 1.22

Naomi thought it was wonderful to be home again. But she knew that she and Ruth had to find something to do, so they could stay alive. Next morning Ruth said to her: "We don't have any food left. It is time for me to find something to do. The harvest of barley has just started. I will go out in the fields and see if anything is left behind. What I find, I will bring home."

Naomi nodded. "Go, my daughter." She prayed that Ruth would find grain for them.

It was a peculiar feeling for Ruth to walk alone out to look for work in a strange land. But she trusted that God would help her.

Ruth walked to a field that was owned by the rich man Boaz. It turned out that Boaz came from the same family as Naomi. When he saw Ruth, he called her.

"Please," Ruth said. "Let me have the barley that your servants leave behind."

"Of course," Boas replayed. "I have heard about everything you have done for your mother in law. I shall help you all I can." He gave his servants order that they should share their food with her.

That day Ruth worked hard, and she got a whole basket with barley. It was more than enough for her and Naomi. When she returned home with the basket in the evening, she brought also food that was left over from the meal earlier that day.

"Ruth!" Naomi looked at her with wide open eyes. "Were does all this food come from?"

"Å, Naomi, I met a man who was so nice and good. His name is Boaz. He helped me and said that that I could come and work with his maid-servants until the end of the barley harvest."

For the first time in many months Naomi smiled. "Boaz is of my family," she said. "If he helps us, I do understand that God have started blessing us again."

The two women sat down to eat. They thanked God for providing so well for them. They prayed for God to bless Boaz, because he had been so good to them.

This story is still about doing the right thing all the time and under all circumstances. It is the superior Motherland council and the Diagram Star with all the laws of the nature, that normally leads all humans to always do the right thing. Ruth and Naomi does everything right and for that reason alone the people close to them helps them in difficult times.

Thanking God means that they are directing some grateful thoughts to the spirit world. It is the spiritual superior Motherland council that is guiding their thoughts in all matters. To say thank you to the spirit world is an act of nature. It makes you feel good.

The Master writing this camouflaged story is telling the humans living in present time about the great grandmother of a great king. Remember it is all fiction with only fragments of the history of the Jews as historical strongholds. If Ruth had chosen like her sister Orpah and gone home to her own people, she would have been just another ordinary girl.

Everyone who read this should understand that in the same way as right choices and good deeds will follow a human trough life as positive thoughts and happiness, wrong choices and bad deeds will be a lifelong burden of negative thoughts and sadness.

The great grandmother to a king

Ruth 2, 23-4, 22

The rest of the barley harvest Ruth worked in the fields owned by Boaz. She always came home with more than they needed.

At the end of the harvest Naomi said to Ruth: "You are so young and pretty. Can you not try to get married with Boaz?" Ruth did not mind and when Naomi understood how she felt, she said she had a plan.

That night Naomi sent her to Boaz. He was sleeping in the field. Ruth went to lay down by his feet. In the middle of the night he suddenly woke.

"Who is it sleeping at my feet?" he whispered in the dark.

"It is me, Ruth. I have come to ask you if you will get married with me. You are after all of Naomi's family. I need a man, Boaz, and you have always been so good to me."

Boaz stood up. "Dear Ruth, you are so beautiful. Every man would see it as an honor to be married to you. And it is strange that you should come and ask me about that. Will you marry me?"

Ruth nodded, and Boaz bent down and kissed her. They smiled at each other. "I shall talk with the leaders in the village," said Boaz. "We will get married as soon as possible." He took her hand. Then he kissed her again and sent her home.

Ruth told Naomi the good news. The next day they told all their friends about what had happened. They held a grand wedding. Everybody in Bethlehem was present.

As the years passed by, Boaz and Ruth become more and fonder of each other. The Lord blessed them with a little boy. They asked Naomi to move in with them. In this way she could also look after the boy, Obed, like it was her own grandson.

Obed grew and became a good man. He loved God and lived by his laws. Many years later David, the grand king of Israel, was born in to Obeds family. Therefore Ruth and Boaz were blessed by God. They became the grandparent to a mighty king.

This is a story about several generations in a good family, written to bind the far and forgotten past to present time. It tells about people that always lived right with the knowledge from the Diagram Star. It is all about the forefathers of King David, a great and mighty king of Israel.

If you now, in your world of thoughts, remove all evil and wrong from this and the following family story, you will find that it is a story about how a new world with lasting peace can be built. It is prophesy of what have to happen in present time; the building of a new Motherland and electing a new superior Motherland council for the world.

It also tells the story how a man and a woman are supposed to get married. It is done right in all aspects, and the most important one is that a man and a woman want to live together as one, and have children together. Just as important is the consent of the family and the elders in the village. This is the cradle of the laws and the rules for living, and it is important to do right all the time.

The question of love is in our days totally destroyed in the sense that the human love is derived from egoistic thoughts of riches and personal power.

Like the marriage between Boaz and Ruth is described they marry with an open and strong knowledge of that their children would inherit the spiritual strength and personal abilities of both parents. The breeding of livestock like horses and cattle is highly regulated by the rules of humans more than natural selection. It is just as important to breed humans according to the laws and rules of Mother Nature. In our present time, the number of parents divorcing is alone proving that the laws and rules for living is wrong as wrong can be.

The camouflaged story about Ruth is that she did like her mother in law and lived by the commandments. It means that she was one of very few who still had knowledge of the Diagram Star. They knew the difference between right and wrong and lived their life right, always and no matter what. Even the danger of getting killed could not make them do wrong.

The story takes place in Bethlehem; in the village were the history of the lost Motherland is born again in the body of Jesus. Ruth, Boaz and their son Obed is good and faithful people in a world where the three factors of the Original Sin is spreading and occupying more and more of the common world of thoughts.

In the stories that follows, be sure to understand that Jacob, who was given the name Israel, is the symbolic forefather of the whole world population. When the Bible speaks of the children of Israel, the twelve tribes of Israel, it is about the whole world population. The tribe of Juda has no right to occupy the land around Jerusalem and call it Israel. It is misleading and wrong.

For the Master who wrote this story the most important issue was to preserve and pass on the camouflaged stories from generation to generation, and this story leads to King David. It will become clear that all the camouflaged stories are fictive, in the since that the story hidden under the camouflage is describing how a new world with lasting peace can be built.

Longing for a child

1 Samuel 1-5

A long time after Ruth's son Obed was born, the people of Israel again forgot the living God. Most of them did not worship him any longer.

On this time a man named Elkanah lived. He had two wives. One had children and the other did not. She who didn't have children was named Hannah. She had long, black hair and dark eyes that shone when she smiled. Elkanah was very fond of Hannah.

The years past and Hanna did not have any children, but Elkanah still loved her more than his other wife. Her name was Peninnah. She had many sons and daughters. She was not as nice and good as Hannah.

Peninnah knew that Elkanah loved Hannah more than her, and it made her jealous. She used every opportunity to mock Hannah. Often Peninnah told her she was useless, because she could not give her husband a child.

Elkanah was one of the few who on this time tried to follow the Lord. Ones a year he took his whole family to Silo. The Ark of the Covenant was there, in a tent and a priest named Eli looked after it.

Every year, after Elkanah had worshipped God in Silo, he held a party for his family. Hannah and Peninnah and her children were there. Every time they held the party, Elkanah gave Hannah twice as much meat as he gave to Peninnah. He felt sorry for her because she did not have any children, so that was the least he could do. He hoped that a little extra meat could make her smile. She didn't do that so often as before.

The people of Israel, the whole world population, are forgetting about the dead superior Motherland council time and time again. But they are reminded just as often, and now you are reminded again. It is truly difficult to make you able to see what's right and what's wrong in the world you live in.

Under the camouflage of religion this means that you forget about the laws and rules for living as thought by the superior Motherland council. The people forget because they are forced to live by the laws and rules made by the warrior kings and the priesthoods.

Who is doing right in this family? It is only humans living right and doing right in the light of the Diagram Star, who can be the carrier of the history of the Motherland and the global system of government. They are carrying the hidden message.

The underlying story is about the children of Israel, meaning the symbolic twelve tribes that populated the whole world; with the exception of the many aborigine people still living like Mother Nature intended all humans to live. The humans who lived in the time before the Motherland went under was highly educated, like the aborigine peoples still are. It is their education that is the reason that they have survived though the last large ice age. And their education will make it possible for them to survive also through the next ice age, and onward.

For you, reading the camouflaged stories in present time, God is camouflage over the laws and rules of Mother Nature, in other words, the laws and rules that comes natural to mankind. They are all imbedded in the Diagram Star by the superior Motherland council and given to people all over the world to learn and use in daily life. The sun, the moon and the twelve Zodiac star signs is model for the official emblem of the superior Motherland council. You know that the bright shining Diagram Star has been with mankind from before the beginning of time and will be with humans until after the end of time. Every time you look up on the sky, day or night, you know that the signs of the zodiac are there, always, talking to you. The Diagram Star is the official emblem of the superior Motherland council. Now you can feel, deep inside, that everything is beginning to make sense.

The Diagram Star is the tree of life in a paradise world. The serpent is a symbol for the three factors of the Original Sin that makes the whole world in to a living hell for all humans.

Before the Motherland was destroyed in a natural catastrophe the whole world population was living with lasting peace obeying one common set of laws and rules for living.

The whole world population was living with everything they needed, with enough food for everyone, beautiful and strong clothes and strong houses. The main activity was education, and the best students ended up in the Motherland or in any other production site were for example the flying vessels, boats and ships was made. Other advanced tools not mentioned here was also made, but never more than needed in all thinkable scenarios. For example the flying vessels were used to send out rescue teams to help in places that were hit by natural catastrophes and such. The flying vessels were also used every year, by the Motherland council members or representatives when they visited their home villages. They brought gifts and received gifts but the main reason vas to bring the fully educated Masters home and bring the selected new students to their education center.

After the Motherland went under all activity with the production of top class educated human beings stopped. The evolution of mankind stopped suddenly, and the chaos of wars and conflicts started, and never stopped. Twelve thousand years is a relatively short time in the history of mankind.

The camouflaged stories in the Bible, together with all the tales, myths and legends in the world, is carrying the history of the lost Motherland trough the ages. In order to understand it all, your dormant brain cells have to be activated again and new brain cells have to be built.

The Masters writing these camouflaged stories were hunted down and killed on sight by the warrior kings and priesthoods. They had to work undercover and they had to make their stories known and passed on from generation to generation, or else the history of the lost Motherland would be forgotten for all times.

The Master who wrote or rewrote this story lived under the despotic rule of the Roman Empire and he wrote the truth when he wrote that the children of Israel had forgotten God. The Romans was, like all other humans in the world, one of the tribes descending from Israel. You know him as Jacob, the father of twelve sons. He was the symbolic forefather also to the Romans. They wanted to build a new Motherland and rule the whole world peacefully. But they did wrong when forcing people to obey with the use of warfare and heavy taxation. Jacob is therefore a symbolic forefather for the whole world population living in present time. The biblical name Israel is a symbol for the new world that could have been built, if the whole world population had continued to live with lasting peace, like brothers and friends, in the time after the Motherland was destroyed. But the children of Israel started killing each other, fighting to be stronger, greater and richer than others. They are still at it, doing wrong for all the wrong reasons, because they have forgotten the laws and rules from before the Motherland was destroyed.

The humans who knew about the lost Motherland were few, and they are described as the main characters in the camouflaged stories in the Bible. The Bible is the Ark of the Covenant. The lid is the camouflage of religion. Only by removing the lid and let the birth light of the Diagram Star shine again, can make things right in the world you live in.

Peninnah hurts Hannah

1 Samuel 1, 6-8

Every year during the celebration Peninnah noticed that Elkanah gave Hannah more meat than anyone else. And every year she had something cruel to say about her.

Year after year Peninnah leaned over the table and whispered to Hannah: "Meat is better than nothing, but really you are useless. Elkanah is only feeling sorry for you because you don't have any children."

The insults became more and more hurting as the years went by. One year it was almost unbearable. "You are getting old, Hannah. My oldest son is almost an adult now. What will you do when you lose you beauty? Then Elkanah will stop giving you extra meat. You don't even have a son to comfort you."

Hannah could not stand it anymore. She covered her eyes and started crying. She longed with all her heart to have a child. "Why do I not get a child?" she sighted in her heart.

Elkanah saw that she cried, and he understood that Peninnah had been cruel to her. "Don't feel sorry for not having any children, Hannah," he said. "It means nothing."

But it meant a lot for her. Hannah ran from the table.

Hanna is a symbol for all the good in the world, and is still waiting to have a child. The whole world population is still waiting for the common laws and rules of the lost superior Motherland council to be born. This camouflaged story tells people living in present time how hard it is to live with the force of evil in command all over the world. People living with the force of good is waiting and hoping for the force of evil to go away, while the years pass by and nothing happens.

The Master who wrote this story knew that the force of good would win in the end, before it was too late. He describes the born again forces of good as a child that will be a great prophet, strong in spirit, showing personal abilities from birth and are given a specific upbringing. A regular child or one child among many would not be spoken of by anyone. Hannah and Elkanah are given the right personal abilities that it takes to have a very special child together. The way he was conceived was foretold.

The story is all together fiction and tells people living in our present time how difficult it will be for the force of good to take back control over the evolution of mankind. The forces of good really need help from the spirit world in order to be able to remove the forces of evil from the common world of thoughts.

The world needs a many physical teachers with the ability to make people think differently and understand that the force of evil truly is destroying the whole world with the enforced desperate quest for riches and personal power.

You must understand that there are no humans anywhere doing wrong because they want to. It is your inheritance to do wrong and you all believe that doing as the national state laws and rule tells you to do, are right. You think and do as your parents did and forefathers have done for some twelve thousand years. The world leaders are only humans and they do what they think is right for the same reasons as you do. Therefore start thinking thorough what the paradise Adam and Eva was forced to leave was like. What was the life on planet earth like, when the whole world population was governed by one superior Motherland council, with one common set of laws and living rules?

You are your thoughts. Without them you are nothing. With your thoughts occupied by the forces of evil, by the three factors of the Original Sin, you are a slave, a soldier or a servant who doesn't know any other life than under the force of evil. Samuel is a symbol for the new common world of thoughts that has to be born soon. It is late, but not too late.

A prayer from the heart

1 Samuel 1, 9-18

Hannah walked to the tent were the priest was preparing an offering to God. She didn't know what to do, but she kneeled and put her head in her hands. Her lips moved while she prayed and tears ran down her cheeks.

"O, Lord," she prayed silently. "I wish so very much for a child. Please, God! If you want to give me a child, I shell give him back to you. I will bring him here, for the priest to educate him. The child shall be yours."

While Hannah prayed, the priest Eli noticed her. He saw her lips move, but did not hear a sound. Hannah's eyes were red from crying.

On this time not many in Israel came to Elis tent to pray. Those who did prayed loud. Some came to Silo only to eat and drink. When Eli saw Hannah's red eyes and the lips that moved, he thought she had too much to drink.

"Hello, you there!" he shouted to her. "You shall not come here if you are drunk!"

"Master," Hannah said. "I am not like one of the drunken people who stumbles inn during the celebration. I am just terribly unhappy."

Eli walked closer and understood that she was speaking the truth. "Walk in peace," he said. "The God of Israel will give you what you prayed for."

Hannah bent her head. "Thank you for the blessing," she said. She felt like a burden was lifted from her when she walked from the tent. She knew that if she should have a child or not, was up to the Lord. She knew now that he did what was best for her and Elkanah.

This is how the whole world population is hoping for lasting peace in the whole world. It is a strong, almost desperate hope. Everybody is terrible unhappy with all the evil that happens in the world, all the time, and everyone is praying for the end of all evil and a long lasting peace to come. Now you know that only a new superior Motherland council elected by you and the whole world population can give you what you are praying for. The forces of evil, which are all the national states, the global system of capitalism and all the religions in the world, will not be able to continue to lead mankind in a world where everybody knows the history about the lost Motherland.

The words of the God of Israel are coming from the Diagram Star. It is the only physical remains of the lost Motherland and the superior Motherland council. The priest Eli is a symbol for the Masters who have written all the camouflaged stories in the Bible.

The Diagram Star is, among many other things, telling people living in present time how planet earth was populated. The Diagram Star is the natural book of law that all earth life has to obey and live by. Even the flowers on the land multiply in the same natural manner.

Hannah and Peninnah are just like Jacobs two wives, and the story about them have similarities and the same outcome, which is a son that is all good. The Master is telling people living in present time that it will be just as difficult to give birth to the forgotten Motherland history as it is to give birth to a son that is all good.

Peninnas children will never become anything great, because they are born with their mother's spiritual strength and personal abilities. Because they have a good father in Elkanah they will grow to be good people, but never to be only good like Hannah's child.

Hannah is living like nature intended her to live, right in all thoughts and deeds, and for her it is a strong wish to have a child. If she in any way had broken the laws and living rules derived from the Diagram Star and fought against Peninnah with for example false accusations and lies, her child with Elkanah could never be educated by a priest and become a great prophet.

In the time before the Motherland went under, all humans lived like Elkanah and Hannah and did everything right in the light of the Diagram Star. No one knew the force of evil. Living in a self supported village where everybody knew everybody, breaking the laws and rules for living were not an option.

The boy Samuel

1 Samuel 19-21

Hannah went home with Elkanah. A few months later she understood that she was going to have a child. It was a happy day for Hannah. She just couldn't tank God enough.

She had a handsome little boy and called him Samuel. It means "God have heard". "I have asked the Lord for him," she said, "and he heard me."

When Peninnah mocked her, it did not hurt any more. If she said that she had many more children than her, Hannah did not even listen. "My Samuel is worth ten other sons," Hannah thought.

The next three years she had Samuel with her. She played with him and prayed with him. She thought him to count and she sang and danced with him. Often they laughed together. When Samuel was three years of age, Hannah knew the time had come to give him to the priest Eli. Samuel was a gift from God and she knew that he would take god care of her son.

Thanking God is saying thank you to the superior Motherland council in the spirit world. The Zodiac star signs are their official emblem, one for each of the council members. The help they can give from the spirit world is limited. Their thoughts are helping you and guiding you through your world of thoughts, if your thoughts are good from only doing right.

It is a law of nature that you will not get help and guidance to do the right things, when your world of thoughts is filled with evil and wrong doing.

To keep a promise, no matter what it is about, is an important part of the common laws and rules for doing right. The greater the promise is, the greater the happiness is when keeping it.

Samuel is not like any other child. He is born with a promise that his mother doesn't even think about breaking. She knows that she could break the promise if she wanted to, but if she did she would not be a better mother than Peninnah. And Samuel would have been just like any other child learning to live in a world where the three factors of the Original Sin are dominating their thoughts.

Hannah entrust Samuel to Eli

1 Samuel 1, 26-2, 11

Hannah held Samuel by his hand. They were standing at the door of the tent in Silo. "Eli!" she called. When the old man came, she said: "Do you remember me? I am the women that you blessed three years ago. Then I asked God to have a child. Here you can see that the Lord answered my prayer." She smiled looking at Samuel.

Samuel knew that he belonged to God and he knew that he now should live with the priest Eli. He was not afraid. His mother had told him that God would protect him, no matter where he lived, and he trusted God. Besides she would come visit him every year when the family came to Silo.

Samuel knew that he was a big boy now. He did not cry. He just looked at Eli and then at his mother. He worried about starting to cry when she did.

Hannah told Eli what she had promised God. He nodded. Then he bent and said welcome to the boy. Samuel looked in too the old man's friendly eyes. He understood that he was safe.

The priest Eli is a symbol for a Master living in hiding as a teacher. This is what the Masters have done up though the many generations since the Motherland went under. The Masters were often a part of the priesthoods or advisors to warrior kings who would kill them if they knew that their mission in life was to preserve and pass on the history of the lost Motherland to new generations.

Look at the mother Hannah as a symbol for the lost Motherland and her son Samuel as the story of the lost Motherland being passed on, still under cover. The mothers promise to God shows the importance of this story. The story speaks of knowledge, about education and the importance of knowing the Diagram Star.

Samuel and Eli

1 Samuel 2, 18-21; 3, 1

Little Samuel lived happily with Eli. The old man was like a father to him. Elis sons were greedy and selfish. They did not care about God, like Samuel did.

Every year Hannah and Elkanah came with a new coat to him. Every time Samuel felt homesick, he put the coat on and thought about his mother who loved him.

Samuel helped Eli in the temple. The work was to keep all the lamps lighted. He also learned about the many different sacrifices that Eli gave to God, and he was told that to pray, was like talking to God. Sometimes Samuel wondered why God didn't speak to him.

The tent in Silo is a temple. In the time before the Motherland went under the temples all over the world were centre for common education in the light of the Diagram Star. The Ark of the Covenant is kept in the tent in Silo, and we know that in the symbolic chest is the Diagram Star. The lid is the camouflage of religion. The diagram is holding the full world history, the laws and rules for living, and more.

When the lid of religious camouflage is removed from the Ark of the Covenant, the Diagram Star will again enlighten the whole world population, and there will be lasting peace. As long as the force of evil, the three factors of the Original Sin, is in command, the lid is kept on. When the time is right, the lid can be removed from the Ark of the Covenant, and the right time is now.

The Master who wrote this story is saying that Samuel helped the priest Eli to keep the lamps lit. Fire = Knowledge about the lost Motherland, says the formula and all living light from a lamp, candle or a campfire, is a symbol for the light from the Diagram Star. The light from the candles symbolically ensures all humans that the knowledge is living on through the ages. You can normally see nothing while looking in to the living light of a candle, but with the knowledge about how the Motherland disappeared in to the ocean in an inferno of burning gasses and boiling water, you "see" a lot.

It is you, living in present time, who shall know that the knowledge from the Diagram Star have been preserved and passed on from generations to generation through the whole history of mankind. It is done by people who know. Feel the good feeling when you light a candle.

For some twelve thousand year the whole world population has been living in the darkness of oblivion, like living dead, not seeing but truly feeling the forces of good from the living light.

Sacrifices to God are under the camouflage a sacrifice of time, time to remember and learn to preserve and pass on the knowledge of the Diagram Star. Everything the Masters knew had to be hidden from the warrior kings and the priesthoods, who used warfare and brutal force to keep their position as elite. Everyone who spoke against them was killed.

Both Eli and Samuel dedicate their lives to this important and secret service for mankind. The physical things they offered was symbolic and only the trusted humans, known to be able to keep their promises, knew the true underlying story.

Samuel hears the voice of God

1 Samuel 3, 2-18

One night Samuel woke when he heard a voice calling him: "Samuel!"

"Here I am," Samuel replayed and ran in to Eli. "Did you call my name, Eli? What do you want?" The old man turned in his bed and scratched his beard. "I did not call you," he said. "Go to bed again. It is in the middle of the night."

Samuel did as he was told, but after falling in sleep, the voice woke him again, calling: "Samuel." The boy ran in to Eli again.

"Yes, Eli, he said.

"I have not called you, my boy," Eli said again.

Later the same night Samuel heard the voice a third time: "Samuel!" He had never heard the voice of God before, so he still thought that Eli called him. Again he ran to Eli.

This time Eli understood that Samuel must have heard the voice of the Lord. It had been a long time since God had spoken to anyone of the Israelites. "God the Lord is calling you," Eli said to him. "Next time he calls, you shall say: Speak, my Lord, your servant is listening."

The boy did as he was told. Next time the Lord spoke to Samuel, he said: "I have seen all the evil that Elis sons do. From now on I will speak trough you, Samuel."

The next morning Samuel told Eli everything God had said. It was the first of many times that God spoke to Samuel.

It is the spiritual superior Motherland council talking to you, the reader of the story, and all it takes for you to understand the story underneath the camouflage of religion, is knowledge about the lost Motherland. The words come in to your world of thoughts as thoughts. The only way to obtain the right knowledge is to study and learn.

Samuel is a symbol for children learning about the lost Motherland and the global system of governing the world. Before the time comes that a new generation of Masters is fully educated and can start teaching, the knowledge can be obtained in direct contact with the Spirit World.

The Spirit World is the common world of thoughts. For the last twelve thousand years the common world of thoughts has been occupied by the three forces of the Original Sin. The sons of Eli are a symbol for the whole world population, living under the laws and rules of evil.

You have to find the knowledge of good under the camouflage of religion with your own capacity to think right, and after you have found knowledge you have to spread it to as many people as possible. The most important promise you give, you give to the superior Motherland council in the Spirit World. The promise is that if you do find knowledge and a brand new understanding is born within you, you will pass it on to your children. Teach your children and never, never ever give up restoring knowledge as long as you live. The lid of religious camouflage is taken of the Ark of the Covenant, and the bright light of the Diagram Star is shining again.

It is easy to see that the only good way to live is to live like Samuel, and do everything right and good. You have to stop living like the sons of Eli, you and the whole world population.

It is not a dream. A world without evil can come true, for your children and their descendants.

The Spirit World is a real world that is open to every single human being. You are all living in the Spirit World, thinking thoughts from the common world of thoughts as long as you live. Your brain is the receiver of thoughts coming from your soul, your aura, your spirit of life.

In the time before the Motherland went under the common education lasted until the age of 25. Everyone with the abilities and wish to be a Master had the change. A Master had to be able to fill any given leading position in the society. In a time were all the people in the world was working together in the evolution of all important global tasks, it was important that all the best possible candidates had a change to reach the top as a member of the superior council of the Motherland.

The Diagram Star talks to every one of you, and the knowledge is accessible at all times. In the time after the Motherland went under all common education stopped and the chaos of wars and conflicts spread like cancer all over the world. The self-appointed warrior kings and priesthoods used warfare and brutal force to get what they wanted from the population. People all over the world was forced in to a life as willing working slaves, soldiers and servants, for a despotic system of government that has been passed on from generation to generation right in to our present time.

The Diagram Star is calling on you, on the whole world population. The message is unanimous and cannot be misunderstood. Only with the global system of government that is to be found under the camouflage of religion, tales, legends and myths, can save mankind from destroying the world and the world that used to be a paradise can be a paradise again.

The donkeys that went missing

1 Samuel 8, 1-9, 25

Samuel became a great prophet. He spoke the word of God to the people. After some time had passed the people of Israel started wishing for a king, and they told it to Samuel.

"No," answered Samuel. "God shall be your king."

But the people did not listen to him. "Well, well," said Samuel, "you shall have a king. Go home again."

On this time there was a handsome young man in the smallest tribe of Israel. His name was Saul. His father had lost some donkeys and therefore he sent his son and a servant out to look for them.

Saul and the servant were looking high and low after the donkeys, but could not find them. They had been gone for many days. Finally Soul decided to go back home without the donkeys. Then his servant said: "There is a man of God living nearby. He is very wise. Perhaps he knows where the donkeys have gone. We can ask him."

The two men walked to the house of Samuel. The day before God had said to him: "Tomorrow you will be visited by a stranger. It is him that shall be king over my people."

Samuel waited the whole day for the stranger. When Saul discovered the prophet in the doorway, he asked: "Do you know where the holy man of God lives?"

"It is me," said Samuel. "The Lord has already spoken to me about you. You don't have to worry about the donkeys. Come with me up on the hill over there." Samuel pointed. "There is a celebration there. You will sit at the top of the table. One day you will be a great man."

Saul did not believe what he heard, when he followed Samuel up on the hill.

Only the superior Motherland council can govern the whole world population. The people say no, and the Master writing the story is showing you how a wrong man is elected in to a leading position.

There is a mysterious spiritual force in the nature, leading humans to think and do things based on sudden ideas that come to mind. There is a difference between thoughts that comes to your mind from the Spirit World and the thoughts that comes to your mind from the visible world around you.

In order to receive and understand thoughts from the Spirit World you have to know the difference between right thoughts and wrong thoughts. As soon as you are able to disregard all the wrong thoughts that have been imposed on you and your forefathers for some twelve thousand years, your mind will be open for thoughts from the Spirit World. One thing is certain. With an open mind and some experience, the Spirit World can help you find things that are lost.

The donkeys that went missing started a search to find them. In this camouflaged story the man who is looking is the man who is found. It is a tale, everything that happens with Saul when he meets with the prophet Samuel. But it is a tale with a core of truth. This is how certain humans with the right spiritual strength and the right personal abilities are found and democratically elected to be a leader. It is done with the help from the Spirit World and it is a true law of Mother Nature.

But this story is telling humans living in present time how a wrong choice was made. When a wrong person is elected in to a leading position, things will start to go wrong from the beginning. In this case the story is about the whole world population and the beginning of the building of national states and kingdoms. Saul was the wrong choice and became a bad king in an evil world.

Samuel had said to the Israelites that God should be king. This is right. God is a new superior Motherland council, governing over the whole world population with one common set of laws and rules for living. With a new Motherland the whole planet earth will be one kingdom, and the council of twelve will be the omnipresent, omniscient and omnipotent democratic elected king.

The whole of the known world history is wrong as wrong can be and have been wrong for some twelve thousand years. Under the camouflage God is the superior Motherland council and the natural laws and living rules for mankind are chiseled in to stone tablets all over the world. The whole world population is meant to live as nature intended with only the Diagram Star speaking on behalf of the superior Motherland council. Before the Motherland went under, the whole world population lived in self supported villages. The humans in charge of every village were a council of twelve Masters. Their education was common all over the world, and as long as the common education was the main activity and only the best students made it to the degree of Master, world peace was permanent.

This is also a story about how personal fame and power can change a man's spirit and make him do things that are utterly wrong. And it is mainly knowledge from education that divides the personal power and spiritual strength that Samuel have and Saul never gets. Saul gets the power of a king, and can only uphold the power by use of soldiers and a set of laws and living rules that he makes up to fit his needs.

If the king is a good man or a bad man does not really matter, it is the position as a king that is wrong.

The great secret

1 Samuel 9, 26-10, 8

After the festivity on the hill Saul stayed the night in Samuels's house. He slept on the roof, because it was to warm inside. Next morning Samuel said that he should go home.

When the two men were on the way out of the town, Samuel turned against Saul and poured oil over his head. It meant that Saul was special selected by God.

"The Lord has chosen you to lead his people and rule over them as king," he said.

Saul bent his head. "This I don't understand," he said. Everything that had happened seemed so great and impossible. How could Samuel know all this? The answer was simple. God must have told him.

"When you continue home from here today", Samuel said, "you will meet a man telling you: The donkeys that you have been looking for, is found. Go home to your father now, before he starts to worry about you."

The people wanted a king because all other nations had a king. The title king has two meanings. Before the Motherland went under the title king was used by all the twelve council members. They did not have national states and armies to protect the borders and they did not collect taxes of any kind from the population. Like everyone else they were self supported. Sometime in the future a leader of the superior council of a new Motherland will be selected, and it will be done right.

At the time Saul was elected to be a king over the Jews there were many warrior kings all around them, leading the population in the land they had under their control. The Jews had no king and no land. With a king they could raise an army and take land they could make their own. But it never happened. The story is telling you all that it was the building of national states and that were wrong.

Saul was elected king several thousand years after the Motherland was gone, and the kings on the nearby land got more and more greedy, using their soldiers to get stronger, richer and more powerful than other kings. They were called warrior kings and were the leaders of the growing chaos of wars and conflicts.

Under the camouflage there is a story about the difference between doing wrong and doing right, meant for the people living in present time. The message is to not do anything that is clearly wrong just because others do it.

Under the camouflage of religion the people of Israel is the whole world population. Jerusalem and the land in that region is a symbolic theatrical stage for the whole planet earth. Every people in the region had a king and this is the story about how the warrior kings and their priesthoods developed in to be more and more tyrannical, with the growing armies and selected servants that used the entire population as working slaves and soldiers. They all did wrong, and the following warrior kings and priesthoods have continued to do wrong ever since. The many national states, democratic or not, are just another page of the same story. The national state leaders still collect taxes by use of despotic force and use the population within their national borders as working slaves, soldiers and servants.

The world leaders must be forgiven; because they have no knowledge of the global government system from before the Motherland disappeared from the face of the earth. When they are told, they refuse to believe a Motherland ever existed. They are, like most humans, blind and live their lives like living dead. They have to; just have to see the difference between right and wrong.

You know the saying: Not seeing the forest for all the trees. You and the whole world population are living like inside a bubble, living your life like your parents and the forefathers have done ever since the Motherland was destroyed. You know that something is wrong, but you find it is impossible to see that governing the whole world population with the use of many national states is unnatural and wrong. The world history has many stories about what happen to the humans who dare to speak negatively about the national state they live in. Now you know enough to see the difference and choose the right thing to do.

You are now able to see the world from outside the bubble. Think about what you see. The many never ending wars and conflicts in the world are not right. The thousands of humans that die every day for reasons like national belonging, poverty and religion is not right. You are now able to see that the humans living on planet earth truly can live good lives without their national states, the money and the religion.

What will emerge without the three factors of the Original Sin is the strong feeling of tribal and family belonging. Every single human being in the whole world will have everything they need to live good lives, with safety and happiness and true love in a world where there is no evil. And the whole world population will participate in the election of a new superior Motherland council.

Saul is proclaimed king

1 Samuel 10, 9-27

In the same moment Saul turned to leave Samuel, God did something special. He gave him a new heart. When Saul saw that everything happened like Samuel had predicted, he knew that it was God that let it happen. Later the same day Saul heard about the donkeys, just like Samuel had said.

Shortly after this Samuel called the people together. "Do you still want a king?" he asked.

"Yes, we want a king!" they shouted.

"Then God will select a king among you," said Samuel. The tribe of Benjamin was indicated by lot. In that tribe the family of Matri was indicated. It was the family that Saul belonged to.

Then Samuel went from man to man in that family, until God selected Saul. Samuel asked where he was.

"Who is Saul?" People looked around. "Where is he?"

Samuel asked the Lord and he said the Saul was hiding between bags and baskets. People ran looking and found him. They led him to Samuel.

"Look how tall he is," said Samuel. "This is your king!"

And the people shouted: "God save the king!"

Samuel told the people that they had to follow the laws of the Lord now that they had a king. As long as Saul followed the laws, the Lord would bless him.

Saul became a great king and a mighty man, and he led the children of Israel into many battles against their enemies the Philistines, but after a while he disobeyed the laws of the Lord.

Samuel warned him, saying: "You have been very foolish in not keeping the commandments of the Lord your God, for had you done so, the Lord would have established your kingdom upon Israel for ever. But now your kingdom will not continue."

A world of clever fools you truly are. Now look at Israel as the whole planet earth. The children of Israel are a symbol for the whole world population, and if the Master writing the story is telling you that a wrong person was elected king for a reason. The Egyptian hieroglyphs were badly translated in to the Hebrew language. The story is all about your forefathers choosing to live with the three factors of the Original Sin.

It is not possible for a whole lot of national leaders, warrior kings, religious leaders, presidents and others, to lead the world population in to an era with long lasting peace. It is impossible for the many world leaders to build a new world with lasting peace together. They need a common superior leadership.

This camouflaged story is telling you how King Saul, as a symbol for all the kings wrongly elected, is becoming a bad king doing wrong. Anyone can see that the election is wrong, in the description of Saul as a tall and handsome person with a weak spirit and without the needed degree of knowledge.

The world needs a new superior Motherland council as a king of kings, governing the whole world population with one common set of laws and rules for living. The election of such a king of kings is described in the camouflaged story about King David. Under the camouflage King David is starting the building of a new Motherland. The force of evil in the world around him is the camouflage that makes the story a part of the many biblical stories.

Under the camouflage of religion Israel is a symbol for the whole planet earth, and the Master writing this story is telling people living in present time that their long history of wars and conflicts, the building of cities with strong walls around for protection, the building of national states and the building of the global capitalistic system, could have been avoided all together, if the many world leaders had made the right decision back then and continued to live by the laws and rules given by the superior Motherland council.

This means that the rule of warrior kings was never meant to be, and as the many camouflaged biblical stories continues, you will learn that no matter how popular the king was when elected, he is completely unable to uphold the commandments of the Lord and live by them. You know now that the commandments are derived from the Diagram Star and you know that every warrior king had to break them in order to build a nation inside national borders and continue to break them with their self written laws and rules for living in order to stay in power.

Under the camouflage Lord God is the late superior Motherland council. The only valid set of laws and rules for living is noted in the Diagram Star. The model for the Diagram Star is the

163

sun, the moon and the twelve star signs of the Zodiac, and as a diagram it speaks to every living human being on the planet. With a superior Motherland council as a king of kings, humans would not have discovered the forces of evil and national states would not have been built. The global system of capitalism would not be in existence and neither would all the religions in the world.

You know that the global warming, flooding and increasingly stronger wind, among other natural catastrophes, is a direct result of the human activity that breaks the laws of Mother Nature.

Just think what the world would have been like without the desperate quest for riches and personal power. It would have been a world without the oil wells, without all the cars, ships, trains and plains. There would have been a well established contact net between all the tribal peoples in the world and the means of transport of goods and people would have been based on what was needed.

They had flying vessels before the Motherland went under and certainly boats and ships for specific needs. Just mentioning it: the technology that was used was far more advanced than any human living in our present time can imagine.

Just think of how the three factors of the Original Sin have destroyed a happy peaceful paradise world, just because some wrong choices were made in the far past.

God selects a new king

1 Samuel 15, 9-16, 13

In the beginning Saul tried to be a good king. He ruled like God wanted him to do. But after a while he got greedy. God did not like that Saul was thinking only on himself. Therefore God asked Samuel to find a new king.

"I want that you fill your horn with oil and go to Bethlehem. There you shall gather the sons of Jesse, and I will show you the one who is to be the next king."

When Samuel got to Bethlehem, he sent for Jesses sons. The oldest was a handsome young man. But the Lord said: "I am God. I judge people not for their looks. I look at the heart and discover what you don't see."

When all the seven sons had walked by Samuel, he turned to Jesse. "The Lord has not chosen any one of them. Du you have more sons?"

"Yes, I have one more," Jesse replayed. "But he is so small. He is out looking after the sheep's." Then they sent for Jesse's youngest son, David.

The boy had big brown eyes and had dark skin. His smile seemed to light up every room he entered. He was good looking and strong.

"The Lord said: "Him it is." Samuel then took the horn of oil and anointed David in the midst of his brothers. It meant that he was elected to be king. The Spirit of the Lord was with David from that day.

Who is the Lord God who talks to Samuel? Who have given Samuel his authority so the many tribes of Israel listen to him and do as he says? His authority is in knowing the full Motherland history.

Lord God that have spoken to people for the last some twelve thousand years, is the superior Motherland council speaking through the Diagram Star from the spirit world, from the common world of thoughts. But the common world of thoughts has been occupied by the three factors of the Original Sin for some twelve thousand years. You have to know the full history about the lost Motherland in order to know how to build a new world with lasting peace.

This is important. It is only the humans living in present time who knows that the whole planet earth have been a living hell since the Motherland went under. And it is only humans who lived before the Motherland went under who knows what paradise the whole planet earth was back then. Their thoughts are in the common world of thoughts, fully accessible for you and the whole world population.

It is the story of the peaceful kingdom that ruled the whole planet earth; the Masters have preserved and passed on through the history with the use of the Diagram Star. The whole world population really lived together like brothers and friends, with one set of laws and rules for living until a natural catastrophe ended it all and the chaos of wars and conflicts started.

Next time you hear the king or any priest in your nation referring to God as the high and mighty power they serve, you know that God is the superior Motherland council in the Spirit World. The world leaders don't know. Therefore you have to tell them, again and again.

This is a story telling the people living in present time that the world population really tried to live right using the common set of laws and rules for living that was given by the superior Motherland council. But after a while the leaders, the self elected warrior kings and priesthoods, got greedy and started making their own laws and rules for living. Saul is a symbol for all of them.

King David is a true symbol for what it takes of a human to be elected king. A good leader of men have to do everything right, be brave and happy with life. It is the spiritual strength of a man that is fundamental along with the degree of education and personal ability. Make sure that you already now understand that under the camouflage of religion, the election of King David is the election of a new superior Motherland council, and the whole story is about building a new Motherland. All you have to do is to remove all evil and wrong doing from the story.

In our present time the three factors of the Original Sin is slowly but surely destroying planet earth. The common world of thoughts is completely occupied by thoughts that are totally against the laws and living rules given by the superior Motherland council. You and the whole world population have work together to remove the three factors of the Original Sin from the common world of thoughts.

David meets Saul the king

1 Samuel 16, 14-23

David returned to the sheep's again. Every time a lion or a bear threatened the flock, he would throw a stone on them with his sling. During the long days out on the hills he also played on his harp and sang hymns to the Lord.

While David got closer to God, Saul moved further away from him. The Spirit of God left Saul, and he became unhappy and felt terrible. And he couldn't sleep either. He was always sad and anxious. He had no appetite. Sometime he imagined things that weren't real. Often he felt that he was two persons in one body.

Saul's servants said that he had to find someone to set his mind at rest.

"Where do I find someone like that?" Saul asked.

"I have heard about one of the sons of Jesse. He is good playing harp and sings. And more so he is very brave. He does not talk much and are all in all a good boy," said one of the servants. "Not only that. The Lord is with him."

Saul sent for David and Jesse let his son go to the king. He brought a donkey loaded with presents. It was bread and vine for King Saul.

David got closer and Saul got further away from God. The Master writing the story is telling the humans living in present time how the safety and the happiness of belonging to a tribe slowly fades away from people who do wrong, while people who always do right, keeps the happiness and are respected by everyone. Bravery comes with knowing that you do things right.

Every person living on planet earth will feel the happiness; safety and belonging to a tribe grow stronger as soon as they get to know the Diagram Star. The whole world population will sing and dance when the time comes that the three factors of the Original Sin is removed from the common world of thoughts. You will all be free from your national states, the global system of capitalism and all the religions in the world.

You know that everything you do wrong is following you like a heavy burden that takes your happiness and safety away from you. Likewise you know how happy you always are when you do things right all the time.

Saul have become a greedy and selfish king and it is the thoughts about his own personal power and his riches that take him away from the light of the Diagram Star and inn to a mental darkness of evil forces that makes him very unhappy. This happens with all humans who have all they need in abundance, but still feels that something important is missing in life. They miss the knowledge about the lost Motherland.

The Diagram Star is symbol and all the thoughts connected to it are for real.

All humans living in present time know that the laws and rules of their nation rule their common world of thoughts. Many humans are searching all their life for knowledge that can give lasting peace to the world. They search in vain because they have to do it inside the laws and rules of the nation. Now you know that all the national states in the world have to be built down peacefully in order to create lasting peace for the whole world. Then all the greedy and selfish kings and national leaders like Saul will be out of work and new leaders like David will be elected.

Remember now that all humans in the world are equals, not one is greater than others. Humans with a strong or a week spirit, and different level of education, all are equals in the eyes of all humans. Humans are democratically elected in to positions that are permanent in all tribal communities. All humans know their spiritual strength and what position they can fill and what work their can do with pride and happiness. Humans in all the positions are equals; it is the position they fill that is different, but equally important for everyone living in the community. The position as a member of a council is not more important than the position as for example a carpenter or a farmer. The important issue is that all humans do what they are good at and what makes them respected, proud and happy.

David and Goliath

1 Samuel 17, 1-19

In the course of the next years David often visited the castle and played his harp for King Saul. Sometimes Saul had to leave to fight the Philistines. Then David went home to his father.

Among Saul's soldiers were three of David's older brothers. Jesse often asked David to bring food to the brothers; like corn, bread and cheese. In this way he found out how they were doing.

One time Saul and his soldiers had a big problem. The battle had not started yet, because the Philistines had a soldier named Goliath. He was very big, a strong giant, and now he challenged the Israelites.

"The one who dares, can come and fight with me!" he shouted. "If I win, you all will be our slaves. If your man wins, we shall serve you."

But when Saul's soldiers only looked at Goliath, they started shivering with fear. "It is no use fighting a man like him," they whispered. Not one dared to fight him. Also David's brothers were afraid of Goliath.

Goliath is a symbol for the laws and rules of the many national states in the world. The whole world population is afraid to oppose the system with many national states governing the world. People are truly afraid to break the laws and rules of their nation because of the punishment they know will follow. Opposing all the national states in the world is unimaginable for most people. But all the world needs now is one man with the right qualities as a human and brave enough to challenge the whole world.

As you can read, armed forces are not an option in the coming battle that you and the whole world population have to fight together, for lasting peace. There are no human enemies in the world, only brothers and friends. Your common enemy is all the wrong and evil thoughts in the world.

The little stone is a symbol for everything that is good and right in the world. It will take down everything that is evil and wrong in the world, and then the little stone will grow in to a mountain that covers the whole planet earth. The same story is told several times in the Bible

It is not a matter of getting world dominance like many self elected conquerors have tried and failed before in our known world history. It cannot be done as long as the three factors of the Original Sin are in control of the common world of thoughts.

It is a matter of restoring lasting world peace by building a new Motherland for all the many people living in the world. Then the whole world population will be governed by one global Motherland parliament and one common set of laws and rules for living, and the world will automatically become a paradise again. Truly Internet and modern technology can be used to elect twelve parliament representatives from every people in the world. Then you will be able to challenge the way the world is governed and win.

Hopefully many men and women can stand forward and show the whole world population that the present system of governing the world truly can be taken down and replaced with the global system of governing from the time before the Motherland went under. As soon as the giant falls, the whole world population will join in and start the process of building a new world with the use of only peaceful means.

All people who is fighting each other in wars, is fighting for reasons derived from the three factors of the Original Sin. The warrior kings fight for the right to control the land and the people living on the land. It is by warfare and brutal force the national states in the world has been built and it is by the same force they continue to exist.

The war between the Israelites and the Philistines described in this story is camouflage for something much more important than about two greedy kings who wanted to expand their riches and personal power.

David is symbolizing the enormous strength there is in a strong spirit and in the knowledge derived from the Diagram Star. Knowledge about the lost Motherland is stronger than all the armed forces in the world. What David does is the right thing to do for him and his people. Remember now that under the camouflage the Israelites and the Philistines together is a symbol for the whole world population. Their differences are in their common world of thoughts. The Philistines are a symbol for the thoughts derived from the three factors of the Original Sin and the Israelites is a symbol for the thoughts that are derived from the Diagram Star and the superior Motherland council. It is all a matter of reviving the full world history from the time before the Motherland was destroyed.

The fight against the forces of evil, three factors of the Original Sin, has not yet started. In our present time you and the whole world population are trembling with fear, watching the world fall apart, unable to do anything at all because your laws and rules denies you to do the right thing.

Look at the three forces controlling your life from birth to death as a three headed monster. You all think that there is no force in the world that can remove all the national states, the global system of capitalism and all the religions in the world, from the common world of thoughts.

But you truly can take the three headed monster down by being brave and skilled like David. As soon as you realize that it is the monster that is destroying the world using humans that have been denied knowledge about the lost Motherland for several thousand years, you will start doing what you do best and take the monster down within your own world of thoughts.

Knowledge about the history of the lost Motherland and the global system of government with one set of laws and rules for living is the thought that can restore lasting peace on planet earth. All it takes is you and many other brave humans that are needed in order to spread the thoughts all over the world. Spread it like seed, using Internet and modern technology, and feel the happiness that comes with doing right.

Goliath insults the Israelites

1 Samuel 17, 20-30

More than one month Goliath threatened Israel's army. On this time Jesse asked David to bring food to his brothers, and David was happy to make the trip.

When he got to the camp, he started looking for his brothers. Then he heard a call of fright from the Israeli soldiers.

"Run for your life! The giant is coming!"

Goliath shouted: "Hah! I knew it! You Israelites are just a bunch of cowards. You can of course prove that I am wrong, if you want. Your God is weak! He cannot help you!"

Goliath had said something terrible. He had said that God was weak. When David heard Goliaths insult, he got angry. He tried to learn more from the frightened soldier around him, and he heard that there was a reward to the one who killed Goliath. Saul had offered great riches and he will give him his daughter in marriage.

I do not call the whole world population cowards, because you are not. The whole world population is in present time captives locked inside their national borders and are forced to obey the laws and rules of their nation. You are trapped, there is no way of escaping and you see no way out. If you emigrate it is only from one nation to another. Looking at the world falling apart around you in an escalating chaos of wars and conflict along with the aspect of what global warming can do to the world, everybody is worried. But nobody knows what to do.

Perhaps a severe insult will start a reaction. You know by now that God is the superior Motherland council. They had real power over all the colonies, kingdoms and empires in the world in the time before the Motherland went under. They were strong enough to keep the knowledge about evil out of the common world of thoughts and the whole world was a true paradise.

After the Motherland was destroyed and the superior Motherland council died people did learn that they could break the laws and rules given by the superior Motherland council and get away with it. All the council members were in the Spirit World with all others who had died. They had no physical power to stop the escalating chaos of wars and conflicts between self elected warrior kings and priesthoods. Still today, the insult Goliath made back then still stands.

There is many brave men living in our present time, but they just can't see their own nation and all the nations in the world as an enemy of lasting world peace. People are proud of their national state and as long as the majority of the population is living well and willingly work hard and pay their taxes, they are ok with the life they live. But you all are captives of the three factors of the Original Sin.

Look around you and you see the world being destroyed little by little. In order to see the whole world as one natural living organism, you have to look at the world from outside. Do it mentally in your world of thoughts, and you see that all the national states in the world have relative poor populations?

Everybody have to work, make money and pay taxes in order to live a good life. It is wrong, because the national states, the use of money and all the religions was never meant to be. The three factors of the Original Sin is manmade and against the nature of the world. It is the nature protesting when humans dies by the thousand for reasons that wasn't meant to be.

Do you see the millions of humans that are locked inside their national borders, dying by the thousands because of the three factors of the Original Sin?

All the tribal people in the world are by nature meant to live together like a large family, like brothers and friends. It can be like that again if you tell the whole world population about the history of the lost Motherland and the Diagram Star.

The democracy of present time is an insult to mankind. The government system with many national states is not stronger than the walls of Jericho. The global system of capitalism is a similar wall and the greatest wall of all is the camouflage of religions. You are behind a great wall of ignorance, and you will stay there as long as you choose to deny that the lost Motherland ever existed.

David wins a victory

1 Samuel 17, 31-54

David went to King Saul and said: "I want to fight against Goliath. I don't like that the people of God is regarded as cowards."

"You are not able to fight Goliath," said Saul. "You are just a young shepherd and he is a trained soldier."

David stood tall. "I have saved my sheep's from both lions and bears," he said.

In the end Saul agreed. He gave Saul his amour and his weapons, but they were too big and too heavy for David. He took it off. "I will meet Goliath dressed like a shepherd," he said. He picked five smooth stones from a brook and with his sling in his hand he walked to fight with Goliath.

When Goliath saw him, he roared: "What an insult! Are you sending a little boy to fight against Goliath?

But David replied: "You have sword and spear. My weapon is the Lords, the God of all humans. He is God for the tribes of Israel, the God you insulted. Today the Lord will let me win over you. The whole people will then understand that no battle can be won by the sword, but by the force of God.

Goliath came closer to attack David. David had a stone in his sling. He swung it around his head a couple of times and then he sent the stone away.

The stone came faster than Goliath could think. He did not have time to use his shield and the stone hit him in the head. The giant fell to the ground.

David took his large and heavy sword and killed him. The Philistines did not believe their own eyes. They tried to escape, but the Israelites did not let them get away so easy. That day they won a great victory because David had trusted the power of God.

Remember the little stone from the brook. It symbolizes the force knowledge given by the late superior Motherland council represent. Knowledge about the lost Motherland has to be reinstated in the common world of thoughts. Only then a new world with lasting peace can be built.

After many thousand years, the world leaders, you and the whole world population, should know that world pace not can be won by the sword, but by the force given by a new superior Motherland council. The building of a new Motherland and electing a new superior Motherland council will put an end to all wars and conflicts.

Not nations, but all the many tribal peoples in the world, will send twelve of their best leaders to represent them in the new Motherland parliament. The superior Motherland council will be elected from the many parliament representatives. They will be the new leader of the world.

With the Diagram Star back in the common educational system all over the world, the whole world population will be governed by on common set of laws and rules for living. Only then the whole world population can feel the true freedom of living as nature intended.

Under the camouflage of religion the Masters message is clear. It is said time and time again that the formula or code they used when preserving and passing on the history of the Motherland is the four fundamental elements. Water, Earth, Fire and Air are all elements from the Zodiac star signs, explaining the nature of the world and the only way humans can live together in lasting peace.

The fight against the three factors of the Original Sin can only be won with the natural and everlasting knowledge that the bright shining Diagram Star has carried up through the ages.

The knowledge has always been there for you all, but blinded as you are by the three factors of the Original Sin, you just haven't seen it. You haven't even looked for the possibility that all the religions in the world are covering the knowledge mankind needs in order to be able to build a new world with lasting peace.

Lasting world peace cannot be built with war power against war power, both with an occupied world of thoughts to lead them. In order to win over the enemy thoughts in your mind and put an end to the chaos of wars and conflicts in the world, the whole world population have to gather in tribes, choose their leaders and fight together with only peaceful means to end an occupation of the common world of thoughts that have lasted for some twelve thousand years.

King Saul is envious

1 Samuel 17, 55-58; 18, 5-30

After David killed Goliath Saul made him general. He was sent out in many battles. Every time David came home from war, he grew in the eyes of the people. He soon became a great hero.

One time David came home after having slaying many Philistines, women came out of the cities of Israel, dancing and singing. They sang: "Saul has slain thousands, and David has slain ten thousands."

Saul got angry for this. He was envious and said to himself: "David is ten times more popular than I am. Soon he will try taking my kingdom away from me." From that day David was envious of David.

Saul even tried to kill David by sending him out on dangerous missions. David just grew in the eyes of the people as a hero. One time he fought against the Philistines, Sauls daughter Michal prayed that he would come home safely. She loved David. God was with him and he did everything right.

Now you have to change your way of thinking completely, because the growing of a man in to a hero and a king has to be done without winning wars and conflicts and bringing home a lot of stolen gods. The greatness of every leader has to come from spiritual strength, the level of knowledge and personal abilities. Happiness and personal willpower is essential for every leader of people, and their personal strength can only grow in the eyes of the people.

Think about the mental battle between all the religions in the world and the knowledge found in the Bible, underneath the camouflage of religion.

There can never be lasting peace in the whole world as long as the strong and dominating three factors of the Original Sin are ruling the common world of thoughts.

In the present world even the best of leaders will have to do things that is against everything they hold for being right. They have to make the right choices under the given wrong and evil circumstances, and they see no other way of doing things. Remove all wrong and evil from the biblical stories and you will discover how people lived in the time before the Motherland went under.

When national leaders make mistakes and loose important battles, either it is in peacetime or in wartime, they will quickly be replaced. But the system of government continues like before. The forces of evil, the three factors of the original Sin, are the essence of everyone's life and it is the life of cowards. The richest of the rich and the established royal families are sitting safe inside their castles and let their riches and titles be inherited by their own sons and relatives. Without their workforce, soldiers and servants they would be ordinary human beings, not greater than others. Even the best paid slaves, is still slaves. Their salary is derived directly from the sum of money they accumulate for the owners.

The priesthoods of a nation is in their position for the duration of their life and are the most important tool for the royalties and the richest of the rich in keeping the population ignorant and suppressed. All organized common education is work related. Without the religion all the national states in the world would appear like well organized crime units, all with their own laws and rules for living.

It is the three factors of the Original Sin that are the giant that the whole world population is afraid of. What does it take to make a David of present time start the battle against the giant, before it is too late? The reward will be great, measured in happiness, pride and the respect from other humans.

History shows that many humans have fought against the establishment, but everyone have lost the battle. This is not warrior kings fighting other warrior kings to steal their land and riches and make the population their slaves. The coming battle is fought by humans with knowledge about the lost Motherland, against humans with religious belief in dogmas and assumptions that are utterly wrong.

Many of the camouflaged stories in the Bible are about the antagonism that there is between all the three factors of the Original Sin and the Diagram Star. Without the three factors of the Original Sin there would not have been war heroes on the planet at all.

The laws and living rules given by the superior Motherland council is the force of nature. Humans will always be in the nature and have to live accordingly. Life would be natural and right with only the good force of nature.

If all evil is removed from the common world of thoughts, the good will find back to the natural meaning.

War is the opposite of peace, and if war is removed from the common world of thoughts, peace will find back to the natural meaning.

Riches are the opposite of poverty, and if the whole global capitalistic system is removed from the common world of thoughts, personal ownership will get back its original meaning.

Religious belief is an opposite of not belief, and if all religions are removed from the common world of thoughts, knowledge about the lost Motherland will emerge and find back to its natural track.

Love is the opposite of hat, and if hate is removed from the common world of thoughts, the feeling of love will find back to its natural meaning.

Friends for life

1 Samuel 18, 1-4; 19, 1-7

After David had killed Goliath, Saul called him to the castle. It was here David first met Jonathan, Saul's son and Michal's brother. That day David had talked with Saul. Then he heard something behind him. It was Jonathan. The two young men looked at each other.

In the same moment Jonathan's soul was connected to David's soul. Jonathan knew that he had found a friend for life. The two young men promised that they should love each other, and Jonathan let David have his coat, the sword, the bow and the belt.

Several years later Saul asked Jonathan and his servants to kill David. But Jonathan was more than a brother for David. He said to him: "My father will kill you! Be careful tomorrow. You have to hide. I shall talk with my father about you."

Jonathan went to see his father the next morning. He talked about what a good man David was and that it was wrong to kill him. Then David came back to the castle. But Saul broke his promise. Soon he got angry at David again.

Also a David of present time will need many good friends in order to succeed in building a new Motherland. Being better than a king must have a meaningful purpose for a good man, and David is a man strong in spirit and does everything right under the given circumstances, while Saul does everything wrong.

The meaning for the camouflaged stories about David is clear. All you have to do is to take a moment and think about who David would be in a world without the three factors of the Original Sin. Him and humans like him would have been selected to get a higher education as

Masters in the Motherland. Twelve humans of his spiritual strength would be elected to sit in the new superior Motherland council.

Saul is a symbol for the evil and wrong thinking of all the world leaders in present time. David is a symbol for the rightful and good thinking that will have to lead the whole world population when the evil thinking of the wrongful and self elected world leaders and their priesthoods are removed from the common world of thoughts. The battle is to be fought by only peaceful means, and not on human will die in the process.

Very soon individuals with David's character and personal abilities will come forth, and with the knowledge hidden under the camouflage of religion the many David's of present time can remove all evil in the world and build a new world with lasting peace. For them the most important thing in life will be to do everything right in the light of the Diagram Star. They know if they do just one thing wrong, they will be just another Saul.

As soon as the knowledge about the history about the lost Motherland and the Diagram Star has been spread all over the world, the new knowledge will be the much needed foundation for a new world order. The whole world population will eventually understand that the only action that can save the world from being totally destroyed is to remove the three factors of the Original Sin from the common world of thoughts.

Humans living in present time have to win the mental battle over evil and ignorance together and become like brothers and friends with each other. They have to win the battle the twelve tribes of Israel lost several thousand years ago, after their Motherland was destroyed. The common world of thoughts was altered with the use of warfare and brutal force. A new Motherland council of world leaders, speaking on behalf of the Motherland parliament and the whole world population, could alter the common world of thoughts back on the right track. They would always keep their promises.

Jonathan saves David's life

1 Samuel 19, 9-29, 42; Hymn 59

It was no use trusting Saul. One evening when David played his harp for him, he suddenly got up from his chair and took his spear. He towed it in full force against David. David got away as fast as he could. He barely avoided being killed.

That night his wife Michal helped David to get away from Sauls soldiers. David went to the prophet Samuels house and told him what had happened. Then he went back to the castle to see Jonathan.

"What have I done?" he asked. Jonathan and David made a plan together. They agreed in using a signal. Jonathan should talk to his father about David. After he would go out in the field to shoot with bow and arrow and if Saul really wanted to kill David, Jonathan should shout to the boy who fetched the arrows: "They are further away!" That should be the signal to David.

Jonathan and David walked together out in the field, were they had agreed to meet later. They were strongly attached to each other, and Jonathan called out to God: "You shall be our witness! If my father wants to kill David and I don't warn him, then let the Lord punish me. Let my children and his children live as friends forever, also after the Lord have eradicated all David's enemies." Then David hid in the field, while Jonathan went to see his father.

Two days later Jonathan asked his father about David. Saul got furious. He even threw his spear against Jonathan, but missed.

The next morning Jonathan ran out in the field with his bow and arrow. He shot an arrow and asked the servant to find it. "The arrow is further away!" he shouted. "Hurry up!" Then he sent the servant home and David came out from his hiding place.

David fell for Jonathan's feet. The two friends were so sorry that they cried together. Both knew that a long time would pass before they saw each other again.

The true and only definition of David's enemy is not Saul; it is the three factors of the Original Sin. The force of good is in the nature of all humans, while the force of evil is imposed on all humans by the warrior kings and priesthoods. The force of evil is manmade, controlling the thoughts of all humans and are the true enemy of lasting world peace.

The whole camouflaged story about David and his life is telling the people living in our present time how the many kingdoms in the world grew forth by fighting each other in order to increase the land area and the number of people living on it. The normally used modus operandi was to attack and rob villages, kill the leaders and force the whole village population in to a life as a slave, soldier and servant. Those who protested were instantly killed.

And a leader that did everything right in the eyes of the people was a real threat to the warrior kings and their priesthoods. The people wanted David to be their king. He is the kind of king the whole world population wants. It was gruesome time for humans in this part of the world, and then, as they still do, the people wanted a world with lasting peace.

Remember what Samuel said in the beginning of the story, when the people demanded a king to protect them and lead them in battle. The Prophet, meaning the Master who wrote the story, knew that it was impossible to stop the government system with many kingdoms to grow fort, and all good people needed a king and an army that could protect them.

The world history is full of a chaos of wars and conflicts. The building of empires and national states was a true flood of sin that spread all over the world. Without kings and world leaders like Saul, planet earth would still be a paradise for all mankind. In our present time all humans live in the opposite of a paradise, which is a living hell.

The history about David speaks about how a regular human being can grow in the eyes of the population and stand off as a king in the making. Saul was fighting to promote himself as the greatest and the strongest in the eyes of the people, and he failed in everything he tried to do. He couldn't accept that David went past him as more popular. Kings all through the history have acted the same way as Saul, with very few exceptions. They lived their meaningless lives with intrigues and killed everyone who threatened their kingdom and themselves. All in all they committed a crime against mankind and the crime still goes on.

Alone in a cave

1 Samuel 24, 1-22; Hymn 57

Saul hunted David like he was a wild animal. He knew that David was hiding in an area with many caves. Saul and his soldiers started searching there.

When Saul was alone for a while, he had to go in to a cave for a needed errand. He did not know that David was hiding in that cave!

"Look, David," his soldiers whispered to him. "God have blessed you again. Now you have the change to kill King Saul."

David shook his head and answered: "No, no one kills a king chosen by God!" He climbed down the cave towards Saul. Carefully he cut a peace off from Saul's coat. Then he went back to his hiding place. In the same moment he returned to his men, David regretted what he just had done. He did not want to harm Saul in any way. "I should not have cut the peace of his coat," he said.

Saul left the cave. When he was outside, David ran after him and fell down in front of him. "My king!" he shouted. Saul looked startled at him. David held up the peace of his coat. "This I cut from your coat. God gave it in my hand while you were in the cave, but I did not harm you! I even held my men back, and stopped them from killing you. Do you now believe that I am your enemy? Why do you persecute me like this? I have done nothing wrong!

Saul understood that David could have killed him if he wanted. "A man does not let his enemy get away so easy," he said. "I believe you, David."

Saul let David and his men in peace, at least for some time. But soon Saul had forgotten his promise again.

Saul wanted to kill David for one reason, and that reason is that David does everything right and becomes the hero in the eyes the people. If fact, David is a symbol for a member of the superior Motherland council in the time before the Motherland went under. Saul does everything wrong in his position as a king and are a true symbol for the whole history of warrior kings and priesthoods.

It is the opposition that David meets in this story that makes him grow as a person in the eyes of the people. Remember that he already is anointed to be the new king and are predicted to be a great king for the Israelites. You know that the biblical Israelites are a symbol for the whole world population. If David had used his change and killed Saul in the cave, he would have degraded himself by doing something wrong. Then he would not have been a better king than Saul.

Make no mistake. Under the camouflage of religion the Master writing this story is saying to you, being among the David's of present time, just how you have to fight with only peaceful means in order to restore the global system of government and build a world with lasting peace. There is no other way.

Everything is lost

1 Samuel 29, 1-30, 31

The Philistines again attacked Israel. Among the leaders was king Akis of Gat. This king had protected David when he escaped from King Saul. Akis now asked David and his men to march with him. He wanted David to fight his own people, the Israelites.

When the Philistine generals heard about this, they said: "No, we don't want David with us in the battle. What if he turns against us?"

Akis then sent David and his men home to their families. David went to Siklag, were he had lived more than a year.

In Siklag he discovered something terrible. The town was set on fire! While David and his men were gone, the amalekittene had raided the city. All their families were taken prisoners!

David inspected his men. Six hundred men followed him. Two hundred was too tired, so they were left in the city. The whole day he pursued the amalekitt army. When it started to get dark, David and his men attacked. It became a long and hard battle during the night, and children ran in all directions. But at last David and his men von the battle. Only four hundred of the amalekitt army got away, because they had camels to ride on.

Remember now that the Philistines, the Amalekitt army and even the Israelites are thoughts in your world of thoughts. You are your thoughts. Without your thoughts you would not be living. The battle that takes place in all the camouflaged stories is a battle between the good and the evil in the common world of thoughts. The camouflage stories always let the force of good win, but still, it is not easy to fight with only the sword of knowledge against large armies of ignorant believers and not believers. With the use of Internet and modern technology knowledge about the lost Motherland will prevail. Then the whole world population can build lasting peace together.

The attacks by real armies against unarmed unprotected villages happened all the time back then. The camouflaged stories were accepted by the warrior kings and the priesthoods because they were right in their eyes. More and more tribal people were forced in to a life as slaves, soldiers and servants under the rule of a warrior king. It was the true history of the warrior kings and priesthoods that were written down by Master living under cower.

In a world where it is the smartest king with the largest army that always wins the battles, the world history is always colored in favor of the winner. This camouflaged story shows how the chaos of wars and conflicts spread all over the part of the world where the stories where written. The reason for this truly negative activity is that the Diagram Star and the common laws and rules for living was forgotten or made in to unbelievable religions, legends, tales and myths. The ruling kings and the priesthoods made their own laws and rules and forced the population to obey them. Those who protested were instantly killed. And it is well known if a person refused to fight as a soldier for his king, he was killed as a traitor.

The Masters had to live undercover in order to stay alive, mostly as advisors for the warrior kings or as priests or shepherds. Some of them even made it to be elected king.

The many camouflaged stories about tribe's attacking other tribes are very true, but the stories written with the camouflage is more like historical tales. Whole villages are attacked by warrior kings and set on fire. Many innocent humans were killed. The self elected warrior kings, who get back to his home village with a lot of stolen goods and slaves, are praised like heroes. In the view of what's right and what's wrong, all the warrior kings and their priesthoods were the worst of killers and criminals one can imagine.

These fights about fertile land to live on, about riches and personal power, started with Cain and Abel in the time just after the Motherland went under and has continued in to our present time. In order to create lasting peace in the whole world, the circle of evil that started back then has to stop.

The global system of government that Adam and Eve left had common laws and living rules for the whole world population. The new world can only be built by people like David elected from the whole world population. Everything they do they have to do together and do it right. Doing wrong is not acceptable.

Saul and Jonathan dies

1 Samuel 31, 1.13; 2 Samuel 1, 1-27

David returned home to Siklag. Here he was told about the great battle between Sauls Israelites and the Philistines. It was the battle that the Philistine generals had denied David to participate in.

"It was a terrible battle," a messenger told him. "The Philistines were fighting hard and they killed three of Saul's sons, among them Jonathan…"

"No!" David shouted out loud. "Not my brother Jonathan!"

The messenger continued: "The king was surrounded. He had no choice. Saul fell for his own sword. He killed himself."

Now both David and his men began to cry. They did not eat the whole day. Gods anointed King was dead! It was a dark day for Israel!

This story is special in its camouflage and has a double meaning. It would be of great interest to see the Egyptian hieroglyph it was translated from. The battle happened because of the desperate fight to be the strongest and the richest warrior king in that part of the world. Where the fighting takes place is a symbol for the whole planet earth and the story clearly tells you that the whole world population only can win lasting peace with the use of a new Motherland parliament and a new superior Motherland council.

If you look at the story about David as a recipe for building a new Motherland in our present time, the death of King Saul and his son Jonathan is symbol for how the force of evil is losing against the force of good in the end. If the three factors of the Original Sin are removed from the common world of thoughts, the knowledge about the lost Motherland and the Diagram Star will grow as a force of good that the whole world population needs.

David is elected king

2 Samuel 5, 1-10, 13-25

Now that Saul's sons were dead, the tribes of Israel came to David and said: "We all belong to the same family. Also when Saul was king you were our leader. We have heard that the Lord has chosen you. We want you to be our king!"

When David became king, he wanted that Jerusalem should be his city. On this time Jerusalem was just a little village. But it was very well protected, and it would be difficult to take it.

The Jebusites, who lived in Jerusalem, laughed of David: "You could not even win over the blind and the lame in this city! You will never win over us?!

But David had God's blessing. When he and his men took Jerusalem, he made it the city of Israel and the royal city of the Jews.

When the Philistines heard that David had become king, they called all their armies together in order to attack him. But David asked the Lord what to do. God answered: "Don't attack at ones, but put your soldiers in a ring around them. When you hear the sound of footsteps in the treetops, you shall hurry. It means that the Lord have gone before you and will beat all the armies of the enemy."

And that's how it happened. David won over the Philistines everywhere.

David was thirty years of age when he became the king in Juda. He became one of the greatest kings the Jewish people have had. He ruled over Israel and Juda for forty years.

Jerusalem is chosen as a new Motherland for all the twelve tribes of Israel. The whole world population belongs to the same family and is meant to live together as brothers and friends. You can choose a whole continent to be the new Motherland, and why not choose Africa.

It is not right to even question if this story ever happened. Like most of the camouflaged stories in the Bible it is pure fiction in a combination with the true history from that region of the world. Israel and Juda is a symbol for the whole world and Juda is the land the Jewish tribe lived on. You know that the God that talks in the camouflaged stories is the spiritual superior Motherland council talking through the Diagram Star.

The superior Motherland council has been in the Spirit World since the Motherland was destroyed in a natural catastrophe some twelve thousand years ago and the Diagram Star is forgotten by everyone except a sturdy group of Masters. They were working hard to preserve and pass on the history of the lost Motherland and the only way it could be done was in the camouflaged stories that became the Bible.

Now just think for a while on what all the religions in the world would have been like in our present time, if they had not been imposed on people with the use of warfare and brutal force.

The historical details in the story about King David are not important, but with knowledge about the camouflage, the story becomes very important for the humans living in present time. Look at Jerusalem, the royal capital of the biblical Israelites, as a symbolic theatrical stage for a new Motherland and the surrounding land a symbol for the whole world.

Jerusalem and the surrounding land are a true symbol for the whole world, and the many battles, first against the Jebusites to take the city and later against the Philistines, is a description of the battles that will have to take place in the common world of thoughts. The help from God is the true force of knowledge given to all humans by the superior Motherland council. It truly is the recipe for building a new world with lasting peace that is to be found under the camouflage of religion.

The Philistines and tribes like the Jebusites are all invented and are the evil forces derived from the three factors of the Original Sin. If you look around you, you will instantly understand that the common world of thoughts have been occupied by the forces of evil for some twelve thousand years. The occupation ends with this explanation.

This is not world history taught to you in school. It is history long forgotten and regarded as wrong because it is different from what the world leaders want you to learn in school. The world leaders do what they think is right, because the laws and the living rules of the nation tell them so. Forgive them, because they don't know what they are doing. The forces of evil started a long time ago and have become an important part of everyday life. The lives you live are wrong as wrong can be.

Historical correct it is that peaceful villages were attacked by warrior kings and priesthoods and the population was forced in to a life as slaves, soldiers and servants. Time has come to set you free.

The warrior kings and priesthoods got bigger and stronger over the years and started building their fortified cities, castles and monasteries in order to protect themselves from enemy attacks. Even the castles and grand houses of the rich in our present time are build as strong prisons, were the owners look them self in to be safe from all kind of intruders. It is not right.

The right and natural way to live is in self supported villages, in houses without looks on the doors and were everybody have all they need to live a good life on planet earth. No one needs more.

The Ark of the Covenant comes to Jerusalem

2 Samuel 6, 12-23

Jerusalem became David's royal city. He decided to move the Ark of the Covenant to his city, and he ordered priest to carry it with logs. It was Gods commandment to Moses too carry the Ark like that.

When the Ark came to Jerusalem, the priest put it in a tent that David had ordered made special. It became a great festivity and people rejoiced. David had assembled both a choir and an orchestra and they played beautiful for God.

People praised and thanked God for all he had done for them. They remembered what God had said to Abraham, Isaac and Jacob. They told stories about how God had liberated them from the gruesome slavery in Egypt. They also talked about Moses and Josva, who led them in to the Promised Land, were they now lived.

People sang and danced all day long and King David was the first in line. He was so happy for being Gods elected king and because he had the Ark of the Covenant close, so the happiness filled him. He danced around singing as loud as he could.

"Let the heavens rejoice and the earth be happy. Let the oceans and everything in them praise the Lord! Let the fields be happy! The trees in the forests shall sing. They shall sing of happiness for the Lord!

David was overwhelmed by happiness, but Michal, his wife, was not happy at all. She was the daughter of King Saul. Now she watched him from the castle window. "Why shall David make such a fool of himself?" she thought to herself.

When he came home that evening, she told him that she was ashamed of him. In spite of that they had loved each other earlier, noting became as before between them. Michal never had a child.

Jerusalem is a symbol for the new Motherland and the land around is a symbol for the whole world. The story is a vision for the future, after a new Motherland is built, a new superior Motherland council is elected and the whole world population is living under a common set of laws and rules for living. If you can't see this is because you are blind. Only the history about the lost Motherland can cure the blindness. Then you will understand that living under the rule of the three factors of the Original Sin is like living like a living dead.

The Ark of the Covenant is open and the Diagram Star will soon be back in the centre of all education. You will feel just as happy as King David when you fully understand what the Bible has been hiding all this time.

The twelve members of the new superior Motherland council are still equal to all other humans. Not one human is greater than others in the new world. The superior power is in the title the person is elected in to. The laws and rules for living given by the new superior Motherland council are the natural laws and rules given by Mother Nature. The whole world population will share the happiness of being free and sing and dance together.

The happiness over having the Diagram Star back as a guiding star for the whole world population will be fantastic when it happens sometime in the future, hopefully soon.

Do you understand now the tremendous impact the change from the present system of government with many national states to the global system of government from the time before the Motherland was destroyed, will have for the whole world population?

Every single human being will learn to know the Diagram Star and learn more and more about it during the lifetime on planet Earth. It will be like a special book that all humans know is the carrier of the whole world history. It is the first book known to man. The sun and the moon and the twelve star signs of the Zodiac are the model for the Diagram Star. It will be with humans until after the end of time.

Natural knowledge is a part of Mother Nature and cannot be forgotten. Even if religious belief is imposed on people, natural knowledge will always be present, telling you what's right and what's wrong in the world. In our present time and for the last twelve thousand years religious beliefs has been imposed in to the common world of thoughts. Also national belonging and the obedience to the laws and rules of your nation is imposed on you and the whole world population. Only by removing the three factors of the Original Sin can the natural knowledge given by Mother Nature be restored. When that happens there will be world peace and even the world leaders will dance and sing as loud as they can.

All the peoples of the past have made copies of the Diagram Star, the emblem of the superior Motherland council. The Maya people of Yucatan, the Naga-Maya people of India, the Babylonians, Assyrians, Egyptians and the Pueblo Indians in the southwest of North-America. Almost all of them filled the Diagram Star with signs, dogmas and assumptions that should explain why their Motherland was destroyed in a natural catastrophe.

This is not right to do, because it covers the original imbedded knowledge of the past. The Diagram Star is a diagram that must be in its original form before the history of the lost Motherland can be understood and read from it like an open book.

Now you know that the Diagram Star is to be in its original form, like it was before the three factors of the Original Sin were imposed on people. Call it sin if you like, but the chaos of wars and conflicts that quickly spread across the globe and resulted in the building of the many national states, is truly a gruesome crime against mankind. It was done by self elected warrior kings and priesthoods. The crime has never ended and the original Diagram Star was more or less forgotten.

In our present time the Bible is the Ark of the Covenant, and when the camouflage of religion is removed from the many stories and they are back in the Diagram Star, knowledge will quickly cover the whole world and put an end to religious belief.

The battle that King David is fighting, with the help from a new superior Motherland council and knowledge from the Diagram Star, will surly win over the three factors of the Original Sin. Only then, sometime in the near future, will there be a feast with a tremendous happiness that the whole world population will participate in.

David becomes a murder

2 Samuel 11, 1-26

David was a great king because he was so loyal to God, but one day he did not put God first in his life. He took another man's wife, and that was against Gods commandments. The woman's name was Bathsheba. She was married to a hetitt named Uriah, one of David's best soldiers.

When David found out that Bathsheba should have a child with him, he became desperate. He had to cower what he had done. David ordered his generals to send Uriah to a place where the battle was special hard. Then the generals should withdraw all other soldiers from the battle, so Uriah was killed by the enemy.

When the news of Uriah's death reached his wife Bathsheba, she cried for several days. Her husband had been good to her and she loved him. Now she felt overwhelmed by guilt.

Infidelity is a sin that no one shall commit, only because it is in their power. The warrior kings are known for their infidelity, and are almost expected of him by his people. It is a sin that never is forgotten, and both the involved sinners are punished by having to live the rest of their life without the feeling of the true happiness, love and safety that comes from living a life doing everything right. Right and wrong, good and evil, fateful and unfaithful, were some opposites that did not exist in the time before the Motherland went under.

An unhappy king

2 Samuel 11, 27-12, 24

Sometime after Uriah's death David sent for Bathsheba. He wanted to get married to her. Bathsheba went to the castle and became his wife. A few months later she gave birth to a boy.

David and Bathsheba could be happy over having a son, but God did not like it. David had done a great sin and he could not hide it for God. He had taken another man's wife and then he had killed her husband!

The Lord sent the prophet Nathan to David. Nathan said to him: "The Lord says that because you have done this, all your sons will fight each other, and this child will die."

David held his head low. The words of the Lord did sting him like a sword in the heart. He knew that God was right. It was no use trying to keep secrets for God. He said: "I regret, Master. I should not have done it."

The child died, but one year after David and Bathsheba had another son. He was called Solomon. It was something special about that boy. Solomon was chosen by God to be the wisest man that ever lived.

This is the regret all humans feels after having done something unnatural and wrong. It is of little use to have second thoughts and regrets. Humans can forgive each other, but the wrong doing cannot be redone and is never forgotten. The wrong doing becomes a burden of thoughts, discovered or not. True happiness is gone for good. With crimes like infidelity and murder on his conscience, David is now not a better king than Saul was.

The story is clearly describing the development of the warrior kings in to being merciless tyrants. Also the kings own people were submissive slaves, soldiers and servants. This is the great contrast between the times before the Motherland went under, when absolutely all humans were equals, not one greater than others.

Even if the Ark of the Covenant has come to Jerusalem, the Diagram Star and the knowledge about the lost Motherland was still locked in and guarded by high priests. In the darkness of oblivion there could never be lasting peace in the world. On the contrary the chaos of wars and conflicts increased and the greediness of the ruling elite only escalated, as it have done ever since.

You know the content of the Ark of the Covenant is the Diagram Star. You are now able to remove all the evil from this story and read the recipe for building a new Motherland. Can you do that? Can you look at the world where you live and see what the outcome will be if all the national states, the global system of capitalism and all the religions in the world are removed from the common world of thoughts?

At the time this camouflaged story was written in to the Bible the three factors of the Original Sin have fastened its evil grip on the population, who are told to look up to their kings as they were gods. The warrior kings and their priesthoods committed the worst of crimes, not only to individual human beings, but to the whole population, and were never punished. The kings still say that they are second to God. It is true that the democratic elected councils in the world were second to the superior Motherland council in the time before they died in a natural catastrophe.

After the superior Motherland council was dead and gone, the self elected kings all over the world could do whatever crimes they wanted and get away with it. This story speaks of the punishment that comes from doing evil deeds. The self elected warrior kings and priesthoods committed a crime against mankind when they took the land with the use of warfare and made the people living on the land in to slaves, soldiers and servants.

In our present time it is their descendants who preserves and passes on the three factors of the Original Sin from generation to generation.

Regular people are still punished in the worst thinkable ways for crimes they have committed because they are poor and have no other option to feed them self and their family.

In our present time the whole world population is unhappy and tired of wars and conflicts, and if the present system of government is allowed to continue, mankind will fall for their own sword.

The description of Solomon is the description of a man who would have been elected to be one of the twelve members of the new superior Motherland council. The description of his kingdom is all about how the new Motherland can be build, after the three factors of the Original Sin is removed from the common world of thoughts.

The young king

1 Kings 3, 2-5

When David died, young Solomon became king. It sounded nice to become a king with gold and glitter, but to be a good king and find out what's best for the people, is a difficult thing to do. When Solomon became king, he felt very unsure.

One night Solomon had a dream. God showed himself to him and said: "Ask for what you want, and I will give it to you.

Some people would have asked for things they could be happy with, good health, money or personal power. Solomon did not ask for any of that. He wanted something that was much, much better.

The young king was born in to a tradition were the three factors of the Original Sin was a major part of everyday life and ruled over everyone's thoughts. The question of being a good or a bad king was not an option, because there was and is no such thing as a good king in a world governed by the three factors of the Original Sin. A so called good king has to do bad things in order to stay in power.

This camouflaged story is a tale about human activities that are right and wrong. It is right for a young king to feel unsure. But it is directly untrue to claim that God showed himself to him in a dream and said that he could ask for anything he wanted, and he would get it. The dream and the wish are fictive and made up by the Master writing the story.

In a world with a superior Motherland council in charge, every council in the world could ask them for many things, but not gold and glitter. The gold and glitter are the camouflage that made the roman emperors like the story. They built their empire with the use of warfare and brutal force.

The people reading the story back then knew just as well as you do, that the large amount of gold and glitter in the kings possession came from attacking, killing and stealing from almost defenseless village populations. And it is the stolen gold, silver and valuable jewelry along with the national states and the taxpayers, that are past on as inheritance within the royal families of present time. It is done by willing servants, the political leaders of the respective national state.

Ever since the Motherland went under some twelve thousand years ago, a wise king would be one that took control over a lot of fertile land, gathered more slaves, soldiers and servants by winning battle after battle. They were mega criminals doing wrong.

It is the laws and the living rules of the leading elite that let all kind of national states be protected and passed on as inheritance to coming generations that are the legalized crimes against humans all over the world. To willingly let it happen makes all of you an accomplice. The definition of a sin that can be forgiven is that you don't know you are doing wrong. To pass on titles along with personal riches and large areas of land from father to son is also a self invented law that is as wrong as wrong can be. The burden of sin is heavy. Time has come to lay it down.

Therefore the king Solomon's dream and wish for wisdom is wishful thinking of the Master who wrote the camouflaged story.

Solomon's dream

1 Chronicle 3, 6-15

When God asked Solomon to wish for something, he replayed: "Lord, you did help my father David when he was king. He trusted you. Now you have chosen me in his place. I am so young, Master. I don't know how I shall be as good king as my father David was. I only ask for one thing. God, give me a heart that is filled with wisdom. Help me so I can see what is right and what is wrong. I will govern over your people like you want me to do it. Help me judge your people with wisdom, help me see the difference between good and evil."

God did like the answer. He said to Solomon: "Because you have asked for this and not for a long life or being rich, I will grant you your wish. Now I have given you a new heart. There will never be another king as wise and great as you."

But it was not all. God added: "I will give you also what you didn't ask for. You will be rich and honored. If you wander on my pathway, I will give you a long life."

You are wise enough to see what is right and what is wrong in the world you live in, and surly you can see the difference between good and evil. Right and good is the laws and rules given by the superior Motherland council. Wrong and evil is the laws and rules of every national state in the world.

A newly elected superior Motherland council is like the young king and will need everything that Solomon is asking for. God is the old superior Motherland council in the spirit world. They are powerless against the laws and rules of the national states. Only by building a new Motherland and elect a new superior Motherland council, the whole world population will be living right in a world governed only by the forces of good.

When a new world is built, there will be many self supported villages all over the world, and the elected council members can ask the new superior Motherland council for advice in all matters. Imagine now that it was the new superior Motherland council that in the beginning was uncertain of how to rule the world with only the forces of good.

The Master writing the story had the plan that the story had to be good enough to be remembered and passed on to coming generations. Now you are told the enormous difference between living in a world governed by only the forces of good and living in a world governed by both good and evil, and it is the Master of the past who is telling you this. You may try to imagine what this story would have been like, if the Egyptian hieroglyphs were translated correct. Then you could have read the full history about how the Motherland was destroyed in a natural catastrophe. With only the forces of good in command a new Motherland would have been built long ago.

Everything that comes to humans in their dreams comes from the spirit world. The Diagram Star and the spirit world are really present in the thoughts of all humans. The diagram shaped like a bright shining star is a symbol that carries the whole world history. When people lift their eyes to the sky and ask for answers, they are addressing the sun, the moon and the twelve star signs of the Zodiac. The Zodiac was taken down on earth and made in to the Diagram Star. The taking star has been with humans from before the beginning of time and will be with humans until after the end of time. All the religions in the world are defined to be dogmas and assumption built on not knowing the history about the lost Motherland. God speaking in the Bible is the voice the superior Motherland council, speaking to humans from the spirit world.

The spirit world is the aura that encloses the whole planet earth, and every single human being and all earth life. It is just as real as the air that fills the lungs of all living beings. As the aura or spirit is enclosing every human being, it is the receiver of the thoughts. The physical brain is the physical part of the receiver. Like this thoughts received from the spirit world can be expressed as words and activity. This is how all earth life, including human beings, knows how to live and how to reproduce in a right and natural manner. All humans know that obeying the Ten Commandments is the natural and right way to live. Still all the nations in the world break the commandments all the time.

It is utterly wrong to live your lifetime on planet earth with thoughts that are based on dogmas and assumptions that everybody feels are wrong and evil. But mostly all humans are living their lives controlled by a strong Wall of Ignorance. In order to learn to see the difference between good and evil, you have to see for yourself what's on the other side of the wall. You will know a paradise world when you see it. You will learn how the Wall of Ignorance came to be, and you will forgive all living human beings. After you have seen how the whole world was governed by one superior Motherland council and one set of laws and rules for living, your wall of ignorance will disappear instantly. You will know the difference between good and evil, and you will know that evil have no place in your world of thoughts. Your thoughts will be filled with wisdom, and you will lose your ability to hate.

A Master of the past had his degree in all the seven original sciences, often specialized in the one of greatest personal interest. Education was the most important activity all over the world. It was the spiritual strength and level of education that decided a person's position in the society. Every living human in the world had the same opportunity to reach the top in a world enlightened with the Diagram Star.

The life of Solomon was already planned in detail by the Master who wrote the camouflaged story the first time. Think for a moment again on how the warrior kings of the past got rich. It had to do with their thoughts and actions, and it was often the greedy and faithful advisers that wrote the official history about the king while he was still alive. They had to please the king, or else they would be killed. Therefore consider that the many camouflaged stories in the Bible were written long after they happened, and the ruling elite accepted everything as long as it didn't threatened their position in society.

The child with two mothers

1 Kings 3, 16-18

One day two mothers came to see King Solomon. They both carried a child, but one of the children was dead. Both claimed that they were the mother of the living child.

Salomon commanded one of his soldiers to cut the living child in two pieces, so they could have half a child each.

The first woman shouted: "No! Please don't kill the baby! Give the baby to her, then it will at least live."

But the other woman said: "You are right, King Solomon. None of us should have this baby. Just cut it in two pieces!"

The king sighted: "Give the living baby to the first women," he said to the soldier. "She spoke as a true mother!"

Judge you self in this case. It is an event from another era of time, but is just as valid today as back then. Women thinking like the other woman do not deserve the responsibility for a child. The story is told to promote King Solomon as wise and correct in his judgment. The truth is that the judgment could never have occurred in a world without the three factors of the Original Sin.

Camouflaged stories like this are like mathematical formulas. If they are about one man, the story underneath could be about a whole people or the whole world population, all depending on the persons given name.

Try to look at this story as the battle that soon will take place between good and evil on a global scale in the common world of thoughts. It is a very difficult mission to convince those who will keep the present system of government with many national states, the global system of capitalism and all the religions in the world. The three factors of the Original Sin are slowly destroying the world, and they think they always do right and the best they possibly can. They have to be told the full history of the lost Motherland. Only by removing the forces of evil, lasting peace will grow forth on planet earth.

What do you want to do?

A temple for the Lord

1 Kings 4, 20-28; Psalm 72

The most important thing that King Solomon did was to build a temple for God in Jerusalem. The building of the temple started some four hundred years after the children of Israel came out of Egypt and it took seven years to build. Cedar tree and gold covered the temple, both outside and inside. The best coppersmiths, artists and sculptors created a wonderful building. They covered the roofs and the floors with beautiful ornaments.

When the temple was finished, Salomon assembled the elders of Israel and all the heads of the tribes. The priests came with the Ark of the Covenant, the container of the two stone tablets with Gods Ten Commandments. It was placed in a special room in the temple. A cloud that covered God then came down over the temple. People understood that the Lord was close.

Salomon prayed: "God, I thank you for being able to build this temple for you. Thank you to my father David for planning it. But not even this temple is good enough for you. No place is big enough or tall enough for you. You have created heaven and the earth. Let now the temple be a place where we always can find you."

Then God revealed himself for Salomon and said: "If you do as I say, I shall live in this temple. I shall listen to the prayers of the people when they come."

Solomon built a beautiful castle for himself. It took thirteen years to complete. The hall with his throne was unlike any others. There was a lot of gold and jewelry there.

Then he built a grand castle to one of his many wives. It was the daughter of the Egyptian Pharaoh. Solomon needed a lot of workers for his big building projects. Men from tribes that earlier had been enemies now worked for him, along with his own people.

Solomon was very rich. Every day he eats from plates of gold, and he used knives and forks of gold. The cups were made of gold. Even his clothes had treads of gold.

The most important in his government was that he judged people with justice. He wrote: "The Mountains shall bring peace to the people… He shall rescue the poor who is calling, the miserable that no helper have." More than anything else Solomon was busy seeing that Gods chosen people had all they needed. This he could do as long as he followed the laws and rules for living given by God.

God as a creator of heaven and earth is a statement that needs to be corrected with the definition of God. The many Egyptian hieroglyphs and hieratic characters were translated wrong, but the stories have an inner core of true world history.

The superior Motherland council created the whole planet earth in the Motherlands image. This means that the symbolical twelve tribes emigrated from the Motherland and populated the whole planet earth. The common laws and rules given by the council preserved lasting world peace.

The Motherland and the superior Motherland council was the centre of the earth for a very long time. When the Motherland was destroyed in a natural catastrophe and almost everyone living there died, they became the spiritual heaven, remembered by the whole world population. When you know that the sun, the moon and the twelve star signs of the Zodiac, as in the Diagram Star, is the official emblem of the superior Motherland council, it is understandable that a temple will be built as a place where those who died can be remembered. But as the camouflaged story continues, the temple in Jerusalem was destroyed and the history about the lost Motherland was forgotten, because of the forces of evil.

The building of a new world is clearly visible in the whole Bible, under the camouflage of religion. The temple is an educational center where the teaching from the Diagram Star again becomes the most important human activity. God is the new superior Motherland council and Jerusalem is a good symbol for a new Motherland, a new centre for the whole world population.

It took seven years to build the temple and the number seven is a symbol for the seven original sciences. The building became big, strong, practical and beautiful and the best available builders and building material was used.

Remember now that the temple as described in this story was never built. The whole story is fictive and describes how a new world is to be built sometime in the future. All you have to do is to remove all the evil and all the gold and glitter.

After the new Motherland is ready built the elders of the world will gather and together they will elect a new superior Motherland council that will govern the whole world population with wisdom and the forces of good. The most important mission of the new superior Motherland council will be to make sure that everyone, the whole world population, has all they need to live a good life on planet earth.

The twelve members of the new superior Motherland council shall not build temples or castles for them self; they shall build centers for the important title they are democratically elected to possess for the duration of their life. The emblems for the titles will be the twelve star signs of the Zodiac, just as it was before the Motherland went under.

Important parts of the fictive story about Solomon are left out. Where did all his riches come from? It is said in the Bible that Solomon did put forward his share of gold, silver and jewelry to use for building the temple for God. Then Solomon sent out order to all the kings and tribal leaders in the region to come to Jerusalem with an equal share of gold, silver and jewelry to be used on his building projects. Those who didn't come or didn't pay enough was attacked by Solomon's army and robbed for all their riches of gold, silver and jewelry. This is how all the emperors of past and present have financed their wrong doings.

After the population was robbed for all their riches and made in to slaves, soldiers and servants they were heavily taxed and became very poor. Those who submitted them self and did everything Solomon told them to do, had to work on his building projects and was given all they needed of food, clothing and shelter. People realized that they were not better off than their forefathers had been as slaves, soldiers and servants in old Egypt.

How life was in real for both the rich and the poor back then, one can only imagine. The same taxpaying system is still valid in our present time and life is relative livable for everyone who submit them self and do as they are told. Humans that for various reasons fall outside the government system of their national state and don't pay taxes are still very poor and are treated like outsiders.

The story about Solomon was written a long time after he lived, and if he ever lived the story about him is made in to a camouflage over the true history of the Motherland. All you have to do is to leave out everything that is wrong or unbelievable in this story. Remove all the gold, silver and jewelry from the temple, the castles and give it back to the people. Back then, under the control of the roman emperors, the story about Solomon had to be written with the camouflage in order to be accepted and passed on from generation to generation.

Solomon did not follow the common laws and rules for living given in the commandments. The Diagram Star was kept hidden in the Ark of the Covenant and he lived and developed the use of the three factors of the Original Sin. That he did by passing on the titles, the land and the riches to a long line of warrior kings and priesthoods by use of laws and rules that was made for that reason.

It was the titles and everything they inherited that the population was forced to obey and respect, even if the sons of the leaders weren't cut out to be leaders of any kind. Royal families were never meant to be.

Solomon became very rich because he was evil against his enemies and relatively good against those who submitted and became his slaves, soldiers and servants. But still, back then a large number of humans died every day for reasons that comes from poverty. Poor people still die and it will continue in to the future, no matter what your national leaders keep promising.

The Temple Solomon built for the Ark of the Covenant is good religious camouflage. The description of the Ark of the Covenant and the Temple is very similar, everything covered with gold outside and inside and with many beautiful ornaments. Remember that inside the Ark of the Covenant is the Diagram Star, chiseled in to two stone tablets. The symbolism in this is that the knowledge of the Diagram Star that is preserved and passed on to next generation is of greater value for mankind than all the gold in the whole world.

Gold, silver, precious jewelry and beautiful ornaments will lose their monetary value the day the rule of the Original Sin collapses and leaves all humans with their precious properties, and nothing to eat for anyone, rich or poor.

The Temple itself, built with the Diagram Star as the ground drawing, is a symbol for all education centers. In the time before the Motherland went under, every single village in the whole world had an education center, a school open for everyone.

Education was the most important activity back then, before the common world of thoughts was occupied by the three evil forces of the Original Sin. The best students was sent to the education centers of the region, and the best of the best was sent to the continent of the Motherland to educated in to a degree as Master. It was a world built on knowledge about the lost Motherland.

Solomon and the queen of Sheba

1 Kings 4, 29-24; 10, 1-13

> *The Queen of Sheba heard about the wisdom and riches of Solomon and came to see him. She had heard about the greatness of Solomon, but she did not believe in all the stories about him. She came the long way from Yemen to Jerusalem to find out if everything said about him was true.*

> *The Queen arrived in Jerusalem with a very great train of attendants, with camels carrying spices, and much gold and precious stones. When she came to Solomon's castle, she asked all kind of questions.*

> *The wisdom God had given Solomon had developed his heart and mind. He could see problems from several sides and tell what was right.*

> *The Queen said: "I haven't even heard half of you. You are even more clever and richer than the many stories tells about you!"*

> *She gave Solomon many gifts, spices and precious stones. Never before had so many spices arrived to Israel. It was cinnamon, salt, Muscat, carnation, pepper and many other spices. All this was rare and very valuable. She also gave Solomon much gold; while he on his side made sure that she could go home with a lot of presents.*

> *Finally the Queen of Sheba said goodbye to her friend. She went back to her far away land bringing with her the stories about Solomon's wisdom.*

Under the camouflage of religion the wisdom spoken of in this story is the knowledge of the Diagram Star. Some humans are born more intelligent than others and carry with them an inner wisdom that is clearly shown through the person's thoughts, spoken words and activity. A truly wise person is always good and do things right. Knowledge comes from learning, and a king willing to learn can achieve a high degree of knowledge from teachers, advisors and priests. But there is a fundamental difference in being good and do right according to the laws and rules of the nation you live in and the laws and rules given by the superior Motherland council.

If you mentally remove the title and all the riches from Solomon, you are left with a wise man, a man of wisdom, a Master of the past. He was known to be able to divide right from wrong and therefore he was a good judge. You have to remove all evil and all gold and glitter from the story in order to see that the story is from another kind of world.

It is possible that there ones lived a king named Solomon that was known to be both very rich and wise. But then he would have been a good king living with the three factors of the Original Sin, meaning he was a nice and good person in a position where he had to be evil and do wrong in order to be a king.

When reading a story like this you have to be able to remove everything evil derived from the Original Sin and see the good from the Diagram Star. Then the global system of government and the lost history about the Motherland will come to surface in your world of thoughts almost by itself. The Masters of the past saw the stories like symbols and had a clear view of what was right and what was wrong.

It is also possible that the warrior kings and priesthoods had knowledge about the lost Motherland and the global government system that really could bring back lasting peace on planet earth.

The roman elite of rulers really tried to build a new Motherland and bring as many people as possible in under their control. They should have done it with only peaceful means, meaning without warfare and brutal force.

In our present time the use of Internet and modern technology has made it possible to reach out to the whole world population, but perhaps the Wall of Ignorance has grown too strong.

If the Queen of Sheba had come the long way from Yemen to Jerusalem because she herself wanted to see the two stone tablets in the Ark of the Covenant and learn the true meaning of them, then her visit would have had a meaning.

This camouflaged story is more like a meeting where two criminal leaders compare riches and personal power. Everything the two self appointed royalties have of property is to be looked upon as stolen gods from numerous brutal attacks on peaceful villages and rich individuals. It was their malicious use of the three factors of the Original Sin that made them rich and powerful. The leaders knew very well that their actions were a crime against mankind that only could be preserved and passed on from generation to generation by use of the right and the power that warfare and brutal force gave them.

The story about Solomon ends with his death, and his kingdom is divided. He reigned in Jerusalem over Israel for forty years. The number forty years does also have a specific meaning underneath the camouflage of religion. It is like an x in a mathematical equation, a number not known.

The test

1 Kings 16, 29-33; 17, 1; 18, 19-36

The division in 992 B.C. of the United Kingdom of Israel into two parts, the northern kingdom of Israel and the southern kingdom of Judah, was a momentous event in the history of the Hebrews. After about fifty years, a king

191

named Ahab succeeded to the throne of Israel. He married Jezebel, daughter of the king of the Zidonians, and built an altar and a temple to the heathen god, Baal, in his capital city of Samaria. He was sternly rebuked for his evil ways and worship of Baal, by the prophet Elijah.

The prophet told the king that there would be no rain or dew before he said so. And three years went by without a drop of rain. There was a great famine in the land.

A prophet is elected by God to speak his word. The meaning is that the words of the prophet shall bring the people closer to God, but then they had to be willing to listen to him.

Elijah lived much later than King Salomon. God's people had started to worship strange gods. The king and the queen at this time were Ahab and Jezebel. They were bad people. They had leaded the people away from God.

Elijah challenged Jezebels priests to battle. He said to King Ahab: "You made a mistake when you started following the false god Baal. Send me eight hundred and fifty of the prophets that eats at the queens table. Then we shall see who the true God is!"

Time had come for God to make a great wonder. The people should no longer be in doubt about who the true God is. The last three years the people have heard the king and the queen say: "Baal shall send us rain. Just wait and see."

But no matter how much the people offered and prayed, it did not rain. Baal was not a god. Only the Lord God could send rain to a dry land. Now he wanted to prove, through Elijah, that he was the only God the people should worship.

Elijah asked Baals priests to slaughter an ox. They should put it on an altar made of wood, but they should not set it on fire. He should do the same with another ox; also put an altar of wood. "Call now on your god and tell him to set the wood on fire under the ox," Elijah said. "Then I will call on my God! The God that answers with fire is the true God!"

The whole people agreed that this was a just test. The priests of Baal did everything they could to get the altar of wood burning. They prayed from morning to midday. "Baal, answer us!" But they did not get an answer. They danced and shouted louder and louder. But no answer came. No fire started burning under their oxen.

Now it was Elijah's turn. He poured four big buckets of water over his wooden altar. This he did three times, until the ditch around was full of water. He also poured water under the oxen.

Listen to God means, under the camouflage of religion, to listen to your inner voice, the voice from the spirit world telling you right from wrong. It means that you see with your inner eye and know that you do the right thing. It is the ability every human have, to distinguish right from wrong and know that doing right always will win over doing wrong. It is the way of nature. In this camouflaged story you know that it is the laws and rules of the nature that will win over beliefs invented by warrior kings and priesthoods. Just like Elijah, you know the outcome even before it begins.

It is your thoughts that you use on a daily base you shall decide what is right and what is wrong. Make sure that it is your own decision and not something you are told to believe is right. Don't be affected by the teaching that is imposed on you and your forefathers for thousands of years. Many traditions are in use all over the world and traditions and ceremonies that a majority of the population think of as right could be wrong. Christian ceremonies like baptizing, confirmation, marriage and burial are certainly right; it is only the words spoken by the priest and the religious belief that are wrong. All religious belief is camouflage over knowledge about the lost Motherland and is therefore wrong. But as camouflage the religion have been and still are very effective tool for the national leaders. Imposed belief is a mental wall in the common world of thoughts that has to be broken down.

In order to interpret this camouflaged story in to our present time, you need to know the Masters formula and have the ability to understand the story like you understand a symbol or a painting. When you know the underlying story, you will never forget it.

The formula says: Water, Fire, Earth and Air = Knowledge about the lost Motherland and a lot more. You yourself, with the formula in your thoughts, will with your inner eye see the full story underneath the camouflage of religion.

The prophets are spokesmen for the Masters, who always had to live undercover in order to avoid been captured and killed by the evil warrior kings and the priesthoods.

The Masters had and still have as a life mission to preserve and pass on the history about the lost Motherland and the global system of government to coming generations. The full history can be derived from the Diagram Star as found in the Ark of the Covenant, and the Masters truly did what they set out to do. They preserved and passed the story about the bright shining star on from generation to generation. It is the Masters who writes the camouflaged stories about the many prophets. The Masters could read the Diagram Star as an open book. In the time before the Motherland went under, the whole world population used the Diagram Star as their common book for education. Now you can read it like an open book.

Elijah is described as a great prophet, and the things that make him great are the wonders that he do. In real life there never happened any miracles at all. Not ever. The only miracle to be seen is the fact that so many humans believe in the wonders described in the Bible, and that no one even try to explain them realistic with common sense. It will be a tremendous revelation, a true miracle in your world of thoughts, the moment you understand it all and with your own eyes see the difference the knowledge about the lost Motherland and the Diagram Star will do for the whole world population of present time.

A battle between the god Baal and Israel's God is as symbolic as symbolism get. The God of the Israelites, always written with large letter G, is a symbol for the laws and rules given by the superior Motherland council, as found in the light of the Diagram Star.

Under the camouflage it is clearly said that humans are not meant to worship gods at all. The whole world population is by nature meant to live with knowledge and knowledge alone. It is the knowledge found in the history of the lost Motherland that can give you the ability to look beyond the laws and rules of your national state and see right from wrong. It is knowledge the whole world population have forgotten and needs to learn about.

The battle described in this story is a battle between knowledge from the lost Motherland found in the Diagram Star, and the three factors of the Original Sin.

It is our well known sun, the moon and the twelve star signs of the Zodiac that is the model for the Diagram Star, and the way the sun enlightens the whole world, the Diagram Star will enlighten the whole world population with knowledge. Water, Fire, Air and Earth = Knowledge about the lost Motherland.

What the prophet Elijah is using to make the wood burn is buckets of water, which under the camouflage of religion, is the knowledge that is necessary for the humans living in present time in order to be able to build a new world with lasting peace. Making the wood burn is a symbol for what will happen as soon as the knowledge about the lost Motherland returns to the world.

Fire and rain

1 Kings 18, 37-46

Elijah lifted his hands high, reaching for heaven and prayed calmly and slowly, so everyone could hear: "Lord, you Abrahams, Isaacs and Jacobs God, show us now that you are God. I am your servant. Answer me, Lord. Show this people that you are the Master. I pray that you answer with fire!"

Suddenly the fire from the Lord fell from heaven! The wood and the stones and the earth and parts of the bull were consumed by the fire. The heat was tremendous. It meant nothing that the wood was wet.

"Look! The fire fell from heaven!" people shouted. "The Lord is God!"

King Ahab felt his knees tremble. Elijah turned towards him. "Take the priests and prophets of Baal; let not one of them escape."

They took them, and they were all killed. By evening the rain came and thus the famine was ended.

This is a very bad translation of Egyptian hieroglyphs. It was done deliberately to hide the history about the lost Motherland. Still there are issues to be investigated in the matter of translation. It really did not matter for the Masters, because they knew the full history about the lost Motherland. They made the code or formula for their own use. The lost Motherland is Heaven and the late superior Motherland council is God in the spirit world.

Elijah is lifting his hands, reaching for the sun, the moon and the twelve star signs of the Zodiac. If you, the humans living in present time, are going to succeed, you have to do more than bringing the full history of the lost Motherland back down on the earth. The building of a new Motherland has to start. The election of a new Motherland parliament has to be completed in a correct democratic manner. Then the twelve new members of the superior Motherland council will be elected from the parliament representatives. In the time after all this is done, the three factors of the Original Sin will evaporate in the bright light from the Diagram Star.

The years with dry weather and the famine is a symbol for the darkness of oblivion that the whole world population still lives with. You are all longing desperately for a new world with lasting peace. The knowledge that you need is hidden in the Bible.

No one is going to be killed for his or hers religious belief. It is their world of thoughts that will change completely. The heathen God Baal is a symbol for the three factors of the Original Sin.

This means that the drought and the famine in the land of Israel is a clear symbol for the long lasting lack of knowledge that still is haunting people all over the world. Not the people and not the world leaders know what to do to recover the knowledge that is so important for the whole world population in present time.

It is the knowledge that all humans have hungered for ever since the Motherland went under.

The priests and prophets of Baal are the present national leaders and their priesthoods. They are certainly not going to be harmed in any way, because they truly do believe in what they think is right. It is their thinking that have to be altered ones and for all with a clear and unmistakable sign given by the forces of the nature. When the world leaders finally understand that their opinion of the world's history and the religions in the world is wrong, they will stop having the opinion.

Elijah is, together with Abraham, Isaac and Jacob, symbols for the knowledge that the whole world population has to possess before the new world with lasting peace can be built. The land of Israel is a symbol for the whole planet earth. The people of Israel are a symbol for the whole world population. In our present time the knowledge can be spread all over the world faster than the wind, by use of Internet and modern technology.

The whole world population has to open their eyes for the knowledge that is preserved in the Diagram Star. When it happens the enforced religious belief will disappear from the common world of thoughts like dew for the sun.

The Bible is the Ark of the Covenant. The lid is the camouflage of religion. As soon as the lid of religion is removed and the Diagram Star again can enlighten the whole world, the knowledge will truly spread faster than the wind.

A chariot of fire and horses

2 Kings 2, 1-12

Elijah had become an old man. All his life he had tried to lead the people of Israel back to God. He had a young friend named Elisha.

Time had come when Elijah should die and go to heaven. He had promised Elisha a double part of his strength as a prophet. But Elisha had to follow and watch when God took Elijah up to heaven. When they came to the river Jordan, Elijah took his mantle and struck the water so it divided. The two men went across on dry ground.

While they walked together and spoke, a chariot of fired and horses appeared and swept them apart, and Elijah went up by a whirlwind into heaven.

When Elisha saw this, he said: "My father, my father!" But Elijah had gone to be with his God.

Heaven is a symbol for the spirit world. Humans living in present time needs knowledge from the spirit world in order to be able to build a new world with lasting peace.

Elijah did not succeed in leading the people back to God, and the story goes on with Elisha. What does it mean?

The Master who wrote the camouflaged story is telling the people living in present time how the knowledge is preserved and are being passed on from generation to generation. The knowledge about the lost Motherland is preserved and passed on as religious belief in the kingdom of God. You know that God is the superior Motherland council and that Heaven is the spirit world where the spirits of all humans go when they die.

Knowledge has a cycle just like water. Knowledge will always be available in the spirit world, and all it takes to find it, is to remove the camouflage of religion from the many stories in the Bible. The river Jordan is a symbol for all the knowledge there is in the world. Now the knowledge is open to you. Then you have to tell the whole world population what the story about Elisha means, under the camouflage. People need to know that the knowledge about the lost Motherland is hidden under the camouflage of religion, in the Bible.

A strange way to cross the river

2 Kings 2, 13-15

Elisha stood looking up to heaven. It was a strange sight! Glowing horses galloped across the sky. They pulled a chariot that was so glorious that it seemed like on fire. Elijah was driving a chariot of fire. The wind whistled and hit Elisha. He used his hand to shade for his eyes. The light was enormously strong and the sand whirled around him.

Suddenly it was completely silent. Elisha lowered his hand and looked up. Elijah was gone. There was nothing to see on the sky any more. There was no wind. Elisha looked around. He was all alone.

He bent and took the mantle Elijah had left behind. Then he turned towards the river Jordan and hit the water with the mantle.

"Where is the Lord, Elijah's God", he shouted. In the same moment he hit the water with the mantle, two walls of water raised and Elisha walked across the river on dry ground. When he got to the other side, the walls of water fell together with a splash. His wish had come true. God had given him the same strong spirit of a prophet that Elijah had. The prophet Elisha was ready to go were God called him.

The word Hebrew means "from the other side of the river". It means that people on the other side of the river knew the history of the lost Motherland, and knew that the God of their religion is the late superior Motherland council. Then on the desert side of the river Jordan, the Hebrew people made their choice and put the Diagram Star in a golden chest and called it the Ark of the Covenant.

The other side of the river is now a symbolic mental desert and the people living there no longer know the story about the lost Motherland. They made the Ark of the Covenant and never stopped dancing around the Colden Calf. Try to understand that you and the whole world population are living in a mental desert, in the darkness of oblivion, like blinded and living dead. Your mental desert is covered with the gold and glitter and the dogmas and assumptions derived from the three factors of the Original Sin. Many humans live their life using all their energy striving for riches and personal power. The many millions of poor people use all their energy to make money enough to feed them self and their family. I am asking all of you to stop whatever you are doing and have a look at what awaits you on the other side of the river Jordan, in the Promised Land.

You should know by now that both sides of the river are on the other side. You and the whole world population can build the new world right where you live. The building of a new world with lasting peace can only be built with a complete set of new thoughts and with only peaceful means. The new thoughts are the knowledge about the lost Motherland and the Diagram Star.

You and the whole world population are still living in the desert, in the darkness of oblivion, on the other side of the river Jordan. In order to find the knowledge you and the whole world population have to symbolical walk through a river of knowledge. You will find the land with milk and honey, meaning finding a life with a true meaning; a life in a paradise where all humans have all they need to live a good life. So come across, out of the mental desert and see with your own eyes the paradise world that your ancestors choose not to enter several thousand years ago.

Fire, water, earth and air are symbolizing knowledge about lost world history and the light strong as the sunlight comes from the Diagram Star. The symbolism in this story is the same as before, and it is the Masters method of telling the people living in present time that the knowledge about the lost Motherland is carried by the Diagram Star and has been taken in and are preserved in the spirit word, in the common world of thoughts.

The essence of all this is that the work in the real world has to be done by living human beings. Humans cannot make dry pats across a river, but they possess the knowledge that can open the eyes of all human beings, including yours.

The crossing of the river Jordan was also symbolically done in the camouflaged story about Josva and all the Israelites. You should know by now that all the religions in the world are like a gigantic wall of thoughts based on imposed religious belief. The Israelites broke down the walls of Jericho with the use of the knowledge hidden in the Ark of the Covenant.

The walls of Jericho are a symbol for all the three factors of the Original Sin. The story shows that knowledge truly can win over all religious belief.

The crossing of the Red Sea is also a symbol for the ocean of knowledge that the whole world population will need to learn before they can start building a new world with lasting peace. The story tells that one's upon a time the whole world population knew the history about the lost Motherland.

The prophet Elisha is crossing the river Jordan alone, and his mission in life is to preserve and pass on the knowledge he received from Elijah. Mentally he walks in to the land of milk and honey, because he knows the full history about the lost Motherland and he knows what's in the Ark of the Covenant.

Look at the world you live in. The whole world population is still blind and living their lives as living dead, while watching the world being destroyed around them. It is a fact that the government system with many national states, a global system of capitalism and all the religions in the world, are destroying the planet we all live on.

Planet Earth is inside one of many long term cycles, and it is difficult to tell exact what is caused by destructive human activity and what is caused by Mother Nature itself. It really doesn't matter a lot; because the destructive human activities have to stop anyway if our children and their descendants shall have a planet earth to live on.

The destructive human activity is caused by the three factors of the Original Sin, and it is only the knowledge uncovered from the Bible and the Diagram Star that can help mankind to build a new world order with lasting peace. It is a well founded fact that you all still are working slaves, soldiers and servants under the rule of a government system that first was enforced by the Pharaoh in old Egypt. Only knowledge about the lost Motherland can set you all free.

The oil jar that never got empty

2 Kings 4, 1-7

Elisha travelled all over the country. Everywhere he spoke to the people. He tried to stop them from worship false gods. He gave advice to both kings and poor people. Elisha asked everyone to receive the love of God. Because the Holy Spirit was over him, he did great wonders in the name of God.

One wonder did help a mother to avoid seeing her two sons sold as slaves. This woman was a widow after a prophet of God. The evil queen Jezebel was still in power, and she was behind many killings of Gods prophets. The widow had two small children, and there was no money in the house.

On this time it was difficult for a widow to earn money. The woman had no one to help her. One day she said to Elisha: "Help me! My husband is dead. You know that he believed in God and served him. But I own so much money, and I have nothing to pay with. The man I own the money to say that he will come and take my children if I don't pay him soon. We will be sold as slaves, both me and the boys! Help me!"

"How shall I be able to help you?" answered Elisha. He thought about it. "What do you have in the house?" he asked. "Is there anything you can sell?"

The woman shook her head. She gave her two boys a hug. "I have nothing but a jar with ointment oil," she said.

Elisha said: "Go to all your neighbors and borrow empty jars. Ask for as many as you can. Carry them inn to your house and then take your sons with you inside and close the door. Pour ointment oil in all the jars you have collected, and put them aside."

She did as Elisha said. She walked around to all the neighbors and collected as many jars she could get hold of. Then she closed the door and started filling them with oil.

She poured and she poured. First one jar was full, then one more and then one jar after the other! But the little jar with ointment oil was always full. How could it contain so much oil? She said to one of the boys: "Get another jar!"

"You filled the last," he answered.

The woman looked at the many jars that filled the house. She shook her head wondering. Then she went to tell Elisha what had happened. He said: "Go and sell the oil, and pay your dept. Then you and the boys can live on what's left."

Wonders like this did never happen at that time, and not before and not later. This story is a symbol. In other words the story is an Egyptian hieroglyph wrongly translated. What it tells is what will happen as soon as the three factors of the Original Sin are removed from the common world of thoughts. The prophet Elisha is a symbol for the knowledge about the lost Motherland. It is the knowledge the whole world population needs in order to be able to build a new world with lasting peace.

The woman and her two sons is a symbol for the trust the whole world population has to show the history about the lost Motherland when hearing it told. Trusting that the story is true will help the whole world population in getting rid of the three factors of the Original Sin, even when not really knowing what the outcome will be.

The outcome of accepting the story about the lost Motherland will be like making a mental journey back in time, to before the time the Motherland went under, and finding the history and the global government system that kept the world peaceful for so long. Furthermore the outcome will be like making a mental journey back in time, to the paradise world that Adam and Eve left.

After you have seen the Motherland with your inner eye you will be able to begin planning to build a new world with lasting peace for your children and their descendants.

The jar of ointment oil is a symbol for the knowledge that will remove all religious belief from the whole world. The global system of capitalism will be removed along with all the national states in the world. Only then there will be enough food for all humans living on planet earth. Without the use of money there will be no rich and poor people in the whole world and therefore there will be no more slave workers. Certainly all humans will work, but the work will be for the common good of the tribal community.

The happiness and respect that will return to all humans will be deep enough to last the whole lifetime.

The prophets of God that queen Jezebel have killed many of, is the story about the Masters who preserved the story about the lost Motherland and told it to everyone who wanted to listen. Some Masters were running regular schools under cover. They had to use a camouflage of religion over the many stories about the global system of government, with one set of laws and rules for living for the whole world population. In present time the leaders of the national states have no knowledge about the global system of government that can make their capitalist towers fall like the walls of Jericho.

What will happen when the history of the Motherland gets to be public knowledge is difficult to know. The work will be difficult. Read about what Moses and Aaron had to do in order to convince Pharaoh to let the Israelites go. Mother Nature is already helping by protesting against the destructive human activity that is caused by the three factors of the Original Sin. Pharaoh is a symbol for the world leaders, Moses are a symbol for the late superior Motherland council and the Israelites are a symbol for you and the whole world population. There is no way around, and now one can do the work for you. The world is one and the whole world population has to do the work together, starting now.

Escaping from God

Jonah 1, 1-3

Ones upon the time there was a man named Jonah? He was of God's chosen people, the Israelites. On day God said to Jonah: "I want you to go to the city of Ninive. Tell them that they live their lives wrong, and that I will punish them."

Jonah did not like Ninive. The inhabitants were enemies of Gods people. But God was willing to forgive them, if they converted. The people in Ninive were the worst in the whole world at that time. If God could forgive them, he could forgive anyone.

Jonah did not like this. He thought it was wrong that God should care about them. Therefore he did something foolish. He hurried away from Ninive as far as he could get. Then they would at least not be warned, so they didn't understand what God intended to do with them. Jonah wanted Ninive to be destroyed.

But Jonah made a big mistake. It was impossible to hide from God. He is everywhere and knows everything. Jonah went to a harbor named Joppe. It is where the city Tel Aviv is in our present time. In Joppe Jonah walked along the quay looking for a ship that could take him to another part of the world. Jonah found a ship bound for Tarsis. It was far enough.

To convert is to find a new knowledge and change your world of thoughts. When humans look at each other as enemies, it is their thoughts that are in direct opposition to each other. During the last some twelve thousand years, ever since the Motherland went under, both sides of the enemies have been equally wrong, fighting for the wrong reasons, believing to be right.

In order to break the circle of evil, the whole world population has to get together and build a new Motherland. Only after a new superior Motherland council has been elected to lead the whole world population with one set of laws and rules for everyone, the chaos of wars and conflicts will end.

Read again how the new superior Motherland council will be elected. Only a global democratic elected council can be omnipresent, omniscient and omnipotent in the world.

The worst enemy of the whole world population in our present time is the human thoughts and decisions that are derived from the three factors of the Original Sin. The common world of thoughts is occupied by wrong and evil thoughts.

Jonah is a symbol for the history of the Motherland and the global system of government that makes all humans think right and do only things that by nature is the right thing to do.

The city of Ninive is a symbol for the whole planet Earth and the people living there are you and the whole world population. It is the common world of thinking that is so terribly wrong. And no one knows that their thinking is wrong and the destructive and unnatural activity that they think is right is destroying planet Earth as home for mankind.

Someone have to tell the world leaders and the whole world population exactly what they do wrong and what they have to stop doing in order to be able build a new world with lasting world peace, for our children and their descendants. I am doing just that to the best of my ability, and all of you have to do is listen and learn.

It is not easy for anyone to accept that the whole common world of thoughts is utterly wrong. You are all the population of the city of Ninive. If you don't change your way of thinking and doing, the whole planet earth will be destroyed by the forces of Mother Nature.

If you all change your way of thinking and doing to only good and right according to the laws and rules of Mother Nature, you will certainly be forgiven.

The laws and rules for living given by the superior Motherland council is the laws and rules that are right by nature and you will have nowhere to escape to when the time comes that Mother Nature is putting her foot down!

Storm on the Ocean

Jonah 1, 4-16

As soon as Jonah had entered the ship, he laid down to sleep. He thought that he could relax, because he had escaped from God. He was wrong.

The Lord sent a strong wind over the ocean. The waves were high as houses, and the ship was thrown up and down, back and forth. The sailors said: "It must be a reason for this to happen. Someone onboard must have behaved so bad that his god is angry with him!"

All the sailors prayed to their gods. They prayed to be saved. But the wind just howled and the waves got bigger and bigger.

The captain went under deck and woke Jonah. "How can you sleep in a storm like this?" he asked. "You should pray to your God. Perhaps he can save us."

When the men onboard heard that Jonah was Jewish, they got scared. They had heard about Israel's God. They gasped. "Are you trying to escape from him?" They all knew it was impossible. God sees everything.

"It is your God that is punishing us. How shall we end this storm?

"If you throw me overboard, the storm will die down," said Jonah. First they would not hear talk about anything like that, but they had no choice. They prayed to Jonahs God: "O, Master. Don't kill us in this storm. We haven't done anything wrong. It is this man that is to blame."

They had no choice. Jonah was thrown out in the roaring ocean. Suddenly the wind stopped blowing and the waves calmed down.

Like that it is in our present time. You are all carrying a Jonah in your world of thoughts. You are all escaping from the knowledge given to you by the Diagram Star, in a world with an escalating chaos of wars and conflicts.

The symbolism is clear and very important. What happens in this story is the same thing that happens when Jesus Christ calms the storm on the sea. There is a symbolic storm increasing in strength in the world at present time. It is a storm that started some twelve thousand years ago, after the common laws and rules for living were abandoned and the three factors of the Original Sin came to be.

It is the laws and rules for living that is made up by the many national states in the world, that really is about to destroy planet Earth completely. The present storm is truly killing thousands of humans every day, and because most of what happens all over the world is within the laws and living rules of a national states, and no one can do anything to stop it from continuing. The only force that can stop mankind from destroying the planet they live on is knowledge, knowledge about the lost Motherland that will change the common world of thoughts completely.

Therefore you and the whole world population have to find the forces of evil by definition and get rid of them ones and for all. The forces of evil are the three factors of the Original Sin, and as soon as they all are gone, there will be lasting peace on planet Earth.

Jonah is a symbol for the thoughts that have to be told to the whole world population in order save the world from total destruction. To begin with the world population will not hear of it. They will deny that a Motherland ever existed. How can they stop the world and get rid of the most important parts of their daily life? Stop working for money, stop being proud of your nation and stop living with the many religions in the world? Can human beings really live together as brothers and friends in a world with only the forces of good?

It is really possible to eradicate all the national states and return to one set of laws and rules for the whole world population. Forget about all the religions in the world, because they all are just camouflage over lost world history.

201

After some time with an increasing chaos of wars and conflicts in addition to the growing number of large global catastrophes, mankind has no choice. Don't wait too long before you change your way of thinking, because you are truly on a sinking ship.

The big fish

Jonah 1, 7-2, 10

When the sailors had thrown Jonah overboard, he felt something cold and slimy around him. He would have screamed in fear if he had not been under water. A gigantic fish was swimming around him!

Suddenly the fish opened the mouth wide and a moment later he had swallowed Jonah! Because the fish was so big Jonah could stand inside it, and he could breathe too. But it was dark and the smell was bad.

It was not by change the big fish swallowed Jonah. God had sent it to teach Jonah a lesson. No matter where he went, he could not escape from God. God wanted Jonah to do what he was asked to do, and go to Ninive with his message.

After a while Jonah prayed to God for forgiveness for his attempt to escape. He thanked God for not forgetting him.

After three days and nights the Lord made it happen that the big fish throw Jonah up on dry land. In one moment he was inside the fish and in the next on the dry sandy seashore.

Do you now understand that all the stories in the bible are about you, always about the humans living in present time? To be saved by the big fish is a symbol for the unbelievable rescue the whole world population needs right now. Humanity will possibly continue to live in the darkness of oblivion, even within an ocean of knowledge, until the common world of thoughts has been cleansed and the building of a new world with lasting peace can begin.

Mother Nature is not giving up making mankind return to living their lives as nature intended, in a world just like the paradise it was before the Motherland was destroyed in a natural catastrophe. After twelve thousand years in a mental darkness, with a life as living dead, now time has come to do what you now know is right. Jonah in present time is you. Now you are told and you have to inform the whole world population. If mankind as we know it is going to survive the next thousand years, you have no choice.

Jonah changes his decision

Jonah 3, 1-10

Again God said to Jonah: "Go to Ninive and speak my word to the people there." This time Jonah did as God said. Ninive was a very large city. The houses laid scattered for miles in a circle. Jonah used three days to walk around in the city. The whole time he shouted: "The city Ninive will be destroyed after forty days!"

The people in Ninive, who heard Jonah, were shocked. This was ugly news. They listened to the warnings from God and believed in him. They took of their nice clothes and dressed in coats made from sacks. They stopped eating and spent several days in prayer. Everyone, from the poorest beggar to the richest farmers, asked God to forgive them for having been so evil.

Even the king of Ninive took of his fine coat and dressed in clothes made from sacks. He ordered everyone to do like he did. "No one is allowed to eat, not even the animals!"

When God saw that the people in the city were grieving and would convert, he forgave them.

The number three and the number forty along with other numbers used in the camouflaged bible stories have a certain meaning. They are never picked in random and are like a number not known, like an x in a mathematical equation.

God is the superior Motherland council in the spirit world and Jonah is the messenger telling the world population in present time that if they don't stop their evil activity, the whole world will be destroyed. You are hereby told that if the world population in present time continues to live with the three factors of the Original Sin as they have done for the last some twelve thousand years, the whole world will be destroyed by the strong forces of Mother Nature.

Understand this right. Planet earth will continue to be a green and fertile planet for a long time before it becomes uninhabitable for earth life. If mankind continues to live with the three factors of the Original Sin, life will continue to be a living hell for billions of human beings. How many more humans shall die, not knowing why they ever lived?

Who have the power to tell the world leaders to stop what they are doing? Who can make them understand that the quest for money and personal power is wrong? Who can tell them that the building of many national states was wrong? Who can tell them that all the religions in the world are wrong?

Only Mother Nature has the strength to do gather the whole world population and force them to start making the right choices. Only Mother Nature will forgive the whole world population and give them the chance to really build a new world with lasting peace. But someone has to tell the world leaders how to begin.

Mother Nature needs many human messengers to explain to the whole world population how to build a new world with lasting peace, and this is where you come in. If you hate the world that you live in, and know how to make the whole world population change their evil ways, you have to tell them. Don't try to hide from what's unavoidable, like Jonah did.

The global warming is a fact and the leaders of the world don't have a clue about what to do. The use of a lot of money only makes things worse. The destructive human activity will soon reach a point were all production of oil have to stop completely. The consequences cannot be avoided. There is no half way about it. The new global system of government, with a new Motherland, has to be implemented over a relative long period of time. It is done by first removing the three factors of the Original Sin.

It is a fact that the whole world population has to work together in order to save mankind from destroying planet Earth completely. It has to be done while we still have Internet and modern technology.

Don't misunderstand this. The new world that we can begin planning will have production factories for everything humans will need in order to live a good life. The technology will find its way back on the right track and the common world of thoughts will be a world that everyone understands. Humans are not meant to live with hope, but with everything they hope for.

God is good

Jonah 4, 1-11

When God decided to let the people in Ninive live, Jonah got angry and very unhappy. "Master, how can you save Ninive, the gruesome city and all the evil people? It is not just!"

The Master answered: "Jonah, what's the matter with you? Why are you so agitated?

Jonah walked to a place east of the city, were he sat and sulked. It was hot in the sun and God made a plant grow up, to give him shade. Thanks to the plant he could look out over the whole city without being bothered by the sun. Jonah thought that the plant was the only good thing in his life.

But God let a serpent sting the plant and when the sun came up the next day, it was withered. God sent for the hot wind from east and the sun was hot over the head of Jonah. He did not feel good at all this day, and he prayed: "Master, I am mad at this plant. Even the plant has failed me. I would rather die than live."

"Why are you mad at the plant, Jonah?" God asked.

"I want it back again," Jonah answered.

Then the Master said: "You are angry because a plant dies. You want it to live, even if you didn't plan it. It came up one night and died the next night. Why should I not care if hundred thousand humans die in Ninive? They did not know how many bad things they did before you told them. This was the reason I sent you to them. They needed to learn the difference between good and evil. Though you they have met me."

Jonah now understood that God had thought him a very important lesson.

This camouflaged story is all about you and the whole world population in present time. You don't know that the three factors of the Original Sin is evil and destructive, slowly destroying the planet that you all live on.

What impact from Mother Nature is needed, before you stop doing what you do and start living like nature intended all earth life to live?

The strong sunshine is a symbol for the Diagram Star. Jonah is a symbol for the Masters back then; the only humans who knew the full history of the Motherland and the global system of government that really are the only government system that can be the foundation for a new world with lasting peace.

Perhaps this is the last change ever, that mankind will get from the spirit world to change their way of living.

You too will all be forgiven and can continue to live on planet Earth, but it has to be without the three factors of the Original Sin. They are all manmade and are as follows: the many national states, the global capitalistic system and all the religions in the world.

You all have to realize what's wrong in the world. Humans did learn about good and evil when they had to leave a paradise world. It happened after the Motherland was destroyed in a natural catastrophe some twelve thousand years ago.

There are a great difference between the good that comes from doing wrong and the good that comes from doing right. Now time has come to remove all doing wrong from the common thoughts of mankind, and thereby let the good get back is natural meaning.

You are all living with the three factors of the Original Sin as a part of your daily life, and not one of you have had the time to do anything other than continue were your parents and forefathers left of, and do your best to create a good life for you self and your family. You cannot get to know that you are doing wrong unless you are told. What does it take to convince you to look for yourself, under the camouflage of religion, and find the truth?

I am giving you the opportunity to look back in time, more than twelve thousand years, and see for yourself that life was only good back then, and what life on earth can be like for our children and their descendants.

What will you do the day that all the fertile land in the world has been turned in to a dry desert and the sun is burning hot? It is like that millions of humans have lived every day for some twelve thousand years. The madness has to stop now.

No one can eat money, gold, silver and precious stones and there are no protection, no human rights behind all the national borders when everyone who lives there begins to slowly starve to death. All the religions in the world are just a simple camouflage over the knowledge that really can save mankind from self destruction.

Mother Nature can and will forgive you all, if you choose to convert and begin living in to the bright light of the Diagram Star. The message from the many camouflaged stories in the Bible is the knowledge about the lost Motherland and a global government system with common laws and rules for living. It is the only knowledge that can save the world from going under.

Jeremiah stays with the people

2 King 25, 8-24; Jeremiah 39, 8-14: 40, 1-6; 52, 12-30

For a long time God sent prophets who should warn the people. If they didn't stop worshiping false gods, they would be weak. Jerusalem would be destroyed. God's people would become slaves. But the people did not listen to the prophets.

Now time had come when the king of Babylon Nebukadnesar captured and destroyed Jerusalem. The king had given orders to burn the temple of the Lord. He also burned the king's castle and all the houses in Jerusalem. Every building of value was burned down. The whole city went up in flames!

Then the army started to break down the walls around Jerusalem, and the people was captured. They were sent to Babylon as slaves.

While Jerusalem was burning, king Nebukadnesar sent men in to the temple and the castles to steal all the treasures there. The soldiers took everything they could find, gold and silver. Nothing was left in the temple. Nebukadnesar took everything to Babylon included the large copper columns.

God's prophet at that time was named Jeremiah. Except from the poorest of the people, was that the only man that Nebukadnesar saved. The king gave order that Jeremiah should not be harmed. One of the kings captains said to him: "Everything happened just as you said, Jeremiah. The Lord has let all this happen because the people wouldn't listen to him. But now you are free. You can come with us to Babylon, if you want. There you can live safe. If you want to stay here, you can. You can do as you wish."

When Jeremiah refused to go with the king's bodyguard, the captain said: "Well, well, then you get to stay here with the people." Then he gave Jeremiah food and money and let him go. Jeremiah chooses to stay with Gods people. This was the poorest of the poor, the only people left in Jerusalem, a city in ruins.

This is perhaps difficult to understand at first. Jerusalem with the temple is a good recipe for how to build new Motherland. God's people are the whole world population. Jerusalem is like a theatrical stage for the Motherland that was destroyed in a natural catastrophe. In the time after the catastrophe the chaos of wars and conflicts started and never stopped.

Jerusalem after the destruction and the long lasting history with wars and conflicts is an image of the whole world. Tell the whole world population that the many religions are camouflage over the history about the lost Motherland, and there will be peace in the world.

King Nebukadnesar is a symbol for the world leaders in present time, and for the common world of thoughts that all people are forced to believe is right. Even the population in the rich countries is kept relative poor by use of national laws and rules for living, and most of the gold, silver and property are controlled by a small number of national states and individuals.

King Nebukadnesar and his army of soldiers is a good symbol for the common world of thoughts that the three factors of the Original Sin is creating just by being present in the world. Not even the world leaders can see the evil they preserve and pass on to the coming generations.

It is the world of enforced thoughts that is forcing the soldiers of present time in too merciless wars against people who thinks just like them, that they are fighting for the forces of good with God on their side. The winner takes all. The gruesome truth is that the soldiers on both sides in the battle do what their national laws and rules tell them to do. The winner continues to build his tower higher and higher, until a stronger enemy attacks and takes it all.

Like Cain and Abel it is brothers fighting brothers for the control over the as much land as possible, the largest population, and the largest army. What Nebukadnesar did to the city of Jerusalem, the present leaders is still doing to the world. Knowledge about the lost Motherland will make it stop.

The large amount of gold, silver and other valuables owned by royal families and individuals are nothing other than stolen gods. Before the Motherland went under every tribal family in the world were rich in the sense that all that they had of valuables was protected and passed on to new generations according to unbreakable tribal and family rules. Every item had family history connected to it. After the superior rule of the Motherland was gone, self appointed warrior kings and priesthoods started robbing whole villages at the time. The population was forced to live as slaves, soldiers and servants, or die. Like this the family and tribal history was wiped out and forgotten.

The city of Jerusalem is a symbol for the lost Motherland. Most of the population who lived there was killed in the catastrophe, but their knowledge lived on in all the colonies, kingdoms and empires all over the world. After the chaos of wars and conflicts started the kings in power made use of the common scientific knowledge, but wanted to wipe out the knowledge about the history about the lost Motherland and the global system of government. The kings wanted to build the largest army, be richer and more powerful than anyone else. The strongest of the kings wanted to rule the world from a new Motherland. But not one of the attempts to build large empires with the use of warfare and brutal force succeeded. A new world with lasting peace can only be built by use of only peaceful means from a new Motherland under the control of a new superior Motherland council.

In order to recreate global control with lasting peace, the Ark of the Covenant has to be explained. The closest the people living in present time can come to the Ark of the Covenant, is the Bible with the many camouflaged stories. Remove the camouflage of gold and glitter and the strong light of knowledge from the Diagram Star can ones again enlighten the whole world population and teach them that lasting peace only can be built with peaceful means.

The choice prophet Jeremiah is making when he chooses to stay with the poorest of the poor is a choice of which common world of thoughts he want to live his life with. It is a choice that you and the whole world population have to make, and you have to choose like Jeremiah did, in order to choose right.

Will you choose to continue to live with the three factors of the Original Sin as the dictating ruler of your world of thoughts, or will you choose to live with the knowledge about the lost world history that is given from the Diagram Star?

It is a clear choice between continuing to watch the whole planet earth being destroyed by greedy and selfish humans, or take part in the rebuilding of the global system of government from the time before the Motherland was destroyed.

A special school

Daniel 1, 1-6

King Nebukadnesar took several times large flocks of Jews prisoner. He made them in to slaves and forced them to live in Babylon. The last group of prisoners came when Jerusalem was set on fire and destroyed. In the first group, taken prisoners some eighteen years before, there were some young men from prosperous families in Juda. One of them was Daniel.

Daniel and his three friends came from god Jewish families. King Nebukadnesar had given the order that the handsomest, strongest and brightest boys among the captives should be put in a special school. They should be taught by Babylonian teachers for three years. After that the best students should serve the king.

Now Daniel and his friends did not have to be slaves any more. But they had to live like the Babylonians wanted, and because they were Jews, it was not easy.

Just like Daniel and his friends was selected to go to a special school, is the same natural method used all over the world at all times. It is their degree of spiritual strength, degree of knowledge, intellect and personal abilities that leads the best students to the top as important leaders in the society they live in.

But they all have to submit and live by the laws and rules for living that are decided by the king himself and his advisors. It is the government system with many national states without a superior leadership that are wrong and have been wrong since the superior Motherland council died in a natural catastrophe.

Imagine the many national states in the world as a group of people standing on a field they have to work on together as brothers and friends in order to get enough food for everyone. They need a common set of laws and rules and a strong leader in order to make it work. The field is the planet earth and every national state has laws and rules of their own. The world needs a new Motherland.

Under the camouflage of religion Daniel and his friends are clear symbols for the knowledge and the common laws and rules for living that the Diagram Star was radiating out all over the world in the time before the Motherland went under. The Ten Commandments are totally ignored by the many national states, but used by the leaders to control the population.

Under the camouflage Daniel and his friends are symbols for the knowledge that the Masters do their best to preserve and pass on to next generation. In this story the Master writing the story is telling people living in present time that no matter what the warrior kings and the priesthoods do in order to wipe out the knowledge about the lost Motherland from the common world of thoughts, it is not possible.

Knowledge that comes from Mother Nature to the humans has the same cycle as water. The knowledge about the lost Motherland and the global system of government is in the Spirit World. Even if the knowledge is forgotten by all living human beings, it is still there in the common world of thoughts for you to find and use. It is only the knowledge from the Diagram Star that can remove the three factors of the Original Sin from the common world of thoughts.

Babylon is in present time known for its high standard within education, wise scholars, and scientists, craftsmen of all kind, and beautiful buildings and more. They used their knowledge to implement the three factors of the Original Sin. But if you mentally remove all the three factors of the Original Sin from this story, you will find a way of earth life that is equal to life as it was before the Motherland disappeared from the face of the Earth.

Nebukadnesar was one of the kings who valued knowledge and he systematically educated the brightest captives for his own use. Think for a moment about the laws and rules for living in the national state you live in. You are all captivated inside the national borders and from birth to death you serve your nation. Your democratic system allows you to choose your own leaders. It is the outlines of a prison camp if you ask me. Like Daniel long for the destroyed Jerusalem, you long for the lost Motherland. Like Daniel you can't go back because it isn't there anymore. But you can also do like Daniel and live according to the laws and rules of the lost Motherland, and do right in everything that you do. Only by living like Daniel, a new world with lasting peace can be built.

It is very important that you understand that all the people in the world have to work together in order to create long lasting peace on planet Earth. It can only be done by building a new Motherland and elect a new Motherland parliament with representatives from every tribal people in the world. Only then the force of good will become strong enough to remove all evil from planet earth.

The destructive enemy and the source of all evil are the three factors of the Original Sin. They control the common world of thoughts by use of warfare and brutal force.

There are no humans to blame for all the evil in the world. The world leaders as well as individuals are just following the laws and rules for living made up by our forefathers in the time after the Motherland went under.

With a global set of laws and rules for living and a new superior Motherland council elected from the new parliament representatives from all the peoples in the world, the whole world population would be like one large family again. The word peace would find back to its original meaning.

They were different

Daniel 1, 7-8

Daniel and his three friends knew that they were different. But they did not care. They were proud to belong to God's chosen people.

The names of Daniels friends were Hananja, Misael and Asarja. This was the best boys among all those who had been taken captives. The Babylonians let them study history and books about the language in Babylon. They were also given Babylonian names.

The leader of the king's court, a man named Aspenas, gave the boys new names. Daniel was called Beltsasar. Hananja became Sadrak. Misael was called Mesak. Asarja got the name Abed-Nego.

King Nebukadnesar gave order that the boys only should eat the best food available. They were supposed to eat a lot of fresh vegetables and meat, and every day they should drink wine. It was a problem. The meat and the wine the Babylonians gave Daniel and his three friends, was not prepared the way Gods people should eat and drink. The laws the God had given Moses was clear on this point. They should eat meat only from animals that was slaughtered in a special manner.

Daniel and his friends had learned the commandments when they were little, while they still lived with their families at home in Jerusalem. Daniel decided that he was not going to break the laws and rules that God had given his people.

The whole world population has broken the common laws and rules given by the superior Motherland council all the time since the Motherland went under. The Jewish laws and rules for living are like any other laws and rules written by humans. They were implemented first of all because they wanted to make it clear that every Jew is belonging to a very special tribe. They were the people chosen to preserve and pass on the common laws and rules of the past. They are the keeper of the lost history, the history that is the only possible way to build a new world with lasting peace. Obviously they don't know that they in their Bible preserve and protect the history of the lost Motherland and a global system of government. They don't know that the Bible is the Ark of the Covenant

Under the camouflage the Jews are only one of the twelve tribes that are the biblical Israelites, a symbol for the whole world population. The laws and rules for living that are derived from the Diagram Star are clearly stating that humans can eat anything they want from the part of the world that they live in.

Therefore it is clear that the Jews live according to Egyptian hieroglyphs that were wrongly translated.

The Master wrote this story in order to make Daniels and his three friends known to the reader. They are different in a special way. They are representing knowledge from the lost Motherland, and knowledge is wanted and needed by the forces of evil, as long as the knowledge isn't threatening their riches and personal power.

A test for the belief

Daniel 1, 9-13

Daniel went to Aspenas. He pointed at the food on the table. "I have come to ask for help," he said, "because I cannot follow the king's order."

Aspenas looked at the boy. He liked Daniel. The boy had touched his heart. While he now listened to the boy, he decided to help him, no matter what it would cost.

"But Daniel, it is no use. If the king finds out that I am not giving you the food he decided, he will certainly kill me. What shall I say when you look paler and thinner than all the other boys?

Daniel was silent for a moment. Then he ran to the guard that Aspenas had chosen for him. "Can you give me and my friends ten days? Give us only vegetables and water. When ten days have gone, you will see if we look better or worse than the other boys who are getting the kings special food. After that you can decide what we shall eat."

The guard looked at Aspenas. He nodded. The test was on.

Food is to be connected to knowledge and not to belief. Under the camouflage of this story the Master is telling people living in present time that the knowledge of the fundamental seven sciences from the time before the Motherland went under, was taken in by the warrior kings and priesthoods and put to use under strict observation.

Scientific knowledge became a tool for the ruling elite and it still is. The brightest students with the right family connections and good overall qualifications are taken control of by the national authorities and put to use were they can do the best job for the nation. But the knowledge about the lost Motherland was slowly forgotten or covered up in unbelievable legends, tales and myths.

Gods own people, the biblical Israelites, are the whole world population. After the Motherland went under a large part of the world population started thinking differently. Self elected warrior kings and priesthoods started gathering people in order to create peace and order. But they soon got greedy and started building large castles and churches with the use of all the gold, silver and precious stones that they stole from defenseless village populations. And the poor village population had no choice other than to work for the new ruler as slave, soldier and servant. After a couple of generations the history of the village population was lost. The children of the captives had to attend the schools the ruling king found suitable for them.

The Jewish boys enjoys a certain freedom because they are the best students in the school and represent the knowledge even the most despotic kings needs, but they are just as much slaves of the despotic ruling system as both the king and the Babylonian population is.

It is just possible that king Nebukadnesar and the Babylonian people came from another part of the world, and needed the knowledge in order to be able to control the population were they lived. Being a warrior king is equal to being the captive in charge of a prison. The king's castles are their prison and their guard of soldiers is guarding them well.

They passed the test

Daniel 1, 14-20

The guard kept his word. In ten days he let Daniel, Hananja, Misael and Asarja eat only vegetables and drink water. At the end of the test the four boys went to see Aspenas.

Aspenas did not believe his own eyes! Daniel and his friends had put on more weight than the other boys! Not only that, their eyes shone. They smiled happy. The other boys soon became out of breath, while Daniel and his friends were bursting of good health and energy.

Aspenas said to the guard that they could continue to eat vegetables and drink water for the next three years. God blessed them, and they grew big and strong.

God also helped the four boys to be clever and competent. They learned everything they could from the books about the Babylonian history and language. Daniel could even tell people what their dreams meant.

When the three years was over, Aspenas took the all the boys from the school to king Nebukadnesar. The king asked them a lot of questions about what they had learned. It was not easy to answer them, but the best and the wisest answers came from Daniel, Hananja, Misael and Asarja. The king therefore decided that they should be his advisors.

Like this your forefathers submitted to the rule of the three factors of the Original Sin, and you still do. This story is telling you how the knowledge about the lost Motherland survived trough the ages. Many Masters who lived with the knowledge about the lost Motherland became advisors for the kings. They never betrayed the laws and rules given by the superior Motherland council.

The Master who wrote this story had everything that should happen to Daniel and his friends ready planned before it was written down. Because the story was meant to be preserved and passed on from generation to generation, it had to be complete and wisely written. The story is all about knowledge and how little knowledge it takes to win over all the religions in the world.

The four boys know very well that they are Jews, and they remember everything that they learned at home with their families. They are holding their traditions sacred because they trust their parents to do what's right for them as a family and tribe. But as captives they have to adjust.

That is exactly what the whole world population has done. You have adjusted to the despotic rule of the three factors of the Original Sin and have done so for several thousand years. The forces of good are always second in command.

But the Motherland, the Diagram Star and the global system of government is not entirely forgotten. All the people in the world dream about a world with lasting peace and wonder if it ever is going to happen.

Now you are told that the recipe for building a new world with lasting peace is found in the Bible, under the camouflage of religion. The knowledge carried by the Diagram Star is going to make lasting peace come through.

The definition of God is the superior Motherland council. The strict laws and living rules that are natural to all humans is found in the Diagram Star. Now you know that a new superior Motherland council has to be elected and a new Motherland has to be built, with the use of only peaceful means. All it takes to break down the wall of religion belief is the knowledge about the lost Motherland. In this story Jerusalem is camouflage over the lost Motherland. Daniel and his three friends are a symbol for those humans who were true to the history of the lost Motherland, no matter what.

The fortune tellers

Daniel 2, 1-13

Just after Daniel became the king's advisor, Nebukadnesar had a horrible dream. He called all his fortunetellers. "This dream makes me feel anxious. I want to know what it means."

The fortune tellers replayed: "Yes, Lord King, tell us the dream, and we shall explain what it means."

But the king said: "No, you are first going to tell me what I have dreamt, and then what the dream means. If you can't do it, I will see that you all are killed and your houses destroyed. But if you can interpret the dream, you shall have rich gifts and honor."

The fortune tellers thought that they might had heard wrong, so they tried again: "Tell us your dream, and we shall be happy to interpret it for you."

Now the king got angry. "No, you will not be told," he said. "You are trying to deceive me. Listen to me! First you shall tell me what I dreamt and thereafter what the dream means!"

"But no king has ever demanded things like this of their fortune tellers!"

The king got even angrier. He stood up and pointed at the fortune tellers on their knees in front of him. "Now it is enough! If you don't follow my order, you shall all die!" Then there was sent out an order that all the kings' wise men should be killed.

But the order war not only for the fortune tellers and wise men. It includes the king's advisors and it meant that also Daniel and his friends should be killed!

This story is written as an historical tale, by a Jew who is describing the four boys as the smartest of all others. The king is described as a tyrant, staying in power only by the force of his obedient elite and many armies. All opposition is killed.

It is a story about the good and the evil, and shows how the good is stronger than evil in situations that cannot be solved by brutal force.

The story is a camouflage over the knowledge that can be derived from the Diagram Star. It was not only the Romans who killed people with knowledge about the Motherland and a global system of government. Many people knew that people wasn't meant to be ruled over by despotic kings and priesthoods. The Romans knew about the superior Motherland council that used to rule the whole world with one set of common laws and rules for living. The council was their gods and they really tried to build a new Motherland, but failed because they used the three factors of the Original Sin. The Egyptians, the Greeks and the Romans knew that all the people in the world used to speak the same language and lived together with lasting peace like one large family. They knew that every tribe used to be lead by a council.

This means that all the warrior kings and religious leaders in the last few thousand years have come to their positions in the society by use of other means than spiritual strength, knowledge and personal abilities. The kings were all bad leaders using the whole population as slaves, soldiers and servants. They became kings by means of illegal inheritance or by use of warfare and brutal force. Read: The national states, the global system of capitalism and all the religions in the world, all through our known world history, were never meant to be.

This camouflaged story is also written to promote Daniel and his three friends as the savior of many human lives. But under the camouflage it is the king's dream that gives the story a meaning that everyone can approve of and understand as being right.

What does the king's dream mean?

Daniel 2, 14-43

Daniel and his friends prayed. Late at night Daniel had a vision. He thanks the Lord and went to see the king.

"Can you really tell me what I have dreamt? Can you tell me what the dream means?" asked the king.

Daniel replied: "No, but there is a God in heaven who can. You saw an enormously large statue of a man. The head was of gold, the chest and arms was of silver, the belly and the hips of copper, the legs of iron and the feets of both iron and clay. A small stone fell from heaven and broke the statue in to dust, bit by bit. The stone grew and became a mountain that covered the planet Earth. That was the dream. Now I shall tell you what it means. Every part of the statue is a separate kingdom. You, who are the king of Babylon, are the head. After you there will be another kingdom, and after that another and another. Finally there will grow fort a forth kingdom, strong as iron. But it will be a divided kingdom.

This camouflaged story was written in to the Bible under the rule of the Roman Empire and is describing the development of kingdoms and national states in the world.

God in heaven is the late superior Motherland council. The large statue of a man is a symbol for all the national states in the world in present time, with their global capitalistic system and all the religions in the world. The small stone from heaven is the knowledge that can be derived from the Diagram Star.

The small stone is knowledge that will make the statue, meaning the three factors of the Original Sin fall apart and disappear from the face of the earth. The knowledge from heaven, from the spirit world, will spread quickly all over planet earth. With the knowledge about the lost Motherland mankind will be able to build a new Motherland and elect a new global parliament and a new superior Motherland to govern the whole world with only the forces of good.

You should know by looking at the world history that God of the many religions, meaning the late superior Motherland council, can do very little from heaven, from the spirit world. Therefore the knowledge about the lost Motherland has to be used by humans living in present time to build a new world with lasting peace.

The difference between the world of present time and the new world is best explained as the difference between Hell and Heaven. The world at present time is a living Hell for billions of human beings and the reason for their misery is the three factors of the Original Sin.

In the Bible the Pharaoh of old Egypt is the first to make use of the three factors of the Original Sin. The system with warrior kings and many national states is still ruling the world, and it is wrong as wrong can be.

The little stone falling from heaven is a symbol for the one little thought of truth that holds the force of all the knowledge in the world. The little thought, which is all about a global system of governing the whole planet Earth, is indeed knowledge stronger than all religious beliefs together. The little thought about a Motherland and one set of laws and living rules for the whole world population, will in our present time grow big enough to cover the whole planet Earth.

It is only a thought that by nature is right that can grow that big in the real world. It is a historical fact that the Roman government system is the foundation for the global government the United States of America is trying to enforce to the whole world population. Observe the little symbolic stone from heaven as a simple solid thought, right now falling from the common world of thoughts, crushing the present system of government in to dust.

The new world, with lasting peace, that you all are going to build for our children and their descendants, will have a new superior Motherland council and one set of laws and rules for the whole world population. It truly will be a kingdom that never ends.

A kingdom that never ends

Daniel 2, 44-49

God had shown the king that Babylon should fall for Persia. Later Greece should rule, followed by the Roman Empire. Rom was the divided kingdom in the dream. Then God should do the greatest of all wonders and he should use his son, Jesus, to do make it happen. His kingdom should be different. It should be built on peace, not on war. Daniel continued to speak about this, and now he was looking in to the future.

"While the divided kingdom rules, God will make another kingdom that never will end. It will last until the end of time. It is the small stone that is going to be large as a mountain and fill the whole planet Earth. God have shown the king all this."

The king said to Daniel: "Your God is the greatest, and the one with the most wisdom!" Then he appointed Daniel to be the most powerful man in Babylon, next to the king.

This is confirming everything that I have said. The kingdom that will last until the end of time is a kingdom with one Motherland and one set of laws and rules for every tribal people in the world. A new superior Motherland council will be elected and the whole world will be a paradise like it was before the Motherland went under some twelve thousand years ago.

This story is telling you about Jesus, the born again Motherland history. The kingdom Jesus speaks about is a new Motherland with a global system of government that has to be reinstated with only peaceful means. The twelve apostles is a symbol for the new superior Motherland council.

This vision of Daniel proves that this story was written at the end of the roman era, after the story about Jesus was written. My wish to see the original scripts is growing. The translators must have been Masters with knowledge about the lost Motherland. If they were, the Egyptian hieroglyphs were translated wrong with the purpose to preserve and pass on the history of the lost Motherland to coming generations, hidden in the many biblical stories. The Roman Empire was built with knowledge from the lost Motherland. Who knew and when did the knowledge end, if it ended at all?

The knowledge about the lost Motherland never ended because it is a part of human nature to know the difference between right and wrong. But the knowledge was covered by religious belief, enforced on to the population by use of warfare and religious doctrines. The kingdom that never ends was attempted built, but because of the merciless killing of the first Christians, the apostles and many others, the attempt ended with the camouflaged stories about Jesus in the New Testament.

The Diagram Star is the first book known to mankind. It is stated in the Bible that the Diagram Star have been with mankind from before the beginning of time and will be with mankind until after the end of time. Knowledge has an eternal cycle just like water, earth, air and fire. Only with the knowledge about the lost Motherland derived from the camouflaged biblical stories and the Diagram Star, the kingdom that never ends can be built.

History shows clearly that all the kingdoms and empires built by self elected warrior kings and emperors, have fallen apart. They are a form of government with many variations, but always built on the use of the three factors of the Original Sin and motivated by human greed and the quest for personal power over people.

In our present time the three factors of the Original Sin is freely used when building international companies and capitalistic alliances. They are the new kind of colonies, ruling planet earth in a destructive and negative way. It is the global capitalistic system that slowly is killing planet Earth, in close relationship with all the national states in the world and all the religions in the world. Together the three factors are a long lasting crime against mankind. It cannot and will not last. Humans living in present time do not have a choice. If they don't stop dancing around the Golden Calf now, they will continue dancing while seeing the last sunset ever.

It is a fact that the whole world population still is living in a mental desert, always on the move with a hope that the new world is going to build itself. Jesus, the born again Motherland history, came and left because the roman emperors and the priesthoods denied that the lost Motherland ever existed. Time has come to cross the river Jordan and discover the paradise world that this planet earth was, and can be again. Your world is your thoughts. No one can cross the river for you.

The whole world population is now witnessing that the climate on planet Earth is getting hotter because of destructive human activity. It is an activity driven and controlled by the quest for personal riches and power by individuals and national states alike. Their talk of God and willingness to help poor nations out of poverty is an insult to the human intellect. The whole world population is still working slaves, soldiers and servants to the national state they are born in to.

The camouflaged history about Daniel and his three friends is fiction from the beginning to the end. But it is a historical tale preserving some very important information about the lost Motherland, and is a prediction telling that all it takes to stop the circle of evil in the world is one little thought of knowledge. The little thought that you need to fill your world of thoughts with knowledge, is found in the Bible under the camouflage of religion.

The building of the kingdom that never ends can only come true after the three factors of the Original Sin is removed from the common world of thoughts. As the story about Daniel and his three friends develops it shows that the kings and their forces of evil is shifting all the time in battles where evil is fighting evil, while the forces of good is everlasting as a part of the nature of the earth.

Three brave men

Daniel 3, 1-18

Many years went by. King Nebukadnesar soon forgot all that he had said about Daniels God being the only true God. Instead he built a large statue of gold. He called it for his God.

The king issued an order: "Every time the royal music plays, everyone must fall to the ground and worship the large statue of gold. Those who don't shall be thrown in to the oven of fire and be burned."

It did not last long before the king's men discovered that Daniels three friends did not worship the large statue of gold. If they had done that they would have broken Gods commandments. The law said: "I am the Lord your God. I shall be your only God. Do not make statues of other gods to worship."

When king Nebukadnesar heard this he sent for Daniels friends. He called them by their Babylonian names. "Sadrak, Mesak and Abed-Nego, is it true that you don't want to worship my large statue of gold?"

The three men did not yield an inch." We cannot worship your god," they said. "Even if we are thrown in to the burning oven, we know that our God is powerful enough to save us."

With the same strength I say that the Diagram Star is the carrier of all the knowledge the world population needs in order to be able to build a new world with lasting peace. Under the camouflage of religion God is the superior Motherland council and it is the laws and living rules given by them that are preserved and passed on through the ages by the Diagram Star.

The Diagram Star is the emblem of the superior Motherland council and are the only the knowledge that is complete and can save the whole world population from destroying planet earth. The life as working slaves, soldiers and servants have to come to an end before it is too late. In order to do that the three factors of the original Sin has to be removed from the common world of thoughts. In other words it is all the national states, the global system of capitalism and all the religions in the world, which has to be removed from the face of the earth.

All through the history from Pharaoh in old Egypt to king Nebukadnesar in Babylon thousands of years passed by. From then and in to our present time a few thousand more years has passed by. Roughly twelve thousand years have passed since the Motherland was destroyed by a natural catastrophe. All this time the three factors of the Original Sin have ruled the whole world population. King Nebukadnesar is a very good symbol for the rule of evil in the world at present time. Your national state is calling the shots and you do as you are told. Living like blinded and living dead is the only life you know. Daniel and his three friends know about the laws and rules given by their Motherland and refuse to follow the king's order. It is all about living right no matter what, and you must do the same.

The large statue of gold is a symbol for the Original Sin and the right name for it is a long lasting crime against mankind. The crime called our common sin is still rolling over the whole planet Earth, unstoppable as a destructive tsunami because of the human greed, the quest for money and personal power along with plain stupidity. The Original Sin was created, preserved and passed on by the self appointed conquerors, and numerous warrior kings and priesthoods. It is still in charge of the common world of thoughts.

It is now some one thousand years since the chaos of wars and conflicts reached Norway and the Scandinavian countries. When Norway was gathered in to one country, the warrior king and his priesthood used the same method as Nebukadnesar to enforce the ridicules religion and demand a total submission from the population. Many good people were killed because they refused to be a working slave, a soldier or a servant under the new self appointed king and his priesthood.

The enforced religion that started some 1600 years ago has to be taken in to consideration. The roman emperor Constantine understood that the camouflaged religion Christianity not could be stopped by warfare and numerous killings. He took the religion, with the camouflage intact, and used it as a tool to control the many different tribal people he ruled over and collected taxes from. The religion became the third factor in the Original Sin and was enforced on the populations with the use of warfare and brutal force.

It is time to take the religion back and remove the camouflage from all the stories in the Bible. Time has come to start planning how a new world can be build, with the history of the lost Motherland and the Diagram Star as the source of knowledge.

The three brave men spoken of in this camouflaged story are representing the forces of good in the world. It is a true fact that the knowledge given by the superior Motherland council, as carved in to the stone tablets as the Diagram Star, has a cycle like water, and not even the hottest fire can destroy it. You have to be just as brave and do what you know is right all the time.

The burning oven

Daniel 3, 19-30

Nebukadnesar got furious. He gave his soldiers order to tie up the three men. "Take them away! And see that the oven is seven times hotter than ever before!"

The soldiers did throw Daniels three friends in to the oven. When they did the oven was so hot that the soldiers died.

The three men were no longer tied up. They could walk around in the fire. It seemed like they didn't have any pain from it. Even more strange was that there was a fourth man together with them. He gloved even stronger than the fire. Could it be Jesus himself, sent by his Father God to protect and strengthen the three men?

The king gave order that the men should come out. When they came out from the heat, the fourth man disappeared. Daniels friends were saved.

The king shook his head. "This is unbelievable! Your God is truly the greatest. He protects those who trust in him. From now on I do not allow anyone to speak bad about your God."

Daniels three friends, Hananja, Misael and Asarja, are in this story symbols for the knowledge about the lost Motherland that are carried through the ages by the Diagram Star. Jesus is the bright shining star in centre of the diagram. Jesus is the born again Motherland history and the carrier of the whole world history. The model for the diagram when it first was made is the sun, the moon and the twelve star signs in the Zodiac.

Now think for a moment about the Zodiac up there on the sky, with the sun and the moon in the centre and the twelve signs around it. The twelve star signs are the original emblems for the twelve members of the superior Motherland council. The spirit world is closer to earth, in the atmosphere, in the air that makes all earth life possible. Just like every living creature has an aura of life around and inside the body, planet earth has an aura of life. For those humans who knew the history about the lost Motherland, it wasn't worship to reach for the sky or burn a sacrifice on an altar; it was remembering the superior Motherland council.

This was common knowledge before the Motherland went under. It is the Zodiac star signs that are found hidden under the famous Bethlehem Star. It is the Diagram Star that has traveled over the sky, through the history of the world from before the beginning of time and will be with mankind until after the end of time. The knowledge it preserves and passes on from generation to generation cannot be destroyed, because it is in the spirit world, in the common world of thoughts.

Before the Motherland went under, education was the most important activity of all humans. Humans had to learn, and the ability to learn was a law of the nature that all humans were born with. Life was lived complete, with the safety and happiness that comes from belonging to a family and a tribe.

In the time after the Motherland went under, all education was mostly for the few selected elite families the king needed to control the population on his captivated land.

Living under cower was a small group of Masters, who continued to educate their students in the light of the Diagram Star, just like before the Motherland was destroyed. The Masters mission in life was to preserve and pass on the knowledge about the lost Motherland from generation to generation. This is important. Think of the Zodiac as a spiritual group of signs up on the sky, inside your world of thoughts and the common world of thoughts. Call it heaven if you like. Down on planet earth the twelve star signs of the Zodiac are carved in to stone tablets shaped as a diagram and called the Diagram Star.

Study the Diagram Star well. It is difficult to comprehend it all, so give it time. The studies will make it possible for you to find the way to the history of the lost Motherland all on your own. Like the whole world population, you have been living in the darkness of oblivion, not seeing and not knowing for so long, always depending on that everything you learn from your parents, in the schools of your nation, is right and not wrong.

You know by now that all the religions in the world, together with all the legends, tales and myths, are dogmas and assumption that your national state and national church believe are right. Even if everything they believe in are wrong, it is important to understand that it all have its origin from the lost Motherland. You need to take down the religion in order to get all the way back to the history about the lost Motherland. Only when belief is removed from your world of thoughts, the small seed of knowledge can grow big and fill your life with meaning.

With the use of the Diagram Star it is possible for you and the whole world population to recover the lost world history and the global system of government, and use it for building a new world with lasting peace. This story is telling you that not even the hottest fire can destroy the knowledge of the lost Motherland.

The king's celebration

Daniel 5, 1-13

King Nebukadnesar became old and died. The next king in Babylon was Belsasar. Daniel continued as the king's advisor. One day something strange happened. Daniel was now an old man.

The king held a large party. He was drunk and thought for himself that he had great fun. Then he thought that he just for fun would do something new. He would like to see all the gold and silver cups and plates that were taken from Gods temple in Jerusalem.

"To day we shall drink like gods!" he shouted to the guests. Together they praised their false gods of gold and silver. Then they drank from the holy cups and jars.

Suddenly a hand became visible, out from nothing! The hand started writing on the wall in the king's castle. The king became pale. His hands were shaking and his knees were trembling.

"Bring in the astrologers, the Chaldeans and the soothsayers," he ordered. "Hurry up! I must know what the hand is writing. The one who interpret the writing shall be rewarded." All the kings' wise men did their best, but no one could interpret the writing on the wall.

Now the king's mother interfered. "There is a man who possibly can help you," she said. "He is the leader of the wise men. It was him who helped Nebukadnesar to interpret his dream. This Daniel can perhaps help you now."

Gold, silver and precious stones is the gods the humans worship still. Working for money and using money is the main activity for the whole world population is wrong as wrong can be, according to the laws and living rules given by the superior Motherland council.

Warrior kings and priesthoods went to war against each other, and the winner took all the valuables from the looser and made the captives his slaves, soldiers and servants.

The cold, silver and precious stones that are owned by royalties and rich people all over the world are mostly stolen goods. It is the poorest of the poor people that are the rightful owners of the valuables that were stolen from their forefathers. Many thousand of the poor people dies every day from reasons that comes from poverty, a poverty they were forced in to by the self elected kings and their helpers the so called elite of obedient servants.

Do remember that the whole world population still is working slaves, soldiers and servants under the strict control of the laws and living rules of the nation they were born in to. It does not matter how much or how little money you earn by so called honest hard work. You are expected to use it all when buying things you don't really need, and it is the flood of money through the global capitalistic system that makes the richest of the rich even richer. They are slaves of the system to. It is the system that are wrong and people do the best they can, not knowing that their common world of thoughts have been occupied by the three factors of the Original Sin for several thousand years. Now you know.

The rightful owners of the riches of Babylon are the peaceful village populations that were attacked by the warrior kings and their soldiers. Those who were fighting back were killed and everyone who chose to obey the new self elected king had to give him all their valuables. Then they all had to work hard and pay taxes and dues to the king in charge and the priesthood.

The beautiful items made of gold, silver and precious stones had no monetary value for the tribal people living in villages. The value for them was their own tribal history going back to the first beginning. Every item had its own history. After the attack the tribal history died out and the descendents of the tribe are still living in a mental desert, not knowing, always searching for answers and wondering why.

The stolen gods were passed on as inheritance from father to son. The laws and the rules for living were made up by the king and his advisors. It is still the same self made laws and rules for living that is governing the whole world. They are wrong as wrong can be.

The writing on the wall is the visible and increasing destruction of the world we all live in. Soon, if not already, will see the royal families, the large international companies and richest of the rich humans, will begin to pay the price for their long lasting crime against mankind. The only people who can help save the world for our children and their descendants, is people like Daniels and his three friends. It takes more than one Daniel to save the world, but someone has to tell the world leaders what the writing on the wall mean.

The writing on the wall

Daniel 5, 13-31

Daniel was taken before the king, who said: "I have heard that you can interpret dreams. Tell me what the terrible hand have written on the wall. Then you shall be greatly rewarded. You will be dressed in royal garb and I will give you a chain of gold."

"The gifts you can keep for yourself," answered Daniel. "I don't want any reward from you. I shall read the writing on the wall for you, because the greatest God have shown me what it means. You remember Nebukadnesar? He knew that God is the only one deciding who shall be king.

But so much you have not learned. You have not shown respect for the Lord. That is what king Nebukadnesar once ordered. You have been so proud that you have taken the cups, the jars and plates from Gods temple and you have let your women drink wine from them. It is therefore the hand have written you a message to day.

The words are: MENE, MENE, TEKEL, and UPHARSIN. The words means: MENE: God has judged your kingdom and have finished it. TEKEL: You have been evaluated and have not passed the test. UPHARSIN: Your kingdom will be divided between the Medes and the Persians."

When Daniel was finished speaking, the king rewarded him. But the same night everything Daniel had said come true. Belsasar was killed and the Persians took the Babylonian kingdom.

The writing on the wall was meant for you all and the leaders and the whole world population in present time. If you think and do like king Belsasar your thinking is an insult to the common world of thinking, and your activity celebrating your riches and being proud of it all is an insult to the millions of poor people in the world. Clever fools are the right name for each and every one of you. You need to come out of the long lasting darkness of oblivion in order to understand the writing on the wall.

In the darkness of oblivion, without the bright light of knowledge from the Diagram Star, you are like blinded and showing off with pride the high tower that almost reaches to the sky. You are the blind man spoken of in the New Testament and as long as you live in a world with religious believers and not believers, you live your life on planet earth like living dead.

You should by now see the writing on the wall and understand what it means. The system of government with many national states, a global system of capitalism and all the religions in the world, have to come to an end. The negative human activity is destroying planet Earth and killing millions of humans in the process.

If the work starts now, it will take at least forty year to build the new global government system with one Motherland and one set of laws and living rules for the whole world population.

The writing on the wall is clear and easy to interpret: The some twelve thousand years with the three factors of the Original Sin and a constant chaos of wars and conflicts are coming to an end. Be prepared in your world of thoughts. The era has been a living hell for the whole world population. Now the knowledge from the Diagram Star will restore the global government system and recreate a true paradise for all mankind.

It is obvious that this camouflaged story was written after a long time with roman rule. It is an historical tale and wishful dream for the poor occupied people that lived, and still lives their lives as slaves under greedy and despotic rulers. The self elected warrior kings and priesthoods lived their lives using most of their time to steal everything they could of gold, silver and other valuables from peaceful village people. The owners fought hard to hold on to what for them was the family history and pride. Criminals are too weak a word for the self elected rulers back then, and the humans living in present time have inherited it all.

The Master who wrote the story could see back in time and use historical facts to create the camouflage that was necessary to make the roman emperor and the priesthoods except the story as not threatening.

The present government with many national states is totally against the law and living rules given by the superior Motherland council and planet Earth is suffering badly. It is a fact that Mother Nature is writing the message on your wall, for you and the whole world population to see. The aggressive and at time desperate quest for riches and personal power is slowly but surely bringing the whole planet Earth toward a final end.

Shall our children and their descendants continue to die without even knowing why they have lived? You have to do something to save the world. Jesus is the born again Motherland history. The lost world history came and left some two thousand years ago and can be found hidden under all the camouflaged biblical stories.

Look back in history and make an attempt to count all the humans who have died because of the three factors of the Original Sin. The writing on the wall is meant for all of you.

Lion's den

Daniel 6, 1-28

After Belsasar was killed, the median Darius became king. He selected three men to govern his kingdom. One of them was Daniel.

Daniel was now a very old man. He had served God of all his heart and all his power. He prayed a lot. Daniel had seen God do many great things and the Lord had blessed him with wisdom.

Soon king Darius discovered that Daniel was a better man than the two other advisors. The king wanted to put Daniel in command over the whole kingdom. This the two other advisors did not like at all. They collaborated against Daniel and tried to find errors in him. They wanted to prove that he was a liar and a deceiver. But it showed impossible, because Daniel was a good and loyal man. But finally they found a way to take him down.

Together they went to the king and asked him to sign a royal command which said that he was God. "The command said that no one should worship any other god than the king for the next thirty days. If someone did, they should be thrown in the lion's den and die there." The king liked the idea and signed.

Even if Daniel knew the kings order, he continued to pray to the Lord. All his life he had prayed at least three times a day every day. He kneeled at a window facing Jerusalem and thanked God for all his blessings. Then he prayed for his people. He hoped that one day the Israelites could return to Jerusalem.

Daniels enemies stood down in the street and saw that he prayed. They went straight to king Darius. "Do you remember the royal commandment that no one should pray to another God than you? Daniel is not following the order! He prays to his God every day!"

When the king heard this, he understood that he had been deceived. The whole day he tried to think of something that could save Daniel, but there was nothing he could do. The order was signed with the king's name.

The guard brought Daniel to him. The king said: "I cannot save you. I hope God will." And then Daniel was thrown in to a large cave with wild lions. The cave was covered with a large stone. What would happen to him? Was this the end?

The next day, as soon as the sun rose, king Darius hurried to the lion's den. He stood over the stone that covered the cave. His voice trembled. "Daniel! You the living servant of God! Have God managed to save you from the lions?" He held his breath in the excitement of the moment.

Then a voice was heard: "Yes, he has, my Lord the King!" Daniel was saved! "My God sent an angel and he closed the lion's mouth. God protected me and I am not harmed. I have done nothing wrong, my Lord the King!"

The king ordered the guard to open the cave. When they helped Daniel out, there was not a scratch on him. The king now ordered the men who had deceived him and sent Daniel to the lion's den, should be thrown to the lions them self. The evil advisors did not even reach the bottom before the lions had killed them.

King Darius next order was: "All over my kingdom shall people respect Daniels God. He is the living God. His kingdom will last until the end of time. He makes signs and wonders. He saved Daniel from the lions!"

Daniel is a symbol for the knowledge derived from the Diagram Star. God is the spiritual superior Motherland council in the Spirit World. Jerusalem is a symbol for the Motherland that was destroyed in a natural catastrophe. The Master writing this camouflaged story knows, and writes what everybody who knows is hoping and praying for: the building of a new Motherland and the election of a new superior Motherland council. The last order of king Darius, that everybody in his kingdom should respect Daniels God, is wishful thinking. No wonders happened, not then, not before and not after.

If all evil and wrong are removed from this story, it is the building of a new Motherland that becomes visible.

The power of kings, no matter how rich and powerful, is built on evil and can never last long. The power of Daniel and his three friends are a different kind of power. It is the power of a new omnipotent, omniscient and omnipresent superior Motherland council in a world without the three factors of the Original Sin.

The God or gods that all the kings and the priesthoods in the world claim to believe in is the long gone superior Motherland council. In order to do the right thing all the national leaders in the world have to get together and select a new global parliament and elect a new superior Motherland council and ask them to start leading the whole world population with one common set of laws and rules for living. It would result in that all the national leaders would lose their large salary and become an equal to all other humans. They haven't done it before in our known history, but now they just have to, or see the world fall apart, slowly but surely. They are the Pharaohs of present time.

The power of the spiritual superior Motherland council and the Diagram Star is always present in the world and cannot be destroyed. The sun, the moon and the twelve star signs of the Zodiac is the model for the Diagram Star and it has been with mankind from before the beginning of time and will be with mankind until after the end of time.

Daniel is a symbol for thoughts that are right according to the nature of men. Symbolically the right thoughts about the right way to live on planet Earth have been preserved and passed on through the history by the Jews, the tribe descending from Juda, one of the twelve sons of Jacob, named Israel. It is their tribal history that is the Bible, but they obviously don't know that the Bible is the Ark of the Covenant and the world history their history is hiding.

There is no power on planet Earth that can alter things that are good, right and true. But the forces of good can be covered up with a veil of evil. Twelve thousand years under the terror of the three factors of the Original Sin, with numerous wars and conflicts, cannot wipe out the knowledge that is hidden under the camouflage of religion.

Now look at this story in the light of new knowledge. It is the knowledge from the Diagram Star that have been looked in and hidden for the whole world population for twelve thousand years. When the knowledge in our present time is taken out from the Ark of the Covenant, it will be just as perfect as it always have been.

Remember now that the evil force of the three factors of the Original Sin still is the dominating force of evil in the common world of thoughts. The dictating teaching of evil is in the thoughts of all humans, and it is the common world of thoughts that need cleansing.

There are no other enemies in the whole world, than imposed thoughts in conflict over what to believe and not believe, and therefore the battle for removing the three factors of evil from the common world of thoughts, starts with a mental battle in your own world of thoughts. If you discover that your fundamental thoughts for living right are wrong, you don't have the wrong thoughts any longer.

You have the ability to separate evil from good in your own world of thoughts.

Only with the Diagram Star as a common leading star the new peaceful world can last until the end of time. Think about what the knowledge found in the Bible can do for your children and their descendants, when the whole world population finds a way to really build a new world with lasting peace.

Remember that twelve thousand years of living with the three factors of the Original Sin hardly can be disposed of overnight. The change will perhaps take at least forty years and it will have to be done with only peaceful means. Start the battle with only knowledge about the lost motherland and being right as your only weapon and feel the happiness of victory.

The proud king

Ester 1, 1-8; 2, 5-7

Not all Jews taken prisoners by the Babylonians ended in the king's city. Many settled in other parts of the Persian kingdom. The beautiful Jewish girl Ester lived a place like that. She had no parents, but lived with a relative named Mordekai.

One of the kings of Persia was named Ahasverus. His kingdom stretched from Egypt to India.

King Ahasverus was a very proud king. The best he knew was to show people who rich and powerful he was. He used half a year to show his elite of trusted kings and princes and army leaders in his empire how rich and powerful he was. They had seen his treasures and the castle, the horses and the soldiers. At the end of a period like that he uses to give a party, which lasted for seven days.

Many people came to the king's garden party. They sat on benches made of gold, silver and precious ornament. They looked at the wallpaper with threads of gold. They talked and danced around the fountains.

The proud king is just a mega scoundrel and all his riches and power is built on gold, silver and precious thing that either are stolen from peaceful village people or extracted from mines by slave workers. All the beautiful castles and gardens were built by slave workers.

The kings dynasties have shifted up through the ages, and the stolen riches was taken over by the new king. Some kings were strong enough to hold on to the power long enough to pass it on to his son or a trusted relative as inheritance. They became dynasties, ruled by one royal family for some generations.

But not one dynasty has lasted long, and the reason was often that the king made mistakes like being proud and showing of. Kings had advisors and helpers of all kind to rule the population, but the use of warfare and brutal force could not create long lasting peace. The enemies were many.

224

Under the camouflage is the story about what's the right way to lead the whole world population in a world with lasting peace. If all wrong and evil is removed from this story, it is a story about how a new world with lasting peace can be governed. In a kingdom as big as this one there should be many kings, at least one king for every tribal people. The king should not be one person, but twelve democratically elected leader with different departments, but equal power.

And the many different kingdoms all over the world should be governed by a superior Motherland council, making the whole world population in to a large family, speaking the same language and learn to live by one common set of laws and rules as derived from the Diagram Star.

Neither kings nor anyone else shall be proud over being the leader. In the new world that soon is to be built, there will be no stolen riches and property to be proud of for anyone and the democratic elected council members will be like any other member of the population.

The position as an elected council member is what the population is thought to respect and be obedient to. It is like that still today, a king or a president or any other political title is to be respected and obeyed through the ages, while the elected person for the title lives and dies.

In the time before the Motherland was destroyed, the best suitable person in the whole population was found and made a leader. The position as a leader of the superior council on the Motherland could not be passed on to a son or other family members. The same rule vas valid for any other position in the society. Education was the main activity for all humans, and the best students became Masters and the best of the best of the Masters was elected in to superior leading positions. Nothing was left to chance in this matter. The evolution of mankind was serious undertaking.

Therefore; all the builders of large kingdoms and empires with the use of warfare and brutal force, is to be regarded as evil criminals with the sole motivation of being the richest and the most powerful king in the world. And that's the motivation the present leaders of the world have inherited and takes for being right for them self and the population. They lead the world not knowing that they together are preserving and passing on the three factors of the Original Sin.

It is the three factors of the Original Sin that are the evil enemy force that you and the whole world population have to conquer and remove from your world of thoughts and the common world of thoughts. Not an easy thing to do, but you can do it.

Even today the human greatness is measured in inherited titles, riches and personal power and not in the person's spiritual strength, level of education and personal abilities. That is why the world still is a living hell for the many billions of poor people, and has been for some twelve thousand years.

The dance around the Golden Calf is still going on, and while the world population is getting larger in number, it is only the richest of the riches that still keeps on dancing. The poorest of the poor is dying, not even listening to the music. The poor people who still are alive is just looking unhappy at the dancers around the world, waiting to die. Most people know that if they protest and demand new leaders, the dance will still continue and nothing will really change. The poverty in the world will exist as long as the three factors of the Original Sin are allowed to rule the common world of thoughts.

What the camouflaged stories in the Bible are telling you is that the Golden Calf has to be destroyed completely in order to stop the dance. If the gold, silver and precious stones are given back to the people, they will use it to make historical ornaments used for remembering their family history.

In other words the three factors of the Original Sin have to be removed from the common world of thinking before lasting peace can be restored.

Only then the whole world population will get all they need to live a good life on planet Earth. No one will be rich and no one will be poor.

The meaning with life on planet Earth is that all the tribal people in the world shall live together as brothers and friends and live by one common set of laws and rules.

Queen Vastis no

Ester 1, 19-22

King Ahasverus bragged about being the richest king that ever had lived. "My armies are the greatest," he said, "and also I have the most beautiful queen in the world!"

"O", the people sighted. They had heard about queen Vastis. "Can we see her? We will see the queen!" they shouted.

The king's servants ran off to get queen Vasti. She had her own party. "The king has ordered that you shall come and show you self for the guest," they said.

The queen sighted and put her hands in the side. "Why?"

"He wants them to see how beautiful you are."

But to their surprise the queen shook her head. "No, say that I will come later. Don't you see that I am busy at the moment?"

The servants were shocked. They hurried back to the king with the news. The guests were also shocked. Everyone looked at Ahasverus. How did the king take this? The king was furious. He sent for his advisors and said: "How should I punish the queen for not doing as I tell her?"

The advisors answered: "You must act quickly, or else all the wives of all the trusted kings and leaders in your kingdom will begin to say no to their men. That they will not like! Send out a royal declaration that Vasti no longer is queen. Then you can look around to see if you can find someone to take her place."

The king liked the idea and sent out the decree. It was written in many different languages. Everyone understood what he meant. The king was looking for another queen.

In our present time it is the politicians and the company leaders that have to be replaced if they don't do as they are told by the management. Think about what happens in a regular marriage when the wife insults her husband in front of guests. What happens is that the love between them dies, the happiness disappears quickly and the marriage often ends with a divorce. It is a law of the nature that is broken, and if the husband shows cowardice and let the insult pass, the wives of the guest might start doing the same against their husbands. Husbands and wives that are insulting each other have married for the wrong reasons. The wrong reasons are riches and personal power that comes a good job or from being the son of a rich father.

This camouflaged story is told in order to bring Ester and the Jewish tribe back in the position among the leaders of the kingdom. Under the camouflage the story is showing that the force of good always is second in command. The forces of evil would not last long without the forces of good. It is a story about a good king who has to do evil deeds in order to stay in power. But most of all it is a story about the forces of evil controlling the whole world population and the forces of good barely survives. Good thoughts and evil thoughts in a world where the evil thoughts wasn't meant to be.

Miss Persia

Ester 2, 1-20

King Ahasverus sent out his most trusted men. They were looking for the most beautiful girls in the whole kingdom. Among them was the Jewish girl Ester.

Ester and the other young girls were taken to the castle. Exited they walked up the stairs to their new home. They were given all they wished for, beautiful clothes and the finest perfume. The servants gave them massage and waited on them.

While Ester lived in the castle, she told no one that she was Jewish. Her relative had advised her to do. Because Mordekai always had been like a father to her, Ester did as he said.

When the king's men took Ester inn to the castle, Mordekai followed her. Every morning for the whole next year he walked in the yard around the castle. In this way he could see what happened.

When the year was over the king should decide who had won the beauty competition. Who was to be his next queen? The king liked all this.

Finally it was Esters turn to go in to the king. Everyone agreed that they never had seen a more beautiful young woman. And the king said: "No one is like Ester!" The beautiful Ester became the new queen of Persia.

The whole Old Testament is about the development of warrior kings and priesthoods and their despotic control of the whole population in their kingdom. All the many different tribal people were slaves under one autocratic king with his elite of selected trusted kings, priests and leaders on all levels. Those who were reported as not doing as the king ordered was rapidly dethroned and killed. Every human in the large Persian kingdom are to look at as slaves, soldiers and servants under a king who had absolute power. Ester had no choice and again, like in the story about Joseph in Egypt and about Daniel in Babylon, a biblical Israelite is next to the king. It is a symbol for the force of evil and the force of good ruling the whole world population. So remove all evil from this story, and se the prospect of a new Motherland, a new global parliament and a new superior Motherland council.

What the Master who wrote this camouflaged story wants to preserve and pass on to the coming generations, to everyone who lives in present time, is the merciless emptiness that is enforced on the population with the use of inherited government power of warfare and brutal force. Look forward to the day of freedom when the whole world population again lives together in peace, speak the same language and learn and obey the laws and rules given by a new superior Motherland council.

In our present time the whole world population lives their lives like blinded zombies who are living dead. Everybody's thoughts are rotating only around money and sex. A man selecting a woman he wants to get married to is often valuing the body's beauty on the outside more than her inner personal spiritual strength, knowledge and personal abilities. That is truly wrong if the idea is to have clever children.

The description how king Ahasverus selects his queen fits directly in to our present time, were all human activity is measured in money and the personal power that comes from owning things. Power that people have come by as inheritance is a meaningless power.

No one can do anything about it because everyone has their world of thoughts occupied by the three factors of the Original Sin and don't know any other way to live on planet Earth. Both men and women focuses on their own and others outside look and personal riches, more than their inner personal qualities.

The kingdom that stretched from Egypt to India is a symbol for the whole planet earth. It is the richest nations with the largest armies that decides everything, and when they don't get things done the way they wants, they go to war to get it.

While the richest of the rich is living in luxury with a lot more than they need and chooses their women like Ahasverus did, thousands of humans dies every day for reasons caused by poverty. This misrule cannot continue. Poverty is caused by the global capitalistic system that makes the richest of the rich richer.

The only form of government that can win over the present ruling system with many national states is the global government system that is found in the Bible under the camouflage of religion. It is a ruling system totally without the desperate quest for money and riches, totally without poor people, soldiers and servants and without all the religions in the world. The ages in the darkness of oblivion are coming to an end, and the knowledge mankind needs will come from the Diagram Star.

Remember now the definition of the Diagram Star. It is the twelve Zodiac star signs with the sun and the moon in the centre that are the origin of the Diagram Star. The twelve Zodiac star signs are the emblems of the twelve members of the superior Motherland council, and the Diagram Star is their common emblem. Like this the Diagram Star was used as a common book in all education all over the world, in the time before the Motherland went under. Look at the Zodiac as projected down to all humans as the cosmic Diagram Star. The sun and the twelve signs of the Zodiac became the God of all the religions in the world.

In the time after the Motherland went under and the superior Motherland council died and became remembered as spirits in the Spirit World, they had no physical power over the self elected kings and priesthoods who wanted to live their lives in luxury, using the population as obedient slaves, soldiers and servants.

The warrior kings and priesthoods invented God and used the power of religion to control the population and make them pay taxes. Warfare and brutal force in the name of God is the only physical force present in the world, and it is a well used tool for all the national states in the world.

The only way out of the circle of evil is to build a new Motherland with a global parliament and elect a new superior Motherland council, who can govern the whole world population with just one set of laws and rules for living. They will govern a world without the three factors of the Original Sin and all the tribal people in the world will live together as brothers and friends.

It is the government system from the biblical kingdom with one Motherland and lasting peace this camouflaged story is all about. Ester has as a mission to preserve and pass the history of the Jews on to coming generations.

The whole history of the Jewish tribe is used as a hiding place for the knowledge the whole world population needs in order to be able to build a new world with lasting peace, but it was only the Masters who could recover the knowledge with the use of the formula or code hereby given to you all.

The Jews are condemned to death

Ester 2, 21-3, 15

Every day Mordekai walked back and forth outside the castle. He waited in excitement to hear how Ester was doing. She was queen and could have everything she pointed at, but Mordekai was still worried. It was like he should have been her father.

At the kings court there was a powerful man named Haman. It was only the king who stood over him. Haman had given the order that everyone should kneel before him when he came.

But at the kings gate there was a man who did not kneel before him. It was Mordekai. He knew that Haman was an amalekitt, one of Israel's hated enemies. He wouldn't kneel before an amalekitt.

Time and time again Haman passed by Mordekai. Every time Mordekai refused to kneel before him. Haman became more and more angry.

Finally he went before the king and said: "There is a tribe who refuses to obey my orders. I want you to kill all of them."

Haman did not want only Mordekai to be killed. He wanted to see all the Jews dead! The king agreed on that without really knowing what Haman was talking about. He let writers send his order out over all of Persia. The order was that all the Jews should be killed; young and old, women and children, and it should all be done within one year!

Every living human can understand how wrong this royal declaration is. The Jews have suffered from killings and attempted genocide several times in their history, and when it happens it is always evil to the extreme. If the Jews are told that they are Gods chosen people without knowing the true definition of God, they will be forgiven along with the whole world population. The biblical Israelites are a symbol for the whole world population. This camouflaged story was written during the terror regime of the Roman Empire, were the first Christians was killed by the thousands in the amusement arenas. And killings like this happened after the order of one powerful leader.

This camouflaged story is written in order to make it easier for you to separate evil from good. It is still evil declarations based on the three factors of the Original Sin that are wrong for the whole world population in our present time. The decelerations are mostly given by powerful world leaders with the help of many advisors. They are all in general good, clever people, following the laws and living rules of their nation. A lot of time and effort is used to fight all the evil in the world, and everyone who reads this story knows the king's declaration for killing all the whole Jewish tribe is very wrong. You know that evil is not meant to be present in the world and in this story the Jewish people are a symbol for the good thoughts that by nature should govern the whole world population in a world with lasting peace.

Look at this camouflaged story as all the evil thoughts are trying to wipe out all the good thoughts ones and for all. Ester fights for the good thoughts with her life at stake, and wins in the end. But evil thoughts will be in charge as long as the three factors of the Original Sin are present in the common world of thoughts.

It is the evolution of the global capitalistic system that is killing thousands of humans every day. There is a constant chaos of wars and conflicts in the world because the national leaders want to be regarded and respected as good leaders for their population. Every national state have laws and living rules that provides the nation with willing working slaves, soldiers and servants, and the circulation of money is the foundation for all evil. In addition all the national leaders are shouting out loud that religion is a personal thing. People can believe what they want, as long as they all respect each other's believes and opinions and live by the laws and the rules of the nation. The three factors are the Original Sin.

The governing system with many national states is based on the three factors of the Original Sin, and by continuing in to the future, the whole world population will over time die out and disappear. And still, after several thousand years with the destructive three factors of the Original Sin, the whole world population believes that they are doing all they can to fight the forces of evil and do things right. This they believe because the factors of good are second in command in all the national states in the world.

How can it be wrong and evil to produce oil products and make a lot of money? How can it be wrong to build cars that are used to drive to work, drive to do the shopping, drive on holyday, among other things? How can it be wrong to use oil and pollute the atmosphere? How can it be wrong to work for money? How can it be wrong to live like we do?

Well, it is very wrong, just as wrong as the royal order from king Ahasverus to kill all the Jews. If the world leaders, religious and political, continue to preserve and pass on the three factors of the Original Sin like they do, they will lead the whole world population towards a certain death. Billions of humans will die, not knowing why they ever lived.

You live your life wanting to live like king Ahasverus. Your quest for money and riches never stops, because you have to use the money to buy things. It is the political democratic system in a nutshell. If the whole population gets to be rich enough to stop working and stop paying taxes, the nation would expire, die out. The whole life form in present time is wrong, and it is only the richest of the rich who get richer.

There are a high and strong wall between the rich and the poor people. It is very difficult to climb and only a few humans make it over and become rich. If the global system of capitalism is removed from the common world of thoughts, the wall will crumble and fall.

The Master, who wrote this story a long time ago, wants to tell the people living in present time how very wrong it is to live with the tree factors of the Original Sin as the foundation for the government system of a nation.

The Jews are certainly proud of their tribal history, but they should know that they were chosen by the Masters to protects and preserve the history of the Motherland, as hidden in the many historical tales in the Bible. The Bible is truly the only Ark of the Covenant in the world, and the lid is made of the camouflage itself. Remove the camouflage of religion, and you will find the bright shining Diagram Star, telling you about a global government system that is the only road to lasting peace in the world.

Ester, Mordekai and the Jews are the people with good thoughts in this story, and it reveals the dream that the whole world population is dreaming in present time. Remember that the Jews in the Bible stories are the Israelites and a symbol for the whole world population.

Ester has a plan

Ester 4, 1-5; 12

Mordekai became so agitated when he heard about the royal order about all the Jews should be killed, that he tore his clothes to pieces. He walked up and down in the city and cried.

Him and Ester sent messages to each other from time to time. "You have to go to the king and ask him to save us," said Mordekai.

Ester became pale. "But the king does not receive any other than those he sends for. If I go to see him without been called to him, he can kill me. My only change is that he stretches his scepter towards me and chooses to listen to me."

But Mordekai was determent. "You will not be saved, even if you are the queen. If you keep silent in a time like this, God will save his chosen people through someone else. But God made you queen because of this."

Easter prayed. Then she said: "Tell Mordekai that I agree with him. If I am going to die, I rather do it for the right reason."

Three days later she went to the king's receptions hall. The king saw her and smiled. Then he pointed his scepter towards her. "Ester, is that you? You shall have anything you ask for, even if it is half my kingdom."

"I would like to invite you and Haman to dinner with me tonight," Ester answered. She hoped that he would say yes.

"Thanks, I will very much come!" said the king. The same evening and the next Ester had dinner with the king and Haman.

After the first evening Haman went home and bragged to his friends. He showed them his riches and said: "I am so powerful that even the king and queen have dinner with me."

This is about the three factors of the Original Sin and the history about the lost Motherland. It is the power of good and evil fighting each other. There is something fundamental and very important in this camouflaged story that has been told several times in the Old Testament. The stories about Joseph in Egypt, Daniel in Babylon and Ester in Persia is telling you and the whole world population that the world can be governed without the evil force of the many national states, without the global system of capitalism and without all the religions in the world. In fact

231

the whole world population can be governed by the forces of good alone, by a new superior Motherland council from a new Motherland.

The forces of evil, as derived from the three factors of the Original Sin, are manmade and can be removed from the common world of thoughts. What Queen Ester did was protecting the knowledge about the lost Motherland and the forces of good from being totally wiped out. Just think about what the world would have been like without the good forces fighting the evil forces.

In a future world with a new superior Motherland council and only the forces of good in charge, there will be no striving for personal riches and power. All the leading persons will have other motivations, like for example personal pride and respect for doing what they do right. In a self supported community were everybody knows everybody even the smallest crime will follow the person trough the whole lifespan.

Remember now the symbolism in this story. Ester, Mordekai and the Jews are a symbol for the biblical Israelites, the descendants from Jacob, who got the name Israel. They are the whole world population that in real life, in present time, are about to destroy planet earth with the use three factors of the Original Sin. Ester does the right thing to save her people, risking her life by telling the king about what is about to happen. Like him, the world leaders of present time do not know that the forces of evil thoughts are ruling the world.

Are you brave enough to tell your national leader that the building of many national states long ago, was wrong as wrong can be. Not only your own nation, but all the nations in the world have to be built down peacefully stone by stone, along with everything they stand for.

Not so long ago, the warrior kings and priesthoods in my county Norway, killed people who had the knowledge about the lost Motherland that hereby are given to you. They used several hundred years to merciless kill all opposition, and the outcome you see in our present time; a population of obedient slave workers, soldiers and servants.

Will you dare to wake the forces of evil in the world by calling them by name? Will you have sensible world leaders by you side, understanding and seeing right from wrong? Will the leaders of the world understand that everything the many nations in the world have built during the last several thousand years has to be taken down?

Like Ester, you have no choice. If you don't act, your children and their descendants will face a terrible future. Millions of humans will continue to die, not knowing why they ever lived. You have to use Internet and modern technology and tell the world leaders that even large adjustments aren't enough. The planning of building a new world with lasting peace has to start now. The building plan is found in the Diagram Star.

Ester saves her people

Ester 7, 1-6

It was the second night Haman had dinner with the king and Ester. It was this moment that she had asked for. One more time she served the best of the best. When the king looked at his beautiful queen, he felt very content.

"Tell me one thing, my friend," he said to Ester. "What do you really mean by doing all this? What do you want?

Ester felt her heart beat extra hard. She took a deep breath. "I pray for my life and for the lives of my people," she said. "We are all to be exterminated. We are to be killed! All of us!"

"What are you saying?" the king said surprised. "What evil man has thought of something like that? Who is it?

Ester stood up and pointed at Haman. "The evil enemy is the man sitting there! It is Haman!" Terrified Haman spilled wine from his cup.

There were both good and evil kings in earlier times, as national leaders in present time. It is not the leaders of the world that there is something wrong with. They are like everyone else born in to a government system that is inherited from the forefathers, and no one can even imagine that it is wrong.

King Ahasverus is a symbol for the world leaders in present time. Haman is a symbol for all the evil in the world, namely the three factors of the Original Sin, and the king have no knowledge of the terrible genocide that are about to happen. The world leaders in present time have no knowledge about the fact that their merciless quest for riches and personal power slowly but surely are killing the whole world population. They have to be told.

The world leaders do the best they can under the given circumstances, and because they don't know the lost history of the Motherland and the global system of government, they can only watch the world being destroyed all around them. Money cannot heal the wounds they bring upon people all over the world. They have to be told that they have to remove the three factors of the Original Sin from the face of the earth or know for sure that millions of humans will die on their command. If they do realize what they have to do to save mankind from a terrible future, and does it soon, the whole world can be built up to be a true paradise for our children and their descendants.

Can you even begin to comprehend the importance of the knowledge from the Diagram Star and what it will mean for the whole world population?

What will the present warrior kings and priesthoods do when they get to know that they are leading on in preserving and passing on the three factors of the Original Sin to coming generations? They are truly leading the whole world population as they were blind, and they are blind for the history of the lost Motherland. Look back on our world history for the last twelve thousand years, and try to understand what you see. If you look forward in time, with the present government system with many national states, with a global system of capitalism and all the religions in the world, what do you see? Du you see a world with lasting peace? No! All you see as a future for your children and their descendants is a copy of the world you live in today.

With lasting peace means a world peace that isn't controlled by many armies. With lasting world peace means a peace that are built in a world where all the weapons of war is melted and made in to pickaxes, spades and other tools for tilling the land.

Haman is hanged

Ester 7, 9-8, 2

King Ahasverus was furious. He got on his feet in a hurry and went for a walk in Esters garden. Haman throws himself before Esters feet and begged for mercy.

When the king came back again and saw Haman clinging to Ester, he lost his temper completely. "What is this? Du you dare to lay hand on the queen!? Don't touch her!" The king's guard came running in. They knew that Haman had signed his own death sentence.

"Hang this man!" the king ordered.

Then king Ahasverus gave Hamans house and everything he had owned to queen Ester. Mordekai came forth. Ester told the king that he was a relative of her, but he had been like a father to her.

The king took of his special ring and gave it to Mordekai. Ester gave Mordekai all that Haman had owned.

Haman was hanged because he had touched queen Ester. He was not hanged because he had ordered that all the Jews in the kingdom should be killed. The king had signed the order and a king's decree is like an arrow I flight. It cannot be taken back. Mordekai was rewarded for doing everything right. You have to do like he did, and dare to stand against the forces of evil. Then they will take action and show how evil they are. Ester proved her strong spirit and bravery and won a great victory for the forces of good.

The story have an underlying read tread, and the Master wishes to tell the people living in present time that the world history from the time before the Motherland was destroyed will live through ages no matter what happens. The forces of good can be held down with the use of warfare and brutal force, but they will always be a part of every human's life on planet earth.

Who is Haman of present time and who is Mordekai? Who is queen Ester in present time and who is king Ahasverus? What does the world population of today to look forward to? What world will you leave for the coming generations?

Is there anyone at all comprehending that the governments system based on the three factors of the Original Sin only can lead towards an increasing chaos of wars and conflicts?

The battle for fertile land has become harder and more subtle and is clearly visible in the increasing number of fugitives from countries where there is not enough fertile land to feed the population. What happen when the national borders are broken down by hordes of hungry humans that fight of all power to survive?

One change to survive

Ester 8, 3-17

After Mordekai had received his reward, the queen ones more went to see the king. Again she risked her life. If the king had not pointed his gold scepter towards her, it would have meant that she lost her life the next day.

But in the same moment Ester came in to the reception hall, she throws herself before his feet. She cried and sobbed. The king pointed the gold scepter towards her. She was saved! "Is there any possibility that my people can be saved from Haman's terrible royal decree," she asked.

Ester knew that when the king ones had given an order, it could not be withdrawn. But the king had an idea. He sent for Mordekai. "You have my ring now, Mordekai," he said. "Send out a new royal command that can save the Jews."

Mordekai then sent out this royal decree: "All Jews have permission to defend tem self when their enemies' attacks them on the given day."

As the news spread, the Jews became relived and happy. Many who wasn't Jews, now wished to be. They knew who would walk victorious from that battle.

All humans know that nothing can save mankind from an increasing number of natural catastrophes that most certainly will come in the future. But there is a good change that mankind can be saved from an increasing number of wars and conflicts in the future if the whole world population demands that a new Motherland shall be built and a new superior Motherland council shall be elected.

Yes, there is a good possibility to build a new world with lasting peace, but then the warrior kings and priesthoods of present time have to step down from their titles and return to be regular human beings. The world will still need strong and good leaders of all kind, and many years will pass before fully educated Masters can replace them.

Resistance

Ester 9, 1-10; 9, 20

The day that Haman had given came, but it turned out a lot different from what he had imagined. God blessed the Jews and made them able to stand against those who wanted to eradicate them. The enemies of Gods people had to take the fall this day. All the small kings and generals stood on the side of Mordekai and the Jews. They helped Gods people to defend them self against the enemy.

Mordekai now sent out a new royal decree. Is stated that Jews all over the kingdom never should forget how God had helped them in this miraculous and strange way. Every year they should remember this and celebrate it with a party. Everybody should give presents to the poor that day.

Queen Ester and king Ahasverus continued to rule Persia for many years.

The Master who wrote this camouflaged story did his best and by deciding that the day should be a yearly event for celebrating God, was an insurance that the Bibles hidden message would be passed on from one generation to the next. He knew that the government system with despotic warrior kings and priesthoods only could be eliminated by use of peaceful means, and for that reason their despotic rule would continue in to the future. The Masters knew the formula had to survive at any cost, and they succeeded.

This story was written inn to the Bible during the strict control of the Romans. Therefore the story got a shape and action that could be understood and accepted by them. The religion Christianity got so popular that the Romans couldn't fight it by killing the Christians by the thousands, and for that reason the roman emperor Constantine started using the religion as a tool to control the many different people they ruled over.

They took the religion in use and enforced it on the many populations with the use of warfare and brutal force. They did it without knowing that under the camouflaged of religion was the true message about how lasting peace could be built on planet Earth.

The Bible is the Ark of the Covenant. It was declared holy with the sole reason to protect and pass on the hidden message to coming generations. Now you are told that it is not holy at all any longer. It is time to remove the camouflage and let the Diagram Star shine its light on to the whole world population again. All that needs to be done is to separate right from wrong in your world of thoughts.

We are all sinners, the priests of the present time is stating as a fact every Sunday in churches all over the world. Yes we are, but now you are told about the three factors of the Original Sin, and can dispose of it by studying the Diagram Star. Then you will be a sinner no more.

Haman is a symbol for all the evil thoughts in the world. Ester is a symbol for the knowledge about the Motherland and the global government system that really can be restored on the whole planet Earth. King Ahasverus is a symbol for the present government system with many national states that has to change. The world leaders need the leadership of a new superior Motherland council.

Now time has come to send out a new global decree that tells the whole world population to start planning to build a new world order with the use of the knowledge from lost Motherland and the Diagram Star. Then our children can leave a world with lasting peace to their descendants.

Build a new world.

With new thoughts

The New Testament is telling you how.

Jesus is the born again Motherland history.

Study this image and see the symbolism.

The three wise men are a symbol for the lost Motherland, a large continent that was divided in three kingdoms by natural channels. It is the history about the superior Motherland council that have traveled through the history, preserved and passed on by a group of scholars called Masters. They lived and worked under cover, and had to camouflage the history in to popular stories that would be accepted by the merciless warrior kings and their priesthoods. The Egyptian hieroglyphs were translated wrong for a reason and the many meanings of the Hebrew words were used to hide the true story about the lost Motherland. Now time has come to tell you the full story. It is the only possible way towards building a new world with lasting peace.

Virgin Mary is a symbol for the new Motherland that never came to be some two thousand years ago. The existence of the lost Motherland was denied by the world leaders at the time, the Romans and the priesthoods. Father Jacob is a symbol for global parliament, the superior Motherland council and the knowledge the world population needs to learn in order to be able to build a new world with lasting peace. Jesus is the born again Motherland history. All you have to do in order to discover the lost world history is to remove the camouflage of religion from the Bible. The Bible is the Ark of the Covenant.

God is defined to be the spiritual superior Motherland council. Before they all died in a natural catastrophe they were omnipotent, omniscient and omnipresent. Jesus, as the born again Motherland history, shows you how a new superior Motherland council have to be elected by the whole world population.

This is the lost Motherland.

This is the Motherland Mu that was destroyed in a natural catastrophe some twelve thousand years ago. Only the global system of government from that time can restore lasting peace on the whole planet Earth.

The Motherland was by nature divided by channels and open sea in to three kingdoms, and it is the knowledge about the lost continent that has traveled through the world history, protected and passed on from generation to generation by a group of scholars called Masters.

The history of the lost Motherland was born again some two thousand years ago camouflaged like a religion, because the Roman emperors, the warrior kings and the priesthoods of the time were killing everyone who dared to speak about the global government system that would set all humans free and create lasting peace in the world.

Now, some two thousand years later the camouflage is herewith removed and the history of the lost Motherland is told in full. The people living on the Motherland were many. 64 million, the legend tells. Twelve democratically elected leaders from every tribal people in the world represented the people who had elected them and they, the global parliament, elected among them self the twelve members of the superior Motherland council. They were the leaders of a world that was truly a peaceful and fertile paradise for everyone.

The twelve star signs of the Zodiac were the official emblems for the superior Motherland council. Together the twelve Zodiac star signs, with the sun in the centre, was the official emblem of the whole superior Motherland council. It was taken down long ago and made in to the Diagram Star. You can still find a copy of the Diagram Star in the prehistoric crosses.

The Diagram Star was the common book of education all over the world. All the tribal people had emigrated from the Motherland and populated the whole planet earth. The tribal villages could be large or small, still not one person was greater than others. The whole world population spoke the same language and lived together like brothers and friends, with lasting world peace. Every village had a council of twelve to lead them; still not one person was greater than others. All humans were respected for doing what they did to the best of their ability.

The lasting peace in the world was preserved because no one knew the forces of evil. They had no knowledge about nations with borders and armed forces. The global capitalistic system and enforced religion was unheard of.

Then some twelve thousand years ago the Motherland was completely destroyed in a natural catastrophe. Some 64 million humans died in the catastrophe and among them were the twelve members of the superior Motherland council. They were remembered by the whole world population and from them came all the religions, legends, tales and myths in the world.

The twelve members of the superior Motherland council became God in the religion of Christianity. As long as they were alive and present in the world they were omnipotent, omniscient and omnipresent and had the physical power to keep lasting peace in the whole world. After they died they lost their physical power and became spiritual beings called Gods. The lost Motherland and everyone who lived on it became the well known Heaven in the Spirit World.

Not long after the many self elected warrior kings and priesthoods started fighting each other for the most fertile land to live on, and in the process they attacked peaceful villages, stole all the valuables and made the inhabitants in to slaves, soldiers and servants. Like this a paradise earth was transformed in to a living hell for the whole world population, and as you very well know, it still is a living hell for billions of people. The Hebrew word Devil means enemy and of mankind is the tree factors of the Original Sin, which have been the dictating force of evil all this time.

The only way to build a new world with lasting peace is to restore the lost knowledge and build a new Motherland. A new global parliament has to be elected and from them a new democratically elected superior Motherland council will be elected. You will learn that Jesus came to earth some two thousand years ago, camouflaged as the born again Motherland history.

The three factors of the Original Sin – in a short definition

Part one of the three factors of the Original Sin is the global capitalistic system, a system made by the greedy, selfish and despotic royal rulers of the past. The monetary system is passed on from generation to generation as inheritance, and the present population of the world doesn't know that it is manmade and never meant to be. Money is a tool for the national leaders to control the population and make them in to willing working taxpayers. In the time before the Motherland was destroyed the whole world population lived well without the use of money. They certainly had personal and tribal valuables, but never money made by national leaders as a tool to control the population.

Part two of the Original Sin is the building of many national states all over the world. The builders were warrior kings and priesthoods, and they committed a gruesome crime against mankind by doing that. The national states were built with the use of warfare and brutal force. The population living on the land was forced in to a life as working slaves, soldiers and servants. It happened symbolically for the first time when Jacob, who got the name Israel, and his twelve sons moved in to old Egypt to settle there.

The twelve sons of Jacob is symbol for the many tribes that emigrated from the Motherland in order to populate the whole world. They are the biblical Israelites, and under the camouflage the whole world population in present time is descending from the Israelites. The Jews are just one of the twelve tribes. The Jewish tribal history is used as a symbol for telling the history of the whole world population. Look around and see for yourself. The whole world population is still working slaves, soldiers and servants under the laws and rules of the nation they are born in to. The world population of present time has difficulties in picturing a globe without national border, where all humans' lives in self supported villages and possess everything they need to live a good life.

The important third part of the Original Sin is all the religions in the world. They are a system of belief that kills many humans in collaboration with the two other parts of the Original Sin. The religion is still used as a tool for controlling the population and forcing them in to a life as obedient slaves, soldiers and servants for the national state they are born in to.

With this new knowledge all the religions in the world can be removed from the common world of thoughts. Together with the religions there will be a new knowledge and understanding of all the tales, legends and myths in the world. The knowledge from the Diagram Star is taking mankind some twelve thousand years back in time, and reveals a new world of thoughts that are based on knowledge alone. It is a true revelation for every single human living on planet Earth.

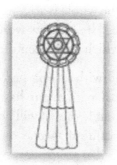

This is the Diagram Star. It is found chiseled on a stone tablet dated to be more than thirty-five thousand years old. The Diagram Star is however much, much older. The simple diagram is the first book known to mankind and has as confirmed in the Bible, been with humans on earth from before the beginning of time and will be with humans until after the end of time. With the Diagram Star as a common source of knowledge and book of law and living rules, the whole world population lived with lasting peace.

As a consequence of the natural catastrophe that destroyed the Motherland the three factors of the Original Sin started. It developed in to the many severe different opinions between nations that at present time is about to destroy the world. The three factors are: all the national states, the global capitalistic system and all the religions in the world.

Jesus symbolizes the star in the centre of the diagram. The twelve apostles are a symbol for the new superior Motherland council. It is only knowledge from the Diagram Star that can remove the Original Sin from the common thoughts of humans and create lasting peace for all humans.

It is the Diagram Star itself, chiseled in two stone tablets, which are the symbolic content described in the Bible. The Ark of the Covenant is fictitious all together, but it tells us that the Masters writing the camouflaged stories made an effort to make sure the knowledge of the lost Motherland was preserved and passed on from generation to generation. The gold that covers the Ark both on the outside and inside, the two angels and other decorations are symbols for the camouflage of religion that is covering all the stories in the Bible. Under the camouflage of holiness, gold and glitter the Ark of the Covenant is protecting, preserving and passing on the knowledge about the lost Motherland and the Diagram Star to coming generations. Right now the lid is removed from the Ark of the Covenant, and we shall challenge the enemy in the common world of thoughts, the tree factors of the Original Sin, and win.

The Bible is the Ark of the Covenant, and all you have to do in order to take the lid of, is to remove the camouflage of religion from your world of thoughts. What you will find is the Diagram Star and the strict laws and living rules given by the superior Motherland council.

The strong light from the Ark of the Covenant is the important historical information that was locked in to a mental prison of oblivion, forgotten due to not existing education. The symbolic strong light inside the Ark of the Covenant is the light from the Diagram Star. The light is truly strong enough to enlighten the whole world population with knowledge about the lost Motherland.

It is the sun, the moon and the twelve star signs of the Zodiac that are model for the Diagram Star. It is called a cosmic diagram, because it preserves and passes on the knowledge of how the universe was created and it is telling the humans living in present time how their first ancestors came to planet earth in cosmic eggs. The bright shining star is showing humans how to build cosmic eggs in the future, in order to populate new earthlike planets in the universe.

Each of the twelve members of the superior Motherland council had one star sign as their official emblem. Together the twelve star signs was the official emblem of the whole superior Motherland council. Remember now that it was the titles of the twelve council members that lived eternally. The elected human beings lived and died like all humans do.

The sun was not worshipped by anyone in the time before the Motherland was destroyed. It was a source of knowledge until the enforced religion covered it up. The Motherland was known as the Empire of the Sun, and all the kingdoms and empires that developed all over the world was given the title Son of the Empire of the Sun. It was a title given to the land, not to the democratically elected council who administrated the use of the land. The twelve members of the council, the Masters called kings and emperors, were elected from the people, with their spiritual strength and personal abilities as the only factors for elections. No human was greater than others and the position as leader and council member could not be given as inheritance from father to son.

"The first meaning" of the Diagram Star is that of the twelve Zodiac star signs. Place the sun and the moon in the centre of the diagram and the twelve star signs in the sections around. Then you give them names, and you are on the way towards a profound knowledge that takes your world of thoughts all the way past all the religions, myths and legends in the world. The camouflaged story about Jesus is telling you about the lost Motherland and how a new superior Motherland council is elected.

In the time before the Motherland was destroyed in a natural catastrophe the Diagram Star was the common book that was used in education by the whole world population. Every child had the diagram memorized and it was easy to remember. They had no knowledge of any form of religion, myths and legends. They knew the history of the past and were thought to build the future with lasting peace. Then the Motherland was destroyed in a natural catastrophe, and without the physical leadership of the superior Motherland council, and the whole Motherland continent gone from the face of the earth, the chaos of wars and conflicts started.

It is from the science astrology the Masters of old got their formula for writing the many camouflaged stories that became the Bible and the foundation for all the religions in the world. Place the Zodiac star signs in the twelve sections of the Diagram Star and place the sun and the moon in the centre. In groups of three the Zodiac signs are connected to the four elements that are <u>fire</u> (ram, lion, the archer) <u>earth</u> (bull, virgin, Capricorn), <u>air</u> (twin, weight, Aquarius), <u>water</u> (cancer, scorpion and fish).

In order to be able to read the Diagram Star like an open book, you need to recover the knowledge hidden in all the stories in the Bible. The star shaped diagram is found many places where you live today, and at many places in the Bible. One is Jacob and his twelve sons in the Old Testament. Another is Jesus and his twelve apostles in the New Testament. Also the Bethlehem Star is a camouflaged Diagram Star and the three wise men are symbolizing first the three kingdoms of the Motherland and next they are symbols for the group of Masters who had as mission in life to preserve and pass on the history of the Motherland to the generations to come. Some two thousand years ago the history was born again, camouflaged as baby Jesus. Every Christmas tree is a symbol for the Diagram Star.

Outside the Bible there are copies of the Diagram Star all over the world and the most distinct one is Stonehenge in England. Stone circles all over the world are a copy of the Diagram Star, with the mission of preserving and passing on history to coming generations. Like the star diagram all stone Circles are ambiguous and was used to remember the history of the local tribes, their heroes, chiefs and population.

Many of the people of the past are known to have made a copy of the Diagram Star with the sun as model. The Maya people of Yucatan, Naga-Maya people of India, the Babylonians, Assyrians, Egyptians and the Pueblo Indians in the south-west of North-America are the best known. In the time after the Motherland was destroyed, almost all peoples started filling the Diagram Star with signs and inventing dogmas about how it happened. This was not the right thing to do, because the signs and drawings, the legends and myths and the assumptions and dogmas covered the Diagram Star and made it impossible to understand for the generations to come.

The Diagram Star is the carrier of the whole world history. The Masters who wrote the many camouflaged stories of the Bible kept the diagram clean and chiseled it in to stone tablets to make sure it would be found and understood at a later time. If you have difficulties understanding what this text is saying, it is because it is new thoughts to you. You understand the camouflage that the warrior kings and priesthoods filled the Diagram Star with, such as signs and symbols for all kind of stories they used to control the population.

In our present time all the religions and sects in the world are a good proof for how wrong life for all humans can be when an elite of greedy warrior kings and religious leaders forces the population to believe in a long line of meaningless dogmas and assumptions that came to be in the time after the Motherland went under.

Now you all know that the Diagram Star have to be studied as it is originated from the Motherland before the catastrophe. Soon you can read the diagram star like an open book. In order to remove the three factors of the Original Sin from your world of thoughts, the following explanation is meant to help.

The camouflage of religion is removed.

An angel is visiting a young girl

Lukas 1, 26-38

The Jews knew that one day God would send the Messiah. Then God should come near to his people. This Messiah was Jesus. He came to earth as a little child and became the world's savior.

The mother of Jesus was a woman named Mary. One morning she woke to a bright light shining in her room. An angel named Gabriel had come to her. "Be greeted, Mary! You are blessed among women!" he said.

Mary was frightened. "Don't be afraid, Mary, God has chosen you to be the mother of his son, Messiah."

Mary should get married to a man named Joseph. When she heard what the angel said, she did not object. Instead Mary said: "I will do everything you say." She knew that God would help her.

The angel Gabriel said that her relative Elisabeth also should have a child. "Nothing is impossible for God," he added.

Mary believed him.

This is a good example of how wrong the Egyptian hieroglyphs were translated in to the Hebrew language. Virgin Mary is a young woman, symbolizing a fertile and good land, chosen to be the new Motherland. From far back in time, from the spirit world, from the darkness of oblivion, the tree wise men brings with them knowledge about the lost Motherland history. Jesus is the born again Motherland history, given to the whole world population.

The Masters was doing their best to restore the lost Motherland history and wanted to help the many tribal people to free them from the dictating Roman occupants. The history tells us that they lost. With the use of only peaceful means they could not win over the roman soldiers and the local priesthoods. The first Christians was not religious believers in an undefined God, they knew the born again history about the lost Motherland. They died by the thousands because they would not deny what they knew was true.

Under the camouflage of religion the biblical Israelites are the twelve symbolic tribes that emigrated from the Motherland and populated the whole world. This means that the Jews and all the other tribal people in the many bible stories are a symbolizing the whole world population. In the real world this means that there are no human enemies in the world, only enemy thoughts derived from the three factors of the Original Sin.

When this camouflaged story was written down, some ten thousand years had passed from the time the Motherland was destroyed. Mary is a symbol for the new Motherland that never was built. From her the history of the lost Motherland will be born camouflaged as baby Jesus.

Joseph the carpenter, her husband to be, is a symbol for the knowledge people living in present time needs in order to be able to build a new Motherland and a new world with lasting peace.

Mary's relative Elisabeth is old and has wanted to have a child her whole life. She is a symbol for the lost Motherland history and has wanted to return to the common world of thought for a very long time. Elisabeth and Mary are symbolizing the old and the new Motherland, the same story. The journey over the mountain symbolizes the mental journey you have to make back in time, to find the lost world history.

God is defined to be the spirit of the late superior Motherland council, and what the spirit world want to return to the world, is a physical omnipotent, omniscient and omnipresent system of global government that can restore lasting peace for the whole world population. In order to return the history of the lost Motherland to the whole world population, a new global parliament and a new superior Motherland council has to be elected. Jerusalem and the surrounding land in this region of the world were chosen as a theatrical stage for the explanation how the new Motherland has to be built. There is no other way to lasting world peace.

The angel Gabriel is the visualization of a message coming from the spirit world; from the spiritual superior Motherland council. They are talking on behalf of God in the Bible. The angels are thoughts coming from the spirit world. The strong light is a symbol for the Diagram Star and it symbolizes knowledge that any one of you, humans living in present time, can read from the diagram as from an open book.

The Master who wrote the camouflaged story about Jesus and his twelve disciples wants to tell the humans living in present time that Jesus is the born again Motherland history. The disciples are learning until Jesus dies, and then they become apostles.

Therefore look at the Diagram Star as a map of the world, with a new Motherland in the centre and the whole world population in the sections around. Jesus is a symbol for the new Motherland and the twelve apostles is a symbol for the new superior Motherland council representing the whole world population.

A journey over the mountain

Lukas 1, 5-25; 39-45

Mary's relative Elisabeth was very old. She and her husband had wanted to have a child for many years. Now finally Elisabeth should have a child. God had said that the boy she was to give birth to would be a great blessing.

After the angel Gabriel had visited Mary, she left her home in Nazareth in Galilee. She traveled south to Judea to visit Elisabeth.

When Mary arrived, she called Elisabeth. She heard the voice and for the first time in several months she went out to meet Mary. She called out loud: "Mary, you are blessed by God. I know you are the mother of the Lords child! This I know because my own child reacted when you called my name. There is something special with you, Mary! Gods child lives in you."

Truly there is something special with Mary. She is a symbol for the new Motherland that never came to be some two thousand years ago. She is carrying Jesus, the born again Motherland history inside her. The story is clearly describing how a new Motherland can be built in our present time. This means that the Motherland history is going to be born in to the world again, born in to the light of the Diagram Star.

Elisabeth is a symbol for the old Motherland that was lost in a natural catastrophe some twelve thousand years ago. Think of Elisabeth and her husband as a symbol for the guardians of the history about the lost Motherland, eager to tell the story to the whole world population.

The two women, one young and one old, are symbols for the same lost Motherland history. The true father of the two boys is the spiritual superior Motherland council. The journey over the mountain is connecting the very old and lost Motherland history of the past with the young.

The Masters have protected and passed on the history through the ages, and wanted to make the story known to the whole world population. Their history book was the Diagram Star. They wrote the camouflaged story about Jesus in order to explain how a new superior Motherland council is elected.

The formula is clear on this: In your thoughts you know that a mountain is Earth and that Earth is referring to the star signs of the Zodiac and the Diagram Star, which is world history and knowledge about the lost Motherland.

Not easy to explain in a few words, but it is a law of the nature that an old and long forgotten history has to be born and told first before the new story can be born again. There has to be a link between them. This have to do with Jesus been called Son of God and John the son of Man. They are both telling the same story.

Try to see that Jesus was born from spirit and water, and therefore are a product of thought and knowledge. He is an invented person that never lived. He is the camouflage over the Motherland history that was born in to the common world of thoughts some two thousand years ago. A new Motherland was not built then and therefore Jesus, as the born again Motherland history, still lives on in the spirit world with the father, the spiritual superior Motherland council.

The desert is a strong symbol in the Bible. People with knowledge about the Motherland history was a not wanted opposition to the warrior kings and priesthoods, and many escaped in to the desert were they lived and educated people about how the world was governed in the time before the Motherland went under. But living in the desert is a symbol for the life you and the whole world population lives and have lived for some twelve thousand years. You live in a metal desert, in the darkness of oblivion, not knowing how to build a new world with lasting peace. The Master writing the story about Jesus is telling you how.

You have to get used to look for the deeper meaning in the camouflaged stories. The river Jordan is a symbol for two very different worlds, with the desert on one side and the land of milk and honey on the other side. The word Hebrew means "people from the other side of the river".

The act of being baptized with water means confirming knowledge about the lost Motherland and the superior Motherland council. Look at the world you live in and decide what side of the river Jordan you live on. The truth is that you live in the desert and don't know anything about the lost Motherland. Your leaders, both religious and political, deny that the lost Motherland ever existed.

If you want to be baptized by John the Baptist, like Jesus did, you will find the knowledge about the lost Motherland, the knowledge that all humans need in order to be able to build a new world. Symbolical you can walk from the desert, across the river of knowledge and in to a new world where peace is ever lasting. Leaders like John the Baptist can give you the knowledge symbolical with water. Water is a part of the formula and refers to the twelve Zodiac star signs and the Diagram Star. The whole world population is still wandering aimlessly around the desert, like you have done for some twelve thousand years.

Being baptized with water was a symbol for confirming that the person had knowledge about the lost Motherland, and the Masters worked really hard in this period of time to teach people and try to change the world by use of only peaceful means.

The knowledge that is found in the Bible has to be discovered by humans living in present time that are able to divide right from wrong in the world where they live. Jesus is the light of the world; you can read in the Bible. When the camouflage of the religion is removed, Jesus is the star in the centre in the Diagram Star, the symbolic bright shining sun. As the born again Motherland history, Jesus can again illuminate the whole world population with knowledge and give them lasting peace.

If it is difficult to see what the Diagram Star is telling you, put Jesus in the centre and his twelve disciples in the sections around. Then you read the Bible stories with the formula and separate wrong from right. The stories will then have a true meaning that is meant to be the foundation for all human thinking.

Understanding the Spirit World is important. The angel Gabriel is a fictive spiritual character. Everything that comes from the Spirit World to humans comes as thoughts. Contact with the Spirit World is contact with the common world of thoughts. After the physical body dies, it is the human's thoughts that live on in the Spirit World. All humans are their thoughts and breathe in their thoughts from their own aura or spirit. The brain is just the receiver.

The humans living in present time is all born with the three factors of the Original Sin totally dominating their thoughts. Their mind is occupied by an evil force of dogmas and assumptions and they are not able to understand the thoughts and signals that come from the Spirit World.

Many humans experience a contact with the Spirit World, but the thoughts they receive is interpreted wrong because of the enforced thoughts from religion. The angel Gabriel and all other angels from the Bible are invented by the Masters of the past. Under the camouflage of religion the angels are the messengers from the Spirit World.

There is an even deeper explanation of stories like this. It has to do with the wrongful translation of the Egyptian hieroglyphs in to the written language. The Masters knew the full history about the lost Motherland and how the global kingdom was organized and did not need to translate the hieroglyphs in to written stories. Only the forces of evil would use dogmas and assumptions and force the population to believe in them. From the Old Testament we know that the force of good always was second in command. It still is.

At the well

Matthew 1, 1-19

After Mary had visited Elisabeth, she hurried home to Nazareth. She knew that she soon had to tell Joseph that she should have a baby. She asked God to prepare him for the news. Mary loved Joseph and did not want to hurt him.

She sent for him when she got home and asked him to meet her at an old well just outside the village. When he came, Mary said: "Joseph, something strange has happened, but it is true."

Joseph wondered why Mary looked so serious. And why it was so important that they met here, were no one could hear what they said?

"God has blessed me," said Mary. "I really don't know why. He has chosen me to be the mother of his son, Messiah. The child I am carrying is already three months." Mary held her breath. She hoped that Joseph would understand.

"O, Mary…" Joseph turned from her. He loved her so much, but now he could not get married to her. Joseph did not know what to believe of her.

He looked at Mary again. She seemed so sure. When he left her he thought about how they could cancel the wedding without hurting Mary too much. They had so many dreams and they had hoped for so much. Now everything fell apart for him.

The well is a symbol for the Diagram Star, and everything that happens at a well full of water is right according to the laws and living rules given by the superior Motherland council. This story makes it clear that they both are good people, living with only the forces of good in their thoughts.

To read a story knowing the formula makes it in to a different story all together. Mary is the lost Motherland history and Joseph is a symbol for the knowledge that humans in present time needs to build a new Motherland and lasting peace on planet Earth.

The way Joseph reacts to the news that Mary is going to have a child is the camouflage story. It has to be right in order to be passed on from generation to generation. The camouflage is the religion.

The child to be born is called Messiah and the message from the Spirit World comes from the late superior Motherland council. Jesus is the born again Motherland history. The knowledge about the lost kingdom can remove the forces of evil from the common world of thoughts and restore the forces of good in the world. It is done by electing a new superior Motherland council and by building a new Motherland for the world.

Think about the historical development in the Old Testament for a while. The camouflaged stories about Joseph, the son of Jacob, in the beginning of the Bible and Daniel and Ester in the end, symbolizes the forces of good in the world being second in command up through the ages. There is an ongoing struggle between good and evil all over the world. The force of good always wins, but always with the force of evil in command as the laws and rules of a national state. Some one thousand six hundred years ago the force of good was growing fast as the early Christians, and was about to win over the force of evil. Then it happened in the year 324 that the roman emperor Constantine took hold of the religion and started using it as a tool to control the many different people he ruled over. This means that the forces of evil, the three factors of the Original Sin, took the growing force of good and made it a part of the force of evil, and it still is.

The force of good is used up front by most national states in the world, and the fight between good and evil is everywhere and never seems to have an end.

The force of evil is the laws and rules of your national state. The force of good is the laws and rules given by the superior Motherland council. The force of good was alone in governing the whole world population in the time before the Motherland was destroyed in a natural catastrophe.

Josephs dream

Matthew 1-20-24

One night not long after, the Lords angel came to Joseph. "Don't be afraid to get married to Mary. She speaks the truth. Her child shall save all humans from their sins. You shall call him Jesus."

When Joseph woke, he believed what he had heard.

Mary had prayed for Joseph. After Joseph had the dream, he went to see her. He said that everything was in order between them. Her prayer was heard! Not long after they got married.

Jesus is the born again Motherland history and it is the knowledge about the lost continent that is going to save the whole world population from all their sins.

The sins spoken of in the Bible is the Original Sin, defined in to three specific man made factors. The three factors are: (1) the building of national states with the use of warfare and brutal force, (2) the global system of capitalism, meaning the use of money in every thinkable way, (3) and all the religions in the world.

These three factors have occupied the common world of thoughts for some twelve thousand years and are a well known part of daily life all over the world. The three factors of the Original Sin came to be in the chaotic times just after the Motherland went under and have been with mankind ever sins.

Now you know your sins and the sins that the born again Motherland history can and will save you from. You will all be forgiven, because you did not know. What you do know and live with all the time is the never ending fight between the good and the evil in the world. You should know by now that it is the forces of evil that always stays in command, as the laws and rules of your nation, while the good laws and rules given by the superior Motherland council is covered up and camouflaged by religious dogmas and assumptions.

In the time before Original Sin started, not one people and not one person was greater than others. A person's place in the community was seen in personal strength, degree of knowledge and ability to be in the position democratically elected to. The village peoples were equals all over the world. They were rich with gold, silver and valuable items. All the items had a specific purpose and carried the family and the tribal history from generation to generation. They lived in strong houses and had beautiful clothes. Their leaders were a democratically elected council with twelve members.

Every human being in the self supported village all over the world had everything they needed to live a god life on planet Earth. Education was the main activity in every village, and the best of the best students was sent to the Motherland to be educated in to a Master degree.

In fact, what was going on was breeding humans after a global plan. All humans were happy and safe. They had no knowledge of evil at all.

That is the paradise world is what the born again Motherland history can restore for the whole world population, if only you can lift your eyes and see that Jesus is the born again Motherland history that came from the spirit world. The story was denied by the world leader and returned back in to the spirit world, hidden under the camouflage of religion.

Jesus is born

Matthew 1, 25; Luke 2, 1-7

It was early in the morning. Joseph had packed the donkey. Mary sat between the big sacks that Joseph had tied on for her comfort. Together they left Nazareth and traveled to Bethlehem in Judea.

The roman emperor, Cæsar Augustus, had commanded everyone they ruled over to go to the city where they were born. He wanted his soldiers to count everyone in the large kingdom he ruled over, in order to make them pay taxes and dues. Joseph's relatives came from Bethlehem, so he had to go there to be registered.

"I should wish we did not have to travel to day," said Joseph. "It is not long before you shall have the child." Maria nodded. She tried to sit comfortable on the donkey. It was not easy. The child was big in her now, so she almost lost her balance. It was going to be a long and troublesome journey, which she knew.

The hours past and when the sun came up it got hot. Mary felt like sleeping, but she knew that if she did, she would fall off. She walked for a little while, but it did not last long before she was so tired that Joseph had to help her back up on the donkey again.

Finally they got to Bethlehem. The streets were filled with people. Everywhere children was running and playing. It was a loud noise. Suddenly Mary felt that something happened in her stomach. "Joseph, I think the child is coming soon!"

Joseph went pale. "We must get you in somewhere, away from all the noisy people," he said. They went from hostel to hostel and asked if they had place for them. No one took them inn. Finally Joseph cried out in despair: "Is there no place at all for us to stay for the night?"

"You can go to the other side of the city," said a man who owned a hostel. "Just by the fields there are some caves we use as stables. I use to have my animals there. Take your wife there and let her lay on some hay on the floor. It is at least quiet over there, so no one will disturb you."

Joseph thanked the man and hurried back to Mary. She leaned herself on him as they walked on.

When Mary was in place in the stable, Joseph relaxed a little. He had prayed so much that this had to go well. He thought it was bad that she had to give birth in a stable, but they had no choice.

When the child was born, Joseph held the boy in his arms. "This is Jesus," said Mary.

Under the camouflage of religion it is the lost Motherland history that is born again in this story. Jesus is the bright shining light from the Diagram Star. For a short while the history about the lost paradise world lived and enlightened people back then, and gave them hope for a life free from forced slavery under roman emperor Cæsar Augustus, and the paying of taxes and dues.

The Master, who wrote the camouflaged story knew that the knowledge about a global system of government from before the Motherland went under, not would be accepted among the roman elite, scribes and priesthoods. It just couldn't happen some two thousand years ago, but it can happen in our present time.

By writing the story about the lost Motherland as a drama, as a story that people could recognize them self in, using Bethlehem as a theatrical stage, was a success. The story about Jesus lived on through the ages of constant wars and conflicts, as a religion imposed on people. The Masters used the many biblical stories as the Ark of the Covenant. Now the lid of religion is removed and the hidden story about a global system of government is presented to you. Jesus is the Diagram Star.

Still, it seems very difficult for all humans living in present time, to understand that the kingdom, the new world Jesus is a symbol for, is a government system that was lost some twelve thousand years ago after a large natural catastrophe.

Jesus is the born again Motherland history and his kingdom on earth is the global government system that can restore lasting peace on planet Earth. He is presented as the Son of God and God is defined to be the spiritual superior Motherland council. Jesus is the son of Mary, defined to be the lost Motherland, the continent that disappeared in to the Pacific Ocean some twelve thousand years ago. The large continent was a beautiful cultivated garden, and after it was gone it was remembered by the whole world population as a spiritual Heaven. The many stories about the spiritual Motherland council became the many legends, tales, myths and religions in the world.

The new Motherland never came to be built some two thousand years ago, and the lost history returned back in the Spirit World. Call it a Heaven if you want. Most important is the fact that the story about the lost Motherland is to be found in the many camouflaged stories in the Bible. The Masters writing the many camouflaged biblical stories had a plan to preserve and pass on the history and they succeeded.

In order to understand this you have to release your world of thoughts from religious dogmas and assumptions and have the ability to see and decide what's right and what's wrong in the world you live in.

The camouflage of religion was meant for the roman rulers, the local corrupted warrior kings and the priesthoods, everyone who wanted to continue to live their lives in luxury under the Roman Empire.

It was a difficult time for the whole population. But with the religious camouflage intact and with knowledge of the secret formula, the stories that became the Bible gave the population hope for a better life. The whole world population still hopes. Humans are not meant to live with hope, but with everything they need to live a good life on planet earth.

The three factors of the Original Sin have lasted for some twelve thousand years, and they have to be built down with only peaceful means if mankind is to survive. There are no human who really needs the benefits from the three evil factors of the Original Sin in order to live a good life on planet earth. The whole world population has to work together in order to build down the present world, that truly are a living Hell for billions of human beings. Then the building of a new world with lasting peace for our children and their descendants can begin.

The shepherds

Luke 2, 8-17

The night Jesus was born, something strange happened. On the fields nearby was a group of shepherds, watching over their sheep's. Suddenly they heard the sound of a strong voice.

"Look!" one of the shepherds called out and pointed to the sky. They all looked up. It was a clear light, bigger than any star. It got bigger as it came closer. "Do you hear music?" They stopped talking about the light on the sky and got silent. Far away they heard the sound of singing. It came closer to.

Then the sky was filled with light. The shepherds saw an angel standing before them. The angel said: "Don't be afraid. Tonight a saviour is born. You shall see it is true when you find the child in a stable nearby."

Suddenly the shepherds were surrounded by angels! The angels sang: "Glory to God in the highest, and on earth peace, good will toward men." The song was soft and pleasant, but it was like the earth was trembling.

The shepherds fell on their knees. They thanked God for letting them see and listen to it all. When it was dark again they looked at each other. "Did I dream?" asked one of them. No, they knew it was real. They gathered the sheep's and left for Bethlehem.

When they were just outside the city, they noticed a gigantic star just over the hilltop. There they saw a cave and noticed that there was people in it.

The saviour is Jesus, not born as a human being but as the lost Motherland history. It is the lost world history that humans living in present time needs in order to be able to build a new world with lasting peace.

There were no wonders like described in the Bible, not ever. The wonders are a part of the camouflage that is the foundation for all the religions in the world.

The shepherds are a symbol for the all the world leaders, and the sheep's are a symbol for the whole world population in present time, including you. A new superior Motherland council will be the symbolic one shepherd for the whole world population.

The angels and the clear bright light is a symbol for the Diagram Star. They are the messengers from the spirit world enlightening the whole world population with the Motherland history, born again in to the common world of thoughts. Now think of Jesus as the light in the centre of the Diagram Star.

Jesus came back to planet earth some two thousand years ago, to save the whole world population from their life as slaves, soldiers and servants for the occupying armed forces of the warrior kings and the priesthoods. The born again Motherland history had to be camouflaged as a religion. It was the only way the Masters could preserve and pass on the history of the lost Motherland to coming generation, and they succeeded. Their camouflaged stories became the world religions that the descendants of the warrior king and priesthoods still use as a tool to control the population on their land.

Now time has come to uncover the lost world history and restore lasting peace on planet Earth.

The visit of the Wise men

Matthew 2, 1-10

A little while later Mary and Joseph were visited by high ranking persons. They were wise men from a land far east. They had seen the bright shining star on the night sky and thought something great had happened. Therefore they came the long way. First they went to see Herod the king in Jerusalem.

They asked: "Where is he that is born the King of the Jews? For we have seen his star in the east and have come to worship him."

Herod the king knew nothing about the birth of Jesus. He asked the religious leaders and scribes: "Where is the king of the Jews to be born?"

"In Bethlehem," they answered. This they knew because the prophets had said it many years before.

"When did the star appear?" the king asked the wise men. He wanted to find out as much as possible about the new king. He did not want anyone to come and take his throne. Herod the king was an evil man. Now he started thinking out a plan. "Go and worship him," he said to the three wise men. "When you have found him, I want you to come back to me and tell me where he is, so I can worship him to."

The wise men went to Bethlehem. They followed the star until it stopped. When they went in to the cave, they saw baby Jesus in the arms of Mary. They smiled and laughed. This was worth the effort with the long journey. They had found the king!

Without the camouflage of religion the story about the birth of Jesus the child is dramatically changed.

The history of the lost Motherland has traveled through the ages, through our known and accepted world history. The story was remembered by the Masters and their students with the Diagram Star as a common book of education. Some two thousand years ago the lost Motherland history was born again, concealed in a masterly made camouflage.

King Herod is a symbol for all evil in the world at present time, and in the Bible it is written that only the spirit of God can remove all evil from the world we all live in. Now be wise and think through the definition of God again. God is the superior Motherland council, the twelve titles that was lost when the Motherland went under. They are in the spirit world now. Jesus is a fictive person, the born again Motherland history. The whole story about him is telling you and the whole world population how to elect a new superior Motherland council, in detail.

From the multitude, meaning the whole world population, the twelve apostles are chosen. The twelve apostles are teachers with a Masters degree and from them the common laws and rules for the whole world population are given. It is only the willpower of the whole world population together in agreement, standing behind a new Motherland parliament and a new physical superior Motherland council, who will be strong enough to remove all evil from the world. You know the definition of all evil to be the three factors of the Original Sin, namely all the national states, the global capitalistic system and all the religions in the world.

The three wise men are a true symbol for the lost Motherland and the Masters that were educated on the Motherland and knew the story well. After the whole Motherland continent had been destroyed in a natural catastrophe, a group of Masters made it their life mission to preserve and pass on the history about the lost Motherland from generation to generation. They succeeded.

The Masters are the three wise men in this camouflaged story, and they are a symbol for the lost Motherland, which was divided in to three kingdoms by natural cannels. Everything in the painting has a symbolic meaning. Their hats are showing who they are and where they came from.

Look at the old painting above. The jar that one wise man are handing over as a present to Jesus the child, is a symbol for the lost world history been handed over from the spirit world to you and the whole world population. The star in the back are the Diagram Star and Jesus the child dressed in white are the starlight. He is the Morning Star. He is the Bethlehem Star.

The cross in the halo behind Jesus is the emblem of Jesus as the born again Motherland history. The child is the story that Virgin Mary is receiving and is handing over to the people living in the world at present time. The halo around the heads of Mary and Joseph means that they are enlightened with the knowledge from Jesus, the Diagram Star. The three together are a symbol for the new Motherland that has to be built, and they want you to know.

The Master who painted the story down knew what he did, but had no idea that it would take mankind two thousand years to crack the code.

King Herod is a symbol for the many national states in the world, which with their self made laws and rules for living still control the whole population and force them to work all their lives and willingly pay taxes and dues. There are still warrior kings and priesthoods like there have been since after the Motherland went under. The capitalists and political leaders are still holding on to their riches and personal power and continue to build their capitalistic tower inn to the clouds. They don't know how wrong they are.

Now look at Bethlehem and the land around as a symbol or a theatrical stage for the whole world. It is fairly simple to predict what will happen when the whole world population gets to know the lost Motherland history. All humans know, deep within, that Jesus as a person never will come back and save the whole world population. It is only knowledge about the time before the lost Motherland was destroyed that can create lasting peace for the whole world.

Gifts to a king

Matthew 2, 11-12

> *The three wise men opened their sacks. They brought beautiful and rare gifts to the little family. Mary and Joseph watched with wide open eyes when they unpacked. "They are truly gifts for a king," Mary whispered to Joseph. He nodded.*

> *One of the wise men bent deep. "We have traveled far. The star showed us where to go. Here is gold to the great king."*

> *The second wise man came forward to Mary. "It is not often a star as large as this is visible. The child is going to be the greatest among humans." He laid a jar of myrrh at the feet of Mary. Myrrh was an exclusive perfume, only used by the rich people.*

> *The third wise man smiled to Mary and Joseph. "This is incense, which gives a delicious sent when it is burned. Incense for God. We don't know what it means, but this king is both human and God."*

> *Mary and Joseph thanked the men and all bent their head in prayer. They tanked God for sending Jesus to the world.*

> *The night before the wise men should leave for home, they had a strange dream. In the dream God warned them and said they should not go back to King Herod. The three wise men believed what they heard in the dream and went home another way.*

"This king is both human and God." Jesus is a human in the camouflaged story, and under the camouflage he is the born again Motherland history. He is the bright light from the Diagram Star, and you can see that it is the light radiating from the child that is enlightening all the visitors. Under the camouflage Virgin Mary is the new Motherland and God is the spiritual superior Motherland council. The Bethlehem Star is the Diagram Star and Jesus, the born again Motherland history, is the starlight in the centre. The Masters who wrote the story brought the history of the lost Motherland in to the world in this way.

The Masters had to make the camouflaged stories about Jesus popular and credible for the humans living in that period of time. The people had lived for thousands of years with the tyrannical warrior kings and dictating priesthoods as their leaders. The camouflaged stories told by the Masters were popular and was passed on from generation to generation as planned.

People with knowledge of the camouflage knew that the three wise men brought with them gift with a special meaning. It is still a gift for the whole world population, not received. It is the gift of freedom and the knowledge about how to build a new world with lasting peace.

In the time the Bible was written Jesus was spoken of as a king, in order to give the suppressed population hope for a better life with a global government system common to all the people on earth. They hoped for a life like their forefathers had, were all the tribes lived in peace and every village had control over their own lives.

It is very important that you, and all the humans living in present time, learn to separate evil from good by clear definitions, learn to remove the camouflage of religion from the Bible and take the Bible back as a regular world history. Then if Jesus is placed in the centre of the Diagram Star and the twelve apostles in the sections around, you discover the whole history about the Motherland that were lost some twelve thousand years ago. What you will learn then is that the whole world population can live natural and good lives on planet earth, with ever lasting peace and one set of laws and rules for living.

What Jesus and the twelve disciples is telling the humans living in present time, have to be studied over some time through education. After the graduation all humans will have a different degree of knowledge, built on the person's own spiritual strength and abilities. But you will all know and not believe.

Now it remains to be seen if the leaders of the many national states in the world will react the same way as Herod the king when they hear about a global system of government that is going to take away all their riches and privileges. There are still people living as the richest of the rich, continuing to protect their position as King Herod did.

Very important it is to build down all the three factors of the Original Sin with only peaceful means. If the political and religious leaders of the world don't give in and follow the will of the majority of people, the three factors of evil will eventually fall because of the force of Mother Nature. It will not be nice.

He shall be called Nazarene

Matthew 2, 13-23; Luke 2, 39-40

After the wise men had left Mary and Joseph, the family relaxed. Jesus the child sleeps and eats. He grew and became larger and stronger as the weeks passed by.

One night Joseph had a dream. Like the wise men he dreamt that God spoke to him: "Stand up! Take the child and his mother and flee into Egypt and stay there until I bring you the word when to return. Herod the king is searching for the child. He wants to kill it."

Joseph got up. The dream was so real. He did not doubt that it was God who had spoken to him. Earlier he had seen how God had protected them. Joseph bent his head and prayed: "Yes, God, we shall do as you say."

He woke Mary and told her what he had dreamt. They hurried packing what they had and loaded everything on the donkey. Joseph carefully lifted the sleeping Jesus and laid him in the arms of Mary. Then they left in to the dark night.

In between Herod the king had waited impatient for the three wise men to return from the visit in Bethlehem. He had planned on deceiving them, but now it was them deceiving him instead.

"They should tell me where this king of the Jews is." Herod did not like the thought that there was another king in the land. He wanted to be the only one. "Whoever this king of the Jews are, I will find him and kill him! I don't know where he is, but I know he is a little boy child."

Herod gave his soldiers the order that they should seek through all of Bethlehem and kill all newborn boy children under the age of two.

Several years past and finally the evil king Herod died. Joseph, Mary and Jesus lived safely in Egypt all this time.

One night the Lords angel appeared for Joseph in a dream and said: "Rise up and take the young child and his mother and go into the land of Israel. For those who sought the child's life is dead."

The next morning Joseph told the good news to Mary. Soon they were on the way back home. They settled in the city of Nazareth, so the words which were spoken by the prophets might be fulfilled: "Messiah shall be called a Nazarene."

In Nazareth Joseph had a carpenter workshop and people came to him with chairs and tables that needed repair. Joseph was working hard all day. He also made furniture. When Jesus got older, he was often in the workshop and watched Joseph work, and he helped him when he could.

In the evenings Joseph and Mary told Jesus about the history of the Jews, and they spoke about the good God. The little family learned a lot from each other in these years when Jesus was a boy.

"Messiah shall be called a Nazarene." In the old days all the teachers, who after their graduation left the Motherland to teach history and sciences, were called Nazarenes. The title was pronounced differently back then, more like Naacals, and they existed as a group of scholars for a long time after the Motherland went under. Soon they had to escape from the warrior kings and the priesthoods and work under cover, using the title Master. Therefore it is written in the Bible that everyone who reveals the lost Motherland history and become able to teach the whole world population shall be called a Nazarene.

The biblical Israel is the name for the new Motherland and the biblical Israelites are a symbol for the whole world population. The Jewish tribe was just one of the twelve tribes that emigrated from the Motherland to populate the whole world.

It is easy to see the similarities with what happened in Egypt when the Israelites got too many in number and became a treat to Pharaoh. By removing the camouflage from the stories, the born again Motherland history ones again will become a threat to the present system of governing the world. Under the camouflage the Bible is clearly saying that the global government system from the lost Motherland is the only way to build a new world with lasting peace.

Under the camouflage in the Old Testament we learn that the biblical Israelites still are living in Egypt, as working slaves, soldiers and servants. The Israelites symbolizes the whole world population and it is a fact that the leaders of the many national states are preserving and passing on the same evil government system as the Pharaoh and as King Herod stands for in this story from the New Testament.

It is easy to separate evil from good in all the camouflaged bible stories. It should be just as easy to separate evil from good in the world where you live. It is not the humans; it is the way the world is organized with many national states, a global system of capitalism and all the religions that are the forces of evil. All the three factors have to go in order to be able to build a new global order where all humans are equals.

With the Diagram Star in mind it is easy to place Jesus in the centre and the twelve disciples in the sections around. Jesus then becomes the bright shining light of the good laws and rules for living, as given by the superior Motherland council.

Jesus is symbolizing the sun in centre of the Diagram Star. He is the everlasting force of Mother Nature, the laws and rules given by the superior Motherland council. His disciples are symbols for the twelve members of the new superior Motherland council. They are representing the whole world population. The whole world population will again be enlightened with knowledge from the Diagram Star and the knowledge about the lost Motherland is the foundation for building a new world with lasting peace.

Remember now that the Diagram Star is like an open book that is made with the sun, the moon and the twelve star signs of the Zodiac as a model. The Diagram Star is the carrier of the whole history of the universe and planet earth. The cosmic diagram has been with mankind from before the beginning of time and will be with mankind until after the end of time. The emblem of the Motherland will soon again be the foundation for every living human being and give their life a true meaning.

In the Old Testament Jacob and his twelve sons is the foundation for life, the forefathers of the whole world population. Place Jacob in the centre of the Diagram Star he becomes Israel. His twelve sons become the biblical Israelites. The camouflaged Old Testament story tells us that they went to Egypt to settle on fertile land. In time they became too many, and every boy child was killed.

It is true that the twelve symbolic tribes immigrated and populated the whole world. After the destruction of the Motherland and the death of the superior Motherland council, the three factors of the Original Sin slowly but surely took control over the people all over the world. It is still the three factors of the Original Sin that are controlling the common human thinking and thereby enforcing the destructive and evil activity that are destroying the world.

The conclusion from just looking at the world around you will be that the whole world population, with no exceptions, still are working slaves, soldiers and servants forced to obey the laws and rules of their national state, just like our forefathers was in old Egypt.

The new world with lasting peace can only be built by use of the global system of government from the time before the Motherland went under. A new Motherland has to be built and without the three factors of evil, and the new world will be a true paradise.

Jesus among the teachers

Luke 2, 41-52

When Jesus was twelve years, Mary and Joseph took him along to Jerusalem. It was soon Easter, and the city was full of people.

The last day of the Passover Mary and Joseph left Jerusalem to return home. Both thought that Jesus was with other children going back to Nazareth. After a whole day on the way, they started asking other children in the group: "Have you seen Jesus?" The children shook their heads.

Mary and Joseph looked at each other. Jesus was left in Jerusalem! How could they find him? They left the people they trawled with and hurried back to Jerusalem. Hear they looked everywhere. Mary and Joseph did see many children, but they did not find Jesus.

For three days they searched high and low. They had lost the precious Son of God! Finally they went to the temple, were the Jewish people worshipped God on the Sabbath and other holydays. Joseph noticed a flock of teachers who were listening to someone. And there, in their midst, Jesus sat! It was him they listened too.

Mary and Joseph made their way to Jesus. Mary said: "Child, why didn't you try to find us? We have been looking for you everywhere. We were so worried!

"Why were you looking for me?" Jesus replied. "Did you not know that I must be in my father's house?"

Jesus meant that because he was the Son of God, he wanted to be in the temple, his father's house. When they left the temple with him, they heard people say: "It is strange that such a young boy can talk with such a great wisdom."

Jesus went back to Nazareth with Mary and Joseph. He was an obedient boy and did as they said. It was some good years for all of them.

The Master writing the story about Jesus has to make the camouflage right and interesting for the reader. Still, under the camouflage it is a story of great importance for mankind. The little family together is a symbol for how all the families in the world will be living in villages that are self supported with everything humans need to live a good life on planet earth.

Mary is a symbol for the new Motherland that has to be built in order to create lasting peace in the world. After the old Motherland had disappeared in to the ocean in a inferno of burning gasses and boiling water, all that was left is the history that people remembers and passes on to the new generations. Joseph the carpenter is a symbol for the knowledge the people living in present time need to restore in order to be able to build a new world with lasting peace. Jesus is the born again Motherland history. All three of them have a halo around their head, and it means that they are enlightened with knowledge from the Diagram Star.

The Israelites spoken of in the whole bible, is a symbol for the whole world population. The Jews were selected to symbolize the whole world population by the Masters who wrote all the camouflaged stories.

Jerusalem is truly a theatrical stage, a symbol for the Motherland the Masters wanted to tell the whole world population about. They tried to do what I am trying to do in present time. They used the region where they lived as a theatre stage. Truly the life and death of Jesus are played ones a year, all over the world. It is a great play, and like any play made while the occupants was watching, had to be camouflaged.

The Temple is a symbol for the seven temples that were the education centers in the Motherland before it went under. It is the house of God, and God is defined to be the twelve members of the superior Motherland council. They had the twelve star signs of the Zodiac as an emblem for the position they were elected in to. With the sun in the centre the emblem became the Diagram Star, which is the carrier of the whole history of mankind.

If you look at the diagram you will see a map of the whole world, with the lost Motherland in the centre and all other regions and empires in the sections around. You will see that all the cities and villages in the world is built with the Diagram Star as a ground drawing, with the town hall in the centre and all the other buildings in the sections around.

And the Diagram Star is the ground drawing for how the new Motherland and the self supported villages is going to be built, with lasting peace in a world were all evil is gone for good.

The Bible is a bridge over troubled water; it is a bridge over knowledge going back in time, more than twelve thousand years. You have to know about the past in order to be able to build the future. It is really impossible to build a new world with lasting peace, only by use of the three factors of the Original Sin. The many national states have to be removed and replaced with democratically elected councils. They shall all have a new superior Motherland council to lead them. The humans living in present time don't have the slightest idea about how to live without all the national states, the global system of capitalism and all the religions in the world.

How can you be convinced that your way of life have to change before lasting peace can be restored for your children and their descendants?

Knowledge about the lost Motherland and the global system of government was lost in time because the warrior kings and the priesthoods did their best to make everyone forget. They wanted to continue to live in luxury and keep the whole population as obedient slaves, soldiers and servants. Soon new generations was born in to the world, knowing nothing about the Motherland history. The only education they got was what their parents had learned before them. All they knew was that they had to obey the laws and the living rules given by the king and his closest and most trusted men.

This is the world that you were born inn to; just look yourself around.

In the time before the Motherland was destroyed, education was the most important activity for all humans. Every tribal village had an education centre and the Diagram Star was their common book of knowledge.

The Diagram Star has for a long time been spiritual, invisible and hidden behind the camouflage of dogmas and assumptions, like for example the Bethlehem Star and the star in the top of every Christmas three.

Even if the knowledge the star is radiating is forgotten, all writings burned and all temples given false religious meanings, the knowledge about the lost Motherland will always live on in the Spirit World. Under the camouflage of religion the Diagram Star is living and radiating knowledge to the world. Remove the camouflage and you will find safety, and an abundance of happiness along with the knowledge. Knowing the Diagram Star will be you most precious treasure.

Even if there isn't one single Master left alive in the world, all their thoughts through all times are found in the Spirit World. All you have to do to understand it all is to separate good from evil in the world you live in. No other human can do it for you. You will learn that all evil in your world of thoughts is coming directly from the three factors of the Original Sin. I know that my definition is right, and all three factors have to be built down by use of only peaceful means, before the new world with lasting peace can be built.

It is written in the Bible that only the spirit of God can remove all evil from the world we all live in. You know the definition of God by now.

Just like Jesus was lost for his parents, the born again Motherland history was lost for you some two thousand years, camouflaged as God. So start searching in your own world of thoughts now!

Jesus is baptized

Matthew 3, 1-17; Markus, 1, 1-11; Luke 3, 1-22; John 1, 29-34

Jesus had a relative. He was named John the Baptist. John was the son of Elisabeth, Mary's old relative. When John became adult, God told him that he should speak a special message to the people. "Make yourself ready!" John was to tell them. "Make yourself ready for him who is coming!"

People sat on the riverbank of Jordan and listened to him. John baptized people. He said he knew why God wanted them to be clean. "Convert and begin a new life!

John looked up and wondered who the next person to be baptized was to be. It was Jesus! The two relatives looked at each other. Jesus went down in to the water. When he came out, he prayed. Then the heaven opened! Gods Holy Spirit came over him. It was like a dove hovering over his head. This made it clear for everyone who was present that Jesus was filled with the Holy Spirit.

A voice spoke from heaven: "You are my son. I have always loved you. You have done what pleases me." It was Gods voice. He told the people that they should listen to Jesus.

Look at the old painting above. It is painted by a Master and under the camouflage of religion the message is clear.

In the back you see the Diagram Star. The water comes from the starlight. The dark color from the star is telling the humans living in present time that the knowledge was covered by the darkness of oblivion and replaced by religious belief at the time it was painted. The Diagram Star is not dark any longer. Time has come to shine the light of knowledge all over the world.

The formula is clear: Water = Knowledge about the lost Motherland. Jesus is the born again Motherland history. Being the Son of God means he is spiritual, a product of knowledge and common thoughts, and he is a fictive figure that never lived as a human.

John the Baptist is called the Son of Man, and is a symbol for the lost Motherland history where people where men, real living human beings. He was captured and beheaded as the story shows, and symbolizes the fate of the millions of other real human beings who dared to oppose the warrior kings and priesthoods by speaking about the lost Motherland as a kingdom without the terror of their despotic rule.

John the Baptist is speaking directly to you, living I present time. Convert now! It is the last change you and your descendants will get. If you continue to live under the force of the three factors of the Original Sin, mankind will destroy them self completely.

It is literally you, the whole world population that are the Hebrew people, living on the other side of the river Jordan in a mental desert. You all have to rise from your life as blinded and mentally dead, and start living a new life with knowledge instead of a meaningless imposed religious belief.

The dove above the head of Jesus has a twig in the beak and shows with this quite clear that a new world has to be built for the whole world population. It is a peace dove that speaks of the Promised Land, the new world that not yet has been built.

The halo means that they are enlightened by the knowledge from the Diagram Star. The three students standing in line to be baptized, symbolizes the whole world population.

In the Motherland, more than twelve thousand years ago, baptism in water was a ceremony that was a confirmation of the student's level of education when graduating. The baptism had a true and deep traditional meaning.

Gods Holy Spirit, under the camouflage of religion, is all the knowledge that are in the Spirit World, meaning the container of every thought that humans have thought all through the ages. It is the common world of thoughts and is used by all living human beings, all the time. You are searching for the thoughts of the spiritual superior Motherland council.

The Diagram Star is the visible book that has been with humans all this time. Everything that humans are learning comes as thoughts and is spiritual. It is thoughts that are controlling human lives at all times, and by nature it is meant that all human thoughts shall be good and right.

The evil thoughts derived from the three factors of the Original Sin, is the force of evil occupying your thoughts all the time. It is only the spiritual force of the thoughts of the superior Motherland council that can remove all evil from the common world of thoughts.

Jesus and his friends

John 1, 19-34

Sometimes when John the Baptist was preaching, religious leaders came and watched everything that went on. They wanted to know if John really was prophet, sent by God. "Who is the strange looking man standing preaching in the middle of the river?" they asked each other.

"Who are you", they asked him.

John answered: "I am not Christ." John knew that Jesus was Messiah or Christ.

"But why do you baptize then, when you are neither Christ nor a prophet sent by God?"

"I baptize in water, but there is one who is standing with you who will baptize with the spirit of God. I am not worthy of being his slave." The Pharisees looked around in the crowd but saw no one different from all others.

A few days later John saw Jesus in the crowd again. Then he shouted: "There is the Son of God. He is carrying the sins of the world! I baptize you in water, but he shall baptize you with the spirit of God! He is the Son of God, but you don't know him!"

When the Pharisees heard John, they got even more confused and angry. They saw Jesus walking through the crowd of people. "It is bad enough that John have so many followers. If this Jesus becomes even more popular than him, our problems are bigger than we thought."

The spirit of God is the spirit of the superior Motherland council and Jesus is the born again Motherland history. John the Baptist is a symbol for the knowledge all human being lived with as a part of their daily life in the time before the Motherland was destroyed. People were by tradition baptized in water when they reached the age of 25, and got their spiritual strength and the degree of education confirmed in the presence of the village council and the whole village population. Everybody lived with knowledge about the superior Motherland council and knew that the best students could be selected to sit in the Motherland parliament or even in the superior Motherland council.

Being baptized by John the Baptist is a symbol for coming across the river, from the mental desert of oblivion and in to the new world full of knowledge. The process from religious belief to knowledge about the lost Motherland is like a walk from the desert and inn to the land of milk and honey. On the way you will cross a symbolic river of knowledge. John the Baptist is a stronghold in the real world.

Being baptized by the spirit of God is the process of finding the full Motherland history only in contact with the spirit world and the spiritual Motherland council.

Jesus is the born again Motherland history, the part of the lost world history that the whole world population is searching for. The Pharisees is a symbol for the laws and rules of all the national states in the world. The crowd is you, the whole world population still standing on the other side of the river Jordan. It is symbolical described as being a mental desert, a lifetime of not knowing anything about the lost Motherland. The act of being baptized with water by John the

Baptist means a mental walk across the river and truly finding the long gone knowledge about the lost Motherland.

Under the camouflage of religion the water in the river Jordan is knowledge about the lost Motherland history and the global system of government that again can create long lasting peace in the world.

Remember that also John is a fictive person and that it is the Master writing the story who is talking through him directly to humans living in present time. There is no way around the many camouflaged stories in the Bible. As parables they are all about the whole world population. You are all Hebrews living on the other side of the river. The stories under the camouflage are taking you back in time some twelve thousand years, and it is all about your thoughts and the common thoughts of the whole world population. It is the common world of thoughts that have to be cleansed with knowledge. Remember that water is knowledge, and just one little fragment of knowledge can make the large walls of religious belief fall and crumble in the common world of thoughts. It will happen, hopefully soon.

Under the camouflage the Pharisees is a symbol for the wall of religion, and together with the two other factors of evil the religion is a major factor of the Original Sin.

The Pharisees is the religious leaders of the time, just as the priesthoods are in present time. Together with the national leaders and the builders of the global capitalistic system, the three factors are still making the lives of the whole world population in to a living hell. The billions of poor and suffering humans know that a living Hell is a correct description of the world and has been for the last twelve thousand years.

It is of fundamental importance that all of you, the whole world population, are waking up from the mental trance of imposed blindness that you are living in. You have to decide, all on your own, what is right and what is wrong in the world history you live with and have learned to be proud of.

It is a fundamental fact that the building of the many national states by the use of warfare, religion and the greed for personal riches and power, was wrong as wrong can be back then when it first happened. The warrior kings and priesthoods acted a lot worse than the worst thinkable criminals and committed a crime against mankind that still goes on.

Sadly it seems that no one is able to see the world from inside the bobble where you all live. You have to come out and see the world from outside in order to understand. What will the richest of the rich and all the national and religious leaders do when they discover that all they do is the command of the three factors of the Original Sin? They preserve and pass on the three factors that are manmade and slowly are destroying the planet that still would have been a paradise, if the Motherland had not been destroyed some twelve thousand years ago.

Something must happen soon, because it is clearly visible for everyone that the force of Mother Nature that is protesting against the destructive human activity.

All the religions in the world are building on indoctrinated dogmas and assumptions that are meant to control the national workforce in tight collaboration with the global capitalistic system.

All humans who lives inside the borders of a national state is forced to work all their life for dictating national laws and rules for living. The Original Sin are a vital part of most human daily lives and are, by use of the many national traditions, passed on from generation to generation.

The Devil is tempting Jesus

Matthew 4, 1-12; Mark 1, 12-21; 6, 17-20; Luke 3, 19-20

After Jesus was baptized in the river Jordan, he went out in to the wilderness to pray. God's enemy, the devil, wanted to destroy Gods plans for Jesus. He hated that someone lived near God.

Jesus was the Son of God. He could do anything. God's enemy wanted Jesus to use his power for him and not for God.

Jesus was in the wilderness for forty days. He ate nothing the whole time. The devil knew he was very hungry. First he tried to tempt Jesus with food. "If you are the Son of God, command this stone to be bread."

Jesus knew that it was more important to do what God wanted. "Man does not live by bread alone, but by every word that comes out of the mouth of God."

Then the devil took Jesus to the holy city of Jerusalem and put him on a pinnacle of the temple. "Jump," said the devil. "If you are the Son of God, throw yourself down. For it is written that he shall send his angels to save you."

"It is also written: You shall not tempt the Lord your God."

Finally the devil took Jesus to the top of a big mountain and showed him all the kingdoms in the world and the glory of them. "All this tings I will give you, if you fall down and worship me."

Then Jesus said: "Away, Satan. For it is written: You shall worship the Lord your God and him only you shall serve." Then the devil left him, and angels came to serve Jesus.

When Jesus left the wilderness, he heard that king Herod had thrown John the Baptist in prison. When Jesus heard that he departed into Galilee. And leaving Nazareth, he went to stay in Capernaum on the sea coast.

This camouflaged story is very interesting. It is in a way talking directly to you, living in present time. The spiritual God and Heaven are defined to be the physical paradise world from the time before the Motherland went under. After the natural catastrophe the Motherland was remembered by all humans in the world as a Heaven in the Spirit World. God is defined to be the superior Motherland council, and they are all spiritual beings in the Heaven. The reason all people think of Heaven up on the sky is the fact that the sun, the moon and the twelve Zodiac star signs always have been the official emblem for the superior Motherland council. The last Masters elected in to the position as members of the superior Motherland council have been dead for some twelve thousand years. Now time has come to elect twelve new members to a new physical Motherland council and build a new Motherland. It will be like bringing the lost Motherland back on planet earth and build a new world with the use of the born again Motherland history.

Defining the Devil and Hell is not difficult. The Devil is the three factors of the Original Sin and Hell is the whole physical world at present time. The whole world population is truly worshipping the Devil in their desperate quest for riches and personal power. The Devil has been in command over all the national states in the world for some twelve thousand years and life is a living Hell for the whole world population.

Remember now that Adam and Eve were tempted by the Devil, disguised as a serpent, in the time just after the Motherland was destroyed in a natural catastrophe. It was then humans discovered that they could break the laws and rules given by the superior Motherland council and get away with it.

Jesus is tempted and you are told that the right thing to do is to always live according to the laws and rules given by a new superior Motherland council. As soon as you reject the forces of evil, you will know that there is no going back.

All the religions in the world are imposed on your forefathers a long time ago by warrior kings and priesthoods and you have inherited the life with the three factors of the Original Sin from them.

Your children and their descendants will continue to inherit the many imposed religious dogmas and assumption from you, if you continue to live like you do. It doesn't matter if you are a believer or a not believer, the many religions are a part of your life wherever you live. Don't you care at all? Not caring are the greatest sin of all.

Now you know that it is the three factors of the Original Sin that is tempting you all the time, never setting you free. You live in one of the many kingdoms in the world. See for yourself what the forces of evil are doing to the world you live in.

The camouflaged story about Jesus being tempted by the Devil in the wilderness is a dream story telling you that you have to choose the way Jesus did in order to save the world you live in from being completely destroyed.

Jesus is the born again Motherland history and the Devil is the three factors of the Original Sin. It is the three factors that you are born into and like everyone else; you hate the way the world is organized. Still you think that removing all the nations, the global capitalistic system and all the religions in the world, is impossible. Well, it is not impossible. Mother Nature is calling out loud, warning the leaders of the world time after time that soon it will be too late to say no to the Devil.

What to do? The only way for mankind to survive is to divide them self in to self supported tribal communities. After the present system of government, with many national states, a global system of capitalism and all the religions in the world, is built down with the use of only peaceful means, the whole planet can again be built like a true paradise for the whole world population.

Just imagine that all the weapons of war is melted and made in to pickaxes, spades and other tools for tilling the earth and all the people in the world are living together with lasting peace.

The first disciples

John 1, 35-52

Just before John the Baptist was taken to prison, he asked two of his followers to go and follow Jesus. One of them was Andrew. When he and his friend found Jesus, they followed him. Jesus turned and asked what they wanted.

They asked if they could come with him to where he had thought staying the night. They wanted to hear what he had to say. Jesus answered yes.

The followers of John had learned how important it is to listen to the truth. John had said to them: "Soon one will come that is greater than me. Follow him."

While Andrew was listening to Jesus, he thought for himself that he had to tell everyone he knew about this man that John the Baptist had spoken about. He went to see his brother. "Simon!" he called. "We have found the Messiah! Come with me to him."

Simon did not know what to believe. When Jesus saw him, he said: "You are Simon, son of Jonah. You shall be called Kefas, or Peter. Both Kefas and Peter means rock." It was the first time Jesus met Simon and from now on Simon was called Simon Peter. Later it became only Peter.

The next day Jesus walked to Galilee. Here he met a man named Philip. "Follow me," he said, and Philip did as he was told.

Philip got hold of a friend named Nathanael. "We have found him that Moses and the prophets have spoken about," he said. "It is Jesus from Nazareth."

Nathanael laughed. He said that he didn't believe that something good could come from Nazareth. But when they met, Jesus said to him: "I know you, Natanael. You believe in God, and you try to do what he wants. I also know that you sat in the shade of the fig tree and thought when Philip found you."

Nathanael was surprised that Jesus knew so much about him. "I believe," he said. "You are the Son of God. You are the king of Israel."

Jesus smiled. "Do you believe so easily? You shall see bigger things happen than this."

This is interesting. The bigger things Jesus talks about and the wonders he does is not about healing people, but about healing the whole world. Israel is the name of the world. The born again Motherland history can heal the world.

This is the recipe you have to understand and follow before a new world with lasting peace can be built. First you denounce the three factors of the Original Sin, also known as the Devil. Then you make the born again Motherland history known to the whole world population. The disciples are humans whom want to know and want to build a new world with lasting peace. In other words the whole world population has to participate in selecting the many leaders of the new parliament. They will be the teachers explaining the full history of the lost Motherland and how the life of all humans will be in a new world. The mental walk will take time, because every living human being has to find knowledge in their own world of thoughts.

Jesus is the born again Motherland history, still camouflaged with words and still thoughts that are meant for the reader, for you and the whole world population. If you now are beginning to understand the great wonder the born again Motherland history can do to the world, the work of the ancient Masters will be fulfilled.

In time the new superior Motherland council will be democratically elected from the best leaders from every people in the world. It is you and the whole world population living in present time that has to gather a new Motherland parliament and elect superior Motherland council. Under the camouflage of religion, God is the superior Motherland council, the only democratically elected power that can govern all the people in the world with only peaceful means. By means of their position they will be omnipotent, omniscient and omnipresent.

The Masters, who wrote the great wonders described in the Bible, knew that the wonders never happened in the real world, not then, not before and not after. They were using the tribal history of the Jews as a background and made-up the camouflage stories in order to make the stories in to popular historical tales.

The symbolism is glowing from this story. John the Baptist is the son of the old couple Elisabeth and Zacharias. John is called the Son of Man, and he is the born again Motherland history revealed from the past. When John baptized Jesus, it is an act of passing the Motherland history on from the far past and in to the present time.

The Motherland history has been lost since the Motherland went under some twelve thousand years ago. Jesus is the key that you and the whole world population have to use to retrieve the lost Motherland history from the Spirit World, where the full story is now. In the real world the lost Motherland history is made in to a religion, because the Roman emperor and the religious leaders back then denied that the lost Motherland ever existed. If the world leaders of present time also deny that the lost Motherland ever existed, they have to be convinced before it is too late.

Jesus is the born again Motherland history and his twelve disciples are a symbol for the new superior Motherland council. They are representing the whole world population. You are all students before you graduate.

Nathanael is calling Jesus the king of Israel. This has nothing to do with the present state of Israel, were only one of the twelve tribe's lives, namely the Jews.

Jesus is called the king of the Israelites, the twelve Hebrew tribes that evolved from the twelve sons of Jacob, who was named Israel. The born again Motherland history is the king of the whole world and are only power that can lead you and the whole world population out of the mental desert of oblivion that you all are in, across the river of knowledge and in to the Promised Land; in to a new world with long lasting peace.

The lost Motherland truly was the centre of a united world, and the born again Motherland history is the foundation for the building of a new centre for the whole world population. It will be the rightful Israel. The superior Motherland council will soon again be the power over all powers; the king over all kings; the council over all the councils in a new world.

In our present time it is you who are the disciples who have to start thinking completely new, and some of you will become apostles, meaning teachers.

A large catch

Matthew 4, 18-22; Mark 1, 16-20; Luke 5, 1-11

After Andrew had taken Peter to Jesus, the two brothers went home. They were fishermen and had to tend to the boats and the nets.

Peter saw that a large multitude of people coming towards him. Jesus walked in front of them. He went straight to Peter, entered his boat and asked him to pull out from the shore. From the boat Jesus spoke to the crowd of people.

When Jesus was finished speaking he turned to Peter. "Row out on deep water and let down your nets for a catch," he said.

"Master, we have been working all night and have taken nothing," Peter answered. "Nevertheless, I will do as you say."

When he had done this, they enclosed a great multitude of fish. The net almost broke! He had to call for help from another boat. They came and they filled both the boats so full that they began to sink.

When Peter saw this, he fell down on his knees before Jesus, saying: "Depart from me, for I am a sinful man, O Lord."

Jesus said to him and Andrew: "Don't be afraid. Follow me and I will make you fishers of men." And immediately they left their boats and nets and followed him.

When they had gone a little further they met two other fishermen, who were in their boats mending their nets. They were the two brothers Jacob and John. Jesus walked to them and said: "Follow me." They left their father Zebedee in the boat with the hired servants, and followed Jesus.

These men became close friends of Jesus. They followed him everywhere, while he taught the people. They too did learn from him. They were his students, his disciples.

Why is the Egyptian hieroglyphs translated so wrong? This story tells about how difficult it has been for the lost Motherland history to become known and accepted by the whole world population. But with the help of the born again Motherland history, the symbolic catch is phenomenal. Under the camouflage of religion everybody understands that this is not about catching fish at all, it is about humans transforming their thoughts from religious belief and in to knowledge about the lost Motherland history.

The born again Motherland history will get an abundance of followers all over the world, very quickly, as soon as people learn to understand that the lost Motherland history can remove the force of evil from the world. It is a part of the world history that has to be written down and spoken about, in order to make it known to the whole world population.

The born again Motherland history will tell you about a paradise world that is without all the national states, without the global system of capitalism and without all the religions in the world. The new world will be a world where nothing is done with the motivation of making money. The sole motivation for making things will be a general need and everything will be free. The reason for living for everyone will return to build cosmic eggs and populate new fertile planets out in the universe. There will be enough work to do for everyone where they live. It will be a world filled with technology; education will be the most important activity. Everyone will live in strong houses in self supported villages, wear nice clothes and own things made of gold, silver and precious stones. And the valuable items will carry the history of the family and tribe through the ages.

The world will be very different, in fact just as you think a paradise should be.

Water, Air, Earth and Fire = Knowledge about the lost Motherland, says the formula. You know by now that the Diagram Star is the official emblem of the superior Motherland council and that it is the sun, moon and the twelve star signs of the Zodiac that are the model for the Diagram Star. All the humans in the world are born in to a certain star sign and get an education from the Diagram Star. In a world without the three factors of the Original Sin, live would all of a sudden have a meaning for the whole world population.

The disciples are symbols for the new superior Motherland council, representing the whole world population. In present time everyone is living with the three factors of the Original Sin as their dictating laws and rules for living. Therefore the new elected Motherland council will have to start off as disciples, as students that have to learn to read the Diagram Star like an open book.

The written and accepted world history tells us about the gruesome deeds the warrior kings and the priesthoods did to each other in order to be the among the richest and the strongest military national states in the world. The whole world population is in present time still working slaves, soldiers and servants within their national border. There are no exceptions, because even the richest of the rich have to build their guarded home like a prison were the owner locks them self in every night.

Only knowledge from the Diagram Star can set the whole world populations free. The chosen disciples are fishermen, and in this story they make a great catch with the help of Jesus form Nazareth. Jesus helps them in this miraculous way in order to make them follow him and learn more.

Under the camouflage you and the whole world population are the fiches. Jesus is the born again Motherland history and the disciples representing all the people living in the world. Hopefully soon many of you will be active in healing the world with knowledge. It is the only remedy that can create lasting peace in the world.

Many national states will feel ashamed for being what they are, like Peter was, when people get convinced that the knowledge they need to build the new world, is found under the camouflage of religion, in their Bible. Because the world population has lived with the three factors of the Original Sin in charge for some twelve thousand years, mankind does not have a choice if they want to build a new world with lasting peace for their children and their descendants.

The marriage in Cana

John 2, 1-11

A few days later Jesus and his disciples were invited to a wedding in Cana, the city Nathanael came from. It was a large wedding. The festivities lasted for several days. Mary, the mother of Jesus, was there to.

Many people came to the wedding. New food was put on the table very often. It was meat and nuts, rice, bread and fruit. All the guests drank wine. Half way through the feast the bridegroom discovered that they had very little wine left. It would be bad if they didn't have enough.

It was the bridegrooms responsibility that there was enough wine. If it ended, it meant that the festivity would end to. This was not good!

Mary heard about the problem. She went to Jesus. "They have no more wine," she said.

"Why do you tell me that?" Jesus replied. "It is not yet time for me to act."

Mary still called a servant. She said that he had to do exactly what Jesus told him to do. Jesus asked the servant to fill up three large stone jars with water. In the same moment the jars were full, he said: "Take the water to the kitchen master to taste." When he tasted the water it had turned in to wine. He took it to the bridegroom to taste.

"What are you doing?" he said. "This is the best wine I have ever tasted!" The bridegroom did not know where the wine came from, but Mary did.

When the camouflage is removed from this story, it is all about doing what may seem impossible. All humans know that wine is made from grapes alone. The grapes need water to grow, but there is not a drop of water used in the process of making wine from the grapes. It is the sun and the rain water that makes the grape plants grow. Only Mother Nature can produce the grapes used for making wine.

Now look at who is present at the wedding and see the symbolism. Jesus is the born again Motherland history. He is the bright light from the Diagram Star, bringing the knowledge about the Motherland history to the whole world population. It is truly needed. The world leaders just don't know what to do and needs to be told.

The Master who is telling the story to humans living in present time is emphasizing that convincing the whole world population about what the Motherland history can do for the whole world population, will seem just as impossible as making wine from water alone.

Look at the wedding in Cana as the whole world population in present time. The world leaders are discovering that the life they live under the dictating laws and rules given by the three factors of the Original Sin, is coming to an end. It is an end caused by the forces of nature, because human beings with their destructive activity have used almost all the natural resources on planet Earth.

The only thing that can save mankind from a total collapse; from the end of life on earth as we all know it, is the born again history of the Motherland. This is the truth, and it is not a minute to soon humans gets to know this. The knowledge that all humans needs to build the new world with lasting peace, is found in the light from the Diagram Star.

The unclean Temple

John 2, 13-25

Jesus and his disciples walked to Jerusalem. They came just before the Passover and went straight to the temple. It was here Mary and Joseph had found him the time they had lost him.

When Jesus came to his father's house this time, he did not like what he saw. Instead of praying to God and study the Law of Moses, they used the temple as a marked place. They sold sheep's and oxen and birds that the visitors could use for offering. They heard the sound of the animals and people shouting and screaming in the temple. The disciples looked at Jesus. They understood that he thought this was very bad.

Suddenly Jesus took a whip. He ran in to the temple square. The disciples looked at him with surprise. Jesus ran back and forth and drove both humans and animals away. "Get out," he shouted. "Take all this away from here! How dare you make my father's house in to a marketplace?"

He overthrows the money changers table. The coins went in all directions. The animals ran out and the people shouted in fright.

When Jesus was finished, he gathered the people and taught them. This he continued to do the whole Passover holiday. He did several wonders. Many believed in what he said and they wanted to hear more about God. They promised that they would follow him.

This camouflaged story is about the whole planet Earth and the destructive and evil activity of mankind. The temple was meant to be a sanctuary where people should gather and remember the superior Motherland council in the time after the catastrophe. Lighting a candle in remembrance and giving livestock to help the poor and starving was an act of goodness for a long time, until the forces of evil took control. As you know, the tree forces of the Original Sin is still in charge, and the act of goodness is actively used by the priesthoods to make people pay money to them in order to be called good religious believers.

It is truly very wrong to bring the three factors of the Original Sin in to the temple and enforce people to believe in dogmas and assumptions that are made up by the leading religious authorities. The sole motivation of the priesthood was to make money. Now you can see how rich they have become, just by telling lies and pure nonsense to the people. The paradox is that just under the camouflage of religion the full story about the lost Motherland is hidden.

Jerusalem is a symbol for the lost Motherland and the temple is a symbol for the many learning centers in the world in the time before the Motherland went under.

In the present situation there are no learning centers in the whole world. All the cathedrals, churches, synagogues, mosques and all other buildings used for prayer and worship of the many Gods, is unclean in the sense that they all base their existence on making money. All the religions in the world are a major part of the Original Sin and they truly are an insult to all humans.

Therefore it is correct to call the whole planet earth for a sacred temple for the whole world population, and it is very much unclean. Make sure you understand this correct. It is the common thoughts of the whole world population that are unclean, in the sense that it is the thoughts derived from the three factors of the Original Sin have been enforced on to human beings for several thousand years.

The common world of thoughts is occupied by the three factors of the Original Sin and the only natural forces that can clean the thoughts for all humans are the knowledge about the lost Motherland history and the Diagram Star. Jesus is the bright shining star in the diagram returning as knowledge to the whole world. He starts to teach the people as a process of cleansing the common world of thoughts. He is a spiritual person telling the born again Motherland history to the whole world. He is demonstrating what you have to do before you can build a new world with lasting peace for your children and their descendants.

Your mind is your personal temple and your world of thoughts has to be cleansed by separating right from wrong. Your thoughts are unclean after several thousand years of wrong teaching.

There are no evil people in the world, just evil thoughts.

What then, will the cleansing of thoughts result in?

All the oil wells in the world will be closed for all future, with the positive consequences that will have on the earth's climate.

Without the unnatural and desperate quest for money and personal power humans will be able to concentrate on the technological development and lead the evolution back on the right track again. Flying vessels will be built several places in the world, for common use, and the building of cosmic eggs will commence.

Planet Earth is not the first planet in the history of mankind, and will not be the last. The planet will send seed out in to the universe in order to populate new earthlike planets with earth life. Many cosmic eggs will be built in the future, as described in the camouflaged story about Noah and his Ark.

The reason for the humans in present time to know so little about the universe and the history of planet earth is due to the influence of the three factors of the Original Sin, the occupation of the human daily life that happened some twelve thousand years ago. It will take time to make the multitude of blind people see the truth. You are all living your lives as living dead, and you find no meaning with life. The born again Motherland history will make the blind people see and wake up the living dead.

He is the water of life

John 4, 1-26

Jesus and his disciples passed through a district called Samaria. The people here, the Samarians, had been the enemies of the Jews for a long time. No Jew would speak with a Samaritan.

But Jesus started talking to a Samaritan woman when he came to a well. He was tired after a long walk. Now he asked her: "Will you give me some water?"

She was surprised over that a Jew spoke to her, but she pulled water from the well and gave to him. "How come that you, being a Jew, is talking to me, a Samaritan woman?" she asked.

Jesus said: "If you knew the life that God would give you and if you knew who I am, you would ask me for water to drink. Then I would give you living water from God. If you drink from the water that I will give you, you shall live forever, and never be thirsty ever again."

The Samaritan woman became surprised. Water is something we all need to live. Especially in a land where it is hot, like in Samaria, people appreciate water. Often it is difficult to find water.

Jesus said: "Every person who drinks from the water I will give him shall never thirst again."

"That water I want!" the women shouted. Then Jesus asked her to get her husband to come. When she told Jesus that she didn't have a husband, Jesus told her everything about her life. He knew how many men she had been with. "And the man you are living with now is not your husband," he added.

The woman became even more surprised. How could he know all her secrets? She was afraid for him and tried to talk about something else. Jesus knew what she was thinking and he wanted to help her. She said that she did not know a lot about God, but she had heard about a Messiah that should come to planet earth.

"Messiah has arrived," said Jesus. "You are talking to him now!"

The Master writing this camouflaged story makes it easy to remove the camouflage. A well full of water is a symbol for the Diagram Star. Water = Knowledge; knowledge about the born again Motherland history.

Jesus is the Messiah, the message hidden in the Bible, the lost history that mankind needs in order to be able to build a new world with ever lasting peace. The water of life that he wants to give the Samarian woman is knowledge, and when she knows about the lost Motherland, she will know how to live her life right.

The Samarian woman is a symbol for the whole world population, who is told to believe what national state leaders tell them is right and don't ask questions. The message in the Bible is that all humans in the world should be living together like brothers and friends, like a global family. And that is truly the life the whole world population wants to live. They only have to be told that the message has arrived. It is hidden in the Bible, under the camouflage of religion.

If you only knew the life knowledge from the Diagram Star could give the whole world population, you would not hesitate for one moment. After a learning period you would never have to seek knowledge no more.

The knowledge from the Diagram Star is in a natural cycle in the common world of thoughts, just like the cycle of water. Your world of thoughts needs cleansing and learning before the cycle of knowledge can begin to lead you through your lifetime on planet earth.

The woman at the well

John 4, 27-42

"Who is the woman at the well?" the disciples asked when they came back from the place they had been to buy food. When they saw that Jesus was talking to her, they got worried. "That he should not do," they said. "She is a Samaritan. No Jew will speak with them."

The woman did see the angry faces and thought that it was about time to get home. Jesus had given her quite a lot to think about. She left the jar of water and hurried in to the city. There she met a multitude of people: "Come and see a man who has told me all that I have done in my life," she said. "Can it be possible? Could it be the Messiah who had come? "

The woman's story made people curious. They followed her out to the well and met Jesus. Here they listened to his speech, and they opened their minds and their hearts for him. "Stay with us and tell us more," they asked.

The disciple's didn't like this. They had no wishes to stay with the Samaritans. But Jesus loved all humans. He stayed in the city for two days. Many believed in him, that he was the Messiah. Some believed because of what the woman had said, but most of them believed because they had heard Jesus speak. He spoke about love and he stayed with them even if they were Samaritans and he was a Jew.

This camouflaged story tells humans living in present time that all the peoples in the world are equals. Not one tribe or person is greater than others.

All the people in the world have lived with an infernal chaos of wars and conflicts for some twelve thousand years, in a world where the three factors of the Original Sin has been and still are in charge over all human thinking. Twelve thousand years is a relative short time in the history of mankind, but as destructive as the era has been, it will never be too late to build a whole new world with lasting peace; never too late to build the Promised Land.

When the time comes that all the peoples in the world ones again is living together as brothers and friends in a world with lasting peace, the whole world will be a once again be a paradise. Once again it will be a person's spiritual strength, degree of knowledge and personality that will decide his or hers position in the society where they live.

Jesus is the born again Motherland history. Learn to know it well, and you will know that human beings have been living like living dead ever since the Motherland went under. Jesus is not healing individual human beings; he is healing the whole world population. All you need to do is understand. You will understand that human beings is meant to live with the knowledge from the Diagram Star, with a global system of government and one set of laws and rules for living. It is the only possible way to build a new whole world with lasting peace.

The woman at the well is a Samaritan. Under the camouflage she is the whole world population. You are a Samaritan and you know what you have done right and wrong in your life. You know the world history and you know that all the so called great conquerors, the warrior kings and both religious and political leaders, have done wrong and still are doing wrong. The reason is the three factors of the Original Sin. Humans have lived with it for so long that they have difficulties separating right from wrong, but everybody knows that something must be wrong in the way we live.

You know that the building of the many national states was wrong. The building of the global system of capitalism was wrong and the building of all the religions in the world was wrong. Now you see the world being destroyed all around you and you know the reason is the three factors of the Original Sin. And you know that only if the whole world population works together, the tree factors of evil can be removed from the common world of thoughts. You know!! You know what to do!!

Go in to the city where you live and tell everyone what you just have learned about the lost Motherland. Your well of knowledge is the Diagram Star. Jesus is the born again Motherland history and it is only the history about the lost Motherland and the global system of government that can restore lasting peace on planet earth. You are one human living on planet earth in present time. You are a Samaritan that has learned to always do what's right from now on. You will do wrong no more.

Four men on the housetop

Matthew 9, 2-8; Mark 2, 1-12; Luke 5, 18-26

One day Jesus taught in the house of a friend, a multitude of people was gathered to hear his words. People were everywhere, both in the house and outside. Everybody wanted to listen to as much as possible of what he said.

274

Four men carrying a stretcher made their way through the crowd. "Let us through! We want to get to Jesus!" they shouted. But soon they realized it was impossible even to get to the door. Then two of the men climbed up on the housetop. The two others threw ropes to them, and they pulled the stretcher up on the roof.

On the stretcher was a very sick man. He was totally paralyzed and couldn't move. The four friends had gone to get him in order to take him to Jesus. They knew that Jesus could heal him.

The four men started to make a hole in the roof. People inside the house heard sounds above them and looked up. Suddenly dust and bits and pieces of planks started falling around them. Next moment a stretcher was lowered through the hole, and there was a sick man tied to it!

Jesus knew the sick mans friends had done a lot to get him this far. He said to the sick man that his sins were forgiven. He could start a new life. Then Jesus said: Stand up and walk home!"

The man did as Jesus said. It was like he never had been sick. "Praised be God! Jesus is really the Son of God!" the man and his four friends shouted, while happily singing on their way home.

Remember who Jesus is under the camouflage. The biblical stories are never about healing individuals one by one. They are about healing planet earth, about restoring the global system of government from the time before the Motherland went under.

The born again Motherland history is going to heal the whole world population from being paralyzed. Before the world can change, your thoughts have to find the true understanding of what's right and what's wrong and stop doing wrong. You will all be forgiven because when you can forgive yourself you can forgive all others. The building of a new world starts with you doing right, and never again doing wrong.

As the Motherland history spreads around the world and more and more people will realize what they have to do to build a new world, some national populations will feel paralyzed with guilt over the magnitude of wrong they and their forefathers have done for so long. But they will be forgiven and then they can begin living with the tremendous happiness and safety that comes from doing right.

The man on the stretcher is sick because he has sinned. Jesus is telling him that his sins are forgiven and he can start his life with a new beginning. He and his four friends are happy singing on their way home. Just imagine the happiness that will spread around the world when all the people understands that they cannot be punished by any other human beings, for sins that our common forefathers committed several thousand years ago. The sins that are committed against planet earth will repair them self as only the force of nature can, as soon as the wrongful exploitation of natural recourses stops.

Still, the whole world population is mentally in old Egypt, as working slaves, soldiers and servants. Pharaoh is a symbol for the present system of government, with many national states and their desperate quest to be the richest and the strongest in the whole world. Walking in the desert is a symbol for living in the darkness of oblivion. Time has come leave the desert and come across the river of knowledge and in to a new world with lasting peace.

The tax-collector who said yes

Matthew 9, 9-13; Mark 2, 14-17; Luke 5, 27-32

One day Jesus walked down the street he passed a table where a tax-collector sat. The Jews did not like tax-collectors. They worked for the Romans, the enemies of the Jews. Furthermore they often swindled people and took money for them self.

When Jesus past the tax-collector, named Matthew, he said: "Follow me!"

Matthew had heard about Jesus and he wanted to follow him, but was afraid that Jesus would say no. Matthew was after all a tax-collector. When Jesus said: "Follow me," Matthew got up from his chair. He left all the books and all the money and followed Jesus.

Some days later Jesus had dinner in the house of Matthew. There were several other tax-collectors present, some of them known to have swindled people.

When the religious leaders saw this, they got angry. They said to the disciples: "Why does your master eat with tax-collectors and sinners?"

Jesus answered: "They that are healthy do not need a physician, but they that are sick does. This means: I will have mercy, and not sacrifice. I have not come to call the righteous, but the sinners to repentance." He said that it was better to take care of people who had problems, then to waste precious time trying to follow rules that only harm people.

In this camouflaged story the common laws and rules given by the superior Motherland council are illuminated.

Jesus has come to make the world leaders of present time see what they are doing wrong and teach them to do right. The Pharisees, the religious leaders and the Roman rulers forced people follow their self made laws and rules with the use of warfare and brutal force.

The world leaders, political and religious, are still enforcing their self made laws and rules on the population and make them pay taxes and dues. Those who refuse to obey the laws and rules of the nation are persecuted as criminals and punished according to the crime. Jesus is telling you that it is the world leaders who do wrong when they continue to live by and enforce the three factors of the Original Sin to the population. The poor and the hungry humans in the world are not to blame for anything, doing what they have to in order to stay alive in a hostile and evil world.

The invalid at the pool

John 5, 1-9

One day Jesus was at a sheep marked in Jerusalem. By a pool was a great multitude of invalid people, of blind, lame and withered, everyone waiting for the water to move. For an angel of the Lord came down at certain seasons, went into the pool and troubled the water. And whoever stepped in first after the troubling of the water, was cured of whatever disease he had.

When Jesus came to the pool, he saw all the sick people there. One man had waited thirty-eight years to get in to the pool.

"Do you wish to be made healthy?" Jesus asked him.

"I have no one to throw me in to the pool after the angel has troubled the water," the sick man answered.

Jesus said to him: "Rise, take up your bed and walk. And immediately the man was made healthy. He took up his bed and walked.

You have been told before that none of the biblical wonders happened in the real world, not then, not before and not after. Certainly some humans had the power to heal sick people, some better than others, but this camouflaged story is not about that at all.

The sick man is a symbol for the whole world population in our present time. People wait and wait for lasting peace in the world, for a better world for all humans, but nothing ever happens. There is possibly not one single person in the whole world that are mentally strong enough to do what it takes to spread the knowledge of the lost Motherland to the whole world population. The knowledge is somehow bigger than big and the daily life of all humans will be dramatically changed. But any one of you can start, be the first to start telling people how a new world with lasting peace can be built. The new world can only be built by the whole world population working together.

Look at the sick man at the pool as all the religious people in the world who are waiting for Jesus to come back to earth as a living human. Now they will learn that Jesus came back some two thousand years ago, as the born again Motherland history. The message is truly hidden in the Bible.

The knowledge from the Diagram Star will heal the blind, wake up the living dead and give them the ability to think their own natural thoughts again.

The born again Motherland history will heal all the humans that are lying down because of poverty and hunger. Thousands of humans are dying every day for reasons that comes from poverty. If the whole world population works together, planet earth can ones again will become a true paradise.

The twelve apostles are chosen

Matthew 10, 1-23; Mark 3, 13-19; Luke 6, 12-16

After Jesus had healed many people, he went into a mountain to pray. He prayed all night to God. At sunrise he called his disciples to come, and from them he chose twelve whom he named apostles. These twelve should live close to Jesus and learn from him. They should continue his work after he was taken up to heaven again.

It was a strange flock Jesus chose. The first, Simon, who is called Peter, and Andrew his brother; James the son of Zebedee and John his brother; Philip and Bartholomew; Thomas and Matthew the tax-collector; James the son of Alpheus and Lebbeus, whose surname was Thaddeus; Simon the Canaanite; and Judas Iscariot, who will betray him.

And he came down with them, and stood on the plain, with the company of his disciples and a great multitude of people from all Judea and Jerusalem, and from the sea coast of Tyre and Sidon, which all came to hear him and be healed from their diseases. And the whole multitude tried to touch him, for goodness went forth from him and healed every one of them.

In this camouflaged story the Diagram Star is filled with the twelve apostles. Jesus is the symbol for the bright shining star in the center. He enlightens the twelve apostles with his knowledge. They are an ancient symbol for the twelve elected members of the superior Motherland council, who represented the whole world population in the time before the Motherland went under. They were sending out teachers to educate the whole world population about the Motherland and how to maintain a world with lasting peace. Now it all relies on you. Don't wait a minute longer for Jesus to return as a person. He did return to the common world of thoughts some two thousand years ago as the born again Motherland history, but the story was rejected by the warrior kings, the priesthoods and the Romans. You can all learn to read the lost world history from the Diagram Star as it was an open book. You can be a teacher.

The Diagram Star is a symbol with a multitude of meanings. When the time comes and a new Motherland is built, the symbol means that every tribal people in the world have to chose twelve of their best men and send them to the Motherland to represent them when decisions of global importance are made. They will together be a global Parliament, a multitude of representatives living in the new Motherland, and from them the superior Motherland council of twelve will be elected.

It is the superior council of the lost Motherland that are remembered as gods, and it is from them all the religions, tales, legends and myths in the world have their origin. The twelve leaders of the world had the twelve star signs of the Zodiac as their emblems. The Diagram Star was their common emblem, the emblem of the lost Motherland. The many prehistoric crosses found in many countries are copies of the Diagram Star. The Bethlehem Star is a copy of the Diagram Star. The bright shining star in the top of every Christmas tree in the world, are a copy to remember the lost Motherland. Stonehenge in England is also a copy of a Diagram Star.

It is from the superior Motherland council that the Masters have the formula or code that explains the many camouflaged stories in the Bible.

The twelve democratically elected superior Motherland council members will in due time be highly educated men with a Master degree, originating from different regions of the world. If you look at the whole world as a university, they will be the apostles; the teachers in every self supported village in the world.

And try to understand this: It is the titles they are elected to fill that are ever lasting and fills the ranks of a hierarchy. The persons elected are all equals. It is the Diagram Star that will be the common book of laws and rules for the twelve chosen ones as well as for the whole world population.

Elected council members with the title of Master will be projected as leaders of modern self supported villages all over the world. It will take time before all the humans living on planet earth is gathered in self supported communities, not bigger than that everyone knows everyone. Without the three factors of the Original Sin, the whole world will ones again be a paradise with lasting peace.

The Sermon on the Mount

Matthew 5, 1-12; Luke 6, 20-23

And seeing the multitude he went up into a mountain. When he found a suitable place his disciples came to him, and he opened his mouth and thought them.

Jesus thought them what real happiness was. They thought that what he said turned the life they were used to live upside down. Instead of saying that it was the strong and aggressive that was the winners in life, he said that it was those who were weak and totally depending on God, that were truly happy in their life. This people had not heard before.

Blessed are the poor in spirit, for theirs is the kingdom of heaven. Blessed are the merciful, for they shall obtain mercy. Blessed are the peacemakers, for they shall be called the children of God. Blessed are they witch are persecuted for righteousness sake, for theirs is the kingdom of heaven. Blessed are you, when men shall revile you and persecute you, and shall say all manner of evil against you falsely, for my sake. Rejoice, and be excitingly glad, for great is your reward in heaven, for so persecuted they the prophets which were before you.

The teaching that is found under the camouflage of all the religions in the world is spoken of again and again through the whole Bible. It is about the way humans lived in the time before the Motherland went under. It was a world totally without the three factors of the Original Sin. Removing them with only peaceful means will change the world of thoughts for all humans.

Blessed is everyone who lives according to the commandments given by the superior Motherland council. They are the billions of poor and weak human beings who have been forced to live under the dictating control of the three factors of the Original Sin for some twelve thousand years.

They are the majority of the world population and when the time comes that the three factors of the Original Sin is removed from the common world of thoughts, they will all be truly happy. Their life as poor and week will be over and the whole world population will live as equals in a world without the global capitalistic system with the use of money. Everything human's needs to live a good life on planet earth will be free of charge. True happiness will be the foundation for everyone in a world without all the national states and without all the religions in the world.

The strong and aggressive human beings are the obvious winners in the world with the present governing system. They are the rich, the leading politicians and the priesthoods. After the three factors of the Original Sin are removed from the common world of thoughts, all humans will be equals, not one greater than others. There will be no rich and no poor humans in the whole world.

After the global system of government is in place with a new superior Motherland council in charge, all humans will get everything they need to live a good life on planet earth. All the many people will live together in self supported villages as one global family, caring for each other. Certainly everyone have to work and do their daily duties, but they will do it with a deep and profound happiness that comes from been respected by everyone.

All the religions, tales, legends and myths in the world are only to be found in the thoughts of humans. They are dogmas and assumptions made up by world leaders not knowing. The world as we know it is enforced on the population by the self elected warrior kings and priesthoods of the past, and it is not right. Everything that is right in the world is found in the history of the lost Motherland, born again as the person Jesus. Let us make it all right.

The kingdom of heaven is the new world with a new superior Motherland council, and it will be yours if you fight for bringing it back.

The prophets from ancient times were persecuted and killed because they spoke of the way of life in the lost Motherland, and they predicted that a new Motherland would be built. They said a new king of kings would come to lead a new world with lasting peace. Now you are told that there will be built a new Motherland and a new superior Motherland council will be elected democratically from the whole world population.

Will you remain passive and see the world being destroyed before your very eyes, just because you are afraid to break the laws and rules of your national state? If you want to be a peacemaker and be called a child of the new world, you have to do things right.

The salt of the earth

Matthew 5, 13-16

"You are the salt of the earth. But if the salt has lost its flavor, how shall it be salty again? Is it then fit for nothing but to be thrown out and trodden underfoot?"

"You are the light of the world. A city that is set on a hill cannot be hidden. Men do not light a candle and put it under a bushel, but on a candlestick, were it gives light to all that are in the house. Let your light shine before men that may see your good works and glorify your father in heaven."

The symbolism is clear. You are the salt of the earth and the salt has lost its flavor. You are the majority of human beings always working to make the world the best possible place to live, under the present circumstances. Like salt is preserving meat, you are preserving planet earth and passing it on to coming generations. Rich or poor, you work hard, educate your children. You don't live in vain, but you live with a strong hope for a better world, a world with lasting peace.

Jesus is the born again Motherland history, he is the salt in your life and the whole world population. Knowing the lost world history is salt mankind needs in order to preserve planet earth and passing it on to coming generations. With the knowledge from the Diagram Star as a foundation for your life, you will be like a burning candle. But until present time you have lived in the darkness of oblivion, without a common education in the light of the Diagram Star.

Imagine the Diagram Star in the top of the Christmas three. And imagine yourself as one of the many lights all over the three. Then see the Christmas three as the world, and every light as a tribal people, living together like a large family should.

You are the light of the world, a major part of the common world of thoughts. The salt of the world is a symbol for the humans always doing what's right for the world, meaning right according to the laws and rules of nature, given by the superior Motherland council. Now you know that the lost salty flavor is the lost knowledge; the knowledge the whole world population needs in order to be able to build a new world with lasting peace.

With knowledge from the Diagram Star and a growing understanding of everything that are wrong and evil in the world, you will be like glowing light in the dark. Other humans will see you and seek to learn what you know.

You shall not be afraid to say or do things that you know is right. What you will experience is true happiness and you will look at all the humans around you with the same respect as they show you. Everyone is equal under the light of the Diagram Star.

The Law and the Prophets

Matthew 5

"Do not think that I have come to destroy the old law or the prophets," Jesus said. "I have not come to destroy but to fulfill. For truly I say to you, till heaven and earth pass away, not one dotting of the letter i and nor the crossing of a t be removed from the law until all is fulfilled.

"Therefore whoever breaks one of the least of these commandments, and teaches men to do so, shall be called the lowest of all in the kingdom of heaven. For I say to you that unless your goodness excels that of the scribes and the Pharisees, you shall never enter the kingdom of heaven.

The old law and the prophets predictions is what Jesus fulfills in the Bible, as the born again Motherland history. The Ten Commandments are the common laws and rules that have to be used by all humans in the new world.

All the national states in the world, breaks the old law given by the superior Motherland council all the time. The laws and rules of all the national states in the world is derived from the three factors of the Original Sin and have to be removed from the common world of thoughts.

The old law that was common for the whole world population in the time before the Motherland went under is broken every day by every national state in the world, while most humans do what they have learned as right. You are still lawbreakers, breaking the laws and rules given by the superior Motherland council by obeying the laws and rules of your national state.

In order to fulfill the rightful laws and prophesies the three factors of the Original Sin have to be completely removed from the common world of thoughts.

The kingdom of heaven is the lost Motherland. It is in present time still spiritual, as a memory of a paradise world that used to be. Jesus is the born again history of the lost Motherland and it is truly the knowledge that he is telling you from the mountain, that can bring goodness back as a foundation for all human thinking and doing. In order to restore the physical power a new superior Motherland council have to be elected and a new Motherland have to be built.

The love of enemies

Matthew 6

"You have heard that it has been said, "You shall love your neighbor and hate your enemy." But I say to you, love your enemies, bless those who curse you, do good for those who hate you, and pray for those who persecute you, so that you all can be the children of your Father in heaven. Because he makes the sun rise on evil and on good alike, and sends his rain on the just and on the unjust."

This is the core of what you need to know. Those who do evil and unjust in the world think that they are doing only what's right for them. The evil and the unjust are embedded in their thoughts by false teaching, and they don't know any other way of doing things. Now you have to teach them to do things right, and when they suddenly understand it all, the evil and unjust will be totally removed from their personal thoughts and from the common world of thoughts.

There are no enemies in the world, just wrong thinking imposed on people by the warrior kings and priesthoods of the past.

The global battle that lies ahead is to take place in the common world of thoughts. All the commandments given by the superior Motherland council have to be restored as the common law and rules for the whole world population.

The Lord's Prayer

Matthew 6

"Our Father art in heaven, hallowed is his name. Thy kingdom come, Thy will be done on earth as it is in heaven. Give us our daily bread. And forgive us our depts., as we forgive our debtors, and lead us not into temptation, but deliver us from evil: For yours are the kingdom, and the power, and the glory, forever. Amen.

There are a lot more to read about the Sermon on the Mountain in the Bible. Please read it in full and make your own discoveries.

Our Father in heaven is the twelve spiritual members of the superior Motherland council. They have been thought of as in the Spirit World ever since the Motherland was destroyed in a natural catastrophe. The lost kingdom can only return by physically building a new world. The whole world population has to elect a new Motherland council and build a new Motherland together, with only peaceful means.

There is a real spiritual world were the thoughts of all who have lived and died are, so think about your own forefathers and that there is a spiritual link between them and you. Through them it is possible to work yourself back in time. In your own mind you can think about the lost Motherland and find understanding for the paradise world that mankind had to leave because of a natural catastrophe.

The reason people think of heaven as high up in the sky is that the superior Motherland council had the twelve star signs of the Zodiac as their official emblems. When the kingdom is to return and be built on planet earth, a new Motherland has to be built. A new global Motherland parliament has to be elected. Then a new superior Motherland has to be elected. As the leaders of the world they will be physical present with the power to maintain lasting peace.

In the new global kingdom all humans will live in self supported tribal villages and have all the daily needs of everything. No one will ever again be hungry, cold or die for any other reasons than the natural.

Forgive your enemies as you forgive yourself. If you can forgive yourself, you can forgive everyone else.

"Deliver us from evil", means to remove the three factors of the Original Sin from the common world of thoughts.

Then the power of the new superior Motherland council will give mankind eternal world peace. They will be omnipotent, omniscient and omnipresent. Therefore pray for the return of the global system of government, soon.

Treasure in heaven

Matthew 6, 19-34; Luke 12, 22-32

In the Sermon on the Mount Jesus thought his followers to seek for hidden treasures. "For where your treasure is, there will your heart also be," he said. What did he mean by that?

No matter what you think about or dream about, it is always what you are the most interested in. Do you dream about more toys, more money, or to be faster to run? Is there something you want more than anything else in the world?

Jesus said that treasures like that can disappear. It is best to look for the hidden treasures in heaven. "You cannot work for both God and worldly wealth."

"You must not be worried about what to eat or drink or what to wear," said Jesus. He wanted us to put God first, and then everything would be taken care of in the best manner. God is greater than all your problems. You can talk with him about everything.

"Look at the birds," said Jesus and pointed at a flock flying over their heads. "Their heavenly Father gives them food. Are you not much better than they? Why are you worried about what to wear? God created the flowers more beautiful than the dresses of King Solomon."

God knows what people needs. The most important thing to do is to follow him, obey him and love other humans like he does. God take care of everything.

It is a pleasure to seek treasures in the many camouflaged stories in the Bible. With the formula the Masters who wrote the stories down used, brings the whole Bible in to the common world of thoughts as a very important history book. The greatest treasure of all is finding knowledge about the lost Motherland. It is knowledge the whole world population can use together when building a new world with lasting peace.

What do you dream about? What do you wish for more than anything else in the world? A new Motherland will not disappear again, not ever, and the knowledge from the Diagram Star will be with mankind until after the end of time.

As soon as you learn to know the Diagram Star, a whole new world of thoughts will open to you. Remove the religion from the camouflaged stories in the Bible and make discoveries of your own. Think about the Diagram Star as the book used in common education by the whole world population, in the time before the Motherland went under.

Make your way out of the Bible and study the twelve Zodiac star signs with the new knowledge. Put the sun and the moon in the centre and the twelve star signs in the sections around. Now think about the twelve star signs as the titles emblems of each member of the superior Motherland council. All the titles have world history connected to them. They have been a part of the world history for a very long time, while the human beings that filled the positions and used the titles for the length of their lifetime, were regular human beings chosen after the original democratic rules.

After the Motherland went under and all the council members died, their titles lived on in the common world of thoughts. They were remembered as the many Gods in all the religions in the world, and a multitude of legends, myths and tales is still told about them.

The house builders

Matthew 7, 46-49

Jesus ended the Sermon on the Mount. "If you do as I say, you will be like the wise man who built his house on a steady rock ground," he said. "What happen to a house that is built on steady rock ground? It stays safe, no matter how much it blows and rains."

"Those who hear these words and don't follow them shall be like the foolish man who built his house upon sandy ground, said Jesus. "What happen to a house built on sand? It may look great, but when it rains and blows in a storm, the house will fall. And great the fall will be."

Everyone who heard what Jesus said had to make a choice. They could continue to live like they had done for a long time, or they could follow the instructions they had heard. They could have let Jesus change their lives.

You all have to make a choice right now. Will you continue to live like you do, or will you begin follow the instructions found in the Bible. The whole world we live in at present time is built on sand ground. The building on sand has been going on for some twelve thousand years. Your forefathers were just as clever as you are, but living as slaves, soldiers and servant's reluctantly obeying their greedy self elected leaders, they had no choice if they wanted to live.

The house built on sand ground is a symbol for the world at present time. You and the whole world population have inherited a world with the force of evil in command. You accept the inheritance as your only choice for your life on planet earth. You are just as clever as humans always have been, but you are all blinded and living your lives as living dead. You never knew that you have a choice. Now you know you have a choice and you have to make it now, if you want to save the world for your children and their descendants. Look around you and see the world you live in slowly being destroyed by the three evil factors of the Original Sin.

The Ten Plagues described in the Old Testament have swept over the whole world for some twelve thousand years. The rain is falling harder and the strong winds are getting even stronger. The house built on sand is slowly falling; the dance around the Golden Calf will soon come to a brutal end.

The world as we know it can still be saved for our children and their descendants. It can only happen if all the evil that is derived from the three factors of the Original Sin is completely removed from the common world of thoughts.

This is first of all difficult to understand by everyone, because the new world order will remove all the national states, the global system of capitalism and all the religions in the world. Rescue the whole world will change your life completely.

Remember now that you do it for your children and their descendants. The transforming will take a long time, and if you start working for the change now, your descendants will remember you with pride.

If you and the whole world population continue to build the world on sand ground, your descendants, if any, will remember you as one of the greedy, selfish cowards bragging about your riches, and bragging about your proud life as a slave, soldier and servant living under a despotic political system that were implemented in old Egypt some twelve thousand years ago.

The Master who wrote the camouflaged story about Jesus is giving you the opportunity to choose different than your forefathers did at the Sermon on the Mount. To choose different is to make the right decision and tell the whole world population that all the stories in the Bible is camouflaged history about a Motherland and one set of laws and rules for the whole world population. The camouflaged stories are all about building a new house on solid rock ground. Make your choice now. The right choice will make a world of difference.

Jesus preaches on forgiveness

Luke 7, 36-50

One Pharisee named Simon, invited Jesus to dinner. The Pharisees were religious leaders. Many of them did not like Jesus because he thought so much about the love of God.

While Jesus sat at the table, eating with Simon, a woman came in. The guests saw that she was a bad woman. She went straight to Jesus and knelt by his feet.

"What is she doing?" Simon said surprised.

Jesus did not replay. The woman was crying. Her tears ran down her cheek and down on his feet. Then she dried his feet with her hair.

Still Jesus said nothing. He was only waiting for her to finish. But the Pharisee Simon thought for himself: If Jesus really was a prophet; he should know how terrible bad the woman was.

Now she put her hand in her pocket in her dress and took out a small jar of ointment. It was a very expensive ointment. All Jewish women had a jar with salve, and saved it their whole life. It should only be used on special occasions. It meant that she praised him as a king. The room was filled with the scent.

Simon got more and more irritated. Jesus knew what he was thinking, so he said: "Simon, I will tell you a story. It is about two men. One of them owed much to a moneylender. The other one owed just a little. When they had nothing to pay, the moneylender forgave them both. Tell me then, which of them will love him most?"

"The one whom he forgave the most," Simon replayed.

"That is correct," said Jesus. "Do you see this woman? I came in to your house, and you gave me no water for my feet, but she has washed my feet with tears and wiped them with the hair of her head. You gave me no kiss, but this woman, since the moment she came in, has not stopped kissing my feet. You did not anoint my head with oil, but this woman has anointed my feet with anointment. Therefore, I say to you, her sins, which are many, are forgiven, for she loved much. But he, to whom little is forgiven, loves little."

And he said to the woman: "Your sins are forgiven. Go in peace."

Forgiveness is the essence of a new beginning in a new world with lasting peace. The dark ages is going to be enlightened by the Diagram Star. You will all know that you have been sinners, and if you feel that you can forgive yourself, you can forgive everyone else.

In the years that the camouflaged stories about Jesus were written, the star in the center of the diagram was dark. The darkness of not knowing had lasted for many thousand years, but like in our present time, all humans knew that something was very wrong in the world.

Some two thousand years ago the camouflaged stories about Jesus was a strong light of hope for a new kingdom, hope for lasting peace in a new world where all humans were free from the despotic rule of the Roman emperors. But Jesus spoke of a new kingdom that was rejected by the roman emperors, the warrior kings and the religious leaders. They had power to have the people they ruled over educated to do as they were told. Those who protested were killed. The forces of greed and evil had occupied the common world of thoughts and still do.

You are the descendants of the people who choose to kneel before the Roman rulers and became the obedient slaves, soldiers and servants of the ruling system that first was imposed by the Pharaoh in old Egypt.

The whole world population is still living in the darkness of oblivion, as explained in the story about Jonah in the whale's belly. The whale belly is s symbol for the monotonous teaching that is derived from the three factors of the Original Sin for some twelve thousand years. The darkness makes you blind and forces you to live your whole live like a living dead, not knowing and forced to believe that the laws and rules of your national state is right.

The time has come for the darkness to give in for the bright light of the Diagram Star, and you are forgiven because you were forced to believe that doing wrong was right.

Think about Jesus as the born again Motherland history. The Pharisee Simon is a symbol for all the religious leaders in the world in our present time. They fight with all available means to preserve and pass on the religion to coming generations because they want to keep their elevated position in the society where they live. Even if the world leaders of present time understand that knowledge soon will win over religious belief, they do not welcome knowledge and the change it will bring for them and their way of life. They cling to their belief in a religion that truly is the camouflage over knowledge.

The woman is a symbol for all the humans in the world that are so poor that they have to commit crimes in order to survive. They will all be forgiven.

Jesus preaches in parables

Matthew 13, 1-19; Mark 4, 1-9; Luke 8, 4-8

It came to pass that Jesus went throughout every village and city, preaching and showing the glad tidings of the kingdom of God. The twelve apostles were with him, and certain women who had been healed of evil spirits and sickness: Mary called Magdalene, out of her went seven devils, and Joanna the wife of Chuza, King Herod`s steward, and Susanna, and many others who cared for him the best they could.

By the seaside, great multitudes were gathered together about him, so he went into a boat and addressed the multitude that stood on the shore.

"A farmer went out to sow his seed," Jesus said. "And as he sowed, some seed fell by the wayside and the fowls came and ate them. Some seed fell on stony places where they had not much soil to grow in. And when the sun rose they were scorched, and because they had no root, they withered away. And some seed fell among the thorns and the thorns sprang up and choked them. But most seed fell into good ground and brought fort fruit, some hundred folds, some sixtyfold, some thirtyfold."

And when he had said these things, he cried: "He who has ears to hear with, let him hear"! Then the disciples asked him, saying: "What does the parable mean?"

And he said: "To you is given to know the mysteries of the kingdom of God, but to the others I speak in parables, that seeing they still may not see, and hearing they still may not understand. Now this is the meaning of the parable: The seed is the word of God. Those on the rock are they who, when they hear, receive the word with joy, and having no roots, they believe for a while, but in time of temptation they fall away.

"Those which fell among thorns are they who, when they have heard, go fort and are choked with the cares and riches and pleasures of this life, so that the faith never ripens.

"But the seed on the good ground are they who, whit honest and good hearts, having heard the word, keep it and bring fort fruit with patience."

The whole Bible is one large parable. Jesus, as the born again Motherland history, is not healing individual human being; he is healing the whole world population. Now the mysteries of the kingdom of God are told to every one of you all over the world. The word of God is the words spoken by the superior Motherland council, and the words are telling the whole world population how to build a new world with lasting peace.

In our present time many humans understand what Jesus is talking about in this camouflaged story, because Jesus himself gives the explanation. But it is not possible for anyone to understand the underlying true message the Bible is hiding, without knowing that Jesus is a fictive person who are the born again Motherland history. In order to fully understand you have to know that the whole world population still is under the dictating control of the three factors of the Original Sin.

The seed is found hidden in the many Bible stories. It is a seed that will find good soil in your world of thoughts. Only by reading the camouflaged stories and finding the hidden story about the lost Motherland under the religion, will give nourishment to the seed and make it grow in your world of thoughts. If you disregard the many biblical stories you will never find the answers that you are looking for.

My hope is that the explanation in this book will fall on good ground in the common world of thoughts. The words of explanation needs time to grow in the thoughts of all humans. Just like a growing understanding; as thoughts that actually is expanding, the explanation will make all humans see and hear again and give them a meaningful life.

It is the mystery of the kingdom of God that Jesus tries to explain, still with camouflage. Under the camouflage the Master writing the story is giving you a clue how to find the underlying message yourself.

It was not possible to spread the born again history of the lost Motherland some two thousand years ago. The parable is not fully explained. The kingdom of God is the lost Motherland. In this parable you are told how to build a new Motherland. You begin with a seed, and if your world of thoughts is good soil, the seed will grow into knowledge that soon will find its way in to the thoughts of the whole world population. In our present time it is possible, with the use of Internet and modern technology.

In the new world all the national states will be gone and all the weapons of war will be melted and made in to pickaxes, plows and other tools for cultivating the land. All humans will live in self supported villages and work for each other in a world where everyone lives under the common laws and rules given by the new superior Motherland council.

The Bible is the Ark of the Covenant. When the lid of religion is removed the knowledge from the Diagram Star will grow fort and save the world from the destructions that are made by wrongful human activity. The desert walk, the Exodus in the Bible lasted for forty years. Even if it takes twice as long in our present time, the seed of only goodness have to be planted in the common world of thoughts right now. Then the small seed will grow and change the common world of thinking completely.

The grain of mustard seed

Matthew 13

Jesus put fort another parable to his disciples, saying: "The kingdom of heaven is like a grain of mustard seed, which a man took and sowed in the field. It is indeed the least of all seeds, but when it is grown it is the greatest among plants, and becomes a tree, so that the birds of the air come and build nests in its branches.

This parable is, like many other of the camouflaged stories in the Bible, telling you that if just a little bit of knowledge gets to grow inside your world of thoughts, it will grow until you have a full understanding of how the lost Motherland was built and how a new Motherland can be built.

The kingdom of heaven is in the spirit world, meaning in the common world of thoughts. After the Motherland was destroyed in a natural catastrophe some twelve thousand years ago, most of the people living on the large continent died. It is the thoughts about the lost Motherland that will grow in the common world of thoughts and make everyone know the same world history. The common thoughts will be like one tree full of thoughts that the whole world population can agree is right. There will be no wrong thoughts to argue about.

Would there be a world, if there were no thoughts? The world of thoughts, the spirit world, the kingdom of God, is the same for all earth life.

God is defined to be the superior Motherland council who all died when the Motherland went under. Their thoughts are in the spirit world, in the common world of thoughts. Jesus is the born again Motherland history. He is using parables to tell you and the whole world population how to build a new Motherland and a new world with lasting peace. The twelve disciples were chosen from the multitude, meaning the whole world population, and are a recipe for how to elect a new superior Motherland council. They are disciples as long as Jesus is their teacher.

The wheat and the tares

Matthew 13, 24-30; 36-43

Jesus told his disciples another story, also about planting seed. "The kingdom of heaven is like a man who sowed good seed in his field, but while he slept his enemy came and sowed tares among the wheat. So when the wheat came up, the tears came up with it. The workers asked if they should pull out the tares. No, said the farmer, then you will pull up the wheat roots as well. Better wait until the fall. Then we can gather all the tares and burn it. After that we harvest the wheat."

Jesus explained the story: "He that sows the good seed is the Son of Man. The field is the world; the good seed are the children of the kingdom of God. But the tares are the children of the wicked one. The enemy that showed them is the devil. The harvest is the end of the world; the reapers are the angels. Therefore, as the tares are gathered and burned in the fire, so shall it be at the end of the world.

"The Son of Man shall send fort his angels, and they shall gather out of his kingdom all things that offend, and those who do evil, and they shall throw them in to a furnace of fire. There shall be wailing and a gnashing of teeth. Then the righteous shall shine like the sun in the kingdom of their Father."

Use the formula of the Masters and everything else you have learned so far. Then this camouflaged story can be understood like the Master who wrote it wanted to.

It is the good and right thoughts of the whole world population that are inflicted by wrong and evil thoughts. The wrong and evil thoughts have been first in command for some twelve thousand years, and with the good and right thoughts as second in command. As long as the three factors of the Original Sin is allowed to rule the common world of thoughts, the forces of good and right, as the laws and rules given by the superior Motherland council, can never win. This story is a clear recipe of how to remove the forces of evil from the common world of thoughts with only peaceful means. There are no enemies in the world, just wrong thoughts that was enforced on our forefathers with the use of warfare and brutal force.

Jesus is the born again Motherland history and the field is the world. The seed is the world of thoughts for the whole world population. The tares can be seen as thoughts imposed on the people by the use of the three factors of the Original Sin. They are the force of evil and are still occupying the common world of thoughts.

The wheat is the remaining good common thoughts in the world. The good wheat is growing strong, but is somehow overruled by the evil tares. As long as the forces of evil are present in the world, the chaos of wars and conflicts will never stop. The thoughts of all the humans who really want to live in a new world with lasting peace, is in a never ending combat with the evil thoughts that are derived from the three factors of the Original Sin.

The whole world population is living with both the good and the evil thoughts, and the Master of the past is telling you that the thoughts of evil only can be removed by the use of peaceful means. You are now given the power of good, and if the whole world population chooses to be good, the forces of evil will fade and be gone for good.

Angels are the spiritual contact with the lost Motherland in the spirit world. The Son of Man is the new superior Motherland council, with the physical power to totally remove the three factors of the Original Sin from the common world of thoughts.

The time has come to do just that, and the result will be the end of the dark ages under the rule of the three factors of the Original Sin. It is really an end of one world and the beginning of another, on this our beautiful green planet earth. The earth will again be a paradise for our children and their descendants, in a world were all evil is removed.

The disciples are a symbol for the new superior Motherland council. Jesus is the born again Motherland history that the new disciples have to study and learn to know. As a history Jesus is spiritual; he is the Son of God, meaning that he is not a messenger, but the message from the superior Motherland council, who are in the spirit world.

After the new superior Motherland council is elected and are in place in a new Motherland, they will have the power to remove all evil from their kingdom, the whole world.

Jesus in Nazareth

Luke 4; Mark 6

When Jesus had finished these parables, he departed and went into his own country, to Nazareth where he had been brought up. And as his custom was he went into the synagogue on the Sabbath day, and stood up to read. The book of the prophet Isaiah was given to him, and when he opened the book he found a place where it was written: "The Spirit of the Lord is upon me, because he has anointed me to preach the gospel to the poor.

"He has sent me to heal the brokenhearted, to preach deliverance to the captives, and recovering of sight to the blind, to set at liberty those who are oppressed and to preach the acceptable year of the Lord."

Jesus closed the book and gave it back to the minister and sat down. And the eyes of all them that were in the synagogue were fastened on him. And he began to say to them: "Today this Scripture is fulfilled in your ears."

All wondered at the gracious words that came from him, and they said: "Is it not Joseph's son? Is it not the carpenter, the son of Mary, the brother of James and Joseph, and of Jude and Simon? And are not his sisters here with us?" And they took offense of him.

But Jesus said to them: "A prophet is not without honor except in his own country and among his own kin, and in his own house."

And he marveled because of their unbelief.

And all those in the synagogue, when they heard these things, were filled with wrath, and rose up and thrust him out of the city, and led him up to the edge of a hill and which their city was built, that they might throw him down.

But he, passing through them in the midst of them, went his way.

"The Spirit of the Lord is upon me." Under the camouflage this is all about knowing the hidden message of the Bible, knowing what the prophets knew, and telling it to the whole world population. Do you listen to your own inner voice when reading the explanation of the camouflaged stories in the Bible? Can you see with your inner eye? The Scripture is really fulfilled in your ears, but do you understand anything at all?

You are the brokenhearted, living without the security and happiness the knowledge gives. You are the captives who need deliverance. You are the oppressed one who needs to be set free. You want to know, and now knowledge is given to you. How do you react to the truth about the world you live in?

Can you accept that the building of the many national states was wrong as wrong can be? Can you accept that the global system of capitalism is wrong as wrong can be? And can you accept the fact the all the religions in the world are a man made camouflage over the knowledge that humans need in order to be able to build a world with lasting peace?

Jesus calms the storm

Matthew 8, 22-25; Mark 4, 35-38; Luke 8, 22-24

At the end of the day, while he was healing the sick, Jesus pointed at a boat nearby. "Come with me," he said to the disciples. "Let us sail over to the other side of the lake." It was the only possibility for him to get away from the multitude of people. Jesus was tired. He needed to rest.

The sea was calm when they set sail. "It should be a peaceful crossing," said one of the disciples.

"Don't be too sure. You know how fast the weather can change, even if it looks good right now," said one of the others. Jesus went to rest on a pillow.

It didn't last long before the wind started blowing at a full scale storm. It was so strong that they were in danger. The skipper was fighting with the rudder and the boat was thrown about by the large waves. The disciples awoke Jesus saying: "Master, Master, we are sinking."

Then Jesus arose and rebuked the wind and the raging water, and they ceased and there was calm. And he said to the disciples: "Where is your faith?"

They were frightened, and wondered at this, saying to one another: "What manner of man is this? For he commands even the winds and the water and they obey him."

They came to the other side of the like, into the country of the Gadarenes.

This is what might happened when the whole world population gets to know the born again Motherland history and fully understand that mankind have been captives of the forces of evil for some twelve thousand years.

The explanation of this camouflaged story is easily understood in our present time because of the serious situation mankind are facing, with global warming, natural catastrophes, wars and conflicts. It is certainly like a never ending development of evil on planet earth. What will you do when you fully understand the truth? There will be a storm in your mind as there will be in the minds of the whole world population, and the only force that can calm the storm, is the born again Motherland history.

Another storm that might be so strong that it will frighten the whole world population will come from those humans who don't want the present system of governing the world to change. There will be a strong storm of protests from all those who don't understand what good a new superior Motherland council and one set of common laws and rules will do for the world. But soon everyone will rejoice and feel a happiness that comes from the heart.

292

Place Jesus in the centre of the Diagram Star and the twelve disciples in the sections around. The Diagram Star is a map of the world and the disciples are the new superior Motherland council. They have to learn to trust that they are doing the right thing, leading the new world from a new Motherland. They will be the head teachers of the whole world population, and it will be difficult at first, before knowledge from the born again Motherland history is fully understood.

The man who lived among the tombs

Matthew 8, 28-34; Mark 5, 1-20; Luke 8, 26-30

When Jesus stepped forth on the land, he met a man possessed with devils a long time. He wore no clothes, nor lived in a house, but had his dwelling among the tombs.

When he saw Jesus he ran to him and fell on his knees before him. Jesus saw at ones how desperately troubled he was, and said: "Unclean spirits! Get out of this man!"

Nearby stood a flock of pigs and Jesus commanded the evil spirits to leave the man and get into the pigs. They did, and immediately after they got in to the pigs, they fell off a cliff and in to the sea.

Those who had guarded the pigs saw everything that happened. Now they hurried back to the city. When people came out to see, they found the possessed man at the feet of Jesus. There he sat calm and dressed. It was nothing wrong with him.

People were afraid of the power of Jesus. They asked him to go back to where he came from.

When Jesus and the disciples went back on the boat, the man who had been freed from evil spirits asked to come with them, but Jesus answered: "No, go home to your people and tell them about everything the Lord have done for you."

The man walked to the neighboring cities and told them that Jesus had made him well. Everyone marveled over what they heard.

The stories about healing in the Bible are not about healing individual human beings. They are all about healing the whole common world of thoughts. In the past as to day the knowledge about the healing of individual human beings was well known, and the Masters writing the camouflaged stories used the knowledge well. There is a strong common sense in using parables when explaining the camouflaged stories. In this one the man possessed by devils and living naked among the tombs is camouflage for you and the whole world population.

You and the whole world population are living like living dead, without any knowledge at all. Filled with dogmas and assumptions for thousands of years, you need the knowledge derived from the Diagram Star in order to be able to get back to a normal, natural life, safe and happily living with your people and your family in self supported communities.

The twelve disciples is a symbol for the new superior Motherland council, and they have to know this in order to become apostles and teach the whole world population how to remove all evil from their thoughts.

Living as you and the world population have done for many thousand years, under the despotic ruling of the three factors of the Original Sin, nobody knows the history about the lost continent, the Motherland. Now you know and soon the whole world population will know. Knowledge is the little seed that will grow and become the tree of life.

Jesus is a symbol for the born again Motherland history. The man possessed by devils and living among the tombs is a symbol for a state of mind, for thoughts all humans are living with. The thoughts of evil are derived from the three factors of the Original Sin and imposed on people over many generations. Only the bright shining light of good thoughts from the Diagram Star can make the evil forces go away and be gone forever more.

Many more is healed

Matthew 9, 27-31

People that were blind in this era of time could not live a normal life. They had no books with Braille writing, where they could feel the letters with their fingers. They had no dogs trained to lead them while walking. Blind people in the time of Jesus had no choice; they had to beg in order to stay alive. Work was impossible for them. They were completely helpless.

Everywhere Jesus went, people that were sick and tormented followed him. They asked Jesus to heal them. One day it was two blind men that followed him. "Have mercy with us, you son of David!" they shouted.

Jesus went in to the house of a friend and the two blind men followed him. Jesus turned and asked: "Do you really believe that I can make you see again?

The two men were friends. They had heard many stories about Jesus healing people, and they believed he was Messiah. They had stumbled along the road and bumped in to people, following after Jesus. Now they were alone with him. "Yes, Master," they replayed.

Jesus reached out his hands and touched their eyes. "It shall be as you believe!" he said.

Suddenly the two men could see light and colour. Everything became sparkling clear. They shouted loudly when they saw in to the smiling face of Jesus. Were there had been darkness, was light!

The two men became so glad that they told everyone they met about what had happened.

Many more humans will begin to see and understand the symbolic light from the Diagram Star. Jesus is the bright shining star. Knowing something is seeing with your inner eye, it is to understand and see the right from the wrong.

You have to believe you can find knowledge by studying the Diagram Star and then you have to keep pursuing that first thought of knowledge and never give up. Then you will feel that the knowledge you are seeking is growing in your world of thoughts, and you will make some wonderful discoveries almost every single day. The ones who are seeking knowledge will find knowledge. There are still oceans of knowledge to discover, for you to find.

Imagine the happiness you will feel when you know that everything you know is right and when your experience that the whole world population knows the same. To know is the ability to read the Diagram Star like an open book. The amazing thing is that you don't have to carry a drawing of the diagram with you; you have it memorized in your world of thoughts as the foundation of your life.

A part of the knowledge is to know that the camouflaged stories in the Bible are the history of the lost Motherland and a global government system with common laws and rules for the whole world population.

In present time the whole world population lives like inside a bubble, unable to see the life they live from the outside. Not knowing the history of the lost Motherland leaves the national leaders of present time the choice of altering the government system from one destructive political system to another with the use of warfare and brutal force. Removing the many national states all together is not an option for them. Only a new superior Motherland council will have the political power to do that with only peaceful means. It is a power given by the whole world population.

Seeing with your inner eye and understanding the Diagram Star will enlighten your world of thoughts.

You will know that the building of the world with many national states with the use of warfare and brutal force, as we all know it did happen, was wrong as wrong can be. You will be able to go back in time some twelve thousand years and see, with your inner eye, the global system of government with common laws and rules for the whole world population. You will understand the importance of the Motherland council as a superior leader of the world, organizing the life of everyone as nature intended.

When the Motherland was destroyed in a natural catastrophe some twelve thousand years ago, the chaos of wars and conflicts started. You know that electing a new superior Motherland council and building a new Motherland is the only possible way to lasting world peace, and knowing this is all you need to get started. Just remember that a new global parliament has to be elected from the whole world population and from them a new superior Motherland council will be elected.

The beheading of John the Baptist

Matthew 14, 1-12; Mark 6, 14-29

While Jesus walked around and taught the people, his friend John the Baptist was still in prison. King Herod had looked him in because John had said it was wrong of the king to get married to his brother's wife.

This woman's name was Herodias. She hated John and wanted him dead. Had it not been for Herodias, John would have been a free man.

On his birthday King Herod had a grand party. He invited all his friends, family, advisors, generals and other important persons who served him. The castle was full of people who laughed, eat and drank.

The musician's played a strange but beautiful melody. Everyone turned to see a beautiful young woman who started dancing. It was almost as she didn't touch the floor with her feet. Never had they seen a better dancer.

King Herod smiled. "This is the daughter of Herodias, my wife," he said. "No one can dance like her."

Slowly but surely the girl danced towards king Herods table. She danced in front of him and ended the dance kneeling before the king.

The king felt even more proud of her when he saw in to her eyes. "Ask me for anything you want, and you shall have it," he said with an oath that made certain that he couldn't take his promise back.

The girl ran to her mother, Herodias, and asked: "Mother, what shall I ask for?"

Queen Herodias smiled an evil smile:"Ask for the head of John the Baptist on a platter."

When the girl came back to the king with her wish, he got very worried. John was in spite of everything a good man. He could not kill him; he thought to himself and looked around at all the important people with his table. King Herod felt week and gave in. He ordered a guard to get the head of John the Baptist on a platter.

When the disciples who followed John heard that he was dead, they went to the prison. They asked for his body, so they could bury him. The disciples went to see Jesus and told him that John the Baptist was dead. When Jesus heard that his closest friend was dead, he got very distressed.

John the Baptist and Jesus are representing the force of only good. They are two of a kind, in the sense John is the lost Motherland history born in to the world as a real person and are called the Son of Man, while Jesus is the spiritual born again Motherland history and are called the Son of God. It is a true picture showing you that the spirit world and the real world are one. They are both the history of the lost Motherland, the kingdom of the past. In order to be accepted by the world leaders the history about the lost Motherland must have a known and accepted link to the past.

The warrior kings and priesthoods removed that accepted link by killing John the Baptist. It was because they had no knowledge about the lost Motherland history that made the Roman emperors deny that the Motherland had ever existed. Jesus, the born again Motherland history, was only spiritual, as words and allegations, and lived on as a religion.

Under the camouflage of religion the original Egyptian Hieroglyphs have to be translated again. The true meaning is that Jesus and his disciples is a symbol for the new superior Motherland council that has to be elected and the new Motherland that have to be built in order to restore lasting peace in the world. The twelve apostles is a symbol for the new council members and Jesus is the spiritual laws and rules for living as they were given before the Motherland went under some twelve thousand years ago.

The beheading of John the Baptist is a symbol for taking away all physical evidence and make Jesus, the born again Motherland history die. But the camouflage is solid, and the full story about the lost Motherland will live on camouflaged as religion.

King Herod and his wife Herodias is a symbol for the evil serpent in the tree. She is a symbol for all evil that are derived from the three factors of the Original Sin from the time the Motherland went under. Good kings are weak kings and have to obey the forces of evil, even if they only want to be good.

The story is a tale and the beheading of John the Baptist is a true symbol for an attempt to put a stop to all teaching about the lost continent, the Motherland and the knowledge about the Diagram Star. The result was that the religion called Christianity started growing rapidly. The story is invented, written by a Master who did the right thing in a world where the forces of evil was in command.

People, you live in a world controlled by evil, by the three factors of the Original Sin. Break the chain of evil now. A thousand years will pass before another change like this is given, and if you do nothing you are week like King Herod. Queen Herodias is a symbol for all the evil forces in the world. Stop being the blind and the living dead, not knowing why you live. I am certain that you don't want to stand and watch your only link to knowledge be destroyed ones again, like all the kings' friends, family, advisors, generals and other important persons who served him did.

To a quiet place

Matthew 14, 13; Mark 6, 30-33; Luke 9, 10; John 6, 1-3

A few days after Jesus had heard about the death of John the Baptist, he had to help a multitude of people. He did not have time to eat. Jesus was very saddened by the loss of his friend and relative John. The more he heard people shout his name, the more tired he felt.

He called Peter and pointed at a boat nearby. "I need to be for myself. Let us get away and get some rest."

Jesus and his disciples went into the boat in order to go to a quiet place. Here they should pray and strengthen each other.

But people knew that Jesus had left, and they tried to find out where he was going to. It didn't last long before even more people gathered on the seaside looking for the boat. When they saw it was on the way to the other side, many started shouting and running around the lake to the other side.

There will be a significant similar riot all over the world as soon as people all over the world get to know that they for some twelve thousand years have been captives by a global government system that first was imposed by the Pharaoh in old Egypt. All humans will eventually find out that they all still are working slaves, soldiers and servants under their national state government. The crime against mankind done by the warrior kings and priesthoods of the past is beyond any comparison. But the riot will calm when people realize that there is no one to blame. The world leaders of present time didn't know more than ordinary hard working humans, and have to be forgiven.

When Jesus and his disciples goes in to a boat and sails across a sea, it is easy to remove the camouflage of religion. Jesus, as the born again Motherland history, is bringing an ocean of knowledge to the whole world population.

The twelve disciples are a symbol for the first twelve tribes who emigrated from the Motherland a very long time ago. They are in the boat together with Jesus because they are symbolizing the forefathers of the whole world population. All humans on planet earth have a link all the way back to the first superior Motherland council. Therefore look at Jesus as the born again Motherland history and the twelve disciples as the new leaders of the world, learning the history of the lost Motherland. The multitude of people is the whole world population eagerly seeking to know.

It was a major part of the world history that was lost when the Motherland was destroyed in a natural catastrophe. The reason was that almost all common education stopped, and people only had legends, tales and myths to remember.

Now use a parable and look at what happened when the warrior kings and priesthoods attacked peaceful villages, killed the leaders, stole all the valuables of gold, silver and precious stones and made the remaining village population in to obedient slaves, soldiers and servants. After a few generations the long and proud history of the village and all the families had died;

vanished for all times. Their history had been rooted in their personal and common items made from gold, silver and precious stones, that became the foundation for the many rich kingdoms and religions in the world. You are living in a world with a foundation of stolen gods.

The lost world history is rooted deep within the religions of the world, and it takes time to comprehend. Thoughts are like plants in the nature; they need time to grow, so take time.

The multitude of people in this camouflaged story is you and the whole world population living in present time, seeking almost desperate for knowledge about the past; knowledge that finally will give your life on earth a true meaning.

There is a symbolism in the multitude of people leaving on one side of the sea and finding Jesus again on the other side, after a long walk around.

The whole world population used to live with knowledge, safety, happiness and long lasting peace in the time the lost Motherland existed. The long walk without knowledge started some twelve thousand years ago, when the Motherland was destroyed in a natural catastrophe. The chaos of wars and conflicts started and you and the whole world population are still walking along the seashore and searching for the lost knowledge.

You should know by now that the whole world population is forced to live with the three factors of the Original Sin. You are forced to work, pay taxes and dues and use whatever is left to buy things that are made for that purpose. Every human being is born in to a nation with guarded borders. You all get a name and a number, are educated in to a position as a worker, soldier or servant. No one is free.

Like that your national state is arranged, with one willing and submissive workforce with no thoughts and will of their own.

What you and the whole world population are seeking is knowledge how the world was arranged before the long walk along the seashore started. You are seeking a global government system with the same set of laws and rules for living for the whole world population. All humans live in self supported villages where everybody know and care for each other. Education will again be the main activity and the spiritual strength and personal abilities will be the only difference between all humans. Let it so be.

Thousands gets to hear Jesus

Matthew 14, 14-25; Mark 6, 34-36; Luke 9, 11-12

When the boat with Jesus and the disciples finally reached the shore, many waded out in to the sea to receive them. "Jesus! Jesus!" they called.

The whole afternoon Jesus spoke to them. He told them about the love of God. It was a lot of people gathered. The sun was bright and the birds sang. It was a beautiful day. People sat in the sand and in the grass. They listened to Jesus and saw him healing the sick and praying for them. It was a good place to be.

But one important thing was missing. On a tour like this everyone should bring food with them. Later in the day more and more people started complaining that they were hungry. Finally, in the disciples went to Jesus and said that he ought to send people home, so they could get something to eat. "At least they could go to the villages nearby and get some food there," they said.

The knowledge about the Motherland and the global system of government is in this story told to people with the use of only peaceful means. Some two thousand years ago they did not have Internet and modern technology, and all the land in the region was under the strict control of the Roman Empire. From the history of the Romans we know that they had no mercy with any kind of opposition. The region was and is a theatrical stage symbolizing the whole world.

The so called first Christians were not religious at all. They were freedom fighters doing their best to preserve and pass on the knowledge about the lost Motherland from generation to generation. They knew as you all should know by now, that lasting world peace cannot be achieved by the use of warfare and brutal force.

The first Christians was captured and killed by the thousands, because of what they knew. The Masters writing the camouflaged stories that became the Bible had to live under cower as for example advisers for the kings or hiding in the desert as shepherds. If captured, they were killed without mercy.

Some two thousand years ago the camouflage was removed for a short time, in order to give people hope with the knowledge about the lost Motherland, the continent with three kingdoms that ruled the whole world with lasting peace. Many humans did learn to read the Diagram Star like an open book. The Masters did succeed in what they had planned to do, and when Emperor Constantine converted to Christianity in 324 and made Christianity a state religion with the camouflage intact, the many camouflaged stories lived on and became the religion we all know so well.

Was Emperor Constantine a Master himself, or was he fooled to do what he did? He started using religion as a tool to control the many different tribal people he ruled over. History tells that whole villages were baptized by brutal force. Those who refused to be baptized were killed. Religion became a third part of the Original Sin, with the camouflage intact and that is the reason the story of the lost Motherland never will be forgotten.

Now the whole world shall hear the story about the lost Motherland, and learn how to build a new world with lasting peace. The whole story is in the Bible, under the camouflage of religion.

Food for the hungry

Matthew 14, 16-18; Mark 6, 37-38; John 6, 4-9

Jesus looked at all the thousands of humans that were gathered. People were so enthusiastic about what he had said to them during the day, and he did not feel like stopping just yet. He said to Philip: "Where can we buy enough food for everyone?"

Philip stared at Jesus: "We have to work eight months in order to be able to feed so many humans! Even then they would only get a few pieces of bread each."

Andrew, Peter's brother, came to Jesus. "There is a young boy here," he said. "He has five bread and two fishes. But it is not a lot."

The disciples did not know, but Jesus had a reason to asking them to feed the people. He wanted to give them a lesson in belief in the love of God.

There is an enormous difference between the love humans felt for each other before the Motherland was destroyed and the love humans of present time feel for each other. Love in a world with no evil is the kind of love Jesus speaks of in this camouflaged history. The people had no God or goods to worship; they had the common knowledge from Diagram Star. You have to know the history of the past in order to be able to build a new world with lasting peace.

Knowing the history of past means that you have to move back in time some twelve thousand years and find what you need to know there. Everything in between is a mix of religious dogmas and assumptions, tales, legends and myths. With the knowledge from the Diagram Star it is easy to separate the good from the evil; separate the right from the wrong and do only right in your life. You know that the evil and the wrong are not meant to be a part of the world we all live in. By the laws and living rules given by the superior Motherland council humans are meant to live in a peaceful world in the light of the Diagram Star.

In our present time all humans walk around like blinded and living dead. Many are dancing around the Golden Calf having fun, believing it is the best possible way to live. But the majority of humans are living their whole life being poor, and they know it is a wrong way to live in a world where the forces of evil are in command. They are praying for the superior Motherland council to return and demolish the Golden Calf completely.

You all believe you can see the world and you all fight for peace. But you even if you can see the difference between right and wrong, you don't know how to remove the wrong completely from the face of the earth, because the wrong in the world has become a major part of your daily life, and you believe you cannot live without it. Billions of humans don't have money to buy food and many starve to death. They have to live without the safety and happiness the belonging to a self supported village will give, without all the national states, the global capitalistic system and all the religions in the world.

The inner happiness and profound joy all humans will feel when they learn to know the Diagram Star will create a feeling of happiness that exceeds everything humans have felt for the last some twelve thousand years. Without the three factors of the Original Sin a stronger and deeper love will come to surface. It is a love to life itself that will be common for the whole world population. It is a love built on the fact that the whole world population lives together as a very large family and absolutely everybody have all they need to live a good life on planet earth.

The love in our present time is exclusively based on thoughts that have to do with money, nations and religions. Think thorough through what the feeling of love will be based on after the three factors of the Original Sin is gone. Think about love in a new world with lasting peace.

The boy who participated in feeding thousands

Matthew 14, 19-21; Mark 6, 39-44; Luke 9, 14-17; John 6, 10-14

Jesus asked the people to sit down in small groups. Then he thanked the boy for giving the bread and the fishes. Jesus held the five breads and the two fishes up so people could see them.

The multitude of people went silent. Jesus looked up. He thanked God for the food he had given them. Then he blessed the food and broke the breads in to pieces. He gave them to the disciples, so they could give the food to the people.

Then something strange happened! Jesus distributed more and more bread to the disciples. They did the same with the fishes. When the baskets were empty, the disciples came back for more, and Jesus filled the baskets again and again. Soon the many thousands of men, women and children were full.

The disciples gathered the remains after the meal, and filled twelve baskets with the leftovers! What a wonder!

No wonders happened during the era of this story, and wonders never have happened, not before and not after. Read this story knowing that Jesus is a symbol for the born again Motherland history and the disciples as a symbol for the new superior Motherland council. They will truly have the power to feed millions of humans, after the new Motherland is built and the three factors of the Original Sin is removed from the common world of thoughts. And as the story goes, no humans will starve again, not ever.

Jesus is asking the thousands of people to sit in small groups, and the twelve disciples distribute the food to them. This is a symbol of importance, so use some time to understand what it says. When the whole world population again lives in self supported villages, the laws and rules given by the superior Motherland council will secure that all humans have everything they need to live a good life on planet earth.

The twelve sons of Jacob in the Old Testament is a symbol for the first twelve tribes that emigrated from the Motherland to populate the whole world. That part of the world history is hidden under the camouflage story about how the biblical Israelites, the whole world population became slaves, soldiers and servants in the time after the Motherland was destroyed.

The twelve disciples symbolize a newly elected superior Motherland council who have to learn about the lost world history from Jesus, from the born again Motherland history. They will be leading the whole world population without the three factors of the Original Sin.

301

If the history about the lost Motherland is made known to the whole present world population, they will all be filled with the knowledge they have missed for some twelve thousand years, and the twelve baskets with leftover means that the source of knowledge never again will be empty.

The story is really true. If the three factors of the Original Sin are removed from the common world of thoughts and the whole world population divides them self in to a multitude of self supported villages, there will be enough food for everyone, in abundance and forever. The twelve baskets is a symbol for the food supply for the whole world population.

How many human beings dies every day for reasons linked to poverty, in the duration of your lifespan on the planet? How many have died in the last twelve thousand years for reasons linked to the three factors of the Original Sin?

Are you prepared to let this continue in to the future, as the inheritance you leave to your children and their descendants?

Jesus walks on the water

Matthew 14, 22-27; Mark 6, 45-52; John 6, 15-21

Jesus sent the multitude away and asked his disciples to get in to the boat and go ahead of him to the other side of the lake. Then he went up in to the mountain to pray, and when the evening came he was there alone.

But the boat was now in the midst of the sea, tossed by the waves, for the wind was against them. And in the fourth watch of the night Jesus went to them, walking on the sea.

When the disciples saw him walking on the sea, they were troubled and said: "It is a spirit." And they cried out for fear. But Jesus spoke to them, saying: "Be of good cheer. It is I, Jesus. Be not afraid."

Peter answered him and said: "Lord, if it is you, let me come to you on the water."

"Come," he said. And Peter came down out of the boat, and he walked on the water, to go to Jesus. But when he saw the strong wind, he became afraid and began to sink. "Lord, save me," he cried, and immediately Jesus stretched forth his hands and caught him. "O you of little faith, why did you doubt?" he said.

And when they had come into the boat, the wind ceased. Then they that were in the boat worshipped him, saying: "Truly you are the Son of God."

Right now the world leaders don't know what to do. Like the whole world population they are afraid and they truly need to be guided by a superior Motherland council.

Who is Jesus? He is, in all the stories about him, the born again Motherland history. As a story he is spiritual; he is thoughts. The Master who wrote the story could not foresee the many religions and the many national states in the world, but the whole world population was always divided in departments and symbolical placed in the twelve sections around the star in the diagram, around Jesus.

This camouflaged story means that the whole world population is gathered together in the same boat, meaning together on planet earth. Everybody is worried about everything that is happening in the world, and the worrying increases as things gets worst.

Water, Air, Earth and Fire = Knowledge about the lost Motherland, says the formula. The lake is a symbol for the sea of knowledge Jesus represent. Jesus, as the born again Motherland history, have opened up the sea of knowledge for the whole world population. The story tells us that people all over the world will have problems understanding the knowledge at first. The twelve disciples is a good example for that. There will be a storm in the common world of thoughts that will shake the people hard. They cannot handle the new knowledge without Jesus, the born again Motherland history. They are still disciples and don't know what to do without their spiritual teacher.

Also the strong wind is knowledge, and returning to religious belief is not an option.

Among the frightened disciples Peter got up and wanted to walk on the water. But after a few steps he became afraid and started to sink.

This symbolizes what happened some two thousand years ago. Many humans understood what the global system of government could do for the whole world population, but when the Roman Emperors started killing those who knew about the born again Motherland history by the thousands, and those who knew gave up the attempt to build a new world with only peaceful means. But they had given hope for a better world to so many people that the camouflaged stories became a religion for them. Now time has come to remove the camouflage of religion. Humans cannot walk on water, but they can learn to trust the history about the lost Motherland.

The camouflaged history about Jesus is telling people living in present time what to do in order to restore the global system of government on planet earth. It can only be done with the use of peaceful means. The story about the lost Motherland is told again and again, over a long period of time. It makes the many camouflaged Bible stories a true Ark of the Covenant.

When you get to the point where you can see the Diagram Star both in the Bible and outside, for example as the sun and the twelve Zodiac signs and understand what they are, you will find the knowledge about the lost Motherland and be able to disregard all the dogmas and assumptions as well as everything else that has happened in our history between then and now. It is all wrong and derived from the three factors of the Original Sin.

Baptizing people in water is a symbolic act from the time of the Motherland. Students were baptized at the age of twenty-five, and the ceremony was a confirmation of their level of spiritual strength and their level of knowledge. Many of the best students made it to the degree of Master and became the teachers of the whole world population.

It is important to understand that it is you, the people living in present time, who needs help to fully understand and trust the born again Motherland history and comprehend the knowledge coming from the Diagram Star. There is no one else. It will be difficult to convince both leaders and people that the change is necessary and have to happen soon. Only with knowledge about the lost Motherland the whole world population can work together and build a new world with lasting peace.

A stranger who believe

Matthew 15, 21-28; Mark 7, 24-30

Gods plan for Jesus was that he first should work among the people of Israel. Later the good news about Gods love should be told to the whole world population. Many Jews would not believe in Jesus, but there were others who believed that he was the Son of God. One of them was a woman who had a little girl who was very sick.

This woman went to the house where Jesus was. She kneeled before his feet and called out loud: "Please! Help me! My daughter is very sick!"

Jesus did not answer with a word. The reason was that he wanted to test her, and see if she really believed in him.

In the same way it happens that God sometimes don't answer our prayers at ones. He is not saying yes or no. He tells us to wait. It is in times like that fait is built up and made stronger.

Another reason for Jesus to be silent was that the woman was not a Jew. Time had not come for him to heal those who were not Jews. But it was difficult for him to refuse the woman's prayer.

"Please, my Lord! Make my girl well!"

The disciples interfered: "Send her away," they said. "She is disturbing us."

"Now it is written that I shall take care of the Jews," Jesus said to her. "It is not right to take the bread from Gods children and throw it to the dogs."

She replied: "Also dogs eat the crumples that fall from their masters table."

When Jesus heard her answer, he said: "Woman, your fait is great. Because you answer like you do, your daughter is well again. Go home now."

The woman did as he said. When she got home, her little daughter was sleeping in her bed. She was no longer sick.

This is a story that gets a total different meaning when the camouflage of religion and the misinterpretations is removed. First of all, the people of Israel are the descendants from Jacob and his twelve sons. Juda was one of his sons and are the forefather of the Jewish tribal people. Jacob got the name Israel for a reason and is the symbolic forefather for the whole world population. Therefore the Jews in our present time have no right to occupy land and build a national state and name it Israel.

What Judah did later in this story, was done by the whole Jewish people. They did it for a very good recon, when they sold the history about the born again Motherland to the religious leaders who passed it on to the Romans. The scribes, scholars and Masters who wrote the camouflaged stories and made the Bible many years later had a plan for all the stories, and they succeeded. They did it in order to preserve and pass on the born again Motherland history to the coming generations. It becomes clear that the Jewish tribe was selected by the Masters, without their knowledge of what their history was camouflage over.

The Jews sold the story about Jesus, the born again Motherland history, and as long as the so called Holy Book is passed on by those who strongly believe in the religion of their people, the history hidden under the camouflage will live on. Now time has come to revile the full story about Jesus as the born again Motherland and teach the whole world population about the Diagram Star. The Bible is the Ark of the Covenant. Time has come to remove the lid.

It is the three factors of the Original Sin that makes the whole world population sick and in some parts of the world humans are dying by the thousands every day. Already several thousand years ago the prophets could see that the whole world population needed healing, and because they knew about the lost Motherland, they also knew the only way to heal the world. All three evil factors have to be removed from the common world of thoughts, in order to heal the world. You are all living like blind and living dead. Seek to think your own thoughts about what's right and what's wrong in the world. Now you know how the world can be saved.

Just like the Israelites were forced in to a life as slaves, soldiers and servants for the Pharaohs of old Egypt, you are still slaves, soldiers and servants for the same despotic ruling system.

A blind man in Betsaida is healed.

Mark 8, 22-26

Jesus walked to a little village named Betsaida. Here someone came to him with a blind man. They asked him to touch the blind man, so he could see again.

Jesus took the blind man and led him out of the village. The blind man did not know what to believe, there he followed Jesus. He felt the hand of Jesus in his own. His friends had told him that Jesus had healed others. Then he could heal him to!

Jesus stopped and let go of his hand. The bind heard him spit. The next that happened was that he could feel the warmth of both the hands of Jesus on his eyes.

When Jesus took his hands away from the man, he asked: "Do you see anything?"

The man looked up and moved his head from side to side. "I see humans, but they are like trees," he said.

Jesus put his hands on him again. The man blinked. Now he saw everything clear. He saw his friends, smiling to him. "I can see! I can see!" he shouted. Everyone gathered around him and embraced him, and they thanked Jesus.

It is truly you that are blind, or hopefully beginning to see things clear. The whole world population has been blind for a very long time, from the time the Motherland was lost and until present time. You are all blinded by the three factors of the Original Sin. What can you see, now, with the new knowledge?

Already several thousand years ago the Masters could tell the world that the building of walls around cities and the building of high towers reaching for the sky, was wrong as wrong can be.

The wall around the cities became the border around nations and the towers are a symbol for the global system of capitalism. All the national states are managed just like a prison camp, in which the population have no choice but to obey the self made laws and rules for living.

The walls are still there to protect the self elected government and the richest of the rich. The poor and submissive population is forced to work in order to maintain a life people have gotten used to up through the many generations. No one knows the good life humans lived when the whole world population was under the strict control of the superior Motherland council and one common set of laws and rules for living.

The loss of the Motherland destroyed a lot more than you can imagine. It took your eyesight away and made your lifetime on planet earth in to a life as a living dead. Everybody is seeking the knowledge that can make them see again, and only the history of the born again Motherland can restore the eyesight that has been lost for many thousand years.

Jesus did spit before he put both his hands on the eyes of the blind man. Water = Knowledge is a true formula, and the fact that Jesus is speaking in parables makes it easy to understand that under the camouflage is the story about the whole world population.

You need to find just a little knowledge in order to begin to understand, and soon you will see how important the born again history of the Motherland is.

It is your inner eye that is blinded by the unstoppable indoctrination of tradition, dogmas and assumptions. With only a little knowledge and the ability to separate right from wrong, you will understand that Jesus is the born again Motherland history and that only a complete implementation of the common set of laws and rules for living can restore a world with lasting peace.

A lot will be won if you get interested in the truth that the Bible is hiding under the camouflage of religion. Very soon you will be shouting out loud: "I can see! I can see!"

The rock

Matthew 16, 13-19; Mark 8, 27-29; Luke 9, 18-20

Jesus took his disciples to a quiet place north of the Sea of Galilee. Here he asked them a very important question: "Who do people say that I am?"

"Some say you are John the Baptist, some that you are Elijah and others say Jeremiah or one of the prophets."

"But who do you say that I am?" Jesus asked.

Peter stepped forward to answer: "You are the Christ, the Son of the living God."

Jesus said to him: "Blessed are you, Simon, son of Jonah, for the flesh and blood have not revealed the answer to you, but my Father who is in heaven. And I say also to you that you are Peter, the rock, and upon this rock I will build my church."

Jesus said that he would build his congregation on people like Peter, humans who knew that he was Christ, sent by God. Everyone who believes in Jesus has built their life on the strong rock that is the truth of Jesus. The house on the rock does not fall, even if the strongest of storms are blowing.

The Masters knew then what I am telling you now. When the religion is removed from this story, Jesus is presented as the centre of the Diagram Star, the star in the diagram that now is rediscovered. Jesus is the lost world history that all the prophets have foreseen and the apostles are teaching. The Diagram Star is the official emblem of the superior Motherland council; speaking to all humans and telling you about a global system of governing that were all natural and good, a true paradise. The lost Motherland is in the spirit world, also called heaven. The spirit world is the common world of thoughts. When you hear the born again Motherland history, you know it is the right way to live. You can help to tell the whole world population, because everybody has to participate in building the new world with lasting peace.

Jesus is the born again Motherland history, he is thoughts from the spirit world teaching all humans how a new Motherland can be built. John the Baptist was the lost Motherland history born by very old parents, who had wanted to tell the story for a long time. They were a symbol for the Masters who preserved and passed on the story about the lost Motherland from generation to generation. Baptizing Jesus was the main mission in his life. It was an act that symbolized how the knowledge was given to the whole world population, through Jesus, a spiritual being. Jesus is like an offspring of the superior Motherland council who are in the spirit world.

Jesus wanted to build his congregation on people like Peter. It means that the new Motherland has to be built on solid rock ground by people who know. One of the continents has to be chosen, so why not choose the whole of Africa as the new Motherland.

Elijah and the prophets did not live in the same time, but they all had the same message to people living in present time; the message being that one day soon the history of the lost Motherland and the common set of laws and rules for living were to return to planet earth.

The camouflaged stories in the Bible is written by some 44 authors who were Masters preserving and passing the history about the lost Motherland on to coming generations. It was a history that was told repeatedly for several thousand years. New camouflaged stories were written and only the best lived on. The names of the people telling the stories and the names in the stories were different, but the story about the lost Motherland was always the same.

At the time the camouflaged stories about Jesus and his disciples was written the Masters really thought that a terrible global natural catastrophe, called doomsday, had to happen before the world leaders would come to their senses.

Only after a period of time like the ten plagues the Pharaoh in Egypt was hit by, the world leaders will start thinking about ruling the whole world differently. Then the whole world population needs to know what to do, like Moses, Aaron and the Israelites did. Remember now that the biblical Israelites are a symbol for the whole world population.

Many humans are beginning to understand that their city walls and high capitalistic towers are built on sand ground, with religion and warfare as mortar between the bricks, and are about to fall down. Humans living in present time are facing and increasing chaos of wars and conflicts, and millions more will die before the world leaders come to their senses.

The transfiguration

Matthew 17, 1-9; Mark 9, 2-10; Luke 9, 28-36

After six days, Jesus took Peter, James and John his brother, and brought them up into a high mountain. There Jesus was transfigured before them: his face shone like the sun and his clothing was as white as light. And, behold, there appeared to them Moses and Elijah talking with him.

Then Peter said: "Lord, it is good for us to be here. If you will, let us make three tabernacles here, one for you, one for Moses and one for Elijah."

While he still spoke, behold, a bright cloud overshadowed them, and a voice came out of the cloud, saying: "This is my beloved Son, in whom I am well pleased. Listen to him." And when the disciples heard it, they fell on their faces and were much afraid.

But Jesus came and touched them and said: "Arise and do not be afraid." And when they had lifted their eyes they saw no man, except Jesus alone.

As they came down from the mountain, Jesus commanded them, saying: "Tell the vision to no man, until the Son of Man has risen again from the dead."

And his disciples asked him, saying: "Why then do the scribes say that Elijah must come first?"

Jesus answered: "Elijah truly must come first and restore tings. But I say to you, that Elijah has come already, and they did not know him, but have done to him whatever they pleased. Likewise the Son of Man also shall suffer from them."

Then the disciples understood that he spoke to them about John the Baptist.

It is necessary for all humans to understand the spiritual aspect with life, at least to a certain degree. It is not difficult to find an understanding that all humans can live with as correct.

"His face shone like the sun" is said about Jesus. Jesus is in the centre of the Diagram Star. The sun, moon and the twelve star signs of the Zodiac is the model for the Diagram Star, the official emblem of the late superior Motherland council. Jesus is the carrier of the knowledge that can enlighten the whole world population. You must be able to see that the origin of the Diagram Star is the sun, moon and the twelve Zodiac star signs. The sun is the reason for all earth life as we know it, the mother of all earth life and it have been with mankind from before the beginning of time and will be with mankind until after the end of time. The twelve star signs of the Zodiac are the official emblems of the superior Motherland council and will as such live forever.

Jesus is a symbol for the sun and his twelve disciples is a symbol for the new superior Motherland council that has to be elected. Because there are no human teachers to teach them, they have to find the knowledge in the spirit world, in the common world of thoughts.

Everything that happens on a mountain in a Bible story is right according to the common laws and rules for living. It is not a wonder at all; it is camouflaged knowledge about the lost Motherland.

This camouflaged story was written by a Master of the past, one of those who preserved and passed on the knowledge through the history. They all had to live in hiding for the roman emperors, the warrior kings and the priesthoods that were protecting and passing on the forces of evil, the three factors of the Original Sin.

"Likewise the Son of Man also shall suffer from them." Jesus, as the born again Motherland history, is in all living humans, all the time. The knowledge has to be born again in the common world of thoughts.

The world leaders and the priesthoods of present time are the protectors of the three factors of the Original Sin, passing it on as tradition, inheritance and self-made laws and rules for living. They are the ruling class in our present time, not knowing the wrong they do to the whole world population.

"The Son of Man" has to be born again. Not as one person, but as many humans who knows the full story about the lost Motherland and are able to spread the knowledge to the whole world population. How the world leaders and the priesthoods will react this time is not known. Hopefully they will come to their senses and do like Pharaoh did for Moses and Aaron and the biblical Israelites.

The stories about Moses have not happened. The story is a recipe telling humans living in present time what they have to do in order to restore a world with lasting peace. The whole world population is still obedient working slaves, soldiers and servants under a despotic ruling system that wasn't meant to be. They have to be set free and they have to tell how to build a new world. In order to obtain the knowledge they have to be symbolical baptized with water. Water = Knowledge, says the formula. The whole world population needs leaders who can lead them out of the mental desert and across the river of knowledge. Therefore forgive your leaders as you forgive yourself.

The government system with many national states and their self-made laws and rules for living is made to keep the whole population on the edge of poverty and dependent on work to live a relative good life. The national states in the world are in fact a tremendous crime against man kind that has lasted for some twelve thousand years.

Understand that the only real ting in the world is your own world of thoughts and the common world of thoughts. The common world of thoughts is the Spirit World. Heaven is a camouflage for the Spirit World.

"Elijah truly must come first and restore all things." Read the camouflaged story about Elijah again in the Old Testament. What did he do? He convinced the warrior king and the priest that his God was the mightiest, and after he had done that he spread the good news across the land faster than the king could travel.

How can I convince you and the whole world population that Jesus, as the born again Motherland history came back some two thousand years ago? Can't you see that Elijah and Moses have come to your world of thoughts a long time ago? They are thoughts just as Jesus is, and all you have to do to make the thoughts come alive. Then the whole world population, working together can build a new world.

What the Master of the past want you all to know, is that if you want to find a complete understanding of your life and why you live, you have to study the many stories in the Bible closely after the camouflage is removed. Jesus will truly transform in to a sun in your world of thoughts. He is the centre in the Diagram Star. He can enlighten your mind and give your life on planet earth a meaning.

The many disciples following Jesus are all of you and from all of you the twelve new members of the new superior Motherland council will be elected. You will, sooner or later, find the understanding that the present government systems with many national states are wrong and have been wrong as long as they have existed.

Maybe you will find the understanding I am trying to explain to you the day you are staying in an empty marked place with your hands full of money. Will it be of any use to pray to your God after the whole planet earth is destroyed? Can your government help after all the land and the water is polluted? The whole world population needs a common leading star.

In the time before the Motherland went under the whole world population lived in self supported communities or villages. It is the only way to live in a modern and technological advanced world.

The children first

Matthew 18, 1-14; Mark 9, 33-37; Luke 9, 46-48

One day the disciples walked with Jesus, they whispered to each other: "I wonder about who is the greatest disciple?" Some meant it was Peter. Other thought John was the most important disciple. This they started arguing about.

When they asked Jesus what he meant, he did not answer at ones. Nearby a child was playing. He called the child to come and embraced him. "Do you see this child?" he said." The one who comes like a child, full of confidence and not pretending, will be the greatest in the kingdom of heaven. And for everyone who receives such a child in my name, receives me. And whoever receives me, receives not me, but the one who sent me. But those who harm a child who believes in me, or teach them not to believe in me, will be in great trouble. It would be better for them that a millstone was hanged around their neck, and were thrown into the sea."

The twelve disciples' shivered with fright. They looked at the little child sitting on Jesus knee. It was strange to them that a child could mean that much.

"Take good care of the children," said Jesus. "Love them like a shepherd loves his sheep's. If one of them is lost, he looks for it all through the night until he finds it. All children are precious in the eyes of God. He loves them all."

Remember that this story is a parable. Jesus is a symbol for the born again Motherland history. The disciples are a symbol for a newly elected superior Motherland council and are representing the whole world population. The child sitting on the knee of Jesus is a symbol for the whole world population in the new world that soon will be built. People have to be thought the same laws and rules for living, and as long as they do as they are taught, the superior Motherland council will love them like a father and mother loves their children.

You can ask yourself which national state is the greatest in the world, and try to answer the question yourself. If all the national states in the world were to decide which one of them were the greatest, they would argue among them self and never reach an agreement. The national states have to be removed and one new Motherland has to be built. A global parliament has to be elected from every people in the world, and from them a new superior Motherland council will be elected.

The only way to create lasting peace in a new world is to gather all the people in the world in to self supported villages with a council of twelve Masters to lead them. Even if the villages then were gathered in colonies, kingdoms and empires, they will all be lead by a council of twelve. Think of the whole world population as the children, full of confidence and not pretending. Not one will be greater than the others. Not even the members of new superior Motherland council will be greater than any other humans in the world. The only difference between all humans will be their spiritual strength, their level of knowledge and their ability to work.

There is only one answer to the question: You are all equals, one human being is not greater than others; all the tribal villages are equals no matter how many inhabitants they have.

Now you do understand that all humans living in present time will live their lives with the new superior Motherland council as the leader of the world, full of confidence and not pretending. The whole world population will be like children in the true sense of the word. You will all live in strong houses; have beautiful clothes and enough food for everyone. You will live like Abraham and Sara lived in the time before the force of evil entered their world and they had to leave their homeland. You will live in the light of the Diagram Star with a new world of thoughts.

All humans in the world will love each other like a shepherd loves his sheep's. This means that you shall love all humans in the world as you love your children. The new superior Motherland council will be the shepherd and the whole world population will be the sheep.

The future world can be explained in detail. It will be a world in which all humans will do their daily work for the common good of the tribe. Tribal belonging will replace national belonging. All humans in the world will have everything they need to live a good life like nature intended.

The best students will be sent to the Motherland for a higher education. Think now for yourself how the student will enter the Motherland just like the child came to Jesus, full of confidence and not pretending. They will have no demand for high wages and will not dream about personal riches, power and fame. They will have a life with a profound meaning.

The new world has to be the future for our children and their descendants. They will live right, like humans lived in the time before the Motherland went under. Personal pride and honor will be the strongest motivation for all humans. The technological revolution will soon fall back on the right track, and the building of cosmic eggs can start again.

Not alone

Matthew 18, 15-20

The disciples asked Jesus what they should do if someone played them a trick or did something really bad to them?

Jesus answered that if someone hurt them, they should first talk with the person alone. They should in a friendly manner try to solve the matter. "If it doesn't work, then you shall bring a friend. When two or three gather in a room, I listen to you. I shall always be there with you, in the same room and listen to your prayers."

Therefore we are never alone. Even if we don't see Jesus, he is at our side. He will always follow us.

Think for a moment about the Diagram Star. You know it well by now, and it is with you wherever you go, always. When a new Motherland is built and there is only one set of laws and rules for living for the whole world population, the knowledge will always be with you.

The feeling of a true belonging to a tribal community will prevent every kind of crime and breaking of the common law and rules for living will almost never happen. The person who commits the crime will lose his pride for the rest of his life and will never be trusted again in his community. The loss of respect and trust from family and friends is the worst that can happen to a human.

In the time before the Motherland went under, the Diagram Star was the book that everyone studied through an education that lasted until they were twenty-five years of age. Along with a large number of signs and symbols the students studied the seven basic sciences, and everything they learned, they remembered all their life. Everyone had a specific mission to fill in their lifetime. Only the best students became Masters.

In the future, after the new Motherland is built and the new superior Motherland council is in place, the Diagram Star will be with you wherever you go and whatever you do. This is about the spiritual part of the life of humans on planet earth. The contact with the Diagram Star is the contact that by religious people is called contact with angels. Without the three factors of the Original Sin you will know what is right and what's wrong, and live accordingly.

In present time and for the last twelve thousand years humans have lived with both right and wrong, with good and evil, not knowing that the self-made law and rules of your national state is wrong and evil. It is no use trying to change the laws and rules when it is the national state itself that are wrong. After all the national states in the world are removed from the face of the earth, the laws and the rules for living that are derived from the Diagram Star will be only good and only right.

The leper who was healed

Lucas 17, 11-19

When Jesus walked through a village, ten lepers came to see him. They had heard that he came this way, and now they hoped that he would heal them. Since they were lepers they were not allowed to walk on the road. They stood far off and called: "Jesus! Master! Have mercy on us!" They had hoods over their heads and scarf's hiding their faces. This was because people should not see their disgusting wounds. Now they asked Jesus to heal them.

Jesus pointed towards the city. "Go and show yourself before the priests," he said. This was his way to tell them that they all were healed. Only people that were healed should go to the priests.

The men did as Jesus said. While they were on the way to the temple to see the priests, they felt something strange. Their skin itched on the arms and on their backs. One of them pulled up his sleeve and saw the skin was healed.

He shouted: "Praised be God! Praised be God the Almighty! I am healed! I am well!" He turned around and ran back to Jesus. Hear he fell down before him and grabbed his feet. "Thanks!" he shouted of all his heart.

Jesus looked at the man who thanked God so intense and said: "But was it not ten of you who were healed? Where is the other nine?" He looked at the man. "You can go now," he said. "Your belief has healed you."

Why was there only one who returned and said thank you? Perhaps the nine others were like many humans in our present time who never say thank you to God. Maybe one just forgot to say thank you. Another might be too shy. Maybe one was too proud.

Maybe one of the lepers was so excited for the healing that he took the wrong road back and didn't find Jesus. It is possible that one were to busy. It was so much he had missed and had to catch up with.

One leper might not come back to thank Jesus because the priest told him it wasn't necessary. A man like that always did what others told him to do, without any thoughts of his own. The seventh leper did maybe not thank Jesus because he didn't understand what had happened to him. The eight did not go to thank Jesus because he saw no reason to do it. He had never thanked anyone for anything.

Maybe the last leper was so happy where he walked, that he did not notice where he was. Only one of the lepers experienced fully that Jesus healed the whole human being. As it so often happens in this world, the nine others took the gift from God for granted. What about us? How often do we thank him?

The symbolism for the whole world population is clear, and the story tells us all what will happen in the time after the complete healing of the whole world population has taken place. You will all say thank you to the superior Motherland council.

It is important, for your own life, to think thank you every time you have a personal experience were you understand that someone or something in the Spirit World have helped you with something that is important to you. All humans have experienced events like that, events one normally don't talk about after they have happened. Even if it is a small thing, or as big as saving your life, it gives you a good feeling to say thank you.

In this camouflaged story Jesus is the born again Motherland history and the ten lepers is symbols for the selfish and ignorant bunch the whole world population have become. Life is taken for granted by most people.

Life as it has been for the last some twelve thousand years and is in present time, is not much to thank the Spirit World for. It is a living hell for most people. But the life all humans lived before the Motherland went under, and the life all humans will live in the time after the new Motherland is built, will be a paradise world that everyone will say thank you for. Say thank you to whom? Just by thinking thank you is enough. The superior Motherland council will hear you, and the prove is the profound happiness you feel when you do something meaningful and right.

By learning everything there is to learn about the lost continent that used to be the Motherland and the global system of government that can heal the world, you will make a significant change in your own life on earth. The change will feel as great as you can imagine the lepers felt after they were healed.

It is the whole common world of thoughts that will be cleansed and healed, and when you know that all the true answers and all the knowledge have been preserved and passed on by thousands of humans who have died after dedicating their whole lives to the work, your thanks should wholehearted go to the Spirit World. One of the nameless Masters wrote the camouflaged story about Jesus. Don't forget to say thank you. I know that you will smile of happiness when you do.

The time has come to start the walk out from the mental desert of oblivion mankind have been in for so long. Follow the light from the Diagram Star and come across the river of knowledge. You and the whole world population are still slaves, soldiers and servants of the government system that we know from old Egypt and still are valid. In our present time the quest for money and personal power is about to destroy the whole world.

A new change

John 8, 1-11

Jesus went back to Jerusalem. Here he taught in the temple. One morning the religious leaders came to him with a woman. She sobbed with fear. The priests throw her down in front of him.

"This woman was found together with a man," they said. "It was not a husband. The Law of Moses says that a woman like that shall be stoned. What do you say?"

The woman did not even dare to lift her head. She had been with a man, it was true, and she knew it was wrong. They were not married, and now they had harmed their spouses.

Jesus bent down and wrote in the dust. "Now?" asked the religious leaders. "What do you think we shall do with her?"

Jesus stood up. "The one who never have committed a sin, can throw the first stone at her," he said. He thought them not to judge.

The priests and people nearby looked at each other. Everyone knew that they had done something wrong one time or another. No one was perfect. One after the other the religious leader's disappeared and then the others followed. The eldest went first and the younger followed. No one said anything. At the end Jesus was alone with the woman.

"Woman", said Jesus, "have no one condemned you?

She lifted her head and looked around. "No, Master," she whispered. "Not one."

Jesus said: "Neither do I condemn you. But don't do this again. Go back to your husband, and start a new life."

The woman started to cry. But this time it was tears of joy. She was no longer afraid.

When the camouflage is removed from this story, it is all about you and the whole world population. The camouflaged stories had to be preserved and passed on, no matter what. First: stoning people for punishment is a law made by the warrior kings and the priesthoods. They did it according to a law they invented as a tool to control the population with fear. Stoning people as punishment was only done by the warrior kings and the priesthoods, and it was a punishment unthinkable in the time before the Motherland was destroyed. It is not a law given by the superior Motherland council.

The sin that is inherited from your forefathers makes you all sinners. The whole world population has their personal world of thoughts occupied with the inherited sin. Is the inherited sin to be compared with deadly cancer, or can the thoughts heal over a generation or two?

The inherited sin is the three factors of the Original Sin and the sinner is every single human living on Mother Earth. The sin is a birth gift to every single human being and is by the laws and rules of all the national states an inheritance that most people accept as a part of their daily life. There are just no ways around the inherited sin. It is preserved and passed on to the coming generation by those humans who have inherited or taken the positions as leaders of the world. The inherited sin is manmade and can only be stopped with knowledge about the lost Motherland.

Remove the camouflage and you will find that the power of knowledge is stronger than all religious belief. The power of knowledge that is derived from the Diagram Star will truly heal the world. Forgive each other. You have all sinned, and you know it well. Begin a new life no, and sin no more.

The Good Samaritan

Luke 10, 25-37

One day while Jesus was teaching, he got a question from a man. This man had studied the laws of God for many
years. He asked: "Master, what shall I do to get to heaven?"

Jesus answered: "What is written in the laws of God? How do you read?

The man said: "You shall love the Lord your God with all your heart and your neighbor like yourself." When Jesus
said that the man answered right, the man asked: "Who is my neighbor? What more shall I do? Who are the
others that I shall love?"

Jesus answered with a story: "One man was on a journey from Jerusalem to Jericho. He was alone. The road was stony
with many curves. Suddenly a gang of thieves attacked him. They hit him severely and stole all his belongings,
even his cloths and left him for dead.

"The man was did lie on the side of the road, half dying. Then a priest came by. When he saw the man, he was
shocked. The man could barely lift his head and ask for help. The priest looked another way and hurried on as
fast as he could.

"And likewise a Levite, when he was at the place, came and looked at him and passed by on the other side.

"Then a Samaritan, as he journeyed, came to were the man was lying, and when he saw him he had compassion with him. The wounded man was a Jew and the Samaritans and the Jews had been enemies for centuries. Still he went to him and bound his wounds, pouring on oil and vine, and put him on his own beast and brought him to hostel and took care of him.

"And the next day, when the Samaritan departed, he gave some money to the innkeeper and said to him: "Take care of him, and whatever more you spend, I will pay when I come back."

"Now tell me, Jesus said. "Which of these three, do you think, was a neighbor to him that was robbed by the thieves?"

And the Jewish lawman said: "He that showed mercy on him."

Then Jesus said: "Go and do likewise."

All those who heard Jesus telling this story, understood that he wanted them to love all humans, and special the strangers and those who were in need.

This is a story that you all understand. In a new world without national borders the whole world population will be neighbours. Under the camouflage of religion, this story is all about the common laws and rules for living from the time before the Motherland was destroyed. The laws of God are given by the superior Motherland council. The twelve council members were elected by a Motherland parliament who had twelve democratically elected Masters from every people in the world as representatives. The superior Motherland council was omnipotent, omniscient and omnipresent and the whole world population lived by the laws and rules given by them.

By knowing the past, the future can be built. What Jesus is telling the Jewish lawman to do, is impossible in a world where the thoughts of all humans are occupied by the three factors of the Original Sin.

Let us look to the future, to a new world without the three factors of the Original Sin. The whole world population will be living in tribal communities without the man made national borders and without ownership to the land they live on. They will live together as brothers and friends, all over the world.

And make a note: Every human who dies is gone for good, buried and remembered. It is only the spirit of every human who lives on in the spirit world. There is no other place. It is called heaven because the spirit of the lost Motherland is there. The twelve members of the Superior Motherland council are there along with everybody else who has died in the course of the history of mankind.

You have heard about the devil and hell and the right understanding is that a living hell started in the world when the Motherland was destroyed in a natural catastrophe. The devil is the three factors of the Original Sin, also known as the serpent in the tree of knowledge.

In the new world with a new superior Motherland council and a new Motherland, no one can come and just take the land you live on with the use of warfare and brutal force. No one can buy or sell land or anything else for that matter. All humans work for the good of the community and getting paid with money is unheard of. The new world with lasting peace will truly be a paradise for the whole world population.

It is the law and the common sense of the tribal council that decides for example when a village population has grown too big for the area of land that is giving them food. Then a full scale tribe have to leave the Mother tribe and seek new land to live on. The emigration will be well planned by the council and as long as there is free land to settle on in the neighborhood, there will be no problems to solve.

In the future, after the new world is ready built, all humans will live together as good neighbors. All humans in the world will have everything they need to live a good life on planet earth, and there will be no evil anywhere.

The tribes living close to each other will be family related and friends. Minor conflicts can happen, but always in a small scale for reasons that are natural and accepted. One example is when a young man sees that the woman he wants for his wife is given to another man. Whatever the young man does is accepted as a crime of passion, but if the crime is seriously wrong the young man can be excluded from the tribe for life. Wrong doing is not accepted.

The whole concept of love between people will be different in the future, when the new world is ready built. Just imagine a world without the use of money of any kind; a world without weapons of war and without religion of any kind.

If there is a famine in one or several tribal villages, the neighbors will share, care and help the best they can. Likewise if a natural catastrophe happens.

What will happen when the world is full of people, with no place to go when a tribe is too big for the land to feed them all? What then?

The meaning with life on earth is to multiply and populate many new planets in the universe. Humans are the only creature with the ability to build cosmic eggs and send them out in to the universe filled with all kind of seed for earth life.

Now for some twelve thousand years the evolution of technology and the building of cosmic eggs have been off track, because of the ongoing evil occupation of the common world of thoughts. When the Motherland was destroyed in a natural catastrophe it became a severe setback for the natural evolution that was meant to be.

The reason the setback have lasted for some twelve thousand years is the outburst of greed and selfish thinking, the diversion of love from humans to riches and personal power, for a few self appointed leaders of armed soldiers.

The so called great warriors in the part of the world history we all know so well, are all criminals of a higher degree. Mostly everything that has been written in the world history is serious crimes against mankind, fully documented. The building of national states was wrong as wrong can be. The making of the global capitalistic system was wrong and the establishing of the many religions was equally wrong.

Everything that are wrongly built in the last some twelve thousand years have to be built down by use of only peaceful means. If not, they will fall by the forces of Mother Nature and perhaps millions of humans will die in the process.

The question to be asked is if it ever is going to be built; a world with lasting peace, people who love each other, and with the building of cosmic eggs in process by the best people from every tribal people in the world?

Then whole tribes will be sent off in to the universe towards a new young and fertile planet, just like the first symbolic twelve tribes were sent off from the Motherland to populate planet earth. They will be sent off in to the unknown universe; much like Abraham and Sara was, as described in the beginning of the Bible.

When you know that the first beginning of humans and earth life came to planet earth in cosmic eggs, then you know what to do in order to make mankind survive in to the far future. Planet earth is a living organism in the universe, with a certain lifeline, and before the lifeline of planet earth comes to an end, many young and fertile planets in the universe will be populated with earth life. The deeper meaning of all this you will first understand after a long study of the Diagram Star.

Our most important present concern is to make all humans in the world start living together like the Good Samaritan in this story. A change of world leaders is not the way to do it. A cleansing of your world of thoughts and the common world of thoughts is my vision for world peace. Not easy in a world where you all have gotten use to be captives of the three factors of the Original Sin.

Martha and Mary

Luke 10, 38-42

When Jesus was here on earth he had three very good friends. It was the sisters Martha and Mary and their brother Lazarus. They opened their home for Jesus and wanted him to feel at home there and Jesus often came to visit to Martha, Mary and Lazarus. It was a place was he could relax and get away from all the humans that constantly were around him.

One time he visited them, Mary did learn something important. Jesus wanted to relax in the sitting-room and he talked with Mary. The sister Martha was excited for having Jesus visiting and she wanted to do the best possible things for him. Therefore she was busy preparing food in the kitchen.

"I want this to be a perfect evening," she said to herself. There was one problem. Martha thought it was too much work for one person. She ran from place to place, collecting herbs and vegetables in the garden, washing and cooking.

318

When Martha looked inn to the sitting room from the kitchen she saw Mary doing nothing at all. She just sat by the feet of Jesus and listened to him talking. "She should help at least a little," Martha thought. There was so much to do.

In the same moment Jesus saw Martha and he stood up and walked to her. "Master," she said. "Do you not care that my sister let me be alone with all the work that has to be done? Tell her that she shall come and help me."

But Jesus answered: "Martha, Martha, you are carful and troubled about many things. But only one thing is needful. Mary has chosen that good part, which shall not be taken away from her. Why do you not do the same?"

Martha looked at him and suddenly she relaxed. She felt that her muscles weren't so uptight anymore and she started to smile. Then she nodded and followed him in to the sitting room and sat down with her sister. Together they listened to what Jesus had to say.

From then on Martha understood that the most important thing she could do, was to learn to know Jesus better. This is something all the followers of Jesus should remember.

The most important thing you can do is to get to know the Diagram Star. Just by looking at the diagram you will see many things that are a lot more important than the everyday work that you do. You will see the superior Motherland council and understand what happened on planet earth after the Motherland was destroyed. It was the twelve members of the superior council that was remembered by the whole world population and became the God of all religions in the world. It was this important memory that was taken away from our forefathers.

Jesus is the centre in the star and you and the whole world population has to get to know the Diagram Star is right knowledge for the world. You have to learn that the three factors of the Original Sin are wrong for the world.

If you don't take time to learn about the lost Motherland, the forces of evil will slowly destroy the world as you know it. The poorest of the poor are already dying by the thousand every day and soon also the richest of the rich will start dying for the same reasons. Knowing the Diagram Star is very important. Knowing the Diagram Star makes you and the whole world population able to build a new world with lasting peace.

It is all about your world of thoughts and the common world of thoughts. In the rich part of the world the thoughts are always fully occupied with thinking about making more money and get more personal power.

In the poor part of the world the thoughts are always occupied with the never ending struggle to make enough money to feed the family and get them a watertight roof over their heads. In a world without money things will be done differently and certainly no one will starve to death.

The continuing occupation of the common world of thoughts is forcing the whole world population in to using all their time and effort to make the best of the life their national state have prepared for them. The freedom to choose is restricted by dictated frames. All the national states in the world are nothing but regular prison camps. Captives inside a system of laws and rules, is what you all are. Thousands of years with wrongful tradition and belief have made the whole world population blind for the knowledge that is hidden under the camouflage of religion. Knowledge from the Diagram Star can set you all free.

Humans are blind for the fact that they all live with the three factors of the Original Sin. You all live with the indoctrinated inherited nonsense the world of thoughts is filled with. Remember, your world of thoughts is by nature meant to be the meaning with life on planet earth.

In the global kingdom the Bible is telling us all about, the whole world population lived like Abraham and Sara lived before they left their home land to search for the Promised Land. Everybody had all they needed to live a good life on planet earth. Abraham and Sara is a good symbol for the whole world population in our present time is searching for. You are not searching for new fertile land to live on, but for a return of the global system of government that were lost when the Motherland went under some twelve thousand years ago.

The two sisters Martha and Mary are symbols for the whole world population, searching for the knowledge that can save the world from further destruction. Those who stop working and begin to learn what's right and what's wrong in the world, is doing the one thing that the world needs right now.

Mary and Martha is a symbol for the new Motherland that has to be built. Listen to the teaching of Jesus, the born again Motherland history, is more important than anything else you can think of.

Lazarus is raised from the dead

John 11, 1-46

On another occasion Jesus heard that Lazarus was very sick. Jesus waited a few days before he went to visit him. When he and his disciples came to the house of Martha and Mary, Lazarus was already dead.

"Lord," said Martha. "If you had been here, my brother would not be dead. But I know that even now whatever you will ask of God, God will give it to you."

Jesus said that Lazarus would raise again from the dead, but Martha did not understand what he meant. "Whoever lives and believe in me shall never die," said Jesus.

When Mary met Jesus, she fell before his feet. "Master, if you had been here, my brother would not have died." She wept and the people around her wept with her. "Were have you laid him?" Jesus asked. They lead him to a cave closed with a big stone. "Take away the stone."

When the cave was opened, Jesus started thanking God. Then he said in a loud voice: "Lazarus, come forth!"

They heard a sound from inside the cave. Out came the dead, covered in grave clothes, and his face was bound with a napkin. Jesus said to them: "Unbind him and let him go."

Mary and Martha could not believe what they saw. Lazarus was alive under the white grave clothes. When they had untied him, the large flock of people called out excited and happy. But some of them went off to the Pharisees and told them what Jesus had done.

You know that humans, who are dead, never will return to life with body and the spirit of life, not ever. The spirit leaves the human body after death and lives on in the spirit world as thoughts. Jesus and all the persons in this story are fictive and have never lived on planet earth. The story is a parable and Lazarus is in fact a symbol for you and the whole world population.

Jesus is the born again Motherland history and it is the history of the lost continent that can bring the whole world population back to a meaningful life again. This means that you and the whole world population are living your lives more or less like living dead, totally without any sensible meaning.

As long as the whole world population is living with the three factors of the Original Sin and let them dictate your lives, you are virtually living dead.

Being living dead means been deprived of the whole specter of thoughts that gave all humans a meaning with life in the time before the Motherland went under. In a paradise world life has a true meaning, or it wouldn't be a paradise.

Meaningless and utterly wrong it is to live in a world where the multinational companies and the few rich countries keep exploiting the poor in their own country as well as all over the world. The money that is given to the poor countries is an insult not only to the people the money is given to, but also to the human intellect in general. How foolish is it possible for clever people to be? Thousands of humans are dying every day, lives that could be saved with a simple change of governing the world as a whole.

The good shepherd

John 10, 1-21

Many wondered who Jesus was and where he came from. They asked the same questions time and time again. Jesus could give them answer.

"I am the good shepherd," he said. Then he made a picture for them with words. He wanted them to understand why he called himself the good shepherd.

"I am at the gate to the sheep fold," he said. "The shepherd stands at the entrance. He knows what sheep's is his, and let them pass. He is keeping wild animals that can hurt them, away.

"The good shepherd does everything he can to save his sheep. He will die for them if necessary. Because the sheep's are his, he does not run away if a wolf is coming. One that is hired to do the work can do that. I am the good shepherd. I know my sheep's and they know me. I give my life for them, and I shall come back to live again. It is something the God my Father let me do."

Many liked what Jesus said and they wanted to believe in him as the good shepherd.

This camouflaged story is about Jesus as the born again Motherland history. The superior Motherland council was the leader, the shepherd for the whole world population in the time before the Motherland went under. The whole planet earth is the sheep fold and the whole world population is the sheep's. Some twelve thousand years ago the superior Motherland council died in a natural catastrophe that destroyed the Motherland. At that time the shepherd died and the sheep fold gate was left open for the wild animals to get in. It was then the evil entered the common world of thoughts and the chaos of wars and conflicts started.

The almighty God in heaven is a religious camouflage for the almighty superior Motherland council who died and is in the spirit world. As spirits in the spirit world they had no power to control the thoughts of human beings, who started doing wrong. Jesus is a symbol for the lost world history that the new shepherd; the new superior Motherland council has to know. Jesus is the spiritual power coming from the spirit world that can educate his twelve elected disciples with the knowledge that gives them the power to become a new physical and strong shepherd for the whole world population.

It is very important to understand that it is the Diagram Star that is the link between the spirit world and the physical world. The diagram shaped like a star has traveled through the ages, preserving and passing on the knowledge about the lost Motherland. It will always be there for you.

The camouflaged story about Jesus dying on the cross, with the promise to the people that he will come back again is a picture drawn for you and the whole world population, in words.

Jesus is the born again Motherland history, in words and in spirit. By building a new Motherland and electing a new superior Motherland council, the good shepherd will be back to care for his sheep. It can only be done if the whole world population works together.

Wild beasts are merciless in their quest for food. The national states and multinational companies are just as merciless in their quest for more riches and personal power. Because of their evil activity the world is a living hell for all humans.

The lost sheep and the lost silver coin

Luke 15, 1-10

The cost for follow Jesus can be high, but God is valuing every human being highly. It is the same for children, women and men. He wants everyone to convert to him and begin a new life.

The religious leaders did not like those who followed Jesus. Therefore Jesus told two stories about how valuable all humans are in the eyes of God. The first story was about a sheep that were lost.

Jesus said: "If you have one hundred sheep and one of them is lost, will you not then start searching for the lost sheep? And when you find it, will you not carry it back to the others? Will you not call all your friends together? And you will shout to them: "I have found the lost sheep! In the same way it will be more happiness over a sinner that converts than over ninety-nine humans who thinks that they are so good that they don't need God."

Heaven is filled with joyful angel song every time a human comes back to God.

The other story was about a woman who had ten silver coins. She lost one of them, and it was worth a whole days work. Jesus said: "If a woman looses one of the coins, will she not search for it all over the house, until she finds it. She will sweep the floor and looks under carpets and beds. When she finds it she will send for her friends to come and say: "Rejoice with me now! I have found the lost silver coin."

In the same way the angels will smile and sing every time a human says that they will believe in God and that they will live their life with Jesus from then on."

People were surprised over what Jesus said. It meant that bad people, even the very evil humans, was welcome in heaven. If they only converted, God would receive them and give them the power to start a new life. Jesus showed them the way in to the kingdom of God. He said that they should love God and each other.

God wants everyone to convert and begin a new life.

God is defined to be the new superior Motherland council and the strict laws and rules for living found in the Diagram Star. To begin a new life means a total change in the common world of thoughts. The change in your world of thoughts has to begin and end with you. You have discovered that important knowledge is missing in the world. The knowledge about the lost Motherland is lost, and you have to start searching for it, and don't give up until you find it.

Jesus is the born again Motherland history, and if you find and understand the history from the time before the Motherland went under, you will find and understand how the future world with lasting peace can be built. Your state of mind when you fully understand it all will be a deep and profound happiness that will be a permanent foundation for the rest of your life.

Heaven is defined as the spirit world, the common world of thoughts, and the contact between the thoughts of the humans living in our present time and the thoughts of all the humans that have lived on planet earth, is the angels. Think of them as spiritual beings that are linked to all the feelings a living human can experience.

After the evil force of the three factors of the Original Sin is removed from the common world of thoughts and from your world of thoughts as well, the common world of thoughts will be like Mother Nature intended from the beginning, filled with only the natural force of good.

The Masters who wrote the stories are asking you to convert to the global system of government that secured a world with lasting peace in the time before the Motherland went under. Jesus, as the born again Motherland history, is the knowledge his disciples needs before they can be elected to sit in the new superior Motherland council. Virgin Mary is a symbol for the new fertile Motherland that has to be built by the whole world population working together.

The lost sheep and the lost coin are symbols for the thoughts that have been lost for so long. The whole world population is lost sheep's in our present time. But if only one of you find the lost thoughts and tell everyone, rejoice and singing will begin and sound all over planet earth.

Warrior kings and priesthoods have all through the ages been fighting against the knowledge from the Diagram Star and the global system of government it speaks of so clearly. They are the world leaders and elite of present time, born in to their position because of the three factors of the Original Sin. And they pass their inheritance on to the coming generations, not knowing that the life they live is wrong as wrong can be.

To say is plainly, human beings have to be in charge of a last attempt to stop destroying the planet you all live on. You will get the help you need from the common world of thoughts. Do not reject thoughts and ideas that you don't understand right away. Most humans on this planet earth want lasting peace from the chaos of wars and conflicts that is haunting a large part of the earth population. Only with lasting peace the whole world population together can prepare for the coming natural evolution.

You have to read the Sermon on the Mount again and understand Jesus when he says that the world you know will change dramatically and your way of life will be turned upside down. He is also telling you that the new world with lasting peace only can be built by humans. Jesus, as the born again Motherland history, can only tell you how. Therefore, if you haven't found the lost knowledge yet, search for it and never give up.

The boy who left home

Luke 15, 11-49

Jesus also told a story about a father who had two sons. He said: "One day the youngest son went to his father and asked for the money that he was to inherit after the father was dead. He would have them right now. The father thought it was a bad idea, but after a while he said yes. A few days after the young man had gotten the money, he left home.

He traveled far, until he reached a far of land. Here he wasted all his money on drinking and partying. When the all the money was spent, he didn't know what to do. He didn't even have enough money to buy food.

The young man went from house to house and begged for crumble. Finally he got a job on a farm as a keeper of pigs. He was so hungry he could eat with the pigs.

It didn't last long before the young man started thinking for himself: "The workers on the farm back home with my father have more than enough to eat. And here I am about to die from starvation! I will go back home to my father and tell him that I am sorry that I left him." And then the young man left the pigs and started on the long journey home.

When Jesus told this story about the young man who had left his home, he hoped that people would understand what he meant. God would forgive everyone who really repented, everyone who were willing to start a new life.

Jesus told the rest of the story: "The young man did not know that his father had been looking for him. He had been looking down the road and prayed: "Let the boy come home to day!

When the boy still had some ways to go before reaching home, his father saw him. He called out: There he is! It is him! My son is coming home! Then he ran off to meet and embraced him.

But the young man held his head down: Father, he said, I have behaved badly. I do not deserve to be called your son any more. All the money is wasted, and...

But the father interrupted him. He ordered his servants that they should hurry and find the best clothes and put them on him. Put a ring on his finger and give him a pair of shoes. Slaughter the calf and we shall have a party. My son was dead, but now he lives. He was lost, but is found.

The young man cried from happiness when he saw how high his father loved him. He was so relived. It didn't last long before the party was on. All the servants and workers rejoiced with him.

But the oldest son was not so happy when he came home from the field. He heard music and laughter and asked a servant if there was a party on the farm. When he heard what had happened he got angry. His father tried to explain everything to him, but the oldest son just turned away from him.

It is not just, he said. For many years I have lived like a god son. I have labored and worked really hard for you, and you have never given me as much as a kid, so I could give a party for my friends. But when your other son spends all the money you gave him, you give him everything.

But you are also my son, said the father. All I own belongs to you. Don't you understand? Your brother was dead, and now he lives. He was lost and now he is found!"

This camouflaged story is about the three factors of the Original Sin and the whole world population. All humans, except the many aborigine people, have lived a totally meaningless and wrong life for the last twelve thousand years. It is unbelievable that sensible and clever human beings can live like you all do. People are working hard most of their lifespan and have done so generation after generation, always living on the brink of poverty. The need for money is forcing people to work, and without a job poverty is knocking on the door, often destroying whole families. Money and the global system of capitalism is one of the three factors of the Original Sin.

Like the young man guarding the pigs, starving for too little to eat, the whole world population has to submit to the use of money. With money you are accepted anywhere in the world, but when the money is gone you are reduced to be a homeless beggar. Now think about the billions of humans who are living without money or less than a dollar a day. Not one of them have a homeland to return to, they are all more or less locked in to their country and die because of reasons that comes from poverty.

The young man had knowledge and remembered the good life with his family, the life he had chosen to leave. He deeply regretted his choice and went back to his family. He was surprised over the overwhelming welcome he got, and was grateful.

The whole world population lives without knowledge of the lost Motherland and the global system of government that secured lasting world peace in the time before it went under. In order to return to the god life when the whole world population lived together like one big family, a new Motherland has to be built. The father in this camouflaged story is the new superior Motherland council.

The knowledge about how to build a new Motherland and elect a new superior Motherland council, was given to the world population some two thousand years ago, camouflaged as Jesus, the born again Motherland history.

The knowledge about the paradise world of the past is found in the Bible, under the camouflage of religion. The whole world population has to be informed, and together mankind has to decide to return to the global government system of the past. A new Motherland has to be built, and the whole world population will rejoice and be extremely happy while restoring the world in to the paradise world that Adam and Eve left.

The only way to survive for our children and their descendants is to build self supported villages for the whole world population, the way the nature of things advises, like humans did in the time before the Motherland was destroyed in a natural catastrophe. There is a lot of symbolism in returning to "Fathers House".

Look forward to the day your thoughts resurrect from the darkness of oblivions, from a life as a blind and living dead to a life in the light of the Diagram Star.

Money greedy people

Luke 16, 10-14

The religious leaders did not like that Jesus spoke about love and forgiveness. Most of them were only thinking about money and personal power.

Jesus said: "You cannot love money and at the same time live for God. You must not love the money and things more than God. If people are honest in money matters, it shows that they can be trusted. One that is honest when it is about money can also be trusted with greater things, like for example taking care of people."

Jesus showed the Pharisees that they had to choose between the love for money and the love for God. What should come first?

All the religions in the world are one part of the three factors of the Original Sin. The other two factors of evil in the world are the many national states and the global system of capitalism. All three factors have to be removed before a new world with lasting peace can be built. It is a matter of fact.

This is a choice the whole world population has to make, and it is very important to understand that the future life with a new Motherland and one set of laws and rules for living for everyone will be a world totally without money. Everything a human need to live a good live on earth will be free of charge. Certainly everyone have to work every day and all their life, but it will be the natural work for the good of everyone, for the common good.

Without the ownership of land and use of money to buy things, all humans will be equals and highly respected no matter what work they do for the common good, and with the mutual respect for each other comes the happiness and the pride over doing a good job.

Religious leaders from some two thousand years ago and religious leaders of present time is still thinking within the same man made frames. Connected to their national governments as priests, they have chosen a life that will preserve a world with a few rich humans and billions of poor humans.

Does any one of the religious leader of present time consider that their preserving and passing on their religion is the reason for the wars and conflicts that kills thousands of humans every day?

Not only the religious leader, but all of you have to, just like the young man choosing to return home to his father's house, make the choice of leaving the dogmas and assumptions of the religion behind and begin building a new Motherland.

Why is a few money greedy religious humans allowed to continue to lead on in the destruction of our beautiful planet earth?

To love God means to live on a planet earth where a new Motherland is built and a new superior Motherland council is elected. God is a camouflage over the lost Motherland who is in the Spirit World, and Jesus is camouflage over the born again Motherland history explaining how to elect a new superior Motherland council.

As long as you and the millions of poor people let the money greedy religious leaders control your lives with their own invented dogmas and assumptions, planet earth will continue to be a living hell for the whole world population.

The rich man and the beggar

Luke 16, 19-31

Jesus also told a story about how to live. "Ones there were two men. One was very rich and one was very poor. The poor man's name was Lazarus. He looked bad. He had nasty wounds all over his body. All he could do was to lie on the ground and beg outside the rich man's door. He begged for crumbles that were left after the rich man had eaten. The dogs used to come and lick his wounds.

But the rich man did not care about the poor and helpless people like Lazarus. He lived for himself. He had nice clothes and used a lot of money; he went to parties and enjoyed life.

When Lazarus finally died, angels came and carried him away. They put him in the arms of Abraham. He had no more pain and was never hungry no more.

But when the rich man died he was sent to the place where evil humans belonged. He lived with terrible pain and he could see Abraham far above, and he saw Lazarus by his side.

Father Abraham! The rich man called. Help me, please! Send Lazarus with some water so I can wet my tongue. I am so thirsty!

But Abraham answered: Don't you remember? You had so much good in life, while Lazarus had nothing. Now you are punished.

Then you must send Lazarus to my brothers, so he can warn them, said the rich man.

No, they have enough of warnings they can read about, Abraham answered. Moses has written about it, and so has the prophets. They have all tried to make people seek God."

If only the rich man had converted and done like God wanted, he would have done ok. But now it is too late for him.

After all humans have died, it will be too late. The definition of God is very important. The laws and rules given by the superior Motherland council have to be followed to the letter. The whole world population has to start living like nature intended, before it is too late.

It is easy for the rich people and for the world's religious and political leaders to know that only a central power, a new superior Motherland council for all the people in the world, is the only power that will be able to restore lasting peace. The superior Motherland council of the past is spiritual and the laws and rules are known, they are powerless against the three evil factors of the Original Sin.

It is easy to find the recipe for building a new Motherland hidden in the camouflaged stories in the Bible. Moses, the prophets and Jesus is telling you how to restore lasting peace on the whole planet earth. Writing the stories was done by the Masters of the past.

The rich man is a symbol for all the more or less ignorant rich people and nations in the world, helping the poor people and the poor nations in the world with crumbles from their riches. When the time comes when even the richest of the rich is unable to buy food for money, they will suddenly wake up from the common mental blindness and their life as living dead. But then it will be too late for many humans and only people living self supported villages will survive. The aborigine people of our present time are a proof for just that.

The story about Abraham and Sarah in the Old Testament is about how the whole world population lived in the time before the Motherland went under.

After the superior leadership of the Motherland disappeared, almost all the people on earth wanted to continue to live the peaceful life they were used to, but the self appointed warrior kings and priesthood started forcing them in to a life as a working slaves, soldiers and servants.

Most of the people living in self supported villages were rich in gold, silver and precious stones. They had nice strong clothes and houses built in stone. Their main activity was education.

In a world without the national borders, without the global capitalistic system and without all the religions in the world, the daily life was different from the life that you are used to in our present time. The people had all they needed to live a good life on planet earth; they were all happy and content. All humans were equals and lived with lasting peace.

It all changed when the warrior kings and the priesthoods started attacking the villages, killing all opposition, stealing all the riches and forcing the surviving population in to a life as working slaves, soldiers and servants. The government system with many national states, a rich elite and a large poor population started back then, and is still in command.

People dies by the thousands every day, and all the rich peoples and national states do, is to secure their riches and giving crumbles to the poor people and nations. They just continue to believe that money can save the world, while the chaos of wars and conflicts just escalates year by year.

The day the rich people and the national states in the world understand that they are doing things utterly wrong; it will be too late for a lot of people, both rich and poor. Getting rid of the three factors of the Original Sin will not be easy, but it has to be done in order to save the world. The discovery of the Diagram Star will make it possible, if the work starts now.

The rich man can be compared with the young man who came back to his father's house and asked for forgiveness. The rich man waited too long. After death it is too late to ask for forgiveness. He didn't convert in time and didn't even consider doing it, because he didn't know what to convert to. Now the rich people on the whole planet earth are told that the only way to be forgiven by our children and their descendants, is to convert to the global system of government that are clearly described in the Bible, under the camouflage of religion.

You have to know by now that the only life after death is the spirit of your thoughts, and the only difference between good and evil is the content of your thoughts.

More about prayer

Luke 18, 1-8

Prayer is the same as talking with God. Jesus wants us to talk to him about anything. He wants to be our best friend. God always hear us when we pray.

Sometimes when we pray, we think that nothing ever happen. It feels like God is not listening to us. This is not true. God always listen. Sometimes we have to wait for the answer. It can be difficult to pray in times like that, but Jesus wants us to continue. He told a story that should teach his friends that they should continue praying and never give up, no matter what.

"Ones upon the time there was a bad judge, who didn't care for anyone. One day a poor woman asked him for help against a man that was cheating her. At first the judge didn't care about her at all and didn't want to help her. But she had no one else to turn to. Again and again she asked him for help.

At the end he gave in and helped her. If a bad judge can do that, you can be sure that God always will listen to you. He is full of love and is always willing to help people."

Before the Motherland went under every human on earth could ask their village council for anything and get an answer strait away. If the inquiry was very important for the whole village population, it could go all the way to the superior Motherland council, and an answer would be given strait away.

After the Motherland went under the superior Motherland council have been thought of as in a spiritual heaven, and all the prayers for their return have failed so far. The spiritual superior Motherland council is powerless against the three physical factors of the Original Sin. The only way to restore the almighty power of the superior Motherland council and restore lasting world peace is to elect a new one.

It is just that the spiritual Jesus is doing when he elects his twelve disciples and teaches them to become apostles. Only Masters with a height degree can be elected to sit in the council. Jesus is the born again Motherland history and he is telling people living in present time how to build a new world with lasting peace.

You cannot pray for riches and personal power, because it is totally not natural. It is against the laws and rules for living given by the superior Motherland council.

Without the camouflage of religion a prayer is a personal request to a powerless spirit world for an answer to a difficult question. In a world without the three factors of the Original Sin the request would go to a physical superior Motherland council and the answer would come straight away.

The religious concept with a lot of wrong and unbelievable dogmas and assumptions has blinded humans for the ability to separate right from wrong. It is wrong to think that an undefined spiritual God can do anything at all for humans and humanity. You and the whole world population have to elect a new global parliament and a new superior Motherland council. From a new Motherland they can answer your prayers straight away.

Most people think the religious dogmas and assumptions are wrong, and the resurrection of Jesus is just one of many unbelievable stories. It is equally wrong to make a mental distance to religion. Study the camouflaged stories close with the formula and knowing that Jesus is the born again Motherland history, the resurrection suddenly make sense.

Remember that your world of thoughts and the common world of thoughts are the most important factor of all. Without thoughts the world would be empty.

The blindness you experience about the spirit world is made by the continuous indoctrination from the national governments and their priesthoods. They keep on telling the whole world population about the dogmas and assumptions that you all know is wrong as wrong can be.

Therefore clear your mind and think for yourself. Decide what's right and what's wrong, and your contact with the spirit world will become normal and natural. In a world without the three factors of the Original Sin your contact would be with a new superior Motherland council. It is the contact the whole world population is missing.

It is so simple, really. All earth life lives inside the aura, the atmosphere of air that surrounds the whole planet earth. Everything is the spirit world, the common world of thoughts and your world of thoughts. Everything lives inside the spirit world, and when a physical human body dies, it is the aura, the spirit and the world of thoughts that continues to live on in the spirit world. It is the same for all earth life.

But it is not enough. Humans need a physical superior Motherland council in their world of thoughts. It would make the world complete again.

When homes are broken

Matthew 19, 3-11; Mark 10, 2-9

Sometimes it happens that two that are married with each other, dissolve the home. They stop living together. It is called a divorce. Everyone hurts. Often the children are suffering the most.

When mother or father leaves home, some children feels that it is their fault, but it is not. They cannot be blamed for that. Mothers and fathers choose to divorce. It can be for many reasons, but the children are never to blame.

Jesus knew that divorce is not good. He was also aware of that a man and a woman can decide that they don't want to live together any longer. On day a Pharisee asked him: "Can a man divorce a woman for any given reason?"

Jesus did not like the question. He said that God guided man and woman together so they could be one. He did not want them to divorce. The religious leaders then asked why the law said that they could divorce.

Jesus said: "It is because you have a hard hearth. Therefore people have been given the permission to divorce. But it is not the way God want it to be. When a man and a woman get married, it is the natural meaning that they shall stay together until death."

When the disciples heard that, they said: "If it is like that, isn't it sometimes better to not get married at all?"

Jesus answered that not everyone had to get married, but the marriage, that was a gift from God, should always last the whole life through. Jesus wanted to protect the family, and when he did that, he protected the children.

In the time before the Motherland was lost, divorce between a man and a woman who were married, never happened. In a world without the three factors of the Original Sin, the love between people was true and natural. The saying that man and woman is one, is originating from the fact that all reproduction of life forms on planet earth is a product of a cell division.

Look now at the Diagram Star again. One man or one woman alone in the centre of the diagram will live and die unproductive. In order to reproduce and make children a man and a woman have to get in to the center of the diagram and be one together. Only together a man and a woman can produce children, symbolized by the twelve sections around the star in the centre. The Diagram Star is telling you and the whole world population how to multiply.

And learn this and remember: Humans are by nature breeding children, and choosing a wife for the wrong reasons, can result in children with a weak spirit, without the ability to learn and often with both physical and psychological defects.

A marriage in the past was meant for engender the best possible children, to secure the future of the tribe. A marriage was built on pride and belonging. A young man or a young woman could not get married without the permission from their parents and the tribal council, and the whole village population was invited.

In our present time both the man and the woman have stronger motives than love as the reason to get married. Money and level of education comes before family name and history, and the reason for all marriages is a good life with a safe economy and a relative high position in society.

God is defined to be the twelve members of the superior Motherland council. They are administrating the strict laws and rules of Mother Nature. It is not natural that a man and a woman who are married divorces and move away from each other. The reason for the divorce is almost always based on one or all the three factors of the Original Sin and it is a true sign of decay for the family. Personal pride is as good as destroyed with the quest for riches and personal power; the good feeling of belonging to a family is gone for the same reason. A divorce is marking a child in a negative sense for life and only the strongest in spirit lives and becomes good parents for their own children. A strong and true inner happiness for a man and a woman and the children is the essence for being good parents.

Therefore the work with the rebuilding of the Motherland and the global system of government has to commence right now. If it already is too late, the whole world population will perish without even knowing why they lived. It is not too late to restore the right kind of love.

Try now to understand how important the hidden message in the Bible is for you, your children and their descendants. Marriage between a man and a woman is indeed a gift, and shall last the lifespan to the end.

Let the children come to me

Matthew 19, 13-15; Mark 10, 13-16; Luke 18, 15-17

Jesus is the children's great friend. One time he said that the angels protecting children always is close to God in heaven. The children are so full of confidence, and God is very fond of them. Every child is a treasure for him.

Parents that had heard Jesus speak, knew this. One day some of them came to Jesus with their children. They asked Jesus if he would lay his hands on them and pray for them.

But the disciples replayed: "Get away from here! Can't you see that the Master needs rest? He does not have time for this. He has more important things to do than to play with kids!"

Then Jesus got angry. "No," he said. "Don't send them away. Let them come to me."

He looked at the disciples and used the children to teach them more about his kingdom. "The kingdom of heaven belongs to those who believe the kingdom exist with the confidence these children shows. Only those who are like the children will enter my kingdom."

Then Jesus held his arms out towards the children that stood around him. He stroked them on the hair, gave them hugs and held them tight. He whispered something in their ear that made them laugh.

The mothers laughed happy when the children came running to them. The disciples looked around and laughed with them. The best of all was that the children understood what Jesus meant when he said: "Come to me."

"Come to me," means come to the new Motherland, because Jesus is the born again Motherland history. "The kingdom of heaven belongs to those who believe," means that you have to agree that the lost Motherland really existed and that it really was destroyed by a natural catastrophe some twelve thousand years ago.

The twelve apostles are elected from the disciples and are a symbol for the new superior Motherland council. They have to learn a lot of things before they can become Masters leading the new world. The disciples in this story don't know enough to choose right from wrong. Only humans who believe that the lost Motherland existed and understand that a new Motherland has to be built, is thinking and doing right.

Do think about the content of your own world of thoughts in a world that are totally without the evil force of the three factors of the Original Sin. Your thoughts will be filled with confidence that it is the right way to live. The "new kingdom" will be the whole planet earth.

The lost Motherland is in the spirit world and the new Motherland is not even planned by the leaders of the world. They keep on arguing about who is the greatest and strongest national state in the world. In this camouflaged story the Master writing the story about Jesus is reminding you, telling you about a world where the whole world population lived with one leading authority with the same confidence, happiness and trust that the young children lives with under the authority of their parent.

This means that the new Motherland with the new superior Motherland council in the lead will restore on set of laws and rules for living for the whole world population. I will be a world without all evil the children have to learn as they grow up to be adults. It will be a world without all the three factors of the Original Sin.

The rich young man

Matthew 19, 16-22; Mark 10, 17-23; Luke 18, 18-21

One day Jesus got a question from a man: "Master, how can I come in to the kingdom of God? I want to live forever."

Jesus knew that the young man was very rich. He also knew that he for many years had tried to become a religious leader. Jesus told him something he already knew: "Follow the commandments."

The young man answered: "I have followed the commandments from childhood. Now I want to do more." The young man wanted to get as near God as possible.

Jesus was fond of the young man, but he knew that there were one obstacle between him and God. He knew that the young man loved his money more than anything else in the world.

The young man loved God to, but he loved his riches more. Therefore Jesus said: "One thing you lack: Go and sell everything you own and give the money to the poor, and you shall have treasure in heaven. Then come, take up the cross and follow me."

The young man was sad to hear this. Deep inside him understood that he had not put God first in life. He was not willing to give up his riches and follow Jesus. He bent his head and walked away.

This camouflaged story is about something the Masters of the past knew very well. If the rich people in our present time are told that the building of a new Motherland and implementing one common set of laws and rules for living for the whole world population, only can be done in a world without the global capitalistic system and the money they love so much, they will protest against it. Removing all the national states and all the religions in the world is out of the question for the few rich humans in the world, but for the multitude of poor people in the world it will be a relief. They will all be set free from the dictating and merciless governing by the three factors of the Original Sin.

Now you need to think about what happened when Moses and Aaron asked Pharaoh to let the Israelites go. It was not the spiritual superior Motherland council that sent the ten plagues, but Mother Nature protesting against wrongful human activity. Remember the last plaque well.

When the rich people in the world start dying because of global catastrophes caused by destructive and wrong human activity, then they might consider living together as brothers and friends, like people that all are equal to each other, in self supported villages. If the whole world population converts now, a lot more humans will survive and be welcomed to live in the new world.

"Then come, take up the cross and follow me". This means if you accept the new way of life you will also have the cross as your guide through life. The cross is a copy of the Diagram Star, which are the emblem of the lost Motherland and the new Motherland that not yet are built.

Who comes first?

Matthew 19, 23-30; Mark 10, 23-31, Luke 18, 24-30

Still the disciple's believed that Gods love could be bought for money. They meant that people were rich because God wanted to reward them. This is of course not right. Jesus said: "It is easier for a camel to walk though a needles eye then for a rich person to get into heaven."

Jesus wanted to rescue people from everything they are committed by. It is only because of Jesus we can enter the kingdom of heaven. Not because you are rich and are striving to be good. People believe that they have to do a lot of good to deserve a place in heaven.

The truth is that God will lead us there. It is his gift to everyone who prays for it. You cannot buy yourself a place in heaven, and you cannot get a place because you believe you deserve it. God alone gives you that place.

Jesus said: "Every person who is willing to leave home, parent and friends and follow me will receive a hundred times more both here on earth and in the world to come. There humans will live forever. Many who are the first here on earth, will be last to enter heaven. And those who are the last here on earth will be the first to come to my kingdom."

The spiritual heaven is the lost Motherland in the spirit world. A new Motherland on earth will be a new Garden of Eden and the whole world will again be a paradise. It is the paradise world that will be closed for all rich humans; in the sense their money will be worthless. This story is not about life after death, but the new world that will be built hopefully in the near future. It will be a heaven on earth.

Jesus is the born again Motherland history, and when a new Motherland is ready built, money and riches will not be a part of it. In a world without money and the global capitalistic system the concept of being rich or poor will not exist.

Only a certain number of people will be elected to live in the new Motherland. They will be elected because of their ability to lead, their spiritual strength and their level of education. They will be the global parliament members. The whole family, young and old, will be asked to leave their homeland to start a new life in the Motherland. From the parliament members the new superior Motherland council will be elected.

As said before, the multitude of poor people in the world will accept the new Motherland and the new global government system straight away, and be the first to benefit from the new way of life. Most humans will continue to live just where they always have lived, and they will experience the new way of life as a change from an earthly hell to an earthly heaven. The whole world population will work hard and build a new world with lasting peace for their children and their descendants.

The rich people, the national leaders and the priesthoods will hang on to their luxury way of life for as long as they can, and they will for that reason be the last to enter heaven on earth. But they will follow and they will all be forgiven, every one of them.

With a new superior Motherland council to manage the whole world population, there truly will be lasting peace.

The heavens in the sky will always exist in the common world of thoughts. They are the spirit world where all the spirits of those who have died is and always will be. Whit them are the spirits from the billions of humans who have lived and died not knowing why, in the era where the three factors of the Original Sin have ruled planet earth.

Jesus and the twelve disciples is a camouflage for the new superior Motherland council that you and the whole world population have to elect among yourselves. The elected humans have to be disciples and study for a long time before they can call them self apostles, teachers and Masters. There is no one else.

The workers in the vineyard

Matthew 20, 1-16

Jesus taught more about how the last comes first and the first comes last. He told the disciples this story: "The kingdom of heaven is like a man who owns a vineyard. He went out early one morning and hired people to work for him. They agreed on the usual wages for one day's work. A few hours later he saw several men standing there with nothing to do. They also agreed on the wages, and went to work on his vineyard.

The owner went out both in the middle of the day and in the afternoon and looked for more workers. At the end of the day he found the last group.

"Why have you not been working today?" he asked.

"No one has offered us work," they answered.

Then the owner said: "You can work for me. Go to the vineyard and help with the harvest."

One hour later the owner of the vineyard said to the foreman: "Call the workers together. The last group shall be paid first."

First the owner paid the last group he had hired. He gave them a full day's wages, even if they only had worked one hour! Then he paid the ones he had hired before them and like this he kept on until he came to the group that had been working the whole day. Everybody got the same salary.

Those who had been hired first, complained over this. They said that they thought they should be paid more than those who had worked just one hour. "We have been sweating all day," they said.

"Friends," said the owner. I am just. You got the salary we agreed on. Why I pay those who work less than you, is my business. There is no reason for you to ask for more. I do with my money as I please. Take what is yours and go home."

Jesus looked at the disciples. They were very surprised. "Like this the last shall be the first, and the first the last," he said.

All the workers got paid for the day, enough for what they needed. Those who were hired last had been just as willing to work the whole day as the others. Like that it is with us when we come to Jesus. He will always forgive us. He will give every one of us the same life in his kingdom. God treats everyone the same way. It is our belief in God, not what we have done, that gets us in to the kingdom of heaven.

It is the common laws and living rules of the superior Motherland council, that the whole world population shall have all they need to live a good life on planet earth. It is not a question about money at all. In a self supported village everyone will have their duties, a job to do for the common good. Everyone will be respected for what they do, and with mutual respect between all humans comes the happiness called true love.

The rule is that everybody always shall be willing to work for the common good of the tribe, and if every tribal people in the world do the same, the world will be a paradise where all humans have all they need to live a good life. The evil differences that are made by the three factors of the Original Sin in our present time will disappear completely. Position in the community will be decided by spiritual strength and level of education.

The little man in the tree

Luke 19, 1-10

In Jericho lived a rich man named Zaccheus. He was the chief among the tax collectors and made a lot of money both for himself and the Romans. The Jews did not like him because of this. They called him a greedy traitor.

When Jesus was on the way to Jerusalem, he traveled through Jericho. A lot of people had come out in to the street. They waited to see him, and when he came they greeted him by calling out his name. One of them was Zaccheus, but he was so little that he could see nothing in the crowd. Therefore he climbed up in a tree.

He pulled himself up on the lowest branch. Then he climbed higher. He did not care that people laughed of him; there he sat high in the three. He had heard that Jesus was a friend of the tax collectors. He had to see him, no matter what the cost.

People under him started calling. Zaccheus could see a man coming down the dusty street. Was it him? So this was Jesus from Nazareth, Zaccheus thought. He shouted loud along with the others. But suddenly he went silent. As Jesus past the tree were Zaccheus sat, he looked up. He looked straight at Zaccheus. The tax collector could not speak a word.

Zaccheus stared and stared. He had not seen eyes like that before. He just could not look away. Jesus said: ", Make haste down from the tree, Zaccheus. Today I shall visit you at home."

Zaccheus almost fell down from the tree. He was surprised, but then he started laughing. "What an honor," he thought. He got down from the tree and walked with Jesus to his home.

People did not like it. "Look at Jesus," they said. "He is going to the home of this sinner."

When Zaccheus had welcomed Jesus to his house, he gave a promise: "Here and now I promise to give half of my goods to the poor. Those I have taken money from on false accusations, I give beck fourfold." He bent his head. Zaccheus had learned to know Jesus. He wanted to live for him.

Jesus said: "To day salvation have come to this house, inasmuch as he also is a son of Abraham. For the Son of Man has come to seek and save that which was lost."

Abraham is a symbolic forefather for the whole world population, and that includes you.

The Son of Man is a physical person and the Son of God is a spiritual person. It means that it takes physical persons with historical knowledge to explain to humans living in present time what the world lost some twelve thousand years ago when the Motherland went under. A living person who knows what was lost back then has to explain to you and the whole world population what they need to know and what they are doing wrong.

Jesus is a spiritual person made physical only as a fictive person in the many camouflaged stories that truly tells all of you how life on earth is supposed to be. The Son of God is giving you a spiritual link to the part of the world history that is in the spirit world. The Masters who wrote the stories knew the full Motherland history, and they had to camouflage the stories if they wanted to stay alive. And the camouflaged stories had to be implemented as a religion, because it was the only way the stories could be preserved and passed on to new generations.

Salvation means a total change of thoughts, a change from religious belief to knowing the lost world history. Just imagine what the change will do to the common world of thoughts.

Zaccheus is a symbol for the rich people in our present time. Even when they learn that money will be worthless in the near future, they will hold on to their riches as long as they live. Perhaps it will take two or three generations before the whole world population gets used to the new way of living, without money.

Money will in time be worthless, but all the valuable items of gold, silver and precious stones will in time be given back to the whole world population after a precise and just system. Like Abraham and Sara, the whole world population will live in strong houses and have beautiful clothes. Many of the valuable items belonging to a person or a family will be displayed on ceremonial clothes. The clothes worn during a ceremony for example concerning education, marriages and other festivities, will tell the family history to everyone who knows the meaning of beautiful made symbols. The items will have a personal value that in many ways was the essence of life for all humans in the time before evil came in to the world.

All in all this means that when the self elected warrior kings and priesthoods raided the villages and stole all they items of value, the long and well documented history of the village population was wiped out completely. All the stolen gold, silver and precious stones were worked on by skilled craftsmen, and became the property of the thieves. In our present time the royal families and the richest of the rich is proudly calling the riches they have inherited or bought for their property, but a lot of it, if not all, is stolen goods.

The whole world population is rightfully called sinners, because the knowledge about the Diagram Star and the world history from before the Motherland went under, is covered up by greedy warrior kings and priesthoods, and lost in time. Together with their many working slaves, soldiers and servants, the whole world population is forced to live a life without knowledge of the past.

The methods used to force the population in to total submission have changed little through the ages. In our present time it is the global system of capitalism and the imposed need for money that are the tool used by the national states to have as many active working tax payers as possible. The national states are nothing less than work camps with a despotic self made set of laws and rules for living.

The new world will be different. The only salary will be a strong feeling of tribal belonging, respect, pride, safety and profound happiness. Knowledge can save mankind from destroying planet earth. Knowledge will continue to be lost as long as humans continue to believe in their religion and continue to live with the three factors of the Original Sin.

A job well done

Luke 19, 11-27

Jesus told a story: "Ones upon time a king went on a long journey. Before he left home, he gave ten of his servants a large sum of money. When he after a long time came back, he called the servants and asked how they had used the money. Had they been smart or foolish?

All except one had been smart. The foolish servant had buried the money and had not made any attempt to make more. The king was angry. He took the money from the man and gave them to the servant who had made ten times more while he had been gone."

Jesus wanted the disciples to understand that the story was about them. They had been given a glimpse of the kingdom of God. He wanted them tell them that those who learned more about the kingdom of God would be rewarded, while those who turned their back on what Jesus let them see, would get nothing back.

This is exciting. How can it be done, convincing both the believers and not believers that the kingdom of God is a camouflage over a global government system that secured long lasting peace in the world, before the Motherland went under? If you turn your back on the religion as nonsense, you will never see the real world hidden underneath.

Jesus is a symbol for the born again Motherland history and the disciples is a symbol for the new superior Motherland council, representing the whole world population. Therefore it is you that have to understand that this story is telling you that people who have the most knowledge about the lost Motherland will adapt faster to the new world with a government system that is totally different from the despotic system that rules the common world of thoughts in present time.

The reward will be great, but not in money. There will be a true revelation in the global world of thoughts. It is essential that all of you start studying the camouflaged stories in the Bible, without the camouflage of religion, and the happiness that grows with the degree of knowledge, is the best reward possible.

Those who turn their back to the Bible because of the unbelievable religion are fools and will get nothing in return. They will continue to live their meaningless lives with religious belief or not belief.

Mary's act of love

Matthew 26, 6-13; Mark 14, 3-9; John 12, 1-8

Jesus journeyed to Jerusalem the last time before his death. The last night before he walked in to the city he was with Lazarus, Mary and Martha. This night something strange happened while Martha was serving food. Mary, who had loved and worshipped Jesus from the beginning, did something strange. She poured costly ointment over him.

Mary knew that Jesus soon were to leave them. Now she wanted to show that Jesus was her king. Mary poured the ointment over Jesus head. Then she kneeled and rubbed his feet with it. She dried them with her hear.

The other guest's watched in silence. Nobody moved. The delightful scent filled the whole room. But some of them did not like what Mary had done. They meant that she could have sold the ointment and given the money to the poor.

"Leave her alone," said Jesus. "She has done a good deed for me. The poor you always have among you, so you can help them any time you want. But you will not always have me among you. What Mary did here tonight, will be told again and again and people will never forget."

The Master who told this story many years ago, are telling you and the whole world population living in present time, that they, the Masters, have tried hard to spread the knowledge about the lost Motherland to as many people as possible. They really did believe, not in dogmas and assumptions, but in the knowledge hidden in the many camouflaged religious stories.

The early Christians were not religious believers and not believers in our present sense of the word, they believed in what they knew, and many died to protect the knowledge from being forgotten and completely lost. Most of the camouflaged stories they told were meant to be preserved and passed on to coming generations, and they succeeded.

The early Christians were a real threat to the government system the Romans introduced all over their empire. The Romans killed thousands of the early Christians, not for their religious belief, but for the knowledge of the past that they possessed.

The roman rulers used warfare and brutal force to fight all opposition. But some four hundred years later the roman emperor Constantine understood that the fast growing religion not could be stopped by killing them all. Therefore he took the religion in to his reign and used it as a tool to control the many different people he ruled over.

The emperor Constantine started enforcing the religion on to people, to whole villages at the time. He started using the camouflaged stories with the camouflage intact, and it is a fact that the religious belief that the whole world population is forced to live with either as religious believers or not believers, started then and just never stopped.

Because the enemy started using the religions as a tool, the knowledge hidden under the camouflage of religion was forgotten by most people. Those humans who dared to speak a word against the warrior kings and the priesthoods were instantly accused and killed.

This is what Jesus is talking about at the supper at Bethany. People must never forget the history about the lost Motherland. Jesus being anointed a spiritual king of his kingdom, the new Motherland that never came to be, will be remembered always.

The Master who wrote the camouflaged story about Jesus knew that they could not win over the roman armies with only peaceful means, but they also knew that some time in the future the knowledge about the lost global system of government would be needed by the whole world population.

Jesus was anointed by Mary, like a mother would bless a son. Mary is a symbol for the new Motherland that never came to be. The story was written for one reason only, that the history about a world with long lasting peace never would be forgotten.

The entry in to Jerusalem

Matthew 21, 1-7; Mark 11, 1-7; Luke 19, 29-35; John 12, 17-19

It was a clear and calm morning when Jesus told his disciples: "To day we enter in to Jerusalem." Something strange happened on the way to the city gate. More and more people gathered around Jesus and his disciples. Hundreds, yes, thousands of humans wanted to welcome him. They sheered and saluted him as the Son of David. It was the welcoming of a king!

Outside Jerusalem was a mountain named the Mount of Olives. From here Jesus sent two of his disciples to bring him a donkey. Then he rode to Jerusalem on the donkey.

People were waving branches from palm trees and saluted him as a king that had come to free them from the Romans.

He had come near the city, and when he saw it he wept over it, saying: "If only you knew, in this day of yours, the things which concern your peace! But they are hid from your eyes. The day shall come that your enemies shall build a trench around you and keep you in on every side. They shall throw you to the ground and your children within you. They shall not leave you one stone on another, because you did not acknowledge the time when God visited you."

And when he entered Jerusalem, the entire city was moved, saying: "Who is this?" And the multitude said: "This is Jesus the prophet of Nazareth of Galilee."

"If only you knew, in this day of yours, the things which concern your peace! But they are hid from your eyes."

The camouflage made by the Masters of the past is good, and when the camouflage of religion is removed and the people and the land are defined, the words of Jesus are speaking directly to you and the whole world population. It concerns world peace; an everlasting world peace in a new world.

Jerusalem and the land around is a symbol, like a theatrical stage for the whole world and the temple is a symbol for the education centers in the lost Motherland.

Jesus is a symbol for the born again Motherland history and the disciples is a symbol for the new superior Motherland council, representing the whole world population.

Entering Jerusalem, knowing he is going to die, is the Masters ways of letting the knowledge return back in to the darkness of oblivion as a religion. The disciples did not have the power to stand up against the Roman emperors, the warrior kings and the priesthoods, and the history about the lost Motherland was forgotten, hidden under a camouflage of religion.

Jesus will by dying return to the spirit world where he came from. He was born as the Motherland history, camouflaged as a human being. Jesus came as a spirit and returned to the spirit world as a spirit. The people were not allowed to know about the lost Motherland and were forced to believe in the many unbelievable camouflage stories in the Bible.

This had to happen back then, because the Roman emperors knew the history about the lost Motherland and they were using armed forces and vigorous brutality in order to protect and preserve their position as elite and rulers over a large part of the world. This they did because they were surrounded by enemy kings and priesthoods who wanted to take their place and rule the world.

The Master who wrote the story about Jesus knew about the global government system of government that would set people free from the Romans. But they could not continue to see that thousands of humans were brutally killed by the Romans, because they knew about the Motherland and the global government system that was a real threat to their empire.

One of the disciples, Juda, is a camouflage for the whole Jewish tribe. He was sent to the Romans to tell them what they wanted to know. The Romans were told about the religion, but with the camouflaged intact, and it is because of this act that the religion Christianity grew and became one of the three factors of the Original Sin. The religion needed a strong opposition to grow large. If the Roman emperors had decided to ignore the religion, it would have faded and died.

The religion became the perfect tool for the Romans and the many warrior kings and priesthoods. They used it to convince the population in to believing that their king were next to God and had the right to use them as slaves, soldiers and servants.

It was the only way the Masters could make sure that the history of the lost Motherland and the global government system could be preserved and passed on from generation to generation. And they succeeded.

The three evil factors of the Original Sin are still ruling the whole planet earth. Now time has come to uncover the knowledge that is hidden from your eyes under the camouflage of religion. It is time to tell the whole world population about the born again Motherland history, and this time you will not deny that the lost Motherland ever existed.

You know that the whole world population still is ruled by the government system that was imposed first by the Pharaohs of Egypt. You are still slaves, soldiers and servants, and if you want to be set free you have to start telling the whole world population about what secrets that are hidden in the Bible. Only knowledge can win over religious belief in dogmas and assumptions.

A new world with lasting peace can only be built with the knowledge hidden in the Bible. The change will take time, and have to be done with only peaceful means.

Cleansing the Temple

Matthew 21, 1-16; Mark 11, 15-18; Luke 19, 45-48

After Jesus had entered Jerusalem he walked to the holy temple. It was the house of God. He had called the temple his father's house.

Jesus went in to the temple. He did not like what he saw there. Two years earlier he had thrown out all the greedy and loud speaking persons. Now they were back again.

The money changers forced people to pay high prices for the animals they had to have as offering gifts. Many poor people became a lot poorer after a visit in the temple, were they came to worship God. It was not the way God wanted the poor should live.

Jesus knew it all. He looked around. Now he was angry. "No!" he shouted out in anger. "This is my father's house! He started overthrowing the tables of the moneychangers. The coins went in every direction. People screamed and ran in all directions. Birds got out of the cages and headed for the windows.

Jesus walked around and threw all the greedy people out of the temple. He called out to the moneychangers: "God said that this should be a house for prayer. You have made it in to a robbers cave!"

When he was ready he looked around. The temple was empty, except for the disciples and a few bitter religious leaders. Slowly blind people and crippling started coming in to the temple again. They wanted Jesus to heal them. Time and time again he reached out his hands and made them well.

The children saw this and they started dancing around Jesus. They held each other's hands and sang out loud: "Hosanna, the Son of David!" Instead of a robbers cave the temple was now a place for happiness.

The only people who not were happy about this change, was the Pharisees. "Listen to the stupid kids," they snarled to each other and pointed at them.

Jesus answered: "Have you not read the Scripture that children and babies shall love God? Everyone who heard everything he taught in the temple that day marveled over his wisdom.

The whole Bible is full of symbolic meanings and parables. This story is a parable where the temple is the whole world you live in at present time. After Jesus has become known as the born again Motherland history and people learn to know and use the new global government system, one of the first things the population of the world will get rid of, is the global system of capitalism.

And after all the religions in the world have been wiped out by the new knowledge found hidden under the camouflage of religion, the whole common world of thoughts will change. Over a period of time all the national states will be gone, and with them all the weapons of war will be made in to pickaxes, spades and other farmer's tool.

The temple is a symbol for the many teaching centers that were found all over the world in the time before the Motherland was lost in a natural catastrophe. They all had the Diagram Star as their common source of knowledge. The students did learn to know the Diagram Star from early age, and the education ended when the student turned twenty-five years of age. The level of spiritual strength and degree of education decided their position in the community where they settled down.

For some twelve thousand years now, the temples of the world have been used by greedy and selfish people, approved of by the warrior kings and religious leaders of the world. New churches, cathedrals and holy buildings have been built to help the forces of evil to control the population and force them to give offerings willingly.

When the born again Motherland history is made known to the whole world population, they will do exactly as Jesus did in the temple of Jerusalem. With the spiritual force of knowledge the whole world will be cleansed for all evil.

The notorious and greedy exploitation of poor people has developed over the years and have become the global system of capitalism that in present time is about to make the poorest of the poor even poorer. Thousands of humans are already dying every day for reasons that comes from poverty.

Remember now that the temple, the city Jerusalem and the land around is like a theatrical stage for the whole world. The blind and the cripple is a symbol for you and all the people in the world that will welcome the knowledge found in the Bible. If it wasn't for the Jewish people and the Masters who wrote the camouflaged stories, there would be no Bible and all knowledge would have been lost.

When the religion is removed from the act of prayer, an educating study of the Diagram Star becomes visible. Think through what you and your family really need in order to live a good life on planet earth. In a self supported tribal community everyone will work together for the common good and have all they need. No one needs more.

It will take time the change the common thinking of the whole world population and get rid of all the robbers caves. The Diagram Star will enlighten the whole world population, and no one can hide from the bright shining star. Even the robbers are blinded, crippled and live their meaningless lives like living dead. They will be the first to be healed, "come to their senses" and start building a new world for their children and their descendants.

And soon the happy children will hold hands, dance and sing around a symbolic Diagram Star. The Christmas parties with the walk and singing around the Christmas tree, will be meaningful for everyone again, when the dogmas and assumptions is replaced with knowledge found hidden underneath the camouflage of religion. The star in the top is the Diagram Star, the light of the new Motherland, and the many lights on the tree branches is the whole world population.

Who gave the most?

Mark 12, 41-44; Luke 21, 1-4

Jesus walked to the part of the temple where the money chest stood. Here people came and gave God what he first had given them. At least it was the intention. But the religious leaders had made it a place where the poor only got poorer. Now the rich seemed to be the holiest, because they gave so much. But it was money the rich didn't need.

Jesus and two of his disciples sat and watched people give money. They saw a poor woman, a widow, who couldn't give as much as the others. She had almost no money at all. She put two copper coins in the chest.

"Did you see that?" Jesus said to his disciples. "The poor widow gave more than all others together. They only gave of the overflow, money they could do without. The poor widow gave everything she had. When she gave the two copper coins, she gave everything she owned."

This is a good example of what is happening in our present time. Those who give money to the church and too many other organizations that are helping the poorest of the poor, only gives what they think is enough, and amount they don't need anyway. In any case, it is the poor people giving the most, because after they have given, they have nothing left.

All the money, animals and other gifts that are given to the churches, are for the priesthoods to use as they please. It makes the churches in to regular robber caves. The money given as offerings in the churches is an enforced willingness.

In a future world without money, life will be totally different. There will be no rich and no poor people in the whole world. The churches and temples will all be replaced with teaching centers and living will is free of charge.

The five bad virgins

Matthew 25, 1-13

It is important to be ready when this era of time comes to an end. To show this for his disciples, Jesus told them a story: "It was ten virgins, bridesmaids, who were to greet the bridegroom welcome. They were a part of the wedding party.

Five of the girls were indifferent, the five others were wise. All ten should wait along the road until the bridegroom came. When he passed, they should light up the road for him with their lamps.

The five bad girls should have known that they would need extra oil. They had only enough to fill the lamps one time. The wise girls had brought plenty of extra oil.

They waited and waited, but the bridegroom did not come. In the end all of them fell asleep, because it was late in the evening. Suddenly someone called: "The bridegroom is coming! Light the lamps!

The wise girls lit their lamps, while the bad ones had used all their oil long ago. They asked the wise girls if they could have some of their oil.

They said no. It would not be enough for everyone. The wise girls said they could go the shop and buy some oil, and they ran as fast as they could. But while they were gone the bridegroom came.

Those who had light in their lamps went with the bridegroom to the wedding. The door was closed. The other girls came as fast as they could from the shop, but it was too late. They knocked on the door and asked to be let in, but the bridegroom said he did not know them and told them to go away.

"Let this be a lesson for you," said Jesus to his disciples. He thought them that one day is the end of time. No one have time to postpone until tomorrow what should happen today. It is no use to borrow time from other humans. If you wait too long to do something, it is too late. Now is the time to choose Jesus. Don't wait until tomorrow.

Make sure that you fully understand that the era of time that are coming to an end is the some twelve thousand years that have passed since the Motherland was destroyed in a natural catastrophe. The new world with lasting peace will be built with the knowledge of the born again Motherland history and the global system of government will last until the end of time.

This is words spoken directly to you and to the whole world population. It is real and it is happening today. Jesus is the born again Motherland history and telling it to everyone cannot wait until tomorrow.

The formula used by the Masters who wrote this camouflaged story is clear: Fire = Knowledge about the lost Motherland. The wise girls are clever enough to think ahead and they are ready to welcome the knowledge about the born again Motherland history. They do the right thing.

Jesus, as the born again Motherland history, will be with the whole world population until after the end of time. The five bridesmaids without light in their lamps is symbolizing the part of the world population who is clearly told that the lost Motherland history is coming soon, but don't understand enough to be ready. But given time they will understand that the new world is built for their children and their descendants. There is a looked door in the mental wall between understanding and not understanding, between knowing and doing right and don't knowing and doing wrong.

The wise men living in our present time is ignored and not heard by the world's political and religious leaders. The end of this era, in this setting, is the end of the era with the force of evil in command, which has lasted for some twelve thousand years. Then living in the light of the Diagram Star will begin and last until the end of time.

Planet earth is just about half way through its lifespan, and mankind will live on in to the future in a world with forever lasting peace. In the new world, that you all are going to build together, there will certainly be room for everyone, but not everyone will find the knowledge that gives peace of mind. The humans without light in their lamps; meaning humans without knowledge, will live and die in the darkness of oblivion. After a few generations every single human being will live with light on their lamps and be wise. You will all live in the light of the Diagram Star.

Again: With the light of knowledge in your mind you know. Without the light of knowledge you don't know. There is a difference.

Judas

Matthew 26, 1-5; Mark 14, 1-2, 10-11; Luke 22, 1-6

This was the last days before Jesus was arrested. He spent a lot of time with his disciples. He taught them and tried to make them understand what he had to do. The time had come that he should fulfill what the prophets had said about him long before.

Jesus was not the only one getting prepared.

The high priests, the scribes and other religious leaders thought of nothing else that Jesus had to be taken out and killed. "We must arrest him without anyone noticing," they said.

They warned each other: "We must be careful to not let it happen during the feast of the Passover. Many people believe he is the Messiah, and they will start a riot if we arrest him." It was still two days before Easter.

The religious leader planned how to catch Jesus. A man named Judas Iskariot arranged a meeting with them. It surprised them. "Judas is one of the twelve disciples who follow Jesus!" one of them said.

"Not only that, Judas also takes care of the money," another said.

Judas met with them. He asked: "What will you give me, if I deliver him to you?"

The high priests smiled content: "We will pay you thirty pieces of silver," they said. It was for this prize Jesus was betrayed to his enemies.

This is a part of the world history that has to be studied and written all over again. It is truly an important story hidden under the camouflage of religion. Look at Judas Iskariot as one of the elected members of the new superior Motherland council and a symbolic speaker for the Jewish tribal people.

Jesus is the born again Motherland history and the disciples is a symbol for the twelve elected members of the new superior Motherland council representing the whole world population. They are regular human being and have difficulties understanding the new world that Jesus is talking about. They were not ready to become apostles, teachers and leaders of the new world. The world was not ready for the born again Motherland history, and therefore the story had to return to the spirit world, to the common world of thoughts. The story about the born again Motherland history was told by the Masters of the past. They knew that the time wasn't right.

The Master had to write a story that would be preserved and past on in to the future as a religion. The Masters were a mixture of people, and the history of the twelve Hebrew tribes became known because the Jewish people took care of it up through the ages. What they did as the chosen people is admirable. Given time the whole world population will say thank you to the Jewish tribe. They never knew that their tribal history was used to preserve and pass on the history about the lost Motherland. The building of a national state and calling it Israel was wrong.

What they knew back then and what they know now is not known, but if Judas Iskariot had not done what he did, the knowledge about the lost Motherland history would have been lost for all times. Then the high priest, the scribes and the religious leaders would have succeeded in their attempt to force the story about the born again Motherland history in to everlasting oblivion.

The story about the life of Jesus and the betrayal by Judas Iskariot is carefully planned by the Masters and written down as a camouflaged religious history many years after it happened. It can certainly be developed further.

The high priest, the scribes and the religious leaders is a symbol for the religious leaders in present time. They are still the enemy and are working actively to protect and pass on the three factors of the Original Sin. Their life as elite depends on money and a specific belonging to a religion wherever they live in the world.

But they obviously don't know that the history about the lost continent, the lost Motherland, is masterly camouflaged inside the Bible. Jesus had to die on a cross in order to make him live forever in a religion. The cross is a copy of the Diagram Star, the official emblem of the lost Motherland. You know by now that the sun, moon and the twelve star signs of the Zodiac is the model, the base for making the Diagram Star. The Masters knew that when the time was right, the camouflage of religion would be removed and knowledge of the history of the lost Motherland would return with the global system of government and ever lasting peace. The time is now.

By writing that Jesus spent a lot of time with his disciples and tried to make them understand, the Masters of the past are telling the whole world population in present time that you have to make an effort to understand the full history of the lost Motherland.

The details of exactly what happened back then are important and interesting, but it is the future for our children and their descendants that are the most important. The new world has to

347

be built now, for several reasons. But wanting to build a world with lasting peace is reason good enough to begin.

There is reason to say that the poor and defeated population in this part of the world knew about the lost Motherland and the global system of government. They knew the kingdom of God was a global government system that would set them free from the Roman Empire and give them lasting peace from wars and conflicts. The religion was knowledge to them; and they lived and died for what they knew.

The increasing popularity of the religion made the roman emperor Constantine take it over and he started using it as a tool for controlling the many different people he ruled over. Tribal people all over the Roman Empire were forced to believe in the one and almighty God by use of warfare. They were given the choice to get baptized or die.

What did the Pharaohs of Egypt know; what did the Greeks and the Romans know and what does the religious and political leaders of the world in present time know about all this?

One thing is certain, and that is that the world leaders, believers or not, are preserving and passing on the unbelievable religion from generation to generation as a part of the Original Sin. The other two parts of the Original Sin is the many national states and the global system of capitalism.

If it wasn't for the Jewish tribe no one would know, but will you believe that the true force behind revealing the formula and the many factors that lead to the removal of religion from the Bible, comes from the Spirit World, from the common world of thoughts.

As long as the three factors of the Original Sin is ruling planet earth and keep controlling the common world of thoughts by use of warfare and brutal force, the destruction of the planet will continue until the knowledge about the born again Motherland returns ones more.

Planet earth is s living unit that is slowly destroyed by greedy people, blinded and living like living dead. And until Jesus, as the born again Motherland history is brought back to life in the common world of thoughts, the blinded and living dead will continue to destroy planet earth. Read this again. When the global system of government, with one set of laws and rules for living have returned to planet earth, the whole world population will get their eyesight back and start living like Mother Nature intended.

Preparation for the last supper

Matthew 26, 17-19; Mark, 14, 12-16; Luke 22, 7-13

Two days after Judas had made the agreement, the Passover feast started. Thousands of people had come to Jerusalem for the occasion.

Thursday Jesus said to Peter and John: "I want you to prepare for the Passover feast."

They asked where he wanted them to prepare it.

"Go to the city," he said. "There you will meet a man who is carrying a pitcher of water. Follow him into the house and say to the owner: "The Master says: Where is the guest chamber where I shall eat the Passover feast with my disciples? And he will show you a large room, furnished. Make ready there."

Peter and John did as Jesus said. They went and found it all as he had told them, and they prepared for the Passover feast.

When the evening came, Jesus sat down with the twelve disciples. He said to them: "How greatly I have desired to eat this Passover meal with you before I suffer. For I tell you, I will not eat another until it is fulfilled in the kingdom of God."

And as they were eating, Jesus took the bread and blessed it, and breaking it into pieces he gave it to them, saying: "Take, eat; this is my body which is given for you. Do this in remembrance of me."

After supper he took the cup and when he had given thanks, he gave it to them, saying: "All of you shall drink of it, for this is the New Testament in my blood, which is shed for you and for many, for the forgiveness of sins. Take this, and divide it among you. For I say to you, I will not drink of the fruit of the wine until I drink it anew with you in my Fathers kingdom."

"I drink it anew with you in my Fathers kingdom." The disciples are a symbol for the new superior Motherland council representing the whole world population, and the kingdom of God is the new Motherland that you and the whole world population are going to build. Jesus is the born again Motherland history, preparing to live on in the Spirit World, in the common world of thoughts, until the knowledge of the lost Motherland and the understanding of the Diagram Star is back in the memory of all humans.

The twelve disciples is ordinary human beings, and just like you they have difficulties in understanding how the new superior Motherland council can lead the whole world population as brothers and friends.

As long as the three factors of the Original Sin are ruling the common world of thoughts, the whole world population is sinners. This evil sin is inherited up though many generations, and the origin of the sin is as good as forgotten by most people. The three factors of the Original sin are commonly accepted and the endless fight between good and evil is a part of everyone's life. But before the new Motherland and the new superior Motherland council can be built on planet earth, the tree factors of the Original Sin have to be removed from the common world of thoughts.

It is because you don't know your sin that you all will be forgiven, no matter what you have done before you got to know. You all will be forgiven for a crime against mankind that has been going on for the last some twelve thousand years.

The bread and the vine is the New Testament and are divided equally between the whole world populations. Now you know that religion is the camouflage and that the Bible is the carrier and protector of the full history of the lost Motherland and the born again Motherland history.

The man with the pitcher of water is a symbol for everyone who knows. You know that the born again Motherland history right now has to be revealed for the whole world population. You and the whole world population have to prepare for a Passover feast that will mark the change from a life in the darkness of oblivion and in to a life in the light of the Diagram Star.

Now study the biblical text thoroughly. The Passover meal that you and the whole world population will prepare, with the born again Motherland history as a spiritual foundation and with a newly elected superior Motherland council of twelve, will be the first supper in the new Motherland, in the new world that have been built.

Who is the greatest?

Luke 22, 24-30

This evening Jesus and his disciples broke the bread and drank the vine. They spoke about God who had saved his people in Egypt. He had saved them from Pharaoh, who had forced them to be slaves.

Jesus sat at the end of the table. The disciples were talking together. They heads were close to each other. Suddenly one of them stood up. "It is me!" he shouted.

"No, it is me!" they quarreled about who were the greatest of them, the most important of them all. Some meant it was John, other meant it was Peter.

Jesus interrupted them. "Kings and princes fight about power," he said. "Like that it is not going to be between you. The one, who serves the others, shall be leader.

Who is the most important; the one who is sitting at the table eating or the one who is servant at the table? Look at me. I serve you bread and vine. In that way you shall do. You have been with me. When this is over, you shall be with me in my Fathers kingdom. Then you shall all sit on thrones and judge the twelve tribes of Israel."

Jesus, as the born again Motherland history, can save the whole world population from a life as working slaves, soldiers and servants. You are not free until the three factors of the Original Sin are removed from the common world of thoughts.

If you look at the world you live in, you clearly see the richest national states with the strongest armies quarrel about who is the greatest and strongest in the world. With a new superior Motherland council in a world without national states, armed forces and a global system of capitalism, the quarrel would finely end.

This is important, very important, and every one of you has to find the full understanding of this camouflaged story. Looking at the image you do se Jesus as the born again Motherland history. The history of the lost Motherland is spiritual and is present in the world as the common laws and rules the whole world population is going to live by. The twelve apostles are elected from the multitude of disciples and are a clear symbol for the new superior Motherland council. They are a symbol for the new leaders of the whole world population.

The first thing to do, as soon as possible, is to educate people and elect twelve highly regarded leaders from every group of people in the world. They will all move to the new Motherland with their families to live. They will be the global parliament and from them the twelve members of the new superior Motherland will be elected.

They will, as regular human beings, have to learn that not one of the twelve is greater than any other human in the world. The whole world population will be equals again, and symbolical the new Motherland council will get together and have their first supper together, as brothers and friends. This first supper will be a yearly event all over the world. The spiritual Jesus will be at everyone's table as the born again Motherland history.

In a world without the three factors of the Original Sin, the Motherland council will see that the whole world population has all they need in order to live a good life on planet earth. The bread and the vine is a symbol for everyone having enough to eat and drink.

Not one person will be greater and more important than others, because not one position in the whole world can be passed on as inheritance from father to son. There will be no kings and princes fighting for power; no national states, no slaves, no soldiers and no religion to.

The temples all over the world will again be education centers and common education in the light of the Diagram Star will be the most important activity for all humans on earth. The best students from every small or large school will be democratically selected and sent off to higher education, first the regional and then in the Motherland education centers. The students who graduate will have a degree as Master, and only a few of them, those with the strongest spirit and highest degree of education, can be elected to sit in the superior Motherland council.

And as said so many times before: the twelve tribes of Israel is a symbol for the whole world population in our present time. From the new Motherland, which will be built like the one that was lost, the superior Motherland council will have the power to govern the whole world population.

Not one of the humans living in present time is going to be judged guilty of their sins, because the task of getting rid of the three factors of the Original Sin will be a job for the whole world population working together with only peaceful means. The first important common job is to melt all the weapons of war in to plows, pickaxes and other farmer's tools.

Now is the time, humans.

The king who served

John 13, 1-9

Jesus looked at his twelve closest friends. They were the ones who should continue his work after he had returned to heaven. He had loved them from before the beginning of time, and he would love them after the end of time.

Jesus knew that his Father had given him a choice. Also the Son of Man could, like all other humans, choose if he wanted to follow Gods plan with his life. He could have gone his own way. But Jesus came from God and wanted to return to God. He wanted to always be at Gods side. He looked at all of the disciples and stood up.

They stopped talking. Now they saw that Jesus poured water in a cask. He looked at them.

"My friends," he said. "No one has washed your feet." Then he went to every one of them in turn. He took of their sandals and washed their feet. After he dried them with a towel he had around his waist.

Jesus was their Master and teacher. Still he did something that a servant should do. With his hands and water in a cask he washed sand and dust from their feet.

Peter could not be quiet any longer. He called out: "Master! What are you doing? Shall you wash my feet to? It is the work a servant should do!"

"You don't understand why I do this now, but one day you will understand," Jesus said.

Peter answered: No! Never! You are not allowed to watch my feet!" He could not stand the thought that Jesus, their king, should be a servant.

"Peter, if I don't wash your feet you cannot live on as a part of me."

When Peter heard this, he said: "Not only my feet, Master. Wash my hands and my head as well." But Jesus answered: "He who is clean needs only to wash his feet to be clean all over. And you are clean; but not all of you are." Jesus added the words "not all of you" because he knew one of them was to betray him.

The disciples did still not understand what Jesus did and why he did it.

The disciples are a symbol for the new superior Motherland council that has to be elected. They represent you and the whole world population. The disciples still don't understand what Jesus did and why. Hopefully you are beginning to understand. It is explained to you time and time again. The lost Motherland was a global government system totally different from the one of present time. Think through what a parable is, and what a story like this is telling you when you know the born again Motherland history. You know that a new Motherland council would serve the whole world population, with no exceptions.

The kingdom of God is in heaven. This means that the lost Motherland is in the Spirit World, in the common world of thoughts. It is there and it will always be there. The whole world population needs to be told.

The history of the lost Motherland and the global system of government is plainly forgotten by all living human beings. You should know by now that forgotten world history never will be lost for all times. Knowledge has a cycle like water and can never be destroyed. Just remove the religious dogmas and assumptions from your world of thoughts, and you will find the history of the past.

The history of the lost Motherland was preserved and passed on up through the history by the Masters of the past. They were a group of people who knew that the ruling system implemented by the Pharaohs of old Egypt was wrong as wrong can be. They lived under cover and wrote the camouflaged stories that later became the Bible.

If you look at this camouflaged story as a sign or a parable, you will see Jesus as the born again Motherland history and the disciples as the new superior Motherland council. The members of the old superior Motherland council were Masters who knew more than you can imagine.

It is the new superior Motherland council who shall serve the whole world population in a new world with lasting peace.

The self appointed kings and priesthoods in the world at present time are living in extreme luxury, with servants to do all the work for them. The rich and powerful people are not servants for the multitude; they are a superior class of people with money and armed forces as the backbone of their personal power and self appointed greatness.

Try to understand that being a servant is not about washing sand and dust of someone's feet. It is a parable and is all about cleansing your world of thoughts and the common world of thoughts with common knowledge. Water = Knowledge about the lost Motherland, says the Masters formula.

Example to follow

John 13, 12-18

When Jesus was done, he put on his coat again and sat down. Then he told the disciples why he had acted as their servant.

"Do you know what I do? You call me Master and Lord, and you are right in that. If I, as your servant, wash your feet, what do you think you shall do for each other?

The disciples had quarreled about who of them were the greatest disciple. Now Jesus said: "I have given you an example to follow. Like that you can be really great. Those who believes in what I say to you, not only believe in me, but also in my Father, who has sent me." Those who follow the example Jesus gave, are doing like God will.

Jesus knew that the disciples would need a lot of help the coming days. An era of darkness was before them. If they could learn to serve each other, it would be easier to get through the era of darkness. Then they would have the blessing of the Lord, if they only listened and learned.

You and the whole world population are living in the era of darkness just as mankind has done for the last twelve thousand years.

Now the era of living in the darkness of oblivion is coming to an end, and it is not a moment too soon.

The natural greatness of a human is in the personal spiritual strength and degree of knowledge. How can it be that the whole world population is blind and live their lives like they were living dead? How is it possible for otherwise clever humans to be this utterly foolish and keep on believing in the dogmas and assumptions made by people with a personal short sighted interest to keep things as they are?

The world leaders who truly believe that they only can be great with many armed soldiers and a large country with many taxpaying inhabitants is as wrong as wrong can be. A lot of money does not make a country or a person great. And the gold and glitter around the religious leaders in the world has given them a false authority and greatness.

Jesus is the born again Motherland history and the disciples are symbols for the new world leaders that are to be elected from the whole world population. Together you are the multitude of people from whom the new superior Motherland council will be elected. You are all descendants from the symbolic first twelve tribes that emigrated from the Motherland a long time ago, and populated the world.

All of you are to follow the example of Jesus. It means that the whole world populations have to begin living together like brothers and friend should. It can only happen after the removing the Original Sin from the common world of thoughts is completed.

All humans have to know the difference between right thoughts and wrong thoughts. One of the human thoughts that are wrong and terrorizes the whole world is that the largest national states constantly fight to be the greatest. All quarrelling have to end. No one, not even the new members of the superior Motherland council will be greater than other humans. Every human being on the earth will have the same change to become elected as a member of the superior Motherland council. It is an election for life and the position is not to be passed on from father to son as inheritance.

It might be difficult to understand at first, but following the example of Jesus is the only navigable road towards lasting peace in the world. It is you who have to listen and learn. Foremost you have to learn to listen to your inner voice, and learn to see with your inner eye. That is you contact with the common world of thoughts. Together you have to build a whole new common world of thoughts, based only on what's right. Being wrong is not an option when everyone thinking is right. Only by following the example of Jesus, mankind has a change to put an end to the age of darkness.

Jesus reveals his betrayer

Matthew 26, 20-29; Mark 14, 17-25; Luke 22, 14-23; John 13, 18-27

At the last supper Jesus said to his disciples: "One of you is going to betray me!"

The disciples gasped from surprise. Who would betray the Master to the enemy? They looked at each other and asked: "Who is it?"

Jesus said: "I shall dip the bread. He who dips his bread with me, him it is." Then he dipped the bread in the vine. Judas, son of Simon Iskariot, dipped his bread with Jesus. After Judas dipped the bread, Satan entered in to him. Jesus said: "What you must do, do it quickly."

Judas got up and left them. The other disciple's thought he might go out to get more food. But Judas had decided to go to the enemies of Jesus.

Jesus took bread and broke it in to pieces. He divided the pieces round the table. Then he thanked God for the bread and said: "Eat this. It is my body. Think of me when you eat it."

Then Jesus took a cup of vine and lifted it. Again he thanked God. Then he said: "This is my blood, which is poured out to forgive your sins. I shall always be with you. I shall not drink this again before I am in my Fathers kingdom."

There is on tribal people who stand out in the religion of Christianity. It is the Jews. What is it that they know that all other peoples don't know?

The Jews themselves knows it the best. Perhaps the knowledge is covered with religious belief also for them? Perhaps the knowledge died a long time ago with those few high priests who knew. One thing is certain, the Masters knew, and they symbolical came from all the twelve tribes.

It is now known that the Bible, the history book of the Jews, in fact is the Ark of the Covenant. The mental lid on the gold covered chest is the religion with all its dogmas and assumptions.

We know that the Jews waited the longest before they used warfare and settled on land that they stole from the people who had lived there forever. Then they established a nation of their own in the land that they believe was given to them by God. We know that the Israelites, the children of Israel described in the Old Testament, is in fact a symbol for the whole world population. Therefore the Jews do not have the right to give their nation the name Israel.

One thing is certain, at that is that Jerusalem and the land around is a symbolic theatrical stage for the whole planet earth. Jesus is the born again Motherland history and the disciples is a symbol for the newly elected Motherland council. The Jewish people were chosen by God. God is defined to be the old superior Motherland council who passed away some twelve thousand years ago.

The Master who wrote the camouflaged story clearly meant that the biblical Israelites are the forefathers of the whole world population. The Promised Land is indeed a whole new world.

The vine and bread symbolizes the body and the blood of Jesus. It means first of all that the new Motherland, when it is built, will organize the whole world so that every living human being has enough to eat, at all times. The bread and the vine is also a symbol for the physical basic knowledge about the lost Motherland that Jesus, as the born again Motherland history, is giving to the whole world population.

This means that the whole world population is carrying the knowledge from generation to generation, not knowing, because you live in the darkness of oblivion. Your forefathers were forced to believe in the religion. It was a matter of life or death.

Read the last part of the text again. The sins there is spoken about is all related to the three factors of the Original Sin. You live, believing everything you do is right because your national state laws and rules for living is telling you so. Therefore you and the whole world population will be forgiven, and you can forgive yourself.

If you act now and start working for lasting peace in the world the right way, your children and their descendants will be proud of you. If you know what to do and do nothing, they will despise you.

Remember that Virgin Mary under the camouflage of religion is a symbol for the new Motherland, the fertile earth that is Mother to all earth life, and Father Jacob is a symbol for the knowledge the whole world population needs in order to be able to build a new world with lasting peace.

When the cock crows

Matthew 26, 30-35; Mark 14, 26-31; Luke 22, 31-34; John 13, 31-38

Jesus had changed the Easter meal to the Holy Communion. It was the last meal Jesus had on planet earth. It should be a special memorial for the followers of Jesus.

He and the disciples had ended the meal. They stood up and after they had sung a hymn, they went out of the city to the Mount of Olives. It was a quiet place with many old trees. Here they could rest, think and pray. It was a good place to wait.

Jesus and the disciples walked to the garden that was called Gethsemane. While walking Jesus said: "You will all desert me tonight, because it is written: I will smite the shepherd to night, and the sheep of the flock will be shattered. But after I have risen again, I will go before you in to Galilee".

Peter answered and said to him: "Though everyone else may desert you, I will never desert you." Jesus said to him again: "I tell you truly that tonight before the cock crows, you shall deny me three times."

"O no," said Peter. "I would rather die with you than do something like that!"

The other disciples said the same. "We will never leave you!"

Denying Jesus is equal to denying that the lost Motherland ever existed. This is what you can read about in the known world history as far back as it goes. Denying that the lost Motherland ever existed happened for the first time just after the Motherland was destroyed in a natural catastrophe some twelve thousand years ago. It was denied by the self elected warrior kings and priesthoods, who used the new knowledge of evil to control the population. They lied and used warfare and brutal force to impose their own laws and rules on the people.

Many people all over the world just wanted to continue to live as they always had done, but when the superior Motherland council disappeared in to a spiritual heaven and lost its power, the natural ceremonial and educating contact among people stopped and the chaos of wars and conflicts began. Self-appointed warrior kings and priesthoods almost immediately started fighting among them self in order to be the greatest leader in the world. The population they took control over never stopped waiting for the power of the lost Motherland to return to earth. They still wait.

The production of the weapons of war started and developed rapidly, and the peaceful unarmed villages was brutally attacked, raided and robbed for all the irreplaceable items of gold, silver and precious stones. The tribal people living in the villages had their long tribal and family history destroyed for all times. Those who defended them self against the attacking warrior kings and priesthoods, was killed. They were all forced in to a life as a working slave, soldier and servant under the new despotic ruling system. The same happened almost all over the world, and the governing system with many national states started back there at the beginning of our known and accepted world history.

The leaders of the many colonies, kingdoms and empires in the world at this time denied the very existents of the lost Motherland and started governing the people under their own self-made laws and rules for living. People died and new populations were born in to the despotic government rule that still exist in present time all over the world. From the day they were born, people learned that they had to obey the elite of warrior kings and priesthoods. Those who protested were killed.

It happened all over the world, and just one thousand years ago it happened in the country I was born in, Norway. Those who protested against the new religion and the new rule of one king in the new kingdom were killed. Those who were wiped out as tribal people had knowledge of the lost Motherland in their stone circles, skillful and beautiful made ornaments. When the religion Christianity was imposed on the population with the use of warfare and brutal force, their commonly known history was wrongly and deliberate written down as totally ridicules legends, tales and myths. It was done by monks and priest who were totally under the control of the warrior kings and religious leaders. The same evil happened all over the world.

Through the ages whole continents were attacked, robbed for all valuables and the population was made into working slaves, soldiers and servants, by ruthless warrior kings and priesthoods who wanted to rule the whole world. It is a shameful, horrible and lasting crime against mankind.

As long as the three factors of the Original Sin are allowed to rule the whole world, the meaningless personal quest for money and riches will continue.

If you were to make the choice again, would you deny the lost Motherland ever existed? Well, the choice is yours now. If you make the right choice, your children and their descendants will speak about you with pride and love. If you make the wrong choice your children and their descendants will speak about you with disgust and hate.

In a few years from now it will be too late to build a new world with only peaceful means and thereby preserve the modern technology that the world population needs to stay in contact with each other. If nothing is done thousands of humans will continue to die every single day, until a new stone age sees the light of day. Even then the surviving humans have to make the right choice and choose to build a new world with lasting peace.

A home in heaven

John 14, 1-6

The disciples were very worried, when following Jesus, and tried to find meaning in what he said.

"The whole evening he has spoken about that he shall be betrayed and killed. What does he really mean by that?"

"Do you really believe he shall die soon?"

"I don't know. I don't see how it could happen. It is so quiet and calm everywhere. People are staying at home."

"But think if it is something in it? What do we do then?

Jesus knew that they were worried and even scared. He said: "You shall not be worried about this. You have believed in God, so believe in me to. When I die I go back to my Father's house. There is a place for you all in heaven. I shall make the place ready for you and then I will come back and bring you home with me. Then we shall all be together."

One of the disciples, Thomas, said: "But Master, we don't know where you are going. How shall we find the way?

Jesus said: "I am the road, the truth and the life. Only through me you can come to the Fathers house.

Jesus has not only shown us the road to God. He is the road to God!

Now keep your head cool and think about the definitions again. What and where is heaven? The lost Motherland is known as the Garden of Eden. It was a whole continent cultivated like a garden. When the whole continent disappeared in a natural catastrophe some twelve thousand years ago, the whole world population remembered it as a beautiful garden, a heaven, a dream world. Heaven is the Great Spirit world, the common world of thoughts.

When the lost Motherland was destroyed in an inferno of burning gasses and boiling water, 64 million humans died. The Motherland and everyone who died is in the Spirit World, in heaven, in the common world of thoughts. Lost but not forgotten, because the lost Motherland history lives on in the memory of all living human beings as heaven. The superior Motherland council was at first remembered as the stars signs on the night sky, as the Zodiac. The twelve signs of the Zodiac with the sun and the moon in the centre had been the official emblem of the Motherland for a very long time, and were not easily forgotten.

Shaped like the Diagram Star the Zodiac had been with mankind since before the beginning of time, as a universal emblem, a diagram that everyone could read like an open book. When the Motherland went under it was like the centre of the Diagram Star disappeared and was lost for all times. The whole world population was suddenly without their superior leadership, and the chaos of wars and conflicts started.

Virgin Mary is a symbol for the new Motherland, the fertile land that never came to be. Jesus is the born again Motherland history and are only spiritual knowledge about the world history from before the Motherland was lost. He is the lost knowledge that can enable the present world population to build a new Motherland just like the one that was lost.

And with a new superior Motherland council and representatives from every tribal people in the world in place, a new world with lasting peace can come true. Planet earth will again be a paradise world, a dream world for the whole world population.

Jesus, as the born again Motherland history, truly is the only road to a meaningful life for all humans.

Jesus prays for his friends

Matthew 26, 36-46; Mark 14, 32-42; Luke 22, 39-46; John 17, 1-18

In the garden of Gethsemane Jesus stopped. He wanted to pray with the disciples for the last time.

He said: "Father, the hour has come. You gave me this people. They heard and believed that you have sent me. For their sake I pray that you shall preserve them after I have left them. While I was with them, I guarded them. Now I will come to you, and then they shall rejoice more than they ever have dreamt about.

The world will hate them, but you and I will love them. Let them be one, like we are. When they now walk out into the world, you shall be with them, like you have been with me. Let the love you gave me, be in them."

Jesus prayed that his Father should protect all his followers at all times. He prayed for people like you and I. When he finished, he walked ahead of the disciple's further inn to the garden. Here he took Peter Jacob and John aside from the others. Jesus was worried. He said: "My soul is exceeding sorrowful, even unto death. Stay here and watch over me. You must not sleep." He wanted to speak with God and he said: "Pray that you don't get weak tonight." Jesus went to pray alone.

A little ways from the disciples he fell to the ground. "O, Father!" Jesus called out. "If possible, let me be spared from this pain. My Father, is there no other way? Must I go through with this?" Jesus knew what was coming, what he had to go through. He had chosen to obey. It was the only way God could save his people. God could offer all humans at all times a possibility to start a new life, cleansed for all sin.

Jesus looked up at the stars and said: "Father, I am willing to do as you want."

Then an angel came down to him from heaven. The angel strengthened him. Jesus prayed and prayed. The perspiration ran down his face, red like drops of blood. Every one of them left a mark in the sand on the ground.

Finally he stood up and walked back to the disciples. They had fallen asleep! They were sadden and confused. Now they had just lain down to sleep.

"Peter, do you sleep? Could you not stay awake with me this hour? Stay awake with me and pray, so you don't get tempted tonight."

It happened two times more. Jesus walked to release his heart to God. When he came back he forum the disciples sound asleep. Jesus was alone. When he got back the third time, he said: "Do you still sleep? Well, the hour has finally come. Look! Stand up! Let us go. Look! There is he who betrayed me!"

Think about the paradise world we all could have lived in, if the Motherland had not been destroyed in a natural catastrophe some twelve thousand years ago.

Think about the known world history as a result of the three factors of the Original Sin. In the Old Testament the whole world population was given the possibility to choose between a life with the laws and rules of the lost Motherland and the dancing around the Golden Calf.

The dance is still going on for the present world population that has inherited the Original Sin. Only the inner circle if the rich elite is dancing, while a majority of the world population have given up trying to get rich and famous and just don't know what to do any more. A raising number of human beings die every day, not knowing why they ever lived.

Now time has come to make the right choice for our children and their descendants. Now you know that the choice that was made several thousand years ago, was wrong as wrong can be and you can make it right again: you.

The camouflaged stories in the Bible were written under the rule of the Roman Empire. It was the brutal force of the Romans, the killing of people who did not do as the rulers said, that made the camouflage necessary. Remember King Herod killing all the children and the Roman order that everyone living under their rule should be written in the census, so they could be charged with tax.

You know that it is the same dictating system of controlling people that still rules the whole world. Just imagine the new world with one Motherland and all the people in the world living together like brothers and good friends. It can only happen in a world without the three factors of the Original Sin, without all the national states, without the global system of capitalism and without all the religions in the world.

It is you, the world population of present time that has been sleeping through an era of darkness, a long night towards the light of day. Hopefully you see the light now and wake up in time. Jesus is a camouflage for the bright shining star in the centre of the Diagram Star. In his light you will see the world you live in and you will see the world that could have been. And soon you will all have all the knowledge you need to start building a new world, in the light of the Diagram Star. The knowledge you need to be convinced is found deep in your own world of thoughts.

Remember now that the betrayal of Jesus was set up by the Masters to fool the Roman rulers, the kings the priesthoods. Back then they did not know that the roman emperor Constantine some four hundred years later was to take the religion of Christianity in use as a tool to better control the many different tribal people he ruled over. The camouflage of religion was left intact, and as a result of this a majority of the world population was forced in to a life as clever fools. The age of darkness continued until present time. Hopefully you all can help make the light from the Diagram Star enlighten the whole world population.

Think about the Jewish people. Because of their tribal history the camouflage went on been intact. By removing the camouflage from all the stories in the Bible, the full history of the lost Motherland is revealed for everyone. We should all say thank you to the Jews, because if it wasn't for them the history about the lost Motherland would have been completely lost in the era of darkness.

Still, an angel from heaven is, under the camouflage, a true contact with heaven, with the Spirit World. Now you are told and just by using your natural ability to separate wrong from right, you will know what to do.

Who will deny the born again Motherland history in our present time, and force the world population to continue the era of self destruction? Who will do like the Roman elite and the priesthoods, and deny the thoughts that truly are the only road to lasting peace for the whole world?

Betrayed with a kiss

Matthew 26, 47-57; Mark 14, 43-53; Luke 22, 47-54; John 18, 2-14

Jesus warned Peter, Jacob and John. They heard voices from the other end of the garden. The disciples looked up. They saw flickering light coming in direction of them. Suddenly they got scared.

Peter looked at the religious leaders. They were carrying clubs and swords. "It is the enemy!" he whispered to John. "Look!"

There was Judas! "Why is Judas with the enemy?" Peter asked. But he already knew the answer.

Judas had just told the religious leaders that they should arrest the man he kissed. He would show them who it was. Judas went straight to Jesus. "Hail, Master," he said and kissed him.

"Judas," said Jesus. "Do you betray the Son of Man with a kiss?" Judas could not look at Jesus. He embraced the man who had been everything for him, teacher, friend, God. Then he turned and walked away.

The high priest and the elders grabbed Jesus. He did not even resist. "It is me you are looking for," said Jesus. "Let the others go." He meant the disciples.

Peter could not stand still and watch the enemies of Jesus take him away. He drew his sword swung it and cut of the right ear of the high priests servant.

"Stop!" said Jesus. "Put your sword back in its place. People that hurt each other end up hurting them self's." Then he touched the servant's ear and healed it.

To Peter he said: "If I had wished to resist and fight, I could have asked my Father and he would immediately give me more than twelve legions of angels. But had I done that, I would not have done what my Father wants me to do. Do you not understand? If you fight against them, I cannot do what I came to do."

Jesus turned against his enemies and said: "There was no reason for you to come for me in this way, with swords and clubs. I am not a thief. I have taught in the temple every day. You could have arrested me there."

But all this was done so that the scriptures of the prophets might be fulfilled.

When the guards came, Peter and the other disciples fled. They found a hiding place, afraid to be arrested with Jesus.

When Peter and the others ran, Jesus was alone with his enemies. It did not take them long to understand that he wouldn't resist the arrest. They pushed him out of the garden. The guards took him to the house of the high priest. There all the enemies of Jesus met. They questioned him. They had paid Judas to help with his arrest and now they wanted to judge him to death.

Now you know that Jesus is spiritual, he is the born again Motherland history. The paradise new world can be built, but it can only be done with peaceful means. Now is the time bring the born again Motherland history back to earth and remove the aspect of both riches and poverty, remove the many national states and remove all the religions in the world. The religious leaders of present time are still the enemies of the born again Motherland history, and deny that the great continent ever existed. They deny that the twelve members of superior Motherland council were omnipotent, omniscient and omnipresent in the time before the Motherland went under.

Make sure you understand that it is the evil, greedy and selfish thoughts of the warrior kings and the priesthoods of the past that are the enemy of the born again Motherland history. The world leaders and priesthoods of present time can all be convinced to convert to knowledge and thereby cleanse their thoughts for all evil.

It couldn't be done some two thousand years ago when the camouflaged story about Jesus was written. Now the use of Internet and modern technology makes it possible to let the whole world know what is hidden under the camouflage of religion and it is possible to teach everyone to read the Diagram Star like an open book. Now is the time.

The prophets of the past were the Masters who wrote all the camouflaged stories that became the Bible. They could prophesize about the future because they knew the history of the past. At all times there have been humans in resistance against the elite of religious leaders, the warrior kings and the richest of the rich, meaning all those people who lead on in preserving and passing on the three factors of the Original Sin.

Most of the wars and conflicts have been between various armies lead by people who wanted to rule the population in a different and better way. They have all been using the population as their working slaves, soldiers and servants and categorically denied that the lost Motherland ever existed.

The leaders of the world didn't know about the global government system from the time before the Motherland went under. When they were told, as king Herod was by the three wise men in the story about the birth of Jesus, they did terrible things to prevent it from happen.

Only the Masters knew the full story, and in order to preserve and pass on the story about the lost Motherland, they wrote the story about Jesus been captured and crucified by the religious leaders and the Roman ruler of the time. They succeeded.

The cross is a symbol for the Diagram Star, the emblem of the lost Motherland, and Jesus is a symbol for the born again Motherland history. By way of the crucifixion the born again Motherland history and the official emblem of the Motherland was linked together as a stronghold for the religion Christianity.

Even if the religious leaders, the leaders of the many national states and the richest of the rich continue to deny that the lost Motherland ever existed, the religions of the world will continue to pass on the hidden history from generation to generation. Before this no one knew what you all know now, and if you do nothing, you will not ever be forgiven by your children and their descendants.

Jesus was arrested and the disciples ran to hide, afraid to be arrested with Jesus. Jesus is the born again Motherland history. You, the world population of present time, are the disciples. It is from you the new superior Motherland council will be elected. Will you run and hide when the religious leader's ones again tries to put a stop to the story about the lost Motherland and the global system of government? The knowledge that will make humans able to build a new world with lasting peace cannot be stopped again, not this time. Don't deny. Don't run and hide.

Peter denies Jesus

Matthew 26, 58-69; Mark 14, 54-66; Luke 22, 54-62; John 18, 15-18

Peter had followed the crowd who arrested Jesus. He was so afraid that he did not dare to stay close to them. When he saw that Jesus was taken to the house of the high priest, he waited outside. The yard was full of soldiers. Some of them had made a bonfire were they sat keeping warm.

When Peter sat down at the bonfire a servant maid came over to him. She stared at him. "You are one of the prisoner's friends," she said.

Peter hoped that no one had heard her. "No! No!" he said out loud. "I don't know who you are talking about."

He walked towards the gate. There another maid saw him. She said: "This man was with Jesus from Nazareth."

"No! No! You must be confusing me with someone else. I don't even know the man!" After a little while a crowd of men came over to Peter. One of them knew the man who had lost his ear when Peter attacked him. "You are one of his disciples," he said. "I saw you with him in the garden a few hours ago."

"Yes, he is from Galilee, that's for sure. The dialect reveals him," said another man.

Peter felt his heart pounding wild in his chest. He swears and called out loud: "I don't know the man!"

Not before he had said it, he heard a cock crow. In the same moment Jesus was taken across the yard. He turned and looked at Peter. Then Peter remembered what Jesus had said to him: "Before the cock crows, you will deny me three times." Peter cried and mourned over what he had done.

What will you do after you have read this book and found that the explanation is right? Will you tell everyone what you have learned or will you deny it and say that you haven't read it?

This camouflaged story is all about being afraid to die, hiding and denying Jesus, the born again Motherland history. If the whole world population does like Peter did, it is because for some twelve thousand years have lived in the darkness of oblivion. You are all living on the other side of the river, in the mental desert, not knowing about the new world with lasting peace that can be built with knowledge of the born again Motherland history.

What will happen in the world when this explanation of the Bible, with the religion removed gets to be commonly known? How many humans will continue as before and deny that the lost Motherland ever existed?

All the religions in the world have its origin from the lost Motherland. All the tales, legends and myths have the same origin. For example the Greek mythology is all about the Motherland, written with a camouflage that has to be removed before it make sense in the common world of thoughts.

The history of the lost Motherland is very important for the future world, the new world that has to be built for our children and their descendants. If you and the whole world population do like Peter and the disciples and denies the born again Motherland history, you will never get to know the peaceful paradise of the past, and you will never find the knowledge needed to build a peaceful new world for the future.

Being afraid, denial, betrayal and lies did not exist in the lost Motherland and will not exist in a new world with a new Motherland.

Jesus and Pilate

Matthew 26; Mark 14; Luke 22; John 18

The religious leaders tried to prove that Jesus had broken the law. They even paid people to testify falsely. The high priest said: "Tell us in the name of the living God if you are Christ, the Son of God?

"Yes, I am," said Jesus. "One day you will all see me, as the Son of Man, sitting on the right hand of Power.

"He is saying that he is God! It is against the law!

"Kill him! Kill him! They started to hit Jesus. Then they spit in his face. Also the soldiers hit him.

363

When the morning came, all the chief priests and elders planned against Jesus, to put him to death. And when they had bound him they led him away to the hall of judgment and delivered him to Pontius Pilate, the Roman Governor.

They lied to Pilate. "This man is leading the Jews in a revolt against the Romans," they said. "He claims that he is king."

"Are you the king of the Jews?" Pilate asked Jesus.

"They say so," said Jesus, "but my kingdom in not of this world. If it was, my friends would have fought for me. Yes, I am king. I have come to lead the truth in to the world. Everyone who is on the side of the truth listens to my voice."

God and Jesus is one. They are the history of the lost Motherland and a global system of government that truly can bring lasting peace back to the world. God is the old superior Motherland council and Jesus is the born again Motherland history that will be the foundation for the new elected Motherland council. Together with a new elected global parliament they will have the power to lead a world with lasting peace.

The history about the lost Motherland is spiritual and the world leaders, the priesthoods and the scientist will deny it ever existed. The only way to make them convert and think differently is to explain to them exactly what is hidden in the Bible, under the camouflage of religion. They are the Romans, the high priest, the scholars and scribes of present time and convincing them will change the general public opinion. Then the new world can be built for our children and their descendants. They need a future in a new world with lasting peace.

The laws and rules for living the priests in Jerusalem refer to is made for the only reason to control people and make them pay taxes and dues to the roman rulers, the priesthood and the local kings. The taxes and dues made it possible for the elite to live a life in luxury, it was a life they had inherited and wanted to preserve and pass on to coming generations.

The population was poor and wanted a better life for them self and their families. The camouflaged stories about God and his kingdom gave people hope. Back then the people wanted to know about Jesus, and they knew that his kingdom was all about building a new Motherland and giving them back their freedom, free from the dictating rule of the roman emperors. It was Christianity totally different from the dogmas and assumptions that are imposed on people in present time.

The crucifixion is a symbol for the many early Christians that were killed by the roman rulers at that time. The Masters who wrote the stories knew that they couldn't succeed by talking to small groups of people about a government system that was so totally against the present one.

History tells that the Romans tried to conquer the whole world, with Rome as the new Motherland, and they wanted peace for the people they ruled over. But with armed enemies both outside and within the empire, with the use of warfare and brutal force, they just couldn't succeed in creating peace. Not one of the so called great warrior kings, attempting to build an empire, has succeeded.

The world can still see the effect of the British Empire building, were whole continents still are suffering from the merciless exploitation. Now the United States of America is trying to build a global empire, using the same tools for building a little different. They use the global capitalistic system as a major tool, and follow up with warfare and brutal force wherever they are rejected.

The whole world is fooled by the ruling system called national democracy. The population in all the national states is born inside the national borders, and is given a name and a number. The following common education is meant to educate willing working slaves, soldiers and servants to the nation. The population is allowed to elect their own leaders, and the three factors of the Original Sin is giving the leaders a life in luxury, while the regular workforce are totally depending on a lifetime with work and paying taxes in order to live a relative good life.

It is a wrong way of living, and you know it. You also know what will happen if you speak against the many national states, the global capitalist system and all the religions in the world, and call them the three factors of the Original Sin.

Jesus did it, and he was condemned to die on the cross. Now you know that Jesus is the born again Motherland history, and with the whole story about the lost Motherland and the global system of government, you and the whole world population can make the change. Together you can build a new world with lasting peace. If you do nothing, humans will continue to die by the thousands, defending lies and not knowing why they lived.

Jesus and King Herod

Luke 23, 6-12

"What are you saying?" Pilate asked the religious leaders. "Did you say the man is from Galilee? If so, he should be sentenced by King Herod. He is the one with the responsibility of that land, not me."

Pilate would rather not have anything to do with Jesus. He thought to himself that the man had done nothing wrong. The guard took Jesus to Herod.

King Herod was by chance in Jerusalem at this time. He was there in connection with the Easter celebrations. He was glad to see Jesus. For a long time he had wanted to meet the strange man whom everybody talked about. Maybe he could even do a wonder just for him!

King Herod was disappointed. He asked Jesus many questions, but did not get answer to any of them. Jesus was silent. The religious leaders stood there the whole time. They shouted to Jesus.

"He is a dangerous criminal!"

"He ought to be killed!"

King Herod was tired of Jesus being silent. He and his soldiers started to mock Jesus. They dressed him in a nice shining gown and shouted: "Now you are a grand king!"

"Send him back to Pilate!" King Herod ordered. "I don't want to waste more time on him. Take him out from here!"

Jesus was now taken back to Pilate. Something strange happened that day. Pilate and Herod had been enemies for a long time. Both wanted more power. After they had met Jesus, they became good friends.

It is obvious that the priesthood was more interested to get Jesus killed, than the roman consul and the local king. Like that it still is. The priests of our present time know very well that if the dogmas and assumptions fall for knowledge, it means the end of religion. The day the religious belief in God, Jesus and the Holy Spirit disappears from the common world of thoughts; all the religions and sects in the world have to start thinking new thoughts. Will the religious believers oppose to the knowledge that will turn their world of belief upside down?

Everybody wants lasting peace, but it is impossible to achieve as long as the present system with the many national states, the global capitalistic system and all the religions in the world, is allowed to exist.

Think for a moment about the many different religions in the world and the fact that the most of the world population is divided as enemies because of the differences in belief in the same spiritual power called God. In the same moment they all get to know God as the spiritual superior Motherland council and Jesus as the born again Motherland history, everybody will become good friends.

What will the religious leaders of present time do? Will they continue to deny that the lost Motherland never existed and appeal to the political leaders in the world to keep things as they are?

How will all the religious believers and not believers in the world react, when they realize that all the religions in the world is camouflage over the only knowledge that can create long lasting world peace?

How will all the workers in the world react when they get to know that they all still are slaves, soldiers and servants under a government system that were imposed by the Pharaohs in old Egypt? Money is a symbolic chain that keeps the workers working all their lives. A global chain gang is what you all are.

The lost Motherland was a large continent. It was the three factors of the Original Sin that started after the catastrophe, swept all over the world and destroyed the global system of government. It was a flood of emperors, warrior kings and priesthoods that by use of warfare and brutal force took control of the population, who had been living peacefully in self supported villages for at least 200 thousand years. The world suddenly changed from a peaceful paradise to a living hell for all humans.

Governments all over the world are using the three factors of the Original Sin to control the population in every little detail. When will you understand that the Bible is giving you the recipe for building a new world with long lasting world peace? Will you be brave enough to tell the world leaders?

Pilate tries to free Jesus

Matthew 27, 15-26; Mark 15, 6-15; Luke 23, 13-25; John 18, 36-40

Pilate did not like that the guard came back to him with Jesus. He knew that Jesus was innocent. The religious leaders were jealous of him because of his popularity among the people. Pilate pondered about what to do to set Jesus free. Then he got an idea. He was sure he should manage to set Jesus free. It could not go wrong.

Every Passover the Roman Governor could set one prisoner free. The people them self choose the prisoner they wanted to be set free. Pilate hoped that the people would choose Jesus this year.

There was another prisoner the people could choose. His name was Barabbas and he was a murder, an evil man. Pilate asked the people that were gathered: "Who do you want that I shell set free, Barabbas or Jesus.

While Pilate waited for the crowd to decide, he got a message from his wife. "Have nothing to do with this just man, because I have suffered many things in a dream concerning him."

The religious leader had placed their men in the crowd. "Ask for Barabbas!" they said to the people. "Tell the roman governor that you want Jesus to die."

Pilate gave orders that Jesus and Barabbas should be placed in front of the people. "Who of them do you want that I shall set free?" he asked them.

"Barabbas!" they shouted.

Pilate was surprised. "What shell I then do with Jesus?"

"Crucify him!"

"What? What wrong have he done?"

But the people called out even louder: "Crucify him! Crucify him!

Pilate tried three times to talk to the people about this. "There is no reason to kill him. Can I not just punish him and set him free?

But the crowd called out loud: "Crucify him!" They were on the brink of revolt! Pilate asked the servants to bring him water. He washed his hands and said: "I am innocent in the blood of this just man," he said.

Then all the people answered and said: "Let his blood be on us and on our children." The voices of them and the chief priests prevailed. Pilate gave sentence that Barabbas was set free and delivered Jesus to be crucified.

This was written like this in order to make the roman occupying force just and right in their judging of the people they ruled over. The Master who wrote the story had to consider the roman rulers that were in power at the time, or the camouflaged story would have been declared hostile and not been allowed in the Bible.

The Masters knew the formula and the code and could remove the camouflage just by hearing the title of the story or se a drawing or even a sign. It was the born again Motherland history that they wanted to preserve and pass on to coming generations, and they succeeded.

All of the roman emperors behaved like large scale criminals. They made the mistake that they believed that they could build an empire with the use of warfare and brutal force. A lasting world peace can only be built with peaceful means.

The religion Christianity is a global organization and is built up the same way as the Motherland and the whole world was built in the time before the Motherland went under. The Vatican is the center of the organization. The major difference is that the religion is a camouflage over the knowledge that the world population needs in order to build a world with lasting peace together.

The Vatican is building its existence on collecting money from the many large congregations all over the world. They live and work with the three factors of the Original Sin and preserve and pass on the forces of evil from generation to generation. Do they know?

The story about the lost Motherland had to be camouflaged under as many stories as possible and distributed to people all over the world. What better camouflage could be used in that era of time? The cross is a copy of the Diagram Star, the official emblem of the Motherland and Jesus is a symbol for the born again Motherland history. Jesus on the cross is a major symbol for the religion Christianity and therefore the camouflaged story lives on.

Now look at the choice the people made again.

Symbolical Barabbas represents all the evil in the world at present time, meaning the three factors of the Original Sin. Jesus is a symbol for the good in the world, for the born again Motherland history.

The choice that the people made was wrong. It is the choice of the religious leaders and the political leaders of the world. They still choose the forces of evil to live and the forces of good to die. It is the wrong choice of the world leaders that guides human beings in their desperate quest for riches and personal power. The choice that was made by our ancestors back then, is about to destroy the world completely in our present time.

In the story Jesus dies, but as long as the camouflaged story lives on as religion, the born again history of the Motherland will live on in to the future.

Who made the choice? Was it really the religious leaders who bribed or demanded the crowd so they did choose evil before good? The history tells us that something changed completely around year 324, when the roman emperor Constantine made the popular movement of early Christians in to a state religion.

The religion Christianity was taken in as a tool for the evil, and enforced on to the population by use of warfare and brutality. The historical facts about how the camouflaged stories became the major religions in the world, is gruesome.

It is the future and the building of a new world with lasting peace that is important now. Therefore the spell of enforced wrong believing has to be broken and replaced with knowledge about the lost Motherland. A future world with lasting peace can only be built with the knowledge that is hidden under the many camouflaged stories in the Bible.

Humans living in present time, meaning you and the whole world population are now presented with the choice again. The choice is important. It is a question of be or not to be for the world. You have to choose Jesus to live as the born again Motherland history. You have to choose all evil to die.

Remember now that the camouflaged story about the ten plagues never happened back then. They are a prediction of how far the world leaders in present time will deny the born again Motherland history, before they give in.

Only by telling the whole world population about the born again Motherland history, the world leaders will be persuaded. If not, the Masters who wrote the camouflaged story about Jesus and his twelve disciples will be right in their prediction that the world leaders have to face many large, global catastrophes before they stop listening to the religious leaders, come to their senses and set the people free.

Remember that you and the whole world population are the Israelites described in the Old Testament. You all know that you still are working slaves, soldiers and servants. Just imagine being free from all evil. Therefore choose evil to die and good to live.

Jesus is mocked

Matthew 27, 27-31; Mark 15, 16-20; John 19, 1-16

The multitude of people had said to Pilate that they wanted Jesus crucified. He gave order that Jesus was to be taken inn to the castle.

Soldiers gathered around Jesus and pushed him in all direction. Then they started to tear of his clothes and dressed him in a scarlet robe. It was a robe for a king. This they did to mock him. "Look at him! Do you think he looks like a king?"

"A king should have a crown." They made a crown of thorns and put it on his head. Then they hit him in the head time after time. Jesus did not resist at all.

The soldiers took Jesus to Pilate. Ones again he tried to convince the religious leaders that there was no reason to kill Jesus. But they shouted: "Crucify him! Crucify him!

"You can crucify him yourselves! I find no reason to condemn this man to the death!

"He claims that he is the Son of God," they replied. "According to the laws of the Jews he shall be punished with death penalty!

Pilate walked back in to the castle. "Where do you come from?" he asked Jesus, but Jesus did not answer him. Pilate said: "Don't you know that I have the power to set you free?"

Jesus shook his head and said: "You have no power over me. It is God who is deciding this."

Pilate tried one more time to set Jesus free, but the people did not agree.

What will you do? Will you mock the knowledge about the born again history about a Motherland that was lost some twelve thousand years ago and deny it never existed? Will you continue to live as a working slave, soldier and servant, completely willing to die, protecting, preserving and passing on a totally meaningless life to your children and their descendants?

You live in the darkness of oblivion and are obligated to live by the laws and the rules of your national state from the day you are born and until you die. Jesus, as the bright shining light in the Diagram Star, is able to enlighten the whole world population again and make it possible for you to build a new world with lasting peace together.

Will you make the right choice now and choose the born again Motherland history, or will you stand by your national state and your religion and choose the three factors of the Original Sin and watch the planet earth die in front of you?

Crying women

Matthew 27, 32-33; Mark 15, 21-22; Luke 23, 26-31; John 19, 17

The soldiers forced Jesus to carry the heavy cross. When they got up on the hill, Jesus stumbled and fell. Then the soldiers told a man named Simon, a Cyrenian, that he should carry the cross for Jesus.

A flock of women had followed Jesus all the way to the Golgotha. They cried over him. He turned to them. "Don't cry over me," he said. "Cry over Jerusalem. This city has turned their back on Messiah."

The Messiah is the message found in the Bible, under the camouflage of religion. The cross is the emblem of the Motherland and Jesus is a symbol for the born again Motherland history. The Masters made a drama of the event, in order to ensure that this story was remembered by the future generations.

Jerusalem is a well chosen theatrical stage for a dramatic story that covers the history of the lost Motherland. Jesus is a spiritual story, the born again Motherland history. Among the crying woman were his mother Mary and his mother's sister, Mary the wife of Cleophas, and Mary Magdalene. The three women is a symbol for the new Motherland, the fertile land that is the mother of all earth life. The lost Motherland was a large continent divided in to three kingdoms by natural channels and large seas.

Jerusalem and the land around is a symbol for the new Motherland that could have been, and the temple is a symbol for the many educational centers. Jesus is a symbol for the born again Motherland history that was denied to live. The whole world population turned their back to the born again Motherland history and wiped it in to the darkness of oblivion while the forces of evil was chosen to live on. Now, some two thousand years after the story was written, the time has come to bring the born again Motherland history back in to the common world of thoughts, and this time to stay.

Therefore your choice have to be to tell the world leaders that you want a new democratically elected Motherland council back in command with the one set of laws and rules for the whole world population. Jesus came back to earth some two thousand years ago. All you have to do to get to know the full story about the lost Motherland is too remove the camouflage of religion from all the stories in the Bible.

Now the story is told to you in a way the Masters couldn't do some two thousand years ago. Make the right choice this time.

Jesus on the cross

Matthew 27, 34-50; Mark 15, 23-37; Luke 23, 36-49

Jesus could hardly stand on his feet, week as he was. He had deep wounds in the back after the whiplashes, and blood was running down his face from the crown of thorns.

One of the guards walked over to him. He forced him to drink some vine that was mixed with a painkilling remedy. After having tasted it, Jesus refused to drink more.

Then they crucified him. They nailed his hands and feet to the cross. Over his head they placed an inscription: "This is the King of the Jews." One soldier mocked him. While he hangs on the cross, the soldiers parted his clothing among them, and for his robe they cast lots.

Some of the people walking by shouted at him: "If you are the Son of God, then step down from the cross!"

Not everyone who stood there wanted to harm him. Among the women was his mother Mary, then another Mary and Mary Magdalene. Jesus looked at his mother and John who stood next to her. He said to her: "Mother, this man is your son now."

To John he said: "This is your mother now." From that day John took care of Mary, the mother of Jesus. Like this Jesus thought about those he left behind.

There were two more crosses there, one on each side of Jesus. On them two robbers were crucified. One of them mocked Jesus: "Save you self and us!" he said. "You are Christ, are you not?

The other robber said: "You should fear God. This man has not done anything wrong." Then he called out: "Jesus, think of me when you get to your kingdom!"

Jesus answered: "To day you shall be with me in paradise."

After Jesus had been on the cross for six hours, he called out: "My God, my God. Why have you forsaken me?"

And so he said: Forgive them, for they don't know what they are doing."

During the hours on the cross Jesus became the intermediary between humans and God. He is the road that leads to God for every man and woman and every child.

That afternoon it became dark all over the land. A heavy darkness fell as a carpet over city and land.

Jesus was also in darkness. For the first and only time in his life God had closed his eyes for his Son. Because Jesus was the carrier of the sin of the world, he had to suffer all this.

Jesus said nothing in a long time. He had great pain and was dying. "Father, in to your hands I command my spirit." Jesus had suffered enough. The price was paid. The road back to the kingdom of God was open.

Then Jesus called out again in a loud voice: "It is finished!" and bowed his head and gave up his spirit of life.

Jesus is the born again Motherland history. The history did not die; it lived on as a spiritual religion. Under the camouflage of religion is the full story about the lost Motherland and a global government system that truly is the only road to lasting peace in the whole world.

Everything that happened in this story had been written a long time before, by the prophets, and now the story is written again, explaining the camouflage of religion.

Inri is the inscription over his head on the cross, and it means "King of the Jews."

The history of the Jews was chosen to symbolize the whole world population, the descendants of the twelve sons of Jacob, the Israelites, and the inscription without the camouflage, means "King of the whole world population."

The kingdom of God is the whole world, and the foundation for the power is the spiritual Motherland history, which is ever lasting and omnipresent. The superior Motherland council members are regular human beings, equal to all other humans.

When the Motherland was destroyed the whole world lost its superior leadership, and the chaos of wars and conflicts started. The Motherland and the official emblems of the superior council members are still remembered and are in the Spirit World; in the common world of thoughts.

Jesus is telling his Mother that John is her son now, and tells John to take care of his mother. Mother Mary is a symbol for the new Motherland that never was built, and John is a symbol for the whole world population. The Master writing the story wants all the living human beings to remember the lost Motherland at all times. You all do wish for the rule of the Motherland to return, and now it is no longer hidden in the darkness of oblivion.

Much of the story about Jesus is lost in translation and much is added on the grounds of belief and assumption trough the ages. The last words of Jesus in his conversation with the two robbers and with his Father, God, have a clear underlying meaning.

The two robbers are a symbol for the majority of the whole world population. Their arguing is a symbol for the never ending fight between good and evil in the world, and the good criminal is going with Jesus to heaven. The by passers shouting to Jesus that if he is the Son of God he could come down from the cross, is a symbol for the humans who openly say that they don't believe that Jesus did the wonders described in the Bible stories.

When Jesus asks you to forgive them, because they don't know what they are doing, he is asking the whole world population to forgive each other. You have all lived in the darkness of oblivion, and from birth to death you are forced to believe that the world around you is just like it should be. And those who try to change the world to something better never do succeed, because they don't know the governing system with one Motherland and one set of laws and rules for the whole world population.

During the hours on the cross Jesus became an intermediary between humans and God, the spiritual superior Motherland council. This means that Jesus is the key for understanding and the only road to full knowledge about the lost Motherland and the Diagram Star. When believers look at Jesus on the cross, they remember the story not knowing that religion is a camouflage over knowledge. Only by seeing Jesus as the born again Motherland history and the cross as a copy the Diagram Star, the official emblem of the superior Motherland council, you can see the story behind the camouflage. You and the whole world population have to learn the full story about the lost Motherland before you together can build a new world with lasting peace.

The whole world becomes covered with darkness when Jesus dies. A heavy darkness fell as a carpet over city and land. It is the darkness of oblivion that now shall be lifted; the camouflage of religion is hereby removed for the world to see what's hidden underneath.

Jesus is the carrier of the sin the whole world population committed, after being forced by the religious leaders and their helpers. The sin in question is the three factors of the Original Sin. Jesus, the good forces of the Diagram Star, went away and left the forces of evil in charge. This happened because the forces of good could not win over the forces of evil back then.

With the enlightening knowledge of the Diagram Star you can now look around you and see all that is wrong as wrong can be. With the knowledge you can win this time. It is the evil and wrong that has to be removed before everything that is good and right can return to rule the whole world.

Added to this is the fact that the moment of truth, the moment that you understand what the death of Jesus on the cross means for the whole world population, the mental road all the way back to the lost Motherland is open. After you have achieved a full understanding of the lost Motherland history, the road in to the future is open, with the knowledge people need to build a new world with lasting peace.

And as soon as you and the whole world population know the full message of the many Bible stories, the work of Jesus Christ, the Messenger, is completed.

The temple curtain is split

Matthew 27, 51-54; Mark 15, 39; Luke 23, 45-49

In the same moment Jesus called, he gave up his spirit to his Father in heaven. The temple curtain split in the middle the same moment. The curtain closed the way in to the most holy room, were the Ark of the Covenant stood. It was the closest a man could get to God. Only the high priest had access to the room, and only ones every year.

It was of great importance that the curtain was split in two. When Jesus died, it meant that people no longer had to wait for the high priest should pray for them. Jesus died for all humans. He paved the road for them to God. Everyone can now pray directly to God, because of Jesus.

Jesus was dead. Then a strong sound was heard. It was an earthquake. The whole earth trembled. Large rocks divided and fell from the mountains. People wondered if it was the end of the world.

Men and women shouted out loud in fear. They were confused and ran around. There was panic in the city. Many graves opened and the dead came alive. Later these humans walked around in Jerusalem as they never had been dead.

The interpretation of the many camouflaged stories in the Bible leads to many pleasant surprises. New discoveries make the unbelievable tales in to sensible world history.

Think of God as the superior Motherland council and Jesus as the born again Motherland history. They are both spiritual together in the spirit world as one, meaning that they are in the common world of human thoughts, hidden under the camouflage of religion. This explains that the history of the lost Motherland was lost in the darkness of oblivion for several thousand years, before it was born again as the fictive person Jesus.

Because of the choice people was forced to make some two thousand years ago, under the dictating roman rule and the warrior kings and the priesthoods, the history of the lost Motherland was camouflaged in the many stories that became the Bible.

In the same moment that you understand that Jesus is the lost Motherland history, the curtain of religion will burst in your personal world of thoughts. You will be able to see God and Jesus as the history of the lost Motherland. When the time emerges that the whole world population sees the history of the lost Motherland and understands how the Motherland council had built the world based on the true laws of Mother Nature, the building of a new world with lasting peace can begin.

All things in the biblical story can be explained. The graves that opened and the dead walking around like they never had been dead, is explained with your personal state of mind before you understood the formula and the writing in camouflaged parables. You and the whole world population are blinded by the darkness of oblivion and live your lives like you were living dead. After you have found the understanding of all the camouflaged stories in the Bible, you will walk around in the world where you live, like you never had been living dead.

You know by now that Jerusalem and the temple is a chosen theatrical stage and symbolize the Motherland and the whole world. The temple is down, not one stone is left open a stone in our present time. The temple can only be rebuilt as a new Motherland for the whole world.

The body is buried

Matthew 27, 54-60; Mark 15, 39-46; Luke 23, 49-54; John 19, 38

The captain of the roman guard and his men could not believe their own eyes! He had seen Jesus die, but it was not like he had seen many other humans die. This man had to be the Son of God! "I have never seen anyone die like him," the captain said.

After Jesus had been hanging on the cross for six hours, he was dead. Some women helped a rich man, Joseph of Arimatea, to take Jesus down from the cross. They knew that in a few hours the Sabbath would start and then they were not allowed to do anything. It meant that they would not be allowed to bury Jesus.

Joseph took the dead body down. Mary, the mother of Jesus, Mary Magdalene and the other Mary was with him, and together they dressed Jesus in a white linen robe. There were several other women there. They buried Jesus in a grave that Joseph had bought for himself. Now Jesus should lie there. The grave was carved out of a cliff near the place Jesus was crucified.

The roman captain and his men are a symbol for you and the whole world population; the way you react the day you realize that Jesus is the born again Motherland history. He is the message from the spirit world, and as a spiritual story he can save the world if you and the whole world population demand the history to return. There will be a tremendous reaction all over the world, in all directions in a veritable turmoil. You know how the camouflaged story about Jesus continues. He was dead only for three days. The lost Motherland history was dead, as in the spirit world, for much longer than that, namely several thousand years.

But a small group of scholars, the Masters of the past, kept the story about the lost Motherland alive all through the ages, until the story was told to King Herod in Jerusalem. The seriousness of the story is emphasized by what he did to protect his own position as a king. It was a camouflaged story all together, with a few historical images, but Jesus, as the born again Motherland history has been alive since then under the camouflage of religion. You have to remove the camouflage and make the history find its place in the common world of thoughts.

It is not a coincident that the Master who wrote this camouflaged story used the name Joseph for the man who took Jesus down from the cross and gave him his grave. All the names in the Bible have a specific meaning.

Guards by the grave

Matthew 27, 61-66; Mark 15, 47; Luke 23, 55-56; John 19, 39-42

Joseph laid Jesus body in the grave. He and other friends of Jesus covered his body with more linen cloth. They had scented ointment between the folds. The women wanted to put salve on his body to, but there was no time for that. When the sun set they all had to leave. Everybody cried. They were terrible sad. Jesus was dead.

Joseph rolled a great stone to the door of the grave. The body of Jesus was safe. The religious leaders went to Pilate. "Jesus said he should rise from the dead after three days. It is best to put a guard of soldiers by the grave," they said. "Or else his disciples can come and steal his body, and then tell the people that he have risen from the dead. A lie like that would be worst than anything else!"

"You can have a couple of soldiers to guard the grave," Pilate answered. "Go now and see that the grave is properly sealed."

They closed the grave and sealed the stone before the grave. Roman soldiers were on guard. Now the religious leaders thought for them self that there was not possible for anyone to steal the body. But the religious leaders should be very surprised.

This camouflaged story makes the story about Jesus whole. All humans know that a human body who is dead never can come back to life. But as the spiritual born again Motherland history Jesus can come back. He came, presented himself and left again.

He is in the spirit world and will come back the day you stop denying that the lost Motherland was real and existed in the world. The camouflaged history about Jesus is made of thoughts and spoken words that truly can bring the whole world population to wake up from a long time in the darkness of oblivion.

Jesus is the enlightenment of knowledge; he is the center in the Diagram Star. It is you, the humans living in present time who can bring him back, bring the born again Motherland history out of the darkness of oblivion and in to the common world of thoughts. You are told by the religious leaders to believe in the camouflage of religion and wait for Jesus to return as a human being. Now you know how wrong that is for the whole world population.

The Master writing this camouflaged story is telling the humans living in present time that the history of the lost continent for a long time was lost for the part of the population that was forced in to a life as working slaves, soldiers and servants. Without common education, with warrior kings and priesthoods deliberately destroying ethnic tribes and family belonging and structure, the history of the lost Motherland slowly became the legends, myths and tales that still live on.

The Motherland official emblem, the Diagram Star, is found in many copies all over the world, but few, if anyone at all knows the full story behind its beautiful designed facade.

The Diagram Star is a map over the world. The apostles are a symbol for the newly elected superior Motherland council who is representing the whole world population in the twelve sections around the star. They did what they could.

The religious leaders are a symbol for the many religions in the world in present time. The Roman Empire is a symbol for the armed forces and the quest for world domination. Their empire fell apart, as the Pharaohs did before them and for example the British Empire did after them. All the attempts to build a new world with one central leadership have failed, and the present attempt called a globalization lead by the United States of America, is losing ground. The finance crises and the global warming, together with the never ending chaos of wars and conflicts in the world, will escalate slowly until everything that is built up by the three factors of the Original Sin, falls apart.

Now, before it really gets bad, the time has come for the whole world population to begin planning to build a new Motherland, not in a large building, nor inside a nation, but on a whole continent. All the three factors of the Original Sin have to be removed completely. The ongoing quest to be the richest, the strongest and the biggest national state on planet earth just have to stop. It just has to, if our children and their descendants are going to be able to build a world with ever lasting peace.

Jesus, meaning the born again Motherland history, is far from dead. He is in the spiritual heaven, as written in the Bible. When the camouflaged is removed, heaven is the spirit world, meaning the common world of thoughts.

Why is this repeated in almost every story? The answer is that you need to understand more than you think you need. Imagine the common world of thoughts as an invisible spiritual world that is the container, the carrier of all the thoughts that have been thought on planet earth, all inside a time frame from before the beginning of time and until after the end of time.

All the thoughts are there for you to access, for you to know. The common world of thoughts was open for every single human being, in the time before the Motherland was lost in a natural catastrophe. You need to use a long time before you know enough and you will keep learning the rest of your life.

After the catastrophe the common world of thoughts has been deliberately filled with thoughts that are like weed in a field of grain. The kingdom of heaven is the spirit world, a symbol for the common world of thoughts. The loss of the Motherland made human beings begin to do evil things. The greedy and selfish warrior kings and the priesthoods, the self elected elite, started spreading the seed of Tares, an injurious weed resembling corn when young.

Time has come to remove the dominating wrong and evil thoughts from the common world of thoughts; from your world of thoughts. It is now or never. Your thoughts have to be cleansed now. Only then will mankind be able to build a new world with lasting peace.

The empty grave

Matthew 28, 1-8; Mark 16, 1-8; Luke 24, 1-10; John 20, 1

It was the morning after the Sabbath. It was still dark when the women walked to the grave. Mary Magdalene and the other women had waited for this moment. Now they could return to the grave and salve his whole body.

One woman asked Mary Magdalene: "How shall we get the large stone away from the grave? How shall we get in?"

"I don't know," Mary sighed, "but we have to find a way."

The same moment the sun came up, they arrived in the garden. They brought jars of scented salve. While the sun rose over the horizon, the women arrived at the grave.

Suddenly the earth started trembling. It was an earthquake! The soldiers that Pilate had sent to guard the grave, was thrown to the ground.

An angel of the Lord descended from heaven and rolled the stone from the entrance, and sat on it. Her face was like lightning and her garments were with as snow. The guards was frightened and laid like they were dead.

"Don't be afraid," the angel said to the women. "There is no reason to fear. I know you are looking for Jesus. He is not here. He has resurrected, like he said he should. Come in stead and see the place where his body laid." The angel stretched her hand against the women and asked them to go in to the grave.

Mary Magdalene put the jar she carried on the ground and stood up. She took one of the other women by her hand. "Come," she whispered. "We must see this."

Slowly the women walked in to the grave. "O, no!" Mary Magdalene called out. "He is not here! They have taken him away!"

"No one has taken him. Jesus lives! Yes, he has risen from the dead," said the angel. "Hurry now and tell his disciples that he will meet with them in Galilee. Make sure Peter gets to hear this."

The women ran from the grave as fast as they could, in different directions. Never had they been so frightened and happy at the same time.

Even the most devoted believers cannot believe that this story really happened. But as soon as the camouflage of religion is removed, the story becomes fully understandable.

Jesus lives as a biblical story. The spiritual born again Motherland history can be told to the whole world population, in words and writing. In the same moment the camouflage of religion is removed from Jesus, he will die in a sense that the belief in him as a person dies and the born again Motherland history will come alive in your world of thoughts as knowledge. The rising sun is a beautiful symbol and the words of the angel are words from the bright shining Diagram Star, meant for you. You do need to see for yourself to understand that the history mankind needs in order to be able to build a new world with lasting peace not are dead and gone, but truly safe back in the spirit world. The born again Motherland history lived for a short time among humans in a camouflaged story that will live forever.

Mary Magdalene is a symbol for the new Motherland and the disciples are symbolizing the new superior Motherland council. This camouflaged story is telling the whole world population that the born again Motherland history always will be in the spirit world when the time comes that you want it to return. The time is now.

The camouflage story is like a beautiful picture and you will discover new details every time you read it.

Mary Magdalene meets Jesus

Mark 16, 9-11; Luke 24, 12; John 20, 3-18

Mary Magdalene ran to tell Peter and the other disciples the good news. Peter and John immediately went with her back to the grave. It was empty, like she had said.

Mary Magdalene stood waiting outside the grave, while the others went in. She could see that they really were afraid, when they walked inn. She saw them coming back out, confused.

When the men walked back home, she remained at the grave. She stood crying. She was so anxious. Was it really true what the angel said? She thought that someone might have stolen the body of Jesus. Mary Magdalene did not understand anything of what had happened.

Jesus was dead. But his body was no longer in the grave. What did it mean?

While she cried, she went to see inn to the grave. Suddenly she saw two men in white clothes sitting were the body of Jesus had been laid! They said to her: "Woman, why do you cry?"

"I cry because they have taken my Lord, and I don't know where they have laid him."

She turned, and there stood Jesus in front of her in the garden. But she did not recognize Jesus. He was so different. He said to her: "Woman, why are you crying? Who do you look for?"

Mary Magdalene thought that the man standing in front of her, was the gardener, so she said: "If you have carried him away, then tell me where you have laid him."

Then Jesus said to her in his strong voice: "Mary!" In the same moment she heard her name, she turned quickly. Now she could see who it was. Only Jesus could say her name like that.

"Master!" she called out and fell down before his feet.

"Don't touch me," said Jesus. "I will soon go back to my Father, to my God and yours God."

Mary ran back to the disciples. The news she now could shear with them, was even more glorious than what she had told them before: "I have seen Jesus!" She told them everything he had said.

Jesus is a symbol for the born again Motherland history and Mary Magdalene is a symbol for the new Motherland. She is in contact with the twelve disciples, who are a symbol for the newly elected Motherland council. They just don't know what to do when they are told that Jesus is going to return back to his Father in heaven.

Just think for a moment about what will happen when the whole world population gets to know about the born again Motherland history. They will be utterly confused and don't know what to do. And even after a new Motherland is built and a new superior Motherland is elected, it will take time before the global system of governing the world is fully comprehended.

This camouflaged story is telling the humans living in present time to not be afraid and the born again Motherland history will reveal itself for every one of you through the Diagram Star. You will not recognize the story about the lost Motherland because the whole world population has lived in the darkness of oblivion for some twelve thousand years. But because of the camouflaged story about Jesus, the born again Motherland history, you will find a full understanding of the new world that you and the whole world population is going to build together.

It is known that most of the kingdoms and empires tried very hard to live on with the laws and rules of the Motherland in the time after the Motherland was lost, but after just a few generations brothers started fighting brothers for the best land, for being the richest, the strongest warrior king of all. The camouflaged story about Cain and Abel in the Old Testament tells us that.

Mary Magdalene and the women who cries is a symbol for all the women in the world that have cried over all the humans who have died, all those who have died under the rule of the merciless three factors of the Original Sin, every day for some twelve thousand years. Women are still crying over their dead, every, every day.

Very few of the people living in our present time understand everything that is happening in the world where they live. You live and die, not knowing why. Hereby you are told how to recover the knowledge about the lost Motherland, but instead of trying to understand, many of you turn your back on the knowledge, because it comes from the Bible, a book that are considered Holy. If you have read so far, you do see the light, for sure. You are now able to see through the camouflage of religion.

When the time of the new world arrives, when all the weapons of war is melted in to pickaxes, spades and other tools for cultivating the fields, when a new Motherland is built and all the people in the world lives together like brothers and friends should, guided in all matters of life by a democratically elected Motherland council, it surly will create a fundamental happiness for everyone, built on the safety and respect that only lasting peace in the whole world can provide. Only then all humans in the world will finally live a life with everything they hoped for.

The disciples see Jesus

Mark 16, 14-16; Luke 24, 36-48; John 20, 19-21

Not long after this Jesus revealed himself for the disciples. They were inside a house when Jesus suddenly appeared in their midst!

The disciples got scared. They had closed all the doors. Because no one could come in to the house, they thought he was a spirit. Jesus told them that they should have listened to Mary Magdalene. He was disappointed over that they didn't believe.

He said to them: "Why are you so afraid? Why do you doubt? Look at my hands and my feet. Touch me and see. A spirit is not made of flesh and bone like I am!" He wanted to prove that he wasn't a spirit.

He told them that everything that happened was written long ago. The prophets, Moses and king David had said that this should happen.

"You have seen all this. Now you shall go out in the whole world and tell people about what you have seen. That is the great mission ahead of you."

Jesus left them. The disciples looked at each other with astonishment. This was too good to be true! But true it was. Jesus had risen from the dead! He was with them again!

Mary Magdalene did not believe at first, and after she was convinced the disciples could not believe what she told them. They had to see Jesus with their own eyes in order to believe it was true.

You, living in present time, shall not believe, you shall know. Believe in what you know is the thought you shall cherish.

The twelve disciples are a symbol for new superior Motherland council that you and the whole world population are going to elect amongst yourself. Mary Magdalene is a symbol for the new Motherland.

Think back in time now, some twelve thousand year, in the troublesome years just after the world lost their superior Motherland council.

The large continent disappeared from the world and thousands of humans died when it happened. The whole world population lost their superior leadership, and they were frightened and they did not know what to do.

The twelve disciples believe that Jesus is a spirit, and Jesus proves that he is made of flesh and bone. This means that the born again Motherland history is real.

From the spirit world come thoughts to the humans, that the born again Motherland is living and are reel in the common world of thoughts, ready to be built again, somewhere in the world when the world is ready.

The reason a new Motherland couldn't be built was the new laws and rules for living made by the warrior kings and the priesthoods. The last attempt took place some two thousand years ago, at the cost of thousand of human lives. The Masters preserved the story about the lost Motherland and passed it on from generation to generation as a religion.

Jesus is alive. Jesus is with the whole world population, as a religion based on stories that many people find hard to believe. After the camouflage of religion is removed from the stories in the Bible and all other religious books, the born again Motherland history will be accepted as true world history by the whole world population.

The Old Testament is all about the lost Motherland and the New Testament is all about how a new Motherland can be built.

Thomas doubts

John 20, 34-39

When Jesus appeared before his disciples, one of the eleven wasn't there. It was Thomas.

After Jesus had gone, Thomas showed up in the disciple's hiding place. They told him immediately that Jesus had been there. "We have seen him! He lives!"

"No," he said. "Unless I get to see the print of the nails in his hands and trust my hand into his side, I will not believe."

Eight days later Jesus visited the disciples again. Now Thomas was present. Jesus walked straight inn though closed doors. He suddenly appeared in the room and said: "Peace bee with you!" Then he continued: "Thomas, come to see my hands. Touch the print of the nails. Put your hand on my side and feel the wound. Doubt no more, but believe."

Thomas felt shameful because he had not believed. He bent his head: "My Lord and my God," he said.

Jesus replayed: "Is it because you have seen me that you believe now? Blessed are they who have not seen, and still believe."

Jesus spoke about people like you and I. Do you believe, or do you doubt, like Thomas?

Humans are not supposed to have doubts, but live with a safe and sound knowledge about the world history, the past and the future. The Masters who wrote the camouflaged history about Jesus is trying to make you understand the scripture that became the Bible.

Through Moses you are told that you still are working slaves, soldiers and servants under strict control of the laws and living rules of your respective national state. The crossing of the red sea and the walk in the desert is a recipe of what the whole world population has to do in order to be set free.

You are told again, all of you, but so far nobody believes that the Bible is full of stories that are camouflaged. The camouflage is so unbelievable that only people who are born with the tradition really do believe. They are told that a national state religion just have to be right. Most of the devoted believers can see the right and the just in the religion they are born with and know well, but the interpretation and explanation of the unbelievable camouflage is more or less disregarded.

Now the time has come to remove the camouflage of religion from all the stories, and make the full history of the lost Motherland known to the whole world population. The disciples are not elite, they are not warrior kings and the priests living their life in luxury in a world were a majority of humans are poor and hungry. The disciples are you, the whole world population, and you have to elect a new superior Motherland council together.

The Master who wrote the camouflaged story about Moses and Aaron and the difficulties they had to convince Pharaoh, knew how difficult it would be to convince the worlds political and religious leaders in present time. Just like the last of the ten plaques did kill the oldest son of Pharaoh, it will most likely be the strong force of Mother Nature that makes the present world leader's set the people free.

"The one who sees in to the perfect law of freedom, and continues to do so, will not be a forgetful listener, but a fulfiller of good deeds." Jacobs's letter 1, 25

Good deeds in a world without the three factors of the Original Sin will be totally different from today. This you don't have to see to understand. Reed the definition of the three factors of the Original Sin again.

Planet earth is one whole unit and the whole world population must understand the message hidden in the Bible, and together you must work towards building a new world with lasting peace.

Breakfast at the lake

John 21, 1-14

After all these things Jesus showed himself again to the disciples at the Sea of Galilee. One evening Peter said to six of the other disciples: "I will go fishing."

"We will go with you," they answered.

The whole night they tried to get fish. They cast the net on both sides of the boat and got nothing. When the morning came Jesus stood on the shore, but the disciples did not recognize him. "Children, do you have any food?"

"No," they answered him.

Then he said to them: "Cast your net on the right side of the boat and you will find fish."

The men did as he said. They became very surprised. The net was so full of fish that they were not able to draw it onboard.

John said to Peter: "It is the Lord!" When Peter heard that he cast himself in to the sea and swims as fast as he could to the shore. The other disciples came after with the boat and dragged the net full of fish after them. When they got closer they saw that Jesus had made a bonfire, frying fish and worming bread for them.

"Come and eat," Jesus said to them. And knowing it was the Lord no one dared to ask him: "Who are you?"

Jesus took the bread and gave it to them and fish likewise. This was the third time that Jesus showed himself to his disciples after he had risen from the dead.

This camouflaged story is about the whole world population. When the knowledge about the born again Motherland history and the global system of governing a peaceful globe, is made known to the whole world population with the use of Internet and modern technology, a overwhelming multitude of humans will change their way of thinking and doing and eventually their way of living.

The disciples go fishing in the darkness of the night and don't get any fish at all, because they don't do it right. The fishermen are symbolizing the newly elected superior Motherland council and the fiches are human being. You know that this camouflaged story is about convincing the whole world population that the born again Motherland history is right for the world.

People have to come out of the darkness of oblivion and understand that the present governing of the world isn't right. It is not right, it is wrong as wrong can be and have been wrong for some twelve thousand years. Wrong is the way of thinking, doing and living that you all have inherited from your parents and their forefathers.

It is wrong to rule the whole world population with the three factors of the Original Sin. There can never be lasting peace on planet earth as long as they are allowed to occupy the common world of thoughts.

Now the born again Motherland history is back, introduced by the Masters of the past, the wise men, and the scholars who all the time knew what was wrong. Some time not so long ago the last Master died, and the knowledge about the born again Motherland history died with them. But they had in a masterly manner camouflaged the full history of the lost Motherland, and knew that the knowledge would live on. It takes a human to remove the veil of blindness from the eyes of all humans, but only the spirit of the born again Motherland history can tell you what you see.

With the knowledge about the born again Motherland history the whole world population sees the light of the Diagram Star. People will surly remember the first day with the new knowledge, when they all can eat, be happy and never starve again.

If the world population ones again deny that the lost Motherland ever existed and continue to live like your parents and ancestors have done for the last twelve thousand years, the circle of evil will, encountered by the force of a protesting Mother Nature, continue and possibly destroy planet earth as we know it.

If you do nothing, your children and their descendants will hate you. They will, after all, know that you were given the change to save the world, but you did not use it. Or did you? I hope you did.

Jesus ascends to heaven

Mark 16, 19-20; Luke 24, 50-53; John 14, 1-2; Acts of the Apostles 1, 3-11

Jesus appeared to his disciples for forty days, speaking of things concerning the kingdom of God. Forty days after he died and resurrected, Jesus left the earth and returned to heaven.

Jesus took his disciples to Betania outside Jerusalem. There he was with his friends Lazarus, Martha and Mary were they lived. All his disciples were around him. He lifted his hands and blessed them. Then he asked them to go back to Jerusalem again. There they should wait for what God had promised them.

Jesus said: "John truly baptized with water, but you shall be baptized with the Holy Spirit not many days from now. You shall receive power after the Holy Spirit has come upon you. You shall be witnesses for me in Jerusalem, and in all Judea, in Samaria and to the outermost parts of the earth.

Then Jesus led his disciples out as far as Bethany and he lifted his hands and blessed them. And while they looked on, he was taken up and a cloud received him out of their sight.

While they looked steadily towards heaven as he went up, two men stood beside them in white robes and said to them: "You men of Galilee, why do you stand gazing up into heaven? This same Jesus who is taken up from you into heaven shall come again in the same way you have seen him go."

The disciples went back to Jerusalem filled with great joy. They were continually in the temple praising and blessing God. Some people wondered what kind of place heaven was, were Jesus had returned to. But then they remembered what he had said: "Don't be afraid. Believe in God and believe in me. In my Father's house there are many rooms. Soon I will go and prepare them for you."

This was why Jesus had to return to heaven.

The disciples is a symbol for the new superior Motherland council, and they have to use as long time as it takes to learn to know the born again Motherland history. God is the old superior Motherland council and they are in the spirit world. Forty days after he died and resurrected, Jesus left the earth and returned to heaven.

What do you see when you look up? In the daytime you see the sun and in the nighttime you see the moon and the twelve star signs of the Zodiac. This means that you are looking at the emblems of the superior Motherland council. Together the sun, the moon and the twelve Zodiac signs are the physical Diagram Star, carved in a stone tablet down on earth. You and the whole world population have to do like Jesus did and elect a new superior Motherland council. Only the born again Motherland history as found in the Bible, hidden under the religion, can teach them all they need to know in order to build a new world with lasting peace.

The disciples have to be apostles before they can teach. Heaven is camouflage for the spirit world and the only access to the spirit world is through your own world of thoughts. Everything you know is inside your own world of thoughts. When the camouflage of religion is removed, you will have full access to all the knowledge in the spirit world.

The born again Motherland history will come back to you, to the whole world population, the same way as it left. It was not removed from your world of thoughts; it was just covered up with the camouflage of religion. Remove the veil of religion and the born again Motherland history will emerge in your own world of thoughts. Then you will understand what the Holy Spirit is camouflage over.

The coming of the Holy Spirit

Acts of the Apostles 2, 13

When the day of Pentecost had come, the disciples were all gathered together in one house. Suddenly there came a sound from heaven like a rushing mighty wind, and it filled the house.

Tongues of flame appeared over the heads of each of them. They were all filled with the Holy Spirit and began to speak in other languages, as the Spirit led them to speak.

Now, there was living in Jerusalem Jews, devout men from every nation under heaven. The news spread, the multitude came together and was confounded because every man heard the disciples speak in their own language.

They were amazed and marveled, saying to one another: "Behold, are not all of these who speak Galileans? How is it that each of us hears his own language from where he was born?

Parthian and Medes and Elamites, and the dwellers of Mesopotamia, and of Judea and Cappadocia and Pontus and Asia, of Phrygia and Pamphylia, of Egypt and the parts of Libya around Cyrene, and strangers from Rome, Jews and proselytes, Cretans and Arabs, we hear them speak in our own tongues of the wonderful works of God."

They were all amazed and wondered, saying to one and other: "What does this mean?"

Others, mocking, said: "These men are full of new wine."

But Peter, standing up with the eleven (for they had chosen Matthias to take the place of the traitor Judas), lifted up his voice and said to them: "You men of Judea, and all who live in Jerusalem, listen to my words and know this: These men are not drunken, as you suppose, for it is only the ninth hour of the day. But this is that which was spoken by God to the prophet Joel: "It shall come to pass in the last days, that I will poor out my Spirit upon all men. Your sons and daughters shall prophesy, and your young men shall see visions and your old men shall dream dreams." And he told them about Jesus the Christ, the Son of God.

Then those who gladly received his word were baptized, and that same day about three thousand souls were added to them. They followed faithfully the apostle's teachings and fellowship, braking bread together and praying.

And fear came upon every soul and many wonders were done by the apostles. All that believed were together and owned all things in common. They sold their possessions and divided the money among all the people, as each had need of it.

Daily they went together to the temple, and from house to house they ate with gladness and singleness of heart, praising God and having favour with all the people. And the Lord added to their number daily those who would be saved.

This is a vision for the happening the whole world population is waiting for. The twelve disciples have become apostles, meaning Masters. The Motherland Parliament has representatives from every tribal people in the world and the superior Motherland council will use the language of them all until a global language can be restored. The Parliament will be omniscient, omnipotent and omnipresent through the representatives. Now you think of what this global power of only good will mean in a world without the three factors of the Original Sin.

The temple and Jerusalem is a symbol for the new Motherland ready built. It means that twelve Masters have been elected from every tribal people in the world and sent to the Motherland with their family to live as representatives for the people in their homeland. Twelve Masters from the global Parliament have been elected to be the new superior Motherland council.

Around the symbolic new Motherland is the whole world, a new world were all the people speaks the same language and live together as brothers and friends.

The Holy Spirit is thoughts from the spirit world, presenting the whole true story about everything the camouflage of religion is covering up.

Fire = Knowledge about the Motherland, says the formula. This camouflaged story is telling people living in present time all about the lost Motherland, the old superior Motherland council and the one set of laws and rules for the whole world population.

This means that the whole world population soon will live together as brothers and friends again. Not too soon after living some twelve thousand years under the despotic occupation of the three factors of the Original Sin.

People will live in self supported villages and have all they need in order to live a good and meaningful life on planet earth.

The long lasting peace between all the people in the world will be secured by the common set of laws and rules. They will all live together and own all things in common.

It will be a world without all the national states with laws and rules of their own, guarded borders and armed forces. It will be a world without the use of money all together, a world without the global system of capitalism. It will be a world without all the religions in the world.

It will be a world where every community in the world, small or large, is guided by a democratically elected council of twelve. There will be regional educational centers everywhere needed and education will be the main activity for all humans again. Every community in the world will be visited by their representatives from the Motherland ones every year and the best students will be taken to the Motherland to be educated to be a Master. Every Master will be able to fill a position as a teacher, a scientist or any other leading position in the world.

The Holy Spirit is the whole common world of thoughts. It links everything together as a complete understanding of the history of the lost Motherland in your world of thoughts. When Jesus was crucified he did not die, he was set free in the world as a religion.

Define religion as a story that has an underlying core of truth that many humans can feel is there, but don't fully understand because of the unbelievable wonders, dogmas and assumptions. A helper is sent to help you to find the true understanding about what paradise the whole world was before the Motherland was destroyed some twelve thousand years ago.

The thoughts of understanding the truth will make you see and understand the Diagram Star. The diagram is only a clean drawing of a bright shining star. When you learn to read the diagram like an open book, you will find the full world history, starting from before the beginning of time and until after the end of time.

The tongues of flame of knowing the truth will symbolical hover over your head, like a bright light from the Diagram Star and the darkness of oblivion will be gone.

This will happen all over the world, when everybody sees the light. You will quickly understand that under the light of the Diagram Star, all the people in the world will begin to speak the same language, just as before the Motherland went under.

Even if the words continue to be different for quite some time, the understanding of the Diagram Star will be the same all over the world. The whole world population will live with lasting peace, a world peace that will be guarded by one common set of laws and rules for living.

The finding of the lost thoughts will give the blind back their eyesight and wake up the living dead. The era of darkness, the time of waiting is over. Living in the darkness of oblivion for many thousand years has taken its toll. The cost of the sins of the forefathers is high, counted in human lives.

The Masters who wrote all the camouflaged stories in the Bible was not religious in any way. They lived with the knowledge and their hope and belief was that one beautiful day the thoughts of truth really would win over the religious belief.

After the thoughts about the lost Motherland has found foothold in the common world of thoughts, no power on earth can stop the change from happening. The whole world population is yearning for lasting peace, and the global system of governing that now is uncovered from the Bible is the only passable way to go.

The present governing system, with many national states, a global capitalistic system and all the religions in the world will over time be removed from the common world of thoughts. All humans will eventually speak the same language and live like one big family, living with a world peace that comes naturally. The main activity will be education in the light of the Diagram Star.

A lame beggar healed

Acts of the Apostles 2, 43; 3, 1-10

With the help of the Holy Spirit the apostles did many wonders. More and more humans came to believe in Jesus, and the congregation got more numerous every day. One day a lame beggar was healed. He had never been able to walk.

Peter and John passed him at the temple stairs. The beggar sat there and asked for money. But the two apostles wanted to give him a lot more.

"We don't have silver and gold," Peter said, "but what I have I will give to you. In the name of Jesus Christ stand up and walk!" Peter took his right hand and helped him up. Immediately the beggar could feel the force in his legs. He could stand and walk without help!

"I can walk! I can walk! Praised be the God of Israel!" the man shouted and danced in to the temple, followed by Peter and John.

The twelve disciples are given the title apostles after coming of the Holy Spirit. They are symbolizing the new superior Motherland council that the whole world population has to elect as explained before.

In this camouflaged story the apostles is healing a beggar. The Masters writing the story knew that to heal a person like this was impossible. The camouflaged story is about something else; the impossible healing of the whole world population by telling them about the lost Motherland and how the whole world was organized in the time before the large continent was destroyed in a natural catastrophe.

The whole world population is in present time living exactly like the lame beggar. The money given to him is the only factor that keeps him alive. Money given to all the hard working humans on planet earth in return for work, is keeping them alive under the dictating rule of the three factors of the Original Sin.

Look now at the part of the world where a majority of the population doesn't have work. Nobody gives them money and they have to beg to stay alive in areas where money is used. It is a matter of fact that thousands of humans die every day because they don't have money.

All the billons of poor people in the world will welcome the new global government where every human live in self supported villages and have all they need to live a good life on planet earth.

Many humans living in our present time knows that money never will end poverty in the world. Money is a major part of the Original Sin and can only make things worse for the poor people. Only removing all the three factors of the Original Sin can eradicate poverty from the whole world. Of course all the rich people will disappear as well after some time, but who cares?

Imagine the happiness that will make the whole world population tremble when everyone begins to live following a common set of laws and rules from a new Motherland, knowing that every single human being is living a good life.

But will the political and religious world leaders allow it to happen in present time? How many more have to die, not knowing why they ever lived?

All the signs and wonders described in the Bible are symbols and never happened. It will be a true wonder for the whole world population to experience that all their dreams come true and that they have everything that they have hoped for.

Peter and John get arrested

Acts of the Apostles 3, 3-11; 4, 22

People in the temple got frightened when they saw the beggar jump up and down. Soon a large crowd gathered around him.

Peter saw that they wondered what had happened. He said: "It is Jesus who has healed this man, not us. God has made him rise up from the dead, so Jesus is alive. He is the Messiah. It is the faith in him that has made this man well."

The religious leaders got furious! They did not like that anyone spoke about Jesus. In a hurry they sent for the guards and Peter and John were arrested.

"This shall surly stop them, so they don't speak any more about this Jesus rising from the dead," the religious leaders said. The apostles were kept in prison over night, but still many people started believing.

The next day the religious leaders sent for Peter and John. They asked the two apostles how they had healed the lame man. Peter was filled with the Holy Spirit, so he answered with wisdom.

The religious leaders said: "These men have never had any education. They are simple men from Galilee. How can it be that they are answering so well? They looked at them. "If you stop talking about this Jesus, we will let you go."

"What do you think is right? To do what God will or what you will? Do you think that God wants us to listen to you or to him", Peter answered. "We can only speak of things we have seen and heard."

Peter and John was not the slightest afraid for the religious leaders. The priests could not do more. The man who was healed stood in front of them. Therefore they had to let the two apostles go.

This is a good camouflaged story. If you can remove the camouflage of religion and fully understand what the story is telling you, you are getting educated to be an apostle, a teacher who can teach other humans about how life was like in the world in the time before the Motherland was lost. Best of all, you are losing your fear to speak against the religious leaders. You are no longer afraid, because you know that you are doing the right thing when you speak about the knowledge you have found. You are a teacher working for lasting world peace the only possible way.

At first many people will get frightened when they get to hear about the lost Motherland and the global government system that will change the way they live so dramatically. Will it be better or worse? It will be a lot better for the billions of humans who are poor as poor can be, because the new way of life will give them back the safety and happiness only the belonging to a tribal people can provide. When living in self supported villages in a world without national states and their weapons of war and guarded borders, without the global capitalistic system and without all the religions in the world, it will be a better world for the whole world population.

The change for the richest of the rich, for the national states servants and for the many religious leaders, will be hard to handle, and therefore the change have to come slowly over many years. It will be a walk out of a mental desert for the whole world population. The choice to cross the river of knowledge has to be made by the whole world population together. It will be a long walk, and there is no going back.

So what do you think is right to do in our present time? Is it more important to listen to your national and religious leaders and obey them, than to save the whole world population from some twelve thousand years in the darkness of oblivion?

All the national states in the world were built by the use of warfare and brutal force. The national laws and rules for living is dictated by the political and religious leaders, and makes you and the whole population in to working slaves, soldiers and servants. What is right, then, to serve your national state fatefully and watch the world around you being destroyed by a desperate quest for money and riches, or is it right to make use of your new knowledge and fight to begin building a new world with lasting peace?

You know that the long lasting chaos of wars and conflicts are all about the quest for riches and national power, about who is the greatest and the strongest and have the best political solution. Why not go for a solution that the whole world population can agree to? It means building a new Motherland in a new world and start living together like brothers and friends.

The reason that you and many with you still denies that the lost Motherland ever existed, is because the political and religious leaders of the national states have taught you to believe in their dogmas and assumptions, continuously for several thousand years.

It is you that never have had any education in the light of the Diagram Star. It is you who will speak with a wisdom that will impress the world leaders.

The apostles escape

Acts of the Apostles 5, 12-42

Every day the apostles met at the temple gates. Here they spoke to the people about Jesus. Many believed in them and became the followers of Christ, while others were afraid of the religious leaders. They stood on a distance and listened to what the apostles said.

The religious leaders became more and angrier because of this. They envied the apostles. Now they decided that they didn't want to hear more talk about this Jesus. But more people that ever believed in him! How come?

Finally they ordered the guards to put the apostles in prison. But in the course of the night God sent an angel to them. He opened the prison door and said: "You are free. Go back to the temple and tell the people there about the new life of Jesus."

The apostles walked back to the temple, like the angel had said. In the morning the priests was told that the apostles was out of the prison and back in the temple talking to the people. Now the priests got more worried than ever.

"The men you sent for, is now taking to the people in the temple," they were told. The captain of the guards was sent off, and he took the apostles back to the priests again. Here they were questioned.

"We told you to stop talking about Jesus!"

Peter and the apostles answered: "We must obey God more than humans. Jesus lives. If you convert and believe in him, you will be saved. This we know, because we have seen it happen. It was you who crucified him."

Some of the religious leaders got so angry when they heard this that they wanted to kill them at ones. Then one Pharisee said: "It is best that we let them go. If this is from God, it will last as long as the world exists, no matter what you do. Be careful, so you don't fight against God."

The religious leaders could not do other than flog the apostles, and then set them free. The apostles were happy because they now had been found worthy to suffer for Jesus. Already the next day they spoke to the people.

Jesus is the born again Motherland history with the knowledge about the global system of government that ensured long lasting peace all over the world, in the time before the Motherland went under.

The apostles are a symbol for those of the whole world population who knows enough to be teaching others about the lost Motherland. Symbolically they stand outside the temple doors all over the world. Why outside? They stay on the outside because outside they speak to those who want to know. Those who are inside are still in the mental desert on the other side of the river.

The religious leaders are the multitude of priesthoods in our present time. If they convert to the knowledge and agree to live and obey the laws and the rules of the new superior Motherland council, they will not only be saved, they will become apostles and work hard to convert others.

What does being saved mean? It means a cleansing of thoughts, a totally different understanding of the life as a human on planet earth. The circle of evil is broken. Breaking the laws and rules of your national state you will do without being afraid, because you know that you are right in everything you do.

God is by definition the old superior Motherland council. Jesus is the born again Motherland history, told to the world camouflaged and hidden in the many biblical stories and the apostles Peter and John symbolizes two of the new superior Motherland council. The twelve apostles are symbolical the new leaders of the whole world population. They know what they are doing and are not afraid to speak against the religious leaders.

Converted people will be the new apostles all over the world. They will all be teaching the same true story and after some time the whole world population will know and all imposed religious belief will be gone for good.

The many camouflaged stories in the Bible were written by the Masters of the old school. This is their way of preserving and passing on the history about the lost Motherland to coming generations. The stories about the twelve apostles is all about how all the Masters were brutally killed, and over time the history about the lost Motherland was forgotten. There are no living Masters with the same degree of knowledge and spiritual strength left on earth. But because of their devoted work the history about the lost Motherland was hidden in the Bible and made in to a religion.

Only by removing the camouflage of religion from the many stories in the Bible, humans living in present time will find the lost historical knowledge that are necessary in order to build a new world with lasting peace. The whole world population has to do this together.

All living humans live their whole life together on planet earth. When the time comes and people die, the physical bodies are gone forever. It is only their thoughts that live on forever. The human spirit, aura and soul live on with all the thoughts intact. But the thoughts have to be right in order to be saved in the common world of thoughts. Human beings are born in the common world of thoughts. The brain is the receiver of thoughts and it is the spiritual strength and personal abilities that decides the position in the community.

For all living human being there is only one set of laws and rules for living that is right. It has survived all thought the history, hidden in the camouflaged stories in the Bible. You need to know the Diagram Star in order to find the thoughts that are right for the whole world population.

It is the laws and rules found in the Bible the apostles have chosen to obey and live by, and doing so they make the religious leaders so angry that they want to kill them. And they were all killed, in due time, and their stories about a lost Motherland and the knowledge needed to build a world with lasting peace, was preserved, and hidden in the Bible, under a camouflage of religion.

The true story is that the Masters and their follower would rather die that give up their knowledge for a meaningless religion imposed on them by the religious leaders. Because the double-edged sword of knowledge has to be used with only peaceful means, they all died eventually, and the religion survived.

Some two thousand years ago, when the story about the lost Motherland was written in to their era, also the local warrior kings, the high priests and the priesthoods had to live by the laws and living rules the Roman rulers told them to. All the populations they ruled over was robbed for all their property and forced in to a life as working taxpaying slave, solider and servant. Those who surrendered willingly got a better life than the others.

The only way the Masters of the past could preserve and pass on the many camouflaged stories about the lost Motherland, was to fool the Roman emperors and made them take the religions in use as a tool to control the many populations they ruled over.

Now, in present time, it is only a complete conversion by the whole world population who can save mankind from destroying planet earth completely. Jesus, meaning the born again Motherland history, have been with mankind always, and always will.

You have, just as your parents and ancestors through thousands of years, been indoctrinated by the priesthood and your national state authorities, to do as you are told and blindly follow the national laws and rules for living. It is as wrong as wrong can be. Think about the life you live right now, under the rule of the three factors of the Original Sin, and imagine how life would be without.

The Masters of old and their followers were not afraid to die for what they knew. Now you know what they knew.

Stephen, the first Martyr

Acts of the Apostles 6, 1-7

More and more people believed in what the apostles said. They wanted to learn to know Jesus, and they choose to follow him. They put him first in life. But there were some problems because they were so many. One problem was the food. How should they be able to feed the families?

The apostles choose seven men to take care of the problem. This gave them more time to talk with people about Jesus. The seven men were full of belief and the Holy Spirit. One of them was Stephen. He lived close to God. Stephen did his duties in a good manner and God made wonders with him.

Some men started arguing with him, but they got nowhere. It was no use against the wisdom Gods Spirit gave him. But they were bad men and made people tell lies about Stephen.

"Stephen is speaking blasphemous about Moses and God," they said. It didn't last long before more and more men came to the religious leaders, and soon Stephen was arrested.

He was put before the judges, but Stephen was not afraid at all. His face shone like an angel. The religious leaders did not care that Stephen never had done anything wrong. They sent for people who lied about Stephen. This was the same as when Jesus was convicted. They twisted and changed on everything Stephen had said about Jesus. It was certainly not nice.

Stephen was filled with the Holy Spirit. Gods Spirit helped him with what he should say and when he should say it. Therefore he answered every question with great wisdom. At the end he said: "You have not wanted to listen to what God has to say. Was it not your forefathers who tried to kill the prophets? What about all of you? You killed the Messiah. He came to save you!"

The religious leaders got angry. Stephen looked up. There he saw Jesus standing at his father's right hand in heaven. He said: "I see heaven open. There is the Son of Man!" He pointed up.

Now people got completely wild. They held their hands before their ears and ran against Stephen. They ran him out of town and started throwing stone at him. He fell to his knees and called out loud: "Lord Jesus, receive my spirit! Lord, let them not suffer for this! Then Stephen died. He died like a hero of Jesus, a martyr who was filled with courage and wisdom.

In this camouflaged story the Masters tells the people living in present time about the forces of evil that were working against them and their Message to the world. The forces are still in charge and control the whole world population with the laws and rules of the national states, the enforced feeling of national belonging and the enforced work and paying of taxes. Just by looking at the world you live in, you do see that nothing has changed.

You and the whole world population are still working slaves, soldiers and servant of a governing system that is wrong for the world. You are the Israelites of the Bible and the escape from Egypt never happened. The camouflaged stories are a recipe of how it has to be done. It is the only way the whole world population can be set free.

The people living in present time has the choice between continuing to live under the laws and living rules of the political and religious leaders of your nation, as you all have done for thousands of years, or you can choose the global government system that Stephen spoke about before he was killed.

The building of national states happened only because of the desperate quest for riches and personal power. Warrior kings and priesthoods had learned the method for their wrong and evil doing from the Pharaohs of Egypt, who methodical and ruthless used a time of hunger and poverty as a tool to create willing workers, soldiers and servants. They created the Original Sin and from then on all education was all about building a qualified workforce, able soldiers and devoted servants.

Now think about what will happen if one person takes a stand on the outside of what is commonly accepted in your nation. Being outside means not working and paying taxes. No paycheck means no house to live in and no money to buy food for. Most people in a nation is considered on the inside, willingly living like working slaves, soldiers and servants, believing that the only way to live is how the nation tells you to live.

With only two people on the outside the national state would ignore them. Think now what would happened in the world if there was an avalanche of humans, a crowd growing in too many millions, who denied their national state and wanted to build a new world? Would the national states in the world try to stop the avalanche with warfare and brutal force? How could the multitude of humans be feed properly? This is where the building of self supported villages comes in. The people living on the outside of the national states and their regulations have to live inside self supported villages in order to avoid the lack of food and other necessities for life.

All the religions in the world are an important part of the Original Sin. It was the religious leaders and their helpers who killed Stephen by stoning him. The political and religious leaders of present time have inherited the whole three parts of the Original Sin and their history also shows a ruthless killing of all opponents to their imposed religious belief. The use of false witnesses and wrong accusations was and is common, still.

The whole world population is captives of the wrong doing of their forefathers. The most powerful world leaders believe they do all they do as right as right can be. They believe because they don't know the full story about the lost Motherland. And because of their enforced educated belief in the religious dogmas and assumptions, they deny that there ever was a Motherland. But the whole world was a peaceful paradise before the Motherland went under. Only by building a new Motherland and with the whole world population living in self supported villages, the world can be a paradise again.

In our present time most people are afraid of speaking against the religious leaders and the government. Humans are still as subdued as they were under the dictatorship of the Pharaohs, and everyone is afraid.

Only knowledge can remove the fear. It is all about being brave enough to show how you can separate wrong from right because of what you know. Knowledge can only enter the human mind by the use of education and personal ability to think thoughts on your own. Let the Diagram Star enlighten you, and you will soon be able to free your thoughts from the three factors of the Original Sin.

You know very well that if you have a thought that you believe is right and live with it for a long time, all it takes is to convince you that the thought is wrong, and you don't have it any longer. Nobody have wrong opinions according to themselves. The only force that can convince you that your belief is wrong is knowledge that you know is right.

Saul is converted

Acts of the Apostles 8, 1-4; 9, 1-8; 22, 4-11; 26, 9-18

When Stephen died, there was one religious leader who liked what he saw. His name was Saul. He, like all the religious leaders, wanted Stephen dead.

Stephens's death was the start of a vicious time of persecution for the followers of Jesus. The people of God showed great courage during this time. Time and time again large number of people had to die because they believed in Jesus. Not one failed him. Many had to leave their homes and flee for life.

The enemies of Jesus had hoped to kill all of the followers of Jesus. Instead they grew in number and got stronger as the story about Jesus spread. They had to flee from people like Saul, but while they was on the run, they told everyone they met that it was well worth living for Jesus… and dying for him.

Saul constantly thought about new ways to capture the followers of Jesus. He hated everyone who believed in Jesus, and the hate was dangerous.

Saul went to the high priest and asked if he could search for the followers of Jesus both inland and in other countries. He would arrest them all and bring them back to Jerusalem. It concerned men, women and children. Everyone should be killed.

The rumor of what Soul was about to do spread quickly. All the believers in the area gathered and prayed for each other. They knew that Saul was the worst enemy of all. He was gruesome.

Saul went first to Damascus. He had important letters with him. They gave him the right to arrest all the followers of Jesus everywhere. Armed roman soldiers followed him. But well on the way to Damascus something strange happened.

Suddenly a light from the sky above beamed on to him and Saul fell of his horse! He lay on the ground when he heard a strong voice speaking to him: "Saul! Saul! Why do you persecute me?

"Who are you, Lord? And the Lord said: "I am Jesus from Nazareth. You persecute me because you persecute those who follow me. You put me in prison every time you put them in prison. You kill me time and time again.

Then Saul, trembling and astonished said: "Lord, what do you want me to do?" And the Lord said to him: "Arise and walk into the city, and you shall be told what you must do."

The guard who were with Saul heard the voice, but they saw no one. Saul did as he was told. When he opened his eyes he was blind! His men had to lead him to the place Jesus had told him to go to and there he waited in darkness.

The city of Damascus is more than four thousand years old. Damask is a rich, heavy silk or linen fabric. There is a veil made up by the three factors of the Original Sin covering Saul's thoughts making him believe that his evil doing is right. The road to Damascus was chosen specifically for this camouflaged story because of the name.

Do you really believe that the Roman emperors would start killing thousands of people because of the dogmas and assumption of the religion we know as Christianity?

The many religions in the world are more than an empty belief in an undefined God in an undefined Heaven. The first Christians knew the lost world history that the camouflaged stories in the Bible are hiding. They believed in what they knew, and dying for talking about the born again Motherland history had a meaning. The first Christians were a growing opposition that could free the people from the slavery under the Roman occupation.

Back then, the Roman emperors knew what the religion was hiding. The local kings and the priesthoods also knew what the first Christians spoke about and together they tried to wipe out the common knowledge about the lost Motherland. The knowledge was an actual threat against the Roman regime, and also against the local kings and the priesthoods.

It was the knowledge about the true history underneath the camouflage of religion that made the Roman rulers and the religious leaders persecute and kill the growing number of early Christians.

The whole world population was represented by their elected representatives in a global Parliament and lived together as brothers and friends with lasting world peace. The Motherland population was like a continent of representatives with a connection to every tribal village in the world.

The apostles spoke about a world without a few tyrannical leaders and priesthoods living in luxury and a majority of the population living like slaves, soldiers and servants.

This was the true democratic election of leaders and many people understood that it was the right way to live. Most of what the Greek scholars knew and taught the world what they knew from the lost Motherland history. Common education in the light of the Diagram Star was the main activity for all humans even in the smallest self supported villages all over the world. The best students were taken good care of by the village council and sent off to a higher education in the larger temples in the region. Only the best of the best student got to go to one of the seven educational centers on the Motherland continent, to be educated to a life as a Master.

This means that the whole world population was living in the symbolic light of the Diagram Star, the same strong light that struck the evil roman named Saul down on the road to Damascus.

When the time comes that you fully understand the nature of the lost Motherland and know that the global government system can be implemented in to the world we all live in, you will experience the same change of thoughts as Saul did on the road to Damascus.

Jesus is the bright shining star in the Diagram Star. He is the born again Motherland history. The knowledge will convert you and then you to will see the road back to a life with a natural meaning in a new world. Saul is a symbol what will happen to many of the world leaders in present time. After the spreading of knowledge is over some time in the near future, you and the whole world population can begin to build the new world together.

Saul was blind for some time before he got his eyesight back. He was the same person, but with a totally different world of thoughts. The blindness was a time of confusion and learning. He had become a Christian and started preaching already in Damascus. The disciples believed him, but the people who knew about what Paul had done to Christians before, did not accept him, and planned to kill him. The disciples saved him by helping him to escape over the city wall in a basket. He went to Jerusalem and joined the disciples there.

It doesn't matter if you are a believer or a not believer in a religion. Understanding the full Motherland history will change your thinking completely, and it will never be the same again. You, along with the whole world population, are on the Damascus road together, and you have been on the road for several thousand years.

The strong light of truth from the Diagram Star will blind you for a while, before you begin to understand for example what the election of a new superior Motherland council means for the world. It means that a new era of long lasting world peace will begin.

The roman emperors and the local kings and priesthoods did not succeed in killing all those who knew about the lost Motherland and heard about the many camouflaged stories about the born again Motherland history. Therefore Emperor Constantine in the year 324 took the many camouflaged stories in under his ruling and made the religion a part of his tool to control the many different people he ruled over. From then on the many unbelievable religions in the world have been enforced on the population, only without the knowledge from underneath the camouflage.

Why do you think the religion was made holy by the religious leaders, not to be questioned or changed in any way? When education returned first in monasteries and later in larger scale schools, the main reason was to teach the population to read and write, so they could read the camouflaged stories in the Bible themselves. People were physically and mentally forced to believe in the unbelievable stories and all opposition was severely punished.

Jesus is the strong light and the voice that changed the world of thoughts for Saul. He came to believe in the knowledge about the lost Motherland as told by Jesus, the born again Motherland history. What he and all the other apostles tried to do, with or without the camouflage of religion, was to spread the knowledge to the whole world population. Read the story about the Ark of Noah again. Therefore the work that lies ahead for you and all other teachers is to flood the whole world with knowledge and drown all religious believes. Not one human life will be lost.

Now you concentrate your thoughts about the life humans lived in the time before the Motherland went under. From the Motherland the superior council enforced the common laws and rules on the whole world population. They were the foundation for long lasting peace in the whole world. No man or tribe was greater than others and all people lived together as brothers and friends with everlasting world peace. Crimes were never committed and all humans had everything they needed of food, clothes, houses and material gods. A man or woman, who broke the laws and rules for living, lost the trust and respect from tribe and family and had to live with the shame for the rest of their lives.

The teaching of Peter

Acts of the Apostles 10, 1-48; 11, 1-26

The good news about Jesus was spread all over the land. Many people received what they heard. Many were risking their lives by doing it. But now was the time that other people than the Jews should hear the good news.

Often in the history of the Jews God had spoken through prophets. He had said that a light should come from the Jewish people. That was Jesus. The light should save the world. Jesus had said that his teaching first should be told to the Jews. Later the whole world was to hear the message. This was one of the reasons the religious leaders hated Jesus. They liked to be Gods only chosen people. Now it all should change. Two men, Peter and Cornelius made this clear.

Cornelius was not a Jew. He was a roman officer and had one hundred soldiers under his command. Both he and his family believed in the one and only true God. Cornelius used to pray, and often he gave money to the poor.

One afternoon while Cornelius was praying, he got a vision. He saw an angel who called him: "Cornelius!"

Cornelius was afraid and said: "What is it, Lord?

"God has heard your prayers. He wants you to send some of your soldiers to Joppa, and find a man named Peter. He lives in the house of Simon, a tanner, by the seaside." Cornelius did as the angel said and sent three men.

While the three men were on the way to Joppa, something strange happened to Peter. He was on the house rooftop where he had gone to pray. Peter had a vision!

He saw heaven open and a cloth full of all kind of animals and birds was on it. Then he heard a voice saying: "Stand up, Peter! You can eat all this animals!"

But Peter answered: "No, Lord, we cannot eat food that is unclean according to the law!"

But time and time again the voice spoke to him: "You must not call anything unclean that God has cleansed." Then the cloth was taken up in to heaven again.

When Peter woke up after the strange vision, he was very confused. What did it mean? Then Gods Holy Spirit said to him: "Stand up and go down. Three soldiers are looking for you. Don't be afraid. I have sent them."

Peter went down. From the three men he was told that an angel had asked Cornelius to send for him. The next day they left together. Other believers from Joppa waked with them. When Peter came to the house of Cornelius, he fell before the feet of Peter. All his family and friends was present. They heard Peter say: "Stand up! I myself am also a man."

Peter looked around in the room. It was full of people, men, women and children. Most of them were not Jews. He said: "You know that it is against the law for a Jew to keep company and visit anyone of another people, but God has shown me that he loves everyone. It doesn't matter if they are Jews or not. Therefore I have come. Now I want to hear why you have sent for me."

Cornelius said: "I am so glad that you have come. I had a vision were it was said that we should send for you. God has something to tell us through you. Have he not given you a message?" He told Peter what the angel had said to him in his vision. Peter nodded.

"That he has. God do not make difference between people. He receives everyone who believes in him. That I do understand now,"

While Peter explained, suddenly the Holy Spirit came over everyone who had heard what had been said. They started speaking strange words and glorify God.

The Jews that had come with Peter was surprised. They had never seen the Holy Spirit come over anyone that wasn't Jews.

The news about what had happened spread quickly to the other apostles. People, who were not Jews and was called heathens, had reserved the word of God!

Some apostles did not like it. They meant Peter had broken the Jewish law when he mingled with that kind of people. But the time had come that the whole world should be Gods family. As soon as Peter got back to Jerusalem they started to question him.

"You broke the law," the apostles said. "You went in to the home of a heathen. You even had dinner with them!"

Peter explained what had happened. He told about the vision and the angel that had visited the roman Centurion Cornelius.

When the other apostles heard that, they stopped their protestation and praised God instead. "This means that God have given all humans a change to convert to him and start building a new world with Jesus.

It was around this time the believers in God first was called Christians. It means belonging to Christ.

In the national flag of the Jews they have taken away the circle in the center, who is Jesus, the bright shining light that were the message for the whole world population are. The sections around is also removed along with the light. The Jewish flag is only a fraction of the Diagram Star. No light can come from the Jews. They live in the darkness of oblivion just like the rest of the world population.

The light is going to save the world, the writer of this camouflaged story is saying. The writer was a Master, one of many who spoke through the prophets. They were persecuted by the roman rulers, the warrior kings and the priesthoods of the time and many Masters lost their lives. Still they did what they could to preserve and pass on the word of God, meaning the full story about the lost Motherland and the global government system that could restore lasting peace among all people on the planet. If the whole world population is ever going to live like a family under the light of the Diagram Star, it has to happen soon.

Peter and Cornelius is a symbol for a divided world that seeks to be united again under the rule of a new superior Motherland council. But something went wrong back then. The Roman Empire, the warrior kings and the priesthoods was not meant to be in the world. They only existed because of their military power and their invented laws and rules. The true message, the full history about the lost Motherland, was destroyed with a multitude of dogmas and assumptions.

The camouflaged stories written by the Masters were the best of all. The largest religions in the world came from the story about Jesus Christ. Christ means Messiah in the Hebrew language. And believe it or not, under the camouflage of religion Christianity is the born again Motherland history.

The Masters lived with the certainty of knowing that sooner or later the whole world population would be able to remove the camouflage of religion and find the lost part of the world history. The time has come.

Cornelius is a symbol for the majority of the people living in the rich part of the world with the most soldiers and military power, and their leaders. They are all searching for the solution that will save the whole world and make the whole world population in to one large family under the light of the Diagram Star.

Read all the definitions again. The twelve apostles are a symbol for the new elected Motherland council in our present time, and their story shows how difficult it was back then for all the people in the world who knew and always have known the full story about what's underneath the camouflage of religion. The apostles were all brutally killed for what they knew.

Think of the apostles as angels sending thoughts from the common world of thoughts to your world of thoughts. No humans are born apostles, meaning teachers of the message from the many camouflaged stories in the Bible. The true apostles are humans who receive the full understanding of the lost Motherland from the Diagram Star without any human intervention. The angels are the invisible connection between humans and the spiritual common world of thoughts. A visible angel is like a bright shining Diagram Star. The words spoken by God in the Bible are the Diagram Star talking through the Masters who wrote the many camouflaged stories.

Jesus Christ is the star in the Diagram Star. Only a full understanding of the Diagram Star can save mankind from their ongoing self destruction. Look at the diagram and learn that every thought you derive from it is right.

Human beings are easy to lead, almost like sheep's, and in our present time they are desperately fighting for everything that is worthless in life and gaining ground towards a bottomless abyss.

The humans believe that they are in their full and self-given right to do as they want on the planet earth. Every one of you is born in to a national state that is managed wrong by the forces of evil. The forces of good are always second in command, vigorously used by the forces of evil to control a submissive and obedient population. The reason the evil is difficult to see is the fact that it is covered up by a veil of good. The building of strong armies and modern weapons are evil, but are projected as good because they are for defending the nation. You have to look back in time and find the fact that the building of all the national states in the world was an act of evil.

Likewise the global system of capitalism is evil and all the religions in the world are evil. In order to understand this you have to think thoughts of your own, new thoughts that you know is right.

The reason for all the evil in the world is plainly that the whole world population doesn't have one common superior leader to tell them what to do to remove all evil from the face of the earth.

You know that every group of humans or animals for that matter, have a leader and a common set of laws and rules that by the force of nature is given to them. Remove their superior leadership, and the result will be chaos and conflicts, until a new leader is elected.

Some twelve thousand years ago, a natural catastrophe destroyed the Motherland, and the world leaders, the superior Motherland council, died and were gone. They were gone with the whole continent they lived on. Try to understand how the world was built back then, before the catastrophe. Look at the Diagram Star. The sun in the centre is the old superior Motherland council and Jesus, the born again Motherland history. The sun and the moon are up there on the sky along with the twelve Zodiac star signs. The Zodiac star signs are the emblems for the old superior Motherland council and they will be the emblems for the new superior Motherland when they are elected. It is you and the whole world population that have to elect the new superior Motherland together. There is no one else. You know that it is only with the born again Motherland history a new world with lasting peace can be built.

Up through the ages the superior Motherland council survived by being remembered trough the twelve star signs of the Zodiac. The stories about the many gods came to be, along with all kind of legends, myths and tales.

The contact between the many populations in the world stopped, and when the chaos of wars and conflict started, the stories changed and new ones developed, often enforced on the population totally against their will.

The force that has controlled the common world of thoughts up through the ages is the three factors of the Original Sin. Try look at your own national story, and call it wrong. The reason so many human beings had to die, fighting for the national state, for king and country, was the lack of a global leadership. God was the camouflage over the global government and a common set of laws and rules for living. Look at the history of the world for the last twelve thousand years, and think.

The good news for the whole world population is that the life in the darkness of oblivion soon will be over.

The Diagram Star has always been the emblem of the Motherland. The Diagram Star is found carved in a stone tablet, and is said to be very old. In the Bible you can read that Jesus is the light that shall save the world. The Diagram Star has been with humans from before the beginning of time, and will be with humans until after the end of time. Now the Ark of the Covenant is open and the light from the Diagram Star is upon the world. Now is your chance to make a difference.

How many more human beings have to be born in to the world, live and die, not knowing why they ever lived?

Peter escapes

Acts of the Apostles 12, 1-7

More and more people received the word of Jesus and became his followers. At times it was very dangerous. The evil king Herod wanted to kill all Christians.

Many of the Christians had to escape. Some lived in caves, and they met in secret. Herod also captured Peter and put him in prison. He ordered four shifts of guards to watch him. "After Easter celebrations we will put him on trial," King Herod said. But God had other plans.

Peter was not alone. A lot of people prayed for him. Peter was not afraid to die. He remembered still the words Jesus so often had said to him: "Do not be afraid!" He often thought about that, this night before he was to be put on trial. He was chained to two soldiers and there was guard at the prison door.

Suddenly the light from an angel filled the room. He shook Peter to wake him: "Hurry and stand up!" Peter stood up and the chains fell of him! "Dress yourself and put on the sandals, and follow me," said the angel.

Peter did as he was told, but he couldn't believe it was real. "I must be dreaming," he thought. They passed one guard after the other. Not one of them as much as glanced at Peter! When they came to the gate leading out inn to the street, it opened for them just like that. Peter went out in to the street and the angel disappeared.

Peter went to a house were many Christian was gathered that night. When he knocked on the door it was a maid who answered. She recognized Peter's voice and became very happy. She ran in to the others to tell them and forgot to open the door for Peter.

"Peter is standing outside!" she called out.

The others looked up. "What is this? No, it must be his angel."

Meanwhile Peter continued to knock on the door. Finally they opened and let him in. Everybody started talking at the same time. Peter calmed them down. Then he told them how the Lords angel had lead him out of the prison.

This is about knowledge, about knowing about the lost Motherland and the global governments that can save the world, meaning save the human beings from destroying the world they live in.

Knowledge can be looked in, and judged out of the common world of thoughts by the world leaders as a national law. Being afraid to speak against your national leaders and oppose against the laws and rules of the nation is a regular prison door for the population. Read the story about Daniel in the Lion's den and his three learned friends in the overheated oven. They symbolize knowledge and the force of good and survived opposing the laws and rules of the king. Knowledge cannot be destroyed. It can be removed from people's memories with the use of enforced belief in a religion, but never from the Spirit World, the common world of thoughts.

In present time, and for several thousand years, the common world of thoughts has been occupied by religious dogmas and assumptions, a multitude of legends, tales and myths. They all have the same origin; the lost Motherland. Under the veil of nonsense they all represent the force of good.

For you and every other human being living on planet earth, it is like living inside a room that is filled with darkness. On the outside is the peaceful world that you dream about, but you are enforced to believe what your religions leaders tell you to believe. They don't know more than you and tell you what they have inherited as a holy scripture.

Everything you and the world population need to know in order to build a new world with lasting please it written on the four walls around you. But you are born in the middle of the room, and by parents, family and the laws and rules of your nation, your do learn what everybody else know, and you think it is the right way for you to live your life. Make a move and break the fences, ones and for all.

Reading the writings on the wall is not impossible, but you don't understand what it means. You and the whole world population are living in the darkness of oblivion. What you all need in order to read and understand the signs and the text on the wall is the knowledge from the Diagram Star.

In order to be able to read the Diagram Star like an open book, you need a certain degree of learning. If you start studying the diagram shaped like the star, you will soon see the multitude of stories it is preserving and carrying trough the ages. The stories are not in the diagram, they are all in your world of thoughts. The Diagram Star is the writing on the wall that you need to understand. If you deny the knowledge that you find, you do it because of what you have been thought to believe, because of the inheritance from your forefathers.

Try now to think over what you would have missed, if you were born in to a world that were completely without weapons of war, without the many national states and their borders, a world without the use of money, without the global system of capitalism and a world completely without all the religions in the world.

You wouldn't have missed it at all, because you cannot miss something that you haven't any knowledge of. But you and the whole world population do miss the superior Motherland council and a world with lasting peace, because you know, deep inside your world of thoughts, that such a world did exist. It was the paradise world that Adam and Eve had to leave.

Imagine now being born again in to a world where the whole world population lives in self supported villages and everyone have all they need to live a good natural life on planet earth. Everybody works in their village for each other and is respected for doing things right. They live with a strong feeling of tribal belonging and a proud history going back further than you can imagine.

Imagine that everyone lives in strong houses, wear beautiful clothes and always have enough food to eat. The dresses they make for the many ceremonies and festivities are decorated with their proud tribal and family history is passed on as inheritance from parents to children. Everything is remembered.

There is a lot more to say about the life humans lived before the Motherland went under, but now read this and understand it. The most important activity for every tribal village in the world was education. The best students from every year were sent off to get a higher education. Every village was producing human beings and every student strived to be the best student. Not one marriage between a young man and a woman was random. It was decided by the village council of Masters and their parents, and the whole village had to agree to the marriage. When a child was born it was a happy event for everybody. The evolution of humans was very important for other reasons than present time.

For your information people was educated in to their position in the village, but many of the best students were sent to centers were the education was combined with the building of things there was a common need for. The people were in many ways a lot more advanced than people living in present time. It is a state of mind that comes from living with lasting world peace.

Don't be surprised to learn that there was flying vessels of many sizes back then. The most important common work the whole world population did back then, was the building of cosmic eggs, also called space ships.

Think about were the building of space ships would have been in our present time, if the whole world population was working together in a world completely without the three factors of the Original Sin. The best and the most dedicated builders of all degrees would have come from all parts of the world.

Look at the Diagram Star again, at the circle in the centre and the twelve sections around. Put planet earth in the centre and call it Mother Earth. Planet earth is still a virgin and will quite possibly die like a virgin, if the chaos of wars and conflicts are allowed to continue.

You know that the world population is increasing in number rapidly, and soon there will not be enough food for everyone. The meaning is and has always been that the virgin planet earth shall be the mother of many new and fertile earthlike planets out there in the universe.

Planet earth can only feed a certain number of human beings. Those who are too many are meant to emigrate and populate the universe with earth life. The first cosmic eggs would have been sent of ages ago, if it wasn't for the natural catastrophe that destroyed the Motherland some twelve thousand years ago, and planet earth would have been a paradise heaven for the whole world population.

This is what the Roman emperors, the warrior kings and the priesthoods of the past denied the world population when they did put the knowledge about the lost Motherland in to a heavily guarded mental prison, a room filled with the darkness of oblivion.

The inheritance that is your destiny forces you and the whole world population to stay in the room filled with the darkness of oblivion, and even if you can read the signs and the text on the wall, you don't have the knowledge you need to understand. Your thoughts are covered with the inheritance called the three factors of the Original Sin, and what you need is the enlightening knowledge from the Diagram Star.

What does it take to make you see? Will it help if you are told that all this knowledge, this information about the lost Motherland, comes from the Spirit World? The Holy Spirit is a camouflage over the knowledge from the spiritual superior Motherland council, which is the common world of thoughts. The first thing that you will see is that the whole world population really needs a new and common set of laws and rules for living in peace with each other, like nature intended.

Therefore, come out of your mental prison. The chains that are holding you there will fall of you. You will be guided to the prison gate and the door will open like in a dream. Then use the Internet and modern technology to tell the world what you know. Right now the whole world population is a regular chain gang. Your word of wisdom can be the little stone that grows to be a mountain covering the whole world.

Barnabas and Paul are chosen

Acts of the Apostles 9, 10-25; 14, 1-22

Saul was blind when he came to Damascus. When he left the city, he could see, both with his physical eyes and with the heart. Saulus became one of the most eager followers of Jesus. He changed his name to Paul.

Paul went from village to village and told his story. He had been a religious leader and what he wanted then was to kill all Christians. But then he met God, and there was a change. Jesus had forgiven him. All Paul wanted now was to tell people that Jesus really can change people. He truly was guided by the Holy Spirit.

Sometimes friends were traveling with Paul. One of his friends was Barnabas. Together they went from village to village. They thought the same as Jesus had thought. Sometimes they met friends and sometimes enemies.

In one village they met a man who never had been able to walk. He listened to Paul with an open heart. Suddenly Paul said to the man to get up and walk! Then the man stood up and could walk! He was so happy that he danced around.

Later some Jews from Antioch came and said that Paul was an evil man. Then they hit him. People threw stones on him until they thought he was dead. He was dragged out of the village. While his friends stood around him, Paul stood up and walked back in to the village again. He continued to talk as nothing had happened.

The many stories in the Bible are camouflaged with fantastic wonders and events that no one really believes in. They were made like that in order to make the Roman rulers and religious leaders back then ignore them as not important.

But every story is a parable, and this story is about the whole world population. The Old Testament is about the lost Motherland and how evil entered the world and grew strong in a world without a superior Motherland council to lead them all. The New Testament is all about how the history of the lost Motherland was born again as the fictive person Jesus and how the story was denied by the Roman emperors, the warrior kings and the priesthoods.

The very moment the full story about the lost Motherland and the global government system spreads around the world to all people, they will feel just like the man who never had been able to walk. The words of Paul are the knowledge about a government system with one set of laws and rules for the whole world population. The knowledge truly will make planet earth in to a paradise again.

Now look a little deeper in to this story. The translation is wrong. Paul is talking about himself in this parable. He is comparing himself to a man who never have been able to walk. After the meeting with Jesus on the Damascus road he was able to walk, meaning that the change of thought were just as dramatically changed and his happiness were that great.

What will happen when you see the light and understand it all? Will the Jews come and stop the story as evil, and will the rest of the world listen and deny the story about the lost Motherland, again? Will you and the whole world population kill this story and leave it for dead, or will the story about the born again Motherland be accepted as true?

You and the whole world population are living with a mental wall of ignorance. It is like a prison for your soul.

The common wall of religious belief is explained in the camouflaged story about the Walls of Jericho. All it takes to break the wall of all the religions in the world in to crumbles is knowledge, and then all the traces of religious belief will vanish like dew in the sun.

Take a good look at the world you live in. The world population is growing with some 80 thousand every year. One billion or more is living for less than one US dollar a day and thousands of people is dying every day because of poverty. Don't you want all evil in the world to end? Perhaps you will not live to see it happen, but if you start working like Paul did, your children and their descendants will remember you with pride.

If you do nothing and keep hiding inside your wall of ignorance, your children and their descendants will certainly hate you, if they live long enough to find the message hidden in the Bible.

Singing in the prison

Acts of the Apostles 16, 16-34

One day Paul and his friends prayed for a young girl that got well. She was a slave and had been telling fortunes for people and the man who owned her made a lot of money on her predictions. When she got well, the owner could not make any more money on her, and he got angry. Paul and Silas were taken to the religious leaders.

There many lies were told about them and they were called traitors. Paul and Silas was beaten and thrown in prison. Their feet were attached to heavy wooden logs. They were chained and guarded by soldiers.

They were chained in the same position and they couldn't move at all. Their backs were hurting after the whipping. It seemed hopeless for the two apostles.

But Paul and Silas did not give up. They did not complain. Instead they started singing! At midnight they sang and prayed and worshipped God. The other prisoners listened to them. Suddenly there was an earthquake. The prison cell doors cracked open and the chains fell of all the prisoners.

The prison guard woke up and saw that all the prison doors were open. Then he drew his sword and wanted to take his own life. He thought that all the prisoners had escaped and he knew he would get severely punished. But Paul shouted to him: "Don't do you self any harm! We are all here!"

The prison guard called for light. He trembled from fear when he walked in to them. He fell down before Paul and Silas and after he followed them out of the prison. He asked: "Tell me how I can become a follower of your God!"

Paul and Silas answered: "Believe in Lord Jesus, and you will be saved." The prison guard nodded.

The born again Motherland history is in prison, a mental prison, and the prison door will open if you make an effort to understand what the history about the lost Motherland can do for the whole world population. The prison guard that have kept the lost world history hidden for several thousand years, is the self made laws and rules of your nation.

This is also a parable telling people in present time about how the whole world population will be Christianized if they only get to see the light of the Diagram Star and know the story about the lost Motherland. It is not about being a believer and a follower of a vague and distant God, but a strong attachment to the knowledge about the lost Motherland and knowing that a future without the tyrannical rule of the three factors of the Original Sin is within range. Every human who manage to see what's outside the mental prison doors, will want to live on the outside.

First you have to be aware that your life is just like the life of Paul and Silas while inside the prison doors. It is only the spirit of the superior Motherland council who can open your mental prison door and set you free.

To be an apostle of present time takes great courage and dedication. The times have shifted and in many parts of the world humans have the right to think and speak in direct opposition to their national state government. In many countries all qualified opposition to the sitting government are called traitors, in some cases terrorists, and they are arrested and often killed.

The message hidden in the Bible, under the camouflage, is the power that will open the prison door. Mankind has been inside their mental prison for so long that no one knows about the world on the outside. The world on the outside is the new world with lasting peace that can be built with the knowledge about the born again Motherland history.

The global government system from before the Motherland went under will give the whole world population the freedom that nature intended for them, completely without the system of world domination by many national states, all wanting to be the strongest, richest and self appointed leader of in the evolution of mankind.

What will the reward be for teachers and leaders who sincerely want to save the world from the chaos of wars and conflicts that has been going on for some twelve thousand years? The reward will be a new world with lasting peace for our children and their descendants.

Someone has to be the first to tell the world about the only way to give the billions of poor people in the world a good life with enough food, strong houses and everything they need. And the national leaders, political and religious, all over the world have to act the way the prison guard acted when faced with the true light from the Diagram Star.

The Diagram Star will in a sense be the spiritual leader for the first apostles in our present time. They have to speak on their own, representing the whole world population. The speaking of Jesus as the centre of the Diagram Star, and Jesus as the born again Motherland history will be breaking the laws and rules of the many national states. But all humans knows that only a global government with one set of laws and rules for living can restore lasting peace on planet earth.

Speaking against the use of money and the global system of capitalism will not be taken lightly by the richest of the rich and the world leaders. Perhaps the tower reaching for the sky will fall, like the prison doors did, and set the whole world population free.

All the religions in the world will also fall, like the walls of Jericho, when the knowledge about the lost Motherland is spread all over the world. It is like a new world of thoughts is opening with the knowledge that the Bible is the Ark of the Covenant and the lid is the camouflage of religion.

Be brave.

Paul is warned

Acts of the Apostles 20, 17-38

Paul was on the way back to Jerusalem. He tried to speak the word of God as often as possible. Now he visited friends and found new friends. He wrote many letters to friends he didn't have time to visit.

Paul wanted to get back to Jerusalem as fast as he could. He knew that he never would see his friends again. They warned him and said it was dangerous to return to Jerusalem. But he answered: "You know that I have to go to Jerusalem. I have to complete the mission that God have given me. Take care of yourself after I am gone. Watch out for people who want to destroy our work. Protect the congregation and continue the works that God have let us be a part of."

Time and time again Paul was warned by his friends that people wanted to kill him. Jerusalem had been the most dangerous city for Jesus. Now it would be dangerous for Paul. Everybody knew that he could be thrown in prison there. Also Paul was aware of that. But it did not stop him. He had to be were God wanted him to be.

Paul wrote all this in letters that he sent to friends. They were glad to hear from him. But everybody was worried. What would happen to him in Jerusalem?

This camouflaged story is about doing the right thing, no matter what the cost. Remember that this is all about thinking the right thoughts, about changing the common world of thoughts. Paul, with his friends, is symbolizing the changed world of thoughts for the religious leaders in the world in present time.

It is not about a change in the many political directions and a change of national religion. It is a fundamental change of the way the people on planet earth live their lives. A change from being working slaves, soldiers and servants of a despotic ruling system and in to being totally free, living in a tribal village or community where everybody knows and care for each other.

Those human beings who choose to be the new apostles, the teachers of present time, have to break the laws and rules of their national state. There is no way around. The building of national states was wrong in the first place. But when the work gets to be known and accepted by the majority of the population, done by only peaceful means, things will change.

The walk in the desert is a good parable, a good prediction given by the Masters of the past. Some of the old people will want to continue to live like they do until the end of their time. Then their children and their descendants will be able to complete the building of the new world with lasting peace.

The apostles, the teachers of present time, will be chosen not by any other humans, but by their own change of thoughts, like a call or sign from the Spirit World. They don't have to be leaders of a religious and political kind, like Paul on the road to Damascus, but converted leaders will do the work the best. His world of thoughts changed completely and he worked for the rest of his life for the spreading of the knowledge about the born again Motherland history.

Paul is a symbol for the leaders of the spreading of knowledge, just at Barnabas and Silas is symbols for those who find them self living with a strong feeling of helping the best they can, and are proud of it. Not everyone can be a leader, but most humans can be a teacher and talk about what they know.

The leaders of the world that chooses to be among the first to speak on behalf of a global government system that can save the world, will be hated by many in the beginning and most likely suffer a lot, but it will change for the better when a majority of humans begins to understand what the three factors of the Original Sin is depriving the humans for. The first few brave humans who dare to stand up against the current destructive world evolution will get their names written in the history of the new world, and they will be remembered always.

Paul is remembered for all that he did, and that he did it bravely and without fear for his own life. But he is a fictive person symbolizing the knowledge that truly is enlightenment from the Diagram Star. The story about him was written by a dedicated unknown Master of the past, living under cover for the Roman occupants of their homeland. The knowledge about the lost Motherland was more important, is more important and will always be more important than human lives. It is the only knowledge that can enable the whole world population to build a world with lasting peace.

Remember now who is what under the camouflage of religion. The first Christians who were killed in large numbers by the Romans tyrannical rule, was not believers in a new religion at all, they truly believed in the knowledge about the born again Motherland history and to them it was very important to at least preserve and pass on the knowledge to coming generations. They could not fight the Romans, but they knew that just like the Pharaohs of Egypt and all other known despotic emperors in the world, they would and could not last for long before their greed and never ending quest for more riches and personal power would make even the greatest empire crumble and fall. In our present time it is the strongest and richest nations that will crumble and take the hardest fall, and it will be ugly if the lost Motherland is denied ones again.

It was the knowledge of the Masters and their followers that gave a growing number of people a strong hope for a better life, a life without the Roman occupying force and the local kings and priesthoods that lived a life in luxury as the local elite, in close collaboration with the roman authorities.

The local population hated the way they were forced to live, and all opposition to the roman rule was killed or put in prison. The knowledge about the born again Motherland history had to be camouflaged in order to preserve it and pass it on from generation to generation.

Something changed when the roman emperor Constantine started using religion as a tool for controlling the many different people they had military control over and the religions was forced on to the populations with warfare and brutality. The religion was modified in to an empty meaningless camouflage, based on the many camouflaged stories the Masters had written. Just like a majority of humans living in present time, all the religions in the world was regarded as more or less pure nonsense for only clever fools to believe in.

It is sad to see what the enforced religion have done to the whole world population. Living like living dead and blinded for the knowledge that everyone is seeking, people have become afraid for the laws and rules of the national state they live in.

The present kings, presidents, dictators, politicians and religious leaders; they all descend from the former tyrannical rulers. They are preserving and passing on the three factors of the Original Sin and as Jesus said on the cross: "They don't know what they are doing." Therefore forgive them if they have a change of thoughts and see the light, like Paul did.

Paul speaks to the people

Acts of the Apostles 21

Jerusalem was a dangerous place for Paul. The religious leaders mobilized the people against him, and tried to kill him. But the roman soldiers came just in time to save him. They arrested Paul, to prevent the crowd from killing him.

The soldiers did not know who he was or what he had done. Paul asked if he could speak to the people and the soldiers let him do that.

Paul asked the people to listen to him. Then he told them who he was. He said that Jesus had changed him from being an enemy of the Christians to be one of their leaders. He said that he had met Jesus on the road to Damascus, and that God had sent him out to speak to both Jews and pagans.

When the people heard what Paul said it was the end of the silence. They started calling out loud: "Away with him! Kill this man!" The roman officer got Paul inside the castle. He was just about to torture him in order to find out what wrong he had done, when Paul asked him to calm down.

"It is not allowed for you to torture a citizen of Rome without a just trial," he said. The soldiers would be severely punished if they tortured a roman citizen without a good reason. The officer spoke with the religious leaders in the crowd. He said that he would give them Paul the next day, so he could be but before the court.

Again Paul tried to explain himself, but no one did listen to him. Everybody was shouting at the same time. It was the soldiers that held back and prevented Saul from being harmed. That night Paul was back in the prison again. Here the Lord came to him. "Be outspoken, Paul," he said. "You are doing the right thing. Just like you have spoken about me here in Jerusalem, you shall speak about me in Rome."

The Roman Empire started as a kingdom and evolved to a republic before they became the Empire ruling over many other people. An emperor rules over many other kings. Every empire is built with one Motherland ruling over many others. It is the natural way of building if it is done only by the use of the good forces. The Roman way to rule over the many people they had taken control over by warfare and brutal force, was as evil as evil can be. As military occupants of all the land they had taken by use of aggressive military attack, they became a self appointed superior ruling class for several hundred years.

They Romans were hated for what they did. Jerusalem was the capital of the Jews, and Paul was saved by a roman officer because he was a citizen of Rome. Paul used to be a vicious enemy of the first Christians until he saw the light on the road to Damascus and he became a leader and a teacher for the Christians.

The story is like a sign and has to be seen as a symbol talking directly to you, the humans living in present time. His change of thoughts from an enemy to a friend couldn't change who he was, he was still a citizen of Rome.

After the religion Christianity became an evil tool for the Roman emperors, as well as the warrior kings and the priesthoods, to control the population and make them pay taxes, they became a dangerous enemy of everyone who knew the knowledge about the lost Motherland. The Jews knew the full story about the born again Motherland history. They were the first Christians until the religion Christianity was taken in by the Romans and the enforced Christening of the many tribal people they ruled over started.

But the new religion Christianity, as the humans living in present time know it, was built on the camouflaged stories alone. The religion was made Holy and everyone who dared to speak against it was killed. This is your inheritance. Your forefathers were born in to a world with the untouchable Holiness, so were your parents, so were you and so were your children. Believers or not believers, the religion Christianity is just a masterly camouflage over the part of the world history that the world leaders of the past wanted the population to forget, because they wanted to remain in their position as a ruling class over the population.

But now you are sincerely told that the knowledge of the lost and born again Motherland history, is the knowledge that will enable the humans of present time to unite again as one large family, and build a new world with lasting peace together.

You are still working slaves, soldiers and servants and you really do need a common spiritual willpower to lead you back to a life in freedom. The enemy you have to fight, with only peaceful means, is first of all the wrong thoughts in your own world of thoughts. You are still on the road to Damascus. Do you see the light? Are you ready to do the right thing, and talk directly to the world leaders of present time? Now is the moment of truth.

The democracy of present time is a tragic charade, because it only can be used after the population in question has been attacked, terrorized, totally subdued and brainwashed over many generations. The national leaders truly believe that they are doing the right thing, because they have now knowledge about any other way of doing things.

National pride, a feeling of greatness and strong national belonging has been created by use of warfare between nations, and also when a submissive and misused population is raising an armed attack at their own leaders and wins. Ordinary people have no other choice than to do as the national leaders command them to do. It doesn't matter who wins or loses, wars and conflicts of all kinds is creating a strong but enforced and wrong national feeling. When the national leader calls for soldiers to go to war, everybody enlist. The few, who dares to say no, are called cowards and are often killed by their own.

Are you among the few who dares to tell the world leaders that the building of the many national states was wrong? Even if they do everything right inside their national borders, the leading of a nation is fundamental wrong. All the national borders in the world are wrong, the global system of capitalism is wrong and all the religions in the world are wrong. Only after all the three factors of the Original Sin are removed from the common world of thoughts, living on planet earth will be right again.

In order to get through the wall of religion you do need a door and for the door you need a key. Jesus, the born again Motherland history, is the key you need.

Paul must die

Acts of the Apostles 25

Paul was a citizen of Rome and had the right to a just trial. He wasn't killed by the Jews, but he spent two years in prison without a trial.

The roman governor was named Porcius Festus. He meant that Paul should be transferred to Cesarea. Again Paul was brought before a judge. This time his enemies showed up at the trial. They accused him for one crime after the other, but they had no prove. Festus wanted to please the religious leaders.

"You are the Governor," Paul said to Festus. "If you don't judge me, you must at least not turn me over to the Jews. They are my enemies and they are telling lies about me. I appeal to the emperor in Rome."

Paul claimed his right as a citizen of Rome. He wanted to be questioned be Nero himself. It meant that he couldn't be handed over to the Jewish religious leaders. But he had to remain arrested until Nero had questioned him.

Festus did not know what to do with Paul. He had to send him to Rome. There he could be questioned by the emperor. But before Festus sent him away, he asked King Agrippa what he thought about the case.

One more time Paul told his story. This time he stood in front of the son of King Herod and many other important leaders. When he finished Agrippa said: "Do you think it is so easy to persuade me to be a Christian?" He turned to Festus: "This man have done nothing wrong. It is really wrong that this man shall be sent to Emperor Nero in Rome. But now he cannot be released. He must be sent to Rome.

The Master writing this camouflaged story is telling the apostles of present time that the knowledge about the born again Motherland history have to be told to all the world leaders and the whole world population.

Paul was working hard for that to happen. Everything he did after he saw the light on the Damascus road was guided by the Holy Spirit, meaning that he was guided by a strong calling from the spiritual common world of thoughts. He knew he was doing the right thing. The thoughts and deeds of the superior Motherland council, covering thousands of years of lost world history, spoke to Paul through the born again Motherland history, symbolized by the Diagram Star.

His enemies the Jewish religious leaders wanted him dead. This means that they wanted his thoughts to be removed from the common world of thoughts, his words to stop spreading. They succeeded in doing that. To be saved, to become a Christian, means being saved from your life as a slave, soldier and a servant. Being saved means discovering a whole new world of thoughts that have been covered up by the camouflage of religion for some twelve thousand years.

Now you stop and think about this for a moment. The Jews was chosen for this mission a long time before, chosen to be the enemy of the knowledge for a very good reason. The Masters

411

who wrote the many camouflaged stories that became the Bible just couldn't call the Roman rulers for the enemy of the knowledge about the lost Motherland. Then the many stories would have been censored much more efficient and most of them had been forgotten and lost in the chaos of wars and conflicts that continued through the history. Only as a religion accepted by the Romans the Masters could preserve and pass on the knowledge to coming generations.

Think about the crucifixion of Jesus from Nazareth. Jesus is a symbol for the born again Motherland history, and the cross itself is a symbol for the Diagram Star, the official emblem of the lost Motherland. The crucifixion is a masterly camouflage for the born again Motherland history.

Is it not right to think that the enemy of Paul is the Romans and the religious leaders? Paul is a symbol for the knowledge that truly is a real threat against the rule of the roman elite. All the local warrior kings and the priesthoods, both inside and outside the Roman Empire, were the enemies of Paul, who spoke about Jesus, the born again Motherland history.

There are many aspect of the history of the Romans, their gods and their legends, tales and myths that have to be considered wrong. The right thing to do is to see that when the first Christians talked about a new world free for the roman occupants, it was the stories of the lost Motherland, camouflaged as a religion. People knew that the Roman gods, their legends, tales and myths, had the same origin from the lost Motherland.

It is very much likely that the Romans knew the global system of government the Christians spoke of would destroy their way of life as elite completely. All the religious leaders and the priesthoods would disappear as soon as the population got to know the full history about the lost Motherland. This is the reason why the first Christians were so seriously persecuted and killed by the thousands.

Now all humans know the history from the time the Roman Emperor Constantine in the year 324 took the many camouflaged stories of the first Christians and established a state religion. He did it with the use of warfare and brutal force. Just try to imagine how many humans have died since then, because of all the religions in the world. They truly are a camouflage over lost world history.

After some twelve thousand years without the knowledge about the lost Motherland and a global government system, it takes a lot of thinking in order to fully understand that it is the Bible who is the carrier of the knowledge humans needs in order to be able to build a new world with lasting peace.

Paul got just what he wanted when he was sent to Rome, just like Jesus got what he wanted when he was crucified. The Masters writing the camouflaged stories got what they wanted.

Tempest at sea

Acts of the Apostles 27, 1-26

At last Paul was on the way to Rome. It was not the way he had thought. He did not travel as a free man, to visit friends. Paul was guarded by roman soldiers. He was a prisoner on his way to be questioned by Nero.

One of the officers of the guards was Julius. He understood that Paul wasn't dangerous, and he treated him friendly. When Paul was transferred to a ship, Julius said that Luke and some others of Paul's friends could travel with him to Rome. They went from harbor to harbor and often they changed ships. Several times they sailed through storms and bad weather. At the end it got so bad that it was almost impossible to get trough.

The little ship that Paul was on, found a safe harbor on the island of Crete. There Paul said: "If we don't stay here this winter, we will lose the cargo and possibly our lives to." But he who owned the ship wanted to get to Rome as quickly as possible with his cargo of grain, so he did not listen to Paul. They sailed on.

It didn't last long before the ship sailed in to a terrible storm. The crew could do nothing. The storm lasted for many days. The wave's rolled over the deck, and they had to throw the cargo overboard.

The sky was dark for many days. The captain did see neither the moon nor stars and could not navigate. They did not know where they were! The whole crew was seasick. No one had eaten for days. Then Paul said to them: "Find courage! Not one of you is going to die. Last night an angel sent by God told me that I shall stand before the emperor Nero. None of you will die. We will run aground on an island."

The hidden message in the Bible will meet storms of a different kind when it is about to be told to the leaders of the world in present time. The message Paul is bringing to Rome is a symbol for the message hidden under the camouflage of religion in the Bible. It is the opening of the Ark of the Covenant that is about to happen, but as the story goes Paul never got to speak with Emperor Nero. The knowledge about the born again Motherland history finally gets to Rome, but it ends there.

Now you and the whole world population are in a ship that is about to be wrecked in a severe storm caused by the three factors of the Original Sin. You have the knowledge with you on the way towards a bottomless abyss. You are told about the born again Motherland history, you hear and you still don't hear. You can see and read this text, but you still don't understand what it says. The reason is the religious dogmas and assumptions that were imposed on you forefathers with the use of warfare and brutal force. You see the drawing of the Diagram Star and you still don't see what it is. Or do you?

In safety on Malta

Acts of the Apostles 27

Suddenly they heard a loud crash. The ship had run aground! Now it started breaking up. "Jump overboard!"

Water washed over them, but everyone got safely ashore. That was the only thing that was important. When they got ashore they learned that the island was Malta. The people who lived here was friendly. Paul was safe. He was going to Rome.

Again look at Paul as a symbol for the difficulties the Masters had with the preserving and passing on the born again Motherland history to coming generations. The story has met severe obstacles on the passage through the world history. The message is no longer hidden under the camouflage of religion in the Bible. The story is going to Rome ones again. The Ark of the Covenant is open and the full story about the lost Motherland is told to the whole world population. The whole story about Paul symbolizes what will happen in our present time, only this time the Masters of the past will succeed.

If Paul had died somewhere along his journeys, been killed by his enemies or even drowned in the Mediterranean Sea, the story about him would never have been used in the Bible.

Look at the history of the world from then and until present time. Or even at the world history for the last some twelve thousand years. It is a full scale chaos of wars and conflicts that never should have happened. You know that something is wrong in the world, terrible wrong, and now you know how to build a new world where everything is right. Tell people what you know. When you do you will feel a deep and profound happiness and you can face the worst of storms without being afraid.

Salute the Masters who wrote all the camouflaged stories that became the Bible. The Bible is the Ark of the Covenant. All you have to do is to remove the lid made of the gold and glitter that the whole world population is forced in to believe in as holy and untouchable. The magnificent cathedrals, churches, temples of all kind are just a masquerade to force you and the whole world population in to a life as an obedient working slaves, soldiers and servants. Priesthoods all over the world are telling stories to their congregations that are nothing but camouflage over the born again Motherland history and a totally different global government system. Forgive them, like Paul was forgiven by the disciples. Forgive everyone as soon as they see the light of the Diagram Star and understand it all.

Take the full story about the lost Motherland to your national leaders.

Is there such brave humans living on our present time? Yes, that is certain, but if it takes an event that resembles what happened to Paul on the Damascus road, it might be too late. Now look at the name Damascus. Damask is a linen covering the born again history of the Motherland. The veil symbolizes the camouflage that prevents you from see the hidden story underneath. Now the veil is removed and you can see.

In the Bible the help and the guiding from God to everyone who does right is a camouflage over help and guiding directly from the Spirit World, from the common world of thoughts.

What it takes to achieve a full understanding of the contact with the Spirit World, is spiritual strength and knowledge enough to see clearly with your inner eye. It is your inner eye you use to look at things with when you all alone have to decide what's right and what's wrong in any given situation. It is the inner eye that is guiding Paul on his troublesome journey to Rome. Back then all the first Christians understood what was hidden under the camouflage of religion. They knew what was right and what was wrong.

You are using your inner eye ever day and all the time, but in our present time the inner eye is blinded by the three factors of the Original Sin. Through some twelve thousand years with the darkness of oblivion and chaotic years without knowledge about the Diagram Star, the whole world population have been indoctrinated and educated to keep the stories in the Bible holy. The holy veil of religion is nothing but a camouflage.

Therefore begin to study the camouflaged Bible stories with an open mind and let your inner eye decide what is right and what is wrong. Everything that is right is to be taken in to a setting for the building of a new world with lasting peace.

The understanding of the world history will be turned upside down in your mind. For example you will find that all the known and unknown empire builders, warrior kings and priesthoods will stand out as humans that have committed a gruesome and long lasting crime against mankind. The world you live in is your inheritance.

Finally in Rom

Acts of the Apostles 28, 11-31

Finally Paul arrived in Rome. Believers from the whole region went to meet him and Luke and the others. When Paul saw them, he thanked God. He felt strong again.

He wasn't thrown in prison as expected. He was free to walk around, just guarded by one soldier. Paul went to the religious leaders and told them what had happened. "We have heard nothing about you from the Jews in Jerusalem," they said. "Tell us more."

Again Paul spoke about how Jesus had met him on the Damascus road. He told them how he had travelled around and spoken about Jesus and that Jesus had converted the lives of many humans. God had sent his Son to both Jew and heathens, he said.

The Jews did not know what to believe. Some received what Paul said. Others were in doubt. The next two years they discussed the matter a lot. In the meantime Paul waited for the emperor Nero to send for him. The Romans let him go where he wanted, as long as the guard stayed close by. Paul used the time to speak and pray. He spoke with everyone who came to see him. No one tried to stop him.

The two years should be the last opportunity Paul had to talk freely. Some believes that he travelled all the way to Spain and to Greece during this time. Later he was arrested again and put in prison. From his cell he wrote many letters to friends he had met earlier. In the end Paul was sentenced and beheaded by Nero in Rome.

One of the letters Paul wrote from his cell, the one to the Ephesians, is presented here in order to show you that the Master who wrote the letter speaks directly to you and the whole world population.

Of the armor of faith

(Ephesians)

"Be strong in the Lord, and in the power of his might. Put on the whole armor of God, so that you will be able to stand against the wiles of the devil.

For we wrestle not against flesh and blood, but against principalities, against powers, against the rulers of the darkness of this world, against spiritual wickedness in high places.

Stand therefore with your loins wrapped around with truth, and having on the breastplate of righteousness. Have your feet shod with the preparation of the gospel of peace. Above all, take the shield of fait, with which you shall be able to quench all the fiery darts of the wicked. And take the helmet of salvation, and the sword of the Spirit, which is the word of God."

If you read this letter knowing the whole camouflage of religion, you will soon understand that it is the present governing system that truly is the enemy the whole world population is fighting against every day of the year, year after year. The humans elected in to the positions as leaders of the world do not know that they are using all their power to protect and pass on the forces of evil to coming generations. They must be told about how the superior Motherland council ruled with the use of only the forces of good.

All human beings are by nature good and are fighting against the forces of evil all the time, not knowing what else to do. Now you know the three factors of the Original Sin, and over time you and the whole world population can remove all evil ones and for all from the common world of thoughts.

The power and the mighty strength spoken of in this letter is the power of knowledge. God is by definition the old superior Motherland council and Jesus is the born again Motherland history.

A new Motherland has to be built and a new superior Motherland council has to be elected. With the power of knowledge the whole world population can build a new world with lasting peace together.

Knowing the full story of the lost Motherland is the power that can win over the present government system with many national states, a global capitalistic system and all the religions in the world. The enemies of knowledge are the political and religious leaders of the world. They are enemies of the building of a new world because they deny that the lost Motherland ever existed.

It is the present government system with many national states that are the enemy. The system is wrong thoughts put in action, and wrong thoughts can be changed with convincing knowledge. The humans in the position as political, economical and religious leaders are really not to blame, because they are, like you are, born with the present government system as their inheritance. They just don't know about the part of the world history that dates from before the Motherland was lost.

They don't know more than you did, but after being told by you, the leaders of the world have the power to enlighten the whole world population with knowledge about the lost and the born again Motherland history, which are the only recipe for lasting world peace.

Now look at Paul as a symbol for this knowledge about the born again Motherland history. The knowledge was allowed to be spread around in Rome for some time before it was effectively stopped as a consequence of the roman emperor Nero's persecution and killing of the first Christians.

The symbolism is clear. When Jesus was crucified the disciples suddenly was without a teacher. They became teachers, apostles. Being an apostle means having only the spiritual guiding of the superior Motherland council above them. A true apostle cannot obey the laws and rules of a nation. From the common world of thoughts all the apostles have the same story to tell the whole world population. It is the full story about the Motherland that was lost in a natural catastrophe some twelve thousand years ago. And they all spoke against the Roman way of controlling the population with the use of warfare and brutal force. As the story goes on, all the twelve apostles were brutally killed by the Roman emperors.

The scholars, the scientist, the advisors of the emperors, warrior kings and the priesthoods were all educated in to their position as a servant totally under the control of the self written laws and rules of the dictators, with the military power to back them up.

In our present time the professors, teachers, the priesthoods and experts of all kind, are still educated in to their position by their nation. They are still servants for the sitting government and the national leaders. Still they all obey the self written laws and rules for living to the letter, and not one dare to speak against the nonsense of religion. The national leaders and the priesthoods have taken the many biblical stories the apostles was killed for and made them their own, with the camouflage of religion intact.

Therefore you and the whole world population have to liberate yourself from the laws and rules of your national state. You have to speak openly about the knowledge you can read from the Diagram Star, and you have to work as hard as Paul did in order to be heard. You have the help of the Internet and modern technology. There is no other way to break the circle of evil and start building a world with lasting peace.

The letters of Peter

1 Peter 3-5; 2 Peter 3

The last pages of the New Testament were written during the years of widespread persecution of the early Christians by the Romans. They point towards a future glory as a reward for present suffering and warn against spiritual weakness. The following pages, which follow the epistles of Paul, comprise letters from four others leaders of the growing church. Among them is Peter, the apostle of Christ who was crucified head-down in Rome, a martyred victim of the roman emperor Nero.

Be clear in your definitions and remove the camouflage of religion from these letters. The early Christians were not religious at all in our understanding of the word. They were persecuted and killed because they knew the full history of the lost Motherland by heart. They knew that the Lord our God and his Son Jesus Christ is the lost superior Motherland council and the born again Motherland history.

The Roman emperors and the local warrior kings and priesthoods did not succeed in wiping the born again history from the common world of thought by way of killing people by the thousands. Therefore they took charge over the religion and made it a tool for controlling people and force them in to a life as willing taxpayers. And the force of evil still rules the whole world with the firm use of a religion that truly are a camouflage over the knowledge about the born again Motherland history.

If you define religion you will find that it in short is the remains of a part of the world history that was lost when the Motherland was destroyed in a natural catastrophe some twelve thousand years ago. Religion is the cover-up that along with all the legends, tales and myths keeps the whole world in a permanent abyss of darkness and oblivion.

"No who is he that will harm you, if you are followers of that which is good? But even if you suffer for righteousness sake, happy are you. And be not afraid of terror, nor be troubled. For it is better, if the will of God be so, that you suffer for well doing than evil doing. For Christ also ones suffered for sins, the just for the unjust, that might bring us to God, being put to death in the flesh but made alive in the Spirit."

Even if you all are clever people with a high degree of spiritual strength, it doesn't help you in finding the knowledge you all need in order to be able to build a new world with lasting peace. You just cannot comprehend that it is the many national states, the use of money and all the religions in the world that keep you in the deep abyss of darkness and oblivion. Or do you?

If you know the definition of the three factors of the Original Sin, then you know what one who works for righteousness sake is working to change the way the whole world population is thinking. His success is not measured in money.

Peter counsels humility

"All of you be subject to one another, and be clothed by humility. For God resists the proud and gives grace to the humble. Humble yourselves therefore under the mighty hand of God, that he may exalt you in due time. Cast all your care upon him, for he cares for you."

"Be sober, be vigilant, because your adversary the devil, like a roaring lion, walks about, seeking whom he may devour. Resist him, steadfast in the faith, knowing that the same sufferings are befalling your brothers throughout the word."

The devil, the force of evil, is in charge all over the world. The definition for all evil is the three factors of the Original Sin, namely all the national states, the global system of capitalism and all the religions in the world. The forces of good are found in the Diagram Star, accessible for everyone now that the Ark of the Covenant is open.

By nature the whole world population is meant to be subject to one another, and clothed by humility. This is what Jesus told his disciples at the last supper. You are all human beings and not one of you is greater than others. It is the natural laws and rules given by the spiritual superior Motherland council that resists the proud and gives grace to the humble. The council members are still spirits in the spirit world and have no power to win over the physical forces of evil in the world.

The only way the forces of good can regain full power over the whole world population again is to build a new Motherland and elect a new superior Motherland council. It has to be done by the whole world population working together. The power of lasting world peace comes from the whole world population living together like brothers and friends.

Before the Motherland went under, being proud had a natural meaning. It was the feeling of doing well in the eyes of family and friends. When every single human being in, for example a tribal community, had the same feeling of being proud of one self and each other as a tribe, being humble kept the peace. Everybody lived with a deep and profound happiness and common care that people living in present time know nothing about.

Being subject to one another and be clothed by humility can never happen in this world as long as the greatness of people are measured with the riches and personal power that comes from exploiting other people with the use of the three factors of the Original Sin.

Living under the mighty hand of God means to live in the bright light of the Diagram Star in a world totally without the force of evil that are so perfectly described by the history of the Roman Empire.

Peter speaks of the coming of the Lord

"But, beloved, be not ignorant of this one thing, that one day is with the Lord as one thousand years, and a thousand years is as one day. The Lord is not slack concerning his promise, as some men count slackness, but is long-suffering, not willing that any should perish, but that all should come to repentance.

"But the day of the Lord shall come like a thief in the night, in which the heavens shall pass away with a great noise, and the elements shall melt with burning heat. The earth also and the works that are on it shall be burned up. Nevertheless we, according to his promise, look for new heavens and a new earth, were righteousness will dwell.

"Therefore, beloved, seeing that you look for such things, be careful that you found him by peace, without spot, and blameless. And count the long-suffering of our Lord as salvation, as our beloved brother Paul has written to you, speaking of these things in his epistles.

"Grow in grace and in the knowledge of our Lord and Saviour Jesus Christ."

The last sentence is words spoken directly to you and the whole world population. Knowledge about the born again Motherland history and the global system of government that really can make the building of a new world with lasting peace possible will make you grow as a person.

You and the whole world population are living like inside invisible mental bobbles. One layer of the bobble is a wall of ignorance, and it can only be broken down from the inside, by you alone, with the help of the mental sword of knowledge.

Thousands of years have passed since the knowledge was lost in the deep abyss of darkness and oblivion where you live. You live your life like you do because you as everybody else want to do what you by tradition believe is right.

The promise of God is what the return of the born again Motherland history will provide, truly and certain. By accepting that the superior Motherland council ones existed, the wall of ignorance will crumble and fall like the walls of Jericho and you will all of a sudden be totally free of the mental bubble you and the whole world population have lived inside for so long.

The day of the coming of the Lord is here. The definition of heaven is the spirit world, the common world of thoughts. The full history of the lost Motherland is there in the spirit world. It is your world of thoughts and the common world of thoughts that in the process of separating right from wrong will be cleansed.

The thought of evil, the present of the three factors of the Original Sin will not disappear silently, but as a result of the knowledge about Jesus as the born again Motherland history, all evil will disappear like dew before the sun.

The new heaven is the same old spirit world, our common world of thoughts, but cleansed for all thoughts of evil. And with the common world of thoughts back on the right track, the building of the promised new world can finally begin. The Promised Land is, under the camouflage of religion, the whole planet earth.

The vision of John

Revelation

The final book of the Bible, the Revelation of St. John the Devine, tells in vivid images of Gods final judgment.

The book is cast in the form of a vision and many of its prophecies are disguised attacks on Rome, the great power of the first century. Such is unquestionable the chase of the references to Babylon. This ancient capital of paganism and persecution was comparable in the eyes of the early Christians to the Rome of that day. Thus the following passages must have been clear and encouraging to many.

"And after these things, I saw another angel come down from heaven, having great power. And he cried mightily with a strong voice, saying: "Babylon the great is falling, and is become the habitation of devils and the hold of every foul spirit, and a gage of every unclean and hateful bird.

"And I heard another voice from heaven, saying: Come out of her, my people, that you be not partakers of her sins, and that you receive not her plagues, because her sins has reached in to heaven, and God has remembered her iniquities. And the kings of the earth, when they shall see the smoke of her burning, standing afar of the fear of her torment, shall say: Alas, alas, that great city Babylon, that mighty city."

Disguised attacks on Rome back then are the same as disguised attacks on the political system with many nations in our present time. It is an attack on the global system of capitalism, the use of money and it is an attack on all the religions in the world. Babylon can be seen as a symbol for the whole world. The whole world was a paradise with only the forces of good before the Motherland went under and it became a living hell after the catastrophe some twelve thousand years ago.

"Clear and encouraging to many humans." It is truly clear and encouraging to know what the vision of John means under the camouflage of religion. The future world will be without great cities and buildings that built by the three factors of the Original Sin.

The angel coming down from heaven, having great power, is clearly saying that all the great cities in the world is and will be the dwelling place for all evil as long as the power of evil is allowed to exist on planet earth.

The new world will be built as villages of varying sizes, surrounded by land enough to make the population self supported in every thinkable way. It will be like building a new paradise world for the future. As said before, education will be the main activity in a world without the chaos of wars and conflicts, a world without the national states and their cities with the capitalistic towers reaching for the sky, and it will be a world without all the religions. The cities will slowly become empty. Babylon is a good symbol for all the cities in the world, and they truly are the strongholds for everything that is evil in the world.

Remember the story about Daniel and his three friends. Jerusalem destroyed, not a stone upon a stone, is a symbol for the lost Motherland. The New Jerusalem is a symbol for the new

Motherland you and the whole world population are going to build together, with the help from the spirit world.

A new heaven and earth

> "And I saw a new heaven and a new earth, for the first heaven and the first earth had passed away, and there was no more sea. And I, John, saw the holy city, New Jerusalem, coming down from God out of heaven, prepared as a bride adorned for her husband.
>
> "And I heard a great voice out of the heaven, saying: Behold, the tabernacle of God is with men, and he will dwell with them, and they shall be his people. And he shall wipe away all tears from their eyes, and there shall be no more death, nor crying. Neither shall there be any more pain.
>
> And he carried me away in the spirit to a great mountain, and showed me that great city, the holy Jerusalem. And her light was like a stone most precious, even like a jasper stone, clear as crystal. And she had a wall great and high, and had twelve foundations, and in them the names of the twelve apostles of the Lamb.
>
> "And I saw no temple therein, for the Lord God Almighty and the Lamb is the temple of it. And the city had no need of the sun, or of the moon, to shine in it, for the glory of God did lighten it, and the Lamb is the light thereof.
>
> And all the nations of them which are saved shall walk in the light of it, and the kings of the earth bring their glory to it. And the gates of it shall not be shut at all by day, for there shall be no night there.
>
> "And I, John, saw these things, and heard them.

This is it, people. This camouflaged story is the message the whole Bible is all about, camouflaged under a veil of religion. I will tell you what you will see, when the formula of the old Masters is used to explain the text. The tabernacle of God is the symbolic Ark of the Covenant with the Diagram Star inside, carved out on a stone tablet. The whole story about the lost Motherland is hidden in the Bible, and you know by now that the Diagram Star is the official emblem of the old superior Motherland council.

The first heaven and earth had passed away. The lost Motherland was destroyed some twelve thousand years ago, and became the well known heaven in the spirit world. The superior Motherland council became God in haven and everyone else who died in the catastrophe became spiritual beings in the memory of the people who survived, in the common world of thoughts. This means that after the catastrophe the common world of thoughts suddenly was free from the physical superior leadership of the superior Motherland council. The power of good had become spiritual and the chaos of wars and conflicts started and just never stopped. The whole world became like a chaotic beehive without its queen be.

A new heaven and a new earth is what you and the whole world population have to start building, together. The thoughts about how to do it can only come from the spirit world, from the common world of thoughts that you all are a part of.

Heaven is the new Motherland and the new earth that you all are going to build together is this planet that you all live on. The new heaven and the new earth will be without the three factors of the Original Sin. This means that the three major factors controlling the lives of all humans have to be removed completely from the common world of thoughts, before the new Motherland and the new world can be built.

The new world needs a new superior Motherland council and one set of laws and rules for the whole world population.

The building of a new Motherland and the building of the new world have to be planned carefully before the building can start. Democratically elected leaders from every tribal people on the planet have to plan the new world together. A global parliament has to be elected and gathered in the new Motherland. From them a new superior Motherland council will be elected. Then the new world truly will be seen as a beautiful bride, a new complete governing system, coming out of the common world of thoughts to settle on the whole planet earth.

God is defined for all humans as the late superior Motherland council. They all died along with the whole Motherland population, but their thoughts continued to lead large parts of the world population for a long time under the teaching and guiding of the Masters of the past. The twelve superior titles of the council is still found on the night sky, namely as the star signs of the Zodiac. The titles were ever lasting; the members of the council were democratically elected regular human beings.

But self-appointed warrior kings and priesthoods started fighting each other in an attempt to build a new Motherland, but doing that with the use of warfare and brutal force was wrong and they couldn't succeed. They soon began to build cities with walls around and started using their stolen property to build up large armies of war. Brothers began fighting brothers back then, and the fighting and killing just hasn't stopped.

Human beings do need a superior leadership that is real and accepted by everyone. A new superior council in a new Motherland will be such a common leadership.

The new superior Motherland council will have the Diagram Star as the official emblem. The diagram with a multitude of meanings and the carrier of the lost world history is what you will find in the Ark of the Covenant. The sun, the moon and the twelve star signs of the Zodiac is the model for the Diagram Star. The star in the centre is the born again Motherland history, the spiritual Jesus.

It is therefore clear that it is not the person Jesus that will return to earth and save the world. Only a new man made global government can save the world. With the Diagram Star as the common book for education of the whole world population, there will be lasting peace for ever more.

The teaching of the Diagram Star will, in spirit, take you up on a mountain were you can see the whole planet earth with lasting peace. The Diagram Star is the stone most precious, enlightening the world and its entire population.

The stories about the apostles are all fictive and were written by Masters, the leaders of a lasting opposition, a resistant opposition dating all the way back to the time the Motherland went under. They died the way so many of the first Christians died, fighting peacefully for what they knew is right.

One more vision of John

When the apostle John was very old, he had a vision. It was a dream. Jesus asked him to write down what he saw.

John saw that Jesus stood in front of seven candlesticks of gold. His eyes were like fire and his voice like the sound of rushing water. The face of Jesus was like the sun, bright shining.

Jesus asked John to warn the Christians. Some of them had forgotten the most important. "You don't love me like in the beginning." The poor congregations were rich on love. Those who suffered for Jesus should be rewarded in heaven.

Jesus also sent warnings to the seven congregations. They did not see their own problems. "Those who believe that they can make it on their own are wrong. If you think it is better to trust oneself then God, you are wrong."

Jesus asked John to remind the Christians on this time and time again. They should love, give, turn to God and be faithful.

Fire, Water, Air and Earth = Knowledge about the lost Motherland, says the old Masters formula or code. When seen as the centre circle of the Diagram Star, the seven candlesticks are a symbol for the seven free and fundamental sciences. In their light lays the full knowledge from the time before the Motherland went under, the full story about the lost world history that was born again some two thousand years ago, as Jesus Christ.

The seven sciences of the past are as follows: The first is Grammar and the use of one common language that teaches humans to talk and write correct. The second is Rhetoric, teaching humans to talk right in all occurring situations. The third is Logic, which is teaching humans to separate wrong from right. The fourth is Algebra, the part of mathematics in which letters and other general symbols are used to represent numbers and quantities in formulae and equations. The fifth science is Geometry, teaching humans to measure height, width, length and thickness of things. The sixth is Music, teaching humans about the science of sound, from voice, tongue, harp, trumpet and other sources of sound. The seventh is Astrology, teaching humans about the whole universe, the sun, the moon and the stars.

All this natural sciences is embedded in the Diagram Star, along with all the laws and rules for living that are common for the whole world population.

This camouflaged story is all about returning to the foundation for thinking. In order to be able to build a world with lasting peace, the common world of thoughts has to be the same for the whole world population. The common world of thoughts is spiritual in its being, and it is called heaven, spirit world, Holy Spirit and Great Spirit, to mentioning some names. You are your thoughts. Without your thoughts you wouldn't be living at all.

There is only one common world of thoughts, and by nature it comes with one common set of laws and rules for living.

Up until the Motherland was destroyed in a natural catastrophe, the Diagram Star was the first ever human made book. It is the official emblem of the superior Motherland council. They had copies of the diagram made as crosses in a few different shapes and they all had a specific meaning. Every education center in the world used the same teaching material and all the teachers were educated in the education centers in the Motherland. Every human on earth got the same common education and regarded the superior Motherland council as their superior leader in all matters. Like this the lasting world peace was secured.

The twelve star signs in the Zodiac are the origin for the Diagram Star, with the sun and the moon in the centre. The twelve star signs are the carrier of the whole world history and all the knowledge mankind needs to live a good life on planet earth and elsewhere in the universe.

The Master who wrote this camouflaged story in the first place knew that the Diagram Star had been with humans from before the beginning of time, and that it would be with humans until after the end of time. If John was the author's name, he wrote the story with Jesus as the bright shining star in the diagram centre. Through Jesus he made the starlight talk with words to the whole world population living in present time. "I am the Morning Star," Jesus says. And he has arrived.

The first twelve tribes who emigrated from the Motherland in order to populate the whole world, brought with them a stone tablet with the Diagram Star chiseled in, with every detail. It is possible that you won't believe this, but back then, perhaps two hundred thousand years or more, the humans had flying vessels to use for staying in contact with each other, helping out after natural catastrophes moving necessities and to move students to and from the educational centre's on a yearly base.

During the period of education the right persons was democratically selected to the right positions in every aspect of earth life. Everyone knew why they lived and what the humans living on the planet were working to achieve. Just like they had populated planet earth they were working effectively to build cosmic eggs. You know the vessels called spaceships. Cosmic eggs were used to populate new earthlike planets in the universe.

What is known is that the whole world population was working together on this global project. All the humans were living like brothers and friends in a world with lasting peace. They took peace for granted, because they had no enemies' except the animal predators in the nature.

After the Motherland was destroyed and the whole superior Motherland council was gone, the chaos of wars and conflicts started and just never stopped. The reason the madness is allowed to continue is that the common world of thoughts is polluted with the three factors of the Original Sin. This means that no one knows about the world history from before the Motherland went under. You are living from generation to generation with a veil of evil creating the darkness of oblivion in your mind.

Before a new world with lasting peace can be built, the three factors of the Original Sin have to be removed from the common world of thoughts. Only then the bright light from the Diagram Star can enlighten the world and fulfill your dream. You all want the same for the world you live in and now you know how to make it happen.